RHS GARDEN FINDER 2002-2003

EDITOR
CHARLES QUEST-RITSON

A Dorling Kindersley Book

LONDON, NEW YORK, MUNICH, MELBOURNE, DELHI

First published in Great Britain in 2002 by
Dorling Kindersley Limited
80 Strand, London WC2R 0RL

A Penguin Company

A CIP catalogue record for this book is available from the British Library.

ISBN 07513 3706 4

The opinions expressed in this work are the opinions of the author and
not of the publishers or the Royal Horticultural Society.

Data management and typesetting by
HWA Text and Data Management, Tunbridge Wells

Printed in England by Clays Ltd, St Ives Plc

See our complete catalogue at
www.dk.com

Step into a world of inspirational gardens

Join the Royal Horticultural Society and enjoy free entry to over 90 inspirational gardens in the UK.

Members can receive advice, ideas and inspiration through free entry to the renowned RHS Gardens - Wisley, Rosemoor, Hyde Hall and Harlow Carr - as well as free entry to 88 partner gardens at carefully selected periods of the year. Members also benefit from the excellent monthly magazine *The Garden*, as well as from a free gardening advice service from the RHS experts, available by phone, fax, letter, e mail or face-to-face. Members also enjoy privileged access and special rate tickets to the world's most famous Flower Shows including Chelsea, Hampton Court Palace and Tatton Park, as well as discounted tickets to RHS talks, events and garden tours across Britain.

RHS Membership Special Offer - Save £5

RHS Membership is normally £37 (£30 including a one-off joining fee of £7) but you can save £5 and pay just £32 by either completing the application form overleaf, or calling the Membership Hotline on

0845 130 4646

(Lines open 9:00am - 5:00pm Monday to Friday)

and quote code 1716

Subscription rate valid until 31 October 2002.   www.rhs.org.uk

Registered charity no. 222879

Royal
Horticultural
Society

Membership Application Form

Please return to:

Membership Department,
The Royal Horticultural Society,
PO Box 313, London SW1P 2PE

In becoming a Member of the RHS, I understand that information relating to my Membership will be passed to carefully selected third parties for processing purposes only and that I will receive information from the RHS relating to RHS events and products. I understand that the RHS will not sell my details to anyone.

Please tick

☐ Individual Membership at £32.

Your details

Title   Initial(s)

Surname

Address

Postcode

Daytime Tel. No.

Email address

Payment Details

Payment by credit or debit card

Card details

☐☐☐☐☐ ☐☐☐☐☐ ☐☐☐☐ ☐☐☐☐

Expiry Date [/   ]   Issue No (Switch only) [   ]

Cardholder's name

Signature

Date [   ]

Payment by Cheque (UK bank/building society accounts only

I enclose a cheque made payable to

The Royal Horticultural Society for [£   ]

☐ From time to time we would like to send you details of products and services provided by carefully selected organisations that may be of interest to you and could provide additional revenue to support our charitable aims. If you do not want your name and address details passed to these carefully selected organisations please tick the box.

If you would like to purchase Premier Gift Membership for gardening friends or relations, please call our Membership Hotline on

0845 130 4646

Code: 171

CONTENTS

KEY TO SYMBOLS

(P) Parking available

(🐕) Dogs permitted

(WC) Toilet facilities

(♿) Access for the disabled

(🌱) Plants for sale

(🎁) Gift shop

(🍴) Restaurant

(☕) Light refreshments

INTRODUCTION

Garden visiting

Welcome to the new edition of *The RHS Garden Finder 2002–2003*. This is a companion volume to the *RHS Plant Finder*. The *RHS Plant Finder* tells you where to find the right nurseries for plants: *The RHS Garden Finder 2002–2003* will tell you where to see the same plants growing in gardens which are open to the public. This is all the more important now that membership of the Royal Horticultural Society brings free access for its members to more than 100 gardens up and down the United Kingdom and abroad.

The aim of this book is to supply sufficient detail to enable readers to decide if and when to plan a visit. The list is not exhaustive. It offers a selection of the different types of garden which are open to the public: ancient and modern, large and small, public and private. We welcome suggestions for additions, deletions or alterations to entries. All major gardens which are open regularly are listed as a matter of course. These include many gardens of the National Trust and the National Trust for Scotland as well as botanic and public gardens and those attached to stately homes. But many gardens do not open to visitors regularly: the National Gardens Scheme lists over 3,500. In this book you will find a selection of these gardens which open only once a year or by appointment. Some guides would omit them on the grounds that it is not worthwhile to give publicity to gardens which so few people can visit but, if a good garden is seldom open, it is all the more important to know when the opportunity to see it will arise. This book also concentrates upon gardens with plants: some of the great historic gardens of the 18th century have comparatively brief descriptions, because their landscapes are rather short on horticultural content. On the other hand, some of the best gardens for plants are those which have large 'living collections' for teaching purposes – botanic gardens, and those attached to horticultural colleges. It is important to stress that almost all such gardens nowadays are extremely conscious of the need to offer ornamental and horticultural features to please visitors. Public amenity is usually the principal justification now for maintaining the historic plant collections which were systematically amassed in the 19th and early 20th centuries.

Nurseries

Because this book is plant-led, it also includes about 200 leading nurseries. Almost all have a demonstration garden attached to them, just as most gardens have a nursery or plant stall. This is a recent development – it started about 20 years ago – but is now quite normal: visitors to a nursery like to see plants growing in a garden before making their purchases, and visitors to a garden like the opportunity to buy some of the plants they have seen there. It would not be right to exclude the inspirational series of model gardens at Bridgemere in Cheshire, Barnsdale in Leicestershire or the National Garden Exhibition Centre in Co. Wicklow just because they are attached to a commercial enterprise that sells plants.

How to use this book

In each section gardens are listed by county or region (for Scotland), and then alphabetically by name. In general, we have stuck to the familiar 1974 counties of England and Wales and to the Scottish regional divisions. There are three exceptions: the county of Avon has been redistributed between Gloucestershire and Somerset, Cleveland has been included with North Yorkshire, and Humberside has been split between Lincolnshire and the East Riding of Yorkshire. We have also divided Hereford & Worcester into its two component parts again. We have been careful to ensure, so far as possible, that gardens are listed in the counties or region in which they actually lie, which is not always the county or region their postal addresses suggest, or where their owners believe themselves to live. Thus the Savill Garden lies in Surrey, even though most of Windsor Great Park is in Berkshire, and the gardens at Burford House near Tenbury Wells are neither in Herefordshire nor in Worcestershire, but across the border in Shropshire. To find out about a specific garden, turn to the index at the back: it should take you straight to the page you need.

Practical details
Our source for practical information about directions, opening times, admission charges, parking, lavatories, disabled facilities and refreshments has been the owners or their staff, backed up by our own enquiries where appropriate. The accuracy of these details is not guaranteed, but is believed to be correct at the time of going to press. We rely to a great extent on information which has been submitted to us by third parties. Not everyone who was approached has replied – or replied in time – and this explains some gaps. A paperless version of the book is on-line as part of the Royal Horticultural Society's website (www.rhs.org.uk) and updates will be made as and when they are available. Inclusion in

this book or on the society's website, or exclusion from either of them, should not be construed as a recommendation or condemnation. And, though this book carries the Royal Horticultural Society's endorsement, its comments and opinions are the editor's, and his alone.

Contacting gardens
In order to assist readers with special needs, or who are hoping to arrange a group visit by special appointment, we list the telephone and fax numbers to which enquiries should be directed. In many cases this is the private telephone line of the owners: readers are urged to respect their privacy. If telephone and fax numbers have been omitted, this is because the owners prefer to receive such requests by letter.

Websites
There has been a great increase recently in the number of gardens and nurseries with dedicated internet sites. Many are beautifully designed and extremely informative. They help to attract visitors, especially groups from gardening clubs and tour operators. Please remember that website addresses change frequently and inexplicably. We have checked all the hundreds in this book during the autumn of 2001 and have only included those which are up and running and seem to us to offer useful information. Many websites are of excellent quality: some of the nursery sites permit on-line ordering. Others exist only as registered names: we have omitted them. And far too many people seem to think that, once they have launched their website, there is nothing more that they need to do. One very important plantsman's nursery was still inviting web customers in November 2001 to download a catalogue described as valid only until 1 September 2000.

Visiting times

Many gardens are attached to other attractions – most typically, a house which is also open to the public. The visiting times we have given relate only to the garden. Please remember that most gardens have a last admission time. Typically it will be 30 or 45 minutes before they close, but it can be much longer. Remember, too, that a pre-booked group can often make a visit at a time or season when the garden is not open to individual visitors.

Prices

As with times, so with prices. The admission prices we have given relate only to the garden. If the house or some other attraction is open at the same time, a supplement may be payable. Some owners insist on you buying a full ticket, though most are more reasonable. It is true that some gardens may seem rather expensive but, generally speaking, the market rules of supply and demand apply and you get what you pay for. And it should be said that for every garden which is over-priced there are ten inspirational plantsman's gardens, run on a strictly non-commercial basis, where you can be certain of wonderful flowers, good design and a genuine welcome.

Many gardens offer special rates to groups and, if details are not given, it may be worth asking whether a reduction is available and what minimum number is acceptable. Please remember, however, that not all gardens permit parties: popular gardens which already suffer from wear and tear may not welcome increased visitor numbers. Special rates for families are sometimes available, especially at larger gardens attached to stately homes, where the garden is only one of many entertainments offered to the visitor. There are endless permutations on the numbers of adults and/or children which constitute a 'family' and the age at which a child becomes an adult and has to pay the full entry price. Season tickets are sometimes available, and good value for people who live near a large garden or stately home.

Entrance fees vary, and a few owners have told us that they may increase fees in the middle of the season. Some have a high season for a month or so – like Exbury in Hampshire, and Leonardslee in West Sussex in spring. Others have a special day of the week or open days for charity when the entrance fee is higher. A few owners had not yet fixed their 2002 times or admission charges by the time we went to press and we have therefore indicated that the times or prices quoted are for 2001. All entrance fees are, in any event, liable to be changed: visitors would do well to take more money than they think they will need. Some gardens have honesty boxes, and it is also important to take lots of change, so that you are not forced to choose between paying too much and paying too little.

It is worth remembering that National Trust members are usually admitted free to Trust properties. Readers are strongly recommended to join the National Trust in any event: its portfolio of blue chip gardens is so comprehensive that no garden tour is complete without a visit to one or more of its properties.

Facilities

This guide uses a variety of symbols to show whether a garden has such facilities as public conveniences or plants for sale. We have indicated whether parking is available: this may be at the garden itself or on a public road very close to it. Parking may be at some distance from the house. At Saltram, in Devon, it is 500 yards away, and this is by no means exceptional. You can however expect better parking facilities at a popular property which offers a wide range of entertainments than at a small plantsman's garden in a country lane.

It is often a condition of admission that no photograph taken within the garden may be sold or used for public reproduction without the consent of the property owner. Visitors should also remember that almost all gardens accept dogs only if they are kept on leads. Some restrict dogs to particular areas of a property, like the car-park, or the woods and parkland rather than the garden proper. Private owners are generally better disposed towards dogs than corporate owners like the National Trust or English Heritage. A few owners go out of their way to say that dogs are actually welcome, but not all have shaded areas for parking.

Disabled visitors
We have generally indicated which gardens are suitable for disabled people, though it is important to stress that access may only be partial. Often an area around the house or entrance is accessible for people in wheelchairs, but the more remote parts of the garden are quite unsuitable. It is best to ring before your visit to check. The same is true of other disabled facilities. We have not specified the nature of those facilities, but in most cases it includes lavatories and ramps which are suitable for the wheelchair-bound. It is best to enquire in advance of a visit if particular items of special equipment are required. The National Trust is especially good at adapting its properties to accommodate the needs of disabled visitors and publishes an excellent free booklet called *Information for Visitors with Disabilities*, which details the many special facilities available at those of its properties which are suitable for disabled visitors. It is available from the National Trust's head office in London.

Size of gardens
We have asked owners to indicate the size of their garden and the number of people who work in it. These statistics help to suggest how intensively a garden is worked and how long you need to allow for your visit. The number of gardeners must be interpreted flexibly. Some owners have told us how many paid gardeners they employ: others have included their own contributions and based their figure on how much time they and their family give to the garden.

The NCCPG
Four common abbreviations are used freely throughout the text: RHS for the Royal Horticultural Society, NGS for the National Gardens Scheme, SGS for Scotland's Garden Scheme, and NCCPG for the National Council for the Conservation of Plants and Gardens. We have noted the NCCPG National Collections held at the gardens and nurseries listed and indexed them separately. Not all genera are the subject of a National Collection: there are still some horticulturally important groups of plants which have not yet been seriously collected and studied under the auspices of the NCCPG. Other genera have been split into a number of different collections. This is particularly necessary for a large genus, such as *Rhododendron*, or those, like *Euphorbia*, which require a great variety of growing conditions. Moreover, the NCCPG has wisely introduced a system of duplicate collections to insure against the risks which face every collection of rare plants, so plants are grown in two or more gardens. The need to maintain duplicate collections and split large genera explains why certain names occur several times in the list of National Collections towards the end of the book. That list is taken from information supplied to us by the NCCPG in October last year. The 2002 edition of the National Plant Collections Directory will shortly be published: copies are available from bookshops or from the NCCPG, The Stable Courtyard, Wisley Garden, Woking, Surrey GU23 6QB (£6.20 including p&p).

Champion trees

For most gardens, we give a brief list of Features. These include general information like 'good collection of trees' and more specific facts like 'tallest *Quercus cerris* in the UK'. Occasionally we have included features which are not strictly plants, but add enormously to the character of a garden and the reasons for making a visit. Information about outsize trees is taken principally from the records kept by that excellent organisation the Tree Register of the British Isles (see www.tree-register.org). There are two ways of measuring trees: height and girth. Sometimes the tallest specimen will also have the thickest trunk – but not always. Both the tallest and the biggest can claim to be the champion tree, and we have sometimes made this distinction when noting record breakers in gardens. Tree measurements can never be fully up to date: some records have not been verified since the great gales of 1987 and 1990.

The 2001 season

Many owners told us that their gardens had fewer visitors in 2001 than in 2000. They tended to attribute this to the widespread effects of foot-and-mouth disease. In 2000, poor visitor numbers were generally blamed on exceptionally wet weather. On the other hand, it was widely acknowledged that, though visitor numbers were down in 2001, visitor 'spend' was actually up. The net result was that most garden-owners were not too disappointed by their final figures.

It remains to be seen whether visitor numbers perk up again in 2002 and 2003. Many gardens consider that they are in competition for visitors with other tourist attractions, other entertainments and other activities like shopping. Their reaction has been to put more emphasis upon special events. These vary from those like plant sales, study days and garden walks which are designed to attract keen gardeners, to broad-based entertainments like concerts, craft fairs and car rallies. Many are listed in the Event Finder on the Royal Horticultural Society's website (www.rhs.org.uk). What nobody can yet gauge is the effect these activities may have upon the numbers of people visiting smaller gardens. Nor it is yet clear whether we are seeing the beginning of a decline in garden visiting, or a temporary variation in visitor numbers caused by circumstances which are unlikely to recur. One hopeful sign is that the British Tourist Authority will feature a number of leading gardens when it launches its 'Hidden Britain' campaign this year. This is designed to attract more foreign tourists, particularly visitors from mainland Europe, to come to Britain and enjoy the British countryside.

Acknowledgements

The editor is very grateful to the many people who have helped in the compilation of this work. First and foremost he thanks all the garden owners, nurseries, horticulturists, colleges, societies and everyone else who has responded to his requests for information. He is greatly indebted to them, and regrets that it is not always possible to give each the personal attention which is their due. Particular thanks go the staff of the staff in the regionals offices of the National Trust. Special thanks are also due to Susanne Mitchell, Geoff Hodge, Rebecca Bowen, Mary-Anne Clothier, Brent Elliott and others at the Royal Horticultural Society and especially to Karen Wilson in the publications department. The editor also acknowledges the considerable input of others who have worked with us on this project: John Hodgson, Barbara Levy, David Lamb and our colleagues at Dorling Kindersley. Finally thanks are due for their endeavours to Madeline Quest-Ritson, Christopher and Katharine Blair and, above all, to Brigid Quest-Ritson whose labours are represented throughout these pages.

GARDENS
TO
VISIT

ENGLAND

The purpose of this short introduction is to highlight some of the considerations which apply to gardens in England, but not to those in other parts of the UK or abroad. The first point to make is that gardens and gardening are essentially an English phenomenon. England has always taken the lead within the British Isles, and gardening is still – to some extent – one of our most important cultural, artistic and scientific exports. Within England there are differences of garden emphasis and style between regions. Alpine gardening has many followers in the north of England; Cornish gardens tend to be rhododendron woodland gardens; the smart designers tend to practice in and around London. Gardening is probably at its strongest as a national pursuit in the south-east of the country, where more than half the Royal Horticultural Society's members live. But there are good gardens of every kind open to the public in every part of the country. In fact they are also fairly evenly distributed throughout England, except perhaps for the east Midlands, which has fewer good gardens than its rich agriculture might suggest. Gardens and garden-making depend as much upon social and economic circumstances as upon soil and climate.

A word about the grading of historic gardens is needed. During the 1980s, English Heritage's predecessors compiled a register of gardens and parks of special historic interest. The aim was to draw attention to the nation's heritage, so that designed landscapes were not overlooked, for example in plans for new development. There are three gradings, each of which assesses the historic layout, features and architectural ornaments. Grade I parks and gardens are 'of exceptional interest'; Grade II* parks and gardens are 'of great quality'. Grade II parks and gardens are 'of special interest'. These gradings reflect the importance of a particular garden or park and compare it with others in England as a whole. The register is in 46 parts, one for each of the 1974 English counties, and copies are available from English Heritage. The information they contain about the individual gardens is very comprehensive. It covers the site, area, dates and designers of key surviving elements, surviving features of the garden or park, and other interesting aspects such as historic associations.

The best source of reference for plants and nurseries is the *RHS Plant Finder*. It shows where the main concentrations of nurseries are – in Surrey, for example – and where there are few, like northern Cornwall. It lists only a handful of garden centres, which is a pity because most people buy their plants at local garden centres rather than specialist nurseries. There is no publication which tells you where to find a good garden centre, though the Garden Centre Association has a very helpful searchable website (www.gca.org.uk). The advantage of buying from one of its 150 members is that all are subject to annual inspections by an independent auditor and must satisfy stringent standards to remain members. The only guide to garden centres of which we know is the *Gardeners' Atlas* (Paragraph Publishing). We have sometimes found that its maps are not as accurate as they ought to be, but it lists over 4,500 places of gardening interest of every kind. A recent publication (1999) on UK nurseries was *Gardeners' Favourite Nurseries* by Leslie Geddes-Brown, who asked all the owners who open their gardens for the National Gardens Scheme or Scotland's Garden Scheme to tell her which nurseries they use and recommend. The result is a directory of over 400 nurseries in every part of the UK with endorsements from many leading garden-owners, though few of the nurseries specialise in genera which the smart set eschews – chrysanthemums, dahlias and fuchsias, for example.

The starting point for visiting English gardens must be the 'Yellow Book' which the National Gardens Scheme publishes annually in February under the full title *Gardens of England & Wales Open to the Public.* The Yellow Book is a best seller. It is wonderfully comprehensive and totally undiscriminating. The owners write their own garden entries, with the result that a really good garden may come across as self-deprecatingly boring, while an exciting description can often lead to disappointment. Beware of self-publicists: you can usually spot the hype. The Yellow Book lists over 3,500 gardens and is the single most important guide to visiting gardens in England and Wales, and the least expensive. Copies of *Gardens of England & Wales Open to the Public in 2002* will be available as from the end of February 2002.

Members of the RHS enjoy free entry to many gardens throughout England. Some are free throughout the year: others for only a month or so. In some cases the privilege applies only to members of the RHS, not to any guests who accompany them. Nevertheless, it is an impressive list, and worth spelling out in full. In addition to the four RHS Gardens at Harlow Carr, Hyde Hall, Rosemoor and Wisley, members have free access to the following gardens in

England: Abbotsbury Sub-Tropical Gardens, Arley Hall, Barnsdale Gardens, Batsford Arboretum, Bedgebury National Pinetum, Beth Chatto Gardens, Bide-a-Wee Cottage, Bluebell Arboretum, Bluebell Cottage Gardens, Borde Hill Garden, Broadview Gardens, Brogdale Horticultural Trust, Burnby Hall, Burton Agnes, Cabbages & Kings, Catforth Gardens, Chiffchaffs, Cholmondeley Castle Gardens, Clovelly Court, Corsham Court, Cottesbrooke Hall, Cranborne Manor, Dalemain, Docton Mill, Duncombe Park, East Ruston Old Vicarage, Fairhaven Garden Trust, Felley Priory Garden, Forde Abbey, Furzey Gardens, Glen Chantry, Goodnestone Park, Harewood House, Holker Hall, Kingston Maurward, Knoll Gardens, Loseley Park, Mapperton, Mill Dene, Millgate House, Muncaster Castle, Newby Hall, Normanby Hall Victorian Walled Garden, Nymans Garden, Parcevall Hall, Penshurst Place, Pound Hill Garden, Probus Garden, Raby Castle, Ripley Castle, Rode Hall, Ryton Organic Garden, Sheffield Park Garden, Stillingfleet Lodge, Tapeley Park, Tatton Park, Abbey House Gardens, Dorothy Clive Garden, Quinta Arboretum & Nature Reserve, Sir Harold Hillier Gardens & Arboretum, Trebah Gardens, Trevarno, Trewithen Garden, Waddesdon Manor Gardens, Waterperry Gardens, Westonbirt Arboretum, Wollerton Old Hall and Yalding Organic Gardens. The list has grown considerably in recent years, and the RHS hopes to expand it yet further.

In addition to its Free Access gardens, the Royal Horticultural Society has a system of running lectures at a number of Partner Nurseries and Garden Centres in England, most of which are listed in this book, with a note of how to find out further details. The Society's own *Members' Handbook 2002* gives full details of these and of the many lectures, demonstrations, workshops, garden walks and other events held at RHS Partner Colleges.

BEDFORDSHIRE

Both the Grade I gardens in Bedfordshire – Woburn Abbey and Wrest Park – are open to the public. Few of its other important gardens remain open to visitors, though every garden-visitor should seek out the gloriously eccentric Swiss Garden (Grade II*). The headquarters of the Royal Society for the Protection of Birds, The Lodge at Sandy, is also rated as a Grade II garden and open daily throughout the year. It is regrettable that Luton Hoo has been closed to the public for some years now, and that there is no immediate prospect of this changing. Although Shuttleworth College at Old Warden is now a RHS Partner College, Bedfordshire is horticulturally underdeveloped. It is not over-endowed with arboreta, though Woburn has a fine collection of trees: there are a number of record-breakers there, as well as at Swiss Garden, Toddington Manor and Wrest Park. Surprisingly few private gardens open for the National Gardens Scheme and the county has only one National Collection. There are few nurseries too: best known is Blom's Bulbs at Melchbourne, close to the border with Northamptonshire, but it is not open to visitors. One para-horticultural curiosity worth seeing is the 'Tree Cathedral' near Chessington Zoo.

The Manor House

CHURCH ROAD, STEVINGTON, BEDFORD MK43 7QB

Tel 01234 822064 **Fax** 01234 825531
Website www.kathybrownsgarden.homestead.com
Location 5 miles north-west of Bedford, off A428.
Opening hours 2 pm – 6 pm; 28 April & 23 June. Plus 6 pm – 9 pm on 3 July, with music. And groups at other times by appointment.
Admission fee Adults £3; Children free.

This is a very interesting newish garden – the owners moved here in 1991 and have designed and planted it with a sense of style that is contemporary rather than nostalgic. Kathy Brown is a garden-writer and cookery-writer, and these interests have overlapped in such titles as *The Edible Flower Garden* (1999). But she has also written books about container gardening, bulbs and cottage gardening – all of which have to some extent been worked out in the garden here. She is very good on structure: the French garden is an essay in formal design. It starts right outside the house, with a terrace that has a *gâteau* of tiles and stone at its centre: box cones and gravelled parterres lead down to a circular fountain. Planting is another of her skills: the containers are exuberantly filled with all kinds of unconventional material – lupins for example – and this is one of the few gardens where groundcover roses have been made to grow well as loosely pendulous container plants. Elsewhere are masses of bulbs, some in grass and others in beds which may later be filled with herbs and roses. Gazebos, pergolas, a parterre leading to a wildflower meadow, a cottage garden and a wisteria walk are among the many other features. Definitely a garden to see now and return to in future, as it develops.

 Features Good modern design; bulbs; old roses; wildflower meadow; containers; succulents; grasses; cream teas.

Owned by Simon & Kathy Brown
Number of gardeners owners only
Size 1.2ha (3 acres)

Seal Point

7 WENDOVER WAY, LUTON LU2 7LS

Tel 01582 611567
Location North-east Luton: turn north off Stockingstone Road (A505) into Felstead Way, then second left.
Opening hours 2 pm – 6 pm; 10 & 11 August. And by appointment.
Admission fee Adults £2.50.

This small town garden on a difficult site has been much praised: 'this garden is definitely different!' says Mrs Johnston. It manages to combine a large number of different features with an overall oriental theme, including a bonsai garden arranged on a slate moraine. Plants are important too: the trees are well-chosen for their ornamental effect, and the Johnstons use foliage plants and grasses to intensify the dramatic impact of the plantings. Mrs Johnston was BBC Gardener of 1999 for the south-east region: all the ornaments in the garden were made by her and her husband.

 Features Interesting design; grasses; tea, coffee & biscuits.

Owned by David & Danae Johnston
Number of gardeners owners only
Size 0.4ha (1 acre)

Swiss Garden

OLD WARDEN, BIGGLESWADE SG18 9EA

Tel 01767 626255   **Fax** 01767 627443
Website www.swissgarden@deed.bedfordshire.gov.uk
Location 1½ miles west of Biggleswade.
Opening hours 1 pm – 6 pm (but 10 am – 6 pm on Sundays & Bank Holidays); daily; March to September. 11 am – 3 pm; Sundays & New Year's Day; January, February & October.
Admission fee Adults £3; Concessions £2. Subject to review.

This rustic, gothic landscape garden was largely developed by the Shuttleworth family in the 19th century. It is a remarkable relic: a pleasure ground of winding paths and sinuous waterways, little cast-iron bridges and picturesque huts, quaint kiosks and soaring ironwork arches, gullies and ferneries, vast conifers and cheerful rhododendrons, and an early grotto-glasshouse (note the small panes of glass) planted as a fernery. In short – most enjoyable to visit.

 Features Picturesque landscape; rhododendrons; Pulhamite grotto; fernery; Swiss cottage; new plantings (2000); publications and souvenirs shop; restaurant.

Owned by Bedfordshire County Council
English Heritage grade II*

Toddington Manor

TODDINGTON LU5 6HJ

Tel 01525 872576 **Fax** 01525 874555
Location Signed from Toddington village.
Opening hours 12 noon – 5 pm; Monday – Saturday;
May to August. Closed 20 July.
Admission fee Adults £3.50; OAPs £2.50; Children £2.

This garden is now in its prime, and has all
been made by the owners since 1979 around
some magnificent old trees. It has some
excellent features, notably a lime avenue
which leads into a cherry walk, and a
wonderfully high standard of maintenance.
The walled garden has long beds of
delphiniums and peonies and a fine garden
of herbs (culinary, medicinal and insect-
repelling), while the double herbaceous
border has recently been extended and is
now 100m long and 6m wide. There is also
good modern rose garden of white and
yellow floribundas interplanted with
philadelphus. Further away from the house
are a wild garden and three small ponds:
visiting children may borrow nets to go
dipping.

Features Woodland walks; roses
(mainly old-fashioned); herbs;
mature conifers; good herbaceous borders;
largest *Tilia tomentosa* 'Petiolaris' in the
British Isles.

Owned by Sir Neville & Lady Bowman-Shaw
Number of gardeners 3
Size 2.2ha (6 acres), plus 8ha (20 acres) of woodland

Woburn Abbey

WOBURN MK17 9WA

Tel 01525 290666 **Fax** 01525 290271
Website www.woburnabbey.co.uk
Location 1½ miles from Woburn on A4012.
Opening hours 11 am – 4 pm; daily; 24 March to 29
September. 11 am – 4 pm; Saturdays & Sundays; 1
January to 23 March, & 30 September to 28 October.
Admission fee Park: £5 per car.

Woburn may not have the reputation of
being a gardeners' garden, but Humphry
Repton, who designed the park, considered
it one of his finest achievements. The deer
park is home to ten different types of deer:
one is the Muntjac deer from China, some
of which escaped during World War II and
have spread through much of England.
Nearer the house are a pinetum and a
quercetum (a collection of oaks), cedars,
redwoods, huge swamp cypresses and such
rarities as mature specimens of the hardy
'rubber tree' *Eucommia ulmoides* and *Acer
triflorum*. Elsewhere are lily ponds,
fritillaries, wild orchids and masses of
naturalised *Narcissus* – more than 100
daffodil cultivars. The private gardens
(closed for restoration but scheduled to re-
open in 2003) are simple and formal, mainly
19th-century and Italianate, but they include
a circular hornbeam maze with a Chinese
pavilion at its centre, herbaceous borders, a
rose garden, a camellia house, and lots of
good statues.

Features Mature conifers; fine
collection of trees; deer park; tallest
Zelkova sinica (17m) in the British Isles; two
shops; lunches & teas.

Owned by The Marquess of Tavistock
Number of gardeners 5
Size 16.8ha (42 acres)
English Heritage grade I

Wrest Park

Silsoe MK45 4HS

Tel 01525 860152 (weekends)
Location ¾ mile east of Silsoe.
Opening hours 10 am – 6 pm; Saturdays, Sundays &
Bank Holiday Mondays; 29 March to September. Plus
10 am – 5 pm; Saturdays & Sundays; October.
Admission fee Adults £3.40; Concessions £2.60;
Children £1.70.

The 'English Versailles' is dominated by a
graceful long canal which runs down to the
classical domed pavilion built by Thomas
Archer in 1710. Capability Brown came here
later, but worked around the earlier design.
The house came later still, in the 1830s.

Many historic garden buildings have
survived, some from as far back as the 1730s
and others from the 19th century, including
the orangery, the Mithraic altar, the bowling
green house and the Chinese temple and
bridge. In the walled garden and around the
house are a rose garden, bedding displays
and glasshouses. In the park are handsome
specimen trees, including a fine example of
the purple-leaved birch (*Betula pendula*
'Purpurea').

Features Grand parterres; long vistas;
largest pink chestnut (*Aesculus ×
carnea*) in the British Isles; gift shop; light
refreshments.

Owned by English Heritage
Size 36ha (90 acres)
English Heritage grade I

BERKSHIRE

Even in its attenuated post-1974 shape, Berkshire is well provided with good gardens. Few of its great historic gardens and landscapes are open to the public, though Berkshire's only Grade I landscape, Windsor Great Park, is of course open all the time, while Inkpen House (Grade II*) and Donnington Grove (Grade II) both open for the National Gardens Scheme. Lutyens's great masterpiece Folly Farm (Grade II*) changed hands recently, and is at present no longer visitable. And the wonderful plantsman's garden at Old Rectory Cottage at Tidmarsh is no longer open to the public, following the death of Bill Baker in 2001. There are good specimen trees in Windsor Great Park and the grounds of Eton College. Nurseries are less common than garden centres: Henry Street Garden Centre at Arborfield is one of the more individual ones, with a special line in roses. Berkshire has comparatively few National Collections, though the Crown Estates have no less than nine of them at the Savill Gardens and Valley Gardens, just over the border into Surrey.

Blencathra

OFF THE RIDGES, FINCHAMPSTEAD, WOKINGHAM RG40 3SS

Tel 0118 973 4563
Location Down a private drive at the north-west end of the Finchampstead Ridges.
Opening hours For National Gardens Scheme & the Red Cross. And by appointment.
Admission fee Adults £3; Children free.

Dr & Mrs Gifford bought this 11-acre plot in 1964, built their house on it and set about making a garden with little or no hired help. Now they enjoy a woodland garden where the natural flowers (bluebells, dog mercury, primroses, orchids) are supplemented by ornamental shrubs – especially rhododendrons, azaleas, conifers and heathers. Three small lakes and a bog garden have increased the opportunities. The result is a model for our times – maximum returns for minimum effort.

 Features A woodland garden in the natural style; rhododendrons & azaleas.
Owned by Dr & Mrs F.W. Gifford
Number of gardeners owners only, plus occasional help
Size 4.2ha (11 acres)

Englefield House

ENGLEFIELD, THEALE, READING RG7 5EN

Tel 0118 930 2221   **Fax** 0118 930 2226
Website www.englefield.co.uk
Location On A340, 1 mile from M4 Jct12.

Opening hours 10 am – 6 pm; Mondays (plus Tuesdays – Thursdays from 1 April to 1 November); all year.

Admission fee Adults £3; Children free.

The garden at Englefield descends dramatically from the hill above the house through open woodland where mature native trees like oak and beech are mixed with Victorian conifers. The underplanting was begun in 1936 with advice from Wallace & Barr and has continued ever since. Here are tremendous collections of camellias, rhododendrons, eucryphias, acers, magnolias, davidias, azaleas (many of them the nearly extinct Ghent varieties) and other unusual trees and shrubs. A water-garden borders the stream which falls from a grotto in the hill. On the lower levels, stone balustrades and staircases make a background for deep borders and small, enclosed gardens of differing character. They date from the 1850s, though Lanning Roper reworked them in 1976. They include a pebble garden and a children's garden with joke fountains springing from four little statues. There are drifts of daffodils and other spring and summer bulbs and wonderful autumn colour. A walled kitchen garden has lately been restored producing many varieties of fruit, vegetables, herbs and flowers. The garden is enclosed by a deer park, with magnificent views over the lake and surrounding countryside.

 Features Woodland garden; roses (mainly old-fashioned); rhododendrons & azaleas; daffodils; good herbaceous borders; deer park; refreshments on NGS days.

Owned by Sir William & Lady Benyon
Number of gardeners 2
Size 2.8ha (7 acres)
English Heritage grade II

Foxgrove

SKINNERS GREEN, ENBORNE,
NEWBURY RG14 6RE

Tel 01635 40554
Location On western edge of Skinner's Green.
Opening hours For National Gardens Scheme. Groups welcome by appointment.
Admission fee Adults £2; Children free.

Foxgrove is a plantsman's garden, linked to Louise Peters' nursery next door: Audrey Vockins is her aunt. Bulbs, alpines and herbaceous plants are Audrey's great interest. The hellebores, crocus and snowdrops give a great display in early spring. There are good shrubs (including more than 50 daphnes), roses and handsome small trees too. Louise's nursery is open from 10 am to 5 pm from Wednesday to Sunday but closed in August. It carries an interesting range of hardy and cottage garden plants, including several new *Saxifraga* cultivars from the Czech Republic. Its speciality is snowdrops, which are sold by mail order 'in the green'. Other specialities – worth visiting the nursery to see – are hellebores, grasses and penstemons, and some newly-planted herbaceous borders. Louise Peters' planted-up troughs have been a great feature of RHS spring flower shows recently.

 Features Snowdrops; good herbaceous borders; primulas; spring bulbs; cyclamen & colchicums in autumn; bluebells; bank garden; tea & cakes.

Owned by Miss Audrey Vockins
Size 0.8ha (2 acres)

The Harris Garden

UNIVERSITY OF READING, WHITEKNIGHTS, READING RG6 6AS

Tel 0118 931 8071 **Fax** 0118 931 6577
Location On A327, 1 mile south-east of Reading.
Opening hours 2 pm – 6 pm; 12 May, 23 June, 21 July & 22 September.
Admission fee Adults £2.50; Children free.

The Harris Garden was begun as recently as 1988, though it occupies what was once part of a famous landscape garden created by the 4th Duke of Marlborough (while still Marquess of Blandford) between 1798 and 1817. The idea was to develop a garden as an adjunct to the teaching of horticulture, landscape and botany by the School of Plant Sciences at the University. It is very much a gardener's garden, full of horticultural interest. Annuals, for example, are grown both in traditional drifts of individual plants, and in experimental mixtures. There is a foliage border of tender plants grown solely for their spectacular sub-tropical effects. The winter garden concentrates upon plants whose flowers, bark or form gives particular pleasure in the dark months of the year. The orchard is not a fruit garden, but a collection of ornamental crab apples underplanted with wildflowers and bulbs which flower from January to the time when apple blossom fills the air. There is a large heather garden, where plants are in turn interplanted with dwarf pines: it is designed to lead naturally to a wildflower meadow. The walled garden has been developed as a traditional kitchen garden, with fruit trained on the walls, vegetables, herbs and flowers. The formal gardens include an area where Gertrude Jekyll's famous flower borders at Munstead Wood have been reproduced to illustrate her ideas on colour planting – Richard Bisgrove is the great expert on Jekyll's planting style and one of the team behind the Harris Garden. But there is much more to see, including the woodland garden, a golden garden, a cherry bowl (flowering cherries around a circular clearing with bulbs which flower at the same time), a primula dell, a pond garden, an autumn foliage bed and a splendid mixed border nearly 150 yards (130m) long. The garden is well supported by a friends organisation – details are available from the Hon. Secretary at the School of Plant Sciences.

Features Sub-tropical plants; roses (mainly old-fashioned); plantsman's collection of plants; herbs; plants under glass; good herbaceous borders; fine collection of trees; Mediterranean shrubs; hardy annuals; heathers; primula dell; new water garden (2002); teas.

Owned by University of Reading
Number of gardeners 4
Size 5ha (12 acres)
NCCPG National Collections *Iris* (species)

Frogmore Gardens

THE HOME PARK, WINDSOR CASTLE, WINDSOR SL4 2JG

Tel 01753 869898 **Fax** 01753 832290
Location Access varies: please contact 01753 869898 ext. 2347.
Opening hours 10 am – 5.30 pm; 3 days in May; for NGS. 10 am – 7 pm; 24, 25 & 26 August.
Admission fee Adults £3; Children free in May. Adults £5.20; Children £3.20 in August. (2001 prices).

Frogmore is a royal residence: most of the house dates from the reign of George III. The grounds were first laid out in 1793, when the lake was excavated and the spoil used to create a series of mounds and banks. The many garden buildings include a gothic temple, an Indian kiosk, a tea house and the royal mausoleum where many members of the royal family have been buried since the middle of the 19th century. During the 1920s and 1930s, the gardens were extensively developed by the planting of ornamental trees and shrubs, underplanted by bulbs. The May openings are less expensive than the August ones, because the price for the latter includes a visit to the house. The house may also be visited in May, but there is a separate charge for it then.

 Features Historic landscape & buildings.

Owned by The Royal Family
Number of gardeners 5
Size 14ha (35 acres)
English Heritage grade II*

The Living Rainforest

HAMPSTEAD NORREYS, THATCHAM, NEWBURY RG18 0TN

Tel 01635 202444 **Fax** 01635 202440
Website www.livingrainforest.org
Location Signed from Jct 13 on M4. From A34 southbound, follow signs to East Ilsey, then Hampstead Norreys.
Opening hours 10 am – 5.15 pm; daily; all year. Closed 25 & 26 December.
Admission fee Adults £4.50; Concessions £3.50; Children £2.50.

The Living Rainforest consists of two large landscaped glasshouses, computer-set to create two different rainforest climates. Each has a thickly planted collection of exotic plants of every kind, many of them rare or endangered. There is a particularly fine and near-comprehensive collection of tropical aroids, including the epiphytic *Anthurium warocqueanum* from Colombia and the terrestrial *A. watermaliense* from Costa Rica. The flowering plants are wonderful in winter when the tropical orchids flower, and in spring when the jade vine (*Strongylodon macrobotrys*) flowers for several months – it has even set seed here. Later, in the summer, *Victoria amazonica* becomes one of the great attractions when it fills one of the pools. But the Living Rainforest is fascinating whatever the season or the weather outside, and there are tropical monkeys, butterflies and birds too.

 Features Tropical plants from the Amazon basin and around the world; gift shop; refreshments.

Owned by The Living Rainforest
Size 1,860 sq.m. (20,000 sq.ft.) under glass

Old Rectory

BURGHFIELD RG3 3TH

Tel 0118 983 3200
Location Right at Hatch Gate Inn & first entrance on right.
Opening hours 11 am – 4 pm on 17 February; 11 am –
5 pm on 2 June (rare plant sale); 11 am – 5 pm on 30 June;
2 pm – 5 pm on 7 July. Groups at other times by
appointment.
Admission fee Adults £2; Children free.

This highly acclaimed garden was designed
by Ralph and planted by Esther Merton, a
first-rate plantswoman who knew exactly
what she wanted to achieve. She had a very
good eye for plants, and collected them
herself all over the world, as well as
exchanging gifts with her gardening friends
throughout Britain. Her legacy includes
wonderful roses, lush summer pots,
quantities of spring bulbs (some of them
rare), tiny alpines and unusual hellebores –
all of them extremely well grown. The *tour
de force* is a double herbaceous border where
plants build up their impact through
repetition, backed by yew hedges which get
taller towards the end, to cheat the
perspective. It leads to a pool framed by
dense plantings of strong foliage – ferns,
hostas, maples.

Features Snowdrops; rock garden;
plantsman's collection of plants; good
late herbaceous borders; stone troughs;
exotic displays in tubs; hellebores; lilies; teas.

Owned by A.R. Merton
Number of gardeners 2
Size 1.8ha (4½ acres)

Scotlands

COCKPOLE GREEN, WARGRAVE,
READING RG10 8QP

Tel 01628 822648
Location Between Cockpole Green & Warren Row, in
triangle between the A4130, the A321 & the A4.
Opening hours By appointment; groups welcome.
Admission fee Adults £3.

The garden at Scotlands has been made by
the owners over many years. The house is an
early barn conversion and the lawns in front
run down to a small lake with a fine swamp
cypress (*Taxodium distichum*) on one side
and a pinewood summerhouse after the
style of Repton on the other. Further down
still are more ponds, a waterfall and
waterside plantings in a woodland garden
where azaleas, camellias and pieris are
underplanted with naturalised bluebells and
primroses. The kitchen garden is partially
walled, with an 18th-century design brick-
and-flint gazebo and planted with rather
more flowers than vegetables: a formal herb
garden and a rose garden are each more
prominent than edible crops. It is formally
laid out in such a way that you appreciate
the dynamism of the design but
linger among the plants. There is one other
very handsome lay-out – a lawn with an oval
swimming pool in the centre, backed by yew
hedges which are stepped and staggered like
a stage-set. The colours are enhanced by
small semicircular herbaceous borders and
terracotta tubs planted with colourful
bedding plants.

Features Good design; good plants;
fine trees, especially grey cedars,
chestnuts and copper beeches.

Owned by Mr Michael & The Hon. Mrs Payne
Number of gardeners 1
Size 1.6ha (4 acres)

BUCKINGHAMSHIRE

Buckinghamshire is wonderfully stocked with large estates and grand, historic gardens. All three Grade I landscapes – Cliveden, Stowe and West Wycombe Park – are regularly open to the public, as are the two Rothschild gardens at Ascott and Waddesdon. These estates also have many fine trees. The National Gardens Scheme is active in the county, and lists over 50 gardens to visit, often in village clusters. Dorneywood Gardens at Burnham are particularly worth seeing on their all-too-rare openings for the National Gardens Scheme. There are comparatively few National Collections in the county, though the *Pleione* species and hybrids at Butterfields Nursery in Bourne End, visitable only by appointment (01628 525455), have long been a feature of RHS shows. There is a good selection of garden centres in the county: Buckingham Nurseries & Garden Centre is one of the best known and there is a large Blooms of Bressingham Garden Centre in the old walled garden at Dorney Court.

Ascott

WING, LEIGHTON BUZZARD LU7 0PS

Tel 01296 688242 **Fax** 01296 681904
Website www.nationaltrust.org.uk
Location ½ mile east of Wing.
Opening hours Garden only: 2 pm – 6 pm; Tuesday – Sunday; 2 – 30 April & 6 August to 13 September. Plus Wednesdays & last Sundays in month; 1 May to 1 August. And 18 & 25 September.
Admission fee Garden only: £4 Adults; £2 Children.

Ascott is an opulent late-Victorian extravaganza. It was largely planned by Leopold de Rothschild and planted with trees and shrubs supplied by Sir Harry Veitch. The Dutch garden, the Venus garden and the topiary sundial date from this period – roughly 1880–1920. The topiary sundial is famous: its Roman numerals are planted in box and the gnomon at the centre is made of golden yew grafted onto green Irish yew. The motto – in Latin – reads 'Light and shade by turn, but love always'. Much in these old gardens has been restored, re-made and re-planted in recent years. The bedding in the Dutch garden relies heavily upon the sumptuous leaves of coleus (*Solenostemon* cultivars), cannas and the ornamental cabbage 'Tokio': all were popular 100 years ago. Other parts of the garden have been re-designed in a more modern idiom. The 'long walk' now has a serpentine shape. The old fern garden has been replanted as a box parterre and is now known as the sunken garden. And there is a new 'planet topiary garden', built to resemble the astrological symbols of the 12 planets and showing their position in the sky at the very moment Sir Evelyn and Lady de Rothschild were each born. But there are fine old trees, and new plantings too, including a young collection of modern magnolias and groups of *Davidia involucrata, Aesculus indica* and *Juglans nigra*.

 Features Woodland garden; topiary; mature conifers; good herbaceous borders; spring bulbs; Dutch garden; tallest *Cedrus atlantica* 'Aurea' in the British Isles.

Owned by The National Trust
English Heritage grade II*

Blossoms

COBBLERS HILL, GREAT MISSENDEN
HP16 9PW

Tel & Fax 01494 863140
Location 2½ miles north-west of Great Missenden by Rignall Road, signed Butlers Cross, to Kings Lane about 1 mile on right, then to top of Cobblers Hill. Right at yellow stone markers and right after 50 yards.
Opening hours By appointment only.
Admission fee £1.50 for National Gardens Scheme.

Ⓟ ⬤

The bones of this fascinating plantsman's garden go back to 1925 when a previous owner started to plant up a 4-acre field and an acre of beech wood filled with bluebells. Dr and Mrs Hytten have lived here since 1975 and have benefited from the substantial windbreaks planted in the 1920s and 1930s. Having once been open – there is still a fine view of the Misbourne Valley – Blossoms is essentially a woodland garden now, with an established apple orchard and some lusty specimen trees including a liquidambar and a fern-leaved *Fagus sylvatica* 'Asplenifolia'. The Hyttens have thickened up the woodland themselves and made good collections of maples, eucalyptus and willows, together with some more unusual trees, such as *Tetradium daniellii, Davidia* and *Metasequoia*. Add on a herbaceous border, a scree garden, a rock

garden, a rare collection of herbaceous plants, a cutting garden, a number of very large climbing roses, a small lake, smaller ponds, patios and statues (mostly wood-carvings) – and the scale and variety of the owners' achievement will be apparent. The owners say that spring and autumn are the best seasons, but like all good plantsman's gardens there is lots of interest throughout the year.

 Features A plantsman's collection of good plants; woodland walks; trees, ponds & wooden sculptures; rock garden; good herbaceous borders; teas by arrangement.

Owned by Dr & Mrs Frank Hytten
Number of gardeners owners only
Size 2ha (5 acres)

Buckingham Nurseries and Garden Centre

10 TINGEWICK ROAD, BUCKINGHAM
MK18 4AE

Tel 01280 813556   **Fax** 01280 815491
Website www.buckingham-nurseries.co.uk
Location 1½ miles west of Buckingham, on A421.
Opening hours Summer: 8.30 am – 6 pm; Monday – Friday. 10 am – 4 pm; Sundays. Winter: 8.30 am – 5.30 pm; Monday – Friday. 10 am – 4 pm; Sundays. Open late on Thursdays: 7.30 pm in summer & 7 pm in winter.

Buckingham Nurseries is a well-established nursery attached to a flourishing garden centre where you can find all the extras which are so much a part of visiting a garden centre today – pots, furniture, retailing areas, a restaurant and an aquatics centre. But the nursery's speciality is hedging – it produces a very wide range of bare-root hedging plants and tree plants for ornamental and forestry use. In the display garden are lots of sample strips of hedging, some mature and others more recently planted: these give customers an opportunity to see how a hedge will develop over the years. The website is helpful, too.

Owned by R.J. & P.L. Brown

Butterfields Nursery

HARVEST HILL, BOURNE END SL8 5JJ

Tel 01628 525455
Location Off B476.
Opening hours 9 am – 5 pm (usually).

Butterfields Nursery has two very different specialities: pleiones and dahlias. Ian Butterfield is far and away the most important breeder and seller of pleiones, having bred and selected forms and hybrids for many years – and creates quite a sensation when he exhibits at shows like the Chelsea Flower Show. Two-thirds of all the species, hybrids, forms and grexes of pleiones sold in England are unique to Butterfields Nursery. The dahlias are chosen primarily as garden plants and range across all the classes.

NCCPG National Collections Pleione

Campden Cottage

51 CLIFTON ROAD, CHESHAM BOIS, AMERSHAM HP6 5PN

Tel 01494 726818
Location Signed from A416 between Amersham on the Hill & Chesham.
Opening hours 2 pm – 6 pm; 3 March, 14 April, 12 May, 9 June, 14 July, 18 August, 8 September, 6 October.
Admission fee Adults £1.50; Children free.

This plantsman's garden crams a vast number of rare and interesting plants into its half acre and, like all good gardens, has lots to enjoy at every time of the year. The owners have given the garden a good structure and placed plants together to show the contrasts and harmonies of their colours and shapes. They say they are busiest at their March opening when people come to see the hellebores.

 Features A plantsman's garden; hellebores.

Owned by Mr & Mrs P. Liechti
Number of gardeners 1
Size 0.2ha (½ acre)

Chenies Manor

CHENIES, RICKMANSWORTH WD3 6ER

Tel & Fax 01494 762888
Location Centre of Chenies village.
Opening hours 2 pm – 5 pm; Wednesdays, Thursdays & Bank Holidays; April to October. Plus special plant sale on 21 July from 10 am to 5 pm (£4).
Admission fee Garden only, £3; House & garden, £5.

The richly planted gardens at Chenies Manor are full of variety but designed to complement the Elizabethan house. Their most spectacular period is spring – April and early May – when 300 different cultivars of tulip come into flower in and around the sunken garden, modelled on Hampton Court. All come from Bloms and all are clearly labelled: each is grown in groups of 10 to 50 bulbs and offers a wonderful opportunity to learn about tulips. Later comes the summer bedding, interspersed with herbaceous plantings – red dahlias with white forms of *Campanula latiloba*, for example. And there are colour borders everywhere: one very easy but effective one mixes *Alchemilla mollis* with catmint and *Sisyrinchium striatum*. Add in a Physic garden for herbs, a grass labyrinth, a yew maze, and some beautiful old lawns and yew hedges, and you have a garden of great harmony.

Features Bulbs; topiary; herbs; fruit; physic garden; award-winning maze; tea, coffee, homemade cakes.

Owned by Mrs A. MacLeod Matthews
Size 1.8ha (4½ acres)
English Heritage grade II*

Cliveden

TAPLOW, MAIDENHEAD SL6 0JA

Tel 01628 605069   **Fax** 01628 669461
Website www.nationaltrust.org.uk
Location 2 miles north of Taplow, M4 Jct7.
Opening hours 11 am – 6 pm (4 pm in November & December); daily; 13 March to 31 December.
Admission fee Adults (Grounds) £6; Children £3.

Cliveden is a vast (and very important) landscape garden, filled with whatever money could buy: balustrading from the Villa Borghese in Rome, the dramatic 'Fountain of Love' and a huge parterre below the house. The best parts are the Arcadian ilex wood, quite magical, and newly restored rose garden, originally made by Geoffrey Jellicoe in 1932. But allow lots of time to visit this garden of wonders.

Features Woodland garden; snowdrops; roses (mainly modern); fruit; good herbaceous borders; bluebells; good autumn colour; tallest *Juglans cinerea* (24m) in the British Isles; National Trust shop, Wednesday – Sunday; light refreshments and meals, Wednesday – Sunday.

Owned by The National Trust
NCCPG National Collections *Catalpa*
English Heritage grade I

Great Barfield

BRADENHAM, HIGH WYCOMBE HP14 4HP

Tel 01494 563741
Location Turn into Bradenham village from A4010 at Red Lion & first right – ½ mile.
Opening hours 2 pm – 4.30 pm on 10 February; 2 pm – 5.30 pm on 7 April; 10 am – 4 pm on 26 & 27 October. And by appointment.
Admission fee Adults £1.50; Children (under 16) free.

One of the best modern plantsman's gardens in southern England, not least because of its fluid modern design and comprehensive labelling. Whatever the season, Great Barfield amazes the visitor by the number and variety of plants in flower and their thoughtful placing.

Features Woodland garden; snowdrops; plantsman's collection of plants; good herbaceous borders; wonderful hellebores in February; good autumn colour & fruits; homemade teas.

Owned by Richard Nutt
Number of gardeners owner only
Size 0.6ha (1½ acres)
NCCPG National Collections *Iris unguicularis*; *Leucojum*

Hughenden Manor

HIGH WYCOMBE HP14 4LA

Tel 01494 755573   **Fax** 01494 463310
Website www.nationaltrust.org.uk
Location 1½ miles north of High Wycombe.

Opening hours 12 noon – 5 pm; Saturdays & Sundays in March; then Wednesday – Sunday plus Bank Holiday Mondays from 3 April to 3 November.
Admission fee Garden only £1.50. Park & woodland free.

Hughenden is not a great garden, but interesting for its association with Disraeli. The garden was made by his wife in the 1860s and has a classic gardenesque planting of specimen trees on the North Lawn and a more Italianate design on the southern side. The National Trust has restored it, using photographs taken in 1881, so that the parterres are once again planted with Victorian annuals and bedding.

 Features Good herbaceous borders; 61 old apple varieties; rolling parkland; formal Victorian parterres with bright bedding out as in Disraeli's day; National Trust shop; new stableyard restaurant.

Owned by The National Trust
English Heritage grade II

Lower Icknield Farm

LOWER ICKNIELD WAY, GREAT
KIMBLE, AYLESBURY HP17 9TX

Tel & Fax 01844 343436
Location On B4009 between Great Kinble & Longwick.
Opening hours 9 am – 5.30 pm; daily; all year. Closed from Christmas to New Year.
Admission fee Free.

The owners say that the display garden attached to Lower Icknield Farm Nurseries is best from July to September when their National Collection of *Argyranthemum* is in flower. They now have over 110 cultivars of these shrubby daisies from Madeira and the Canaries: this is at least four times as many as any other nursery offers. But they also

have a good collection of tender salvias, mainly the Mexican species like *S. greggii* and the *S.* × *jamensis* hybrids, and a fair list of hardy grasses. All the plants they sell are raised on the nursery – none is bought in – and they sell no sundries apart from their own brand of growing compost. Plants are what they raise, and there is a succession of half-hardy patio- and houseplants for sale throughout the year, as well as hardy bedding and a good range of unusual hardy perennials.

 Features Good display garden; salvias; argyranthemums.

Owned by Mr & Mrs J. Baldwin
Number of gardeners 1
Size 0.8ha (2 acres)
NCCPG National Collections *Argyranthemum*

The Manor House

BLEDLOW, PRINCES RISBOROUGH
HP27 9PB

Tel 020 7584 4243   **Fax** 020 7823 1476
Location Off B4009.
Opening hours 2 pm – 6 pm; 5 May & 23 June for National Gardens Scheme. And by appointment.
Admission fee £4.50.

This is one of the greatest gardens of our times: beautifully planted and well maintained, it has all been made on thin chalk soil since 1969. There are four parts: first, the garden 'proper' round the house, enclosed by hedges of beech, hornbeam or yew. Best is the armillary garden, an exercise in topiary with the sphere at its centre, surrounded by four cubes of yew, smaller hedges and labels of box. Next comes the walled garden with a gazebo in the centre whose eight trellised posts are planted with clematis and rambling roses. The central grass walk is lined with apple trees trained as spheres around a wire globe: they rise from parterre boxes of teucrium, each planted with a different herb – sage, chives, Greek oregano and so on. The third part of the garden is quite different – 2½ acres of sculpture garden started in 1991 and already remarkably mature. The land has been contoured to maximise the movement of the surface, and give contrast of height and depth. Its fluid modern design is a great foil to the formal gardens around the house. The presiding spirit is a life-size gorilla by Michael Cooper. The fourth part of the garden is different again – 4 acres of water garden, started in 1979 on the site of three old watercress beds. The 13 springs which issue from its sides are the headwaters of the River Lyde, a tributary of the Thames. The steep valley sides are thickly planted with shrubs and herbaceous plants. A wooden walkway, Japanese in style, takes you round the edge of the lakes at the bottom. The muddy banks are planted with candelabra primroses, gunneras, hostas and astilbes. Unlike the rest of the garden, this part is open daily (and free) from dawn to dusk.

Features Good herbaceous borders; sculptures; new water feature by William Pye.

Owned by Lord & Lady Carrington

Stowe Landscape Gardens

STOWE, BUCKINGHAM MK18 5EH

Tel 01280 822850 **Fax** 01280 822437
Website www.nationaltrust.org.uk
Location 3 miles north-west of Buckingham.
Opening hours 10 am – 5.30 pm or dusk (last admissions 4 pm); Wednesday – Sunday plus Bank Holiday Mondays;
3 March to 28 October. Plus 10 am – 4 pm; Wednesday – Sunday; 1 to 22 December. Closed 25 May 2002.
Admission fee Adults £4.60.

This mega-landscape is considered by some the most important in the history of gardens. William Kent designed the Temple of Venus (1731), the Shell Bridge (1733), and the highly original Temple of British Worthies (1734) which has statues of Alfred the Great, the Black Prince, Queen Elizabeth, John Milton and 12 further historic persons. Capability Brown laid out the Grecian Valley in the 1740s: it was while he was head gardener at Stowe that he developed his skill in simplifying formal gardens and creating the distinctive curves and contours which we now recognise as an essential feature of the English landscape garden. The National Trust has undertaken extensive restoration and renovation since it took over in 1989. Go if you have not been already, and go again if you have: from the start, Stowe was a highly fashionable garden with a political message. Stroll round slowly, and contemplate the history and symbolism of each feature. Read the National Trust's excellent guide and then go round again, this year, next year, every year, and commune with the *genius loci*.

Features Tallest *Fraxinus angustifolia* var. *lentiscifolia* (24m) and largest × *Crataemespilus grandiflora* (9m) in the British Isles; National Trust shop; light meals.

Owned by The National Trust
English Heritage grade I

Turn End

Townside, Haddenham, Aylesbury
HP17 8BG

Tel 01844 291383
Location Turn at Rising Sun in Haddenham, then
300 yards on left. Park in street.
Opening hours 2 pm – 5.30 pm; 24 March & 6 May for
NGS. Groups by appointment.
Admission fee Adults £2; Children 50p.

Peter Aldington was once a young architect,
much influenced by Le Corbusier and James
Stirling. In 1963 he and his wife bought this
plot and built their house – a modern
architectural classic, much photographed,
cited, visited and copied (and now listed).
Aldington believed that his job as an
architect was to make connections and
create forms which enclosed spaces for
people to use and enjoy. He then set out to
apply the same principles to his garden,
drawing upon his love of textures and
materials to design and plant it. The garden,
like the house, became one of the most
acclaimed to be made in the latter half of the
20th century. Over the years he was able to
increase its size by small additions. It still
covers less than 1 acre, but never was space
so used to create an illusion of size. A
brilliant series of enclosed gardens, sunken
or raised, sunny or shady, each different and
yet harmonious, contrasts with lawns,
borders and glades. The story is told in *A
Garden & Three Houses* by Jane Brown
(Garden Art Press, 1999). Visitors are
requested to park well away from the house.

Features Brilliant design – a series of
spaces; roses (mainly old-fashioned);
rock garden; a plantsman's collection of
plants; ferns; grasses; refreshments on
NGS days.

Owned by Mr & Mrs Peter Aldington

Waddesdon Manor

Aylesbury HP18 0JH

Tel 01296 653203   **Fax** 01296 653212
Website www.waddesdon.org.uk
Location A41 Bicester & Aylesbury; 20 miles from Oxford.
Opening hours 10 am – 5 pm; Wednesday – Sunday &
Bank Holiday Mondays; 28 February to 22 December.
Admission fee Grounds only: Adults £3; Children £1.50.
RHS members free in March, September & October.

The garden at Waddesdon was laid out in
the 1870s and 1880s for Baron Ferdinand de
Rothschild by the French landscape designer
Elie Lainé: it is one of the finest Victorian
gardens in Britain. A grand Victorian park,
splendid formal gardens, a rococo aviary
and extravagant bedding are the first fruits
of restoring the grounds of this amazing
Rothschild palace. Last year (2001) they
planted a 3m wicker pannier with a
profusion of vegetables. This year (2002),
they are working to celebrate the Queen's
Golden Jubilee. On one side of the house
(where Oscar de la Renta's bedding plan
was last year) they are planting a ERII
monogram in yellow and green. On the
other side will be two enormous (15ft)
three-dimensional crowns based on the
crown jewels and decked with bedding
plants in red, white and blue. Baron
Ferdinand would most certainly have
approved.

Features Daffodils; good herbaceous
borders; new spring walk with 80,000
crocuses (1998); new tropical mound
(1998); gift & wine shop; tea-room.

Owned by The National Trust
English Heritage grade II*

West Wycombe Park

WEST WYCOMBE HP14 3AJ

Tel 01494 513569
Website www.nationaltrust.org.uk
Location West end of West Wycombe on A40.
Opening hours 2 pm – 6 pm; Sunday – Thursday;
April to August.
Admission fee Adults £2.60.

This park, with a lake in the shape of a swan, was made by Sir Francis Dashwood between 1735 and 1782, in a rococo style that was modified by later generations. It has been well restored and embellished by modern additions, including three modern eye-catchers designed by Quinlan Terry.

Owned by The National Trust
English Heritage grade I

CAMBRIDGESHIRE

Cambridgeshire has a good number of historic gardens. Though only Wimpole Hall is rated as Grade I, there is a great cluster of Grade II* and Grade II landscapes in Cambridge itself: these include the Botanic Gardens and the following colleges – Christ's, Emmanuel, King's, Queen's, St John's and Trinity (including Trinity Hall). The Backs are also rated Grade I – and one of the few places in the country where the strange but beautiful parasite *Lathraea clandestina* has naturalised (RHS Garden Wisley is another). The Cambridge University Botanic Garden has by far the most exciting and comprehensive collection of plants in the county, especially for those trees which grow particularly well in the dry climate: many are the tallest of their kind in the British Isles. The National Gardens Scheme is well-supported in Cambridgeshire, and has quite a number of villages where several smaller gardens open together. In Cambridge itself, several colleges open for the National Gardens Scheme, including Clare, Emmanuel, King's, Newnham, Selwyn and Trinity. The county is thinly supplied by nurseries and garden centres, but Monksilver Nursery is a magnet for keen plantsmen and of international importance as a source of rare plants. Cambridgeshire has its fair share of National Collections – here too the lead is set by the University Botanic Garden with no less than nine National Collections from *Alchemilla* to *Tulipa*.

Abbots Ripton Hall

ABBOTS RIPTON PE28 2PQ

Tel 01487 773555   **Fax** 01487 773545
Location Off B1090.
Opening hours 2 pm – 5 pm; 19 May, 23 June, 7 July, 21 July & 4 August, for various local charities.
Admission fee Adults £3; Children (under 16) £1.50.

Humphrey Waterfield, Lanning Roper and Jim Russell all worked here, and few garden owners have had as many gardening friends as the Lord De Ramsey's parents, who made and re-made this garden over more than 50 years. The result is a garden of stylish individuality – as witness the gothic trellis work and the bobbles of yellow philadelphus – but also of great unity. The present Lady De Ramsey has retained the unity of style while replanting many of the borders. In early summer it can fairly claim to be the most beautiful garden in England.

Features Irises; grey border; Chinese bridge; trellis work; splendid herbaceous borders; tallest *Pyrus pyraster* (12m) in the British Isles; new arboretum of rare oaks; teas.

Owned by Lord De Ramsey
Number of gardeners 1, plus 2 part-time
Size 3.2ha (8 acres)
English Heritage grade II

Anglesey Abbey

LODE CB5 9EJ

Tel & Fax 01223 811200
Website www.nationaltrust.org.uk/angleseyabbey
Location Off B1102, signed from A14.
Opening hours 10.30 am – 5.30 pm (or dusk if sooner, last entry 4.30 pm); Wednesday – Sunday, plus Bank Holiday Mondays; 27 March to 27 October. Plus Mondays & Tuesdays from 1 July to 1 September. Winter Walk open Wednesday – Sunday from 2 January to 24 March & from 30 October to 22 December.
Admission fee Gardens: Adults £3.85, but £3.25 in winter.

Seventy years old, no more, but the grounds at Anglesey already deserve to be famous, for they are the grandest made in England during the 20th century. Majestic avenues and 35 acres of grass are the stuff of them: visit Anglesey when the horse chestnuts are out and tulips glow in the meadows. Large formal gardens, carved out of the flat site by yew hedges, house the 1st Lord Fairhaven's collection of classical and renaissance sculpture. Then there are smaller gardens, said to be more intimate, where thousands of dahlias and hyacinths hit the eye: glorious or vainglorious, Anglesey has no match.

Features Snowdrops; good herbaceous borders; landscaping on the grandest scale; long avenues of trees; dahlias; cyclamen; good autumn colour; winter walk; National Trust shop; licensed restaurant & picnic area.

Owned by The National Trust
English Heritage grade II*

Clare College Fellows' Garden

CLARE COLLEGE, CAMBRIDGE CB2 1TL

Tel 01223 333222   **Fax** 01223 333219
Website www.clare.cam.ac.uk
Location Enter from Clare Old Court, Trinity Lane or Queens Road.
Opening hours 10 am – 4.30 pm; daily; April to September.
Admission fee £2.

Two acres of views and vistas, walks and Hidcote-style enclosures filled with exquisite spring bulbs, spectacular hot-colour borders dating from the 1950s and seasonal bedding. The features include a pond garden, a scent garden and fine examples of taxodiums, metasequoias and *Tilia* 'Petiolaris'. The garden is rather low-lying and has suffered much from flooding (in October 2001, for example), so please telephone the porter's lodge on 01223 333200 before visiting.

Owned by The Master & Fellows
Number of gardeners 5
Size 0.8ha (2 acres)
English Heritage grade II*

Crossing House Garden

MELDRETH ROAD, SHEPRETH, ROYSTON SG8 6PS

Tel 01763 261071
Location 8 miles south of Cambridge off A10.
Opening hours Dawn – dusk; daily; all year.
Admission fee Donation to National Gardens Scheme.

Cambridge University Botanic Garden

CORY LODGE, BATEMAN STREET, CAMBRIDGE CB2 1JF

Tel 01223 336265   **Fax** 01223 336278
Location Entrance on Bateman Street, 1 mile to the south of the city centre & 5 mins from railway station.
Opening hours 10 am – 4 pm in winter, (5 pm in spring & autumn, 6 pm in summer); daily, except 25 December to 1 January.
Admission fee Adults £2.50; OAPs & Children £2.

This exceptionally attractive botanic garden is essential visiting for any garden lover: you could spend all day here and not be bored. Cambridge's is also one of the most beautiful and best maintained botanic gardens in the country. The limestone rock garden is one of its major attractions, where the plantings are arranged geographically. It overlooks the small lake whose surface is covered by waterlilies. Late spring is the time to see the nearby woodland garden. Here are fine tree specimens, including *Dipteronia sinensis*, *Tetracentron sinense* and the hardy paw-paw *Asimina triloba*, and a dawn redwood (*Metasequoia glyptostroboides*) grown from the original introduction of seed into the UK in 1948. Along the sides of the little stream which runs through the wood are candelabra primulas, astilbes, irises and a bed of the giant horse tail *Equisetum telmateia*. Late spring is also the time to see the horse chestnuts in flower, the Persian lilacs and the National Collections of shrubby *Lonicera* and *Ribes*. The garden has a very good collection of peony species, which are in some places interplanted with its hardy geraniums: perhaps one reason why the garden is so attractive is that its National Collections are of supreme

horticultural value. The garden also maintains 2 acres of (mainly herbaceous) systematic beds, created by the first curator Andrew Murray in 1845. A more modern addition is the genetic garden, whose scientific purpose is to demonstrate the natural effects of genes on plant morphology. Everywhere, too, are wonderful trees: was there ever a tree more beautiful than the type specimen of *Quercus* 'Warburgii'? The winter garden, planted in 1978, is the best in England, and draws on stems, leaves, bark and flowers to create its unique beauty. The superb series of linked glasshouses are a blessed sanctuary to horticulturally smart undergraduates during winter, but every aspect of the garden's existence is educationally aware and it attracts and interests school children too.

Features Good herbaceous borders; important rock garden; species roses; dry garden; genetics garden; British wild plants; winter garden; tallest *Catalpa* × *erubescens* 'Purpurea' (11m) in the British Isles (and 21 other record trees); shop in summer months; light refreshments.

Owned by University of Cambridge
Number of gardeners 21
Size 16ha (40 acres)
NCCPG National Collections *Alchemilla*; *Bergenia* (species & primary hybrids); *Fritillaria* (European species); *Geranium* (species & primary hybrids); *Lonicera* (species & primary hybrids); *Ribes* (species & primary hybrids); *Ruscus*; *Saxifraga* (European species); *Tulipa* (species & primary hybrids)
English Heritage grade II*

One of the wonders of modern gardening, the Crossing House celebrates the achievements of its makers since 1969, on an unpropitious site right beside the main railway line to Cambridge. Box-edged beds separated by granite paths contain thousands and thousands of different plants, densely planted in the cottage style. Shrubs, herbaceous plants, alpines and bulbs are planted in the same beds, to maximise the effect at all seasons. Peat beds, screes, arches, topiary, pools and raised beds are some of the features which add variety to the most intensely and intensively planted small garden in England. And every few minutes a London express whizzes past.

 Features Plantsman's collection of plants.

Owned by Mr & Mrs D.G. Fuller and Mr J. Marlar
Number of gardeners owners only
Size 0.1ha (¼ acre)

Docwra's Manor

SHEPRETH, ROYSTON SG8 6PS

Tel 01763 260235/261557
Location Off A10 to Shepreth.
Opening hours 10 am – 4 pm; Wednesdays & Fridays; all year; 2 pm – 5 pm, first Sunday of month from April to October. Plus 2 pm – 6 pm on 9 June for the NGS. And by appointment.
Admission fee Adults £3; Children free.

This is very much a plantsman's garden, whose lush profusion defies the dry, cold, alkaline site. Docwra's Manor is a series of small gardens – walled, wild, paved and so on – each brimming with interesting plants and good combinations. There is a sense of abundance, whatever the season. Interesting seedlings are encouraged and nurtured. Everything you see has been made by

Mrs Raven since she and her late husband bought the house in 1954. Do read John Raven's charming and erudite *The Botanist's Garden*, available from Mrs Raven by post for £10 and one of the classics of 20th-century garden-writing.

 Features Plantsman's collection of plants; good herbaceous borders; Mediterranean plants; teas for NGS openings.

Owned by Mrs John Raven
Number of gardeners ½
Size 1ha (2½ acres)

Elsworth Herbs

AVENUE FARM COTTAGE, 31 SMITH STREET, ELSWORTH, CAMBRIDGE CB3 8HY

Tel & Fax 01954 267414
Location Smith Street is the road through the middle of Elsworth; the garden is towards the western end.
Opening hours By appointment.
Admission fee free
Ⓟ ✿

This is an excellent example of a small boutique nursery attached to a National Collection – in this case two of them, *Artemisia* and *Nerium oleander*. Its range is wide – over 50 oleanders, for example, which is twice as many as anyone else – but the owners do not carry large stocks, so they are happy to propagate to order. The list of *Artemisia* species is quite unique – a triumph of plantsmanship.

Owned by Dr J. Twibell
NCCPG National Collections *Artemisia; Nerium oleander*

Elton Hall

Peterborough PE8 6SH

Tel 01832 280468   **Fax** 01832 280584
Location A605, 8 miles west of Peterborough.
Opening hours 2 pm – 5 pm; Wednesdays; June to August. Also Thursdays & Sundays in July & August, 3 & 4 June and 26 August.
Admission fee Garden only: Adults £3; Children free.

The house is a castellated extravaganza, but the Victorian gardens have been energetically restored in recent years and make Elton highly visitable. The knot garden and the collection of old roses are the high spots, best in June.

Features Roses (mainly old-fashioned); good herbaceous borders; fine collection of trees; handsome hedges; good colour plantings; new Gothic orangery (2000); Bressingham Plant Centre on site; tea-room.

Owned by Mr & Mrs William Proby
Number of gardeners 2½
Size 10.3ha (26 acres)
English Heritage grade II*

Hardwicke House

HIGH DITCH ROAD, FEN DITTON, CAMBRIDGE CB5 8TF

Tel & Fax 01223 292246
Location ½ mile east of village.
Opening hours 2 pm – 5 pm; 12 & 26 May. And by appointment.
Admission fee Adults £3; Children 50p.

This is an excellent plantsman's garden with an emphasis on herbaceous plants, roses and bulbs. The owner has a particular interest in Asia Minor, as witness an area devoted to Turkish plants and bulbs.

Features Plantsman's collection of plants; good herbaceous borders; bulbs.

Owned by John Drake
Number of gardeners owner only
Size 0.8ha (2 acres)
NCCPG National Collections Aquilegia

Monksilver Nursery

OAKINGTON ROAD, COTTENHAM CB4 8TW

Tel 01954 251555   **Fax** 01223 502887
Website www.monksilver.com
Location North of Cambridge: between Oakington & Cottenham.
Opening hours 10 am – 4 pm; Friday – Saturday; March to June, & October.

This remarkable nursery is deservedly fashionable. Monksilver specialises in finding and rescuing really rare plants. They say that their areas of speciality include *Anthemis*, *Arum*, *Astrantia*, *Aster*, bulbs, *Euphorbia*, ferns, *Galanthus*, grasses and sedges, *Hemerocallis* species, herbaceous perennials, *Lamium*, *Lathyrus*, *Monarda*, Pink Sheet plants ('pink sheets' are NCCPG search lists), *Pulmonaria*, *Ranunculus ficaria*, *Sedum*, *Solidago*, *Vinca*, rare shrubs and trees, variegated and wild collected plants. But the truth is that they list hundreds of other plants which are equally interesting. Many nurseries claim to have 'rare and unusual' plants: in the case of Monksilver, the boast is consistently true. A fifth of the catalogue changes each year.

Owned by Alan Leslie & Joe Sharman
NCCPG National Collections Vinca

Netherhall Manor

TANNERS LANE, SOHAM, ELY
CB7 5AB

Tel 01353 720269
Location In middle of Soham: turn right off the main road into Tanners Lane.
Opening hours 2 pm – 5 pm; 31 March, 5 May, 4 & 11 August.
Admission fee Adults £2.

This is an unusual garden, worth seeing for its individual collections of genera and plant groups which offer something of interest at every season. The hellebores are good in spring: a 30-year old bed is devoted to the true *Helleborus* 'Potter's Wheel' and another to white seedlings from Helen Ballard. Elsewhere are the seldom-seen *Helleborus* 'Günther Jürgl' (the first of the upright-facing cultivars), *H.* 'Circe' (long thought to be extinct) and *H.* 'Taurus'. Other goodies include *Primula auricula* 'Duke of Edinburgh' (also thought to be extinct) and a complete collection of *Fritillaria imperialis* cultivars. Better still is the collection of 19th-century *Pelargonium* cultivars, including 'Turtle's Surprise', and 'Sophie Dumaresque': all are grown from cuttings every year. Calceolarias, heliotropes, turban ranunculus and hyacinths are other specialities. The garden is immaculately maintained – its lawns are completely weedless – and includes a neat kitchen garden area.

 Features A great plantsman's garden; hyacinths; Victorian pelargoniums; florists' tulips.

Owned by Timothy Clark
Number of gardeners 1 part-time
Size 0.4ha (1 acre)

Padlock Croft

PADLOCK ROAD, WEST WRATTING
CB1 5LS

Tel & Fax 01223 290383
Location 2½ miles off B1307 (was A604) between Linton & Horseath.
Opening hours By appointment on weekdays.
Admission fee £1.

Less than an acre of plantsmanship, Padlock Croft is 'interesting' rather than 'exquisite' say the owners. But they do themselves an injustice, because this is a fascinating garden. Plants are crammed in, growing where they will do best. Until they retired last year, the Lewises had four National Collections of *Campanulaceae* – *Adenophora*, *Platycodon*, *Symphyandra* and *Campanula* itself. They still have very good personal collections of these genera and the *Campanula* collection itself includes every section of the genus. Visit the garden from mid-June onwards, when the campanulas are a knock-out.

 Features Rock garden; plantsman's collection of plants; all organic.

Owned by Peter & Susan Lewis
Number of gardeners owners only
Size 0.3ha (¾ acre)

Peckover House

NORTH BRINK, WISBECH PE13 1JR

Tel & Fax 01945 583463
Website www.nationaltrust.org.uk
Location Signed from Wisbech.
Opening hours Garden only: 12.30 pm – 5 pm; Saturday – Thursday; 31 March to 4 November.
Admission fee £2.50.

Peckover is a charming example of a not-too-grand Victorian garden, complete with monkey puzzle, fernery and spotted laurel shrubberies. Three of the orange trees in the conservatory are 300 years old.

 Features Victorian shrubberies; orangery; fernery; good bedding; herbaceous borders; roses.

Owned by The National Trust
Number of gardeners 1½
Size 0.8ha (2 acres)
English Heritage grade II

Wimpole Hall

ARRINGTON, ROYSTON SG8 0BW

Tel 01223 207257   **Fax** 01223 207838
Website www.wimpole.org
Location On A603, south-west of Cambridge.
Opening hours 10.30 am – 5 pm; daily except Monday & Friday (but open Good Friday & Bank Holiday Mondays); 23 March to 3 November. Open on Fridays in August.
Admission fee Garden: £2.50. Park: free.

Wimpole is an important classical 18th-century landscape where Bridgeman, Brown and Repton have all left their mark. It has a fine 19th-century collection of trees in and around the park, and grand Victorian parterres, where 72 flower-beds are arranged as eight Union Jack patterns and brightly arrayed with 24,000 bedding plants. There is a lot of new horticultural interest in the old kitchen garden, where fruit and vegetables are grown on a big scale to supply the National Trust restaurant, and flowers are grown for traditional decoration. An improving garden.

 Features Woodland garden; daffodils; Chinese bridge; parterre; major replanting of traditional greenhouses restored in walled garden (2000); National Trust shop; restaurant & tea-room.

Owned by The National Trust
Number of gardeners 3
NCCPG National Collections *Juglans*
English Heritage grade I

CHESHIRE

Cheshire has a fair number of important historic landscapes, including Adlington Hall, Arley Hall, Eaton Hall, Lyme Park and Tatton Park, but none is important enough to be accorded Grade I status by English Heritage. Nevertheless, Cheshire has a good reputation for gardens and gardening: it is a prosperous county, with rich soils and plenty of rainfall. This makes it a good area for nurseries and garden centres; probably the best known are Bridgemere Nurseries and Stapeley Water Gardens, both at Bridgemere, where the International Water Lily Society also has its base. Collinwood Nurseries at Mottram St Andrew is one of the leading growers of chrysanthemums, with an exceptionally comprehensive list of cultivars. Other specialist nurseries are Caddick's Clematis Nursery at Thelwall and the two rose nurseries C. & K. Jones at Tarvin and Fryer's Roses at Knutsford. The National Gardens Scheme lists a fair number of middle-sized gardens: azaleas and rhododendrons are particularly popular. Reaseheath College near Nantwich is a RHS Partner College. The RHS Flower Show at Tatton Park will take place from 17 to 21 July 2002.

Adlington Hall

MACCLESFIELD SK10 4LF

Tel 01625 829206   **Fax** 01625 828756
Website www.adlingtonhall.com
Location 5 miles north of Macclesfield off A523.
Opening hours 2 pm – 5 pm; Wednesdays; 19 June to 4 September. Also by prior appointment at any time for groups of 20 or more: telephone the guide on 01625 820875.
Admission fee £4.50 per person; £4 for groups of 20 or more.

It is good to see this important historic garden regularly open to the public again, and to know that the owners are adding their own improvements in another part of the estate. These include a young maze and a rose garden: a 'Father Tiber' water garden is planned for this year (2002). Many of the historical features have been restored: some are still awaiting their turn, but the owners' intention is to repair and rebuild them as soon as possible. One of the oldest is an avenue of yews planted in 1660. An ancient avenue of lime trees, planted in 1688 to celebrate the accession of William and Mary, leads to a woodland wilderness with follies. These include a Shell Cottage (1750s), a Temple to Diana, a Chinese bridge and a Hermitage.

 Features Historic landscape; ancient lime avenue; woodland garden.

Owned by Mrs C.J.C. Legh
Number of gardeners 4½
English Heritage grade II*

Arley Hall

GREAT BUDWORTH, NORTHWICH
CW9 6NA

Tel 01565 777353   **Fax** 01565 777465
Website www.arleyestate.zuunet.co.uk
Location 5 miles west of Knutsford.
Opening hours 11 am – 5 pm; Tuesday – Sunday;
31 March to 29 September.
Admission fee Adults £4.50; OAPs £3.90; Children £2.25.
RHS members free, except during special events.

Arley has pleached limes, red *Primula florindae*, clipped ilex cylinders (10m high) and pretty old roses. But its claim to fame is the double herbaceous border, backed and buttressed by yew hedges, perhaps the the oldest and certainly still one of the best in England.

 Features Topiary; avenues; two walled gardens; roses (mainly old-fashioned); good herbaceous borders; HHA/Christie's Garden of the Year in 1987; shop; lunches & light refreshments.

Owned by Viscount Ashbrook
Number of gardeners 4
Size 5ha (12 acres)
English Heritage grade II*

Bluebell Cottage Gardens & Lodge Lane Nursery

LODGE LANE, DUTTON,
WARRINGTON WA4 4HP

Tel & Fax 01928 713718
Website www.bluebellcottagegardens.co.uk
Location Turn off A533 midway between Runcorn & Northwich.

Opening hours Nursery: 10 am – 5 pm; Wednesday – Sunday & Bank Holidays; mid March to mid September. Garden: 10 am – 5 pm; Friday – Sunday & Bank Holidays; May to August.
Admission fee Adults £2; Children free. RHS members free. Nursery free at all times.

Lodge Lane Nursery is a RHS Partner Nursery selling more than 1,800 different herbaceous plants: it is particularly strong on penstemons, but there are big collections of achilleas, alliums, asters, campanulas, digitalis, euphorbias, gernaiums, nepeta, salvias and ornamental grasses too. Bluebell Cottage Gardens are the nursery's show gardens, well worth a visit in their own right. Both were started as recently as 1993. The gardens have been developed as a series of smaller gardens-within-the-garden. Each has a different theme: among them are the herb garden, the yellow garden, the ornamental grass garden and the scree bed. Large island beds are used to display herbaceous plants: the owners believe that there is nothing to beat them for colour (and sheer garden value) from early to late summer. The wildflower meadow was started in 1994 – three acres of native flowers (mainly perennial) among the grasses, including ox-eye daisies, yarrows, clovers and meadow cranesbill. At the far side of the meadow are three more acres of native woodland, carpeted with bluebells in May. Four RHS special events will take place during 2002: details from 020 7821 3408.

Features Wildflower meadow; 3,000 different plants.

Owned by Rod & Diane Casey
Number of gardeners owners, plus a little part-time help
Size 0.6ha (1½ acres), plus meadow & woodland.

Bridgemere Garden World

BRIDGEMERE, NANTWICH CW5 7QB

Tel 01270 521100   **Fax** 01270 520215
Location M6 Jct 15 & 16: follow signs.
Opening hours 8 am – 7 pm (5 pm in winter); daily; all year except 25 & 26 December.
Admission fee free, but under review.

More than 20 immaculate show gardens in different styles and the television set of *Gardeners' Diary* are just some of Bridgemere's many attractions. All have recently been re-made, together with a complete replica of the garden which won top prize at the RHS Tatton Park Flower Show in 1999. Further improvements and additions are planned for 2002. Definitely worth a visit, whatever the season. Bridgemere will be hosting a two events in conjunction with the RHS in 2002: a talk by Roy Lancaster on 'A Plantsman's Garden' on 25 May, and another by Penelope Hobhouse on 'Gardening History' on 3 October. Full details are available on the RHS website www.rhs.org.uk

Features Woodland garden; roses (ancient & modern); rock garden; plantsman's collection of plants; herbs; plants under glass; fruit; good herbaceous borders; flowering cherries new to UK; several shops, as well as the famous garden centre; refreshments.

Owned by J. Ravenscroft
Number of gardeners 3
Size 2.2ha (6 acres)
NCCPG National Collections *Cimicifuga*

Capesthorne Hall

SIDDINGTON, MACCLESFIELD SK11 9JY

Tel 01625 861221   **Fax** 01625 861619
Website www.capesthorne.com
Location A34, 3 miles south of Alderley Edge.
Opening hours 12 noon – 5 pm; Wednesdays, Sundays & Bank Holidays; April to October.
Admission fee Adults £4; OAPs £3; Children £2.

There are lots of interesting things to see at Capesthorne Hall, provided you are prepared to explore the grounds and find them. Fine trees are certainly a feature: the Victorian arboretum contains some very vigorous wellingtonias and chestnuts, supplemented by recent plantings over the last 50 years. Vernon Russell-Smith designed the formal lakeside gardens in the 1960s: mixed borders of shrub roses and herbaceous plants. Along the rhododendron walk is a splendid mixture of hardy hybrids interspersed with *Rhododendron ponticum* and the sweet-scented *R. luteum*. They flourish under a canopy of tall English oaks and wild cherries. Here too are two cork trees, *Quercus suber*. By the time you have discovered the rose arbour, the avenue of American hawthorns, the ice house and the golden glade (planted to commemorate the golden wedding of Sir Walter and Lady Bromley-Davenport in 1983), you will have some measure of just how much the garden has to offer.

Features Woodland garden; fine collection of trees; historic park; tea-room.

Owned by W.A. Bromley-Davenport
Number of gardeners 2

Cholmondeley Castle Gardens

MALPAS SY14 8AH

Tel & Fax 01829 720383
Location Off A49 Tarporley-Whitchurch road.
Opening hours 11.30 am – 5 pm; Wednesdays, Thursdays, Sundays & Bank Holiday Mondays. 29 March to 29 September.
Admission fee Adults £3; Children £1.50. RHS members free in June.

The gardens below this handsome early 19th-century castle set in rolling parkland have been redeveloped since the 1960s with horticultural advice from Jim Russell. The new plantings have been well integrated into the classical landscape and have added an entirely new horticultural dimension to the landscape. The exquisite temple garden, curling the whole way around a small lake, is breathtakingly beautiful. Highly recommended.

Features Woodland garden; rock garden; good herbaceous borders; fine collection of trees; azaleas & rhododendrons; gift shop; tea-room, light lunches, homemade teas.

Owned by The Marchioness of Cholmondeley
English Heritage grade II

Dorfold Hall

NANTWICH CW5 8LD

Tel 01270 625245   **Fax** 01270 628723
Location 1 mile west of Nantwich on A534.
Opening hours 2 pm – 5 pm; Tuesdays & Bank Holiday Mondays; April to October. Also 2 pm – 5.30 pm on 19 May for National Gardens Scheme.

Admission fee House & gardens: Adults £5; Children £3. National Gardens Scheme day: Adults £3; Children £1.

William Andrews Nesfield designed the formal approach but the main reason for visiting the gardens at Dorfold Hall is the new woodland garden of rhododendrons and other shrubs, leading down to a stream where *Primula pulverulenta* has naturalised in its thousands. Do not miss the incredible hulk of an ancient Spanish chestnut in the stable yard.

Features Spring woodland garden; camellias; magnolias; rhododendrons & azaleas; daffodils & bluebells; good summer herbaceous borders.

Owned by R.C. Roundell
Number of gardeners 2
Size 7.2ha (18 acres)
English Heritage grade II

Dunge Valley Hidden Gardens

KETTLESHULME, HIGH PEAK SK23 7RF

Tel & Fax 01663 733787
Website www.dungevalley.co.uk
Location 1 mile south of Kettleshulme: follow brown tourist signs and turn down a minor road in the village.
Opening hours 10.30 am – 5 pm; daily; April to August.
Admission fee Adults £3; Concessions £2.50; Children 50p.

These hidden gardens 300m up in the Pennines are a surprise and a delight: few are so high, and fewer still so full of colour. It is not only the number of plants which gives such pleasure, but the surprise of finding so many that one might suppose too tender – embothriums, desfontainias and mahonias, for example. But there are also fine rhododendrons, old-fashioned roses and flowering borders in an almost Himalayan setting.

 Features Rhododendrons & azaleas; roses; hardy trees & shrubs; tea-room.

Owned by David & Elizabeth Ketley
Number of gardeners 6
Size 2.2ha (6 acres)

Granada Arboretum

JODRELL BANK, MACCLESFIELD SK11 9DL

Tel 01477 571339   **Fax** 01477 571695
Location On A535 between Holmes Chapel & Chelford.
Opening hours 10.30 am – 5.30 pm; daily; March to October. 11 am – 4.30 pm; Tuesday – Sunday; November to February.
Admission fee Grounds, Science Centre & Planetarium: Adults £4.90; Concessions £3.50; Children £2.50.

The Granada Arboretum at Jodrell Bank was founded by Sir Bernard Lovell in 1971 with funding from the Granada Foundation. This wonderful arboretum specialises in alders, birches, crab apples, pine and *Sorbus*. Long straight drives lead spaciously into the distance, by way of large collections of heaths (*Erica*) and heathers (*Calluna*). The plantings are young and vigorous, the groupings imaginative. A huge radio telescope dominates the site: an awesome presence.

 Features Heather Society's *Calluna* collection; shop; self-service cafeteria.

Owned by Manchester University
Number of gardeners 2
Size 14ha (35 acres)
NCCPG National Collections *Malus; Sorbus*

Hare Hill Garden

GARDEN LODGE, OVER ALDERLEY, MACCLESFIELD SK10 4QB

Tel 01625 828981
Website www.nationaltrust.org.uk
Location Between Alderley Edge & Prestbury.
Opening hours 10 am – 5.30 pm; Wednesdays, Thursdays, Saturday, Sundays & Bank Holiday Mondays; 1 April to 30 October. Open daily from 10 to 30 May for rhododendrons & azaleas and also on 4 June.
Admission fee Adults £2.50; Children £1.25.

Hare Hill is a woodland garden, thickly planted with trees and underplanted with rhododendrons, azaleas and shrubs by Jim Russell in the 1960s. In the middle is a walled garden which has been developed as a flower garden with a pergola, arbour and tender plants against the walls. Planting continues: much *Rhododendron ponticum* has been cleared recently and replaced by new cultivars. Perhaps best in May, there are still some rhododendrons to flower with the roses in July.

 Features Woodland garden; rock garden; plantsman's collection of plants; good herbaceous borders.

Owned by The National Trust
Number of gardeners 1½
Size 4ha (10 acres)

Little Moreton Hall

CONGLETON CW12 4SD

Tel 01260 272018
Website www.nationaltrust.org.uk
Location 4 miles south of Congleton on A34.
Opening hours 11.30 am – 5 pm (or dusk, if earlier); Wednesday – Sunday & Bank Holiday Mondays & 4 June;

23 March to 3 November. 11.30 am – 4 pm; Saturdays & Sundays; 9 November to 22 December.
Admission fee Adults £4.50; Children £2.25.

Little Moreton Hall is the handsomest timber-framed house in England. When the National Trust asked Graham Stuart Thomas to design and plant a suitable period garden, he specified box-edged parterres with yew topiary and gravel infilling – and very fine they are too. In the kitchen garden, a speciality has been made of old varieties of fruit and vegetables. Peaceful, charming and orderly.

 Features Herbs; fruit; good herbaceous borders.

Owned by The National Trust
Number of gardeners 1
Size 0.4ha (1 acre)
English Heritage grade I

Lyme Park

DISLEY SK12 2NX

Tel 01663 762023 **Fax** 01663 765035
Website www.nationaltrust.org.uk
Location 6½ miles south-east of Stockport on A6, just west of Disley.
Opening hours 11 am – 5 pm (but 1 pm – 5 pm on Wednesdays & Thursdays); daily; 29 March to 30 October. 12 noon – 3 pm; Saturdays & Sundays; 1 November to 18 December.
Admission fee Garden only: Adults £2.50; Children £1.20. Plus £3.50 for car (National Trust members free).

There is much of horticultural interest at Lyme, as well as the razzmatazz of a country park: traditional bedding out, two enormous camellias in the conservatory, and a Jekyll-type herbaceous border by Graham Stuart Thomas where the colours run from orange to deepest purple. Best of all is the sunken Dutch garden whose looping box and ivy parterres contain the most extravagant bedding displays. The National Trust has now assumed full control of the garden and restored the structure in line with the original Lewis Wyatt design. Lyme Park featured as Pemberley in the BBC's dramatisation of *Pride & Prejudice*.

 Features Roses (mainly old-fashioned); good herbaceous borders; spring bulbs; bedding out; orangery by Wyatt; 'Dutch' garden.

Owned by The National Trust
Number of gardeners 5
Size 6.7ha (17 acres)
NCCPG National Collections Vicary Gibbs plants
English Heritage grade II*

Mellors Garden

HOUGH HOLE HOUSE, RAINOW, MACCLESFIELD SK10 5UW

Tel 01625 573251 **Fax** 01625 572389
Location In Sugar Lane.
Opening hours 2 pm – 5 pm; 3 June & 26 August. And by appointment.
Admission fee £1.50.

This remarkable small garden was laid out in the 19th century as an allegory of Christian's journey in *Pilgrim's Progress* and originally planted only with plants that are mentioned in the Bible. Features represent such places as the Way of Salvation, the Cave of the Holy Sepulchre, Vanity Fayre, the Dark River, the Delectable Mountains, Doubting Castle and the Celestial City. A spiritual and historical experience more than a horticultural one.

Owned by Mr & Mrs A. Rigby

Ness Botanic Gardens

NESTON CH64 4AY

Tel 0151 353 0123 **Fax** 0151 353 1004
Website www.merseyworld.com/nessgardens
Location Signed off A540, Chester to Hoylake.
Opening hours 9.30 am – 4 pm (5 pm from March to October); daily; all year. Closed from 23 December 2002 to 2 January 2003.
Admission fee Adults £4.70; Concessions £4.30. £3.70 from November to January.

Ness was the creation of a rich Liverpool cotton merchant, Arthur Bulley, who laid out the garden in 1898 and started to plant it with new species from abroad. He was particularly interested in Himalayan and Chinese plants: he believed that many could become established in cultivation in Britain and he therefore sponsored such plant collectors as George Forrest and Frank Kingdon Ward. It is to Bulley that we owe such plants as *Gentiana sino-ornata* and *Pieris formosa* var. *forrestii*, and it was at Ness that many Chinese plants were first grown in Europe – notably the candelabra primulas. Ness was presented to the University of Liverpool by Bulley's daughter in 1948 and has continued to develop as a public amenity, a tourist attraction and a teaching garden, while still retaining the 'feel' of a private garden. It is beautifully laid out in a sequence of incidents: both its design and plantings have continued to improve year by year. The main features are as follows: a 'sorbus lawn', where the type plant of *Sorbus forrestii* grows; a laburnum arch; a herb garden; a rhododendron border (long and deep) underplanted with many lilies; an excellent heather garden; sandstone terraces where tender plants like *Ribes speciosum* and two wild-collected forms of *Lobelia tupa* flourish; a rock garden with an enormous range of different environments, south-facing and north-facing, limestone and sandstone, sunny, shaded and damp; a water garden; a camellia collection; an arboretum; a willow collection recognised by the NCCPG as a National Collection; a rose garden which illustrates the history of the rose; herbaceous borders; and a series of glasshouses with temperate, arid and tropical sections for such plants as *Lonicera hildebrandiana*, the crown of thorns (*Euphorbia milii*) and important economic plants like cotton, sugar cane, kapok and papyrus. As with all botanic gardens, there is no end of things to see whatever the season, and your visit can be as short or as long as it suits. In practice, however, Ness is one of those gardens where you tend to spend much longer than you intended. The website is very comprehensive.

Features Roses (mainly old-fashioned); mature conifers; fine collection of trees; 30m laburnum arch; new Camellia Walk (2000); notable collections of *Sorbus, Betula, Salix* & *Cotoneaster*; tallest *Alnus cremastogyne* (3.3m) in the British Isles; gift shop; tea-room.

Owned by University of Liverpool
Number of gardeners 12
Size 26ha (64 acres)
English Heritage grade II

Norton Priory Museum & Gardens

TUDOR ROAD, RUNCORN WA7 1SX

Tel 01928 569895
Location Well signed locally.
Opening hours 12 noon – 5 pm (but 4 pm in March, & 6 pm at weekends & Bank Holidays from April on); daily; March – October.
Admission fee Adults £3.75; OAPs £2.50.

The old walled garden at Norton Priory has a new lay-out modelled on 18th-century precedents and intended to instruct and please visitors. A cottage garden border, a medicinal herb garden and orchard rub shoulders with colour borders, children's gardens and a scented garden. Beyond are 16 acres of woodland garden with Georgian summerhouses and glades by the stream.

Features Roses (ancient & modern); rock garden; herbs; fruit; good herbaceous borders; current holder of Sandford Award; garden produce shop; refreshments at museum site.

Owned by Norton Priory Museum Trust (Cheshire County Council)
Number of gardeners 2
Size 15ha (38 acres)
NCCPG National Collections Cydonia oblonga

Peover Hall

OVER PEOVER, KNUTSFORD WA16 6SW

Tel 01565 722656
Location 3 miles south of Knutsford.
Opening hours 2 pm – 5 pm; Mondays & Thursdays; April to October.

Admission fee Adults £3; Children £2.

First a classic 18th-century parkland, then an Edwardian overlay of formal gardens – yew hedges and brick paths. Now Peover has modern plantings too – borders in colour combinations, a herb garden, and a rhododendron dell in the woods.

Features Topiary; roses (mainly old-fashioned); herbs; walled garden; landscaped park; rhododendrons.

Owned by R. Brooks Ltd.
English Heritage grade II

The Quinta

SWETTENHAM VILLAGE, CONGLETON CW12 2LD

Tel 01270 610180   **Fax** 01270 610430
Website www.wildlifetrust.org.uk/cheshire
Location Access through the garden of the Swettenham Arms.
Opening hours Dawn – dusk; daily; all year.
Admission fee Adults £2; Children £1. RHS members free.

The Quinta Arboretum was created by Sir Bernard Lovell, originator of the Jodrell Bank Radio Telescope, and is now owned by the Cheshire Wildlife Trust. The garden features more than 5,000 trees and shrubs, with beautiful views over the River Dane meanders. Grand avenues lead to the ancient woodland nature reserve with flower-rich meadows grazed by rare-breed sheep. A wonderful site to visit in all seasons.

Features Nice young arboretum; wildflowers; woodland garden.

Owned by Cheshire Wildlife Trust
Size 16ha (40 acres)
NCCPG National Collections Fraxinus; Pinus

Reaseheath College

NANTWICH CW5 6DF

Tel 01270 625131 **Fax** 01270 625665
Location 1 mile north of Nantwich on A51.
Opening hours 2 pm – 4 pm; Wednesdays; 22 & 29 May, & 5 June. College Open Day 11 am – 5 pm on 19 May.
Admission fee Donation to NGS.

Reaseheath has been thoroughly replanted recently: there is an enormous amount to enjoy and learn here. Highlights include a woodland garden, a model fruit garden, a heather garden, a rock garden, good bedding on the formal terraces and splendid mixed borders.

Features Woodland garden; rhododendrons & azaleas; good herbaceous borders; fine collection of trees; heather garden; formal bedding; Reaseheath Garden Centre, open daily, all year; shop, restaurant & coffee lounge.

Owned by Reaseheath College

Rode Hall

CHURCH LANE, SCHOLAR GREEN, STOKE ON TRENT ST7 3QP

Tel 01270 882961 **Fax** 01270 882962
Location 5 miles south-west of Congleton between A34 & A50.
Opening hours 2 pm – 5 pm; Tuesday – Thursday & Bank Holidays; 1 April to 26 September. Plus 1.30 pm – 5.30 pm on 12 May for National Gardens Scheme & 12 noon – 4 pm from 6 to 24 February for snowdrops.
Admission fee Garden only: Adults £2.50; OAPs £1.50. RHS members free (not snowdrop walks).

Stand on the terraces at Rode Hall and take in the prospect: Nesfield's 1860s rose garden and Repton's landscape beyond. The 'pool' is nearly a mile long and 150 yards wide. But horticulture is also here in abundance: take the boathouse walk past the old stew pond (pretty marginals and a waterfall) to the wildflower garden (terraced rock garden – early 19th-century – *very* early for this sort of garden) where snowdrops, sarcococcas, hellebores (lots), ferns, primroses and soldanellas flourish in the lee of rhododendrons. Note the splendid Loderi crosses, which smell of sugared almonds and extend the flowering season into early June. Admire Professor Pratt's scented azaleas (would that more people knew and grew them) and note how the plantings of rhododendron species are being extended into the adjacent Old Wood. Then visit the walled kitchen garden (about 2 acres) and see the rows of decorative vegetables set between cornflowers, poppies, marigolds and flowers for drying. Espaliered fruit trees cover the walls between 4m abutilons: Cheshire has a mild climate. Look inside the greenhouses and see the many geraniums with scented leaves. And ponder the industry of the head gardener, Kelvin Archer, who grows over 40 cultivars of gooseberry here and holds the world record for the largest gooseberry fruit.

Features Woodland garden; topiary; snowdrops; roses (mainly old-fashioned); fruit; mature conifers; ice house; rhododendrons; grotto; laburnum walk; fully functional 2-acre walled kitchen garden; garden produce.

Owned by Sir Richard Baker Wilbraham
Number of gardeners 2
Size 2.2ha (6 acres)
English Heritage grade II

Stapeley Water Gardens

LONDON ROAD, STAPELEY,
NANTWICH CW5 7LH

Tel 01270 623868   **Fax** 01270 624919
Website www.stapeleywatergardens.com
Location A51, 1 mile south of Nantwich.
Opening hours 9 am – 5.30 pm (5 pm in winter); daily;
all year except 25 December. Nursery opens at 9 am
Monday – Friday & 10 am on Saturdays & Sundays; closes
at 6 pm (but 4 pm on Sundays, 7 pm on winter
Wednesdays & 8 pm on summer Wednesdays).
Admission fee Palms Tropical Oasis: Adults £3.85;
OAPs £3.40; Children £2.15.

Part entertainment, part nursery and part
display garden, the Palms Tropical Oasis is
worth a visit in its own right. A long
rectangular pool in the Moorish style is
flanked by tall palms, strelitzias and other
showy tropical flowers. The display gardens
outside are fascinating all through the year,
especially the water gardens where all the
waterlilies grow.

Features Plants under glass; collection
of hardy waterlilies; *Victoria regia*, the
giant waterlily; major nursey & garden
centre; cafeteria & terrace restaurant.

Owned by Stapeley Water Garden Ltd
NCCPG National Collections *Nymphaea*

Tatton Park

KNUTSFORD WA16 6QN

Tel 01625 534400   **Fax** 01625 534403
Website www.nationaltrust.org.uk
Location Off M6 Jct 19 & M56 Jct 7 – well signed.
Opening hours 10.30 am – 6 pm (but 11 am – 4 pm from
October to March); Tuesday – Sunday, plus Bank Holiday
Mondays; all year.
Admission fee Telephone for prices. RHS members free.

Humphry Repton laid out the parkland at
Tatton. Joseph Paxton designed both the
formal Italian garden and the exquisite
fernery, claimed as the finest in the UK.
Later came a Japanese garden (restored for
the Japanese festival in 2001) and Shinto
temple (1910), such follies as the African
hut, and the mass plantings of
rhododendrons and azaleas. Work on
restoring the walled garden should be
finished during the course of the year
(2002): tomato houses, fig houses, orchid
houses and pot plant houses will be rebuilt.
Tatton Park is wonderfully well organised
for visitors, and gets better every year. Be
prepared for a long and absorbing visit. The
RHS Flower Show at Tatton Park will take
place from 17 to 21 July 2002.

Features Good herbaceous borders;
fine collection of trees; rhododendrons
& azaleas in May; biggest *Quercus* ×
schochiana in the British Isles; current
holder of Sandford Award; Europa Nostra
award for restored orangery & fernery; shop;
restaurant open daily except Monday.

Owned by The National Trust (managed by Cheshire
County Council)
Number of gardeners 13
Size 20ha (50 acres)
NCCPG National Collections *Adiantum*
English Heritage grade II*

Tirley Garth Trust

UTKINTON, TARPORLEY CW6 0LZ

Tel 01829 732301   **Fax** 01829 732265
Location 2½ miles north of Tarporley, just north of
Utkinton on road to Kelsall.
Opening hours 2 pm – 6 pm; 12, 19, 26 & 27 May,
2 June, and possibly some other dates.
Admission fee Adults £3; Children 50p.

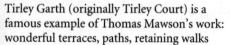

Tirley Garth (originally Tirley Court) is a
famous example of Thomas Mawson's work:
wonderful terraces, paths, retaining walks
and garden buildings. It is this structure
which underpins the planting, including
the rhododendrons and azaleas in the
woodland below. Restoration, replanting
and improvement have continued in
recent years.

 Features Woodland garden; roses
(mainly modern); rock garden;
rhododendrons & azaleas; good herbaceous
borders; cream teas.

Owned by The Tirley Garth Trust
Number of gardeners 2, plus one trainee
Size 15.5ha (39 acres)
English Heritage grade II

CORNWALL

Many of the great historic gardens of Cornwall are also the most interesting horticulturally. Mount Edgcumbe and Tresco are both rated Grade I gardens of national importance, while Caerhays Castle, Lanhydrock, Tregrehan and Trewithen are Grade II* and Antony, Carclew, Chyverton, Cotehele, Glendurgan, Heligan, Lamellen, Pencarrow, Penjerrick, St Michael's Mount, Trebah, Trelissick and Trengwainton are all Grade II. It is a proud list, unmatched by any other county, and evidence of how the big estates have always dominated the gardening scene in Cornwall. The county still has its own horticultural organisation, the Cornwall Garden Society: its spring show is a showcase for camellias and rhododendrons. About 80 gardens open every year for the Cornwall Festival of Spring Gardens which runs from mid-March to the end of May: details from the Cornwall Tourist Board on 01872 322900. Almost all the gardens have fine collections of trees too: those at Trebah, Tregrehan and Trewithin are particularly noted for the age and size of their specimens, while the woodlands of Caerhays contain an exceptional number of well-grown rarities. A new type of Cornish garden has, however, been emerging over the last 25 years, where the owners have taken advantage of the climate to grow a very wide range of newer plants: Pine Lodge, Lamorran and Bosvigo are good examples and will doubtless be followed by others. The county's National Collections reflect the opportunities which the mild climate makes possible: among them are *Escallonia* at Duchy College (a RHS Partner College), *Azara* at Trelissick, *Grevillea* at Pine Lodge and *Acacia* at Tresco. Finest of all is the National Collection of *Dahlia* at Varfell Farm at Long Rock, just off the A30, where some 2,000 species and cultivars can be seen by prior appointment (further details from 01736 710744). Cornish nurseries cater well for the local market: the Duchy of Cornwall Nursery at Lostwithiel has the largest stock of all, while tender exotica are the speciality of Trevena Cross Garden Centre near Helston and Lower Kenneggy Nurseries near Penzance. Best known is Burncoose & South Down Nurseries, a regular winner of Gold Medals for its spectacular displays of flowering trees and shrubs at RHS shows throughout the year.

Antony House

TORPOINT PL11 2QA

Tel & Fax 01752 812364
Website www.nationaltrust.org.uk
Location 5 miles west of Plymouth, 2 miles north-west of Torpoint.
Opening hours 1.30 pm – 5.30 pm; Tuesday – Thursday & Bank Holidays; 26 March to 1 November; also 1.30 pm – 5.30 pm on Sundays from June to August. Last admissions 4.45 pm.
Admission fee Adults £4.40; Children £2.20.

Antony has been an historic and important garden for centuries – and every generation has left its mark. Its classic late 18th-century landscape is superb, though there is considerable debate as to whether Humphry Repton designed it or the Pole-Carews (as they were then called) listened to Repton's advice but followed little of it. The yew walk with its lead statues of a shepherd and his shepherdess and the huge Burmese temple bell, flanked by stone lanterns, date from the 19th century. Much of the horticultural interest was created by Sir John Carew Pole in the middle of the 20th century – masses of bulbs, the lime-tree avenues, over 600 early *Hemerocallis* hybrids from the USA, a 10m loquat tree (*Eriobotrya japonica*) against the house, the vast cork oak (*Quercus suber*) (another record-breaker), the venerable old "Black Walnut" (*Juglans nigra*) on the main lawn and the beautiful spring-flowering *Magnolia denudata*. The position is superb – an elevated promontory above the Tamar estuary, just across Plymouth Sound from Devon. Sir Richard and Lady Carew Pole, who now live at Antony, have continued to intensify and extend this plantsman's garden: more spring-flowering trees and shrubs have been planted, alongside the creation of gardens for summer and autumn interest. The

Summer Garden is particularly effective: hybrid musk roses are underplanted with lilies, irises, phlox and peonies and its walls are covered in clematis, climbing roses, lemon-scented verbena and *Cytisus battandieri*. But there is much to see at every season – the magnolia walk in spring, the knot garden, the terraces m high summer with giant catmint (*Nepeta* 'Six Hills Giant') mingling with the floribunda rose 'Iceberg' and free-standing fig-trees *Ficus carica* 'White Marseilles' in autumn. And it is a large garden, so you need to allow a lot of time to do it justice.

Features Mature conifers; good herbaceous borders; magnolias; yew hedges; tallest Japanese loquat *Eriobotrya japonica* (8m) in the British Isles (and two other tree records); tea-room open at 12.45 pm.

Owned by The National Trust
Number of gardeners 5
Size 14ha (35 acres)
NCCPG National Collections *Hemerocallis*
English Heritage grade II

Antony Woodland Garden

ANTONY HOUSE, TORPOINT PL11 2QA

Tel & Fax 01752 812364
Location 5 miles west of Plymouth, 2 miles north-west of Torpoint.
Opening hours 11 am – 5.30 pm; daily except Mondays & Fridays (but open on Bank Holidays); March to October.
Admission fee Adults £3; Accompanied children free.

This is the 'Cornish' part of the grounds at Antony, still controlled by the Carew Pole family rather than the National Trust. It is a garden of considerable botanical interest

divided into two main areas. First comes the Wilderness, a wooded area to the north-west of the house which runs down to the banks of the River Lynher. Three vistas frame the house from the river: Humphry Repton's influence is clearly apparent here. The Wilderness has been planted with trees and shrubs like Japanese maples, a tunnel of *Camellia* × *williamsii* 'Donation' and *Camellia japonica* 'Lady de Saumarez', *Magnolia obovata*, rhododendron species and hybrids including the strongly scented 'Loderi' and *R. griffithianum*. There is a conifer dell with giant redwoods *Sequoiadendron giganteum*, *Cryptomeria japonica* and *Taxus baccata* 'Dovastoniana' and three ponds cascading down a valley to the salt pans and the Bath House pond. The second area is Westdown, where the planting consists mainly of camellias of considerable variety (including the National Collection of *Camellia japonica*) interspersed with Asiatic magnolias and rhododendron species, thriving in the deep valley. The magnolias include specimens of 'Charles Raffill', *M. dawsoniana*, and *M. campbellii* subsp. *mollicomata* 'Lanarth'. The two areas are joined by the Garden Field where ornamental trees have been underplanted with flowering shrubs and daffodils. A path through deep-scented shrubs and birches completes the link along the river's edge.

Features Woodland garden; plantsman's collection of plants; mature conifers; camellias; magnolias; rhododendrons & azaleas; tea-room.

Owned by The Carew Pole Garden Trust
Size 26ha (65 acres)
NCCPG National Collections *Camellia japonica*

The Barbara Hepworth Museum & Sculpture Garden

2 BARNOON HILL, ST IVES TR26 1TG

Tel 01736 796226 **Fax** 01736 794480
Website www.tate.org.uk
Location In town centre.
Opening hours 10.30 am – 5.30 pm; daily; March to October. 10 am – 4.30; Tuesday-Sunday; November to March. Closed 24-26 December.
Admission fee Adults £3.75; Concessions £2.

Dame Barbara Hepworth's studio and garden have been run by the Tate Gallery since 1980. Hepworth died in 1975, and asked (in her will) that Trewyn studios and the subtropical garden should become a permanent setting to exhibit her works. Visiting it gives you a remarkable insight into one of the 20th century's most important sculptors.

Owned by Tate Gallery & Hepworth Estate
Number of gardeners 2
Size 0.2ha (½ acre)
English Heritage grade II

Bosvigo

BOSVIGO LANE, TRURO TR1 3NH

Tel & Fax 01872 275774
Website www.bosvigo.com
Location Turn off A390 at Highertown just west of Sainsbury's roundabout, then 500 yards down Dobbs Lane.
Opening hours 11 am – 6 pm; Thursday – Saturday; 1 March to 28 September.
Admission fee Adults £3; Children (5–15) £1.

Not a typical Cornish garden, the emphasis at Bosvigo is upon herbaceous plants, chosen for their individual qualities and planted in fine colour combinations. The woodland garden is more traditional, and underplanted with snowdrops, hellebores, wood anemones, erythroniums and epimediums, but the rest of the garden is at its best in summer and keeps well into the autumn. Over the last 20 years or so, Wendy and Michael Perry have created a series of small walled or hedged garden 'rooms' around the mainly Georgian house. Each has its own colour theme: the walled garden heaves with polite blues, mauves and pinks while another is mainly of gold and white. Reds and oranges co-exist in a 'hot' garden which, according to Patrick Taylor in the *Daily Telegraph*, 'will blow your socks off'. Many of the plants are rare, and some are sold in the small specialist nursery.

 Features Woodland garden; plantsman's collection of plants; good herbaceous borders; unusual perennials; Victorian conservatory; colour borders; excellent small herbaceous nursery.

Owned by Wendy & Michael Perry
Number of gardeners owners only
Size 0.8ha (2 acres)

Burncoose Gardens & Nurseries

GWENNAP, REDRUTH TR16 6BJ

Tel 01209 860316   **Fax** 01209 860011
Website www.burncoose.co.uk
Location Directly on the A393 Redruth to Falmouth road between the villages of Lanner & Ponsanooth.
Opening hours 8.30 am – 5 pm (11 am – 5 pm on Sundays); daily except 25 December; all year.
Admission fee Adults £2; Children free.

Burncoose Nurseries specialise in rare and unusual plants: they list over 3,500 different ones – mainly ornamental trees and shrubs – which makes them one of the best for sheer choice in all Europe. Their real specialities are camellias, rhododendrons, magnolias and conservatory plants. Burncoose has won 17 gold medals at the last 21 Chelsea Flower Shows and, over the last 3 years, has won more gold medal awards at UK flower shows than any other exhibitor. It is a RHS Partner Nursery. The garden is a woodland garden, carpeted with bluebells, primroses, snowdrops and wild violets in spring. Two monkey puzzles *Araucaria araucana* are over 30m (100ft) high and a *Eucryphia* × *nymansensis* reaches 13m (40ft). Most of the ornamental plants have been planted since 1900 and the older ones have been matched in recent years by substantial additions.

 Features Woodland garden; rhododendrons & azaleas; plantsman's collection of plants; camellias; bluebells; magnolias; rare trees & shrubs; important nursery (major RHS gold medal winner); teas & light refreshments.

Owned by Charles Williams
Number of gardeners 1
Size 12ha (30 acres)

Carclew Gardens

PERRAN-AR-WORTHAL, TRURO TR3 7PB

Tel 01872 864070
Location A39 east at Perran-ar-Worthal, 1 mile to garden.
Opening hours 2 pm – 5.30 pm. 21 & 28 April, 5, 12, 19 & 26 May. And at any time by appointment.
Admission fee Adults £2.50; Children 50p.

Caerhays Castle Gardens

GORRAN, ST AUSTELL PL26 6LY

Tel 01872 501310 **Fax** 01872 501870
Website www.caerhays.co.uk
Location Between Mevagissey & Portloe.
Opening hours 10 am – 5.30 pm; daily; 11 March to
31 May. Charity openings: 31 March, 14 April & 6 May.
Admission fee Adults £4.50 (£2.50 on charity days);
Children £1.50.

Caerhays has belonged to the Williams family since 1853, but it was not until the young J.C. Williams took over the estate in the 1890s that they began to develop the gardens. It seems that the original inspiration came from a RHS daffodil conference: it sparked JCW's lifelong interest in hybridising. By 1903 he was sponsoring E.H. Wilson's collections in China and this was followed by a partnership with George Forrest. Of the many plants that these expeditions introduced, Caerhays is best known for its magnolias, but JCW is also remembered as a great hybridiser of rhododendrons and camellias. *Camellia × williamsii* was named for him: some of the original plants still flourish at Caerhays, including 'J.C. Williams', 'Mary Christian' and 'St. Ewe'. The present owner, and his son Charles Williams, have been no less involved in conserving and improving the remarkable plant collections at Caerhays. They make a point of trying to accommodate rare and unusual plants, whose cultural requirements take precedence over the niceties of garden design. And the Williams are still involved in wide scale plantings – especially since the garden suffered serious damage in the 1990 great gale. Magnolias remain a major interest and almost all the new forms and cultivars coming out of Australia, USA and

New Zealand have been added to the garden and have grown away well. One of the joys of Caerhays is to stumble upon magnificent old specimens deep in its 100 acres of woodland. Among the many rare trees are fine specimens of *Laurus azorica, Lithocarpus cleistocarpus, L. henryi*; magnolias like *M. delavayi, M. nitida, M. robusta* and *M. salicifolia*; and such oaks as *Quercus acuta, Q. crassifolia, Q. glauca, Q. ilicifolia, Q. lamellosa, Q. lanata, Q. lodicosa, Q. oxyodon* and *Q. phillyreoides*. Almost all these species are known to few of us: this litany of names is a measure of the importance of Caerhays. There is much to discover, so you should allow plenty of time. And see the website – very informative.

Features Woodland garden; plantsman's collection of plants; mature conifers; fine collection of trees; camellias; magnolias; rhododendrons; tallest specimen of *Emmenopterys henryi* (17m) in the British Isles, and 37 other record-breaking trees (including eight *Acer* species); tea-room & beach shop/café in car-park.

Owned by F.J. Williams CBE
Number of gardeners 4
Size 22ha (60 acres)
English Heritage grade II*

Carclew's garden first opened to the public in 1927 and has continued to do so for charity every year since then. It was once the greatest rhododendron garden in the south-west: some of the oldest rhododendrons were grown from Sir Joseph Hooker's Himalayan collections nearly 150 years ago. The many fine trees include a large ginkgo and a form of *Quercus × hispanica* which is *not* 'Lucombeana'. Mrs Chope has been busy replanting and restoring the garden: the waterfall has recently been repaired.

 Features Woodland garden; roses (mainly modern); rhododendrons; tallest *Pseudolarix amabilis* (23m) in the British Isles; homemade teas.

Owned by Mrs Robert Chope
English Heritage grade II

Carwinion

MAWNAN SMITH, FALMOUTH TR11 5JA

Tel 01326 250258   **Fax** 01326 250903
Website www.carwinion.com
Location From Mawnan Smith, turn left at Red Lion, 500 yards up hill on right.
Opening hours 10 am – 5.30 pm; daily or by appointment; all year.
Admission fee Adults £2.50; Children free.

(P) (🐕) (WC) (☘)

Twelve acres of Cornish jungle, exotically thick with vast rhododendrons, camellias, *Trachycarpus fortunei*, drimys, gunneras, lysichitons, ferns, hellebores and the largest collection of bamboos in the south-west. The Towan Nursery collection of camellias and hydrangeas has recently been planted out in the garden and will add yet further interest in future.

 Features Woodland garden; sub-tropical plants; mature conifers; 160 species of bamboo; gunnera; bluebells.

Owned by Anthony Rogers
Number of gardeners 1
Size 4.6ha (12 acres)

Chyverton

ZELAH, TRURO TR4 9HD

Tel 01872 540324
Location 1 mile south-west of Zelah on A30.
Opening hours By appointment at any time.
Admission fee Adults £5; Children (under 16) free; Groups (20+) £4. Visits are personally conducted.

(P) (🐕) (WC) (☘)

Chyverton started out as a Georgian landscape garden. Later owners planted a pinetum in the 1830s and the first rhododendrons in 1890. The horticultural plantings have however been very much extended since the 1920s, initially with some advice from Sir Harold Hillier, but latterly by the owners themselves. Nigel Holman is a distinguished plantsman: Hugh Johnson calls his garden 'a magic jungle'. Magnolias are a particular interest: several Chyverton seedlings now bear cultivar names. Many other established plants have also been grown from seed: rhododendron hybrids from Brodick, for instance. But there is much more to interest the plantsman. A lanky red-stemmed hedge of *Luma apiculata* below the house is outstanding. The planting continues and is now accompanied by the placement of statues in suitable sites.

 Features Woodland garden; plantsman's collection of plants; mature conifers; magnolias, including four record-breakers; nothofagus; new herbaceous plantings (2000); tallest

Rhododendron 'Cornish Red' (16m) in the British isles; lunches & teas for parties.

Owned by Nigel Holman
Number of gardeners 1
Size 50ha (120 acres)
English Heritage grade II

Cotehele

ST DOMINICK, SALTASH PL12 6TA

Tel 01579 351346   **Fax** 01579 351222
Website www.nationaltrust.org.uk
Location 14 miles from Plymouth via Saltash.
Opening hours 10.30 am – dusk; daily; all year.
Admission fee £3.60.

Broad Victorian terraces below the house support many tender climbers such as *Jasminum mesnyi*, while the beds beneath have wallflowers and roses. Down the wooded valley are camellias, rhododendrons and shade-loving plants which thrive in an ancient woodland, kept damp by a small stream. The National Trust has undertaken much gentle restoration and renewal in recent years.

Features Woodland garden; topiary; roses (mainly modern); daffodils; fine collection of trees; palms; ferns; pretty dovecote; National Trust gift shop; restaurant (23 March – 3 November) for meals and drinks.

Owned by The National Trust
Number of gardeners 3, plus 2 students
Size 5.6ha (14 acres)
English Heritage grade II

Duchy of Cornwall Nursery

COTT ROAD, LOSTWITHIEL
PL22 0BW

Tel 01208 872668   **Fax** 01208 872835
Website www.duchyofcornwallnursery.co.uk
Location 1½ miles off A390 at Lostwithiel.
Opening hours 9 am – 5 pm; Monday – Saturday.
10 am – 5 pm; Sundays. Closed Bank Holidays.

The Duchy of Cornwall nursery stocks an extensive general range of all types of plants, and will interest even the most discriminating plantsman. Its policy does not compromise on quality: it offers the cultivars which it considers the best. These range from reliable old favourites to rare and recent cultivars. It was recently described as resembling 'a series of specialist nurseries in one nursery' because of the depth and breadth of its range. It is especially good on hardy fuchsias, and hopes that its collection will one day be recognised by the NCCPG. It is also one of the few nurseries which still supply bare-rooted stock in winter.

The Eden Project

BODELVA, ST AUSTELL PL24 2SGE

Tel 01726 811911   **Fax** 01726 811912
Website www.edenproject.com
Location Signed from A30, A390 & A391.
Opening hours 10 am – 6 pm; daily; all year. Closes at 4.30 pm from November to March.
Admission fee Adults £9.50; OAPs £7.50; Children £4.

The promoters of this imaginative project hope to provide visitors with an understanding of the world of plants, and their importance to human welfare. The area under glass is described as being the size of 30 football pitches. One of the gigantic conservatories – all made in a disused clay-pit near St Austell – is landscaped as a rainforest, while others are Mediterranean, South African and Californian. Staples like cocoa, coffee, bananas and rubber are grown alongside plants used in paper, wine, scent and brewing. Outside are collections of camellias, lavender, sunflowers and hemp.

 Features Giant glasshouses; exotic plants.

Owned by The Eden Trust
Size 14.7ha (37 acres)

Glendurgan Gardens

HELFORD RIVER, MAWNAN SMITH, FALMOUTH TR11 5TR

Tel 01326 250906   **Fax** 01872 865808
Website www.nationaltrust.org.uk
Location 1 mile west of Mawnan Smith, west to Trebah.
Opening hours 10.30 am – 5.30 pm (last admissions 4.30 pm); Tuesday – Saturday, plus Bank Holiday Mondays; 16 February to 2 November. Closed Good Friday.
Admission fee Adults £3.90; Children £1.95.

Glendurgan is a steep, sub-tropical valley garden on the Helford River with a good collection of old rhododendrons and camellias. It also boasts an extraordinary 1830s maze of clipped cherry laurel, recently restored and best seen from the new viewing platform above. Indeed, the whole garden is almost best when viewed from the top – but the temptation to wander down and into it is irresistible.

 Features Woodland garden; sub-tropical plants; mature conifers; laurel

maze; wild flowers; huge tulip tree; tallest *Eucryphia lucida* (13m) in the British Isles; new Bhutanese valley planting (1996); small shop; teas & light lunches.

Owned by The National Trust
Number of gardeners 4
Size 14ha (35 acres)
English Heritage grade II

Headland

POLRUAN-BY-FOWEY PL23 1PW

Tel 01726 870243
Location Find Polruan: go to the bottom of Fore Street, along West Street, left up Battery Lane to end.
Opening hours 2 pm – 6 pm; Thursdays; 2 May to 12 September.
Admission fee Adults £2; Children £1.

A cliff garden with the sea on three sides and a sandy beach, Headland is a lesson in what will tolerate salt-laden winds: eucalyptus, acacias, foxgloves, columbines and junipers, but especially cacti and succulents – agaves, aloes, echeverias, sedums and crassulas. The design and the variety of the planting make it seem much larger than its 1¼ acres.

 Features Cacti & succulents; salt-spray resistant plants; cream teas in garden.

Owned by Jean & John Hill
Size 0.5ha (1¼ acres)

Heligan Gardens

PENTEWAN, ST AUSTELL PL26 6EN

Tel 01726 845100   **Fax** 01726 845101
Website www.heligan.com
Location St Austell to Mevagissey Road, following brown tourist signs.

Opening hours 10 am – 6 pm; daily; all year except 24 & 25 December.
Admission fee Adults £6; OAPs £5.50; Children £3.

Heligan calls itself 'The Lost Gardens of Heligan' but its 80 acres have been spectacularly rescued since 1990 from a jungle of neglect. The owners emphasise that it is 'definitely not just another pretty garden' but best described as a whole series of gardens within a garden. Its kitchen gardens – there are four walled gardens – are of particular interest: they contain over 300 cultivars of fruits, herbs and vegetables, some of them no longer commercially unavailable. Many of the working buildings are once again carrying out their original functions – fruit stores, tool and potting sheds, pineapple pits, peach, vine and melon houses, manure-heated frames and the bachelor gardeners' bothies. Newly recovered features emerge with incredible speed: recent restorations include the 30-acre 'Lost Valley.' The enthusiasm of the restorers is infectious and their achievements are already substantial. The owners are brilliant at getting financial support and publicity – with the result that the garden can get very crowded.

Features Woodland garden; sub-tropical plants; rock garden; rhododendrons & azaleas; beautiful ferny gully; splendid kitchen garden; tea-room.

Owned by Heligan Gardens Ltd
Number of gardeners 25
Size 32ha (80 acres)
English Heritage grade II

Ken Caro

BICTON, LISKEARD PL14 5RF

Tel 01579 362446
Location Signed from A390, midway between Callington & Liskeard.
Opening hours 10 am – 6 pm; Sunday – Thursday; 14 April to 29 August.
Admission fee Adults £3; Children £1.

Ken Caro was started in 1970 as 2 acres of intensely planted formal gardens in different styles, and extended in 1993 by taking in a further 2 acres. It is very much a plantsman's garden with good herbaceous plants and shrubs, not at all a traditional Cornish garden. All-round colour is important here, and so are the panoramic views. The owners are flower-arrangers: look for architectural plants and original combinations.

Features Plantsman's collection of plants; mature conifers; good herbaceous borders; new garden extension (2000).

Owned by Mr & Mrs K.R. Willcock
Number of gardeners 2
Size 1.8ha (4½ acres)

Lamorran House

UPPER CASTLE ROAD, ST MAWES TR2 5BZ

Tel 01326 270800   **Fax** 01326 270801
Location ½ mile from village centre.
Opening hours 10.30 am – 5 pm; Wednesdays, Fridays & the first Saturday of the month; April to September.
Admission fee Adults £3.50; Groups £3; Children free.

The garden at Lamorran has been almost entirely made since 1980, on a steep site above Falmouth Bay. It is tightly designed in the Italian style, but also full of unusual plants – an English Mediterranean garden in Cornwall, say the owners, or a mainland Tresco, though it is closest to the great English garden at La Mortola on the Italian Riviera. One of their latest ventures has been a bank planted with cacti and succulents: another has seen an increase in the number of cycads in the garden. But tender rhododendrons from Asia are yet another interest, and plants from Australia too. The collection of unusual plants is simply amazing: very adventurous. The planting is guided by a desire to experiment with hardiness and tempered by the aesthetic demands of the whole garden. So the garden is not a *botanic* collection, but an extremely good *horticultural* one, and the plants are chosen and placed for their decorative merit and their contribution to the whole.

 Features Sub-tropical plants; plantsman's collection of plants matched to a firm design; good herbaceous borders; fine collection of trees; extensive plantings of Australian & South African plants; over 25 different palms; new gazebo (2000).

Owned by Mr & Mrs Robert Dudley-Cooke
Number of gardeners 2
Size 1.8ha (4½ acres)

Lanhydrock

BODMIN PL30 5AD

Tel 01208 73320   **Fax** 01298 74084
Website www.nationaltrust.org.uk
Location 2½ miles south-east of Bodmin.
Opening hours 10 am – 6 pm (dusk, if sooner); daily; all year.

Admission fee   Garden only £3.80.

Lanhydrock is a grand mansion, mainly 19th-century, with one of the best formal gardens in Cornwall – clipped yews, box parterres and bedding out, as well as large herbaceous borders which contain a good collection of *Crocosmia* (a National Collection until recently). The woodlands behind are impressive for their size and colourful rhododendrons in spring. But it is the magnolias which impress the visitor most: 140 different species and cultivars.

 Features Woodland garden; topiary; good herbaceous borders; bluebells; Victorian parterres; spring bulbs; National Trust shop; restaurant & bar, cream teas from 16 February to 3 November.

Owned by The National Trust
Number of gardeners 5
Size 12.5ha (31 acres)
English Heritage grade II*

Mount Edgcumbe Gardens

CREMYLL, TORPOINT PL10 1HZ

Tel 01752 822236   **Fax** 01752 822199
Location At the end of the B3247 in south-east Cornwall, or by ferry from Plymouth.
Opening hours Formal gardens & park: dawn to dusk; all year. House & Earl's Garden: 11 am – 4.30 pm; daily; April to September.
Admission fee House & Earl's Garden: Adults £4.50; OAPs £3.50; Children £2.25. Formal gardens & park: free.

A long, stately grass drive runs down from the house to Plymouth Sound, through oak woods interplanted with large ornamental trees. The formal gardens are right down on the waterside, protected by a clipped ilex hedge 10m high. There are no less than 10 acres of gardens here, including an Italian garden (made in the 1790s), a French garden (Regency), a modern American garden, a New Zealand garden complete with geyser, the 18th-century Thomson's Seat, an orangery with newly acquired orange trees, and the fern dell recently replanted with ivies and tree ferns. The 2-acre Earl's Garden has recently been restored and planted: highlights include a 400-year-old lime tree and a Victorian shell seat among the herbaceous borders, summerhouses and statues. Allow plenty of time to do justice to these majestic pleasure gardens.

Features Sub-tropical plants; plants under glass; daffodils; good herbaceous borders; fine collection of trees; summer bedding; deer park; formal gardens; fern dell; genuine Victorian rose garden; tallest cork oak *Quercus suber* (26m) in the British Isles; gift and book shops; camellias for sale; orangery restaurant in formal gardens.

Owned by Cornwall County Council & Plymouth City Council
Number of gardeners 3
Size 4ha (10 acres), plus huge park
NCCPG National Collections *Camellia*
English Heritage grade I

Pencarrow

WASHAWAY, BODMIN PL30 3AG

Tel 01208 841369   **Fax** 01208 841722
Website www.pencarrow.co.uk
Location 4 miles north-west of Bodmin – signed off the A389 at Washaway.
Opening hours Dawn – dusk; 3 March to 31 October.
Admission fee Adults £3; Children free. Groups welcome by appointment (discounts usually available).

The mile-long drive at Pencarrow leads to an avenue of rhododendrons and rare conifers before you eventually come to the pretty Anglo-Palladian house. On one side are the outlines of an Italian garden, complete with fountain, laid out in the 1830s, and next to it a great granite rock garden where vast boulders from Bodmin Moor lie strewn among the trees and shrubs. Pencarrow is famous for its conifers: an ancestor planted one of every known variety in the mid-19th century and the survivors are so venerable that the great Alan Mitchell wrote a guide to them. Since about 1970 the owners have steadily retrieved the garden from the state of dereliction in which it was left at the end of World War II and added a further 200 or so conifers. Recent plantings have involved the addition of over 700 of the best modern rhododendrons, 70 camellias and many other broad-leaved trees and shrubs. It is good to see the fortunes of such a distinguished garden revived.

Features Rock garden; important collection of mature conifers; Italian garden; rhododendrons; camellias; great granite Victorian rock garden; blue hydrangeas; ice-house; monkey puzzle avenue; craft gallery; light lunches, cream teas.

Owned by The Trustees of the Molesworth-St Aubyn Family
English Heritage grade II

Penjerrick

BUDOCK WATER, FALMOUTH TR11 5ED

Tel 01872 870105 or 01326 25074
Location 3 miles south-west of Falmouth, entrance at junction of lanes opposite Penmorvah Manor Hotel.
Opening hours 1.30 pm – 4.30 pm; Wednesdays, Fridays & Sundays; March to September.

Probus Gardens

PROBUS, TRURO TR2 4HQ

Tel 01726 882597   **Fax** 01726 883868
Website www.probusgardens.org.uk
Location Off the A390 just east of the village.
Opening hours 10 am – 5 pm (or dusk); daily; March to October. 10 am – 4 pm; weekdays; 7 January to 28 February, and 1 to 24 December.
Admission fee Adults £3; OAPs £2.50; Children free. RHS members free from August to October.

Probus likes to call itself the 'Gardener's Garden' or the 'Really Useful Garden'. Both nicknames are correct: Probus is quite simply the best place in Cornwall to learn about gardening. Everything is clearly labelled: everyone will gain more from a visit than they ever imagined possible. Within it are innumerable garden rooms which illustrate and demonstrate the attraction of gardening with plants: among them are the ornamental grass garden, the seaside garden, the plantsman's garden, the exotic garden, the Japanese garden and the scented garden. The winter garden has a fine array of hellebores, primulas, narcissi and heathers, planted amongst pieris and cornus. There are collections of bamboos, camellias, clematis, conifers, dye-plants, eucalyptus, hebes, herbs, hollies, hydrangeas and many others. Nor is the garden just about plants: it has many demonstration plots for lawns, methods of cultivation, composting and shelter. There are nine greenhouses dedicated to demonstrating techniques of propagation and water-saving: the garden has its own rainwater collection system and is completely independent of the mains. Fruit and vegetables are also grown under glass, together with a range of unusual tender shrubs and perennials – Probus is not in the balmiest part of Cornwall. The low

allergen garden shows which plants will help asthma- and hay-fever-sufferers. The fruit and vegetable gardens grow modern cultivars of particular use to amateurs, and serve as part of the *Gardening Which?* trials. A recent addition is a large millennium herbaceous garden, set within low stone walls and planted as a Celtic colour wheel. One highly original feature is a geological map of Cornwall, made from rock specimens from all over the county. Here too are many of the *Salvia* collection (130 cultivars) which the garden hopes may one day be recognised as a National Collection by the NCCPG.

Features Plantsman's collection of plants; fine collection of trees; alpine plants; herbaceous gardens; winter gardens; grasses; gift shop; coffee shop.

Owned by The Friends of Probus Gardens
Number of gardeners 1, plus 20 part-time volunteers
Size 2ha (5 acres)

Admission fee Adults £2; Children £1.

The garden at Penjerrick was begun by the Fox family in the mid-19th century. It is a great plantsman's garden, famous in particular for its Barclayi and Penjerrick hybrid rhododendrons. Some of the original plants still survive in the peaceful woodland garden, thick with exotics: tender plants thrive in the lush, sheltered valley. The garden is recovering well from a period of neglect: it sums up all that was best about private Cornish gardens 100 years ago

Features Woodland garden; rhododendrons; camellias; tree ferns; ponds & bamboos.

Owned by Mrs Rachel Morin
Number of gardeners ½
Size 4ha (10 acres)
English Heritage grade II

Pine Lodge Gardens & Nursery

CUDDRA, HOLMBUSH, ST AUSTELL PL25 3RQ

Tel & Fax 01726 73500
Website www.pine-lodge.co.uk
Location East of St Austell between Holmbush & Tregrehan.
Opening hours 10 am – 5 pm; daily; 25 March to 31 October.
Admission fee Adults £4; Children £2.

This modern 30-acre garden is rather different from the typical Cornish garden. It has several different styles and contains over 6,000 different plants, all of which are labelled. In addition to the rhododendrons, magnolias and camellias so familiar in Cornish gardens there are Mediterranean

and southern-hemisphere plants grown for year-round interest, herbaceous borders, a fernery, a formal garden, a Japanese garden, a woodland walk and shrubberies. The water features include a large wildlife pond, an ornamental pond, a lake with an island and marsh gardens. Trees are a particular interest: Pine Lodge has an acer glade, a young 4-acre pinetum, and an arboretum. And a new wildflower meadow has just been planted with over 7,000 bulbs and flowers. The pace of the garden's development is very exciting and the owners' appetite for new plants grows even stronger every year.

Features Woodland garden; good herbaceous borders; fine collection of trees; marsh gardens; new Japanese Garden maturing well; good water features; fernery; garden nursery with plants from wild-collected seed; tea-room.

Owned by Mr & Mrs Raymond Clemo
Number of gardeners 4
Size 12ha (30 acres)
NCCPG National Collections Grevillea

St Michael's Mount

MARAZION TR17 0HT

Tel 01736 710507   **Fax** 01736 711544
Website www.stmichaelsmount.co.uk
Location 1 mile south of Marazion.
Opening hours Gardens: 10.30 am – 5.30 pm; daily (weather & tide permitting); April & May. Plus most weekends in summer as part of castle ticket.
Admission fee £2.50 in April & May.

St Michael's Mount is a triumph for man's ingenuity in the face of Atlantic gales, salt spray and bare rock – with sand for garden soil. Careful experiment over the generations has enabled the owners to plant a remarkable garden of plants which resist

Trebah Garden Trust

MAWNAN SMITH, FALMOUTH TR11 5JZ

Tel 01326 250448   **Fax** 01326 250781
Website www.trebah-garden.co.uk
Location 4 miles south-west of Falmouth, signed from Treliever roundabout at A39/A394 junction, through Mawnan Smith to garden.
Opening hours 10.30 am – 5 pm (last admission); daily; all year.
Admission fee Adults £4.50; OAPs £3.50; Children (5 – 15) & disabled visitors £2.50; Children (under 5) free. RHS members free at all times. National Trust members free, November to February.

Trebah has been vigorously restored and improved since the Hibberts bought it in 1980. The view from the top is magical – a beautiful, secret, wooded valley which runs right down to the Helford estuary. A stream cascades over waterfalls, through 2 acres of blue and white hydrangeas, and spills out over the beach. Vast trees, natural and exotic, line the steep sides, while the central point is held by a group of elegant tall palms. Glades of huge sub-tropical tree ferns mingle with giant gunneras, puyas and echiums, while along the sides and overhead is the rolling canopy of 100-year-old rhododendrons. The nursery was re-made in 2001 and a new visitor centre funded by the Heritage Lottery Fund will open in May this year (2002). A paradise for plantsmen, Trebah is also popular with children, whose curiosity is aroused by trails, quizzes and educational games. It is a garden for all people and for all seasons – open every day of the year.

Features Woodland garden; sub-tropical plants; plantsman's collection of plants; fine collection of trees; massed hydrangeas; lilies and candelabra primulas;

extensive new plantings of palms & succulents at the top of the garden; tallest hardy palm *Trachycarpus fortunei* (15m) in the British Isles and three other tree records; excellent nursery; private beach on Helford river; coffee shop & picnic area.

Owned by The Trebah Garden Trust
Number of gardeners 9, plus volunteers & students
Size 10ha (25 acres)
English Heritage grade II

the elements: *Luma apiculata*, Rugosa roses, correas, nerines, Hottentot figs and naturalised agapanthus. On the north side, a sparse wood of sycamores and pines gives protection to camellias, azaleas and hydrangeas. Nigel Nicolson calls it 'the largest and loveliest rock-garden in England'. There is nothing rare about the plants: the wonder is that they grow at all.

 Features Woodland garden; sub-tropical plants; rock garden; good herbaceous borders; wild narcissus; naturalised kniphofias and agapanthus; refreshments.

Owned by Lord St Levan & The National Trust
English Heritage grade II

Tregrehan

PAR PL24 2SJ

Tel 01726 812438   **Fax** 01726 814389
Location 1 mile west of St Blazey on A390.
Opening hours 10.30 am – 5 pm; Wednesday – Sunday (except Easter Sunday); mid-March to mid-June. Then 2 pm – 5 pm on same days to end of August.
Admission fee Adults £3.50; Children free.

Ⓟ ⓦⒸ ⓖ ⓨ ⓔ

An old Cornish garden whose 20 acres of woodland date back 200 years and include a fine range of Victorian conservatories, tall conifers and lanky rhododendrons. Tregrehan is best known for the camellias bred there by the late Gillian Carlyon, especially 'Jenefer Carlyon' which won her the Cory Cup from the RHS. But Tom Hudson's collections in warm temperate regions have also made a big impact on the garden which, under his guidance, has become an important living gene bank of known source plants.

 Features Woodland garden; camellias; pinetum; walled garden; sunken garden; phytogeographic planting; teas.

Owned by T.C. Hudson
Number of gardeners 2
Size 8ha (20 acres)
English Heritage grade II*

Trehane

PROBUS, TRURO TR2 4JG

Tel & Fax 01872 520547
Location Signed from A39 by Tresillian Bridge
Opening hours By appointment only.

Ⓟ ⓦⒸ ⓨ

Trehane has a fine collection of camellias, and many other good things, including magnolias, crocosmias, geraniums and other herbaceous plants. The new owners of Trehane have not yet decided whether, or when, they might start to open the garden on a regular basis, but are quietly optimistic.

Features Woodland garden; plantsman's collection of plants; mature conifers; camellias; bluebells.

Owned by Mr & Mrs John Connell
Number of gardeners 2
Size 4ha (10 acres)

Trelissick Garden

FEOCK, TRURO TR3 6QL

Tel 01872 862090   **Fax** 01872 865808
Website www.nationaltrust.org.uk
Location Take B3289 off main Truro – Falmouth Road.
Opening hours 10.30 am (12.30 pm on Sundays) – 5.30 pm (or dusk, if earlier); daily; 16 February to 3 November.

Admission fee Adults £4.50; Children £2.25.

Once famous as 'the fruit garden of Cornwall', and still maintained by the National Trust, Trelissick is particularly colourful in August and September when the hydrangeas are in full flower. There are over 100 cultivars, some in a special walk. But venerable conifers and tender plants are also features: *Erythrina crista-galli*, cannas and hedychiums are among the many good things that over-winter outside, not to mention daffodils, rhododendrons and camellias in spring.

 Features Woodland garden; plantsman's collection of plants; mature conifers; aromatic plant garden; fig garden; hydrangeas; tallest tree fern *Dicksonia antarctica* (6m) in the British Isles; gift and plant shop; refreshments.

Owned by The National Trust
Number of gardeners 4
Size 12ha (30 acres)
NCCPG National Collections *Azara*; *Photinia*
English Heritage grade II

Trengwainton Gardens

MADRON, PENZANCE TR20 8RZ

Tel 01736 363148 **Fax** 01736 368142
Location 2 miles north-west of Penzance, ½ mile west of Heamoor.
Opening hours 10 am – 5.30 pm (5 pm in February, March & October); Sunday – Thursday & Good Friday; 17 February to 3 November.
Admission fee Adults £3.90; Children £1.95.

Trengwainton has one of the best collections of tender plants on the Cornish mainland, all thanks to the Bolitho family who started planting seriously only in 1925. Much came from original seed from such collectors as Kingdon Ward: some rhododendrons flowered here for the first time in the British Isles, among them *R. macabeanum, R. elliottii* and *R. taggianum*. The plants in many Cornish gardens are past their best. Not so at Trengwainton, where many are in their prime. It is a garden to wander through slowly, giving yourself as much time as you need to enjoy its riches.

 Features Woodland garden; sub-tropical plants; roses (mainly old-fashioned); lilies; acacias; *Myosotidium hortensia*; tree ferns; tallest *Xanthoceras sorbifolium* (7m) in the British Isles (and two record trees); National Trust shop; coffee, snacks, teas; new restaurant (2000).

Owned by Lt.Col. E.T. Bolitho & The National Trust
Number of gardeners 4
English Heritage grade II

Trerice

KESTLE MILL, NEWQUAY TR8 4PG

Tel 01637 875404 **Fax** 01637 879300
Website www.nationaltrust.org.uk
Location 3 miles south-east of Newquay – turn right off A3058 at Kestle Mill.
Opening hours 11 am – 5.30 pm (5 pm in October & November); daily except Tuesdays & Saturdays (but open every day from 16 July to 10 September); 24 March to 3 November.
Admission fee House £4.40; Garden free.

A perfect West Country manor house with pretty Dutch gables, Trerice is unusual among Cornish gardens. It is small and comparatively formal: the design and herbaceous plantings are its best points. It is not surrounded by swirling rhododendron woodland. There is a perfect harmony between the Elizabethan architecture and

Tresco Abbey

ISLES OF SCILLY TR24 0QQ

Tel 01720 424105   **Fax** 01720 422868
Website www.tresco.co.uk
Location Direct helicopter flight from Penzance, or boat from St Mary's.
Opening hours 10 am – 4 pm; daily; all year.
Admission fee Adults £7.50; Children free.

The sub-tropical gardens on Tresco are unique in the British Isles. They were first designed and planted by Augustus Smith in 1834: his successors have been equally passionate in their search for tender plants that will grow outside on Tresco's south-facing terraces as nowhere else in Britain. The collection is especially strong in plants from South Africa, Australia and New Zealand but, even though any account of Tresco reads like a list of plants, it is still very much an ornamental garden which strives for horticultural effect. The oldest specimens include Canary Island palms, a large number of aeoniums from both the Canary Islands and Madeira, agaves from America and puyas from Chile. Since the great gale of 1990, the gardens have been extensively replanted, with hundreds of exotic plants from Kew, all protected by extensive new shelterbelts. No matter what time of the year, there is always a lot of colour and much of interest: proteas and acacias in winter; the shrubby foxglove (*Isoplexis sceptrum*); mesembryanthemums and agapanthus in summer. There is also a shady area where tree ferns and *Musschia wollastonii* flourish. Many people come here year after year to admire the displays of plants which cannot be seen elsewhere in Britain. The standards of maintenance are exemplary. There is only one disadvantage: the helicopter service may make access from the mainland easier and quicker than ever, but the noise from its arrivals and departures does distract you while actually visiting the garden.

Features Sub-tropical plants; plantsman's collection of plants; mature conifers; cacti; succulents; South African, Australian and New Zealand plants; tallest *Luma apiculata* (20m), *Metrosideros excelsa* (20m) and *Cordyline australis* (15m) in the British Isles; shop; light refreshments.

Owned by Robert Dorrien Smith
Number of gardeners 5, plus 2 students
Size 6.7ha (17 acres)
NCCPG National Collections *Acacia*
English Heritage grade I

the gardens. Somewhat anomalously, it boasts the largest collection of mid-Victorian to current-day lawn mowers in the country. They are both interesting and fun to visit.

 Features Colour borders; good collection of apple trees; lawn-mower museum; National Trust shop; restaurant & tea-room.

Owned by The National Trust
Number of gardeners 1
Size 5.6ha (14 acres)

Trevarno Gardens

HELSTON TR13 0RU

Tel 01326 574274 **Fax** 01326 574282
Location 3 miles west of Helston, signed from the junction of A394 & B3302.
Opening hours 10.30 am – 5 pm; daily; all year. Closed 25 December.
Admission fee Adults £3.50; OAPs £3; Children £1.25. RHS members free from 1 January to 28 March.

Trevarno is an interesting new project – an old estate which has been restored and developed since 1997 and which promises to become one of the great gardens of Cornwall again. The old woodland gardens have been cleared, the lake dredged, the 19th-century Italian garden restored and the fountain conservatory refurnished. Work continues: there are plans for a series of stylishly themed gardens dedicated to the flora of different parts of the world. Meanwhile the museum has a vast and fascinating collection of old garden tools and horticultural equipment of every sort.

Features Garden restoration; museum of gardening; shop; refreshments.

Owned by M. Sagin

Trewithen

GRAMPOUND ROAD, TRURO TR2 4DD

Tel 01726 883647 **Fax** 01726 882301
Website www.trewithengardens.co.uk
Location A390 between Probus & Grampound.
Opening hours 10 am – 4.30 pm; Monday – Saturday (& Sundays in April & May); March to September.
Admission fee Adults £4; Children £2. RHS members free from July to September.

Trewithen's setting is magnificent. Instead of the steep terraces of most Cornish gardens, there is a spacious flat lawn that stretches for 200 yards into the distance, with gentle banks of rhododendrons, magnolias and rare shrubs on all sides. It sets the tone for the garden's grandeur, which was largely the work of George Johnstone in the early 20th century. Johnstone was a great plantsman. Note how he used laurel hedges to divide up the woodland and give structure to the garden. He also had an eye for placing plants to advantage. As a breeder, he gave us *Rhododendron arboreus* 'Alison Johnstone', *Ceanothus arboreus* 'Trewithen Blue' and *Camellia saluensis* 'Trewithen White'. There is an excellent guidebook written by Nigel Holman.

 Features Woodland garden; rhododendrons & azaleas; plantsman's collection of plants; camellias; good herbaceous borders; fine collection of trees; magnolias; quarry garden; cyclamen; new fountain (1999); tallest *Magnolia campbellii* subsp. *mollicomata* (19m) in the British Isles and 16 more record-breaking tree species; excellent nursery & garden shop.

Owned by A.M.J. Galsworthy
Number of gardeners 4
Size 12ha (30 acres)
English Heritage grade II*

CUMBRIA

Cumbria came into being in 1974, an amalgam of the old counties of Cumberland, Westmorland and the northern part of Lancashire. Gardening in Cumbria is dominated by the Lake District: both Wordsworth's garden ay Rydal Mount and Ruskin's at Brantwood are open to visitors. There are good historic gardens of the grander sort, too. Though few in number, almost all the most important are open to the public: Levens is rated Grade I, while Dalemain, Holker, Muncaster and Sizergh are all Grade II*. Cumbria's acid soils and the highest rainfall in England are very favourable to the growth of conifers: many of the older gardens have fine specimens of *Abies*, *Picea* and *Pinus*, while Muncaster also offers an extensive collection of *Nothofagus* species. The National Gardens Scheme is active in the county, and particularly successful in persuading garden-owners in and around the Lake District to open for charity. Cumbria has comparatively few nurseries, but the ones we list below are exceptionally good. The county has its fair share of National Collections, with clusters of genera at three of the larger gardens: *Halesia*, *Pterostyrax*, *Styrax*, *Sinojackia* and other *Styracaceae* at Holker; *Astilbe*, *Hydrangea* and *Polystichum* at Holehird; and *Asplenium scolopendrium*, *Cystopteris*, *Dryopteris*, and *Osmunda* at Sizergh. Newton Rigg near Penrith is a RHS Partner College, with lectures, demonstrations and garden walks throughout the year.

Acorn Bank Garden

ACORN BANK, TEMPLE SOWERBY, PENRITH CA10 1SP

Tel 01768 361893 Fax 01768 361467
Website www.nationaltrust.org.uk
Location North of Temple Sowerby, 6 miles east of Penrith on A66.
Opening hours 10 am – 5 pm; Wednesday – Monday; 23 March to 3 November.
Admission fee Adults £2.50; Children £1.25.

Acorn Bank claims to have the largest collection (250 cultivars) of culinary and medicinal plants in the north, but it is almost better visited in spring when thousands and thousands of daffodils fill the woodland slopes, and the fruit trees flower in the old walled garden. Best of all is the huge quince tree, a wondrous sight in flower or fruit.

Features Woodland garden; roses (mainly old-fashioned); herbs; fruit; good herbaceous borders; spring bulbs; woodland walk past Mill; National Trust shop; tea-room.

Owned by The National Trust

Brantwood

CONISTON LA21 8AD

Tel 01539 441396 **Fax** 01539 441263
Website www.brantwood.org.uk
Location East side of Coniston Water, 2½ miles from Coniston, 4 miles from Hawkshead.
Opening hours 11 am – 5.30 pm; daily; 18 March to 18 November. 11 am – 4.30 pm; Wednesday – Sunday; rest of year.
Admission fee Adults £2; Children £1.

This woodland garden was laid out by John Ruskin from 1871 onwards but somewhat altered and neglected after his death in 1900. Working with the natural materials of the site, Ruskin developed a series of experimental gardens within the ancient woodland and on the high moor behind. When the Brantwood Trust began the task of reclamation, it decided to restore the garden partly as it was in Ruskin's lifetime, and partly as a modern re-interpretation of his ideas. Work has recently begun on restoring the 'zig-zaggy garden' and the Victorian 'viewing terrace'. Below Ruskin's 'living laboratory', exotic ornamental plantings frame wonderful views across Coniston Water. There is a regular passenger ferry service from Coniston Boat-buildings: the steam yacht *Gondola* also calls from May to October.

Features Rhododendrons & azaleas; daffodils; bluebells; cottage garden; extensive native fern collection; new native herb & physic garden (2000); bookshop & craft gallery; meals, light refreshments & drinks all day.

Owned by The Brantwood Trust
Size 10ha (25 acres)

Charney Well

HAMPSFELL ROAD, GRANGE-OVER-SANDS LA11 6BE

Tel 01539 534526 **Fax** 01539 535765
Website www.charneywell.com
Location Turn right at Crown Hill roundabout, right at crossroads, and find Hampsfell Road car-park on left.
Opening hours 11 am – 4.30 pm, 22 & 23 June. Groups by appointment at other times between 17 & 28 June.
Admission fee Adults £2.50.

The Mediterranean effects of this tiered and terraced modern classic have been achieved since 1988 by planting lots of phormiums, together with cordylines, palms, yuccas and pittosporums. Bold foliage and a flamboyant personality is what the owners seek in their plants, so they are chosen for such seasonal highlights as striking bark or foliage. It follows that Charney Well is full of evergreen foliage – eucalyptus, acacia, bamboos, corokias and fatsias, for example. The underplantings too are rich and every patch is thickly covered. Do not expect to see anything so conventional as a lawn, but mulches of gravel, slate and bark instead. The site is steep and stony, with panoramic views across Morecambe Bay, splendid air-drainage and a southerly aspect. It may not be a promising place for traditional English gardening, but its situation and the influence of the Gulf Stream make it perfect for the exotic plants the owners choose to grow. This year sees new plantings of further yuccas, alliums, eryngiums and grasses. And the garden is forever changing, especially after trips to see real Mediterranean gardens.

Features Exotic plantings; structural & architectural plants; teas.

Owned by Christopher Holliday & Richard Roberts
Number of gardeners 1
Size 0.2ha (½ acre)
NCCPG National Collections *Phormium*

Dalemain

PENRITH CA11 0HB

Tel 01768 486450 **Fax** 01768 486223
Website www.dalemain.com
Location M6 (Jct 40), A66, A592.
Opening hours 10.30 am – 5 pm; Sunday – Thursday;
24 March to 13 October.
Admission fee Gardens only: £3.50. RHS members free
from 3 June to 13 July.

Dalemain has belonged to the Hasell family
since 1679. The history of the garden starts,
however, with a 16th-century terrace, of
which very few remain anywhere in the
British Isles. Then comes a kitchen garden
with fruit trees planted 250 years ago,
though the overall 'feel' of Dalemain is
Edwardian. Most of the plantings are
modern, including the formal knot garden
and the long and richly planted herbaceous
border which overlooks the park and the
Lakeland Fells. The mixed borders and roses
are dreamily English, particularly the Rose
Walk, which boasts more than 100 old-
fashioned roses. Nearby is the wild garden
with drifts of meconopsis and martagon
lilies in late spring, but this is a garden
which looks good at all seasons. Plants are
well labelled and well grown.

Features Woodland garden; roses
(mainly old-fashioned); herbs;
meconopsis; old flower and fruit varieties;
good herbaceous and mixed borders; biggest
Abies cephalonica in the British Isles.

Owned by Robert Hasell-McCosh
English Heritage grade II*

Graythwaite Hall

ULVERSTON, HAWKSHEAD LA12 8BA

Tel 01539 531248 **Fax** 01539 530060
Location Between Newby Bridge & Hawkshead.
Opening hours 10 am – 6 pm; daily; April to June.
Admission fee Adults £2; Children free.

Graythwaite shows Thomas Mawson on
home ground and at his best. Formal
gardens in the Arts & Crafts style by the
house drop down to sweeping lawns;
beyond the stream is a woodland of
rhododendrons and azaleas. The yew topiary
is good – some castellated and some with a
mixture of green and gold cultivars.

 Features Topiary; roses (ancient &
modern); rock garden; fine trees.

Owned by Graythwaite Estate Trustees
Number of gardeners 1
Size 2.2ha (6 acres)

Hartside Nursery Garden

ALSTON CA9 3BL

Tel & Fax 01434 381372
Location ¼ mile south-west of Alston on the
A686 to Penrith.
Opening hours 9.30 am – 4.30 pm; Monday – Friday.
12.30 pm – 4 pm; Saturdays & Sundays. March to October.
Other months by appointment.

This high-level (over 300m) nursery
specialises in alpines, particularly primulas
(lots of interesting forms of *P. gracilipes*, for
example), dwarf shrubs, conifers and hardy
ferns: all are home-grown in the cold North
Pennines. The display gardens are worth a
visit and maintained in a relaxed style.

Holehird

LAKELAND HORTICULTURAL SOCIETY, PATTERDALE ROAD, WINDERMERE LA23 1NP

Tel 01539 446008
Website www.cragview.demon.co.uk
Location 1 mile north of Windermere town, off A592.
Opening hours Dawn – dusk; daily; all year.
Admission fee Donation (min. £2).

Holehird is a demonstration and trial garden, maintained entirely by some 70 volunteers, all members of the Lakeland Horticultural Society. The society's aim is to 'promote and develop the science, practice and art of horticulture, particularly with regard to the conditions prevailing in the Lake District'. The gardens have recently been extended to about 10 acres and occupy an old walled garden, rockery and the formal gardens in front of the mansion. The interesting thing for visitors is to see what flourishes at every season in a cool damp climate: alpines, azaleas, heathers, bulbs, ferns and much, much more.

Features Woodland garden; rock garden; herbs; plants under glass; heathers; roses; hostas; ferns; Victorian garden; walled garden; spring bulbs; plants for sale on Wednesdays; rhododendrons & azaleas.

Owned by Lakeland Horticultural Society
Number of gardeners about 70 volunteers
Size 4ha (10 acres)
NCCPG National Collections *Astilbe*; *Hydrangea*; *Polystichum*

Holker Hall

CARK-IN-CARTMEL, GRANGE-OVER-SANDS LA11 7PL

Tel 01539 558328   **Fax** 01539 558378
Website www.holker-hall.co.uk
Location Jct 36 off M6, follow brown & white tourist signs.
Opening hours 10 am – 6 pm (last admission 4.30 pm); Sunday – Friday; Easter to October.
Admission fee Adults £3.95; Children £2.25. Prices subject to review. RHS members free, excluding special event days.

The 19th-century formal gardens below the house are scrumptiously planted as herbaceous borders, the first of many imaginative modern designs and plantings throughout this extensive garden. The woodland has foxgloves, rhododendrons and splendid trees: Joseph Paxton supplied a monkey puzzle and Lord George Cavendish the cedars grown from seeds he brought back from the Holy Land. The Gulf Stream enables many exotic trees and shrubs to flourish and flower which might not otherwise be hardy in this northerly climate.

Features Formal & woodland gardens; roses (ancient & modern); rhododendrons; fine limestone cascade & fountain; HHA/Christie's Garden of the Year in 1991; tallest *Ilex latifolia* (15m) in the British Isles (and two other tree records); shop; cafeteria (licensed).

Owned by Lord Cavendish of Furness
Number of gardeners 6
Size 10ha (25 acres)
NCCPG National Collections Styracaceae (incl. *Halesia*, *Pterostyrax*, *Styrax*, *Sinojackia*)
English Heritage grade II*

Hutton-in-the-Forest

PENRITH CA11 9TH

Tel 01768 484449   **Fax** 01768 484571
Location 3 miles from Exit 41 of M6 on B5305.
Opening hours Gardens: 11 am – 5 pm; all year except Saturdays.
Admission fee Gardens only: Adults £2.50; Children free.

The charm of Hutton-in-the-Forest derives from its many architectural, gardening and landscape styles which span 400 years but come together as an historic and romantic whole. The pale pink sandstone house is old, handsomely sited and built onto a mediaeval pele tower. Salvin refashioned it in the 19th century and Gilpin restored the terraces at about the same time: the fine topiary is a little later. Beyond the terraces is a woodland garden where conifers are underplanted by billowing rhododendrons. In the walled garden, a double herbaceous border runs from end to end, screened from the growing vegetables by thick yew hedges. This is a very traditional garden of great serenity.

 Features Woodland walk; herbaceous borders in the walled garden; terraces with topiary; 17th-century dovecote; refreshments when house open, from noon.

Owned by Lord Inglewood
Number of gardeners 1
Size 4.2ha (11 acres)
English Heritage grade II

Levens Hall

KENDAL LA8 0PD

Tel 01539 560321   **Fax** 01539 560669
Website www.levenshall.co.uk
Location 5 miles south of Kendal on A6.

Opening hours 10 am – 5 pm; Sunday – Thursday; 31 March to 10 October.
Admission fee Adults £5; Children £2.50.

Levens means topiary: huge overgrown chunks of box and yew. Some is said to be left over from a simple formal parterre laid out in 1694 and supplemented by golden yews in the 19th century. Some is more recent – successive generations have been good about replacing plants and restoring the garden when necessary. The arbours and high yew hedges, some of them crenellated, are spangled with *Tropaeolum speciosum* and the parterres planted annually with 15,000 plants, which makes Levens one of the best places to study the expensive art of bedding out. Well maintained.

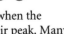 **Features** Topiary; spring & summer bedding; new fountain garden; HHA/Christie's Garden of the Year in 1994; gift shop and plant centre; light lunches & teas.

Owned by C.H. Bagot
English Heritage grade I

Muncaster Castle

RAVENGLASS CA18 1RQ

Tel 01229 717614   **Fax** 01229 717010
Website www.muncastercastle.co.uk
Location A595 1 mile east of Ravenglass on west coast.
Opening hours 10.30 am – 6 pm; daily; all year.
Admission fee Adults £5.50; Children £3.50. RHS members free from March to November.

Visit Muncaster in May, when the rhododendrons are at their peak. Many are grown from the original seed introduced by such plant hunters as Forrest and Kingdon Ward in the 1920s and 1930s. The owners have made an excellent job of identifying them and labelling them: some have turned out to be the tallest of their kind in England. Alongside this vigorous work of restoration, Muncaster also has a developing collection of hardy hybrid rhododendrons and a nursery which sells 500+ cultivars. The castle was revamped by Salvin in the 1860s: stand on its wonderful long curved terrace (*very* long – half a mile) above the steep slopes and soak up the intensely romantic landscape of the Lakeland hills around. Ruskin called it 'the gateway to Paradise'. The new MeadowVole (*sic*) Maze will appeal to younger visitors.

 Features Woodland garden; mature conifers; camellias; maples; masses of new plantings; bluebells; tallest *Nothofagus obliqua* (31m) in the British Isles; lots of new plantings; two gift shops; good specialist plant centre; snacks & full meals.

Owned by Mrs P.R. Gordon-Duff-Pennington
Number of gardeners 4, plus some part-time help
Size 31ha (77 acres)
English Heritage grade II*

Rydal Mount

AMBLESIDE LA22 9LU

Tel 01539 433002 **Fax** 01539 431738
Website www.wordsworthslakes.co.uk
Location 1½ miles north of Ambleside on A591, turn up Rydal Hill.
Opening hours 9.30 am – 5 pm; daily; March to October. 10 am – 4 pm; daily, except Tuesdays; November to February.
Admission fee Adults £1.75.

Ⓟ ⓗ ⓌⒸ

Kept very much as it was in the poet's day, the garden at Rydal Mount is a memorial to William Wordsworth. He believed that a garden should be informal in its design, harmonise with the country and keep its views open.

 Features Daffodils; bluebells; trees; rhododendrons; Dora Wordsworth's terrace undergoing restoration (1997).

Owned by Rydal Mount Trust (Wordsworth Family)
Number of gardeners 1
Size 1.6ha (4 acres)
English Heritage grade II

Sizergh Castle

KENDAL LA8 8AE

Tel 01539 660070 **Fax** 01539 561621
Website www.nationaltrust.org.uk
Location 3½ miles south of Kendal.
Opening hours 12.30 pm – 5.30 pm; Sunday – Thursday; 24 March to 31 October.
Admission fee Garden only: Adults £2.50.

Ⓟ ⓌⒸ ♿ ❀ 🎫 ☕

Sizergh has lots of interest from wild daffodils and alpines in April to hydrangeas and a hot half-hardy border in September – *Beschorneria yuccoides* and *Buddleja colvilei*. Best of all is the 1920s rock garden, made of local limestone, and home to an important (and beautiful) collection of ferns – over 100 hardy species and cultivars. Some of the 60 dwarf conifers have grown to a remarkable size.

Features Good herbaceous borders; wildflower meadow; tender plants.

Owned by The National Trust
NCCPG National Collections *Asplenium scolopendrium*; *Cystopteris*; *Dryopteris*; *Osmunda*
English Heritage grade II*

DERBYSHIRE

Derbyshire has no less than five historic gardens which are listed as Grade I: Chatsworth, Haddon, Hardwick, Kedleston and Melbourne. All are regularly open to the public. The National Gardens Scheme is very active in the county, with a good number of medium-sized and small gardens listed in the Yellow Book. Nevertheless it is the larger gardens on old estates which offer the most horticultural interest. Much of Derbyshire is high and cold in winter, yet it also has some excellent nurseries and garden centres. Bluebell Nursery & Arboretum, right in the south of the county, has one of the most exciting new collections of trees and shrubs in the British Isles, while Abbey Brook Cactus Nursery in Matlock has for long been the UK's leading specialist nursery for cacti and succulents. Its National Collections of *Conophytum*, *Haworthia* and *Lithops* are unmatched by any other collection holder. Begonias and gladiolus are popular in Derbyshire, and fine displays are often seen at local flower shows. Broomfield College at Morley is a RHS Partner College with a wide range of workshops and lectures throughout the year: details from 01332 836600.

Abbey Brook Cactus Nursery

BAKEWELL ROAD, MATLOCK DE4 2QJ

Tel 01629 580306 **Fax** 01629 55852
Website www.abbeybrookcacti.com
Location On A6, 2 miles north of Matlock.
Opening hours 1 pm – 4 pm; daily, except Tuesday. Opens 12.15 pm on Sundays. Closed 1 January, 25 & 26 December.
Admission fee Free.

Abbey Brook is the UK's leading cactus nursery, now 90% wholesale and with 1,000,000 plants in stock. The retail list is remarkable – it offers over 2,000 cultivars, and has at least the same number again among its stock plants. The nursery is worth a visit at any time of the year – so is the website, which offers a full-colour catalogue and on-line ordering. Cactus buffs need no introduction to Abbey Brook, but the nursery is also extremely interesting for those whose gardening interests are quite different. It displays the wonder and beauty of these plants in such a way that you cannot help responding to them – and their extraordinary diversity. There are two special open weekends for the NCCPG this year: 30 & 31 March and 28 & 29 September.

Owned by Brian Fearn
NCCPG National Collections *Conophytum*; *Echinopsis* hybrids; *Gymnocalycium*; *Haworthia*; *Lithops*

Bluebell Arboretum & Nursery

ANNWELL LANE, SMISBY, ASHBY-DE-LA-ZOUCH LE65 2TA

Tel 01530 413700   **Fax** 01530 417600
Website www.bluebellnursery.com
Location 200 yards south of Smisby Church. Follow brown tourist signs to arboretum.
Opening hours 9 am – 5 pm (4 pm from November to February); Monday – Saturday; all year. 10.30 am – 4.30 pm; Sundays; March to October. Closed from 24 December to 4 January.
Admission fee Adults £2.50; Children free. RHS members free.

Bluebell Nursery (a RHS Partner Nursery) has been a stalwart supporter of RHS shows for some years now and has won many medals for its displays of rare trees and shrubs. The 6-acre arboretum has expanded every year since it was first planted in 1992 and is already remarkably mature, but the owners are keen to emphasise that 'you should not expect to find a Westonbirt, Wisley or Wakehurst' yet. Nevertheless, it is a most interesting place to visit, not least to see what will grow in the cold Midlands. Most visitors are intrigued by the many cultivars of dogwoods (*Cornus*), maples (*Acer*) and beech (*Fagus sylvestris*). Other highlights include an avenue of witch-hazel cultivars (*Hamamelis*), fine specimens of *Quercus castaneifolia* 'Green Spire' and the very rare *Quercus rhysophylla* from Mexico, and the largest collection of deciduous hollies *Ilex verticillata* in Europe. The website allows on-line ordering: the nursery sells many more plants than those listed in its excellent catalogue.

Features Fine collection of trees & shrubs; important tree & shrub nursery.

Owned by Mr & Mrs Robert Vernon
Size 2ha (5 acres)

Calke Abbey

TICKNALL DE73 1LE

Tel 01332 863822   **Fax** 01332 865272
Website www.nationaltrust.org.uk
Location 10 miles south of Derby on A514 in village of Ticknall.
Opening hours 11 am – 5.30 pm; Saturday – Wednesday; 23 March to 3 November. Closes at 7 pm on Tuesdays & Wednesdays in July & August.
Admission fee Adults £3; Children £1.50.

The 'sleeping beauty' house is not really matched by its garden, but there are interesting glasshouses in the walled garden, a 19th-century ice-house, a bothy and a kitchen garden. The drive runs along a magnificent avenue of ancient limes. In the walled garden is the only surviving Auricula Theatre, originally built to display the perfection of these beautiful 'florist's' plants.

Features Vegetables; fruit; good herbaceous borders; dahlias; good Victorian-style bedding; deer park; horse-chestnut trees; local varieties of apples & soft fruit; National Trust gift shop; licensed restaurant.

Owned by The National Trust
English Heritage grade II*

Chatsworth

BAKEWELL DE45 1PP

Tel 01246 582204   **Fax** 01246 583536
Website www.chatsworth.org
Location 8 miles north of Matlock off B6012.
Opening hours 11 am (10.30 am from June to August) –
6 pm (last admissions 5 pm); daily; 20 March to
27 October.
Admission fee Adults £4.50; OAPs £3.50; Children £2;
Family ticket £11.

Chatsworth sits near the bottom of a high valley on the edge of the Peak District surrounded by over 100 acres of beautiful landscaped park – the work of Capability Brown. Into this naturalistic setting successive Dukes of Devonshire have inserted formal designs, flower gardens and magnificent garden buildings. Despite their piecemeal history, the gardens at Chatsworth all come together as a single ornament for the house. They have been open to the public for nearly 200 years. The glory days of Chatsworth's garden were the 1830s and 1840s when Sir Joseph Paxton and the 'bachelor Duke' built the Emperor fountain, the rock garden (huge boulders surrounded by conifers), the arboretum, the pinetum and the 'conservative wall', which was intended to keep the heat and ripen fruit trees (and protects an enormous *Camellia reticulata* 'Captain Rawes' with trunks 80cm thick). The present Duchess has been responsible for some stylish additions such as the serpentine hedges which lead from the Victorian ring pond to a bust of the 6th Duke. Perhaps the best known features at Chatsworth today are the Great Cascade, built in about 1700 and unique in England and the Canal, dug at the same time as a formal sheet of water to set off the southern façade of the house. But there is much of

horticultural interest too: a tulip tree avenue, the bamboo walk, Victorian yews of different hues, the rose garden, the cottage garden, the kitchen garden, the blue-and-white and the orange borders and record trees like *Pinus peuce*. Chatsworth has also long been famous for its camellias and glasshouse grapes, both of which have won many prizes at RHS shows. But perhaps the greatest joy of Chatsworth is the sense, which still pervades the entire estate, that it is a private garden in which every visitor feels that he is a welcome guest.

Features Woodland garden; topiary; roses (mainly modern); rock garden; rhododendrons & azaleas; fine collection of trees; pinetum; maze; tulip tree avenue; millennium planting of 100 oaks in 50 different varieties; tallest *Pinus strobus* (42m) in the British Isles; plants for sale in stable yard; licensed self-service restaurant.

Owned by Chatsworth House Trust
Number of gardeners 21
Size 42ha (105 acres)
English Heritage grade I

Dam Farm House

EDNASTON, ASHBOURNE DE6 3BA

Tel 01335 360291
Location Turn off A52 to Bradley, opposite
Ednaston Lane end.
Opening hours 11 am – 4 pm on 28 April (plant sale).
2 pm – 4.30 pm on 26 May, 23 June, & 11 August. Parties
by arrangement from April to October.
Admission fee Adults £3; Children free.

Mrs Player (born a Loder) has made this outstanding garden on a greenfield site since 1980. The design is firm, and the planting exuberant. Clipped hedges enclose a series of separate gardens which flow into each other, but in contrast to the firm design, the planting belongs to the cottage garden tradition. There is a formal garden by the house which ends in a delicate white wire gazebo. The borders are richly planted with the best of modern plants – *Cercis canadensis* 'Forest Pansy' for example and *Viburnum sargentii* 'Onondaga'. Clematis are a favourite and there is a surprisingly large number of plants which one might suppose too tender for Derbyshire – cistus, ceanothus and penstemons. This garden is now in its prime: the trees are semi-mature and the plants have lost none of their youthful vigour. Rare plants abound and are always being added, but it is their treatment which makes the garden such an exciting place to visit and learn from: their planting, training and cultivation are a model for our times.

Features Roses (mainly old-fashioned); fine collection of trees; scree garden; young arboretum.

Owned by Mrs Jean Player
Number of gardeners part-time help
Size 1.2ha (3 acres)

Elvaston Castle

BORROWASH ROAD, ELVASTON DE72 3EP

Tel 01332 571342   **Fax** 01332 758751
Location 5 miles south-east of Derby. Signed from
A6 & A52.
Opening hours Dawn – dusk (Old English Garden,
9 am – 5 pm, but 4 pm in winter); daily; all year.
Admission fee Gardens free. Car park 70p midweek,
£1.30 weekends.

This is an historic garden, once famous for its topiary: it was saved from oblivion by Derby County Council some 25 years ago. The parterres have been replaced and the walled garden replanted with roses and herbaceous plants, and renamed the Old English Garden. However, there is a possibility that it might be sold later this year.

Features Topiary; roses (mainly old-fashioned); good herbaceous borders; two gift shops; restaurant open all year 10 am – 4.30 pm, closed Mondays.

Owned by Derbyshire County Council
Number of gardeners 6
English Heritage grade II*

Haddon Hall

BAKEWELL DE45 1LA

Tel 01629 812855   **Fax** 01629 814379
Website www.haddonhall.co.uk
Location 1½ miles south of Bakewell on A6.
Opening hours 10.30 am – 5 pm; daily; 28 March to
30 September. Plus Monday – Thursday in October
(closes at 4.30 pm). Closed 14 July.
Admission fee House & garden: Adults £6.75; OAPs
£5.75; Children £3.50.

Haddon Hall is a substantial house which dates mainly from about 1600. The gardens, however, are less than 100 years old, having been laid out by the 9th Duchess of Rutland in the 1910s and 1920s along the much older terraces. The Duchess planted formal features like yew trees to add to the structure, but her great passion was for roses, and it is for these most beautiful of flowers that the garden is now known. The collection is a good one and, though it lacks any real rarities, it is kept up to date by the addition of all the best repeat-flowering cultivars, which means that there is a good selection of modern roses among the older ramblers and noisettes. The hybrid teas include the bright crimson 'Royal William' and pink 'Paul Shirville' and among the floribundas are yellow 'Arthur Bell' and the dark red 'The Times' rose. But shrub roses and wild rose species are also well represented. There are 60 different cultivars of delphinium in the herbaceous borders, which are supplemented by tender perennials and annuals, hardy and half-hardy. In June and July there is no more beautiful and romantic garden in England.

Features Topiary; good herbaceous borders; roses of every kind; clematis; delphiniums; coffee, lunch, afternoon teas.

Owned by Lord Edward Manners
Number of gardeners 2
English Heritage grade I

Hardwick Hall

DOE LEA, CHESTERFIELD S44 5QJ

Tel 01246 850430   **Fax** 01246 854200
Website www.nationaltrust.org.uk
Location Signed from M1 Jct 29
Opening hours Gardens: 11 am – 5.30 pm; Wednesday – Monday; 27 March to 27 October.

Admission fee Garden only: Adults £3.40; Children £1.70.

The formal gardens are extensive: avenues of hornbeam and yew and a newly restored 'Elizabethan' (actually 1970s) herb garden (lavender and eglantine) in the kitchen garden. Hardwick has wonderful old fruit trees, nutteries, a mulberry avenue, old roses and modern borders in the Jekyll style. In the park are fine cedars and Hungarian oaks. This is one of the best National Trust gardens, and getting still better.

Features Roses (mainly old-fashioned); herbs; good herbaceous borders; daffodils; fine hedges; mulberry walk; hollies; weekend plant sales only; refreshments Wed/Thurs/Sat/Sun when Hall is open.

Owned by The National Trust
NCCPG National Collections Scabiosa caucasica
English Heritage grade I

Kedleston Hall

DERBY DE22 5JH

Tel 01332 842191   **Fax** 01332 841972
Website www.nationaltrust.org.uk
Location 5 miles north-west of Derby, signed at A38/A52 roundabout.
Opening hours 10 am – 6 pm; Saturday – Wednesday; 23 March to 3 November.
Admission fee Park & garden only: Adults £2.40; Children £1.10.

Kedleston is an important historic garden. The 18th-century landscaped park runs down to a long lake. The house is matched by a Robert Adam summerhouse in the circular garden: impressive and important. Lord Curzon moved it to its present position at the side of the lawns. The park has some splendid trees, most notably a fern-leaved beech (*Fagus sylvatica* 'Aspleniifolia').

 Features Roses (mainly modern); rhododendrons & azaleas; handsome Adam orangery; National Trust shop; lunches & teas.

Owned by The National Trust
Number of gardeners 2½
Size 7ha (17½ acres)
English Heritage grade I

Lea Gardens

LEA, MATLOCK DE4 5GH

Tel 01629 534380   **Fax** 01629 534260
Location 3 miles south-east of Matlock.
Opening hours 10 am – 5.30 pm; daily; 20 March to 30 June.
Admission fee Adults £3; Children 50p; Season ticket £5; wheelchair-bound free.

These rhododendron gardens were started in 1935 by John Marsden-Smedley who was so inspired by his visits to Bodnant and Exbury that he decided to plant his own rhododendron collection. He was then aged 68: by the time he died aged 92 in 1959, the garden contained some 350 cultivars of rhododendron and azaleas. Since that time, it has belonged to the Tye family, who have continued to maintain and develop it. The standard of maintenance is extremely high and it is one of the most beautiful gardens to visit in season. Much is on a steep slope and some of the paths are narrow, but the principal areas are fairly open and there are large numbers of modern, low-growing rhododendron and azalea hybrids underplanted with naturalised bluebells. Little attempt has been made to segregate the colours but the plants are graded for

height, so you stand on a path and look at a mass of rhododendrons of every imaginable hue rising from knee level right back to huge giants far behind. There have been some interesting interplantings with other plants in recent years – ornamental trees, especially conifers, and herbaceous plants like gunneras, celmisias, *Dactylorhiza foliosa* and *Meconopsis betonicifolia*. It should also be said that the garden is extremely well organised for visitors to enjoy themselves.

 Features Rhododendrons & azaleas; light lunches & teas.

Owned by Mr & Mrs J. Tye
Number of gardeners 3
Size 1.8ha (4½ acres)

Melbourne Hall

MELBOURNE DY3 1EN

Tel 01332 862502   **Fax** 01322 862263
Location 8 miles south of Derby.
Opening hours 1.30 pm – 5.30 pm; Wednesdays, Saturdays, Sundays & Bank Holiday Mondays.
Admission fee Adults £3; OAPs £2.

Melbourne is a near-perfect example of an early 18th-century garden, influenced by Le Nôtre. Much has been simplified over the centuries and the original plantings (some by the royal gardener Henry Wise) are rather overgrown now. But there are terraces, circular *bassins*, palisades of limes, intersecting *allées*, lumpy old hedges and the famous yew tunnel to fire the visitor's imagination. The lead statues (from Jan van Nost's foundry in Piccadilly in about 1710) are unique: so is the large urn known as the Four Seasons, which was originally cast for Queen Anne.

Features Good herbaceous borders; turf terracing; grand avenues; shop; refreshments.

Owned by Lord Ralph Kerr
Number of gardeners 2
English Heritage grade I

Renishaw Hall

RENISHAW, SHEFFIELD S31 9WB

Tel 01246 432042 **Fax** 01246 430760
Website www.sitwell.co.uk
Location 2½ miles from M1 Jct 30.
Opening hours 10.30 am – 4.30 pm; Friday – Sunday, plus Bank Holiday Mondays; 29 March to 29 September. Plus Thursdays in July & August.
Admission fee Adults £3; Concessions £2.50.

The gardens at Renishaw were laid out in around 1900 by Sir George Sitwell, grandfather of the present owner. Sir George was an expert on Italian gardens and his book *On the Making of Gardens* (1909) is a gardening classic. He applied the principles of Italian renaissance gardens to the garden he made at Renishaw: symmetry, proportion, scale and shadow. What we see today are yew hedges, pools, fountains, grass and statues – a garden which would not be out of place in Tuscany or the Veneto.

Gertrude Jekyll advised Sir George on the planting, but he did not follow her advice. The modern plantings are mainly herbaceous, and kept within pastel shades to emphasise the line of the formal garden: scarlet pelargoniums, for example, would bring those lines too far forward. The soft colours of old-fashioned roses are perfect: Renishaw has three separate rose gardens with over 1,000 roses. In the woodland garden and against the walls of the kitchen garden, tender plants thrive that seldom survive in Derbyshire – acacias, *Cytisus battandieri* and dendromecons. Renishaw is also worth visiting in the spring, when daffodils fill the lime avenue: they were first planted in 1680 on the advice of no lesser authority than John Evelyn. In the recently restored orangery, the National Collection of yuccas is displayed against an Arizona landscape.

 Features Yew walks & pyramids; clematis; woodland walks; roses (ancient & modern); mature conifers; good herbaceous borders; daffodils; Italian garden; small tea-room.

Owned by Sir Reresby Sitwell
Number of gardeners 4
Size 2.8ha (7 acres) formal gardens, plus woodlands
NCCPG National Collections *Yucca*
English Heritage grade II*

DEVON

No county has such an abundance of good gardens and nurseries as Devon: Devonians maintain that it is the best place in the world for gardening with plants. Rich soils ('Devon acres') and high rainfall make for excellent growth, but the county's microclimates are immensely variable, from the cold, windswept uplands of Dartmoor to valleys along the southern coast which are virtually frost-free. The Royal Horticultural Society's West Country flagship at Rosemoor shows what can be done to develop a major horticultural garden in little more than 10 years. And there is no private garden in England to match the lifetime achievements of Dr Smart at Marwood Hill. Devon has some fine general nurseries and garden centres, like Hill House near Ashburton, but surely no county ever had such an abundance of specialist nurseries. Their specialities include hostas (Roger and Ann Bowden near Okehampton), rare perennials (Carol Klein's Glebe Cottage Plants – a favourite at RHS shows), violets (Devon Violet Nursery at Rattery), clematis (Peveril Clematis Nursery near Exeter), rare trees (Thornhayes Nursery near Cullompton) and penstemon (Shirley Reynolds at Seaton). Devon has more National Collection holders than any other county, including many tender genera like *Azara* and *Agapanthus*. There are comparatively few top-class historic gardens and – such as they are – they tend to date from the 19th century like Bicton. Nevertheless the history of Devon gardens is extremely well documented and the Devon Gardens Trust has a large and vigorous membership. Bicton, Killerton and Endsleigh have splendid collections of old trees: in Edwardian times the avenue of monkey puzzles (*Araucaria araucana*) at Bicton was one of the wonders of English horticulture. Bicton College of Agriculture is a RHS Partner College. The National Gardens Scheme also does exceptionally well in Devon, with more gardens open for its charities than anywhere else in the south-west. Devon is indeed a county of horticultural superlatives.

Arlington Court

ARLINGTON, BARNSTAPLE EX31 4LP

Tel 01271 850296 **Fax** 01271 850711
Website www.nationaltrust.org.uk
Location 8 miles north of Barnstaple on A39.
Opening hours 10.30 am – 5.30 pm; Wednesday –
Monday; 23 March to 3 November. Plus 10.30 am –
4.30 pm on Tuesdays from June to September.
Admission fee Gardens only: Adults £3.50.

Arlington offers mature parkland on a level
site in front of a fine Georgian house. It has
a pretty Victorian formal garden:
herbaceous borders and basket beds with
bedding plants on three grass terraces
around a handsome conservatory. In the
recently restored walled garden, 19th-
century fruit and vegetables grow alongside
local cultivars.

Features Mature conifers; huge old
rhododendrons; National Trust shop;
restaurant & tea-room.

Owned by The National Trust
Number of gardeners 2
Size 12ha (30 acres)
English Heritage grade II

Bicton Park Gardens

EAST BUDLEIGH, BUDLEIGH
SALTERTON EX9 7DP

Tel & Fax 01395 568465
Website www.bictongardens.co.uk
Location On A376 north of Budleigh Salterton.
Opening hours 10 am – 6 pm (5 pm in winter); daily
except Christmas Day.
Admission fee Adults £4.75; OAPs £3.75; Children £2.75;
Dogs £1.

Sixty acres of fascinating features, including:
an Italian garden; a classical orangery;
important trees; the oriental garden; three
walled gardens; historic parkland; formal
gardens; an American garden; a collection of
dwarf conifers; more than 2,000 heathers; an
avenue of monkey puzzles; a hermitage; and
the finest pre-Paxton palm house built
c.1820 from 18,000 tiny panes of glass. The
Bicton College of Agriculture has National
Collections of *Agapanthus* and *Pittosporum*
and is a RHS Partner College.

 Features Woodland garden; roses
(ancient & modern); plantsman's
collection of plants; plants under glass;
mature conifers; good herbaceous borders;
fine collection of trees; tallest monkey puzzle
Araucaria araucana (30m) in the British
Isles (and nine further record-breaking
trees); garden shop; restaurant.

Owned by Simon Lister
Number of gardeners 6
Size 25ha (63 acres)
English Heritage grade I

Ann & Roger Bowden

HOSTAS, STICKLEPATH,
OKEHAMPTON EX20 2NL

Tel 01837 840481 **Fax** 01837 840482
Website www.hostas-uk.com
Location Near Okehampton, in centre of Sticklepath,
near turning signed 'Skaigh'.
Opening hours By appointment only.
Admission fee Adults £1.50; Children free

Ann and Roger Bowden know everything
there is to know about hostas: they are the
UK's leading ambassadors for these useful
and easy-to-grow beauties. They sell them
from a handsome catalogue with excellent
photographs. Prices are fair and range from

£2.50 for basic species to £15 for the latest imported hybrids. But the choice is magnificent: some 320 different hostas, of which a large number are new or re-introduced. Their garden at Cleave House in Sticklepath (NB there are two Sticklepaths in Devon – this is the Okehampton one) has been developed over the last 30 years with mixed plantings for year-round interest. But the display beds for their National Collection of hostas are here too – an incredible 800 cultivars.

Owned by Mr & Mrs Roger Bowden
Size 0.4ha (1 acre)
NCCPG National Collections *Hosta* (modern hybrids)

Buckland Abbey

YELVERTON PL20 6EY

Tel 01822 853607   **Fax** 01822 855448
Website www.nationaltrust.org.uk
Location Signed from A386 at Yelverton.
Opening hours 10.30 am – 5.30 pm; Friday – Wednesday; 23 March to 3 November. 2 pm – 5 pm; Saturdays & Sundays; 4 November to March 2003. Closed 23 December 2002 to 21 February 2001.
Admission fee Adults £2.50.

Originally a Cistercian Abbey, then the house of Sir Francis Drake, the main interest for garden lovers is the charming herb garden along the side of the Great Barn. It has over 50 different culinary and medicinal herbs. The new Elizabethan garden has topiary bushes, box-edged beds, plants from Tudor times and a small orchard of old fruit cultivars.

 Features Herbs; current holder of Sandford Award; refreshments.

Owned by The National Trust
Number of gardeners 1½
Size 1.2ha (3 acres)

Burrow Farm Gardens

DALWOOD, AXMINSTER EX13 7ET

Tel 01404 831285   **Fax** 01404 831445
Website www.burrowfarmgardens.co.uk
Location Turn north off A35 at Taunton Cross: follow brown tourist signs for ½ mile.
Opening hours 10 am – 7 pm; daily; April to September.
Admission fee Adults £3; Children 50p.

There are 7 acres of plantsmanship at Burrow Farm Gardens, and long views over the sweeping hills. A formal pergola walk is lined with old-fashioned shrubs and climbing roses, while the woodland garden is underplanted with rhododendrons, azaleas and interesting herbaceous plants. The candelabra primulas have naturalised all through the bog garden. And the garden is still growing – both in its size and in the intensity of its planting. A recent addition was the rill garden, lined with luxuriantly colour-themed plantings of shrubs and unusual herbaceous plants.

 Features Rhododendrons & azaleas; plantsman's collection of plants; primulas; woodland garden.

Owned by Mr & Mrs J. Benger
Number of gardeners 2
Size 2.8ha (7 acres)

Castle Drogo

DREWSTEIGNTON EX6 6PB

Tel 01647 433306   **Fax** 01647 433186
Website www.nationaltrust.org.uk
Location Drewsteignton village: signs from A30 & A382.
Opening hours 10.30 am – dusk; daily; all year.
Admission fee Adults £2.90 (gardens only).

This is a major 1920s garden, made to match the last castle built in Britain – a granite folly which was one of Lutyens's most remarkable works. The gardens too are grand and grandiose and, up on the edge of Dartmoor, the highest gardens owned by the National Trust. They are mainly within a large enclosed area, tightly hedged against the wind by thick, clipped yew. The design is formal and terraced with granite steps and walls. Both the rose garden (planted with Hybrid Teas and Floribundas) and the vast and vivid herbaceous borders are a contrast with the austere castle on its windy bluff. Weather-beaten, lichen-heavy Japanese cherries, rhododendrons and acers survive in the woodland spring garden on the slopes below.

 Features Woodland garden; roses (ancient & modern); rock garden; good herbaceous borders; tallest *Acer capillipes* (16m) in the British Isles; National Trust shop; self-service tea-room, waitress-service restaurant.

Owned by The National Trust
Number of gardeners 2½
Size 5ha (12 acres)
English Heritage grade II*

Clovelly Court

CLOVELLY, BIDEFORD EX39 5SZ

Tel 01237 431200 **Fax** 01237 431205
Website www.clovelly.co.uk
Location Signed in village.
Opening hours 10 am – 4 pm; daily; March to October.
Admission fee Adults £1; Children 20p.

Clovelly Court Garden is a classic example of the Victorian Kitchen Garden tradition. Lean-to greenhouses with original manual levers house apricots, melons, peaches, nectarines, a vine, citrus and a fig tree. New espalier fan and cordon trees line the walls enclosing the garden, which also shelter the vegetables grown organically and in rotation. Flower borders form the lower half of the walled garden. From the village of Clovelly a woodland walk know as the Long Walk leads an elegant and beautiful path to the gardens. Many tender plants flourish within the unique maritime microclimate of the gardens.

Owned by The Hon. John Rous
Number of gardeners 1, plus 2 part-timers
Size 0.6ha (1½ acres)

Coleton Fishacre Garden

COLETON, KINGSWEAR, DARTMOUTH TQ6 0EQ

Tel 01803 752466 **Fax** 01803 753017
Website www.nationaltrust.org.uk
Location 3 miles from Kingswear off Lower-Ferry Road.
Opening hours 11 am – 5 pm; Saturdays & Sundays in March. 10.30 am – 5.30 pm (or dusk, if earlier); Wednesday – Sundays & Bank Holidays; 23 March to 3 November.
Admission fee Adults £3.80.

The Lutyens-style house at Coleton Fishacre was built by Oswald Milne for Sir Rupert and Lady Dorothy D'Oyly Carte in 1925. Rare bulbs flourish in the warm terraces which surround it. The woodland garden, thickly planted with rhododendrons, azaleas and camellias, crashes down a secret valley to the sea. A stream runs down the valley, dammed to make small pools along the way, where damp-loving perennials luxuriate. Almost frost-free, the range and size of Southern Hemisphere trees and shrubs is astounding – *groves* of mimosa, for example.

Features Woodland garden; sub-tropical plants; plantsman's collection of plants; good herbaceous borders; rhododendrons; rare trees; tallest *Catalpa bungei* in the British Isles (and two other record trees); interesting new plantings in the 'Holiwell' area; visitor reception area & tea room.

Owned by The National Trust
Number of gardeners 3
Size 10ha (25 acres)
English Heritage grade II

Dartington Hall

DARTINGTON, TOTNES TQ9 6EL

Tel & Fax 01803 862367
Website www.dartington.u-net.com
Location 2 miles north-west of Totnes.
Opening hours Dawn – dusk; daily; all year. Groups by prior appointment only.
Admission fee Donation (£2 suggested).

Dartington is one of the best examples of grand mid-20th century gardening in England: it was made with American money at a time when few Englishmen could afford to spend on such a scale. Some famous designers are associated with it: Beatrix Farrand designed the courtyard and influenced the woodland plantings. Percy Cane built the long staircase, excavated the grassy 'tiltyard', planted the yews known as the 'twelve apostles' and opened up some of the long vistas. Henry Moore deposited a reclining woman. The scale is magnificent, and wholly appropriate to the house and landscape. The gardens are very well maintained and full of horticultural interest, but the detail is never allowed to obscure the greater scheme of it. Dartington also has fine mature trees and some interesting modern additions like the quietly contemplative Japanese garden.

 Features Woodland garden; topiary; magnolias; rhododendrons; camellias; dry-landscape Japanese garden.

Owned by Dartington Hall Trust
Number of gardeners 4
Size 11.1ha (28 acres)
English Heritage grade II*

Docton Mill

LYMEBRIDGE, HARTLAND, BIDEFORD EX39 6EA

Tel & Fax 01237 441369
Website www.doctonmill.co.uk
Location Take road from Hartland to Stoke & follow signs towards Elmscott.
Opening hours 10 am – 6 pm; daily; March to October.
Admission fee Adults £3.50; OAPs £3; Children (under 14) £1. RHS members free in March & April, September & October, and on Saturdays in between.

The main attraction at Docton is a working water mill, but the garden is developing quickly and the new owners have already made improvements. First they planted up a small field with magnolias (25 cultivars) and flowering shrubs. Last year they filled a large new glasshouse. This year (2002) they have made a new herbaceous border 70m long and planted 2000 daffodils. Much of the garden is natural bluebell woodland, into which shrubs like rhododendrons have been planted over the last 20 years. But there is also a fine bog garden (candelabra primulas in late spring) and a collection of old roses underplanted with herbaceous and ground-cover plants.

Features Apple orchards; new David Austin rose bed; some young magnolias; many new plantings, including a woodland garden (2001–2002); light refreshments & cream teas.

Owned by Mr & Mrs J. Borrett
Number of gardeners 2
Size 3.4ha (8½ acres)

Escot

OTTERY ST MARY, EXETER EX11 1LU

Tel 01404 822188   **Fax** 01404 822903
Website www.escot-devon.co.uk
Location Signed from A30 at Fairmile.
Opening hours 10 am – 6 pm; daily; Easter to October.
Admission fee Adults £3.95; OAPs & Children £3; under fours free.

Ⓟ Ⓗ Ⓦⓒ 🎔 🚻 ☕ 🍴

Escot is an up-and-coming low-budget old/new garden, responding well to vigorous replanting. It surrounds an aquatic centre and incorporates a wildlife centre. The house is an elegant Regency sugarlump, with distant views to East Hill (Capability Brown advised on the prospect), but the woodlands around the house are full of good Victorian rhododendrons and the walled garden sports a basic collection of old and English roses. Ivan Hicks has been asked to work on the garden in 2002: watch this space.

Features Snowdrops; rhododendrons & azaleas; mature conifers; bluebells; water-plants for sale; home-cooked lunches & cream teas.

Owned by John-Michael Kennaway
Size 10ha (25 acres)

Exeter University Gardens

EXETER EX4 4PX

Tel 01392 263059   **Fax** 01392 264547
Website www.ex.ac.uk
Location 1 miles north of city centre: gardens throughout the main campus.
Opening hours Dawn – dusk; daily; all year.
Admission fee Free.

 Ⓟ Ⓗ

From the horticultural point of view, Exeter has the most interesting university campus in England: the gardens are educational, attractive and important. At the centre are the gardens around Reed Hall, laid out by Veitch in the 1860s at the then phenomenal cost of £70,000. This explains the framework of splendid mature trees and shrubs which give such character to the whole site – especially conifers, rhododendrons, magnolias and hardy palm trees. Modern plantings have kept pace: there is a particularly fine collection of Australasian plants including acacias, callistemons and eucalyptus. Other tender plants that grow outside include *Albizia julibrissin,* cacti like *Opuntia humifusa* and the beautiful parrot-bill plant (*Clianthus puniceus*) from New Zealand. The gardeners also practise with great artistry the Victorian art of bedding out.

Features Tender plants; heathers; summer bedding; conifers; rhododendrons.

Owned by The University of Exeter
Number of gardeners 25
Size 100ha (250 acres)
NCCPG National Collections *Azara*

The Garden House

BUCKLAND MONACHORUM, YELVERTON PL20 7LQ

Tel 01822 854769   **Fax** 01822 855358
Website www.thegardenhouse.org.uk
Location Signed off A386 on Plymouth side of Yelverton.
Opening hours 10.30 am – 5 pm; daily; March to October.
Admission fee Adults £4; OAPs £3.50; Children £1.

The Garden House was first developed by the late Lionel Fortescue, a retired Eton 'beak' between 1945 and 1981. The setting is awesome: a ruined ecclesiastical site on the edge of Dartmoor, with stupendous views. Fortescue was responsible for much of the design and planting as we still see it in the walled garden. He was a great plantsman and insisted upon growing only the best forms and cultivars. He also believed that plants should be well fed and firmly controlled: they still flourish on the treatment and Fortescue's plantings have continued to fulfil their early promise. Over the last 20 years, however, the Garden House has developed in quite a different way under the guidance of the curator Keith Wiley. He has developed six acres of inter-connected gardens, each dedicated to a single theme. The South African garden is intended to replicate the spring flowering of the South African veldt, though mixed with some Californian annuals which pick up the same bright colours – eschscholtzias among the arctotis and osteospermums: it is probably best in July and August. Nearby is the quarry garden where natural outcrops have been covered with such plants as rock roses and creeping thymes, due for major redevelopment in spring 2002 and usually at its best in May and June. The Cretan cottage garden is a pan-European wildflower meadow where the native campions and ox-eye daisies are joined by such plants as *Alchemilla mollis* and astrantias. There is an maple glade underplanted with thousands of naturalised crocus in March, followed by azaleas in April and May: the autumn colour is spectacular. Elsewhere are a lime avenue, a spring garden, a herbaceous bed, a wisteria bridge, a peat garden, a bulb meadow and the prairie garden which uses a lot of grasses as well as ground orchids and *Verbena bonariensis*. But this is a garden in an active state of evolution, full of new features and stimulation at every time of the year.

Features Plantsman's collection of plants; good herbaceous borders; alpine bank; flowering cherries; wisterias; a developing naturalistic extension with *Acer* glade, spring garden, quarry garden, wildflower meadow & South African garden; tea-room with light lunches.

Owned by Fortescue Garden Trust
Number of gardeners 5
Size 4ha (10 acres)

Gidleigh Park Hotel

CHAGFORD TQ13 8HH

Tel 01647 432367 **Fax** 01647 432574
Website www.gidleigh.com
Location 20 miles west of Exeter. Approach from
Chagford: do NOT go to Gidleigh.
Opening hours Guests of the hotel & restaurant only.
Admission fee free to hotel & restaurant clients.

Gidleigh has 45 acres of woodland (much of
it recently replanted) on the edge of
Dartmoor. Most of the rhododendrons and
conifers were planted in the 19th century
and are wonderfully mature. Around the
Tudorised house – now a top hotel – is a
1920s garden. Below is a fine 1930s water
garden. The garden contains nothing very
rare or special, but the position is
stupendous and the sense of space, even
grandeur, is enhanced by immaculate
maintenance. The hotel and restaurant have
received innumerable awards over many
years. Finding it needs careful map-reading:
in Chagford Square turn right at Lloyds
Bank and, after 150 yards, take the first fork
to the right and follow the lane for two miles
to its end.

 Features Woodland garden; delicious
food in Hotel.

Owned by Paul Henderson
Number of gardeners 4
Size 18ha (45 acres)

Glebe Cottage Plants

PIXIE LANE, WARKLEIGH,
UMBERLEIGH EX37 9DH

Tel 01769 540554
Location 4 miles south-west of South Molton.

Opening hours 10 am – 1 pm & 2 pm – 5 pm;
Wednesday – Friday. The garden is also open 2 pm – 5 pm
in aid of the National Gardens Scheme on 17, 29 & 31
March; 1, 26 & 28 April; 10 & 12 May; 9 June; 12 & 14 July;
4, 23 & 25 August; 6, 8 & 20 September.
Admission fee £2.

Carol Klein has a sharp eye for worthwhile
new introductions, yet does not forget the
reliable old classics: her talents have brought
her television popularity and five Gold
Medals at Chelsea 1992–96 (and again in
2000). Her nursery has an exceptional list of
perennials, including lots of newly
discovered species and promising cultivars.
The garden – always good – is now
developing fast and will be open to the
public more frequently than ever in 2002.
The Open Days on 17, 29 & 31 March and
on 1 April are 'Hellebore Days', to study and
appreciate the hellebores and pulmonarias.

Owned by Carol Klein

Gnome Reserve & Wild Flower Garden

WEST PUTFORD, BRADWORTHY
EX22 7XE

Tel 01409 241435
Website www.gnomereserve.co.uk
Location Between Bideford & Holsworthy, signed from
A39, A386 & A388.
Opening hours 10 am – 6 pm; daily; 21 March to
31 October.
Admission fee Adults £2.45; OAPs £2.20; Children £1.90.

There are four reasons to visit this
remarkable conservation centre which has
been featured on television more than 50
times: first, the 2-acre gnome reserve in a
beech wood with a stream; second the 2-acre

pixies' wildflower meadow, with 250 labelled species; third, the kiln where pottery gnomes and pixies are born; fourth, the museum of rare early gnomes. A large slice of gardening history is displayed in this garden and its museum, while the wildflower meadow is one of the best in the country.

 Features Wildflower meadow; large shop selling gnomes; sandwiches, drinks & ice-creams.

Owned by The Atkin Family
Number of gardeners 3
Size 1.6ha (4 acres)

Greenway

GREENWAY ROAD, GALMPTON, CHURSTON FERRERS TQ5 0ES

Tel 01803 842382
Website www.nationaltrust.org.uk
Location 6 miles east of Brixham, on the Dart estuary.
Opening hours Not yet decided.
Admission fee Not yet decided.

Greenway is one of the National Trust's newest acquisitions, which it hopes to open for the first time this year. However, the existing facilities are fairly limited, and it will be some time before the infrastructure is in place. At present, for example, you need to ask permission to bring and park a car. The garden is a wonderful collection of subtropical exotica: among the best specimens are mimosas, clianthus, myrtles, mahonias and puyas. The collection of camellias (over 200 different cultivars, most of them in the sensational camellia walk) is exceptional, and there are more than 50 different *Eucalyptus* species.

 Features Camellias; subtropical plants; eucalyptus.

Owned by The National Trust
Number of gardeners 3
Size 13ha (30 acres)

Higher Knowle

LUSTLEIGH, NEWTON ABBOTT TQ13 9SP

Tel 01647 277275   **Fax** 0870 131 5914
Location 3 miles north-west of Bovey Tracey.
Opening hours 2 pm – 6 pm; Sundays & Bank Holiday Mondays; 31 March to 2 June.
Admission fee Adults £2.50; Children free.

Higher Knowle was built by a pupil of Lutyens on a wooded slope on the south-eastern edge of Dartmoor: a stream flows down towards the Bovey valley – the views are stupendous. The first plantings date from the late 1950s – mature azaleas and magnolias around and above the house. The present owners bought the house in 1966 and have since planted up the lower woodland area with camellias, modern magnolias and rhododendrons. Bluebells, primroses and huge boulders of natural granite add to its charm, especially in spring.

Features A plantsman's garden; good rhododendrons and azaleas; magnolias and camellias.

Owned by Mr & Mrs David Quicke
Number of gardeners owners only
Size 1.2ha (3 acres)

Hill House Nursery & Garden

LANDSCOVE, ASHBURTON, NEWTON ABBOT TQ13 7LY

Tel & Fax 01803 762273
Location Off A384, follow signs for Landscove.
Opening hours 11 am – 5 pm; daily; all year (including bank holidays).
Admission fee Free.

This Victorian Old Vicarage was made famous by Edward Hyams' *An Englishman's Garden* but for many years now it is has been the centre of a distinguished plantsman's nursery. Family-owned and family-run, the 3-acre nursery has an excellent range of unusual or 'hard-to-find' plants – a list of over 3,000 in all, most of them available at any one time. In the glasshouses are handsome large specimens, particularly of fuchsias and passion flowers. Most of the stock is raised in the nursery. Raymond Hubbard also breeds plants: this is where *Nemesia* 'Bluebird' originated. He is also the breeder of *Dianthus* 'Old Mother Hubbard' and *Plectranthus argentatus* 'Hill House'.

Features Mature conifers; daffodils; cyclamen and snowdrops; herbaceous borders; pond garden; conservatory; garden shop; Mother Hubbard's Tea-Room (home made cakes) March to September.

Owned by Raymond, Valerie & Matthew Hubbard

Killerton

BROADCLYST, EXETER EX5 3LE

Tel 01392 881345 **Fax** 01392 883112
Website www.nationaltrust.org.uk
Location West side of B3181, Exeter to Cullompton Road.
Opening hours 10.30 am – dusk; daily; all year.
Admission fee Adults £3.90 (but reduced rate in winter).

Killerton is an historic giant among gardens. Its long connections with Veitch's Nursery have bequeathed it a great tree collection. These include innumerable record-breaking specimens, many from collectors' seed, though one's sense of awe may be a little spoilt by droning traffic on the M5 below.

Features Snowdrops; rock garden; rhododendrons & azaleas; daffodils; fine collection of trees; bluebells; tallest *Ostrya carpinifolia* (22m) in the British Isles (and eight further record trees); magnolia; drifts of *Crocus tommasinianus*; National Trust shop; small well-run plant centre; waitress-service restaurant and self-service tea-room.

Owned by The National Trust
Number of gardeners 5
Size 8.7ha (22 acres)
English Heritage grade II*

Knightshayes Garden

TIVERTON EX16 7RG

Tel 01884 254665 **Fax** 01884 243050
Website www.nationaltrust.org.uk
Location Off A396 Tiverton – Bampton Road.
Opening hours 11 am – 5.30 pm; daily; March to 3 November.
Admission fee Adults £3.90; Children £1.90.

Knightshayes is a garden in a wood – one of the best of its kind in the world. Much of the original canopy is there – notably some very fine oaks – but it is now supplemented by magnolias, birches, nothofagus and sorbus. The garden unveils as a series of walks and glades, with beautiful rhododendrons, camellias and rare shrubs underplanted by hellebores, erythroniums, foxgloves, cyclamen and bluebells. Closer to the house are the stately formal gardens, enclosed by immaculately clipped yew hedges. Here alpine treasures and small bulbs grow in raised beds. The old bowling lawn is filled by a vast circular pool and a single weeping pear, *Pyrus salicifolia* 'Pendula', which is pruned to thin out its canopy of branches. The walled garden, near the stables, is being restored and run organically. In the surrounding park is a very fine collection of trees, including several record breakers. The Douglas firs are particularly impressive.

Features Woodland garden; topiary; good herbaceous borders; hellebores; cyclamen; bulbs; peat beds; centenary planting of 100 trees along visitors' entrance; tallest *Quercus cerris* (40m) in the British Isles; National Trust shop; licensed restaurant; coffee, lunch & teas.

Owned by The National Trust
Number of gardeners 6
Size 20ha (50 acres)
English Heritage grade II*

Lukesland

HARFORD, IVYBRIDGE PL21 0JF

Tel 01752 893390   **Fax** 01752 896011
Location 1½ miles north of Ivybridge on the Harford road.
Opening hours 2 pm – 6 pm; Wednesdays, Sundays & Bank Holiday Mondays; 14 April to 16 June.
Admission fee Adults £3.20; Children free.

(P) (Ɔ) (wc) (&) (☕)

Lukesland is a woodland garden in a stream-fed valley on the southern edge of Dartmoor: it offers the perfect conditions for growing rhododendrons, azaleas and many other flowering shrubs. The house and the earliest plantings date from the 1880s, but most of what we see now has been planted by the present owners since 1975. The family's policy is to try to regenerate poor or over-mature areas, so that the quality and display of plants are improved: during the 1990s, for example, the Howells planted a good selection of late-flowering rhododendrons at the north end of the pinetum. Here too, in 1992, they built a striking reverse suspension bridge, designed by the Scottish architect Sir James Dunbar-Nasmith. The many paths and bridges crossing the stream open up different views as you progress through the garden. The fine examples of rhododendron species include the large-leafed *R. sinogrande*, *R. macabeanum*, *R. falconeri* and *R. arizelum*. The Exbury hybrids include 'Cornish Cross', 'Hawk Crest' and 'Jalisco'. Youngish camellias are starting to make an impact, while other good shrubs include *Drimys lanceolata*, *Michelia doltsopa*, hoherias and eucryphias. There are some very fine specimen trees: *Ginkgo biloba* at 22m, *Davidia involucrata* var. *vilmoriniana* planted in 1936 and now a broad 17m specimen, and a magnificent *Magnolia campbellii* planted at the same time and now about 23m high – its exceptionally wide spread makes it one of the largest in the country.

Features Small pinetum; rhododendrons & azaleas; stream, ponds & waterfalls; tea-room.

Owned by Mr & Mrs B.N. Howell
Number of gardeners family, plus part-time help
Size 6ha (15 acres)

Marwood Hill Gardens

BARNSTAPLE EX31 4EB

Tel 01271 42528
Location Signed from A361 Barnstaple to Braunton Road.
Opening hours Dawn – dusk; daily; all year except Christmas Day.
Admission fee Adults £3.

Marwood Hill is a remarkable plantsman's garden, conceived on a grand scale and fast maturing, though it is still expanding along the long sheltered valley which gives such vigorous growth to its plants. It is exciting for its scale and variety, and for the energy and enthusiasm of its owner, which are an inspiration to many. There is no better place in the South West to learn about plants of every kind. It is moreover a garden of year-round interest. Late in the year, *Galanthus reginae-olgae* flowers with the last of the *Cyclamen hederifolium*: these are followed in midwinter by many other snowdrops and *Cyclamen coum*. There is a wonderful collection of camellias at this season too – some in the open, and others (huge bushes of Reticulata Hybrids) under glass. Magnolias are numerous, including many of the Jury hybrids from New Zealand, the dark form of *M. campbellii* called 'Betty Jessel', *M. sprengeri* var. *diva*, *M. dawsoniana*, *M.* × *wieseneri* and the home-grown 'Marwood Spring'. Many are underplanted with drifts of narcissi. Come the spring, and the pergola draped with 12 different wisterias starts into flower (the colour is extended by interplanted clematis and climbing roses) and the walled garden begins to make an impact with ceanothus, *Clianthus puniceus* and the poppy bush (*Dendromecon rigida*). In early summer the bog garden comes into its own, starting with drifts of candelabra primulas and continuing

with astilbes from the National Collection: in fact the bog garden is full of colour right through until autumn. Hydrangeas are another success story: a very large number of cultivars is planted throughout the garden. As the soil is acid, the 'mopheads' come out in many shades of blue, alongside the cultivars of *Hydrangea paniculata* (Dr Smart considers 'Pink Diamond' one of the best) and *Hydrangea quercifolia* whose oak-shaped leaves change to brilliant colours in the autumn. Leaves and bark are important elements of the garden: Dr Smart has planted the birches close to the eucalyptus so that the contrasts of bark can be enjoyed together – he has planted large numbers of both *Betula* and *Eucalyptus* species. He also has a high regard for the seldom-seen *Amomyrtus lechleriana* in the walled garden. And there is a fine collection of rhododendrons, including large plants of *R. macabeanum*, *R. sinogrande*, *R. eximium*, *R. arizelum*, *R. arboreum* and *R.* 'Sir Charles Lemon'. The garden is constantly changing, improving and maturing: new for 2002 are some extensive plantings of astilbes and a new border for grasses and perennials.

Features A supreme example of a plantsman's collection of plants; roses (mainly old-fashioned & climbers); rhododendrons & azaleas; plants under glass; daffodils; good herbaceous plants; fine collection of trees; alpine plants; birches; *Eucalyptus*; camellias; hebes; teas.

Owned by Dr J.A. Smart
Number of gardeners 5
Size 8ha (20 acres)
NCCPG National Collections *Astilbe; Iris ensata; Tulbaghia*

Nicky's Rock Garden Nursery

BROADHAYES, STOCKLAND, HONITON EX14 9EH

Tel 01404 881213
Location 6 miles east of Honiton, off midpoint of north-south road between A30 & A35.
Opening hours 9 am – dusk, daily. Please telephone first.
Admission fee free

This nursery is one of few in the south-west which specialise in alpines, but the owners are both distinguished members of the Alpine Garden Society. They are keen plantsmen and therefore sell a wide selection of alpines and dwarf plants for rock gardens: bulbs, conifers and shrubs. Almost everything can be seen growing in their show garden. The owners enjoy looking at the garden with visitors and talking about the problems of growing and propagating rock plants.

 Features Rockeries; troughs; scree; raised beds.

Owned by Bob & Diana Dark
Number of gardeners owners (part-time!)
Size 0.2ha (½ acre)

The Old Glebe

EGGESFORD, CHULMLEIGH EX18 7QU

Tel & Fax 01769 580632
Location South (& uphill) of Eggesford for ⅔ of a mile; right into bridleway.
Opening hours 2 pm – 6 pm; 18, 19, 25 & 26 May for National Gardens Scheme. All customers by appointment.
Admission fee Adults £2 & Children £1 on NGS days.

This is a great rhododendron collection, well-known to the *cognoscenti*. Nigel Wright grows over 6,000 plants and 750 different cultivars, and his nursery sells over 200 of them. It is one of the best lists in the UK. The house is an old rectory, with fine lawns, mature trees, walled herbaceous borders, a bog garden and a small lake.

 Features Rhododendrons.

Owned by Mr & Mrs Nigel Wright
Number of gardeners 1 part-time
Size 2.8ha (7 acres)

Overbecks Museum & Garden

SHARPITOR, SALCOMBE TQ8 8LW

Tel 01548 843238 **Fax** 01548 845020
Website www.nationaltrust.org.uk
Location 2 miles south of Salcombe.
Opening hours 11 am – 8 pm (or dusk, if earlier); daily; all year.
Admission fee Adults £3; Children £1.50.

Overbecks has a small, intensely planted, almost jungly garden, perched above the Salcombe estuary. The formal terraces (rather 1930s) are stuffed with interesting tender plants: *Musa basjoo*, phormiums, agapanthus, self-sown *Echium pininana* and every kind of South African daisy, all held together in a framework of hundreds of *Trachycarpus* palms.

Features Sub-tropical plants; bluebells; palms; mimosas; cyclamen; *Magnolia campbellii*.

Owned by The National Trust
Number of gardeners 2
Size 2.2ha (6 acres)
English Heritage grade II

Paignton Zoo & Botanical Gardens

TOTNES ROAD, PAIGNTON TQ4 7EU

Tel 01803 697500   **Fax** 01803 523457
Website www.paigntonzoo.org.uk
Location On A385 Totnes Road, 1 mile from Paignton.
Opening hours 10 am – 6 pm (or dusk, if earlier); daily; all year. Closed 25 December.
Admission fee Adults £8; OAPs £6.50; Children £5.75.

Once a private garden devoted to blue-flowered and blue-leaved plants, this is now an inspiring combination of zoo, botanic collection, public park and holiday entertainment. Themed plant collections are one of its more recent features: among them are economic plants, medical plants; Mexican oaks; palm species. There are tropical, temperate and desert-plant glasshouses.

 Features Mature trees & shrubs; unusual exotics; glasshouses with tropical plants; shops; large self-service restaurant.

Owned by Whitley Wildlife Conservation Trust
Number of gardeners 6
Size 30ha (75 acres)

Plant World Botanic Gardens

ST MARYCHURCH ROAD, NEWTON ABBOT TQ12 4SE

Tel 01803 872939   **Fax** 01803 875018
Location Follow brown tourist signs from Penn Inn roundabout at Newton Abbot.
Opening hours 9.30 am – 5 pm; daily; Easter to September.

Admission fee Adults £2; Children free.

This plantsman's nursery sells a selection of alpines, perennials and shrubs. There is an illustrated seed list with fresh material from the gardens and some interesting collected species. The National Collection of *Primula* extends only to the Cortusoides section of the genus, but the nursery used to collect the *Capitatae* and *Farinosae* too, and it still grows many from those sections. The mature 4-acre gardens are planted out as special habitat zones and burgeon with rare trees and shrubs: worth a long journey to visit in their own right.

 Features Cottage gardens; geraniums; aquilegias; small self-service café.

Owned by Ray Brown
Number of gardeners 2
Size 1.6ha (4 acres)
NCCPG National Collections *Primula* (Cortusoides section)

Pleasant View Nursery & Garden

TWO MILE OAK, DENBURY, NEWTON ABBOT TQ12 6DG

Tel 01803 813388
Location Off A381 at Two Mile Oak pub towards Denbury: then ¾ mile on the left.
Opening hours Garden: 2 pm – 5 pm; 28 April, 19 May & 23 June, 2 & 7 August, 4 & 6 September, for NGS. Nursery: 10 am – 5 pm; Wednesday – Friday; mid March to end of September.
Admission fee Adults £2.

This garden is a remarkable achievement: the collection of trees and shrubs is exceptionally comprehensive – enough to be called an arboretum – and it has all been achieved from open pasture since 1988. Ceanothus and abelias flourish despite being some way inland from the south coast. The nursery has lots of interesting shrubs, both for garden planting and for conservatories, with a special emphasis upon salvias from the National Collection. Pleasant View is the only place to offer some of the rarer species of every kind from all over the world.

Owned by Mr & Mrs B.D. Yeo
Size 1.6ha (4 acres)
NCCPG National Collections Abelia; Salvia

Powderham Castle

EXETER EX6 8JQ

Tel 01626 890243 **Fax** 01626 890729
Location Off A379 Dawlish to Exeter Road at Kenton.
Opening hours 10 am – 5.30 pm; Sunday – Friday; 1 April to 28 October. Also on Sundays in March in aid of the RHS.
Admission fee Adults £5.85; OAPs £5.35; Children £2.95. Charges include guided tour of Castle.

Powderham is not a major garden, though it has some good trees – notably the cork oak (*Quercus suber*) and its Devon hybrid *Q. × lucombeana*. Nevertheless the 18th-century landscaped park is serenely English, the woodland garden is stupendous in March and there is a cheerful modern rose garden all along the front of the house. The greenhouses in the Victorian walled garden are now back in commission after recent restoration.

 Features Roses (mainly modern); woodland walks; plant centre; licensed restaurant.

Owned by Earl & Countess of Devon
Number of gardeners 3
Size 22ha (60 acres), including grounds
English Heritage grade II

R.D. Plants

HOMELEA FARM, TYTHERLEIGH, AXMINSTER EX13 7BG

Tel 01460 220206
Location On A358, just inside the county boundary.
Opening hours 9 am – 1 pm, 2 pm – 5.30 pm, February to September. Phone first (between 8.30 am & 9.30 am only).

This nursery specialises in good herbaceous plants for damp and shady places – woodlanders from all over the world. It is particularly strong on anemones and modern developments of *Helleborus orientalis* – especially scented cultivars and doubles.

RHS Garden Rosemoor

GREAT TORRINGTON EX38 8PH

Tel 01805 624067 **Fax** 01805 624717
Website www.rhs.org.uk
Location 1 mile south of Torrington on A3124 (formerly B3220).
Opening hours 10 am – 6 pm (but 5 pm October to March); daily; 2 January to 24 December.
Admission fee Adults £4.50; Children £1; Groups (10+) £3.50. RHS members free.

The Royal Horticultural Society's garden at Rosemoor is situated in the delightful setting of the Torridge Valley, nestled within extensive surrounding woodlands. After 12 years of development all of the projects envisaged in the original garden masterplan for Rosemoor are now complete. Many of the new garden areas are reaching maturity and these, together with Lady Anne's unique and delightful garden, ensure that a visit to Rosemoor will provide something for all tastes and interests, at every season of the year. Rosemoor is rich in variety: the formal garden demonstrates a wide range of plants and planting styles in a series of individual garden 'rooms', with lots of ideas to inspire visitors for their own gardens. Included are two rose gardens, for modern and shrub roses; two colour-themed gardens – the spiral garden with its soft, pastel theme and the square garden with its searing, hot-coloured plantings; the ever-popular cottage and herb gardens; the *potager*, with decorative vegetable planting; a foliage garden, where leaf form and colour are dominant; a winter garden, full of colour during the colder months, and the model gardens, demonstrating three contrasting design solutions for the average domestic plot. Other attractions include the stream garden and lake; a richly planted fruit and vegetable garden; large areas of parkland and arboretum, and newly developed woodland walks.

Features Woodland garden; roses (ancient & modern); plantsman's collection of plants; stream and bog garden; foliage garden; colour theme gardens; fruit and vegetable gardens; herb garden; cottage garden; tallest *Eucalyptus glaucescens* (21m) in the British Isles (and seven further record trees); good range of book & gifts; licensed restaurant.

Owned by The Royal Horticultural Society
Number of gardeners 16
Size 16ha (40 acres)
NCCPG National Collections *Ilex*; *Cornus*

Rowden Gardens

BRENTOR, TAVISTOCK PL19 0NG

Tel 01822 810275 **Fax** 01822 810275
Location 1 mile west of North Brentor.
Opening hours 10 am – 5 pm; Saturday – Sunday & Bank Holiday Mondays; April to September. And at other times by appointment.

Rowden Gardens is a nursery with a show garden attached. Its speciality is aquatic plants, and the remarkable thing about the garden is that it is made in old watercress beds – long, rectangular tanks. More than 3,000 different plants grow in the garden, which provides the propagating material for the nursery. Almost all its stock is of aquatic or moisture-loving plants: there is a good choice of *Iris ensata* cultivars, for example, many of them raised by the nursery and amounting to the largest collection in the country. Its list of non-aquatic herbaceous plants now totals nearly 2,000 cultivars, with a particularly strong hand of grasses, ligularias, rheums and rodgersias. But Rowden is also *the* place for celandines from its National Collection of *Ranunculus ficaria*: it grows and offers for sale many more cultivars than anyone else. It is also a reliable source of unusual species and selected forms of *Persicaria*. The nursery prides itself on being an introducer of new plants. Until recently it was also a regular exhibitor at RHS shows, where its displays were always much admired for their variety.

Owned by John Carter
Number of gardeners 2
Size 0.4ha (1 acre)
NCCPG National Collections *Fallopia*; *Persicaria*; *Ranunculus ficaria*

Saltram

PLYMPTON, PLYMOUTH PL7 3UH

Tel 01752 333500 **Fax** 01752 336474
Website www.nationaltrust.org.uk
Location 2 miles west of Plympton.
Opening hours 11 am – 5 pm; Sunday – Thursday (plus Good Friday); 24 March to 3 November. 11 am – 4 pm; Sunday – Thursday; 4 November – 19 December and January to March 2003.
Admission fee Adults £3; Children £1.50.

Twenty acres of beautiful parkland, whose huge and ancient trees are underplanted with camellias and rhododendrons. Best in spring when the daffodils flower in hosts.

Features Rhododendrons & azaleas; camellias; parkland; handsome orangery; lime avenue; 'melancholy' walk undergoing restoration (1998); tallest *Acer palmatum* 'Osakazuki' (13m) in the British Isles.

Owned by The National Trust
Number of gardeners 3
Size 8ha (20 acres)
English Heritage grade II*

Sherwood

NEWTON ST CYRES, EXETER EX5 5BT

Tel 01392 851216 **Fax** 01392 851870
Location 2 miles south-west of Newton St Cyres, at the end of a signed road.
Opening hours 2 pm – 5 pm; Sundays; 17 March to 17 November.
Admission fee Adults £2.

This is an important rhododendron and magnolia garden with much more than the collection of Knap Hill azaleas to see and enjoy. The magnolias are good, and there are handsome collections of buddlejas, berberis, cotoneasters and maples which take the garden right through the year.

 Features Good collection of ornamental shrubs.

Owned by Sir John & Lady Quicke
Number of gardeners 1½
Size 5.6ha (14 acres)
NCCPG National Collections *Rhododendron* (Knap Hill azaleas)

Tapeley Park

INSTOW EX39 4NT

Tel 01271 42371
Location Off A39 between Barnstaple & Bideford.
Opening hours 10 am – 5 pm; daily, except Saturdays; 18 March to 1 November.
Admission fee Adults £3.50; OAPs £3; Children £2. RHS members free from 8 June to 8 July.

Tapeley's fame rests on its fine Italianate formal garden laid out on several levels in about 1900 and planted with such tender plants as *Sophora tetraptera* and *Myrtus communis* subsp. *tarentina*. Beyond are palm trees and a rhododendron woodland: worth exploring. All parts are undergoing restoration and replanting with advice from Mary Keen and Carol Klein.

 Features Woodland garden; plants under glass; fruit; gift shop; teas.

Owned by NDCI Ltd.
Number of gardeners 2½
Size 14ha (35 acres)
English Heritage grade II*

Thornhayes Nursery

DULFORD, CULLOMPTON EX15 2DF

Tel 01884 266746   **Fax** 01884 266739
Website www.thornhayes-nursery.co.uk
Location 10 minutes from M5, Jct 28.
Opening hours 8 am – 4.30 pm; Monday – Friday.

This nursery (retail and wholesale) was founded in 1991 with the aim of growing a wider range of ornamental and fruit trees than was generally available in the West Country. Thornhayes has some interesting ornamental trees: they include *Fitzroya cupressoides*, *Betula* 'Conyngham' and good collections of sorbus, pyrus and crataegus: dendrophiles should take a closer look. Hard-to-get West Country apples for cider, cooking and eating are another speciality: these include 'Chorister Boy', 'Peter Lock' and 'Royal Somerset'.

 Features Rare ornamental trees; West Country apples.

DORSET

Both Dorset's Grade I gardens – Abbotsbury and Athelhampton – have plenty of horticultural interest to offer their visitors as well as their historic importance. Abbotsbury has an especially good collection of old trees, including several UK record-holders. Minterne and Forde, too, are good for specimen trees, while one of the tallest specimens in the British Isles of the dawn redwood (*Metasequoia glyptostroboides*) is a twin-stemmed specimen more than 25m high in Bournemouth's Central Park. Most of Dorset's leading nurseries are close to the coast – the chalk hinterland can be cold in winter – and there is a cluster of eminent nurseries on the sandy soils in the southeast of the county. The National Gardens Scheme is very well supported and lists over 100 gardens – a remarkable number for such a small county. The NCCPG has a very active group in the county, but there are comparatively few National Collections – among them *Hoheria*, *Ceanothus* and *Penstemon* – all benefiting from the mild climate along the Dorset coast. Kingston Maurward is a RHS Partner College: the estate once belonged to Sir Thomas Hanbury, who gave Wisley to the Royal Horticultural Society.

Abbotsbury Sub-Tropical Gardens

ABBOTSBURY, WEYMOUTH DT3 4LA

Tel 01305 871387 **Fax** 01305 871902
Website www.abbotsbury-tourism.co.uk/gardens.html
Location B3157, on coast, in village.
Opening hours 10 am – 6 pm (dusk in winter); daily; all year. Closed 1 January, 25 & 26 December. Free to RHS members from January to February & from October to December.
Admission fee Adults £5.30; OAPs £4.90; Children £3.50. RHS members free from October to February.

Abbotsbury is a woodland garden of splendid trees and shrubs of great rarity which has enjoyed a spectacular renaissance in recent years. Palms, eucalyptus, pittosporum and camellias all grow lushly in the sheltered valley and romantic walled garden. Among the trees are many exceptionally large specimens of species that are normally too tender to grow even in southern England – including *Buxus balearica*, *Ilex fargesii*, *Photinia nussia*, *Picconia excelsa*, and *Pittosporum crassifolium*. As well as the collection of hoherias, the gardens' comprehensive display of large-leaved hebes was until quite recently designated a National Collection by the NCCPG. There has been a lot of good planting in recent years, including many new species introduced by such collectors as Roy Lancaster. A stylish Visitors' Centre designed as a Colonial Teahouse and an excellent nursery make for added value.

Features Sub-tropical plants; fine collection of trees; magnolias; candelabra primulas; rare trees; free-standing loquat *Eriobotrya japonica*; excellent collection of rare trees and shrubs; camellias; rhododendrons & azaleas; bluebells; sub-tropical rarities; tallest English oak *Quercus robur* (40m) in the British Isles; five other record trees; shop; restaurant.

Owned by Ilchester Estates
Number of gardeners 5
Size 8ha (20 acres)
NCCPG National Collections *Hoheria*
English Heritage grade I

Athelhampton

DORCHESTER DT2 7LG

Tel 01305 848363 **Fax** 01305 848135
Website www.athelhampton.co.uk
Location 5 miles east of Dorchester, off A35 at Northbrook–Puddletown junction.
Opening hours 10.30 am – 5 pm; Sunday – Friday; March to October. Plus 10.30 – dusk on Sundays from November to February.
Admission fee Garden only: £4.40.

Inigo Thomas designed these gardens about 100 years ago as the perfect complement for the perfect manor house. Sharply cut pyramids of yew, a long canal with waterlilies, and rambling roses in early summer are some of the main features, alongside tulips, magnolias and clematis. The overall effect is most satisfying and harmonious.

 Features Gazebos; beautiful walls and hedges; topiary; winner of HHA/ Christie's Garden of the Year Award for 1997; two *Metasequoia glyptostroboides* from the original seed; shop; restaurant; refreshments.

Owned by Patrick Cooke
Number of gardeners 3
Size 4ha (10 acres)
English Heritage grade I

Bennetts Water Lily Farm

WATER GARDENS, PUTTON LANE, CHICKERELL, WEYMOUTH DT3 4AF

Tel 01305 785150
Website www.waterlily.co.uk
Location 2 miles west of Weymouth, signed off B3157 Bridport road.
Opening hours 10 am – 5 pm; Tuesday – Sunday; April to August. 10 am – 5 pm; Tuesday – Saturday; September. Open on Bank Holidays.

Bennetts Water Lily Farm is the leading nursery in the south-west for aquatic plants: waterlilies, pond plants and marginals in abundance. The flowering season is from to June to late September, which coincides with the tourist season. The gardens have been developed as a visitor attraction: thousands of waterlilies and a 'Monet' bridge.

 Features Waterlilies; tea-room; museum.

Owned by J.L. & A.J. Bennett
Number of gardeners 2
Size 2.2ha (6 acres)
NCCPG National Collections *Nymphaea*

Chettle House

CHETTLE, BLANDFORD FORUM
DT11 8DB

Tel & Fax 01258 830209
Location 6 miles north of Blandford; 1 mile west of the A354.
Opening hours 11 am – 5 pm; Sundays; Easter to September. Ask English Tourism for other opening times. Groups by appointment.
Admission fee Adults £3; Children free.

Chettle House is stunning – built by Thomas Archer in the 1710s and actually improved in the 1840s: it is full of beautiful architectural detail. The gardens are old and formal in structure, but have been re-planted in the English style since about 1970. A croquet lawn fringed by herbaceous plantings fills the foreground to the park, while the borders in the main garden surround a sunken lawn. The plantings are effective, and include a variegated liriodendron, a stauntonia growing over an old yew, a holboellia, a small rose garden, a fine display of *Campsis* in late summer, some 60 clematis cultivars and 23 cultivars of lonicera. A walnut planted in 1957 is already nearly 60ft high. This garden is the original home of the very pretty (and popular) *Campanula persicifolia* 'Chettle Charm' which is white with a blue edge. But the really inspirational thing about the garden is that it is all maintained by the husband-and-wife owners who inherited the estate in 1967 and have devoted themselves to restoring both house and garden.

 Features Fine borders; small tea-room.

Owned by Patrick Bourke
Number of gardeners owners only
Size 1.6ha (4 acres)

Chiffchaffs

CHAFFEYMOOR, BOURTON,
GILLINGHAM SP8 5BY

Tel 01747 840841
Location At Wincanton end of Bourton, off A303.
Opening hours 2 pm – 5 pm; Wednesdays & Thursdays; March to October. Plus 3 & 31 March; 7, 21 & 28 April; 5, 12 & 26 May; 2, 9 & 23 June; 14 July; 25 August; 8 September; 6 October.
Admission fee Adults £2; Children 50p. RHS members free in April, May & August to October.

A pretty cottage, with an excellent small nursery attached, and just off the A303. Started in 1978, the garden has a flowing design, exploits a great variety of habitats and burgeons with good plants. Spring bulbs, herbaceous borders, shrub roses, lilies and clematis are among its key features. A bluebell-lined path leads to the woodland garden, which boasts a splendid collection of rhododendrons, drifts of daffodils and candelabra primulas, and yet more carpets of bluebells. It was originally a dank and scrubby alder copse – on a spring line – but the Potts have cleared it, drained it and planted ornamental trees and shrubs, with autumn colour in mind as much as spring flowers. Here are about a dozen cultivars of *Liquidambar styraciflua* and groups of *Disanthus cercidifolius*, as well as magnolias, meconopsis, maples and gunneras. The nursery is open at the same times as the garden.

Features Woodland garden; plantsman's collection of plants, designed for all seasons; spring bulbs; dwarf rhododendrons; excellent nursery attached; refreshments for groups (15+), by appointment.

Owned by Mr & Mrs K.R. Potts
Number of gardeners part-time help
Size 1.4ha (3½ acres), including woodland

Compton Acres Gardens

CANFORD CLIFFS ROAD, POOLE BH13 7ES

Tel 01202 700778   **Fax** 01202 707537
Website www.comptonacres.co.uk
Location Well signed locally.
Opening hours 10 am – 6 pm; daily; March to October.
Admission fee Adults £5.75; OAPs £5.25; Children £2.95. (2001 prices).

Very touristy, very Bournemouth and very 1920s, Compton Acres offers ten totally unconnected but highly entertaining gardens, all in different styles but joined by tarmac paths. They include an Egyptian Court garden, the Spanish water garden, the Roman gardens and the Canadian Woodland Walk. Best are the Italian garden and the stupendous Japanese Garden. The gardens are undergoing extensive renovation, and the views across Poole Harbour have been opened out again. The atmosphere is still fairly commercial, but the standards of maintenance are among the highest in any garden: no visitor could fail to be cheered up by the bravura of it all.

Features Conifers; rock plants; modern roses; woodland walks; sub-tropical plantings; several shops; tea-room & light lunches.

Owned by Red Sky Leisure Ltd
Number of gardeners 4
Size 4ha (10 acres)
English Heritage grade II*

Cranborne Manor

CRANBORNE, WIMBORNE BH21 5PP

Tel 01725 517248   **Fax** 01725 517862
Website www.cranborne.co.uk
Location 10 miles north of Wimborne on B3078.
Opening hours 9 am – 5 pm (7 pm in May & June); Wednesdays; mid-March to September.
Admission fee Adults £3.50; Concessions £2.50; Children 50p. RHS members free.

Much of the garden at Cranborne is modern, laid out and planted by Lady Salisbury in the 1960s and 1970s, though you would never know it. The Jacobean-style features are designed to complement the old house, which dates principally from the early 1600s, and to remind us that the first gardener was John Tradescant the Elder. You enter the garden through a large (and excellent) garden centre, passing through a small walled kitchen garden where apple trees are trained as 5 ft espaliers. Espaliered apples appear almost as a *Leitmotif* in many other places in the garden. It is fairly simply planted, though you leave through a pretty double border with windows cut into the yew hedge on one side, and on through a herb garden. Everywhere are neat yew hedges and a little topiary. There are no horticultural rarities, but bulbs and polyanthus in spring and a cyclamen bank in autumn, and everywhere a sense of spaciousness, order and age. The classic view is of the narrow cottage-garden walk, backed by more apple-trees, leading towards the pretty flint church. Cranborne also has some fine old trees, notably beeches, limes and a vast low-branching ilex close to the house. The garden is better maintained now than a few years ago: it has clearly been taken in hand and is looking good again.

Features Topiary; roses (mainly old-fashioned); good herbaceous borders; Jacobean mount; new lavender garden (22 cultivars); garden centre.

Owned by Viscount Cranborne
Number of gardeners 2½
Size 3.2ha (8 acres)
English Heritage grade II*

Dean's Court

WIMBORNE BH21 1EE

Tel 01202 888478
Location 2 mins walk from central Wimborne.
Opening hours 2 pm – 6 pm (but 10 am – 6 pm on Bank Holiday Mondays); 31 March; 1 April; 5 & 6 May; 2, 3, 9 & 23 June; 21 July; 3, 4, 25 & 26 August; 15 September.
Admission fee Adults £2; OAPs £1.50; Children 50p.

Ⓟ ⓌⒸ 🌳 🏛

A very wholesome garden: everything, including 150 different herb varieties, is grown without artificial fertilisers, pesticides or herbicides. The new rose garden is also maintained entirely without spraying.

 Features Monastery fishpond; good trees; all organic; herb garden; old roses; organic herb plants and vegetables.

Owned by Sir Michael & Lady Hanham
Number of gardeners 4
Size 5.2ha (13 acres)

Edmonsham House

EDMONDSHAM, WIMBORNE BH21 5RE

Tel 01725 517207
Location Off B3081 between Cranborne & Verwood.
Opening hours 2 pm – 5 pm; Wednesdays & Sundays; April to October.

Admission fee Adults £1.50; Children 50p.

Ⓟ ⓌⒸ 🌳 🌳

The walled garden is maintained organically, with borders round the sides – go in August to see the vast patches of white crinums. It is intensively cultivated and brims with interesting vegetables and fruit houses. There are fine trees around the main lawns and masses of spring bulbs.

 Features Grass cockpit; herbaceous borders; fine kitchen garden; herbs; old roses; old grass cockpit; spring bulbs.

Owned by Mrs Julia E. Smith
Number of gardeners 1, plus 3 part-time
Size 2.2ha (6 acres), plus 0.4ha (1-acre) walled garden

Forde Abbey

CHARD TA20 4LU

Tel 01460 220231 **Fax** 01460 220296
Website www.fordeabbey.co.uk
Location 4 miles south of Chard.
Opening hours 10 am – 4.30 pm; daily; all year.
Admission fee Adults £4.40; OAPs £4.15; Children free.
RHS members free from October to April.

Ⓟ 🐾 ⓌⒸ 🌳 🏛 ☕

The gardens of Forde Abbey surround the 12th-century Cistercian Monastery, a rambling private home since 1650, part Jacobean and part Gothic. They extend over 30 informal acres, with plants of interest and beauty throughout the year, set off by ancient and mellowed stone walls. Trees survive from 1700, although much has been planted in recent years: rhododendrons, azaleas, acers, magnolias, irises, meconopsis and candelabra primulas. But there are also mature Victorian conifers (*Sequoia sempervirens* and *Calocedrus decurrens*), lakes, ponds, streams, cascades, bogs and such oddities as a Beech House.

Features Good herbaceous borders; fine collection of trees; rock garden planted by Jack Drake; Ionic temple (Ham stone); 17th-century vistas opened up (2000); bog garden; working kitchen garden; HHA/Christie's Garden of the Year in 1993; tallest *Cornus controversa* (16m) in UK; gift shop; cafeteria.

Owned by The Trustees of the G. D. Roper settlement
Size 12ha (30 acres)
English Heritage grade II*

C. W. Groves & Son

NURSERY & GARDEN CENTRE, WEST BAY ROAD, BRIDPORT DT6 4BA

Tel 01308 422654   **Fax** 01308 420888
Website www.users.zetnet.co.uk/c.w.grovesandson
Location South of town centre, by river, next to the Crown roundabout on A35.
Opening hours 8.30 am – 5 pm; Monday – Saturday. 10.30 am – 4.30 pm; Sundays.

This modern, up-to-date garden centre (rose beds, Koi carp) also has a traditional nursery attached. Founded in 1866 by the present owner's great-great-grandfather, it specialises in Sweet Victorian Hardy & Parma Violets. These are available from the garden centre as well as by mail order and include a large number of rarities.

 Features Old-fashioned violas; café with home cooking.

Owned by Clive & Diana Groves

Ivy Cottage

ALLER LANE, ANSTY, DORCHESTER DT2 7PX

Tel & Fax 01258 880053
Location Midway between Blandford & Dorchester.
Opening hours 10 am – 5 pm; Thursdays; May to September. Groups welcome by appointment at other times.
Admission fee Adults £2.25; Children free.

This cottage garden has been made (and immaculately maintained) by the present owners since the mid-1960s and is crammed with interesting things, particularly moisture-loving plants. Springs and streams, combined with greensand soil, multiply the possibilities – drifts of marsh marigolds, astilbes and candelabra primulas. Many are chosen with wildlife in mind.

 Features Plantsman's collection of plants; good herbaceous borders; small kitchen garden.

Owned by Anne & Alan Stevens
Number of gardeners owners only
Size 0.6ha (1½ acres)

Kingston Lacy

WIMBORNE MINSTER BH21 4EA

Tel 01202 883402   **Fax** 01202 882402
Website www.nationaltrust.org.uk
Location 1½ miles from Wimborne on B3082 to Blandford.
Opening hours 11 am – 4 pm; Saturdays & Sundays; February & March. Then 11 am – 6 pm; daily; 30 March to 3 November. Then 11 am – 4 pm; Friday – Sunday; 8 November to 22 December.
Admission fee Adults £3; Children £1.50.

The magnificent home of the Bankes family sits among 400 acres of parkland, filled in all directions as far as the eye can see with single specimen trees of great spread – beech, oak and chestnut. Nearer the house are a wonderfully gloomy cherry laurel walk, a lime avenue, and a cedar avenue planted piecemeal over the centuries to commemorate visits by everyone from the Duke of Wellington to the Kaiser. Next to the house is a pretty formal garden, first laid out in 1899 and still planted with the original scheme of pink begonias and blue heliotrope in summer. Nearby is a fern garden under a canopy of hollies, aucubas and yews: gravel paths run between irregularly shaped raised beds planted with male ferns and hart's tongues. There are snowdrops and daffodils in spring and some pretty roses near the stables restaurant – notably 'Cardinal Hume' and 'Anna Zinkeisen' – in summer. There are also many handsome trees, including a cut-leaved beech and several Lebanon cedars. The garden ornaments are however exceptional: they include an Egyptian obelisk (Ptolemy VII) and some first-class 19th-century marbles from Italy.

Features Snowdrops; mature conifers; Victorian fernery; Dutch parterre; huge cedars of Lebanon planted by visiting royalty; lunches & teas.

Owned by The National Trust
Number of gardeners 4, plus 2 part-time
Size 12ha (30 acres)
NCCPG National Collections *Anemone nemorosa*; *Convallaria*
English Heritage grade II

Kingston Maurward Gardens

KINGSTON MAURWARD COLLEGE, DORCHESTER DT2 8PY

Tel 01305 215000   **Fax** 01305 250001
Website www.kmc.ac.uk
Location 1 mile east of Dorchester from A35: signed.
Opening hours 10 am – 5.30 pm (or dusk, if earlier); daily; 6 January to 23 December.
Admission fee Adults £4; Children £2.50; Family £12. RHS members free.

Kingston Maurward belonged to the Hanbury family who owned La Mortola on the Riviera, and laid out the formal garden here in the Arts & Crafts style (with an Italianate overlay) in the 1920s, but much of the present planting is modern. The 'Grecian' temple was restored in 2000, and the hardy salvias in the National Collection have just been planted in a new parterre. The old kitchen garden is a splendid modern teaching garden with innumerable demonstrations of what can be grown in Dorset. Highly instructive.

Features Cyclamen; autumn crocus; fine borders; daffodils; topiary; parkland; cakes & drinks.

Owned by Kingston Maurward College
Number of gardeners 6
Size 14ha (35 acres)
NCCPG National Collections *Penstemon*; *Salvia*
English Heritage grade II*

Knoll Gardens

STAPEHILL ROAD, WIMBORNE
BH21 7ND

Tel 01202 873931 **Fax** 01202 870842
Website www.knollgardens.co.uk
Location Signed from B3073 at Hampreston.
Opening hours 10 am – 5 pm (or dusk if earlier); daily; all year. Closed over Christmas period, and on Fridays & Saturdays from October to March.
Admission fee Adults £4; OAPs £3.50; Children £2. RHS members free from April to October.

This garden was once an intimate and enclosed collection of tender exotics, many of them Australian trees and shrubs which now form the framework for extensive newer plantings. It was here, too, that the first owner, John May, bred the hybrid *Phygelius* × *rectus* 'African Queen'. In recent years, the garden has been enormously expanded as a horticultural visitor attraction. The modern plantings have come together well and provide much to admire: this is a garden to interest the plantsman as much as the less horticulturally minded. The many different areas, winding pathways, and constantly changing views give an impression of a much larger area than its 4 acres. The owners continue to develop the garden and its plant collections, particularly of hardy perennials and grasses – in which the adjoining nursery specialises. There is a fine open area of lawn at the bottom which gives onto the gravel garden, a conifer collection, a small pond and sinuous herbaceous plantings. The garden is maintained to a high standard.

Features Rock garden; mature conifers; good herbaceous borders; *Eucalyptus*; new gravel garden (1998) recently extended (2002); ornamental grasses; refreshments.

Owned by John & Janet Flude, & Neil Lucas
Number of gardeners 2
Size 1.6ha (4 acres)
NCCPG National Collections Ceanothus (deciduous); Phygelius

Macpennys Nurseries

154 BURLEY ROAD, BRANSGORE,
CHRISTCHURCH BH23 8DB

Tel 01425 672348
Location On the Burley Road, on the north-west edge of Bransgore.
Opening hours 9 am – 5 pm; Monday – Saturday. 2 pm – 5 pm; Sundays. Closed at Christmas & New Year.
Admission fee Donation to NGS.

This long-established nursery ('old-fashioned' in the best sense) has a reliable general range across the plant spectrum, plus a few rarities. It is particularly good for conifers, rhododendrons and shrubs. The large woodland garden next to the nursery is open for the National Gardens Scheme and full of interesting plants. Many have grown to a considerable size. The garden is perhaps at its best in late spring, when the rhododendrons and azaleas overlap with the last camellias.

Owned by Mr & Mrs T.M. Lowndes
Size 1.6ha (4 acres)

Mapperton Gardens

BEAMINSTER DT8 3NR

Tel 01308 862645 **Fax** 01308 863348
Website www.mapperton.com
Location 2 miles south-east of Beaminster.
Opening hours 2 pm – 6 pm; daily; 1 March to 31 October.

Admission fee Adults £3.50; Children £1.50 (under 5, free). RHS members free.

Mapperton has spectacular hanging gardens that you see laid out in their entirety from the lawn beside the house. First comes an enchanting steep formal valley garden, running down from a pinnacled orangery to a handsome pool surrounded by terracing and gardens of clipped yew. Below are two canals and finally a long dell garden, with an excellent collection of spring-flowering trees and shrubs, some of them rare and many with good autumn colour.

 Features Topiary; fine collection of trees; small gift shop; licensed café.

Owned by The Earl & Countess of Sandwich
Number of gardeners 3
Size 5.6ha (14 acres)
English Heritage grade II*

Minterne

MINTERNE MAGNA, DORCHESTER DT 7AU

Tel 01300 341370 **Fax** 01300 341747
Location On A352, 2 miles north of Cerne Abbas.
Opening hours 10 am – 7 pm; daily; 1 March to 10 November.
Admission fee Adults £3; Children free.

A woodland garden, best in spring, and well integrated into the park around the handsome Edwardian house. The valley was landscaped in the 18th century with a series of small lakes and cascades. The oldest rhododendrons came from Hooker's collection, but the remarkable Lord Digby (father of the present owner) supported Farrer, Forrest, Rock and Kingdon Ward, which makes Minterne one of the best

Himalayan collections. The circular walk down a greensand valley to the woodland stream and back again is ravishing: magnolias and Japanese cherries are underplanted with camellias and azaleas, while candelabra primulas and astilbes line the pools at the bottom. The fine collection of trees includes exceptional specimens of *Corylus avellana* 'Heterophylla' and *Cercidiphyllum japonicum*, while the many handkerchief trees (*Davidia involucrata*) are sensational in late May.

 Features Cherries; cyclamen; *Lathraea clandestina*; rhododendrons & azaleas; fine woodland walks; tallest *Chamaecyparis pisifera* 'Filifera' (25m) in the UK.

Owned by Lord Digby
Number of gardeners 3
Size 11.5ha (29 acres)
English Heritage grade II

Snape Cottage

BOURTON SP8 5BY

Tel & Fax 01747 840330
Website www.snapecottagegarden.co.uk
Location At west end of Bourton, ¼ mile up Chaffeymoor Hill.
Opening hours 10.30 am – 5 pm; Wednesdays; April to July, plus September. Also 17 & 24 February and 10 March.
Admission fee Adults £2; Children free.

This small cottage garden is crammed with several thousand plants and organically managed to attract wild life. It is therefore especially inspirational for visitors who garden with plants in a small space. Plant specialities include hellebores, pulmonarias, auriculas, geraniums, dianthus, irises and asters, but perhaps the most impressive collection is of snowdrops (*Galanthus*

Sticky Wicket

BUCKLAND NEWTON, DORCHESTER DT2 7BY

Tel & Fax 01300 345476
Location 11 miles from Dorchester & Sherborne.
Opening hours 10.30 am – 8 pm; Thursdays; June to September. Plus 17 June & 19 August for National Gardens Scheme (2 pm – 8 pm).
Admission fee Adults £2.50; Children £1.50.

Sticky Wicket is a highly original garden and worth revisiting frequently. The owners are both designers and conservationists, and their devotion to ecology guides their garden-making: they understand the need to attract birds, insects and other wild life. Yet it is also one of the most photographed and admired of modern gardens, because of the subtlety and integrity of Pam Lewis's colour combinations. She and her husband began the garden in 1987 but the plantings are constantly reworked, so that you find new compositions and combinations every year. Berrying trees and shrubs and those with interesting winter stems are supplemented by plants chosen for their scent, decoration and usefulness to wildlife. The planting is increasingly naturalistic and draws upon a choice of native British plants. There are four principal wildlife gardens: the Frog and Bird gardens where ponds, bird baths, nesting boxes and feeders are thickly incorporated into the design, to attract wildlife close to the house where they can be seen; the beautiful Round Garden, whose colours move from pastel tints to richer hues and back again, but where the plants are chosen for the nectar and pollen they offer to insects; and the White Garden, where ornamental grasses and flowers in loosely planted borders echo the grassy effect of the meadows beyond. The half-acre wildflower meadow, started in 1997, was sown with seed of local provenance and is managed as a traditional hay meadow, at its most glamorous in June and July. Throughout the garden, information boards explain how the Lewises preach and practice 'gardening in tune with Nature'.

Features Wide collection of interesting plants; strong ecological interest; many ornamental grasses; made since 1987; good colour associations; tea, coffee & home-made cakes.

Owned by Peter & Pam Lewis
Size 1ha (2½ acres)

species and cultivars) – over 300 different ones. There is a special emphasis on plant history and the conservation of 'old' cultivars of every sort.

 Features Lots of plants for plantsmen.

Owned by Mrs A .Whinfield
Number of gardeners 1
Size 0.2ha (½ acre)

Stapehill Abbey

STAPEHILL, WIMBORNE BH21 2EB

Tel 01202 861686 **Fax** 01202 894589
Location Signed from A31.
Opening hours 10 am – 5 pm; daily; Easter to September. Plus 10 am – 4 pm; Wednesday – Sunday; February to Easter & October to December.
Admission fee Adults £7; OAPs £6.50; Children £4.50.

A modern leisure development with vintage tractors to admire and lots of plants to sell. The design is rather unco-ordinated but the individual gardens are richly planted and there are some handsome features: a small rose garden, a laburnum pergola, a water garden, a small tropical house and an extensive rock garden, more noteworthy for its design and size than for its plantings. Not a botanical collection, but a good horticultural one.

 Features New Japanese garden (2000); gift shop & many craft shops; licensed coffee shop.

Owned by Stapehill Enterprises Ltd
Number of gardeners 4

Trehane Camellia Nursery

STAPEHILL ROAD, HAMPRESTON, WIMBORNE BH21 7ND

Tel & Fax 01202 873490
Location Between Ferndown & Wimborne, off A31. Next to Knoll Gardens.
Opening hours 9 am – 4.30 pm; Monday – Friday; all year. 10 am – 4.30 pm; Saturdays & Sundays; late February to end May. And by appointment.

This is a wholesale and retail camellia nursery in a woodland setting. They have a wide choice of *Camellia* hybrids, plus a good range of magnolias, pieris, rhododendrons, azaleas and blueberries (plus 'pick-your-own' blueberries in August!).

 Features Camellias; blueberries.

Owned by The Trehane family
Size 4ha (10 acres)

CO. DURHAM

Durham is too often – and wrongly – considered a horticultural wasteland, though it is true that in the 1980s the Royal Horticultural Society had fewer members in Durham than any other English county – less than 100. Things have come a long way since then. English Heritage has drawn attention to the importance of historic landscapes like Raby Castle and the Bowes Museum, and there are now five National Collections in the county. Horn's Garden Centre at Shotton Colliery has the National Collection of coleus (*Solenostemon* cultivars) and a large collection of *Streptocarpus* and pelargoniums too. The city of Durham itself has two outstandingly good gardens for learning about plants – the University of Durham Botanic Garden and the gardens attached to Houghall College, a RHS Partner College.

Barningham Park

BARNINGHAM, RICHMOND
DL11 7DW

Tel 01833 621202 **Fax** 01833 621298
Location 10 miles north-west of Scotch Corner off A66.
Opening hours For NGS. And parties by appointment.
Admission fee Adults £2.50; Children free.

This early 19th-century landscape runs up from the terrace to the old bowling green and down to the skating pond. Humphry Repton had a hand in it. Some Victorian ancestors planted a pinetum, then some keen horticultural Milbanks got to work in the 1920s. They designed the splendid rock garden and diverted a stream to form cascades and pools through it. Unknown and perhaps underrated, if Barningham were in the Home Counties everyone would rave about it.

 Features Hillside rock garden with stream; good herbaceous borders;
terraced gardens; rhododendrons; woodland walks; homemade teas.

Owned by Sir Anthony Milbank Bt.
Number of gardeners 1
Size 1.6ha (4 acres), plus 24ha (60 acres) of woodland

The Bowes Museum Garden & Park

BARNARD CASTLE DL12 8NP

Tel 01833 690606 **Fax** 01833 637163
Website www.bowesmuseum.org.uk
Location In Barnard Castle town.
Opening hours Dawn – dusk; daily; all year.
Admission fee Free.

Twenty-one acres of Victorian splendour, now maintained by the trustees as a public amenity. The formal gardens around the fountain are good – a vast oval parterre re-made in the French style in 1982 – and mature trees pepper the park. Almost all were planted in the 1870s: some of the conifers are particularly fine.

 Features Roses (mainly old-fashioned); fine collection of trees; parterre; large monkey puzzle; gift shop; museum café.

Owned by Trustees of the Bowes Museum
Number of gardeners 1
Size 8.3ha (21 acres)
English Heritage grade II

Houghall

DURHAM DH1 3SG

Tel 0191 386 1351   **Fax** 0191 386 0419
Location Follow A177 from A1 to Durham.
Opening hours 12.30 pm – 4.30 pm; daily; all year.
Admission fee Free.

Houghall is a well-run teaching garden, originally attached to Durham's horticultural college. There is much to see here: a fine arboretum (more than 500 different trees), a young pinetum, good displays of perennial plants and shrubs (one of the best in northern England), and a wildflower meadow for summer interest. Many trials are conducted here, for example on the hardiness of fuchsias: the garden staff say that 'if it grows at Houghall it will grow anywhere'.

 Features Roses (mainly modern); rock garden; plants under glass; good herbaceous borders; alpine plants; heathers; hardy fuchsias; seasonal bedding; excellent young pinetum & arboretum; shop; refreshments available.

Owned by East Durham Houghall Community College
Number of gardeners 6
NCCPG National Collections Sorbus; Meconopsis

Raby Castle

STAINDROP, DARLINGTON DL2 3AH

Tel 01833 660202   **Fax** 01833 660169
Location On A688, 1 mile north of Staindrop
Opening hours 11 am – 5.30 pm; Sunday to Friday; June to August. Plus Wednesdays & Sundays in May & September.
Admission fee Adults £3; Concessions £2. RHS members free, except during special events.

The 18th-century walled gardens at Raby Castle are set within a 200-acre deer park in the heart of Teesdale. Designers such as Thomas White and James Paine have worked on these magnificent gardens, which incorporate herbaceous borders, shrub borders, yew hedges, a conservatory, formal rose gardens and informal heather and conifer gardens. The gardens were considerably altered during the 20th century but many of the original features remain, notably the two fine 200-year-old yew hedges and the ornamental pond that dominates the central garden.

 Features Deer park; walled garden; fine yew hedges; cafeteria.

Owned by Lord Barnard
English Heritage grade II*

University of Durham Botanic Garden

HOLLINGSIDE LANE, DURHAM DH1 3TN

Tel 0191 374 7971   **Fax** 0191 374 7478
Website www.durham.ac.uk
Location In the south of the City of Durham.
Opening hours 10 am – 5 pm; daily; March to October. 11 am – 4 pm; daily; November to February.

Admission fee Adults £1.50; Concessions 50p.

Moved to its present site in 1970, this garden impresses with its youthful energy. The 'North American arboretum' was planted in 1980 to copy natural associations. A woodland garden dates from 1988, a wetland one from 1989, and 1992 saw the opening of the 'Prince Bishop's Garden' with statues transferred from the Gateshead garden festival.

 Features Roses (mainly old-fashioned); fine collection of trees; New Zealand plants; primulas; meconopsis; autumn colour; woodland plants; sculpture by Ian Hamilton Findlay; tea, coffee, cold drinks & snacks.

Owned by University of Durham
Number of gardeners 3, plus volunteers

Westholme Hall

WINSTON, DARLINGTON DL2 3QL

Tel 01325 730442   **Fax** 01325 730946
Location On B6274 north towards Staindrop.
Opening hours For NGS.
Admission fee Adults £2; Children 50p.

Westholme has 5 acres of late-Victorian gardens, recently restored and revived, around a beautiful Jacobean house. They were designed and planted for all seasons: parts are for spring display (bulbs and azaleas), and other for summer (roses and lilacs) and autumn (herbaceous borders). All is maintained by the owners' own hard work and enthusiasm. The garden is worth a long detour to see: would that it were open more often.

Features Roses (mainly old-fashioned); rhododendrons; tea-room.

Owned by Mrs J.H. McBain
Number of gardeners owners only
Size 2ha (5 acres)

ESSEX

Considering its proximity to London, where fortunes have for centuries been made, Essex has few famous historic gardens: Audley End is the pre-eminent exception, and as important horticulturally as historically. It is the county's only Grade I garden. Few of the county's other historic gardens are open to the public. Essex's most famous gardener was Miss Ellen Willmott of Warley Place, Great Warley, but her house was demolished shortly after her death in 1934 and the garden (what remains of it) is now a nature reserve: arrangements to visit it may be made through Essex Wildlife Trust. It has one of Essex's few record trees, an *Umbellularia californica* 20m high. Low rainfall and hot summers define Essex gardening: Beth Chatto has made a study of dry gardening at her nursery near Elmstead Market. Other nurseries of exceptional interest to keen plantsmen are Glen Chantry and Langthorns Plantery. The National Gardens Scheme has a fair number of gardens opening for the Yellow Book, most of them medium-sized and good for seeing plants. There are 14 National Collections in the county. Writtle College near Chelmsford is a RHS Partner College, with lectures and workshops on a wide range of hands-on topics throughout the year. The garden at Hyde Hall has proved an interesting acquisition for the Royal Horticultural Society and much improved by the Society's input – new design features and many new plants.

Amberden Hall

WIDDINGTON, SAFFRON WALDON
CB11 3ST

Tel 01799 540402
Location In Amberden, turn down Cornells Lane: house is 1 mile along.
Opening hours By appointment only.
Admission fee £3.

This much praised modern garden around a handsome old house is open only by appointment at the moment. The single-colour borders contain a wide range of unusual plants and a fine collection of climbing plants backed by attractive old walls. A small 'secret garden' has recently been added, complete with pond, rill and dovecote.

Features Bog garden; good collection of fruit and vegetables; unusual plants; an ivy walk.

Owned by Mr & Mrs David Lloyd
Number of gardeners ½

Audley End

SAFFRON WALDEN CB11 4JF

Tel 01799 522842/520052 **Fax** 01799 522131
Website www.english-heritage.org.uk
Location On B1383, 1 mile west of Saffron Walden.
Opening hours Garden: 11 am – 6 pm; Wednesday – Sunday, plus Bank Holidays; 29 March to 31 October. Closes at 4 pm in October.
Admission fee Gardens: Adults £4; OAPs £3; Children £2.

Capability Brown landscaped the park (rather too many Canada geese) in 1763 but work on rejuvenating the garden at Audley End started some years ago with the formal garden behind the house towards the Temple of Concord. This dates from the 1830s and has 170 geometric flower beds crisply cut from the turf and planted with original varieties of perennials, bedding plants and annuals for spring and summer. Nearby are the Elysian Garden, designed in the 1780s by Placido Columbani, and the Victorian pond garden in the 'picturesque' style, whose walls and pergola are clad with climbing shrubs and roses. Work continues: the kitchen garden is now run as a joint venture with the Henry Doubleday Research Association as a working organic garden. It looks much as it would have done in late Victorian times with vegetables, fruit, herbs and flowers to supply the household. The cultivation is, of course, entirely organic. The vinehouse is one of the earliest and largest in the country, with vines nearly 200 years old.

 Features Bedding out; parterre; magnificent plane trees; organic kitchen garden; ancient trees; shop; restaurant & picnic site.

Owned by English Heritage
Number of gardeners 9
Size 40ha (100 acres), including parkland
English Heritage grade I

County Park Nursery

384 WINGLETYE LANE, HORNCHURCH RM11 3BU

Tel 01708 445205
Location 2½ miles from M25, Jct 29. Off Wingletye Lane, in Essex Gardens, Hornchurch.
Opening hours 9 am – 6 pm, Monday – Saturday; 10 am – 5 pm, Sundays; from March to October. Closed Wednesdays. Open in winter by appointment only.

This small nursery specialises in antipodean plants, many of them grown from native seed and not available from any other nursery in the UK. There is no show garden to speak of, but every tiny corner seems covered in pots of unusual plants. There are lots of hebes and parahebes, as well as New Zealand *Clematis* species, *Coprosma* and other shrubs like leptospermums. They also have a long list of podocarpus cultivars, selected by themselves for their spreading habit and unusual leaf colours. Very interesting.

Features Plants from New Zealand & Australia.

NCCPG National Collections *Coprosma*; *Parahebe*

Easton Lodge

WARWICK HOUSE, GREAT DUNMOW CM6 2BB

Tel & Fax 01371 876979
Website www.eastonlodge.co.uk
Location Signed from A120 at Great Dunmow.

Beth Chatto Gardens

ELMSTEAD MARKET, COLCHESTER CO7 7DB

Tel 01206 822007   **Fax** 01206 825933
Website www.bethchatto.co.uk
Location 7 miles east of Colchester.
Opening hours 9 am – 5 pm; Monday – Saturday; March to October; 9 am – 4 pm; Monday – Friday; November to February. Closed on Bank Holidays.
Admission fee Adults £3; Children free. RHS members free in February & March.

Beth Chatto's garden is a superb example of modern planting, with a very wide range of different plants to see and study, and all chosen for their foliage as much as their flowers. There are two main types of planting here and it is the contrast between them which makes the garden. First there are the parts on dry gravelly soil, where Mediterranean plants flourish; second, there are the water- and bog-gardens on clay. All have been made since 1960. Around the modest house, where the soil is thin and dry, Beth Chatto planted a Mediterranean garden: cistus, *Cytisus battandieri*, salvias, euphorbias, potentillas, verbascums and a tree-like *Genista aetnensis* have come together on the warm slopes. A short walk leads down to a water-garden of remarkable luxuriance, made by damming a damp ditch to create a series of ponds in the valley. The lush and clumpy plantings are quite untypical of Essex, where rainfall averages 50 cm a year. Here are gunneras, astilbes, lysichitons, hostas, phormiums, water-irises, *Rheum palmatum* and the ostrich fern *Matteuccia struthiopteris.* They have a continuous background, not too intrusive, of conifers, specimen trees and shrubs – but the emphasis throughout the garden is on the herbaceous plants for which the adjoining nursery is famous. A copse has

been developed as woodland garden: a canopy of young oaks underplanted with shade-lovers. Here, and in the long shady border above the water garden, are rich plantings of bulbs, woodlanders and ground-cover – aconites, cyclamen, erythroniums and dicentras. The most recent development is the gravel garden, made in 1992 on the site of the old car park, where drought-resistant sun-lovers appear to have been planted straight into gravel in a fluid sequence of island beds. But garden-making is only one of Beth Chatto's gifts: her writings and nursery have made her famous. And the standard of maintenance is impeccable.

Features Colour contrasts; gravel garden; luxuriant water gardens; woodland garden; big nursery adjacent to the garden; tea-room (seasonal).

Owned by Beth Chatto
Size 2.8ha (7 acres)

Opening hours 12 noon – dusk; daily; February to early March (ring for exact dates) for snowdrops. Then 12 noon – 6 pm; Friday – Sunday & Bank Holiday Mondays; Easter to October.

Admission fee Adults £3.80; OAPs £3.50; Children £1.50.

The garden was laid out by Harold Peto in 1902 for the Countess of Warwick (Edward VII's 'darling Daisy'), fell into serious neglect, and has been wonderfully restored since 1993. Much remains to be done, as the owner is the first to admit, but the Lime Grove has now been cleared and the Peto shrubbery was rejuvenated in 2001. Work has begun on re-paving the Italian garden and will be finished this summer.

Owned by Brian Creasey
Number of gardeners 2
Size 9.2ha (23 acres)
English Heritage grade II

The Gibberd Garden

MARSH LANE, GILDEN WAY, HARLOW CM17 0NA

Tel 01279 442112
Website www.thegibberdgarden.co.uk
Location Leave Harlow on B183. Marsh Lane is on left.
Opening hours 2 pm – 6 pm; Saturdays, Sundays & Bank Holidays; April to September
Admission fee Adults £3; Concessions £2; Children free.

This was the private garden of Sir Frederick Gibberd, the master planner of Harlow New Town. It was designed as a series of distinct rooms, and filled with sculpture, pots and architectural salvage. One of the most important architectural gardens of the 20th century, it is being restored with aid from the Heritage Lottery Commission. The castle moat has been dredged and repaired; the top lawns and beds have been replanted; and

work will begin this year on restoring the wild garden. There is an active Friends Organisation: details from Ken Collins on 01279 726047.

 Features Good modern design; wild garden; lime avenue; 'Roman Temple' vistas; light refreshments.

Owned by Gibberd Garden Trust
Number of gardeners 3 part-time plus volunteers
Size 2.8ha (7 acres)

Langthorns Plantery

LITTLE CANFIELD, DUNMOW CM6 1TD

Tel & Fax 01371 872611
Location Between Takeley & Great Dunmow, signed off A120.
Opening hours 10 am – 5 pm; daily. Closed Christmas to New Year.

Langthorns Plantery is a go-ahead modern nursery with an eye for good plants. Though best known for their wide range of hardy herbaceous plants, the owners apply their discriminating taste to all their stock – alpines, shrubs, trees and climbers, especially clematis. The garden is worth a visit in its own right but not always open, so check before you visit.

Olivers

OLIVERS LANE, COLCHESTER CO2 0HJ

Tel 01206 330575   **Fax** 01206 330366
Location 3 miles south-west of Colchester between B1022 & B1026.
Opening hours 2 pm – 6 pm; 5 & 6 May, & 4 August. And by appointment.

Glen Chantry

ISHAMS CHASE, WICKHAM BISHOPS, WITHAM CM8 3LG

Tel & Fax 01621 891342
Location Turn off B1019 just south of A12 towards Benton
Hall golf course & Wickham Bishops: immediately left after
bridge & up track ½ mile.
Opening hours 10 am – 4 pm; Fridays & Saturdays;
6 April to 6 October.
Admission fee Adults £2; Children 50p. RHS members
free.

This remarkable garden has been made on
a bare hillside since 1976: the owners
have an excellent eye for good plants and for
how to use them. You enter past a very
pretty new *potager* and through the
immaculately tidy nursery, itself a
plantsman's treasure-house for alpine and
herbaceous plants. Then you step down into
the garden, filled with endless micro-
habitats, some exploiting the opportunities
offered by dry, stony acid soil, and other
defying it. Scree beds, peat beds, raised beds
and an artificial stream are part of the story,
but so is a winding pattern of ebbing and
flowing island beds. Along the centre of
these beds are trees and shrubs which screen
the two faces from each other and make it
possible to plant both sides of a path with
the same colour. The owners also practice
'vertical planting', which means that season
after season different displays are possible
from the same patch: in one small area, for
example, the spring-flowering fritillaries,
erythroniums and corydalis are covered in
summer by hostas, grasses and rushes. Glen
Chantry is a model of what devoted
plantsmanship can achieve: educational,
functional and beautiful all at once. There is
one formal garden near the house, white and
green in summer with 'Yvonne Rabier' and
'Iceberg' roses, campanulas, lilies,
eryngiums, alliums and geraniums, but the
rest of the garden is fluid, however
disciplined may be the controlling hand. In
fact, very little seeding around is allowed –
perhaps a few plants of Martyn Rix's form of
Eryngium giganteum 'Silver Ghost' – because
the planting is intended to slow you down
and stop you on your way, to admire
individual plants. Besides, the standards of
maintenance are immaculate.

Features Alpines; herbaceous plants;
bulbs; special habitats; masses of
fascinating plants for plantsmen; light
refreshments.

Owned by Sue & Wol Staines
Number of gardeners owners only
Size 1ha (2½ acres)

Admission fee Adults £2.50; Children free.

Quite a modern garden, started in 1968 around three small lakes, with an eye-catching walk to one side leading down to a statue of Bacchus. Good plants and planting everywhere, from the parterres by the house to the woodland where roses and rhododendrons flourish. The main borders underwent a highly successful major re-design in 1998 and are looking very good now. This is the garden of enthusiastic and energetic owners: an inspiration.

 Features Roses (ancient & modern); bluebells; rhododendrons; fine borders; refreshments for pre-booked parties.

Owned by Mr & Mrs David Edwards
Number of gardeners 1

Rhodes & Rockliffe

2 NURSERY ROAD, NAZEING EN9 2JE

Tel 01992 451598 **Fax** 01992 440673
Location ½ mile west of Lower Nazeing along B194; turn right into Nursery Road.
Opening hours By appointment only.
Admission fee free

David Rhodes and John Rockliffe have the finest collection of *Begonia* species and hybrids in Britain. Their occasional exhibits at Chelsea and other RHS flower shows have won them well-deserved gold medals and contributed immensely to popularising the genus in recent years. Their knowledge of begonias is prodigious – as are the size of their collection and the vigour of their plants.

NCCPG National Collections *Begonia*

RHS Garden Hyde Hall

RETTENDON, CHELMSFORD CM3 8ET

Tel 01245 400256 **Fax** 01245 402100
Website www.rhs.org.uk
Location South-east of Chelmsford, signed from A130 bypass. Exit for the Rettendon turnpike, north through Rettendon village and follow the brown tourist signs.
Opening hours 10 am – 6 pm (5 pm from September to November); daily; 18 March to 10 November.
Admission fee Adults £4; Children (6 – 16) £1; Groups (10+) special rates. RHS members free.

From the original six trees on a windy hill with beautiful views to the delightful and imaginatively planted garden of today, Hyde Hall is the result of 40 years of dedication, endeavour and inspiration. Home to the National Collection of *Viburnum*, the garden has also become well-known as a plantsman's garden and for its superb collection of roses. Both modern and old-fashioned roses are displayed in a new rose garden designed by Robin Williams and completed in 2000, together with a large number of climbers and ramblers, many of which are pruned and trained in interesting and unusual styles. The sheltered woodland garden on the northern side is a triumph of cultivation and there are interesting examples of hardiness throughout: *Eriobotrya japonica, Eucalyptus urnigera* and *Pittosporum tenuifolium* are grown in the open, *Buddleja officinalis* and *Crinodendron patagua* against a wall of the yard and *Acca sellowiana* against the house. Hyde Hall was donated to the Society in 1993 and much work has since been carried out. The new Entrance Garden, with its distinctive oak pergola and water feature was extended in spring 1999 with new plantings around the Upper Pond and Hyde Hall Farmhouse. The long herbaceous border has been reworked – backed by new shelter hedges of yew and tongues of yew which divide the border into bays. In spring, there is a delightful mix of bulbs and blossom throughout the garden, particularly in the old stable-yard and Hermione's Garden, and towards the end of the year colour is provided in large part by viburnums and crab apples (*Malus*), both of which are particularly noted for their autumn foliage and fruit. Recent developments include the Dry Garden, with over 4,000 plants representing 740 different species and cultivars, and the Millennium Avenue, 300m long and 20m wide, planted with *Fraxinus excelsior* 'Westhof's Glory' for short-term effect and *Quercus frainetto* 'Hungarian Crown' for 100 years hence.

Features Woodland garden; plantsman's collection of plants; good herbaceous borders; magnolias; South African bulbs; peonies; spring bulbs; ponds; heathers; new garden of drought-tolerant plants (2001); information centre & garden library; licensed restaurant serving hot & cold lunches, afternoon teas, tea/coffee.

Owned by Royal Horticultural Society
Number of gardeners 9, plus students
Size 9.6ha (24 acres)
NCCPG National Collections *Viburnum*

Saling Hall

GREAT SALING, BRAINTREE
CM7 5DT

Location 2 miles north of the Saling Oak on A120.
Opening hours 2 pm – 5 pm; Wednesdays; May, June & July. Groups by appointment on weekdays.
Admission fee Adults £2.50 (for National Gardens Scheme); Children free.

A thinking man's garden, Saling also provokes thought in its visitors. The plantsmanship is impressive, particularly the choice and placing of trees and shrubs. Few modern gardens are conceived on such a scale, or mix classical and Japanese elements so smoothly. The moods, and the lessons, are endless.

Features 17th-century walled garden with fruit trees & borders; oriental touches; fine standing stone; Temple of Pisces, moat & water gardens.

Owned by Mr & Mrs Hugh Johnson
Number of gardeners 2
Size 5ha (12 acres)
English Heritage grade II

GLOUCESTERSHIRE

Gloucestershire is rich in nurseries and large important gardens. Six of its nine Grade I historic gardens (a remarkable number for one county) are regularly open to the public – Batsford Park, Frampton Court, Hidcote Manor, Sezincote, Stanway House, and Westonbirt Arboretum – while a seventh, Stancombe Park, is open by appointment. Almost all the county's Grade II* gardens also welcome visitors, including Abbotswood, Berkeley Castle, Kiftsgate Court, Miserden Park, Painswick House, Rodmarton Manor, Sudeley Castle and Westbury Court. Most have important collections of plants as well as attractive design features. Indeed, almost all Gloucestershire's leading historic gardens have been highly graded precisely because of their horticultural attractions. Rich clay soils account for some of the popularity of gardening in Gloucestershire, though the inland, upland parts of the county can be very cold in winter. Among garden centres and nurseries, the Batsford Garden Centre has a very good general range and makes a speciality of ferns, while Hunt's Court is excellent for roses of every kind. A very large number of gardens open for the National Gardens Scheme though, slightly confusingly, the southern part of the county which used to belong to Avon, is still separately organised: both continue to be very successful in persuading garden-owners to open their gardens and visitors to visit them. Permission to visit HRH The Prince of Wales's garden at Highgrove House near Tetbury may be given to garden clubs and similar organisations. In addition to the world-famous Westonbirt Arboretum, there are important collections of trees at Highnam Court, Batsford Park, and Tortworth Court. The NCCPG is active in Gloucestershire and accounts for 20 National Collections.

Abbotswood

STOW-ON-THE-WOLD, CHELTENHAM
GL54 1LE

Tel 01451 830173
Location 1 mile west of Stow-on-the-Wold.
Opening hours 1.30 pm – 6 pm; 31 March, 14 April, 26 May, 9 June & 7 July.

Admission fee Adults £2; Children free.

Abbotswood is one of the most interesting gardens in the Cotswolds – very Lutyens, very photogenic – with handsome formal gardens in front of the house. A stream meanders through a magnificent rock garden set with a alpine meadows, bogs and moraines, past dwarf azaleas, primulas, lysichitons, heaths and heathers until it disappears. There is also a small arboretum, with some unusual cultivars dating from about 100 years ago, fascinating to browse around: it is being cleared and replanted. The kitchen garden is worth the long walk on the occasions when it too is open.

Features Interesting topiary; fine collection of trees, including conifers; magnolias; heather garden; good borders; roses ancient & modern; good for plants; teas.

Owned by Dikler Farming Co.
Size 8ha (20 acres)
English Heritage grade II*

Barnsley House Garden

BARNSLEY, CIRENCESTER GL7 5EE

Tel 01285 740561   **Fax** 01285 740628
Location On B4425 in Barnsley village.
Opening hours 10 am – 5.30 pm; Mondays, plus Wednesday – Saturday; February to Christmas. Closed on Good Friday. Parties by appointment only.
Admission fee Adults £4; OAPs £3.50; Children free.

Rosemary Verey's famous garden was started in 1952 and more-or-less finished 25 years later. The bones were a pretty house (1697), an 18th-century wall ending in an original Gothick summerhouse and ha-ha, and some fine 19th-century trees. Her architect husband David helped with the design, and together they commissioned sculptures by Simon Verity for important focal points. The result was compact, neat, thickly planted, fairly labour-intensive – and very influential. Mrs Verey reflected the aspirations of many garden-owners in the difficult post-war years, so that when people had more money to spend again in the

1970s and 1980s, Barnsley was available to teach and inspire. The scale is surprisingly intimate – one of the garden's strengths – and the small decorative *potager* spawned many imitations. Barnsley is interesting at all seasons, particularly in early spring when it seems to have much more colour than other people's gardens, and again at midsummer rose time and when the salvias and asters flower in autumn. But it is probably at its best – and certainly at its most photographed – in late spring when the little laburnum walk and the purple alliums underneath are in flower together.

Features Good borders; old roses; ornamental *potager*; gift shop; garden furniture; teas & light refreshements from Easter.

Owned by Mr & Mrs Charles Verey
Number of gardeners 2½
Size 2.2ha (5½ acres)

Batsford Arboretum

MORETON-IN-MARSH GL56 9QF

Tel 01386 701441   **Fax** 01386 701829
Website www.batsford-arboretum.co.uk
Location Off A44 between Moreton-in-Marsh & Bourton-on-the-Hill.
Opening hours 10 am – 5 pm; daily; 15 February to 15 November. Plus 10 am – 3 pm at weekends in winter (hot punch on Boxing Day!).
Admission fee Adults £4; OAPs £3; Children £1. RHS members free except in October.

Batsford has an openness which makes its hillside a joy to wander through, passing from one dendrological marvel to the next. Begun in the 1880s, the Arboretum also has several oriental curiosities brought from Japan by Lord Redesdale – a large bronze Buddha and an oriental rest-house for

instance. But the arboretum is mainly the work of the late Lord Dulverton, who added a large number of new plantings between 1956 and 1992. These include nearly 100 different magnolia cultivars, a comprehensive collection of Japanese cherries, some very beautiful conifers, and excellent collections of such genera as *Acer*, *Betula* and *Sorbus*. Some are already record-breakers: all are in the prime of their life, well-grown and vigorous. The underplantings of spring bulbs are worth seeing, but visit Batsford at any season and you will find much to admire and enjoy.

 Features Mature conifers; fine collection of trees; maple glade; bluebells; aconites; snowdrops; tallest *Betula platyphylla* (19m) in the British Isles (and 12 other tree records); shop; light meals & refreshments.

Owned by The Batsford Foundation
Number of gardeners 2
Size 20ha (50 acres)
English Heritage grade I

Berkeley Castle

BERKELEY GL13 9BQ

Tel 01453 810332
Location Off A38.
Opening hours 2 pm – 5 pm; Tuesday – Sunday; April & May. 11 am – 5 pm, Tuesday – Saturday; also 2 pm – 5 pm, Sundays; May to September. Plus Mondays in July & August. 2 pm – 4.30 pm; Sundays; October. 11 am – 5 pm; Bank Holiday Mondays.
Admission fee Garden only: Adults £2; Children £1.

The grim battlements of Berkeley Castle are host to an extensive collection of tender plants. On three terraces are *Cestrum*, *Cistus* and *Rosa banksiae* among hundreds of plant varieties introduced by the owner's

grandmother, a sister of Ellen Willmott. An Elizabethan-style bowling green and a waterlily pond fit well into the overall scheme.

 Features Roses (mainly old-fashioned); plantsman's collection of plants; mature conifers; good herbaceous borders; shop at Castle Farm; light lunches & afternoon tea.

Owned by R.J.G. Berkeley
Number of gardeners 2
Size 2ha (5 acres)
English Heritage grade II*

Bourton House

BOURTON-ON-THE-HILL, MORETON-IN-MARSH GL56 9AE

Tel 01386 700121   **Fax** 01386 701081
Location On A44, 1½ miles west of Moreton-in-Marsh.
Opening hours 10 am – 5 pm; Wednesday – Friday; 22 May to 31 August. Plus 2–4 June, 25 & 26 August, and Thursdays & Fridays in September & October.
Admission fee Adults £3.50; Children free.

First laid out by Lanning Roper in the 1960s, but consistently improved by the present owners, the gardens at Bourton House are both fashionable and a delight. They include a knot garden, a small *potager*, a raised pond, the topiary walk, trellis work, a croquet lawn, and borders bulging with good colour schemes – purple-leaved prunus with yellow roses, for instance.

 Features New 'moonlight' border (2001); new sub-tropical border (2000); topiary; good colour plantings, especially of herbaceous plants; lots of unusual and little-known plants; homemade cakes with tea & coffee.

Owned by Mr & Mrs Richard Paice
Number of gardeners 2, plus 2 part-time
Size 1.2ha (3 acres), plus 2.8ha (7-acre) arboretum
English Heritage grade II

Dyrham Park

CHIPPENHAM SN14 8ER

Tel 0117 937 2501
Website www.nationaltrust.org.uk
Location On A46, 8 miles north of Bath.
Opening hours 11 am – 5.30 pm; Friday – Tuesday; 22 March to 3 November. Closed 5 to 8 July.
Admission fee Garden only £3; Children £1.50.

Dyrham is fascinating for garden historians, who can study the Kip plan and trace the lines of the 17th-century formal garden which Charles Harcourt Masters turned into classic English parkland. It is not a Mecca for the dedicated plantsman, but the impressive orangery is full of colour and scent.

 Features Good herbaceous borders; deer park; handsome orangery; tea-room.

Owned by The National Trust
Number of gardeners 2
Size 3.2ha (8 acres), plus park
English Heritage grade II*

Ernest Wilson Memorial Garden

HIGH STREET, CHIPPING CAMPDEN GL55 6AF

Tel 01386 841298
Location North end of main street.
Opening hours 9 am to dusk; daily, except Christmas day; all year.

Admission fee Collection box for donations.

A collection of plants all introduced by Ernest H. Wilson, the greatest of European plant hunters in China: Chipping Campden was his birthplace. *Acer griseum, Clematis montana* var. *rubens* and the pocket-handkerchief tree (*Davidia involucrata*) are among his best-known introductions: all are represented here.

 Features Herbaceous borders; trees & shrubs.

Owned by Chipping Campden Town Council
Number of gardeners 1
Size 0.1ha (¼ acre)

Frampton Court

FRAMPTON-ON-SEVERN GL2 7EU

Tel 01452 740267 **Fax** 01452 740698
Location Signed to Frampton-on-Severn from M5 Jct 13 (3 miles).
Opening hours By appointment all year.
Admission fee House & garden £4.50; Garden £1.

Beautiful and mysterious garden, little changed since 1750. The Dutch water garden – a long rectangular pool – reflects the orangery of Strawberry Hill Gothic design. But do also ask to see the collection of botanical water colours known as the Frampton Flora.

 Features Gothic orangery.

Owned by Mrs Peter Clifford
Number of gardeners 1½
English Heritage grade I

Hidcote Manor

HIDCOTE BARTRIM, CHIPPING CAMPDEN GL55 6LR

Tel 01386 438333   **Fax** 01386 438817
Website www.nationaltrust.org.uk
Location Signed from B4632, Stratford/Broadway Road.
Opening hours 10.30 am – 6.30 pm (5.30 pm in
October & November); Saturday – Wednesday; 23 March to
3 November. Plus Thursdays in from 5 June to 30 July. Last
admission one hour before closing.
Admission fee Adults £5.80; Children £2.90. RHS
members free from April to October.

One of England's great gardens, Hidcote is an arts-and-crafts masterpiece created by the American plant-collector Major Lawrence Johnston. It was designed as a series of outdoor rooms, each with a different character and separated by walis and hedges of many different species. Hidcote therefore has a firm architectural structure – many of Lawrence Johnston's ideas came from France and Italy – combined with a great love of plants. The planting is exuberant but always considers the contrasts and harmonies which can be obtained by planting different things together. Some of the rooms are very small, like Mrs Winthrop's garden – no more than a courtyard with a potted cordyline at the centre – and others like the long walk and the great lawn give a great sense of space – though in fact the garden is no more than 10 acres in size. Among the most famous features are: the mixed borders down the middle of the kitchen garden richly planted with old roses and companion plants; the red borders, which were one of the first single-colour borders in the country when first planted in 1913; the cottage garden, planted like an Edwardian flower painting where *Campanula latiloba* 'Hidcote Amethyst' is prominent; the sunken garden

where a huge circular swimming pool fills a hedged compartment; and the woodland area known as Westonbirt where Johnston planted long vistas which run from end to end, but which disappear and reappear as you follow the paths back and forth. The National Trust has just begun a programme of renewal and regeneration and it fair to say that Hidcote will shortly be looking better than ever.

Features Woodland garden; topiary; roses (ancient & modern); rock garden; plantsman's collection of plants; good herbaceous borders; tallest pink acacia *Robinia × ambigua* 'Decaisneana' (19m) in the British Isles; National Trust shop; licensed restaurant; teas.

Owned by The National Trust
NCCPG National Collections *Paeonia*
English Heritage grade I

Goldney Hall

LOWER CLIFTON HILL, CLIFTON,
BRISTOL BS8 1BH

Tel 0117 903 4873   **Fax** 0117 903 4877
Location Top of Constitution Hill: entrance on Lower Clifton Hill.
Opening hours 2 pm – 6 pm; 28 April & probably again in August (ring for dates).
Admission fee Adults £2; Concessions £1.

A Bristol merchant's extravagance, nearly 300 years ago. Ten acres in the middle of the City, with an elegant orangery, a gothic folly tower and the gorgeous Goldney Grotto, which sparkles with crystalline rocks among the shells and follies.

Features Plants under glass; good herbaceous borders; holm oak hedge; many varieties of fruit; the *Chronicles of Narnia* were filmed in the grotto; cream teas in the Orangery.

Owned by The University of Bristol
Number of gardeners 6
English Heritage grade II*

Highfield Nurseries

SCHOOL LANE, WHITMINSTER,
GLOUCESTER GL2 7PL

Tel 01452 740266   **Fax** 01452 740750
Location Off A38, ½ mile from M5, Jct 13.
Opening hours 9 am – 4 pm, Monday – Friday. Closed Saturdays & Sundays.
Admission fee Free.

Highfield is a large nursery, specialising in fruit trees and bushes: it offers a good choice of the best and most reliable cultivars. It also has a good list of roses, ornamental trees, shrubs and herbaceous plants – something for everyone, in fact.

Owned by Joan Greenway

Highnam Court

HIGHNAM, GLOUCESTER GL2 8DP

Tel 01452 511303   **Fax** 01452 308251
Location Entrance on A40 roundabout.
Opening hours 11 am – 5 pm; first Sunday of the month; April to September.
Admission fee Adults £2.50; Children free.

Little remains of the original Highnam, laid out when the house was built in 1658. The garden was however very famous 100 years ago for the features designed or commissioned by Thomas Gambier-Parry in the middle of the 19th century: the terraces, the broad walk, the arboretum and, above all, the winter garden where natural stone is supplemented by pulhamite – the largest and earliest surviving example of the artificial stone. The estate was neglected for nearly 100 years, but restoration – slow and painstaking – began in 1994, so this is a garden to watch and revisit as the work continues.

Features Pulhamite rock garden; fine conifers; tallest *Quercus acutissima* and *Fraxinus excelsior* 'Jaspidea' in the British isles; historic garden in restoration; tea & cakes.

Owned by Roger Head
Number of gardeners 2
Size 12ha (30 acres)
English Heritage grade II*

Hodges Barn

SHIPTON MOYNE, TETBURY GL8 8PR

Tel 01666 880202   **Fax** 01666 880373
Location 3 miles south of Tetbury on Malmesbury Road
from Shipton Moyne.
Opening hours For NGS: 2 pm – 6 pm; 12 & 13 May and
9 & 10 June. Plus 10 am – 5 pm; 1, 2 &. 5 July. Groups
welcome by appointment.
Admission fee Adults £4; Children free.

This is a large garden – six acres
surrounding a converted 15th-century
columbarium – all intensively planted. The
terraces, courtyards and gardens are divided
into rooms (surrounded either by walls or
by tapestry, laurel or yew hedges) to give
year-round colour. Old-fashioned rose beds
are underplanted with tulips for spring and
with alliums and campanulas for summer.
There is a formal herbaceous border, a water
garden and a swimming pool area with large
planted pots. Shrub roses and climbers are
another Hornby passion and are to be found
winding up walls and trees. The plantings
reflect a desire to create an informal feeling
within a formal framework. The woodland
garden is almost an arboretum of
ornamental trees (especially birches, maples,
whitebeams and many different magnolias),
underplanted with spring bulbs. In summer
the grass is left long in the wood and
wildflowers are encouraged to naturalise.
Hodges Barn is a garden of great energy and
diversity.

Features Woodland garden; topiary;
roses (mainly old-fashioned &
climbers); plantsman's collection of plants;
good herbaceous borders; daffodils;
bluebells; cyclamen.

Owned by Mrs Charles Hornby
Number of gardeners 2 part-time
Size 2.2ha (6 acres)

Just Phlomis

SUNNINGDALE, GRANGE COURT,
WESTBURY ON SEVERN GL14 1PL

Tel & Fax 01452 760268
Website www.manntaylor.com/Phlosale.html
Location 600 yards east of Northwood Green, on the left
hand side.
Opening hours By appointment.

The list of *Phlomis* from the National
Collection holder is remarkably long –
nearly 30 species and cultivars. Some are
herbaceous, like the sturdy and reliable
Phlomis russeliana and *P. tuberosa*, while
others are shrubby – the pink *P. italica* will
grow to two metres. But there are stunners
like *P. bovei* subsp. *maroccana* and little-
known species, originally from wild-
collected seed, like *P. platystegia* from Syria
and *P. atropurpurea* from Yunnan.

Owned by Jim Mann Taylor
NCCPG National Collections *Phlomis*

Kiftsgate Court

CHIPPING CAMPDEN GL55 6LW

Tel & Fax 01386 438777
Website www.kiftsgate.co.uk
Location 3 miles from Chipping Campden opposite
Hidcote Manor.
Opening hours 2 pm – 6 pm; Wednesdays, Thursdays,
Sundays & Bank Holiday Mondays; April, May, August &
September; plus 12 noon – 6 pm on Wednesdays,
Thursdays, Saturdays & Sundays in June & July.
Admission fee Adults £4.30: Children £1.

Famous for its roses, especially the
eponymous *Rosa filipes*, Kiftsgate is all about
plants and the use of colour. The best
example is the yellow border, where gold

Hunts Court

NORTH NIBLEY, DURSLEY GL11 6DZ

Tel 01453 547440   **Fax** 01453 549944
Location Signed in centre of village. Or turn across front of Black Horse pub & bear left for ¼ mile.
Opening hours 9 am – 5 pm; Tuesday – Saturday & Bank Holiday Mondays in spring; all year, except August. Also 16, 23 & 30 June and & 1 & 8 September for National Gardens Scheme.
Admission fee Adults £2; Children & RNRS members free.

Features Roses (mainly old-fashioned & climbers); roses of every kind, especially 19th-century cultivars; many other plants of interest to the plantsman; first-rate nursery attached; refreshments on NGS days.

Owned by T.K. & M.M. Marshall
Number of gardeners 1
Size 1ha (2½ acres)

The garden at Hunts Court has been planted since 1976 by something of a horticultural rarity – a plant-loving farmer, and his wife. Keith and Margaret Marshall say they have 'the collector's touch of madness': the result is a garden which is charming, peaceful and educational. Their first love was old-fashioned roses, and they moved their garden fence out into the surrounding fields as the collection of Gallicas, Damasks and Hybrid Perpetuals began to grow: it is now the best in the west of England, and still expanding. The 450 cultivars include climbers, species and a few modern shrub roses. Many are underplanted by the Marshalls' next great passion – hardy geraniums and penstemons, each of which is represented by over 100 cultivars. The fence has been moved out further several times now to accommodate a large collection of ornamental trees and shrubs, underplanted in turn by more unusual herbaceous plants. These are the stock plants for the thriving nursery they now run in their old stock-yard. It is surrounded by a fine plantsman's garden with something for all seasons, including good autumn colour and winter-flowering shrubs. But the Marshalls have just moved the fence again – to plant a mini-arboretum.

and orange are set off by occasional blues and purples. After some dull years, everything about Kiftsgate has revived again: new thinking, new plantings and new enthusiasm have more than restored its excellence. The latest addition (2000) is in marked contrast to the rest of the garden: the tennis court has been transformed into a contemporary water garden, full of movement and sound, by Simon Allison. Structure and form predominate here over Kiftsgate's traditional themes of colour and texture. And the garden as a whole is remarkable for its tender plants – abutilons, echiums, azaras and wonderful tree peonies in May.

Features Roses (mainly old-fashioned); colour plantings; good borders; many interesting plants; tea-room in the house.

Owned by Mr & Mrs J. Chambers
Number of gardeners 2
Size 1.6ha (4 acres)
English Heritage grade II*

Lydney Park Gardens

LYDNEY PARK GL15 6BU

Tel 01594 842844   **Fax** 01594 842027
Location Off A48 between Lydney & Aylburton.
Opening hours 11 am – 6 pm; Sundays, Wednesdays & Bank Holidays; 24 March to 9 June. Plus daily 6 to 10 May and 3 to 7 June.
Admission fee £3, but £2 on Wednesdays; Children 50p.

A remarkable collection of rhododendrons planted over the last 50 years is the backbone to this extensive woodland garden. And not just rhododendrons, but azaleas and camellias too – all are carefully planted to create distinct effects from March to June. The numbers are still growing, and

include plants grown from collected seed and hybrids from distinguished breeders, many as yet unnamed, while others have yet to flower. Lydney is now recognised as one of the best rhododendron gardens in England.

Features Woodland garden; mature conifers; deer park; daffodils; some souvenirs for sale; light teas.

Owned by Viscount Bledisloe
Number of gardeners 2, plus part-time help in season
Size 3.2ha (8 acres) of woodland garden

Mill Dene Gardens

BLOCKLEY, MORETON-IN-MARSH GL56 9HU

Tel 01386 709457   **Fax** 01386 700526
Location In School Lane.
Opening hours 10 am – 6 pm; Monday – Friday; 3 April to 31 October. And by appointment.
Admission fee Adults £3; Children £1. RHS members free in March & October.

This Cotswold water-mill garden has been designed and planted by the owner in an English country-garden style. Steep terraces rise from the mill-pond, stream and grotto. Paths wander through the rose walk, flanked by standard 'Sander's White Rambler' roses and lavender, to the cricket lawn. At the top of the garden, the *potager* and the 'fantasy fruit garden' (all greys and blues) have the church as a backdrop and views of the hills.

Owned by Mr & Mrs B.S. Dare
Size 1ha (2½ acres)

Miserden Park

MISERDEN, STROUD GL6 7JA

Tel 01285 821303 **Fax** 01285 821530
Location Signed from A417, or turn off B4070 between Stroud & Birdlip.
Opening hours 9.30 am – 5 pm; Tuesday – Thursday; April to September.
Admission fee Adults £3.50; Children free.

The Cotswold house at Miserden (Jacobean, with a Lutyens addition) has wide views across the Golden Valley, while the spacious peaceful gardens lie to the side. Most were laid out in the 1920s – a charming rose garden, a long yew walk and expansive herbaceous borders. Recent additions include a rill and summerhouse, a parterre of lavender and hebes, and a shrub border. In the walled garden near the entrance is an interesting nursery with a stock of good herbaceous plants.

 Features Topiary; good trees; good herbaceous borders; martagon lilies; roses; domed yew walk; cyclamen; excellent garden nursery by entrance.

Owned by Major M.T.N.H. Wills
Number of gardeners 2
Size 5ha (12 acres)
English Heritage grade II*

Owlpen Manor

ULEY, DURSLEY GL11 5BZ

Tel 01453 860261 **Fax** 01453 860819
Website www.owlpen.com
Location Off B4066 near Uley.
Opening hours 2 pm – 5 pm; Tuesday – Sunday & Bank Holiday Mondays; April to September.
Admission fee Adults £4.50; Children £2.

Owlpen is a dreamy Cotswold manor house whose loveliness depends upon its site. It also has a small terraced garden with box parterres, overgrown topiary yews and plantings of roses and herbs, most of them added since 1980 by the present owners. The aim is to suggest an earlier garden 're-ordered conservatively' in about 1700. Owlpen is perhaps not worth a special journey by keen plantsmen, but the restaurant, the setting and the house all add up to a good place for an outing.

 Features Topiary; roses (mainly old-fashioned); standard gooseberries; guidebooks & postcards for sale; licensed restaurant (noon – 5 pm).

Owned by Nicholas Mander
Number of gardeners 2
Size 0.8ha (2 acres)
English Heritage grade II

Painswick Rococo Garden

THE STABLES, PAINSWICK HOUSE, PAINSWICK GL6 6TH

Tel 01452 813204 **Fax** 01452 814888
Website www.rococogarden.co.uk
Location Outside Painswick on B4073.
Opening hours 11 am – 5 pm; daily; 10 January to 31 October. Then Wednesday – Sunday in November.
Admission fee Adults £3.60; OAPs £3.30; Children £1.80.

Only 15 years of restoration work lie behind the unique rococo garden at Painswick which has re-emerged from back-to-nature woodland. A white Venetian gothic exedra, a Doric seat, the plunge pool, an octagonal pigeon house, a gothic gazebo called the Eagle House, a bowling green, the fish pond and a gothic alcove have all been reconstructed in their original positions thanks to the efforts of Lord Dickinson and the Painswick Rococo Gardens Trust. Recent additions include the Exedra Garden (18th-century herbaceous plantings in an informal structure, best in early summer) and the kitchen garden (best in late summer). A remarkable garden and a brilliant theatrical achievement.

 Features Woodland garden; snowdrop wood; new plant nursery; new maze (planted 1998); gift shop; licensed restaurant, coffee, teas & light snacks.

Owned by Painswick Rococo Garden Trust
Number of gardeners 4
Size 2.2ha (6 acres)
English Heritage grade II*

Rodmarton Manor

RODMARTON, CIRENCESTER GL7 6PF

Tel 01285 841253 **Fax** 01285 841298
Website www.rodmarton-manor.co.uk
Location Off A433 between Cirencester & Tetbury.
Opening hours 2 pm – 5 pm; Wednesdays, Saturdays & Bank Holiday Mondays; 6 May to 31 August.
Admission fee Adults £3; Children free.

(P) (WC) (&)

A splendid Arts & Crafts garden, with a strong design and exuberant planting. Simon Biddulph says there are 18 different areas within the garden, from the trough garden for alpine plants to the famous double herbaceous borders, now entirely renovated, which lead to a Cotswold summerhouse. Highly original – contemporary, but made without any contact, with Hidcote.

 Features Interesting plants; old-fashioned roses; topiary; much renovation and replanting, including the fine herbaceous borders, white border & wild garden (1998).

Owned by Simon Biddulph
English Heritage grade II*

Sezincote

MORETON-IN-MARSH GL56 9AW

Location On A44 to Evesham, 1½ miles out of Moreton-in-Marsh.
Opening hours 2 pm – 6 pm (or dusk, if earlier); Thursdays, Fridays & Bank Holiday Mondays; January to November.
Admission fee Adults £3.50; Children £1 (under-5s free).

(P) (WC)

The house at Sezincote was the model for the Brighton Pavilion, and seems inseparable from the cruciform Moghul garden that sets off its Indian façade so well: yet this brilliant formal garden was designed as recently as 1965. On the other side are sumptuous borders planted by Graham Thomas and a luscious water garden of candelabra primulas and astilbes around the Temple to Surya, the Snake Bridge and Brahmin bulls. Humphry Repton had a hand in the original landscape, but the modern gardens are even more satisfying than the classical, 18th-century, parkland setting.

 Features Fine collection of trees; good, bold plantings in the water garden; tallest maidenhair tree *Ginkgo biloba* (26m) in the British Isles and 5 other record trees. These include the blue-leaved noble fir *Abies procera* Glauca Group, the weeping hornbeam *Carpinus betulus* 'Pendula' and the yellow-leaved beech *Fagus sylvatica* 'Zlatia'.

Owned by Mr & Mrs D. Peake
Number of gardeners 3
Size 4ha (10 acres)
English Heritage grade I

Snowshill Manor

BROADWAY WR12 7JU

Tel & Fax 01386 852410
Website www.nationaltrust.org.uk
Location In Snowshill village.
Opening hours 11 am – 5.30 pm; Wednesday – Sunday; 29 March to 3 November. Plus Bank Holiday Mondays, 3 & 4 June, and Mondays in June & July. Then 12 noon – 4 pm on Saturdays & Sundays from 9 November to 15 December.
Admission fee Gardens only: £3.50.

The garden at Snowshill has often been praised for its changes of levels and collection of curious artefacts – an armillary sphere and a gilt figure of St George and the Dragon, for instance. Snowshill is as curious as its maker, Charles Wade, and the spooky bric-a-brac which fills his house, but many visitors find it 'charming' or 'interesting'. Snowshill was the National Trust's first all-organic garden.

 Features Roses (mainly old-fashioned); good herbaceous borders; National Trust shop; restaurant.

Owned by The National Trust
Number of gardeners 2
Size 0.8ha (2 acres)
English Heritage grade II

Special Plants

HILL FARM BARN, GREENWAYS LANE, COLD ASHTON, CHIPPENHAM SN14 8LA

Tel 01225 891686   **Fax** 01225 852528
Website www.specialplants.net
Location Near Bath, just south of junction of A46 & A420. Not in Cold Ashton.

Opening hours 10.30 am – 5 pm; daily; March to September. And by appointment. The garden is open for the National Gardens Scheme from 2 pm to 6 pm on 20 June, 18 July, 15 & 18 August & 19 September 2002.
Admission fee Adults £1.50.

The collection of hardy plants at this connoisseur's nursery is excellent, but it is for her tender perennials that Derry Watkins's nursery is best known. Diascias, salvias, pelargoniums and streptocarpus are among her top lines, together with conservatory climbers and shrubs. A three-month visit to South Africa has introduced some interesting novelties – both plants and seeds are available. There are also one-day courses at the nursery in autumn. The new garden is open monthly for the National Gardens Scheme and a useful adjunct to the nursery. In 1996, Derry Watkins and her architect husband bought a derelict barn with three acres of steeply sloping fields. Around the barn he designed bold shapes in gravel, water and grass, terraced with dry stone walls. Then she planted it up with drills of colour using many unusual plants (not a rose or a clematis in sight, alas). There is a 'black and white' border, a sizzling hot red-and-orange bed and a cooler lemon-and-lime slope, as well as a gravel garden, grass garden, bog garden, ponds, vegetable garden and now an orchard and a woodland walk, all set off by wonderful views down the valley.

 Features Unusual plants.

Owned by Derry Watkins

Stancombe Park

DURSLEY GL11 6AU

Tel 01453 542815
Location Off the B4060 between Dursley &
Wotton-under-Edge.
Opening hours Groups by appointment.
Admission fee Adults £3; Children (under 10) £1.

Stancombe has everything: a handsome
house above a wooded valley, a flower
garden of wondrous prettiness, and a gothic
horror of an historic Folly Garden at the
valley bottom. Start at the top. Peter Coats,
Lanning Roper and Nadia Jennett all worked
on the rose gardens and mixed borders by
the house: there is more to learn about good
modern design and planting here than any
garden in Gloucestershire. Then wander
down the valley where the path narrows and
the incline steepens to a ferny tunnel, and
start the circuit of the follies, best described
as an open-air ghost-train journey without
the ghosts. Highly recommended.

Features Fine collection of trees;
excellent borders; fine spring bulbs;
lots of roses; some interesting and unusual
plants; new bog garden (2000) backed by
two sprouting Ms for the millennium.

Owned by Mrs Basil Barlow
Size 6ha (15 acres)
English Heritage grade I

Stanway House

STANWAY, CHELTENHAM GL54 5PQ

Tel 01386 584469   **Fax** 01386 584688
Location On B4077.
Opening hours 2 pm – 5 pm; Tuesdays & Thursdays;
July & August. And groups by appointment. On 24 March
and 12 May for NGS.

Admission fee Adults £3.50; OAPs £2.50; Children £1.

The important water-gardens at Stanway are
undergoing restoration. A pyramidal folly
dominates the hillside behind the house.
Repairs have begun on the 170m cascade
which runs down to a long still tank known
as the Canal. On the way up to the top are
some interesting trees and shrubs. Worth
another visit.

 Features Woodland garden; mature
conifers.

Owned by Lord Neidpath
Number of gardeners 1½
Size 8ha (20 acres)
English Heritage grade I

Stowell Park

NORTHLEACH GL54 3LE

Tel 01285 720308   **Fax** 01285 720360
Location A429 between Cirencester & Northleach.
Opening hours 2 pm – 5 pm; 20 May, 24 June &
9 September.
Admission fee Adults £2.50 (£3 in September);
Children free.

The most important feature at Stowell is its
peach house, 180ft long, which has been in
constant use since the early 19th century.
Nowhere in England does such a glasshouse
produce fruit in the manner perfected by
our Victorian ancestors. Stowell also has an
historic landscape in a magnificent position,
with terraced gardens in front of the house
looking down over the Coln valley and
landscaped woodlands dating from the 18th
century. The pleached lime avenue at the
entrance to the house was planted in 1983
and is now fully established. In the superb
traditional walled gardens are substantial

herbaceous borders and some notable plantings of old-fashioned roses.

 Features Climbing roses; good herbaceous borders; plants for sale on 20 May only; excellent teas.

Owned by Lord Vestey
Number of gardeners 4
Size 3.2ha (8 acres)
English Heritage grade II

Sudeley Castle & Gardens

WINCHCOMBE GL54 5JD

Tel 01242 602308   **Fax** 01242 602959
Website www.stratford.co.uk/sudeley
Location 8 miles north-east of Cheltenham B4632.
Opening hours 10.30 am – 5.30 pm; daily; 2 March to 27 October.
Admission fee Adults £5; OAPs £4; Children £2.75.

This large commercially-run garden has features by many top garden designers: Jane Fearnley-Whittingstall did the roses and Charles Chesshire replanted the 'secret garden' (originally designed by Rosemary Verey) in the Mediterranean style. The whole garden is organically managed. There are fine old trees, magnificent Victorian topiary (mounds of green and gold yew) and a raised walk around the pleasure gardens that may be Elizabethan in origin. Popular and successful.

 Features Topiary; roses (ancient & modern); herbs; mature conifers; good herbaceous borders; ruins of banqueting hall, now a pretty garden; new wildflower meadow (2001); HDRA heritage seed garden; good shop; restaurant & tea-rooms.

Owned by Lady Ashcombe
Number of gardeners 5
Size 5.6ha (14 acres)
English Heritage grade II*

University of Bristol Botanic Garden

BRACKEN HILL, NORTH ROAD, LEIGH WOODS, BRISTOL BS8 3PF

Tel 0117 973 3682   **Fax** 0117 974 1929
Website www.bris.ac.uk/depts/BotanicGardens
Location Take M5 Jct 19 towards Clifton, left into North Road before suspension bridge.
Opening hours 9 am – 5 pm; Monday – Friday; all year except public holidays. Plus 10 am – 5 pm on 23 June & 1 September for the National Gardens Scheme.
Admission fee free, except when open for National Gardens Scheme.

Ⓟ ⓦⓒ ⓦ

This is an educational and accessible garden that bridges the gap between botany and horticulture. The Pulhamite rock garden is listed by English Heritage as Grade II, 'of special interest'. The unusual climatic conditions in its position high above the River Avon have made possible some fine new plantings of South African and New Zealand plants. The collection of *Aeonium* is the most comprehensive in the UK, and the collections of *Pelargonium* species and Central American *Salvia* species are also very good. The rare endemic *Sorbus bristoliensis* grows in a part of the garden dedicated to the flora of the Clifton Gorge. There is an active Friends group: winter lectures, summer visits, a seed scheme and a good newsletter – all for £20.

 Features Rock garden; plantsman's collection of plants; plants under glass; fine collection of trees; cistus; hebes; sempervivums; peonies; aeoniums; salvias;

Chinese medical plants; rare & threatened plants of south-west Britain; teas & plants for sale on NGS days.

Owned by University of Bristol
Number of gardeners 6½
Size 2ha (5 acres)

Westbury Court

WESTBURY-ON-SEVERN GL14 1PD

Tel 01452 760461
Website www.nationaltrust.org.uk
Location 9 miles south-west of Gloucester on A48.
Opening hours 10 am – 5 pm, Wednesday – Sunday & Bank Holiday Mondays, plus 3 & 4 June; 1 March to 27 October. Daily in July & August.
Admission fee Adults £3; Children £1.50.

Westbury was restored in the 1970s to become the best example of a medium-sized 17th-century Dutch garden in England. An elegant pavilion, tall and slender, looks down along a long tank of water. On the walls are old apple, pear and plum cultivars. Parterres, fine modern topiary and a T-shaped tank with a statue of Neptune in the middle make up the rest of the garden, with an opulent rose garden (old varieties only, including the 'true' *Rosa moschata*) underplanted with pinks, tulips and herbs. All the plants were known to cultivation before 1720. Immaculately maintained.

Features Topiary; herbs; biggest holm oak (*Quercus ilex*) in the British Isles; new restoration of pool & fountain as shown by Kip in 1712; picnic area; hot drinks.

Owned by The National Trust
Number of gardeners 1
Size 1.6ha (4 acres)
English Heritage grade II*

Willow Lodge

LONGHOPE, GLOUCESTER GL17 0RA

Tel & Fax 01452 831211
Location On A40, 10 miles from Gloucester & 6 miles from Ross-on-Wye: ½ mile west of Dursley Cross.
Opening hours 1 pm – 5 pm; 28 & 29 April; 5, 6, 12, 13, 26 & 27 May; 9, 10 & 30 June; 1, 14, 15, 28 & 29 July; 4, 5, 11 & 12 August. Groups and private visits by appointment.
Admission fee Adults £2; Children free.

This garden has been entirely made by the owners, enthusiastic plantsmen, since they moved here in 1987. At first they developed just an acre around the house: it remains a good garden of mixed herbaceous and shrubby plantings. Then they started to plant the adjoining field as an arboretum, underplanted with native daffodils, snowdrops and ground orchids. Here are some extremely interesting plants collected on their travels in China and North America – *Sinocalycanthus chinensis* for example, and several *Lespedeza* species. The stream that runs from end to end of the garden has been used to create a bog garden (lots of primulas) and a pond, alongside a large alpine bed. There is much to enjoy and learn throughout the garden.

 Features A good young arboretum; bog garden; maples.

Owned by Mr & Mrs J.H. Wood
Number of gardeners 3
Size 1.6ha (4 acres)

Westonbirt The National Arboretum

WESTONBIRT, TETBURY GL8 8QS

Tel 01666 880220 **Fax** 01666 880559
Website www.westonbirtarboretum.com
Location 3 miles south of Tetbury on A433.
Opening hours 10 am – 8 pm (or dusk if earlier); daily; all year. Visitor centre open 10 am – 5 pm; daily; March to December.
Admission fee Adults £4.50; OAPs £4; Children £1. But Adults £6 & OAPs £5 between 8 June & 8 September, and Adults £5 on 9 September. RHS members free.

Westonbirt is the finest and largest arboretum in the British Isles: it contains one of the most important collections of trees and shrubs in the world. There are 18,500 of them, representing 4,000 species and cultivars, planted from 1829 to the present day, and covering some 600 acres of beautifully landscaped grounds. The maple glade is famous, and so are the bluebells in the part known as Silk Wood. Magnificent spring displays of rhododendrons, azaleas and magnolias, wildflowers in summer and architectural winter beauty are matched by the spectacular autumn colouring for which Westonbirt is justifiably famous. Westonbirt is also one of the best gardens in England for a winter walk but, with 17 miles of paths, you can find quiet areas even in the third week of October when the maples are at their most colourful. The arboretum is brilliantly managed by the Forestry Commission, whose Visitor Centre is a marvel of helpfulness.

Features New Westonbirt International Garden Festival from 8 June to 8 September 2002; over 1000 species of record-breaking trees, including 24 maples (*Acer* species) and 16 *Sorbus*.

Other champion trees include the red horse chestnut *Aesculus × carnea* at 27m; the upright birch *Betula pendula* 'Fastigiata' at 29m; the handkerchief tree *Davidia involucrata* at 24m; the home-sprung *Pinus* 'Holfordiana' at 36m; and the large-leaved deciduous oak *Quercus macranthera* at 31m; gift shop; cafeteria.

Owned by Forestry Commission
Number of gardeners 8
Size 220ha (600 acres)
NCCPG National Collections *Acer* (Japanese cultivars.); *Salix*
English Heritage grade I

HAMPSHIRE

For such a prosperous county, Hampshire has comparatively few historic gardens of the highest importance: only Hackwood Park (not open to the public) and Highclere Park (right in the north) are listed as Grade I. But Hampshire compensates with a wealth of 20th-century plantsman's gardens and nurseries. Indeed, the Sir Harold Hillier Gardens & Arboretum at Ampfield – the world's greatest collection of temperate trees and shrubs – is less than 50 years old and grew out of the commercial activities of Hillier's Nursery. When modern gardens like Brandy Mount, Exbury, Longstock, Spinners, Longthatch and Meon Orchard are taken into account, and some of the small specialist nurseries like Blackthorn and Langley Boxwood, Hampshire emerges as one of the best places in Europe for plants and gardens, plantsmen and gardeners. The National Gardens Scheme is extremely well represented in the county, with a very large number of gardens (160 last year) opening for charity. There are many good gardens which do not open often enough for us to list in this guide: Pylewell Park, Moundsmere Manor and Conholt Park among them. And deep in the New Forest, at Rhinefield, is the best late-Victorian pinetum in southern England. The gardens at Stratfield Saye House, however, will be closed this year for essential renovation: they expect to re-open in 2003. The Hampshire Group of the NCCPG is strong – always a good measure of the interest in gardening with plants – with 24 collection holders responsible for no less than 43 different collections. And the Hampshire Gardens Trust, founded more than 20 years ago by the energy and foresight of Gilly Drummond, has been the model for every county-based gardens trust since then. Sparsholt College, between Winchester and Stockbridge, is a RHS Partner College.

Abbey Cottage

RECTORY LANE, ITCHEN ABBAS,
WINCHESTER SO21 1BN

Tel & Fax 01962 779575
Location On B3047, 1 mile east of the Trout Inn at Itchen Abbas.

Opening hours 12 noon – 5 pm; 7 April, 5 & 6 May, and 3, 4, 25 & 26 August. Also 2 pm – 7 pm on 2 July.
Admission fee Adults £2.50; Children free.

Abbey Cottage would be a fine garden by any standards – it has a firm design, beautiful flint-and-brick walls, good lines, interesting plants, good colour schemes and immaculate standards of tidiness – but what makes it especially interesting is that Colonel Daniell is a recent convert to organic gardening. His says that 'organic gardening was the element missing from my gardening ... now the garden feels complete'. The garden is maintained as much for the pleasure of his many friends and visitors as for his own pleasure.

 Features Organic garden; good structure; excellent maintenance; teas.

Owned by Col. Patrick Daniell CBE
Number of gardeners 1 part-time
Size 0.6ha (1½ acres)

Apple Court

HORDLE LANE, HORDLE, LYMINGTON SO41 0HU

Tel 01590 642130   **Fax** 01590 694220
Website www.applecourt.com
Location South of New Forest, just north of A337 at Downton crossroads.
Opening hours 9.30 am – 1 pm & 2 pm – 5 pm; daily except Wednesdays; March to September.
Admission fee Adults £2; Children 50p.

The display gardens attached to this hosta and hemerocallis specialist nursery are firmly designed and would be worth a visit even without plants. The white garden is especially original: at its heart is an oval-shaped lawn, surrounded by pleached hornbeams. The white plantings lie *outside* this oval of limes. Elsewhere are about 120 cultivars of *Hosta*, many of them – like the daylilies – bred in USA and offered for sale by Apple Court but by no other UK nursery. There are 120 *Hemerocallis* cultivars too, including spider and other unusual forms. Grasses are a third feature and, here too, the

nursery has introduced many from across the Atlantic.

Owned by Diana Grenfell & Roger Grounds
Number of gardeners 2
Size 0.6ha (1½ acres)
NCCPG National Collections *Hosta* (small leaved); *Rohdea japonica*; *Woodwardia*

Blackthorn Nursery

KILMESTON, ALRESFORD SO24 0NL

Tel 01962 771796   **Fax** 01962 771071
Location 1 mile south of Cheriton, off A272.
Opening hours 9 am – 5 pm; Fridays & Saturdays; 1 March to 29 June. Plus Hellebore Days 9 am – 4 pm on 15 & 16 February.

Blackthorn's plants tend to be spring beauties: the nursery's three specialities are hellebores, epimediums and daphnes, all of which they breed, as well as introducing new species. Their most striking hellebores are semi-doubles called 'Party Dress' hybrids. The list of epimediums is the best in England – over 40 different names: their rarities include a large number of collected species like *E. fargesii* Og. 93057 and *E. franchetii* 'Brimstone Butterfly' Og. 87001. The daphnes are no less remarkable: over 50 different names, including such little-known hybrids as *D. × thauma* and no less than 7 cultivars of *D. × hendersonii*. Their general list of alpines and herbaceous plants is equally exciting: they have a covetable and ever-changing selection of good plants. For dedicated plantsmen, a visit to Blackthorn on an open day in February or March is one of the social highlights of early spring: every fellow-plantsman in the country seems to be there too.

Owned by R. & S.White
Size 0.1ha (¼-acre) woodland walk

Bramdean House

BRAMDEAN, ALRESFORD SO24 0JU

Tel 01962 771214 **Fax** 01962 771095
Location On A272, between Winchester & Petersfield.
Opening hours 2 pm – 5 pm; 31 March, 14 April, 12 May, 16 June, 14 July, 11 August, 8 September, & by appointment.
Admission fee Adults £2.50; Children free; for National Gardens Scheme. Otherwise Adults £4.

The gardens at Bramdean are much admired, and rightly so. Against a backdrop of mature trees, two wide mirror-image borders lead away from the back of the house. At the end of the central axis, steps lead to a 1-acre walled kitchen garden whose central beds are planted with a range of herbaceous plants, roses, perennials and bulbs. The vista runs yet further, through an orchard under-planted with massed daffodils to an apple-house some 300 yards from the house. The views in both directions are stunning.

Features Climbing roses; herbaceous plants; peonies; ornamental shrubs; bulbs of every sort; climbing roses; clematis; sweet peas; vegetables; fruit; tender nerines; refreshments.

Owned by Mr & Mrs H. Wakefield
Number of gardeners 2
Size 2.6ha (6½ acres)
English Heritage grade II

Broadlands

ROMSEY SO51 9LB

Tel 01794 505010 **Fax** 01794 505040
Website www.broadlands.net
Location On Romsey by-pass by town centre roundabout.

Opening hours 12 noon – 5.30 pm (last admissions 4 pm); daily; 10 June to 1 September.
Admission fee Adults £5.95; OAPs £4.95; Children (12–16) £3.95.

Classic Capability Brown landscape, handsome old trees and an open park which runs slowly down to a lake and the River Test. The main horticultural interest comes from the massive taxodiums and plane-trees growing luxuriantly alongside the leat. The house majors on the estate's association with Earl Mountbatten of Burma. The shrub borders rely heavily on *Aegopodium podagraria* for their underplanting.

Features Tallest swamp cypress *Taxodium distichum* (36m) in the British Isles; gift shop; tea-room & picnic area by river.

Owned by Lord & Lady Romsey
English Heritage grade II*

Exbury Gardens

EXBURY, SOUTHAMPTON SO45 1AZ

Tel 023 8089 1203 **Fax** 023 8089 9940
Website www.exbury.co.uk
Location 3 miles south of Beaulieu.
Opening hours 10 am – 5.30 pm (or dusk if earlier); daily; 2 March to 3 November.
Admission fee Adults £3.50; OAPs £3; Children £2.50. But Adults £5; OAPs £4.50; Children £3 in high season (approximately mid-March to mid-June).

Rhododendrons, rhododendrons, rhododendrons: over one million of them in 200 acres of natural woodland. More than 40 have won awards from the Royal Horticultural Society. But there are magnolias, camellias and rare trees too, many grown from the original seed

Brandy Mount House

EAST STREET, ALRESFORD SO24 9EG

Tel 01962 732189
Website www.brandymount.co.uk
Location Left into East Street from Broad Street, 50 yards first right.
Opening hours 11 am – 4 pm; 2, 3 & 6 February. Then 2 pm – 5 pm; 3 March, 7 April, 5 May, & by appointment.
Admission fee Adults £2; Children free.

Brandy Mount is the garden of plantsmen – but plantsmen who are also distinguished cultivators and exhibitors of alpine plants. The first surprise is to find quite such a large and secluded garden so near the centre of a busy town. Then you discover that, although the underlying soil is chalky, a great variety of the rarer shade-loving plants thrive in the rich soil under the trees – as well as the snowdrops, for which the garden is famous among galanthophiles. The herbaceous borders in the sunnier parts support the many species of geranium, peonies, daphnes and spring-flowering bulbs which are happy in the warm, free-draining soil. The planting of all these areas is informal, with wide sweeps of lawn between the borders. The vegetable area has just been re-organised as a formal *potager* with traditional box hedges and small beds to allow the owners to grow a greater variety of salad crops and more unusual vegetables, interspersed with flowering plants. Alpines have always been a speciality: they flourish around the terrace in front of the house, where there are over 30 kinds of smaller daphnes. Many alpines are also grown in troughs and sinks, which have recently been reorganised as a group and replanted as small crevice gardens. These support many rare and tricky species which are also grown in frames and in the Alpine House. There is a fine collection of European primulas, saxifrages and dwarf narcissi which are also exhibited from time to time. This garden is fascinating, immaculately maintained, and forever changing, as the collection of rare plants grows ever larger. Strongly recommended.

Features Plantsman's garden; woodland and herbaceous plants on a chalk soil; terrace and troughs for alpines; snowdrops; daphnes; peony species; European primulas; Alpine House; new *potager* (2000); extensive plant sales area full of good plants; teas (but not in February).

Owned by Caryl & Michael Baron
Number of gardeners part-time (very)
Size 0.5ha (1¼ acres)
NCCPG National Collections Daphne; *Galanthus*

introduced by famous plant collectors. A place of wonder in May. The collection of nerines which Lionel de Rothschild bred between the wars was dispersed after his death but reassembled and developed by Sir Peter Smithers in Switzerland. A few years ago he returned them to Exbury where they may be seen once again in October. A new garden has been created in the style of Piet Oudolf and James Van Sweden – huge swathes of herbaceous perennials and grasses within a strong woodland structure.

 Features Good herbaceous borders; candelabra primulas; rare trees; rose garden; water garden; daffodils; massive 2-acre rock garden; *Nerine* hybrids; steam railway; tallest shagbark hickory *Carya ovata* (21m) in the British Isles (and five other tree records); plant centre; gift shop; artist's studio; hot & cold lunches, cream teas; new tea-room.

Owned by Edmund de Rothschild
Number of gardeners 8
Size 80ha (200 acres)
English Heritage grade II*

Fairfield House

HAMBLEDON, WATERLOOVILLE
PO7 4RY

Tel 023 9263 2431
Location East Street, Hambledon.
Opening hours For NGS, and by appointment.
Admission fee Adults £2.50; Children free. (2001 tariff).

Fairfield is one of the best private rose gardens in England. Old roses and climbers were the late Peter Wake's main interest and he grew them unusually well. The shrubs are trained up a cat's cradle of string drawn between five wooden posts. The results make you gasp – 'Charles de Mills' 3m high.

 Features Mature conifers; good herbaceous borders; beautifully grown roses, ancient & modern.

Owned by Mrs Peter Wake
Number of gardeners 1½
Size 2.2ha (6 acres)

Furzey Gardens

MINSTEAD, LYNDHURST SO43 7GL

Tel 023 8081 2464   **Fax** 023 8081 2297
Location Off A31 or A337 to Minstead.
Opening hours 10 am – 5 pm (dusk in winter); daily except 25 & 26 December.
Admission fee March – October: Adults £3.50; OAPs £2.80; Children £1.50. Reductions in winter. RHS members free from March to October.

Furzey demonstrates how woodland garden effects can be created in quite small areas. Parts are a maze of narrow curving paths running between hedges of Kurume azaleas, unforgettable in April and May, but the late summer flowering of eucryphias runs them close and the autumn colours of nyssas, parrotias and enkianthus are worth a visit in October.

Features Rhododendrons & azaleas; mature conifers; camellias; bluebells; naturalised dieramas; heathers; spring bulbs; new 'sensory garden' in raised beds (2000); small shop.

Owned by Furzey Gardens Charitable Trust
Number of gardeners 2 horticultural instructors with teams of students with learning difficulties
Size 3.2ha (8 acres)

Gilbert White's House

HIGH STREET, SELBORNE, ALTON
GU34 3JH

Tel 01420 511275   **Fax** 01420 511040
Location In centre of Selborne, on B3006.
Opening hours 11 am – 5 pm; daily; 1 January to
24 December.
Admission fee Adults £4; OAPs £3.50; £1 Children.

The house was bought some years ago, and
the museum founded to commemorate the
life and work of Gilbert White, author of
*The Natural History & Antiquities of
Selborne.* The garden provides a very good
example of how a person of modest means
might construct a scaled-down landscaped
park in the mid-18th century. The orchard
and vegetable garden have been restored to
the same period and planted with cultivars
that White himself knew and wrote about.
Lawns, a rose garden, a 'wine pipe' and a
herb garden complete the idyll.

Features Plants associated with
Gilbert White; gift shop; tea parlour.

Owned by Oates Memorial Trust
Number of gardeners 2, plus volunteers
Size 12ha (30 acres)

Hardy's Cottage Garden Plants

PRIORY LANE, FREEFOLK,
WHITCHURCH RG28 7NT

Tel 01256 896533   **Fax** 01256 896572
Website www.hardys-plants.co.uk
Location Off B3400 Whitchurch to Overton road: 1½ mile
on left, up Priory Lane, past Watership Down pub.

Opening hours 10 am – 5 pm; daily; March to October.
Evening visits by appointment.

This family-run RHS Partner Nursery offers
over 1,400 different cottage garden
perennials. Its attractive exhibits have been a
great feature of RHS shows in recent years –
including Chelsea and Hampton Court
Palace. It is one of the best nurseries in
southern England for a really wide choice
of good plants. Many may be seen in the
woodland garden and the new (2002)
herbaceous borders.

Owned by Rosy & Rob Hardy

Heathlands

47 LOCKS ROAD, LOCKS HEATH,
SOUTHAMPTON SO31 6NS

Tel 01489 573598   **Fax** 01489 557884
Location Locks Road is the main north-south road
through the middle of Locks Heath.
Opening hours 2 pm – 5.30 pm; 17 March, 14 April,
12 May & 25 August.
Admission fee Adults £2; Children free.

Since building his house in 1967, Dr Burwell
has filled his acre of deep gravelly stoney soil
with a wonderful choice of immaculately
grown plants of every type. It is the
embodiment of careful plantsmanship, a
garden to go round slowly – looking,
studying and thinking. Your first sight is an
80m line of *Paulownia tomentosa* grown
from seed in about 1970, flowering (in May)
all along the road and thought to be the
longest line in England. Next comes *Garrya
elliptica* trained as a small tree. Round the
side of the house is a tall yew hedge, topped
by a brooding topiary peacock. The design is
a mixture of formal and informal, with a
large number of different habitats. Under a

canopy of light oak woodland thrives a shady fernery with orchids and *Rhododendron sinogrande. Iris confusa* flourishes against a wall of the house. Cyclamen and bulbs are everywhere. The climate is mild – the sea is only a mile or so away – so there are hedges of griselinia, a plant of *Pittosporum* 'Garnettii' 5m high, and *Cleyera japonica* growing in the open. In a narrow alley between tall hedges of yew and rhododendron is the National Collection of Japanese Anemones. Dr Burwell will tell you that, though first described in 1695, they were not introduced (from mainland Asia) until the 1840s by Robert Fortune. The collection has about 40 cultivars, including a seedling which will shortly be introduced as 'Heathlands Ruby'.

 Features Many different habitats; a very wide range of plants of every kind; some good combinations of colour & form.

Owned by John Burwell
Number of gardeners owner only
Size 0.4ha (1 acre)
NCCPG National Collections *Anemone* (Japanese anemones)

Highclere Castle

HIGHCLERE, NEWBURY RG15 9RN

Tel 01635 253210 **Fax** 01635 255315
Website www.highclerecastle.co.uk
Location South of Newbury off A34.
Opening hours 11 am – 5 pm (3.30 pm on Saturdays); daily; 2 July to 1 September. Plus 30 & 31 March, 5 & 6 May, and 1-4 June.
Admission fee Gardens only: Adults £3; Children £1.

A major historic garden – when Capability Brown landscaped it in the 1770s he left intact the avenues and follies of the early 18th century, but the park is dominated now by hundreds of huge cedars. Jim Russell advised on the planting in the walled garden, though the 'Secret Garden' is not among his best.

 Features Rhododendrons & azaleas; good herbaceous borders; good collection of cedars; long avenues; shop; good restaurant.

Owned by The Earl of Carnarvon
Number of gardeners 2
Size 220ha (600 acres) of parkland
NCCPG National Collections *Rhododendron*
English Heritage grade I

Hinton Ampner House

BRAMDEAN, ALRESFORD SO24 0LA

Tel 01962 771305 **Fax** 01962 793101
Website www.nationaltrust.org.uk
Location On A272 1 mile west of Bramdean.
Opening hours 11 am – 5 pm; 17 & 24 March. Then Saturday – Wednesday; 30 April to 30 September.
Admission fee Adults £4; Children £2.

The gardens at Hinton Ampner were laid out by the scholarly Ralph Dutton in the middle of the 20th century with great regard to line, landscape and historical propriety. Statues, buildings, axes and views have been placed with exquisite judgement to lead you subtly along the exact route that Dutton intended. He was also careful to choose plants which would do well on chalk and then planted lots of them – using always the best forms: among them are buddlejas, lilacs, philadelphus, cotoneasters, weigelas and shrub roses. It is now one of England's best mid-20th-century gardens, maintained to a high specification.

 Features Topiary; daffodils; yew trees; good plants; teas & homemade cakes.

Owned by The National Trust
Number of gardeners 3
Size 5ha (12 acres)
English Heritage grade II

Houghton Lodge

HOUGHTON, STOCKBRIDGE
SO20 6LQ

Tel 01264 810912   **Fax** 01264 810177
Website www.hydroponicum.co.uk
Location Off A30 at Stockbridge.
Opening hours 2 pm – 5 pm; Mondays, Tuesdays, Thursdays & Fridays. 10 am – 5 pm; Saturdays, Sundays & Bank Holidays. March to September. And by appointment.
Admission fee £5 for garden & hydroponicum, including free tea/coffee. Groups at special rates. Children free.

A lovely gothic *cottage ornée* on a ledge above the River Test, with long spacious views down the river and across the watermeadows. Part of the BBC's dramatisation of *David Copperfield* was shot here. The owner has just begun to restore the 18th-century shrubbery: this means clearing seedling trees to open up the view across the river and re-planting with trees and shrubs which were grown there 200 years ago. Houghton also boasts the leading hydroponic greenhouse in England, where plants are grown in nutrient-rich solutions instead of soil – salad vegetables and some 50 different herbs, as well as bougainvilleas and bananas. The garden makes a great effort to be educational and entertaining. This year (2002) the owners have planted 3,000 more tulips.

Features Plants under glass; daffodils; cyclamen; topiary snorting dragon; tropical orchids; hydroponics shop; refreshments; windfall apples (free!).

Owned by Martin Busk
Number of gardeners 2 part-time
Size 2ha (5 acres)
English Heritage grade II*

Langley Boxwood Nursery

RAKE, LISS GU33 7JL

Tel 01730 894467   **Fax** 01730 894703
Website www.boxwood.co.uk
Location 5 miles north of Petersfield, ring for map or directions (B2070).
Opening hours 8 am – 4.30; Monday – Friday. Plus 10 am – 4 pm on Saturdays.
Admission fee free

These specialist growers of box have a comprehensive range of box plants for hedging, edging and topiary. There are over 50 cultivars of *Buxus* in their delightful catalogue, and some yew *Taxus* also. Both are available in a wide variety of topiary shapes, from simple balls to complex crowns and animals, and (given sufficient notice) they will create individual designs. Rare free-form specimens are also offered.

Features Box, yew & evergreen topiary.

Owned by Elizabeth Braimbridge
NCCPG National Collections *Buxus*

Little Court

CRAWLEY, WINCHESTER SO21 2PU

Tel 01962 776365   **Fax** 01962 776842
Location On main street through Crawley village, 300 yds from church/pond.
Opening hours For NGS, and by appointment.

Admission fee £2 (in 2001)

Little Court crams a lot into its 1½ acres: the design allows for several distinct areas which are linked by spacious vistas and judiciously placed seats to emphasise the many views and axes. A sunken lawn, flint walls, orchards, fine trees, a copse and a 'proper' old-fashioned kitchen garden are some of the features. The plantings are colour-themed, but some plants (like cyclamen and *Crocus tommasinianus*) have naturalised, too. The range of herbaceous plants, in particular, is fairly impressive. There is much to be learned and enjoyed here.

 Features Plantsman's plants; herbaceous perennials.

Owned by Professor & Mrs A.R. Elkington
Size 0.6ha (1½ acres)

Longmead House

LONGPARISH, ANDOVER SP11 6PZ

Tel & Fax 01264 720386
Location 1½ miles from junction of A303 & B3048.
Opening hours 2 pm – 6 pm; 9 & 16 June. And by appointment.
Admission fee Adults £1.50.

Longmead House is an organic showcase: Wendy Ellicock is on the council of the Henry Doubleday Research Association. She and her husband started the garden when they returned from overseas in 1987. The wildflower meadow was one of their first endeavours, begun by planting plugs into areas cleared of turf: now it provides colour from February to November. The kitchen garden has 25 deep beds, much enriched by compost. There are also wildlife areas, a woodland walk, fish pond and wildlife pond, as well as herbaceous and shrub borders.

 Features Wildflower meadow; kitchen garden; all organically maintained.

Owned by Wendy & John Ellicock
Number of gardeners 2
Size 1ha (2½ acres)

Longthatch

LIPPEN LANE, WARNFORD, SOUTHAMPTON SO32 3LE

Tel 01730 829285
Location 1 mile south of West Meon on A32, turn right by George & Falcon, & right again. 400m on right.
Opening hours 10 am – 5 pm; Wednesdays; 6 March to 26 June. And 2 pm – 5 pm; 3, 10 & 17 March, 21 April, 26 May & 23 June for National Gardens Scheme.
Admission fee Adults £2.50; Children free.

The Shorts have gardened at Longthatch since 1955, though in their early years they were busy with the farm around their 16th-century thatched cottage. They started to develop the garden seriously in 1968: it is now a great favourite among dedicated plantsmen. Over the years they have built up large collections not only of hellebores, but also of herbaceous plants (especially hardy geraniums), unusual trees and shrubs. Some of the trees they planted in the early days are now spectacularly mature. There are two central features: first an acre of woodland filled with wonderful small plants, from snowdrops and pulmonarias in winter through to cyclamen in late autumn; and, second, the River Meon which flows through the garden. This is supplemented by numerous spring-filled ponds throughout the garden, one of which helps to maintain the bog garden where *Gunnera manicata* and many other damp- and shade-

Longstock Water Gardens

LONGSTOCK, STOCKBRIDGE SO20 6EH

Tel 01264 810894 & 01264 810904   **Fax** 01264 810924
Website www.longstockpark.co.uk
Location 1½ miles north-east of Longstock Village.
Opening hours 2 pm – 5 pm; 1st & 3rd Sunday in the month; April to September.
Admission fee Adults £3; Children 50p.

Longstock has quite the most extraordinary and beautiful water garden in England, a little Venice where dozens of islands and all-but-islands are linked by an apparently endless number of small bridges and intensely planted with water-loving plants: drifts of astilbes, primulas, kingcups, hemerocallis, musks, water irises and lilies. The ground is so soft that the islands seem to float, and a remarkable accumulation of peat has allowed such calcifuge plants as *Meconopsis betonicifolia* to flourish in this chalky valley. But the garden as a whole has an exceptional variety of habitats: parts are very dry. A seam of acid soil supports a collection of *Rhododendron orbiculare* and *R. williamsianum* cultivars and their hybrids like 'Temple Belle'. Around the perimeter are swamp cypresses and liquidambars: further away are oaks and Scots pines. On the other side of the road lies the splendid arboretum, open at the same time and with a vast collection of well-spaced specimen trees now approaching the prime of their life. Both the water gardens and the arboretum are open only rarely, so that they can be maintained principally for the benefit of partners of John Lewis, but up at the top, along a wooded drive, is an excellent nursery which is open daily throughout the year (afternoons only on Sundays). It specialises in rare trees and shrubs, and has a constantly changing stock of interesting plants. Nearby is a beautiful rose and clematis pergola, but you need permission to see the National Collection of *Buddleja*. 2002 sees the start of a new 'Buddleja Butterfly' garden. Every part of the Longstock estate – water gardens, arboretum, nursery and walled garden – are models of their kind, beautifully maintained and in top condition.

Features Woodland garden; plantsman's collection of plants; good herbaceous borders; arboretum.

Owned by John Lewis Partnership
Number of gardeners 3 at water garden; 3 in arboretum
Size 4ha (10 acres) of water garden; 26ha (65 acres) in arboretum
NCCPG National Collections *Buddleja*; *Clematis viticella*

loving plants flourish. The owners say that their best season is spring – *Narcissus* is another of their many special interests – but there is much to see throughout the year. Birds are encouraged – as is all wildlife, including the trout in the river and waterfall pool.

 Features A plantsman's collection of plants; primulas; meconopsis; hostas; pulmonarias; azaleas and rhododendrons; large gravel bank used as a scree bed; tea & coffee; cake on NGS days.

Owned by Peter & Vera Short
Number of gardeners keen owners only!
Size 1.4ha (3½ acres)
NCCPG National Collections *Helleborus* (part)

The Manor House

UPTON GREY, BASINGSTOKE
RG25 2RD

Tel 01256 862827 **Fax** 01256 861035
Website www.gertrudejekyllgarden.co.uk
Location In Upton Grey village above & beside the church.
Opening hours By appointment only: 9 am – 4 pm; weekdays.
Admission fee £4, to include a copy of the guidebook; £3.50 for groups of 20+.

(wc) (🌱) (🍴)

Ros Wallinger has restored this Jekyll garden since 1984 using the original planting plans (now at Berkeley University, California). She has gone to great pains to recreate it exactly in all its Edwardian loveliness. Some of the roses were extinct here until re-introduced from private gardens in France and Italy after years of searching. The rich herbaceous borders drift from cool blues, white and pinks at either end to hot reds, oranges and yellows in the middle. There is no better place to study Gertrude Jekyll's plantings, but what makes it so special is that it is a

'young' garden again. And the restoration continues. Read more about it in Ros Wallinger's *Gertrude Jekyll's Lost Garden* (Garden Art Press, 2000).

 Features Roses (mainly old-fashioned & climbers); good herbaceous borders; refreshments for groups.

Owned by Mrs John Wallinger
Number of gardeners 1, plus very keen owners
Size 2ha (5 acres)
English Heritage grade II

Meon Orchard

KINGSMEAD, WICKHAM, FAREHAM
PO17 5AU

Tel & Fax 01329 833253
Location Take A32 north from Wickham for 1½ miles; turn left at Roebuck; ½ mile on left.
Opening hours 2 pm – 6 pm; 9 June, 28 July, 1 September, for NGS. Groups welcome by appointment.
Admission fee Adults £2.

(P) (🐕) (♿) (🌱) (🍴)

This stylish garden is a plantaholic paradise. The emphasis is upon difficult and tender plants which look their best in late summer. An extraordinary number of plants survive the winter outside with a little protection: bananas, hedychiums, *Impatiens tinctoria* and *Dahlia imperialis* for example. The Smiths bought the property in 1986 and designed the garden as a series of interlinking paths and glades which radiate out and give the whole lay-out the impression of being much larger than it really is. It is not a quiet or refined garden, but exuberant and experimental, full of dramatic plants and contrasts. The 40 or so *Eucalyptus* species in their National Collection have grown quickly and give the garden an air of maturity. Cordylines, Italian cypresses and *Ligustrum japonicum*

'Rotundifolium' also recur throughout the garden and bind it together. A vast number of pots are planted out for the summer or grouped together. Some may be put in a strategic position for only a few weeks while their flowers associate well with another plant. The owners' plantsmanship is very broad and encompasses hardy plants and alpines plants too: a laburnum hedge as you come down the drive, bulbs of every kind, a quincunx of Japanese anemones, a water garden, a pond, and hundreds of hardy trees and shrubs too. This is a most imaginative and creative garden to visit for ideas about what to grow and how to display it.

 Features Southern hemisphere plants; tea, coffee & biscuits.

Owned by Dr D.J. & Mrs L.A. Smith
Number of gardeners owners only
Size 0.6ha (1½ acres)
NCCPG National Collections Eucalyptus

Mottisfont Abbey

ROMSEY SO51 0LP

Tel 01794 340757   **Fax** 01794 341492
Website www.nationaltrust.org.uk
Location 4½ miles north-west of Romsey.
Opening hours 11 am – 6 pm; Saturday – Wednesday; 23 March to 3 November. Plus Good Friday, and Thursdays from July to August. 11 am – 8.30 pm; daily; 8 to 23 June, for the roses.
Admission fee Adults £6; Children £3.

The park and gardens near the house are stately: Russell Page, Geoffrey Jellicoe and Norah Lindsay all worked here. A broad chalk spring surges out in the grounds and runs down to feed the River Test. One of the London planes (*Platanus × hispanica*) near the river has two huge trunks fused together, though nobody can work out whether the two stems are on the same roots. But it is the old rose collection in the walled garden which has made Mottisfont's name. It is Graham Stuart Thomas's best known work, a collection of all the roses he has discovered, assembled, preserved and made popular through his writings. Mottisfont is surely the loveliest rose garden in Britain, but expect some temporary slippage as it is thoroughly overhauled for the first time since the walled garden was planted in 1972.

 Features Roses (mainly old-fashioned & climbers); plantsman's collection of plants; good herbaceous borders; guided walks and 'rose clinics' in season; tallest *Platanus × hispanica* (42m) in the British Isles; good shop selling books; licensed restaurant.

Owned by The National Trust
Number of gardeners 4
Size 11.1ha (28 acres)
NCCPG National Collections Platanus; Rosa
English Heritage grade II

Oakleigh Nurseries

PETERSFIELD ROAD, MONKWOOD, ALRESFORD SO24 0HB

Tel 01962 773344
Website www.oakleigh-nurseries.co.uk
Location In the middle of Monkwood.
Opening hours 10 am – 4.30 pm (10.30 am – 4 pm at weekends); daily; March to September.

The main specialities of this interesting nursery are fuchsias, penstemons and epiphyllums, with a special emphasis upon pelargoniums – regal, angel, ivy-leaf, zonal, stellar, cactus and scented. But the nursery also has a line in double primroses. A new introduction for 2001 was the angel pelargonium 'Sarah Don': two more are promised for 2002. The website is excellent.

Petersfield Physic Garden

16 THE HIGH STREET, PETERSFIELD

Tel 01730 233371
Website www.hants.gov.uk/leisure/attractnature.html
Location Behind 16 The High Street.
Opening hours Dawn – dusk; daily except Christmas Day.
Admission fee Free.

This is a small town garden, surrounded by walls and planted with the fruit trees, roses, herbs and other plants which were known in the 17th century. It is an initiative of that most energetic and successful organisation, the Hampshire Gardens Trust.

 Features Herbs; new Visitor Centre.

Owned by Hampshire Gardens Trust

Sir George Staunton Country Park

MIDDLE PARK WAT, HAVANT
PO9 5HB

Tel 023 9245 3405   **Fax** 023 9249 8156
Location North of Havant on B2149.
Opening hours Glasshouses 10 am – 5 pm (4 pm in winter); daily; all year. Park dawn to dusk.
Admission fee Free.

The historic heart of this landscape garden is a Regency walled garden and *ferme ornée*, but the local authority has also restored and developed the Victorian glasshouses as an educational resource. Here you can see useful plants like tea, coffee, pineapple, coconut palms, papyrus and rice plants, as well as such ornamentals as *Victoria*

amazonica, passion flowers, sarracenias, *Nepenthes* and strelitzias.

 Features Chinese bridge; good trees; shell-house; lakes; Regency farm; Victorian glasshouses; tea-room; light lunches & refreshments.

Owned by Hampshire County Council
English Heritage grade II*

Spinners

BOLDRE, LYMINGTON SO41 5QE

Tel 01590 673347
Location Signed off A337 between Brockenhurst & Lymington.
Opening hours 10 am – 5 pm; Tuesday – Saturday; all year. Other days by appointment.
Admission fee £2 from 14 April to 14 September; free at other times.

Only 2 acres, but what a garden! Spinners is a plantsman's paradise, where the enthusiast can spend many happy hours browsing at any time of the year. The habitat plantings and plant associations are particularly interesting to study. Much of the garden is light woodland, so it has good collections of hydrangeas, lilies, hostas, rodgersias and ferns. Peter Chappell's RHS Partner Nursery sells an extraordinary range of good plants: you always come away with a bootful of novelties. The trilliums are of course one of the nursery's specialities: they include such rarities as *T. chloropetalum* var. *giganteum* (which has an Award of Garden Merit from the RHS) and *T. parviflorum*. The list of magnolias is perhaps even more impressive: about 90 cultivars, including a great range of *M. acuminata* hybrids, Gresham hybrids and the new *M. stellata* × *M. liliiflora* hybrids, as well as such introductions as *M. dawsoniana* 'Chyverton Red' and *M.* × *loebneri* 'Donna'.

The Sir Harold Hillier Gardens & Arboretum

JERMYNS LANE, AMPFIELD, ROMSEY SO51 0QA

Tel 01794 368787 **Fax** 01794 368027
Website www.hillier.hants.gov.uk/
Location Signed from A3090 & A3057.
Opening hours 10.30 am – 6 pm (dusk if earlier); every day except 25 & 26 December.
Admission fee Adults £4.25; Concessions £3.75; Children (under 16) free. RHS members free.

This is quite the most important modern arboretum in UK. The gardens have the greatest collection of wild and cultivated woody plants in the world: over 12,000 taxa in 180 acres, totalling 40,000 plants. The arboretum was established in 1953 by the late Sir Harold Hillier: Hillier's Nursery aimed at the time to offer for sale every cultivar of every tree or shrub that was hardy in the British Isles. Sir Harold himself was an active importer and collector of new species from all over the world, at a time (of relative economic depression) when few British horticulturists had the impetus to look outside the United Kingdom for plants of any kind. Every part of the arboretum is an education and a pleasure, whatever the season or weather. It has so many unique features that the visitor needs all day to see more than a fraction of its riches: the collection of poplar trees called the Populetum; more than 100 pines (*Pinus* species), including the 'big cone' pine *P. coulteri* whose cones may weigh as much as two kilos; a maple valley; the largest Winter Garden of its kind in Europe and a Gurkha Memorial Garden. But it is the sheer number of trees and shrubs here that makes the most lasting impression: every time you visit, and wherever you walk, you see interesting plants that you have never seen before. The labelling is exemplary and a helpful guide is available. Hilliers' nursery shares a car park with the arboretum. Details of seasonal special events, workshops, evening talks, guided tours and children's activities can be obtained on request.

Features A plantsman's collection of trees and shrubs; mature conifers; also good herbaceous plants; mixed borders; 51 record trees, including 11 *Sorbus*; light refreshments.

Owned by Hampshire County Council
Number of gardeners 14, plus volunteers
Size 72ha (180 acres)
NCCPG National Collections *Carpinus*; *Cornus*; *Corylus*; *Cotoneaster*; *Hamamelis*; *Ligustrum*; *Lithocarpus*; *Photinia*; *Pinus* (excl. dwarf cultivars.); *Quercus*; 'Hillier' plants

Features Woodland garden; an important plantsman's garden; fine collection of trees; rhododendrons; magnolias; woodland plants; rarities and novelties; new peat beds & bog garden; biggest *Eucalyptus perriniana* in the British Isles.

Owned by Diana & Peter Chappell
Number of gardeners part-time help
Size 0.8ha (2 acres)
NCCPG National Collections *Trillium*

Steven Bailey Ltd

SILVER STREET, SWAY, LYMINGTON
SO41 6ZA

Tel 01590 682227   **Fax** 01590 683765
Location East of Hordle, not in Sway.
Opening hours 10 am – 4 pm; Monday – Friday; all year. Plus Saturdays & Sundays from March to June. And Saturdays in December.

This long-established nursery built its reputation on breeding and introducing carnations and pinks. *Dianthus* 'Michael Saunders' and 'Sandra Neal' are among several excellent cultivars to which the RHS has awarded its Award of Garden Merit kitemark but which are available only from this nursery. Its exhibits have for long been a feature of RHS shows. The nursery shop has a good selection of bedding and summer pot plants, alstroemerias and seasonal flowering perennials.

The Vyne

SHERBORNE ST JOHN, BASINGSTOKE
RG24 9HL

Tel 01256 883858   **Fax** 01256 881720
Website www.nationaltrust.org.uk
Location 4 miles north of Basingstoke.
Opening hours 11 am – 5 pm; Saurdays & Sundays; February & March. Then 11 am – 5 pm; Saturday – Wednesday, plus Good Friday; 23 March to 3 November.
Admission fee Adults £3; Children £1.50.

This historic garden has many fine features, including a 17th-century summerhouse which is said to be the earliest domed garden building in England. The horticultural interest lies in its fine old trees, an avenue of red-twigged limes, walnuts, and a venerable tree known as the 'Hundred Guinea Oak' because that was the price which a passing timber-merchant offered for it nearly 200 years ago. In the 1960s, Graham Stuart Thomas added herbaceous borders and old shrub roses.

Features Herbaceous borders; annuals; good trees; wild garden; restaurant.

Owned by The National Trust
Number of gardeners 3½
Size 5ha (13 acres)
English Heritage grade II

Tudor House Garden

BUGLE STREET, SOUTHAMPTON
SO14 2AD

Tel 023 8063 5904   **Fax** 023 8033 9601
Website www.southampton.gov.uk/leisure/heritage
Location Bugle Street runs parallel to the High Street in the old town.

Opening hours 10 am – 12 noon & 1 pm – 5 pm (4 pm on Saturdays); weekdays. Plus 2 pm – 5 pm on Sundays. Open all year.
Admission fee Free.

Sylvia Landsberg's unique reconstruction of a Tudor garden has a knot garden, a fountain, a secret garden and contemporary plantings of herbs and flowering plants all crammed into a tiny area. Some call it a pastiche, others a living dictionary of Tudor garden language.

 Features Tudor-style knot garden; herbs.

Owned by Southampton City Council
Number of gardeners 1
Size 30m×30m (100ft×100ft)

Water Meadow Nursery and Herb Farm

CHERITON, ALRESFORD SO24 0QB

Tel 01962 771895 **Fax** 01962 771985
Website www.plantaholic.co.uk
Location Just off the A272, on the B3046 to Alresford.
Opening hours 9 am – 5 pm; Wednesday – Saturday; March to October. And by appointment.

This nursery offers a good list of waterlilies – *Nymphaea* culitvars, of which they have 70 – and oriental poppies. Many of the hardy plants and herbs in the general list are unusual. The display garden is beautifully laid out – the nursery offers a design and landscaping service – and opens several times from May to July to show off its collection of more than 100 cultivars of *Papaver orientale*.

NCCPG National Collections *Papaver orientale*

West Green House

HARTLEY WINTNEY, BASINGSTOKE RG27 8JB

Tel 01252 844611
Location In West Green village.
Opening hours 11 am – 4.30 pm; Thursday – Sunday & Bank Holiday Monday; May to August. Also for the National Trust.
Admission fee Adults £4; Children £1.

Marylyn Abbott is restoring and re-making the garden at West Green with all the energy she showed in the garden she made in her native Australia. Formality, variety, invention and sheer beauty are here in abundance. The *potager* is especially stylish. Visit it, if you can, and see one of the greatest modern gardens come to life again.

 Features Exuberant plantings; colour combinations; woodland garden; parterre; great sense of style.

Owned by Marylyn Abbott
Number of gardeners 3
Size 3.2ha (8 acres)

White Windows

LONGPARISH, ANDOVER SP11 6PB

Tel & Fax 01264 720222
Location In village centre, opposite village school.
Opening hours 2 pm – 6 pm; by appointment from April to September on Wednesdays. And on 5 & 6 May and 21 & 22 July for National Gardens Scheme.
Admission fee Adults £2; Children free.

White Windows is one of the best small modern plantsman's gardens on chalk, remarkable for the way Jane Sterndale-Bennett, past Chairman of the Hardy Plant

Society, arranges her material. Layer upon layer, White Windows bulges with good plants, well grown and controlled, so that the balance is kept between sun and shade. Leaves and stems are as important as flowers, especially in the combinations and contrasts of colour – gold and yellow, blue and silver, and crimsons, pinks and purples. Much use is made of evergreens and variegated plants. Perhaps the most luxuriant chalk garden in Hampshire and all made since 1979.

Features A plantsman's garden; good herbaceous borders; euphorbias; pulmonarias; hardy geraniums; sedums.

Owned by Mrs J. Sterndale-Bennett
Number of gardeners owner only
Size 0.3ha (0.7 acres)
NCCPG National Collections *Helleborus* (part)

HEREFORDSHIRE

There is, of course, no such county as Herefordshire – not any more. It was dissolved in 1974, when the old county was linked to its neighbour as 'Hereford & Worcester'. This was never a popular union, and Herefordshire people were always quick to point out that they retained their own identity and Lord Lieutenant. Herefordshire is now a District Council but, so distinct does it consider itself, that we list it as a county again. It is a pity that so few of its historic gardens are open to the public. Hergest Croft has by far the most important collection of trees, with a large number of 'record breakers' among them: Eastnor Castle also has some fine trees, the largest of their kind in England. There are comparatively few top-class modern gardens – Elton Hall and the Lance Hattatt Design Garden are memorable exceptions (as is Sir Roy Strong's private garden at Much Birch) – and the county does not do conspicuously well for the National Gardens Scheme. Likewise, it has comparatively few National Collections and National Collection holders and no RHS Partner Colleges or Partner Nurseries. But good nurseries exist – Kenchester Water Gardens and Rickard's Hardy Ferns are two of the best – and the extensive fruit orchards testify to the county's suitability for horticulture. The NCCPG group has worked with the Marcher Apple Network to identify old trees, propagate them and establish new orchards to preserve them.

Abbey Dore Court Garden

ABBEY DORE, HEREFORD HR2 0AD

Tel & Fax 01981 240419
Location 3 miles west of A465, midway between Hereford & Abergavenny.
Opening hours 11 am – 5.30 pm; daily except Mondays & Wednesdays (open Bank Holidays); 30 March to 30 September.
Admission fee Adults £3; Children 50p.

This is a splendid plantsman's garden on a difficult site, with fine borders leading down to the ferny river walk and a meadow planted with interesting trees. Mrs Ward says her 'rambling garden' has 'stopped getting any bigger', but the truth is that the garden grows, changes and improves with every visit and she has just taken in another acre of field: very exciting.

Features Good herbaceous borders; handsome wellingtonias; ferns; hellebores; good nursery.

Owned by Mrs Charis Ward
Number of gardeners 1
Size 2.2ha (6 acres)

The Bannut

BRINGSTY WR6 5TA

Tel & Fax 01885 482206
Website www.bannut.co.uk
Location On the A44, 2½ miles east of Bromyard.
Opening hours 2 pm – 5 pm; Wednesdays, Saturdays, Sundays & Bank Holidays; Easter to September.
Admission fee Adults £2.50; Children £1.

Unlike many plantsman's gardens, the plants at The Bannut have been used to great decorative effect. The best example is the knot garden made from the contrasting leaf colours of different heathers, though the Everetts are fond of all heathers and grow a large number (over 10,000) in the summer heather garden. They are, however, interested in all types of plants and how to display them in the garden. The beds and borders are planted for colour harmonies and contrasts, mainly of herbaceous plants near the modern house, but with more shrubs towards the little copse where cowslips flower in spring. Near the house are a formal yellow-and-white garden and an 'arbour garden' in silver, pink and blue. An old paddock is now planted with rhododendrons, azaleas, camellias and pieris, plus hydrangeas for late-summer interest. Recent additions include a white wisteria walk and a 'secret' garden.

Features Heathers; colour-themed plantings; island beds of shrubs and herbaceous plants; knot garden; cowslips.

Owned by Maurice & Daphne Everett
Number of gardeners owners, plus very part-time help
Size 1ha (2½ acres)

Berrington Hall

LEOMINSTER HR6 0DW

Tel 01568 615721   **Fax** 01568 613263
Website www.nationaltrust.org.uk
Location On A49, 3 miles north of Leominster.
Opening hours 12 noon – 5 pm (4.30 pm in October & November); Saturday – Wednesday, plus Good Friday; 23 March to 3 November.
Admission fee £3.

This majestic park is classic Capability Brown. The National Trust has laid out a one-mile parkland walk which takes in the best vantage points and shows you how the landscape would have looked when young. In the old walled garden, a comprehensive collection of Hereford Pomona is supplemented by old pear varieties, quinces and medlars.

Features Fruit; classic parkland; apples & pears; National Trust shop; licensed restaurant for lunch & teas.

Owned by The National Trust
Number of gardeners 2
Size 4.6ha (11½ acres)
English Heritage grade II*

Bryan's Ground

STAPLETON, PRESTEIGNE LD8 2LP

Tel 01544 260001   **Fax** 01544 260015
Website www.hortus.co.uk
Location On minor road between Stapleton & Kinsham.
Opening hours 11 am – 5 pm; 1 to 4 June and 6 & 7 July. (4 June is for NGS). Open for Hellebore Weekends at the end of February or early in March: ring for details. Groups by appointment between 11 May & 14 July.
Admission fee Adults £3; Children £1.

A young garden: incredibly, the owners moved here as recently as 1993. They have made wonderfully good use of the inherited structure (yew hedges and mature trees around the 1912 Arts & Crafts house) and filled it with good plants. Developments include an auricula theatre, a belvedere, a mirror pool and a 4-acre arboretum. Full of original ideas, Bryan's Ground is already an influential and fashionable garden. David Wheeler is the editor of the elegant gardening quarterly *Hortus*, of which Simon Dorrell is the art editor.

 Features Good modern design.

Owned by David Wheeler & Simon Dorrell
Number of gardeners 2 part-time
Size 2.8ha (7 acres)

Eastnor Castle

EASTNOR, LEDBURY HR8 1RL

Tel 01531 633160 **Fax** 01531 631776
Website www.eastnorcastle.com
Location 2 miles east of Ledbury on A438.
Opening hours 11 am – 5 pm; Sundays & Bank Holiday Mondays; 31 March to 6 October. Also daily except Saturdays in July & August.
Admission fee Adults £3.50; OAPs £2.75; Children £2.

Eastnor is all about trees. The arboretum planted by Lord Somers from 1852 and 1883 is now mature, and full of champion specimens. Many are rare, including a tall American beech (*Fagus grandifolia*) and an enormous red hickory (*Carya ovalis*). It is however the conifers which dominate the setting for the castle, largely because they were planted so thickly and in such great numbers. Michael Hadfield wrote that Eastnor was 'embowered by vast conifers – plantations which spill out into the surrounding hills and fields'. Quite apart

from the many hundreds of cedars, the record-breakers include the Shensi fir (*Abies chensiensis*), the purple-coned fir (*Picea purpurea*) from south-east China, and *Pinus hartwegii* from Mexico.

 Features Mature conifers; spring bulbs; tallest deodar *Cedrus deodara* (38m) in the British Isles, plus 11 more record trees; teas.

Owned by Mr James & The Hon. Mrs Hervey-Bathurst
Number of gardeners 2
Size 16ha (40 acres)
English Heritage grade II*

Elton Hall

LUDLOW SY8 2HQ

Tel 01568 770218 **Fax** 01568 770753
Location Between Wigmore & Ludlow.
Opening hours For National Gardens Scheme, and by appointment for clubs & groups.
Admission fee Adults £2 (in 2001).

Into this historic landscape (home 200 years ago to Thomas Andrew Knight, President of the not-yet-Royal Horticultural Society) the Hepworths and their gardener Anthony Brooks have since about 1990 set a remarkably original and beautiful new garden. Huge herbaceous borders, clear design, rare plants and great sensitivity to form and colour are the essence of it. But what makes it exceptional is the range of quirky follies and fancies with which the garden is strewn – the Tortoise Fort, for instance, and the Moorish sheep palace. Recent additions include a gazebo and a hermitage.

Features Plantsman's collection of plants; good herbaceous borders; teas.

Owned by Mr & Mrs James Hepworth

The Lance Hattatt Design Garden

WEOBLEY HR4 8RN

Tel & Fax 01544 318468
Location 1 mile from Weobley: off Wormsley road, signed Ledgemoor & second right, first house on left.
Opening hours 2 pm – 5 pm; Wednesday – Sundays; April to September.
Admission fee Adults £3.75. Unsuitable for children.

The Lance Hattatt Design Garden used to be known as Arrow Cottage, a name which Lance Hattatt felt to be misleading: he specialises in 'contemporary garden design in the best English tradition' and believes that the new name is more appropriate. The garden is a good example of a modern design where a series of gardens in different styles exhibits a fair measure of plantsmanship. But there is still a problem of naming: though all are to some extent explained, it may be difficult for visitors to see the connection between the names and the gardens. Akademia, Luxor, Andrassy, Indigo Yard, Solomon and Easter Island are just some of them. It should be said, however, that all are maintained to the highest standard. Moreover, the keen plantsman will find *Iris confusa* 'Martyn Rix' flourishing outside, and pots of *Agapanthus africanus* along the rill in summer. Few such gardens combine plantsmanship and artistry so well.

Features Good herbaceous borders; stream; wildflower orchard (2000); fifty-metre, yew-enclosed rill; good plants throughout; old roses; refreshments.

Owned by Jane & Lance Hattatt
Number of gardeners 1½
Size 0.8ha (2 acres)

Hergest Croft Gardens

KINGTON HR5 3EG

Tel 01544 230160 **Fax** 01544 230160
Website www.hergest.co.uk
Location Signed from A44.
Opening hours 1.30 pm – 6 pm; daily; 30 March to 31 October.
Admission fee Adults £4; Children free.

Hergest Croft is an extremely important woodland garden and arboretum around a whopping Edwardian house. It has over 4,000 rare trees and shrubs, but there seems no end to the garden's marvels: huge conifers, magnificent birches, scores of interesting oaks, many acres of billowing rhododendrons – Hergest Croft is one of the best rhododendron gardens in Britain. But it is also worth visiting for its double herbaceous borders, alpine collections, roses, autumn gentians and kitchen garden, all on a scale that most of us have forgotten.

Features Fine collection of trees; rhododendrons; tallest *Cercidiphyllum japonicum* (25m) in the British Isles, among some 50 record trees; homemade teas.

Owned by W.L. Banks
Size 25ha (56 acres)
NCCPG National Collections *Acer; Betula; Zelkova*
English Heritage grade II*

How Caple Court

HOW CAPLE, HEREFORD HR1 4SX

Tel 01989 740626 **Fax** 01989 740611
Location Signed on B4224 & A449 junction.
Opening hours 10 am – 5 pm; daily; Easter to September.
Admission fee Adults £2.50; Children free.

Spectacular formal gardens laid out about 100 years ago (some Italianate, others more Arts & Crafts), and now undergoing restoration. Pergolas, loggias, dramatic terraces and *giardini segreti* with stunning views across a lushly wooded valley. How Caple is a garden of national importance, but little known even locally.

 Features Mature conifers; Italian terraces surrounded by restored pergola; old roses; topiary; woodland gardens.

Owned by Mr & Mrs Roger Lee
Number of gardeners 1
Size 4.2ha (11 acres)

Kenchester Water Gardens

CHURCH ROAD, LYDE, HEREFORD HR1 3AB

Tel 01432 270981   **Fax** 01432 342243
Location On A49 between Hereford & Leominster.
Opening hours 9 am – 6 pm (5.30 pm from October to March); daily; all year. 10.30 am – 4.30 pm on Sundays. Closed Christmas Day.
Admission fee Free.

The gardens and the nursery at Kenchester are equally important for anyone interested in waterplants. The range of plants grown and offered for sale is excellent, and includes nearly 210 cultivars of *Nymphaea*. The gardens have pools and ponds over a large area – well worth a longish visit. This is a dynamic nursery which is getting bigger and better all the time.

 Features Water plants and water gardens; light lunches & teas.

Owned by Mr & Mrs M.R. Edwards
Number of gardeners 2
Size 2.2ha (6 acres)
NCCPG National Collections *Nymphaea*

Kingstone Cottage Plants

WESTON UNDER PENYARD, ROSS-ON-WYE HR9 7PH

Tel 01989 565267
Location North of Weston under Penyard, on the road to Rudhall.
Opening hours 10 am – 5 pm; Monday – Friday; 7 May to 6 July.
Admission fee Adults £2 for National Gardens Scheme.

The garden's main feature is its National Collection of old *Dianthus* cultivars which flower in early summer. This is the place to see such rarities as *D.* 'Fenbow Nutmeg Clove' and *D.* 'Cranborne Seedling'. Mr & Mrs Hughes also sell plants which they have propagated from their collection – the best way to promote a wider interest in old cultivars and guarantee their future survival.

 Features Ponds; grotto; summerhouse; pinks.

Owned by Michael & Sophie Hughes
NCCPG National Collections *Dianthus*

Lakeside

GAINES ROAD, WHITBOURNE, WORCESTER WR6 5RD

Tel 01886 821119
Location 9 miles west of Worcester off A44 at County boundary sign.
Opening hours Parties of 10+ by appointment only between April & September.

Admission fee Adults £2.50; Children free.

These six acres were dramatically planted by Chris Philip, who founded the *RHS Plant Finder*. Tender plants flourish against the old kitchen garden walls. Daffodils bred by Michael Jefferson-Brown run down to the lake, where clean-limbed alders stretch gothically heavenwards. Throughout the garden are good plants, used well: Lakeside is an inspiration to new gardeners, and a place from which all can learn.

 Features Woodland garden; small maturing pinetum; unusual plants; good herbaceous borders; ferns; hollies; heathers; lake; bog garden; teas.

Owned by Denys Gueroult
Number of gardeners 1 part-time
Size 2.2ha (6 acres)

Marston Exotics

BRAMPTON LANE, MADLEY,
HEREFORD HR2 9LX

Tel 01981 251140
Location 7 miles south of Hereford.
Opening hours 8 am – 4.30 pm; Monday – Friday; all year. 1 pm – 5 pm; Saturday – Sunday; March to October. 11 am – 5 pm; Bank Holidays.

Marston Exotics are the leading nursery for carnivorous plants in the UK – perhaps in Europe. The range is formidable: the list of sarracenias, droseras, and pinguiculas is extremely comprehensive. Marston Exotics have been regular exhibitors at RHS shows over many years and have done a lot of selection and hybridisation. Their National Collection of *Sarracenia* has about seven species and over 60 cultivars.

NCCPG National Collections *Sarracenia*

The Picton Garden

OLD COURT NURSERIES, WALWYN
ROAD, COLWALL, MALVERN
WR13 6QE

Tel 01684 540416 **Fax** 01684 565314
Website www.autumnasters.co.uk
Location 3 mile west of Great Malvern; 5 miles east of Ledbury on B4218.
Opening hours 11 am – 5 pm; Wednesday – Sunday; August to October.
Admission fee Adults £2 for NGS.

The Picton Garden at Old Court Nurseries holds the National Collection of Michaelmas daisies (*Aster*). This is also the nurseries' speciality: the extensive collection is fully described in Paul Picton's excellent book *Gardener's Guide to Growing Asters* (1999). But there are also many other interesting perennials and cottagey plants here. When the Michaelmas daisies are in flower, the banks of colour, graded for height, recall the grandest of Edwardian gardens and the Picton Garden becomes one of the great showpieces of English horticulture.

 Features Magnificent collection of asters; herbaceous plants.

Owned by Paul & Meriel Picton
Number of gardeners 2
Size 0.6ha (1½ acres)
NCCPG National Collections *Aster* (autumn-flowering)

Queen's Wood Arboretum & Country Park

DINMORE HILL, LEOMINSTER HR6 0PY

Tel 01568 797052   **Fax** 01568 879305
Location Midway between Leominster & Hereford on A49.
Opening hours 9 am – dusk; daily; all year.
Admission fee free, but small charge for parking.

A vigorous young arboretum, planted over the last 40 years with public amenity in mind. Wonderful for walking, whatever the season, and well run in a friendly, efficient manner so that visitors get the most from it. The rangers say that spring and autumn are the best time for colour, but there are lots of early purple orchids and spotted orchids in summer too.

 Features A fine collection of trees, including mature conifers; bluebells; wood anemones; gift shop; light meals from 9 am – 5 pm.

Owned by Hereford Council
Number of gardeners 4
Size 22ha (60 acres)

Rushfields of Ledbury

ROSS ROAD, LEDBURY HR8 2LP

Tel 01531 632004   **Fax** 01531 633454
Website www.rushfields.co.uk
Location ½ mile south-west of Ledbury off A449.
Opening hours 11 am – 5 pm; Wednesday – Saturday; & by appointment.
Admission fee free

Rushfields specialise in 'choice garden plants', most of them herbaceous. They are particularly good for hostas, and for hellebores, of which they have been developing their own Helen Ballard strains. Other specialities include geraniums, euphorbias, penstemons and monardas, but the nursery is a good place to see and buy a wide range of well-chosen herbaceous plants. More plants may be seen in a large undercover area. Rushfields are consistent gold medal winners at RHS shows.

 Features Hostas.

Owned by B. Homewood

Whitfield

ALLENSMORE HR2 9BA

Tel 01981 570727   **Fax** 01981 570641
Location 8 miles south-west of Hereford on A465.
Opening hours For NGS. And parties by appointment.
Admission fee Adults £2.50; Children free.

Whitfield has magnificent trees, most of them planted by the Clives over the last 200 years. *Zelkova serrata*, a weeping oak, and a ginkgo planted as early as 1778 are some of the highlights, but there is nothing to beat the grove of 20 or so *Sequoia sempervirens* now pushing 150ft (46m) in height.

Features Topiary; mature conifers; fine collection of trees; huge grove of redwoods; tallest dwarf alder *Alnus nitida* and durmast oak *Quercus petraea* in the British Isles.

Owned by Mr & Mrs Edward Clive
Size 5.2ha (13 acres)
English Heritage grade II

HERTFORDSHIRE

Hertfordshire has two great historic gardens (Hatfield House and St Paul's Walden Bury) which are open to the public, and a couple of lesser ones (Ashridge and Knebworth) but few of the others admit visitors. Nor does Hertfordshire have as many good modern gardens as its proximity to London might suggest. Both the Beale Arboretum and the Gardens of the Rose are less than 50 years old, and of interest mainly for their specialist collections. The only garden with really good herbaceous plantings is Benington Lordship. There is a sprinkling of fine trees at such gardens as Bayfordbury (sometimes open for the National Gardens Scheme) and Aldenham – both relics of keen gardening owners in the past – but no old-established arboretum or pinetum of special merit. The National Gardens Scheme can muster only about two-thirds of the number of gardens which open for charity in such a county as Northamptonshire and there are only six National Collections in the county. But Hertfordshire has some good nurseries and a large number of excellent garden centres. The presence of the Royal National Rose Society and its spectacular display gardens is a considerable asset to the St Albans area, as is the nearby horticultural college at Oaklands. Nevertheless, it remains difficult to explain why a county so close to London should not be endowed with horticultural wealth on anything like the scale of Surrey or Kent.

Aylett Nurseries Ltd

NORTH ORBITAL ROAD, LONDON COLNEY, ST ALBANS AL2 1DH

Tel 01727 822255 **Fax** 01727 823024
Website www.martex.co.uk/hta/aylett
Location On A414, on left-hand side when driving towards Hatfield.
Opening hours 8.30 am – 5.30 pm; Monday – Friday. 8.30 am – 5 pm; Saturdays. 9.30 am – 5 pm; Bank Holidays. 10.30 am – 4.30 pm; Sundays.
Admission fee Free

This huge (and very busy) general garden centre has a prime trading position with a vast range of plants and every imaginable sundry. It also offers a design service and delivery. But Ayletts also has a speciality – its award-winning dahlias which have been a feature of RHS shows for many years. The growing fields are a mile or so from the nursery and well worth a visit in late summer or early autumn. All the different classes of dahlia hybrids are represented in both quantity and quality.

Owned by The Aylett family
Size 2.8ha (7 acres)

Beale Arboretum

WEST LODGE PARK HOTEL,
COCKFOSTERS ROAD, HADLEY WOOD
EN4 0PY

Tel 020 8216 3904   Fax 020 8449 9916
Website www.bealeshotels.co.uk
Location A111 one mile south of M25 Jcn 24.
Opening hours 2 pm – 5 pm; Wednesdays; April to
October. Plus: 19 May & 13 October for National Gardens
Scheme.
Admission fee £2 on Wednesdays; £2.50 for National
Gardens Scheme. Children free.

The Beale Arboretum has been developed
since 1963 by adding to the original
plantings in the park which surrounded the
house when it was a private residence. It is
already an exceptional collection: young
trees have been planted among much older
specimens – Victorian cedars and
redwoods – with a view to the overall effect.
There are fine collections of oaks,
hornbeams, liquidambars and nyssas, as well
as shrubby elaeagnus and underplantings of
rhododendrons. Little known as yet, and
maintained primarily as a facility for hotel
guests, the Beale Arboretum is undoubtedly
to be reckoned among the great late 20th-
century arboreta.

Features Eight-acre arboretum;
mature conifers; a fine collection of
young trees; 200-year-old *Arbutus unedo*;
refreshments in hotel.

Owned by Beales Hotel
Number of gardeners 2
Size 8ha (20 acres)
NCCPG National Collections *Carpinus betulus* culitvars;
Elaeagnus

Benington Lordship

BENINGTON, STEVENAGE SG2 7BS

Tel 01438 869228   Fax 01438 869622
Website www.beningtonlordship.co.uk
Location Off A602 Stevenage to Hertford, in Benington
village.
Opening hours Snowdrop week in February (ring for
exact dates): 12 noon – 4 pm. Spring & Summer Bank
Holiday weekends: 2 pm – 5 pm on Sundays & 12 noon –
5 pm on Bank Holiday Mondays. Herbaceous borders
week: 12 noon – 5 pm, daily, 1 to 7 July.
Admission fee Adults £3.50; Children free.

Benington Lordship is a Georgian house
with an Edwardian add-on, a mock Norman
gateway and the ruins of a real Norman
castle in the grounds. The extensive gardens
have been revived and replanted in recent
years without destroying the older features:
a Pulhamite folly, an Edwardian rock garden
and a sense of spacious parkland. But the
highlight of a visit today is the stupendous
double herbaceous border that Mrs Bott
has planted in gentle pastel shades: the best
we know.

Features Roses (ancient & modern);
rock garden; very good herbaceous
borders; heather garden; cowslip bank;
water features (& kingfishers); kitchen
garden.

Owned by C.H.A. Bott
Number of gardeners 2
Size 2.8ha (7 acres)
English Heritage grade II

The Gardens of the Rose

Chiswell Green, St Albans AL2 3NR

Tel 01727 850461   **Fax** 01727 850360
Website www.roses.co.uk
Location 1 mile from junction of M1 & M25; 2 miles south of St Albans.
Opening hours 9 am – 5 pm (10 am – 6 pm on Sundays & Bank Holidays); daily; 1 June to 29 September.
Admission fee Adults £4; OAPs £3.50; Children £1.50; Members free.

This is the most comprehensive rose garden in Britain, and the best in which to learn about roses of all kinds. Its design and lay-out is something of a 1960s hangover – lots of beds cut out of the turf and filled with bushes of a single cultivar. This was the way that roses were commonly grown until about 1980, and it is fair to say that the Royal National Rose Society has not made enough effort to underplant its garden with other plants: this would enable it to open earlier in the season and attract garden visitors in the peak garden visiting months of April and May. Every class of rose is well represented in the gardens. The old roses – Gallicas, Damasks and Mosses – are concentrated in a garden with sweeping curves designed by Graham Stuart Thomas. Elsewhere are collections of Bourbons and Hybrid Perpetuals. The greatest impact comes from the Hybrid Teas, Floribundas and climbing roses: the view down the central avenue from the house in which the Society has its offices is one of the greatest sights among all English gardens. It is a paved walk down to a pool, backed by a pergola of climbing roses and flanked with modern roses in every imaginable colour. It celebrates quite unashamedly the glory of the rose as a good value, easy-to-grow plant that gives greater beauty over a longer period than any other. Yet further parts of the garden are devoted to wild species of roses, groundcover roses, miniatures and special types such as those which have received leading awards from the Rose Society's trials. Some 600 unnamed cultivars at any one time are undergoing trialling, a process which lasts three years. The greatest excitement of recent years was the first appearance of the bluest rose ever seen – 'Rhapsody in Blue' – which will be introduced in 2002. In the main garden itself are 30,000 rose bushes and 1,750 cultivars: no place can beat the Gardens of the Rose in June and July for colour and fragrance. The Rose Society has ambitious plans to expand its gardens to some 60 acres. These began with the opening of the Peace Garden in 1995 (designed to show the importance of the 'Peace' rose in the history of modern rose breeding) but were held up pending a planning appeal. Planning permission to develop the garden has at last been received, and the society hopes to start on the expansion shortly, but inevitably the new development does depend upon funding. Meanwhile, the standards of cultivation in the existing garden have recently given cause for concern.

Features Roses of every kind; iris garden; major collection of clematis; substantial plantings of bulbs and spring-flowering plants; shop with rose books & souvenirs; licensed cafeteria.

Owned by The Royal National Rose Society
Number of gardeners 7
Size 10.7ha (27 acres)
NCCPG National Collections *Rosa* (species & cultivars)

Hatfield House

HATFIELD AL9 5NQ

Tel 01707 287010   **Fax** 01707 287033
Website www.hatfield-house.co.uk
Location Off A1(M) Jct 4.
Opening hours 1 pm – 5.30 pm; daily; 30 March to
30 September. East gardens open only on Fridays
('Connoisseur's Days').
Admission fee House, park & garden: Adults £6.60, but
£10 on Fridays.

The gardens at Hatfield are mainly late
19th- and 20th-century. An 1890s
parterre called the East Gardens is the
outstanding feature: in 1977 Lady Salisbury
enclosed it on either side with avenues of
evergreen oaks – they are grown on two-
metre stems and clipped like lollipops – and
replanted the formal beds. Two years later
she started on the Knot Garden, an historical
recreation in front of the old palace. The
designs are extracted from traditional
English patterns in such herbaries as
Parkinson's. Four central beds surround a
small pool: the corners of the beds are
marked by pyramids of box. Three are knots;
the fourth is a gravel maze, to remind us that
Hatfield already had a maze when Queen
Elizabeth I visited it. The Elizabethan fruit
garden is represented by pomegranates
which are put out in the summer, another
link to the earliest gardens at Hatfield. The
planting is true to the period too: every plant
is one that would have been introduced to
England before 1620. They include clove
carnations, ancient roses and a collection of
historical tulips given to Lady Salisbury by
the *Hortus Bulborum* in Holland. Lady
Salisbury has tried to re-make the gardens as
they might have been, and bring them back
into sympathy with the great unchanging
house. 'It is my dream' she wrote 'that one

day they will become again a place of fancies
and conceits, where not only pleasure and
peace can be found but a measure of
surprise and mystery'.

 Features Good herbaceous borders;
knot gardens and good topiary; physic
garden; organic kitchen garden (whole
garden organically managed); souvenirs and
gift shop; licensed restaurant, coffee shop,
snacks & hot lunches.

Owned by The Marquess of Salisbury
Number of gardeners 7
Size 16.8ha (42 acres)
English Heritage grade I

Hill House Garden

STANSTEAD ABBOTS, WARE
SG12 8BX

Tel 01920 870013
Location Next to the Parish Church in Capell Lane.
Opening hours 2 pm – 5.30 pm on 9 & 16 June. Groups at other times by appointment.
Admission fee Adults £3; Children 50p.

Outstanding plantings in the old kitchen garden include colour borders weeping pears, and vegetables all as neat as imaginable. Pretty woodland garden and lush growth around the pond.

 Features Woodland garden; 20ft high original Victorian conservatory; good herbaceous borders; rose species; homemade teas.

Owned by Mr & Mrs Ronald Pilkington
Number of gardeners 1
Size 3.2ha (8 acres)

Hopleys

HIGH STREET, MUCH HADHAM
SG10 6BU

Tel 01279 842509   **Fax** 01279 843784
Website www.hopleys.co.uk
Location 50 yards north of The Bull pub.
Opening hours 9 am (2 pm on Sundays) – 5 pm; daily except Tuesdays. Closed in January & February.
Admission fee Adults £1.50, but free to those spending £20 in the nursery.

Hopleys has a fine 4-acre garden with some excellent plants (some notable conifers and an ash tree said to be the fourth largest in the UK), but the nursery is its principal draw. It offers an extensive choice of hardy shrubs and perennials, with many half-hardy plants too – being particularly strong on diascias, osteospermums, penstemons and salvias. Since its foundation in 1968, the nursery has been responsible for numerous introductions: the most famous are *Lavatera* 'Barnsley' and *Potentilla fruticosa* 'Red Ace'. The tradition continues with its new *Abelia* × *grandiflora* 'Hopleys'. The website is excellent – very comprehensive and informative.

Owned by Aubrey Barker
Number of gardeners ½
Size 1.6ha (4 acres)

Knebworth House

KNEBWORTH, STEVENAGE SG3 6PY

Tel 01438 812661   **Fax** 01438 811908
Website www.knebworthhouse.com
Location Off A1(M) Jct 7.
Opening hours 11 am – 5.30 pm; daily; 23 March to 7 April, 1 to 9 June & 6 July to 3 September. Plus weekends & Bank Holidays from 13 April to 26 May & weekends only 15 to 30 June & 7 to 29 September.
Admission fee £5.50.

Most of the garden was laid out by Lutyens, who married a daughter of the house. It has been well restored over the last 15 years with Jekyll plantings where appropriate. Inventive and harmonious, few gardens make such good use of space and perspective.

Features Rose garden with herbaceous borders; sunken lawn; gold garden; wilderness; maze; ponds; brick garden (restored 2000); culinary herb & vegetable garden (2001); licensed tea-room.

Owned by The Hon. Henry Lytton Cobbold
Number of gardeners 4
Size 10ha (25 acres)
English Heritage grade II*

St Paul's Walden Bury

WHITWELL, HITCHIN SG4 8BP

Tel 01438 871218   **Fax** 01438 871229
Location B651 5 miles south of Hitchin.
Opening hours 2 pm – 7 pm; 21 April, 12 May & 9 June.
And groups by arrangement.
Admission fee Adults £2.50; Children 50p. Groups £5 per person.

St Paul's Walden Bury is highly important as a unique example of the French 18th-century style – three hedged *allées* lead off into the woodland towards temples, statues and pools. The present owner's father (the Queen Mother's brother) was a past President of the Royal Horticultural Society, and started to blend rhododendrons, azaleas, maples and magnolias (plus much more besides) into parts of the woodland. Other areas major on shrub roses and herbaceous plants. It is therefore a garden that appeals to historians, plantsmen and artists alike.

 Features Woodland garden; formal French landscape; teas & homemade cakes.

Owned by St Paul's Walden Bury Estate Co
Size 24ha (60 acres)
English Heritage grade I

The Van Hage Garden Company

GREAT AMWELL, WARE SG12 9RP

Tel 01920 870811   **Fax** 01920 871861
Website www.vanhage.co.uk
Location On A1170.
Opening hours 9 am – 6 pm; Monday – Saturday.
10.30 am – 4.30 pm; Sundays. Opens at 9.30 am on Mondays.

This long-established and award-winning garden centre is particularly strong on house plants, though it offers a large choice of hardy plants too. Van Hage are also seed merchants: they sell their own flower and vegetable seed, including the record-breaking carrot 'Flak' and some untreated seed which is suitable for organic gardeners. There are display gardens, and a maze maize in summer. They have two other garden centres, one at Chenies near Rickmansworth and the other at Bragbury End on the south-east edge of Stevenage.

ISLE OF WIGHT

The Isle of Wight ('the island' to its residents) may be small and deficient in wealth-creating industries, but it has two exceptional gardens: the 19th-century royal palace of Osborne which overlooks the Solent on the northern shores of the island, and the modern botanic garden at Ventnor on the sunny southern side. The two gardens have an unusual link: the head gardener at Osborne is married to the head gardener at Ventnor. The Isle of Wight also has some fine plantsman's gardens (most notably John Harrison's at North Court), an active Historic Gardens Trust and NCCPG group, several National Collections and some good nurseries. In addition to those listed below, there is a magnificent choice of daylilies available from A la Carte Daylilies (Little Hermitage, St Catherine's Down, Ventnor PO38 2PU – by appointment only), including many of the new American hybrids: the nursery has two National Collections of *Hemerocallis*, large flowered cultivars which have received awards since 1960, and miniature and small-flowered cultivars. Another National Collection is held by Springbank Nurseries (Winford Road, Newchurch, Sandown PO36 0JX), whose nerines have won several awards at RHS shows in recent years and extend to over 600 cultivars.

Barton Manor

WHIPPINGHAM, EAST COWES
PO32 6LB

Tel 01983 292835   **Fax** 01983 293923
Location Next to Osborne House on East Cowes Road (A3021).
Opening hours 10 am – 5 pm; 2 June, 7 July, 4 August, 1 September.
Admission fee Adults £2.50; Children £1.

Laid out by Prince Albert, Barton was for many years part of the Osborne estate. He planted some of the best trees, including the cork plantation near the house. The collection of kniphofias is the main modern attraction for garden-visitors: many are available by mail order.

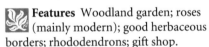 **Features** Woodland garden; roses (mainly modern); good herbaceous borders; rhododendrons; gift shop.

Owned by R. Stigwood
Size 10.3ha (26 acres)
NCCPG National Collections Kniphofia

Deacon's Nursery

MOOR VIEW, GODSHILL PO38 3HW

Tel 01983 840750/522243   **Fax** 01983 523575
Location Moor View is next to school, down School Crescent.

Opening hours 8 am – 4 pm (2 pm on Saturdays);
Monday – Friday; October to April. 8 am – 6 pm (4 pm on
Saturdays); Monday – Friday; May to October.

Deacon's is one of the leading fruit-tree nurseries in England, with tree- and soft fruit of every size and variety. The very comprehensive list includes over 300 apple cultivars, many which are not listed elsewhere – including such regional specialities as 'Devonshire Crimson Queen' and 'Welsh Russet'. All rootstocks are of virus-free origin.

Owned by Brian & Grahame Deacon
Size 6.7ha (17 acres)

Mottistone Manor

NEWPORT PO30 4ED

Tel 01983 741302
Website www.nationaltrust.org.uk
Location On B3399 west of Brighstone.
Opening hours 11 am – 5.30 pm on Tuesdays &
Wednesdays; 2 pm – 5.30 pm on Sundays & Bank Holiday
Mondays; 24 March to 30 October.
Admission fee Adults £2.60; Children £1.30.

Mottistone has a cleverly designed modern garden on a difficult site – steep and narrow. Much has been terraced and enclosed to allow a rose garden and good herbaceous borders. Most of the rest is given to a wide variety of fruit trees, trained to make avenues and underplanted with vegetables or spring bulbs. It is a model for this type of planting, and made long before the current fashion for ornamental *potagers*.

Features Roses (mainly modern); fruit; mature conifers; good herbaceous borders; bluebells; irises; teas.

Owned by The National Trust
Number of gardeners 2
Size 2.2ha (6 acres)

North Court

SHORWELL PO30 3JG

Tel & Fax 01983 740415
Location 4 miles south-west of Newport, off B3323.
Opening hours For National Gardens Scheme & by
appointment.

The Harrison family which owns North Court inherited fine grounds with some magnificent trees and a clear stream at the bottom. John Harrison has extensively replanted it with a plantsman's enthusiasm and a special interest in tender exotica. Definitely a garden to watch in future.

Features Woodland garden; sub-tropical plants; roses (ancient & modern); plantsman's collection of plants; fruit; good herbaceous borders; large plane trees; B & B for garden-lovers; new subtropical walled garden (1998); refreshments.

Owned by Mr & Mrs John Harrison

Nunwell House

BRADING, RYDE PO36 0JQ

Tel 01983 407240
Location Signed off A3055, 1 mile to the west of Brading.
Opening hours 1 pm – 5 pm; 26 & 27 May; then
Monday – Wednesday from 1 July to 4 September. Plus
2 pm – 5 pm on 2 June for National Gardens Scheme.
Admission fee Gardens only: £2.50.

The garden at Nunwell, with its peaceful views across the Solent, dates back to about 1600. The walled garden was built about 100 years later and still has its original paths, flanked by excellent double herbaceous borders. Vernon Russell-Smith planted a small arboretum about 30 years ago. The present owners have added some highly attractive garden ornaments and are restoring the fabric and the plantings after some years of neglect. The mass of 'Frensham' roses and the long stone steps lined with lavender are two of the more striking features. Work continues.

Features Roses (old-fashioned and modern); a plantsman's collection of plants; herbs; a fine collection of trees; statuary; 50m border of 'Frensham' roses.

Owned by Colonel & Mrs J.A. Aylmer
Number of gardeners owners, plus ½
Size 2.2ha (6 acres)
English Heritage grade II

Osborne House

EAST COWES PO32 6JY

Tel 01983 200022   **Fax** 01983 281380
Website www.english-heritage.org.uk
Location Follow the brown tourist signs.
Opening hours 10 am – 6 pm (5 pm in October); daily; April to October.
Admission fee Garden only: Adults £4; Concessions £3; Children £2.

Prince Albert laid out the stupendous Italianate terraces between this elegant Florentine palace and the parkland below. Starting in 1847, he embellished the terraces with balustrades, urns, steps, statues and fountains, all based on designs he had seen in northern and central Italy. The seasonal displays of massed bedding are still impressive, especially as they reach their peak in April-May and September-October: they employ period plants and Victorian designs. In the park are many fine trees, including a great avenue of cedars and a fastigiate form of *Cupressus macrocarpa* planted by Queen Victoria. The walled kitchen garden has recently been restored to use: English Heritage has repaired the wall and the old glasshouses, reinstated the original paths, started to train fruit trees against the walls (including 'Lane's Prince Albert' apples), and filled the beds with vegetables and flowers for cutting. Heritage vegetables and fruit are grown organically at the royal children's gardens surrounding Swiss Cottage.

Features Italianate terraces; working walled garden – cut flowers & fruit; Victorian pleasure gardens; English Heritage shop; tea-room.

Owned by English Heritage
Number of gardeners 10
Size 20ha (50 acres)
English Heritage grade II*

Ventnor Botanic Garden

UNDERCLIFF DRIVE, VENTNOR PO38 1UL

Tel 01983 855397   **Fax** 01983 856154
Website www.botanic.co.uk
Location 1½ miles west of Ventnor on A3055.
Opening hours Dawn – dusk; daily; all year. Temperate House & plant sales open 10 am – 5 pm; Visitor Centre open 10 am – 6 pm.
Admission fee Garden: free. Small charge to visit Temperate House. Car-parking charges.

Originally an offshoot of Hilliers Nursery, the Ventnor Botanic Garden is devoted to exotic plants. It is not strictly a *botanic* garden, but it has a remarkable collection. Many of the plants – perhaps most – are from the southern hemisphere but flourish in the unique microclimate of the Undercliff: widdringtonias from Zimbabwe and Tasmanian olearias, for instance, as well as astelias, *Sophora microphylla* and *Griselinia lucida* from New Zealand. *Geranium maderense* has naturalised on the sunny slopes and so has an amazing colony of 4m *Echium pininana*. Elsewhere are such Mediterranean natives as acanthus, cistus and *Coronilla valentina*, and a remarkable area called the Palm Garden, where stately foliage-plants like yuccas, cordylines, phormiums and beschornerias are underplanted with watsonias, cannas and kniphofias. Almost destroyed by the gales of 1987 and 1990, the collections were rapidly re-made and the garden now looks wonderfully vigorous again. Last year (2001) saw some extensive re-landscaping of the Mediterranean garden. The energetic head gardener has a splendid eye for planting. A magnificent new visitor centre opened recently: it offers the venue for exhibitions and a programme of events as well as a restaurant for visitors. The nursery sells some very interesting and often tender plants which are surplus to the garden's own requirements. Most are seed-raised and come from all around the world wherever there is a Mediterranean-type climate.

Features Sub-tropical plants; plantsman's collection of plants; good herbaceous borders; palms; olives; bananas; medicinal herbs from all over the world; new xerophytic garden (1998); largest collection of New Zealand plants in UK; new nursery specialising in rare plants from the garden; cafeteria & bar with snacks, tea/coffee, lunches.

Owned by Isle of Wight Council
Number of gardeners 8
Size 8.7ha (22 acres)
NCCPG National Collections *Pseudopanax*

KENT

Kent is thick with good gardens and nurseries: the Garden of England has the oldest market gardens in the country. These were developed in the 16th century to supply fresh fruit and vegetables to the fast-growing population of London: the men of Kent filled their barges up with the capital's night soil on the return journey and applied this bounty to their orchards. Kent has long been a rich county, not only because of its soil and climate, but also because many Londoners have traditionally spent the fortunes they made in the City on the acquisition of houses and gardens there. The exceptional number of arboreta and record-sized trees in Kent testifies to its long tradition of ornamental gardening. Not only does it have an exceptional number of important historic gardens, but all six of those which are rated Grade I by English Heritage are open regularly to the public – Godington, Hever, Knole, Penshurst, Scotney and Sissinghurst. Many of the other graded gardens are also open throughout the summer – among them are Chartwell, Emmets, Goodnestone, Leeds Castle, Port Lympne, and Walmer Castle. It is however a matter of regret to garden-historians that the owners of Long Barn have decided not to open it again in 2002: Long Barn was the first English garden of Harold Nicolson and Vita Sackville-West, where the strong designs and exuberant plantings of Sissinghurst were first worked out. Kent's historic gardens are supplemented by fine modern ones with important horticultural collections: the national pinetum at Bedgebury, for example, and the stupendous fruit collections at Brogdale. The gardens at Yalding, Broadview and Cabbages & Kings are important examples respectively of organic gardening, a teaching garden and good modern design. The National Gardens Scheme thrives in Kent. Gardens and gardening flourish in every town and village: a great number of good garden centres and nurseries exist to satisfy the demand for plants. The nurseries include some of the leading specialists in their field: Brenda Hyatt, for example, has won many awards over the years for her auriculas, while Downderry Nursery (another regular at RHS shows in season) has National Collections of lavender and rosemary. The RHS runs lectures at Bedgebury and Cabbages & Kings and, in particular, at Hadlow College which is one of its Partner Colleges.

Bedgebury National Pinetum

GOUDHURST, CRANBROOK TN17 2SL

Tel 01580 211044 **Fax** 01580 212423
Website www.forestry.gov.uk
Location 1 mile east of A21 at Flimwell on B2079.
Opening hours 10 am – dusk; daily; all year.
Admission fee Adults £3; OAPs £2.50; Children £1.50.
RHS members free from January to March and from
October to December.

Bedgebury Pinetum is the national conifer
collection: the International Dendrological
Research Institute considers it the best
conifer collection in the world. It was
founded as a joint venture between the
Forestry Commission and the Royal Botanic
Gardens at Kew: the first plants for the
pinetum were raised at Kew in 1921 and
planted out at Bedgebury four years later.
The collection boasts of over 2,300 different
species or cultivars growing in landscaped
woodland around a series of lakes and
streams. But Bedgebury is not just for
conifer lovers. The woodland garden is also
well known for its deciduous trees: it has
fine collections of oaks and maples, azaleas
and rhododendrons. A new Japanese glade
was added in 1996. Bedgebury is also good
for its autumn colour and one of the best
places we know for a winter walk. The new
plantings are promising.

Features Mature conifers;
rhododendrons; fungi; new Japanese
maple glade; 18 record tree species,
including two broadleaves; tea-room.

Owned by Forestry Commission
Number of gardeners 6
Size 100ha (250 acres)
NCCPG National Collections *Chamaecyparis lawsoniana*
cvs.; *Juniperus*; *Taxus*; *Thuja*; × *Cupressocyparis*
English Heritage grade II*

Belmont Park

BELMONT, THROWLEY, FAVERSHAM
ME13 0HH

Tel 01795 890202
Location Signed from A251 at Badlesmere.
Opening hours 2 pm – 5 pm; Saturdays, Sundays & Bank
Holiday Mondays; 30 March to 30 September.
Admission fee Garden: Adults £2.75; Children £1.

Quiet parkland and the relics of a 200-year
old arboretum surround this handsome
Samuel Wyatt house. The pleasure gardens
are so obviously for the pleasure of the
owners, not for display, that they add
considerably to the sense of domesticity: a
rock garden, a rose garden, and a
Coronation Avenue planted in 1953 of
chestnut and walnut. The old kitchen
garden was restored for the millennium.

Features Rock garden; shell grotto;
rhododendrons; pinetum; teas.

Owned by The Harris (Belmont) Charity
Number of gardeners 3
Size 16ha (40 acres)
English Heritage grade II

J. Bradshaw & Son

BUSHEYFIELDS NURSERY, HERNE,
HERNE BAY CT6 7LJ

Tel & Fax 01227 375415
Location 2 miles south of Herne on A291.
Opening hours 10 am – 5 pm; Tuesday – Saturday &
Bank Holidays; March to October. And by appointment.
Admission fee free. Tours by appointment.

This small family nursery (established in
1910) specialises in clematis, wisteria,
honeysuckles and other climbing wall-
plants – ivies, roses, jasmines and shrubs

which adapt well to walls, including fremontodendrons, garryas and raphiolepsis. Until recently, the nursery had National Collections of climbing honeysuckles (*Lonicera*) and *Clematis montana* cultivars, and this interest is reflected in its excellent list. Many of the species and cultivars it offers are unique to it and not available elsewhere in the British Isles – *Lonicera pilosa* CD&R 1216 and *L.* 'Simonet', for example.

Broadview Gardens

HADLOW, TONBRIDGE TN11 0AL

Tel 01732 850551   **Fax** 01732 853207
Location Signed from A26, 3 miles north-east of Tonbridge.
Opening hours 10 am – 5 pm; daily; April to October.
Admission fee Adults £2; Children free. RHS members free in September & October.

These new gardens attached to Hadlow College include a series of model designs and plantings which are intended to help students to learn the skills of garden design and horticulture. They are, of course, extremely interesting and inspiring for ordinary visitors: they include a sub-tropical garden, a low-maintenance garden, long herbaceous borders, a Japanese garden and a cottage garden. The college also has a good garden centre.

Owned by Hadlow College
Size 3.2ha (8 acres)
NCCPG National Collections *Anemone* (Japanese); *Helleborus*

Brogdale

BROGDALE ROAD, FAVERSHAM ME13 8XZ

Tel 01795 535286   **Fax** 01795 531710
Website www.brogdale.org.uk
Location 1 mile south-west of Faversham.
Opening hours 9.30 am – 5.30 pm; daily; spring & summer. 10 am – 4.30 pm; daily; winter. Closed on Mondays & Tuesdays from 1 January to Easter.
Admission fee Adults £4.50; OAPs £3.50; Children £2. RHS members free from Easter to November.

Brogdale describes itself as 'a living museum' and claims to have the largest collection of fruit cultivars in the world: more than 2,300 apples, 400 pears and 360 plums. There are demonstrations, exhibitions, workshops and events throughout the year. Fruit from the collections is sold, and scion wood supplied.

Features Hardy fruit of every kind – the biggest collection in Europe; excellent shop with rare fruit varieties for sale in season; light lunches & teas.

Owned by Brogdale Horticultural Trust
Size 12ha (30 acres)
NCCPG National Collections apples, including cider & ornamental *Malus*; pears; plums; cherries; bush fruits; blackcurrants, other currants & gooseberries; cobnuts & filberts; strawberries; vines

Chartwell

WESTERHAM TN16 1PS

Tel 01732 866368   **Fax** 01732 868193
Website www.nationaltrust.org.uk
Location A25 to Westerham then signed from B2026.
Opening hours 11 am – 5 pm; Wednesday – Sunday & Bank Holiday Mondays (plus Tuesdays in July & August); 23 March to 3 November.

Admission fee House & Gardens: Adults £5.60; Children £2.80.

The spacious and extensive gardens are well laid out and planted in a slightly old-fashioned style. One of the rose gardens has the variety 'Winston Churchill' but every part has a deep sense of history and all is maintained to a very high standard.

 Features Roses (mainly modern); National Trust shop; restaurant.

Owned by The National Trust
Number of gardeners 5
Size 33ha (81 acres)
English Heritage grade II*

Church Hill Cottage Gardens

CHARING HEATH, ASHFORD
TN27 0BU

Tel & Fax 01233 712522
Location Church Hill is in the middle of Charing Heath.
Opening hours 10 am – 5 pm; Tuesday – Sunday & Bank Holidays; February to September.
Admission fee £2

This is a true cottage garden nursery. It specialises in hardy herbaceous perennials, but there are many dianthus, alpines, hostas, violas, ferns and shrubs to choose from too. The garden has six distinct areas and some island beds but they are unified by the profusion of cottage plants, bulbs, alpine and herbaceous plantings in each of them. Ornamental trees like birches give added structure, and there is a pretty woodland area with yet more interesting plantings.

 Features Cottage garden plants; dianthus; good borders.

Owned by Mr & Mrs M. Metianu
Number of gardeners 2
Size 0.6ha (1½ acres)

Copton Ash Gardens

105 ASHFORD ROAD, FAVERSHAM
ME13 8XW

Tel 01795 535919
Location On A251, opposite M2 eastbound exit.
Opening hours 2 pm – 6 pm; Tuesday – Sundays. And by appointment.
Admission fee free to nursery visitors.

This is a first-rate plantsman's garden, attached to a nursery specialising in real rarities. Started in 1978, the garden now has over 3,000 different plants growing in 1½ acres – the fruit of Tim Ingram's constant quest for new things to try out. His interests can be seen in the large collection of rare Mediterranean plants, a fascinating collection of umbellifers (many of them new to cultivation) and good plants from the Southern Hemisphere which he tests for hardiness. Recent developments include extensive plantings of small bulbs like snowdrops, cyclamen and crocus (species only – no hybrids) and the best woodland perennials, especially hellebores, erythroniums and trilliums. The nursery is excellent, offering the best of these rarities, and with a catalogue that is based on Tim Ingram's own observations, not the recycled nursery-speak of others.

 Features Important collection of dryland plants of every kind.

Owned by Tim & Gillian Ingram
Number of gardeners 1½
Size 0.6ha (1½ acres)

Doddington Place Gardens

SITTINGBOURNE ME9 0BB

Tel & Fax 01795 886101
Location Follow brown tourist signs from A2.
Opening hours 10.30 am – 5 pm; Tuesday – Thursday & Bank Holiday Mondays; Easter to September. And 2 pm – 5 pm on Sundays.
Admission fee Adults £3.50; Children 75p.

The house and garden both date back to the 1860s: Markham Nesfield had a hand in the original formal gardens. The handsome *Sequoiadendron giganteum* and billowing yew hedges are also 19th-century, but this is a garden to which every generation has added something. From the Edwardian era dates the rock garden of local stone: cyclamen have naturalised all through it. The woodland garden was developed in the 1960s on a small outcrop of greensand: rhododendrons, camellias, styrax, eucryphias and maples flourish here as nowhere nearby. More recent are a paved rose garden (*very* pretty), an avenue of *Sorbus aucuparia* 'Beissneri' planted for its winter bark, and excellent colour borders (red and white). And the present owners are adding architectural features and new plantings with great verve.

Features Woodland gardens (4 acres); magnificent lumpy yew hedges; fine old wellingtonias; rhododendrons & azaleas.

Owned by Mr & Mrs R. Oldfield
Number of gardeners 2, plus 2 part-time
Size 4ha (10 acres)
English Heritage grade II

Downderry Nursery

PILLAR BOX LANE, HADLOW, TONBRIDGE TN11 9SW

Tel 01732 810081   **Fax** 01732 811398
Website www.downderry-nursery.co.uk
Location Follow Tourist signs off A26 north-east of Hadlow.
Opening hours 10 am – 5 pm; daily; May to November.
Admission fee Free. Tours available at £5 per adult.

This nursery in an old walled garden has the widest imaginable list of lavender and rosemary cultivars. Almost all the species are here, including the most unusual ones, and a wide number of hybrids and selections, some of them bred or chosen by the owner Dr Charlesworth himself. His exhibits at the major RHS summer shows have been a source of inspiration to many gardeners, and hurried them to visit his nursery, where his display garden has come together very well. Customers speak well of the quality of his plants.

Features Lavender & rosemary.

Owned by Dr Simon J. Charlesworth
Size 0.4ha (1 acre)
NCCPG National Collections *Lavandula*; *Rosmarinus*

Edenbridge House

MAIN ROAD, EDENBRIDGE TN8 6SJ

Tel 01732 862122   **Fax** 01732 867385
Location On B2026, 1½ miles north of Edenbridge, near Marlpit Hill.
Opening hours 2 pm – 6 pm; 14 & 28 April, 5 May, 9 June, 7 & 14 July, & 22 September. Plus 1 pm – 5 pm on 15 May & 19 September, & 6 pm – 9 pm on 12 June. Plus 2 pm – 5 pm; Tuesdays & Thursdays; April to September. And groups by appointment.

Admission fee Adults £2.50; Children 25p.

This 1930s garden has been renewed and replanted by the present owner as a series of garden rooms to offer something of interest at every season. The spacious terraces are home to a rich mix of tender plants, many of them put out in pots for the summer months. A stream with bog plants along its edges runs down to a small pool. In the kitchen garden is a fine greenhouse and small collection of ornamental trees, as well as apples and an appetising vegetable garden.

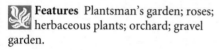 **Features** Plantsman's garden; roses; herbaceous plants; orchard; gravel garden.

Owned by Mrs M.T. Lloyd
Number of gardeners owners, plus 3 part-timers
Size 2ha (5 acres)

Emmetts Garden

IDE HILL, SEVENOAKS TN14 6AY

Tel 01732 750367   **Fax** 01732 750490
Website www.nationaltrust.org.uk
Location Between Sundridge & Ide Hill off B2042.
Opening hours 11 am – 5 pm (last ticket 4.15 pm); Wednesday – Sunday & Bank Holiday Mondays; 23 March to 30 June. Then Wednesdays, Saturdays, Sundays & Bank Holidays from 3 June to 3 November.
Admission fee Adults £3.50; Children £1.75.

A stiff walk up (or buggy ride) from the car-park brings you to this windswept hilltop garden, laid out in Edwardian times and maintained on a slim budget. The formal Italianate rose garden is pretty in July, but better still is the informal woodland garden laid out with trees and shrubs in the William Robinson style. Good in the autumn, but perhaps best in bluebell time.

 Features Rock garden; bluebells; Italianate rose garden; rare trees and shrubs; autumn colour; azaleas; tea-room.

Owned by The National Trust
Number of gardeners 2
Size 7ha (18½ acres)
English Heritage grade II

Godington Park

ASHFORD TN23 3BP

Tel & Fax 01233 632652
Location Godington Lane, Potters Corner A20.
Opening hours 2 pm – 5.30 pm; Thursday – Monday; 16 March to 6 October. House opens on 29 March.
Admission fee Adults £2; Children £1. House extra.

Godington is the prettiest house in Kent, a Jacobean mansion reworked in the 1920s by Sir Reginald Blomfield who advised on the garden for over 20 years. The charming Italian garden is his: statues, loggia, summerhouse, box-edged quincunx and Italian cypresses. The magnificent yew hedge – said to be the longest in the country – dates from his first plantings in the 1900s: Dutch gables have been cut along its top to match the architecture of the house. Elsewhere are an avenue of sorbus and cherry, a sunken pool, a formal rose garden, herbaceous borders, sweeping lawns and an 18th-century park. The trees include a pair of *Prunus* 'Tai Haku' (one of them reputed to be the largest in the country) and a vast specimen of the tulip tree (*Liriodendron tulipifera*). Planting continues: the owners are keen plantsmen and have for many years been making the woodland garden. Part of the walled garden has just been planted as a wildflower mix with common arable flowers, like cornflowers, corn marigold and corn cockle. Meanwhile the Delphinium Society has planted a border with rare cultivars and there is a growing collection of *Clematis montana* cultivars, taken over from the Kent nursery of J. Bradshaw & Sons. And the reason that the garden opens several weeks before the house is so that visitors can see the daffodils and fritillaries: the owners have their priorities right.

 Features Topiary; daffodils; formal Italianate garden; waterlilies; redesigned rose garden (2002).

Owned by The Godington House Preservation Trust
Number of gardeners 3
Size 5ha (12 acres)
English Heritage grade I

Goodnestone Park

WINGHAM, CANTERBURY CT3 1PL

Tel & Fax 01304 840107
Website www.kenttourism.co.uk/goodnestone
Location Follow brown tourist signs from B2046.
Opening hours 11 am – 5 pm; Mondays, Wednesday – Friday; 25 March to 25 October. Plus 12 noon – 6 pm on Sundays from 31 March to 20 October.
Admission fee Adults £3.30; OAPs £2.80; Children (under 12) 50p; Disabled in wheelchairs £1; Group (20+) £2.80; Guided Group £4.50. RHS members free in April, May & September.

Goodnestone is a handsome Palladian building. Jane Austen's brother married a daughter of the house: she will have known the fine chestnut avenue dating from about 1800 and the 18th-century parkland beyond. Later came the formal 19th-century terraces around the house, a 1930s woodland garden (maples, camellias, azaleas, cornus), a 1980s holly walk, and good mixed plantings in the old kitchen garden. A formal parterre in early 18th-century style has just been replanted in front of the house, to celebrate

the millennium. Now the woodland garden is being expanded to take in another three acres which will be planted as an arboretum. It is inspired by the passionate plantsmanship which has imbued the present owners since they first started to garden here nearly 50 years ago. Much of the garden is accessible by wheelchair, but not all.

 Features Woodland garden; topiary; snowdrops; roses (mainly old-fashioned); good herbaceous borders; cedar walk; rhododendrons; teas.

Owned by Lord & Lady FitzWalter
Number of gardeners 2 full-time, 2 part-time
Size 5.6ha (14 acres)
English Heritage grade II*

Great Comp

ST MARY'S PLATT, BOROUGH GREEN, SEVENOAKS TN15 8QS

Tel 01732 886154
Website www.greatcomp.co.uk
Location 2 miles east of Borough Green: take B2016 off A20.
Opening hours 11 am – 6 pm; daily; April to October.
Admission fee Adults £3.50; Children £1.

Great Comp is a monument to the energy and enthusiasm of Eric Cameron who has built up the garden over the last 40 years. The plant content is of considerable horticultural interest and includes some 30 magnolia cultivars and a good range of rhododendrons, conifers, heathers and herbaceous plants: over 3,000 different plants in all. But the most interesting thing about the garden is the way in which large areas have been planted for minimum maintenance. There is much to learn and admire here.

Features Woodland garden; plantsman's collection of plants; good herbaceous borders; ground cover; dwarf conifers; salvias; gifts, plants and souvenirs; refreshments.

Owned by Great Comp Charitable Trust
Number of gardeners 3
Size 2.8ha (7 acres)

Groombridge Place Gardens

GROOMBRIDGE, TUNBRIDGE WELLS TN3 9QG

Tel 01892 863999   **Fax** 01892 863996
Location On B2110, 4 miles south-west of Tunbridge Wells.
Opening hours 9 am – 6 pm; daily; 29 March to 24 October.
Admission fee Adults £8; OAPs £7; Children £6.50.

Groombridge has lots to offer: a drunken garden where the yews lean at tipsy angles, an oriental garden, a 'draughtsman's garden' and a chessboard garden. Ivan Hicks has been at work in the 'Enchanted Forest', where the gardens are said to be 'interactive'. Best of all are the brilliant colour plantings, among the best we know. But the entry price is high, and some may question whether the garden offers good value.

 Features Good colour plantings; gift shops; light lunches & teas.

Hever Castle

EDENBRIDGE TN8 7NG

Tel 01732 865224   **Fax** 01732 866796
Website www.hevercastle.co.uk
Location 3 miles south-east of Edenbridge, signed from M25 Jct 6.
Opening hours 11 am – 5 pm (4 pm in winter); daily; March to November.
Admission fee Adults £6.50; OAPs £5.60; Children £4.30.

Hever is one of the most important Edwardian gardens in England. The pretty moated castle sits in a park of oaks and firs (underplanted with rhododendrons) with a yew maze and formal neo-Tudor garden to one side. The best part is a spectacular 5-acre Italian garden where a long pergola (cool dripping fountains all along) leads past a series of exquisite Italian gardens, stuffed with outstanding sculptures, urns, sarcophagi and other loot brought by William Waldorf Astor from Rome; it finally bursts onto a theatrical terrace and a 35-acre lake, hand-dug by 800 workmen in less than two years.

 Features Woodland garden; topiary; 3,000 roses (old-fashioned and modern, with some climbers too); rhododendrons & azaleas; snowdrops; crocus; daffodils; bluebells; tulips; dahlias; autumn colour; Christie's/HHA Garden of the Year in 1995; plant centre; shop; two restaurants.

Owned by Broadland Properties Ltd
Number of gardeners 10
Size 16ha (40 acres)
English Heritage grade I

Hole Park

ROLVENDEN, CRANBROOK TN17 4JB

Tel 01580 241344 **Fax** 01580 241882
Location Off B2086 between Rolvenden & Cranbrook.
Opening hours 2 pm – 6 pm; 14 & 28 April; 5 & 19 May;
2 & 16 June; 21 July (Hardy Plant Society summer plant
fair); 13 & 20 October. Plus Mondays & Wednesdays in
April, May, June & October. Guided tours & groups by
appointment.
Admission fee Adults £3.50; Children 50p.

This great garden is far too little known. The
drive runs under an avenue of horse
chestnuts through classical parkland with
wonderful views. The pleasure garden is
Edwardian in origin, but has been revived
and replanted by the present owner. Solid
hedges and clipped specimens of yew are
everywhere: backing the excellent
herbaceous borders, around the waterlily
pond and framing a croquet lawn with
standard wisterias. The flowery woodlands
have palm trees in the dell, surrounded by
purple rhododendrons and orange azaleas.
Daffodils abound in April and the millions
of bluebells in the woodland walk never
cease to astonish in early May. Autumn
colours are good, too.

Features Good design and good
plants; new millennium water garden;
plant stall on Sundays.

Owned by David Barham
Number of gardeners 2
Size 6ha (15 acres)

Iden Croft Herbs

FRITTENDEN ROAD, STAPLEHURST
TN12 0DH

Tel 01580 891432
Website www.herbs-uk.com
Location Signed from A229, south of Staplehurst.
Opening hours 9 am – 5 pm; Monday – Saturday; all
year. 11 am – 5 pm; Sundays & Bank Holidays; March to
September only.
Admission fee Adults £2; Concessions £1.50;
Children 50p.

The owners have developed this substantial
nursery over the last 30 years and planted a
series of demonstration gardens. These
incorporate a 16th-century walled garden,
originally attached to Staplehurst Manor.
Other gardens include a cottage garden near
the café, and a 'sensory garden' which shows
how herbs may be arranged and appreciated
for their scent, colour, shape, form and
texture. The intention is to provide design
and planting ideas for all visitors, whatever
the size of their garden. Insects and birds are
encouraged and the catalogue which the
nursery produces lists plants under both
their Latin and common English names.

 Features New medicinal herb garden
(2001).

Owned by David & Rosemary Titterington
Number of gardeners 2
Size 0.6ha (1½ acres)
NCCPG National Collections Mentha; Origanum

Ightham Mote

IVY HATCH, SEVENOAKS TN15 0NT

Tel 01732 810378 **Fax** 01732 811029
Website www.nationaltrust.org.uk
Location Signed from A25 in Ightham village.

Opening hours 10 am – 5.30 pm; daily except Tuesdays & Saturdays; 24 April to 3 November.
Admission fee Adults £5.40; Children £2.70.

Ightham is a moated mediaeval manor in a wooded Kentish valley, with borders of pinks, old roses and lilies. These were re-made about 100 years ago in a dreamily English style. In the woodland parts are thicketed rhododendrons.

Features Woodland garden; National Trust shop; light refreshments.

Owned by The National Trust
Number of gardeners 3
Size 5.6ha (14 acres)
English Heritage grade II

Keepers Nursery

GALLANTS COURT, EAST FARLEIGH, MAIDSTONE ME15 0LE

Tel & Fax 01622 726465
Location At East Farleigh, 4 miles west of Maidstone, on B2010.
Opening hours By appointment at all reasonable times.

Less than 20 years old, Keepers is now the leading fruit tree nursery in the UK. It offers over 600 cultivars – apples, pears, plums and cherries, as well as the more unusual fruits like quince, medlars and mulberries. The owners have an excellent on-line ordering facility and a wide choice of rootstocks. They claim – proudly and correctly – to have made a significant contribution to the conservation of old cultivars of fruit. More than 100 of their apples are not available from any other commercial source.

Ladham House

GOUDHURST TN17 1DB

Tel 01580 212674
Location Left at Chequers Inn on Cranbrook road, then right to Curtisden Green.
Opening hours 1.30 pm – 5.30 pm; 21 April & 19 May. And by appointment.
Admission fee Adults £2.50; Children (under 12) 50p.

Ladham was laid out by a botanist Master of the Rolls in the mid-19th century, and has been enthusiastically restored and updated by the present owner. There is a good mixture of new plantings and old: the latter include the deep red form of *Magnolia campbellii* which has been named 'Betty Jessel' and is now available commercially.

Features Woodland garden; good herbaceous borders; fine collection of trees; magnolias; new 200m ha-ha (1998); new 'hot' garden (2000); teas.

Owned by Alastair Jessel
Number of gardeners 2
Size 4ha (10 acres)

Leeds Castle

MAIDSTONE ME17 1PL

Tel 01622 765400 **Fax** 01622 735616
Website www.leeds-castle.com
Location Jct 8 off the M20.
Opening hours 10 am – 5 pm, March to October; 10 am – 3 pm, November to February. Closed on 29 June, 6 July & 25 December)
Admission fee Castle, park & gardens: Adults £11; OAPs & Students £9.50; Children £7.50. £1.50 off all prices in winter.

More a romantic castle than a garden, Leeds is best seen across the lake (the 'Great Water') which Russell Page created in the 1930s. Page also designed and planted the Culpeper Garden, which takes its name partly from Sir Thomas Colepeper, who bought the castle in 1632, and partly from Nicholas Culpeper, the 17th-century herbalist. It could be said that the Culpeper Garden does not show the 20th century's greatest garden designer at his best: informal plantings of old garden flowers – roses, pinks, lavender, poppies and lupins. Here too is the National Collection of bergamot (*Monarda*) cultivars. The latest development is the 'Lady Baillie Garden', a series of sheltered terraces between the Culpeper Garden and the lake. In this part of the garden the planting is more Mediterranean in character. The nearby maze, planted in 1988, is fun to visit: it resembles a topiary castle with towers and bastions and, when you get to its centre, you find the entrance to an underground grotto. The 'wood garden' is planted with rhododendrons and azaleas and underplanted with daffodils and anemones and there are further rhododendrons to the west of the moat. The greenhouses, built about 1900, include a fuchsia display and a nectarine house. Leeds is run by a high profile charitable trust with a big advertising budget, which may help to explain the high entry charges. Are they worth it for someone who is principally interested in gardens and plants? The answer – paradoxically – is yes, provided you also visit the castle and some of the many other attractions here. The owners say you need at least three hours to experience and enjoy them properly.

 Features Woodland garden; roses (mainly old-fashioned); herbs; good herbaceous borders; vineyard; tallest *Acer cappadocicum* 'Aureum' (23m) in the British

Isles; plant centre; refreshments in the 17th-century tithe barn.

Owned by Leeds Castle Foundation
Number of gardeners 20
NCCPG National Collections *Monarda*
English Heritage grade II*

Madrona Nursery

PLUCKLEY ROAD, BETHERSDEN
TN26 3DD

Tel 01233 820100   **Fax** 01233 820091
Location Half way between Bethersden village & Pluckley railway station.
Opening hours 10 am – 5 pm; Saturday – Tuesday; mid-March to end October.

This is a first-rate general nursery, with a good choice of unusual cultivars across the range. Trees and shrubs are perhaps its main speciality – it is particularly strong on hydrangeas, *Aesculus* and unusual conifers like Prince Albert's yew (*Saxegothea conspicua*) – but Madrona also offers a fine choice of herbaceous perennials. All are well-grown and well-displayed: a thoroughly satisfying nursery to visit.

Marle Place Gardens

BRENCHLEY, TONBRIDGE TN12 7HS

Tel 01892 722304   **Fax** 01892 724099
Location Follow tourist signs from Brenchley.
Opening hours 10 am – 5 pm; daily; 1 April to 7 October. And by appointment.
Admission fee Adults £4; Concessions £3.50.

The gardens around the Jacobean house are mainly formal. They were imaginatively designed and planted in the 1930s and have

been well preserved and improved by the present owners over many years. The sunken garden, laid out with scented plants, is particularly charming. The Victorian greenhouse (recently restored) holds a collection of orchids. Recent additions include some fun sculptures, a 'mosaic terrace', a *potager*, avenues running into the wildlife woodland and a young nut 'plat.' And all around are orchards of Kentish apples.

 Features Good herbaceous borders; some unusual plants; a Victorian gazebo; an Edwardian rock garden; tea, coffee & cake.

Owned by Mrs Lindel Williams
Number of gardeners 2
Size 6ha (15 acres)

Penshurst Place

PENSHURST, TONBRIDGE TN11 8DG

Tel 01892 870307　**Fax** 01892 879866
Website www.penshurstplace.com
Location Follow brown tourist signs from Tonbridge.
Opening hours 10.30 am – 6 pm, Saturday & Sunday, 2 to 23 March; then daily, 23 March to 3 November.
Admission fee Gardens only: Adult £5; OAPs £4.50; Children £4. RHS members free in April, September & October.

(P) (WC) (&) (⊞) (☕)

This is an historic garden of great importance: it has substantial genuine Tudor remains. Nevertheless, much of what we see now was developed in the mid-19th century as a re-creation of the ideal Elizabethan garden, divided into small self-contained garden rooms each with its own style and character. They have been well restored and developed in recent years. A vast Italianate parterre dominates the immediate pleasure garden: it is planted with scarlet polyantha roses – another is planted as a Union Jack. There are borders by Lanning Roper and John Codrington, a 100m bed of peonies, and a garden for the blind, bought off the peg at the Chelsea Flower Show in 1994. One impressive statistic: the garden has over one mile of yew hedging.

 Features Roses (mainly modern & climbers); daffodils; good herbaceous borders; formal Italian garden; spring bulbs; plant centre; tea-room.

Owned by Viscount De L'Isle
Number of gardeners 6
Size 4.2ha (11 acres)
English Heritage grade I

Plaxtol Nurseries

THE SPOUTE, PLAXTOL, SEVENOAKS TN15 0QR

Tel 01732 810550　**Fax** 01732 810149
Website www.plaxtol-nurseries.co.uk
Location On the east side of Plaxtol, off A227.
Opening hours Nursery open 10 am – 5 pm, daily. Closed for a fortnight after Christmas. Gardens open by appointment.

(P) (WC) (&) (❀)

This excellent family-run garden nursery offers about 1,500 different plants, with an emphasis on flowers and foliage for flower arrangers. The main garden reflects this interest and sets out to produce the effects that you would achieve in different flower arrangements: a series of small garden rooms in widely contrasting styles. There is also a small garden made in the Japanese style: the family's other speciality is Japanese plants and garden ornaments. The nursery has a good website.

Owned by Donald, Tessa & Jenny Forbes
Size 0.2ha (½ acre)

Port Lympne

LYMPNE, HYTHE CT21 4PD

Tel 01303 264647   **Fax** 01303 264944
Location Exit 11 on M20 & follow brown tourist signs.
Opening hours 10 am – 5 pm in summer; 10 am – 4 pm in winter; daily except 24 December.
Admission fee Adults £9.80; OAPs & Children £7.80.

More than a zoo, Port Lympne is a stylish and luxurious house, with a seriously important 20th-century garden. It was laid out by Philip Tilden for Sir Philip Sassoon in 1911 on the steepest of slopes above Romney Marshes and worked on by Russell Page in the 1950s. The modern approach is nothing if not dramatic – an absolutely straight 100m walk lined with hydrangeas which brings you suddenly to the top of the stupendous long stone staircase known as the Trojan stairs. Around the front door is a forecourt with 13 statues acquired from the sale at Stowe, in Buckinghamshire, in 1921; castellations in the yew hedges give views to the south. The slopes are terraced into five levels and include a vineyard and 'figyard'. The chess board garden – oblong rather than square – has squares of grass and gravel contrasted with beds for bulbs and annual displays: it is matched by a 'striped' garden on the other side of the main terrace. Down one side are the Long Borders, planted as mixtures of shrubs and perennials, and leading to the magnolia walk, the bowling green, the rose terrace, the dahlia terrace and the herbaceous border. Standards of maintenance remain high: a good garden for grandparents who want to see something more than animals.

 Features Topiary; good herbaceous borders; bedding out; dahlias; shop; restaurant.

Owned by Howletts & Port Lympne Estates Ltd
Number of gardeners 6
Size 6.2ha (15½ acres)

Riverhill House Gardens

SEVENOAKS TN15 0RR

Tel 01732 452557   **Fax** 01732 458802
Location 2 miles south of Sevenoaks on A225.
Opening hours 12 noon – 6 pm; Wednesdays & Sundays, plus Bank Holiday weekends; Easter to June.
Admission fee Garden only: Adults £3; Children 50p. House open by appointment to groups.

Riverhill is a handsome Queen Anne house with grand views over the Weald: the garden suffered badly in the Great Storm of 1987. In the middle of the 19th century it belonged to John Rogers the botanist, who planted many of the surviving conifers and specimen trees. The vast billowing rhododendrons include original introductions by Hooker and Fortune. Rogers's descendants made the rock garden and rose walk.

Features Rhododendrons & azaleas; mature conifers; bluebells; tallest *Magnolia* × *soulangeana* (13m) in the British Isles; small gift shop; homemade teas.

Owned by The Rogers Family
Number of gardeners 1
Size 3.2ha (8 acres)
English Heritage grade II

Rosewood Daylilies

70 DEANSWAY AVENUE, STURRY,
CANTERBURY CT2 0NN

Tel 01227 711071
Location Off to the right of Herne Bay Road, the main
road leading north out of Sturry.
Opening hours By appointment.
Admission fee free.

Here is a splendid place to see more than
600 different daylilies, especially those bred
and introduced since 1970. These include
many of the hundreds of modern American
hybrids: the owners trial new cultivars and
then offer the best for sale. The nursery's list
grows every year: a lot of cultivars with an
RHS Award of Garden Merit have recently
been added. It also offers a range of
companion plants: agapanthus (80 cvs),
crocosmias, and hardy geraniums.

 Features *Hemerocallis; Agapanthus.*

NCCPG National Collections *Hemerocallis* cultivars
post-1970

Scotney Castle Garden

LAMBERHURST, TUNBRIDGE WELLS
TN3 8JN

Tel 01892 891081   **Fax** 01892 890110
Website www.nationaltrust.org.uk
Location On A21, south of Lamberhurst.
Opening hours 11 am – 6 pm; Wednesday – Sunday &
Bank Holiday Mondays; 23 March to 3 November.
Admission fee Adults £4.40; Children £2.20.

The house was built by Salvin in the late
1830s: the quarry where they extracted the
stone for building it is now a sheltered
woodland dell. During the 19th century,
many specimen trees were added to the
parkland – cypresses, cedars and
wellingtonias; those that survived the gales
of 1987 still give structure to the gardens in
their maturity. But the slopes between the
house and the moated and abandoned castle
at the bottom are now covered with
ornamental trees and shrubs planted by
Christopher Hussey in the 1950s – among
them are many rhododendrons, azaleas,
hydrangeas, kalmias and maples. The ruined
castle is now the focus of the whole
picturesque composition and the way it has
been richly draped in wisteria, clematis,
honeysuckles and roses is both romantic and
photogenic. Among the ruins are a herb
garden and a cottage garden designed by
Lanning Roper in about 1970, surprisingly
appropriate and effective. The views of the
castle as you meander round the edge of the
moat are little short of miraculous.

Features Woodland garden;
plantsman's collection of plants;
rhododendrons; azaleas; waterlilies; wisteria;
good autumn colour; plantings in ruins of
14th-century castle; shop.

Owned by The National Trust
Number of gardeners 4
Size 8ha (20 acres)
English Heritage grade I

Sissinghurst Castle Garden

SISSINGHURST, CRANBROOK
TN17 2AB

Tel 01580 715700   **Fax** 01580 713702
Website www.nationaltrust.org.uk
Location 1 mile east of Sissinghurst village, ½ mile off
A262. Cross-country footpath from village.

Opening hours 11 am – 6.30 pm; Friday – Tuesday; 23 March to 3 November. Opens at 10 am on Saturdays, Sundays and Bank Holidays.
Admission fee Adults £6.50; Children £3.

So important, influential and well-known is Sissinghurst that it comes as a shock to realise that Harold Nicolson and Vita Sackville-West began to make the garden there as recently as 1930. Her writings made it famous right from the beginning so that it is possible to trace the history of such features as the white garden in her many books still in print. Harold Nicolson was a careful designer who understood the importance of line and measure: he was very much a classicist in taste. Vita Sackville-West was a romantic, exuberant, poetic plantswoman. It was the combination of these two complementary talents that made the garden a source of wonder and inspiration. Sissinghurst is now part of every English gardener's education, and one to which it is important to return time and again. The garden is always changing and developing. It was the Nicolsons' intention that the garden should continue to develop after they gave it to the National Trust, and this principle – that the garden must be kept up to date with new plants – is inherent in the way that it has been managed. The design is unaltered and unalterable, and the plantings continue to be governed by the Gertrude Jekyll principles of which Sissinghurst is a supremely beautiful interpretation. But the plants are always changing and Sissinghurst therefore remains an influential plantsman's garden too.

Features Roses (mainly old-fashioned); plantsman's collection of plants; herbs; good herbaceous borders; National Trust gift shop; self-service restaurant.

Owned by The National Trust
Number of gardeners 7
Size 2.2ha (5½ acres)
English Heritage grade I

Squerryes Court

WESTERHAM TN16 1SJ

Tel 01959 562345 **Fax** 01959 565949
Website www.squerryes.co.uk
Location ½ mile from A25, signed from Westerham.
Opening hours 12 noon – 5.30 pm; Wednesdays, Saturdays, Sundays & Bank Holiday Mondays; April to September.
Admission fee Garden only: Adults £3; OAPs £2.50; Children £1.50.

The gardens have been excellently restored with advice from Tom Wright since 1987, guided by a Badeslade plan of the original garden made in 1719, before they were landscaped later in the century. The main feature is a formal garden behind the house, where box-edged beds are filled with santolina, lavender, sage and other sweet-smelling herbs, alongside the beautifully planted Edwardian borders. Beyond are rose gardens and shrub borders, with rhododendrons and azaleas in the woodland, and the 18th-century park. The modern design and planting are inevitably a compromise, but Squerryes is place of great beauty and variety.

Features Parterres; topiary; roses (mainly old-fashioned); herbaceous borders; formal design; gazebo; dovecote; woodland walks; lake; small shop in house; teas.

Owned by J. & A. Warde
Number of gardeners 1, plus 2 part-time
Size 10ha (25 acres)
English Heritage grade II

Starborough Nursery

Starborough Road, Marsh
Green, Edenbridge TN8 5RB

Tel 01732 865614 **Fax** 01732 862166
Location On B2028 Edenbridge to Lingfield Road.
Opening hours 9.30 am – 4 pm; Monday – Saturday.
Closed on Wednesdays in January, July & August.

Starborough has for long been an important
nursery for its wide range of trees and
shrubs and, since it took over G. Reuthe Ltd,
in the 1990s, of rhododendrons and azaleas
too. Its list of liquidambars, cornus,
camellias and magnolias is particularly good.

Owned by Mr & Mrs C.B. Tomlin

Stoneacre

Otham, Maidstone ME15 8RS

Tel 01622 862871 **Fax** 01622 862157
Website www.nationaltrust.org.uk
Location 1 mile south of A20; north end of Otham village.
Opening hours 2 pm – 6 pm; Wednesdays & Saturdays;
23 March to 16 October.
Admission fee Adults £2.60; Children £1.30.

Stoneacre is particularly interesting because
the tenant until 2000 was Rosemary
Alexander, Principal of the English
Gardening School at the Chelsea Physic
Garden. It was where she worked out her
ideas and showed her students how the
principles of design and planting look 'on
the ground'. The new tenants intend to
preserve and develop the garden still further.
It is one of the most exciting new gardens in
southern England, and in perfect harmony
with the Tudorised house.

Features Spring bulbs; autumn
colour; strong design.

Owned by The National Trust

Tile Barn Nursery

Standen Street, Iden Green,
Benenden TN17 4LB

Tel & Fax 01580 240221
Website www.tilebarn-cyclamen.co.uk
Location 2 miles south of Benenden; turn left at
crossroads in Iden Green.
Opening hours 9 am – 5 pm, Wednesday – Saturday.

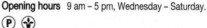

This is a splendid garden-nursery devoted to
one genus – *Cyclamen*. Cyclamen are
everywhere: they have spread through the
lawns and into the drive, as well as under the
shelter trees, shrubs and hedges. In the
glasshouses are rows and rows of every
imaginable hardy species and cultivar of
cyclamen of different ages, all pot-grown
and all of flowering size – a wonderful sight
from August to April. Visitors will also find
pots of some other unusual bulbs species,
particularly the smaller, daintier colchicums,
crocus, fritillarias, snowflakes and narcissus.

Owned by Peter & Liz Moore

Walmer Castle & Gardens

Kingsdown Road, Walmer, Deal
CT14 7LJ

Tel 01304 364288 **Fax** 01304 364826
Location Follow brown tourist signs.
Opening hours 10 am – 6 pm (5 pm in October,
& 4 pm from November to March); Wednesday – Sunday.
Closed January, February, 24-26 December & when the
Lord Warden is in residence.

Admission fee Adults £5; Concessions £3.80; Children £2.50.

The gardens at Walmer Castle are well worth a visit, partly for their horticultural interest and partly for their many historical associations – William Pitt, the Duke of Wellington and Winston Churchill were all Wardens of the Cinque Ports. The castle looks onto the Broad Walk, 100m long, on either side of a wide path backed by massive mature yew hedges (3m tall and 2m wide), and lined with fine herbaceous borders. Beyond are a croquet lawn, magnificent 19th-century terraces, and Penelope Hobhouse's new Queen Elizabeth the Queen Mother's Garden. To the north of the Broad Walk is the Kitchen Garden – an enclosed orchard with espaliered fruit trees, a cutting garden and glasshouses. Further away are drifts of daffodils, a lawnful of specimen trees planted by famous visitors from the 19th century onwards, a wildflower meadow, a thickly wooded quarry and a holm oak avenue planted in 1866.

Features Magnificent old yew hedges; new garden by Penelope Hobhouse; English Heritage shop; tea-room.

Owned by English Heritage
Number of gardeners 4
Size 3.2ha (8 acres)
English Heritage grade II

Yalding Organic Gardens

YALDING, MAIDSTONE ME18 6EX

Tel & Fax 01622 814650
Website www.hdra.org.uk
Location On B2162, ½ mile south of village.
Opening hours 10 am – 5 pm; Wednesday – Sunday; May to September. Also weekends in April & October & all Bank Holiday Mondays.
Admission fee Adults £3; Children free. RHS members free.

Yalding has a series of 14 historically themed gardens run organically by the HDRA. They include an apothecary's garden in the 13th-century style, a late-19th-century artisan's garden and a post-war allotment: all very stylish and educational. Others show the influence of William Cobbett and Gertrude Jekyll through the centuries. There is a central hop-pole pergola – a good example of how design features should come out of their surrounding landscape. A recent addition is tall wooden henge. The HDRA sets out to inspire, to educate and to give pleasure – and succeeds.

Features Gardens through the ages – modern reconstructions; café open from mid-morning to tea-time.

Owned by Henry Doubleday Research Association
Number of gardeners 4
Size 2ha (5 acres)

LANCASHIRE, GREATER MANCHESTER & MERSEYSIDE

There are few historic gardens in this industrial corner of the north-west, but several public parks whose importance is both historical and contemporary: Sefton Park in Liverpool was designed by Edouard André, Birkenhead Park by Sir Joseph Paxton, and Heaton Park in Manchester by William Emes. The public gardens at the seaside resorts of Blackpool and Southport are famous for their summer displays. Few private gardens are open to the public, though the National Gardens Scheme has in several villages managed to persuade a cluster of gardens to open simultaneously and make up a good afternoon's visiting. Myerscough College near Preston is a RHS Partner College, with lectures and workshops all through the year. It also has a National Collection of *Eryngium*. There is a handful of other National Collections in the three counties, but this is not a corner of England with any established interest in plants apart, perhaps, from alpines: Reginald Kaye at Carnforth and Holden Clough near Clitheroe are both long-established nurseries specialising in plants for cold climates.

Catforth Gardens

ROOTS LANE, CATFORTH, PRESTON
PR4 0JB

Tel 01772 690561
Location M6 Jct 32, then north up A6 & follow brown tourist signs.
Opening hours Farm gardens open 10.30 am – 5 pm; daily; April to August. Bungalow gardens open same times & dates but only Thursday – Sunday & Bank Holidays.

Admission fee Adults £2.50; OAPs £2; Children 50p. RHS members free.

Catforth Gardens incorporate the gardens of two separate but adjoining houses, those of Cherry Tree Lodge and Willow Bridge Farm. The garden around Cherry Tree Lodge is planted with trees, shrubs and herbaceous plants to give year-round colour. Rock gardens, bog gardens, ponds, woodland and island beds support a wide variety of plants, and it is home to a National Collection of *Geranium*. Willow Bridge Farm has a cottagey garden, but its main features lie in the large paddock garden, designed as a summer flower and water garden with sweeping herbaceous beds, roses, ponds and dry banks. Both gardens contain a wide variety of plants, many rare and unusual, and the nurseries specialise in the herbaceous plants which grow in them, such as phlox, crocosmias, lythrums, monardas, campanulas and agapanthus.

Owned by Judith & Tony Bradshaw
Number of gardeners 4
Size 1.2ha (3 acres)
NCCPG National Collections *Geranium*

Croxteth Hall & Country Park

CROXTETH HALL LANE, LIVERPOOL
L12 0HB

Tel 0151 228 5311   **Fax** 0151 228 2817
Location Muirhead Avenue East.
Opening hours 11 am – 5 pm; daily; Easter to September.
Admission fee Adults £1.15; OAPs & Children 65p for walled garden (subject to review). Grounds free.

Very much a public amenity, Croxteth Hall has a fine woodland trail along the River Alt, but the main interest for gardeners is the Victorian walled garden. There are lines of trained fruit trees, growing either against the walls or free-standing, a large vegetable garden (lots of varieties grown from the HDRA), an area for soft fruit, a herb garden, and a mushroom house – to remind people how mushrooms were once cultivated in grand gardens. These are interplanted with more ornamental features – a bedding

display, a rose garden, some herbaceous borders and the collection of fuchsias. There are also working greenhouses and some beehives.

 Features Herbs; plants under glass; fruit; good herbaceous borders; current holder of Sandford Award; cafeteria.

Owned by City of Liverpool
NCCPG National Collections *Fuchsia*
English Heritage grade II

Dunham Massey

ALTRINCHAM WA14 4SJ

Tel 0161 941 1025   **Fax** 0161 929 7508
Website www.nationaltrust.org.uk
Location 3 miles south-west of Altrincham off A56, well signed (Dunham Massey Hall & Park).
Opening hours 11 am – 5.30 pm (4.30 from 27 October); daily; 23 March to 3 November.
Admission fee Gardens only: Adults £3.50; Children £1.75.

Ⓟ ⓌⒸ ⓖ 🎁 🍵

Dunham Massey's 250 acres include an ancient deer park, a mediaeval moat made into a lake in the 18th century, an Elizabethan mount, an 18th-century orangery and some early landscape avenues. All remain, but the National Trust has decided to major on its even more interesting Victorian relics – evergreen shrubberies, ferns and colourful bedding-out schemes. Even that does not preclude the Trust from planting the most modern forms, such as the hybrids of *Rhododendron yakushimanum* and latest *R. occidentale* azalea hybrids. The result is a potent cross-section of historical and modern styles with a solid core of Victorian excellence, while the standard of maintenance is one of the highest in any Trust garden.

Features Topiary; good herbaceous borders; hydrangeas; skimmias; Edwardian parterre; current holder of Sandford Award; garden shop.

Owned by The National Trust
Number of gardeners 5
Size 10ha (25 acres) of garden & 90ha park
English Heritage grade II*

Fletcher Moss Botanical Gardens

MILL GATE LANE, DIDSBURY M20 8SD

Tel 0161 434 1877
Location In East Didsbury, off A5145.
Opening hours 8 am (9 am at weekends & Bank Holidays) – dusk; daily; all year.
Admission fee Free.

Fletcher Moss is a model municipal botanic garden, beautifully maintained but open for free. In the rock garden, substantially constructed on three levels with a pool at the bottom, is a rich collection of alpine plants, small conifers, maples and aquatics. The woodland areas have excellent autumn colour, but are almost as good in spring.

 Features Rock garden; mature conifers; bulbs; heathers; rhododendrons; cafeteria.

Owned by Manchester City Council
Size 5ha (12 acres)

Hoghton Tower

HOGHTON, PRESTON PR5 0SH

Tel 01254 852986   **Fax** 01254 852109
Location A675 midway between Preston & Blackburn.

Opening hours 11 am – 4 pm; Monday – Thursday; July to September. 1 pm – 5 pm; Sundays; July to September. Also Bank Holiday Mondays from Easter to August.
Admission fee Adults £2; Children (under 5) free.

A series of spacious courtyards and walled gardens surround this fierce castellated house which is approached up a long avenue. Its garden is not among the greatest, but the setting is impressive and there are fine spring walks in the rhododendron woods below. The rose garden was restored last year and is very colourful.

 Features Good herbaceous borders; rhododendrons & azaleas.

Owned by Hoghton Tower Preservation Trust
English Heritage grade II

Holden Clough Nursery

HOLDEN, BOLTON BY BOWLAND, CLITHEROE BB7 4PF

Tel & Fax 01200 447615
Website www.holdencloughnursery.co.uk
Location 8 miles north-east of Clitheroe, off A59.
Opening hours 9 am – 5 pm; Monday – Saturday: all year. Plus 1.30 pm – 5 pm on certain Sundays in April & May. Other times by appointment.

This long-established nursery (founded in 1927) has a large range of interesting alpines, perennials, dwarf conifers, shrubs, ferns, grasses and foliage plants. It is well-known at shows, all over the country. One of its best introductions is the hardy and vigorous hybrid *Iris* 'Holden Clough'.

Leighton Hall

CARNFORTH LA5 9ST

Tel 01524 734474 **Fax** 01524 720357
Location Signed from A6 junction with M6.
Opening hours 2 pm – 5 pm; daily except Saturday &
Monday; May to September. Open at 11.30 am in August
Admission fee Adults £4.50; OAPs £4.

The handsome semi-castellated house is set
in lush parkland with the Lakeland fells as a
backdrop: the Victorian conservatory to the
side of the house has just been restored. The
main garden features are in the 19th-century
walled garden, whose formal paths contrast
with the exuberant informality of the
planting. Here are herbaceous borders, a
herb garden, fruit trees, a vegetable plot and
masses of climbing roses – as well as the
unusual gravel maze.

 Features Roses (mainly old-
fashioned); herbs; fruit; good
herbaceous borders; 'caterpillar' path maze;
restored Victorian conservatory.

Owned by R.G. Reynolds

Rufford Old Hall

RUFFORD, ORMSKIRK L40 1SG

Tel & Fax 01704 821254
Website www.nationaltrust.org.uk
Location 7 miles north of Ormskirk on A59.
Opening hours 11 am – 5.30 pm; Saturday – Wednesday;
23 March to 30 October.
Admission fee Garden only: Adults £2.

One of the National Trust's most successful
re-creations, the gardens are laid out in the
Regency style around a 15th-century
timber-framed house. The garden had little

character when the Trust took over, but
Graham Stuart Thomas was charged with
adding the exotic shrubs and plants to make
it more interesting to visitors: old roses,
rhododendrons and ground-cover plants.

 Features Roses (mainly old-
fashioned); rhododendrons & azaleas;
good herbaceous borders.

Owned by The National Trust
Size 2ha (5 acres)

Speke Hall

THE WALK, LIVERPOOL L24 1XD

Tel 0151 427 7231 **Fax** 0151 427 9860
Website www.nationaltrust.org.uk
Location 1 mile off A561, surrounded by Liverpool Airport.
Opening hours 11 am – 5.30 pm (4 pm from mid-October
to March); Tuesday – Sunday, plus Bank Holiday Mondays;
all year. Closed 1 January, 24-26 & 31 December.
Admission fee Adults £2.50; Children £1.50. Plus £3
for car park.

The garden is mainly modern, a sympathetic
restoration of the one which a rich Liverpool
merchant made in the mid-19th century. On
the south lawn, three Victorian island beds
have recently been re-made. The nearby
rose-garden was planted in 1984 with shrubs
and Floribundas. All around are daffodils,
rhododendrons and bluebells in spring.

Features Roses; spring bulbs; summer
borders; stream garden; tea-room.

Owned by The National Trust
Number of gardeners 3
Size 7ha (17½ acres)
English Heritage grade II

LEICESTERSHIRE

One of the reasons why there are so few historic gardens in Leicestershire (no Grade I and only two Grade II* gardens) is that much of the county was open and unenclosed until the latter half of the 18th century. Even today, it is not as rich in interesting gardens as its neighbours, Northamptonshire and Warwickshire. However the National Gardens Scheme offers a respectable number of gardens to visit in its Yellow Book, and there are interesting plantsman's collections at Wartnaby and Long Close, as well as the excellent University of Leicester Botanic Garden. Leicestershire has some good garden centres, and a handful of first-rate specialist nurseries. Brooksby Melton College is a RHS Partner College with a fine teaching garden and collection of plants. It also has two National Collections: *Liriope* and *Ophiopogon*. Contrary to local belief, there is no such county as Rutland: it was dissolved in 1974 and absorbed into Leicestershire.

Barnsdale Gardens

THE AVENUE, EXTON, OAKHAM
LE15 8AH

Tel 01572 813200   **Fax** 01572 813346
Website www.barnsdalegardens.co.uk
Location The Avenue is on the south west edge of Exton.
Opening hours 9 am – 5 pm (7 pm June to August); daily; March to October. 10 am – 4 pm; weekends only; November to February. Last entry 2 hours before closure. Closed for two weeks at Christmas & New Year.
Admission fee Adults £5; Groups £4; Children free. RHS members free.

Barnsdale was famous for 20 years as Geoff Hamilton's *BBC Gardener's World* garden. Within it are 37 individual small gardens, laid out and maintained with the same intention – to encourage people to make the most of their opportunities as garden-owners. The gardens are of every kind. Some have descriptive names like the Tranquil Garden and the Town Paradise: others are more specific like the Plantsman's Garden, the Fruit Orchard, the Rose Garden, the Stream and Bog Garden. But for many visitors the most interesting are those which match their own particular circumstances and inspire them to become better gardeners – the First Time Garden, the Small Town Garden, the Ornamental Kitchen Garden and the Allotment Garden. All are maintained to the highest standard and continue to educate, delight and inspire. The attached nursery sells over 1,500 different plants, often in small quantities. Run by Geoff Hamilton's son, its policy is to offer the widest possible choice of good plants to its customers.

Owned by Sue & Nick Hamilton
Number of gardeners 7
Size 3.2ha (8 acres)

Belvoir Castle

BELVOIR, GRANTHAM NG32 1PD

Tel 01476 870262   **Fax** 01476 870443
Website www.country-focus.co.uk/belvoir/castle
Location 6 miles west of Grantham.
Opening hours 11 am – 5 pm; daily; 28 March to 7 April; 14, 21 & 28 April; May to September. Then Sundays only in October.
Admission fee Castle & gardens: Adults £7; OAPs £5; Children £3.50.

Belvoir has formal gardens along the Victorian terraces beneath the castle, and a Broad Walk overlooking the 19th-century rose garden. Some way off is a hedged enclosure with seven statues by Colley Cibber. The Spring Garden, a pretty woodland garden, has recently been restored to its early 19th-century form and is open by appointment to groups at any time of year.

Features Woodland garden; roses (mainly modern); tallest bird cherry *Prunus avium* (28m) and yew tree *Taxus baccata* (29m) in the British Isles.

Owned by The Duke of Rutland
Number of gardeners 4
English Heritage grade II

Goscote Nurseries Ltd

SYSTON ROAD, COSSINGTON LE7 4UZ

Tel 01509 812121   **Fax** 01509 814231
Website www.goscote.co.uk
Location 5 miles north of Leicester, on B5328.
Opening hours 9 am – 5 pm; Monday – Saturday. 10 am – 5 pm; Sundays. Closes at 4.30 pm in winter and between Christmas & New Year.
Admission fee Free

Goscote has a wide range of reasonably-priced plants of all types – more than 1,500 are produced on site. They offer an extensive collection of trees and shrubs, including acers, azaleas, clematis, conifers and rhododendrons, many of them rare or unusual but suitable to the cold Midlands. Plants can also be seen in the show gardens, laid out as island beds. The website is helpful and comprehensive.

The Herb Nursery

THISTLETON, OAKHAM LE15 7RE

Tel 01572 767658   **Fax** 01572 768021
Location In the middle of the village.
Opening hours 9 am – 6 pm (or dusk); daily; closed from Christmas to New Year.

This family-run nursery lists nearly 500 herbs and wildflower plants, with a special emphasis upon lavender, mint and thyme. The range of scented-leaf pelargoniums is particularly good (80+ cultivars), and there is a extensive range of cottage garden plants. Local gardeners speak well of it. The demonstration beds and borders around the nursery are a bonus.

Owned by Peter & Christine Bench

Kayes Garden Nursery

1700 MELTON ROAD, REARSBY, LEICESTER LE7 4YR

Tel 01664 424578
Location On A607, north-east of Leicester.
Opening hours 10 am – 5 pm (but 12 noon on Sundays); Tuesday – Sunday; March to October. 10 am – 4 pm; Fridays & Saturdays, November to February.
Admission fee Garden £2; Nursery free.

This popular nursery has an excellent, mature display garden, densely planted with a wide range of interesting plants. It also opens for the National Gardens Scheme. New this year (2002) is an enclosed garden devoted to clematis and other climbers, underplanted with an enormous variety of eryngiums. The nursery's specialities are hardy herbaceous plants, grasses, aquatics and climbers. Hazel Kaye has a plantsman's eye for quality, and the list includes many of the best forms of a wide range of plants.

 Features Eryngiums; tradescantias; teas.

Owned by Hazel Kaye
Number of gardeners 2
Size 0.6ha (1½ acres)

Long Close

MAIN STREET, WOODHOUSE EAVES, LOUGHBOROUGH LE12 8RZ

Tel 01509 890616 (daytime)
Website www.technophobia.com/longclose
Location 4 miles south of Loughborough.
Opening hours 9.30 am – 1 pm & 2 pm – 5.30 pm; Monday – Saturday; March to July. Groups welcome at other times by appointment. Plus 2 pm – 5.30 pm on 7 April (plant fair) and 19 May (plants for sale).
Admission fee Adults £2.50; Children free. Tickets from Pene Crafts Gift Shop, opposite.

This is a plantsman's garden, made over many years and now magnificently mature. Some of the plants might be thought too tender for so far north: the owners like to call it 'a Cornish garden in Leicestershire'. The terraced lawns lead to a fine woodland garden, underplanted with bulbs, magnolias, camellias and massed rhododendrons and azaleas. Elsewhere are good herbaceous plantings, penstemons (quite a collection),

a parterre, waterlily ponds and a *potager*. The adjacent wildflower meadow is also pretty in late spring.

 Features Woodland garden; rhododendrons; azaleas; spring bulbs; penstemons; lots of other interesting plants; plants for sale, especially penstemons; refreshments for groups by arrangement.

Owned by John Oakland & Pene Johnson
Size 2ha (5 acres)

Philip Tivey & Son

28 WANLIP ROAD, SYSTON LE7 1PA

Tel 0116 269 2968
Location About 500 yards from culmination of Leicester western bypass and 200 yards west of junction with Station Road.
Opening hours 9 am – 5 pm; Monday – Friday. 9 am – 3 pm; Saturdays.
Admission fee Free.
Ⓟ ✿

These growers of dahlias are well-regarded by specialists. They also have a good list of Korean and hardy chrysanthemums. The dahlias are at their peak from August to October.

Owned by Philip Tivey
Size 0.8ha (2 acres)

University of Leicester Botanic Garden

BEAUMONT HALL, STOUGHTON DRIVE, OADBY LE2 2NA

Tel 0116 271 7725
Location 3 miles south of Leicester on A6 London Road opposite Racecourse: visitor entrance at The Knoll, Glebe Road.

Opening hours 10 am – 4 pm; Monday – Friday; all year. Plus Saturdays & Sundays from 16 March to 10 November. Closed 1 January, 25 & 26 December.
Admission fee Free.

The University of Leicester Botanic Garden moved to its present site in 1947. It fills the grounds surrounding four houses, which were built early in the 20th century and are now used as student residences. The four (once separate) gardens have been merged into a single entity, the University Botanic Garden with some 16 acres. They now support a wide variety of plants from historic trees to an 1980s ecological meadow. A pretty Edwardian pergola draped with roses, a well-planted rock-garden and a splendid display of hardy fuchsias from the National Collection all add to its interest. In 1997 the garden opened an out-station at Knighton, known as the Attenborough Arboretum. Though its plantings are still few and the trees very young, it is designed to display the native tree flora of England in an historical sequence of arrival dates – ending with beech (*Fagus sylvatica*) after the last ice age.

Features Roses (ancient & modern); rock garden; rhododendrons & azaleas; plants under glass; mature conifers; cacti; succulents; heathers; fuchsias; tallest red hawthorn *Crataegus laevigata* 'Paul's Scarlet' (12m) in the British Isles.

Owned by The University of Leicester
Number of gardeners 6
Size 6.4ha (16 acres)
NCCPG National Collections *Aubrieta*; *Chamaecyparis lawsoniana*; *Fuchsia*; *Hesperis*; *Skimmia*

Warren Hills Cottage

WARREN HILLS ROAD, COALVILLE
LE67 4UY

Tel 01530 812350
Location On B587 near the schools on the Copt Oak to Whitwick road.
Opening hours 12 noon – 5 pm; 31 March, 26 May, 14 July, 25 August & 15 September. And by appointment.
Admission fee Adults £1.50; Children 50p.

This young garden is attached to a small nursery specialising in herbaceous plants: the owners describe it as 'a plantaholic's garden'. It has been landscaped and planted to provide year-round interest. The main interest is the collection of over 40 different astrantias, each growing in its own labelled bed. Other features include raised beds, screes, gravelled areas, a cottage garden area, a pergola and a bank of rhododendrons underplanted with hellebores, bulbs and perennials. A garden to watch.

Features Astrantias; campanulas; penstemons; salvias; cream teas on open days.

Owned by Mr & Mrs G. Waters
Number of gardeners 3 part-time
Size 0.8ha (2 acres)
NCCPG National Collections *Astrantia*

Wartnaby Gardens

WARTNABY, MELTON MOWBRAY
LE14 3HY

Tel 01664 822549 **Fax** 01664 822231
Website www.wartnabygardens.co.uk
Location 3 miles north of Melton Mowbray on A606. Left at A6 Kettley then 1 mile.
Opening hours 11 am – 4 pm; 28 April, 19 May & 23 June & by appointment (not mid-week).

Admission fee Adults £2.50; Children free.

Wartnaby is the garden of someone who loves roses and is prepared to make them one of the principal elements of her garden design: the result is one of the best modern examples of how to grow roses in mixed borders. Even in the so-called rose garden, the roses do not dominate: they are interplanted instead with other shrubs, like ceanothus, hebes and tree peonies, and underplanted with geraniums and bulbs. Foliage, shapes, colours and textures take over when the roses are not in flower. The long central path in the substantial kitchen garden is flanked by massed plantings of hybrid musks, including 'Felicia', 'Prosperity' and 'Pink Prosperity', underplanted with the grey-leaved *Stachys byzantina* and *Lychnis flos-jovis*, and edged with lavender and box. Wartnaby is a garden of enormous interest and charm: if only it were open more often!

Features Roses (mainly old-fashioned) used in mixed borders; fruit; fine collection of trees; colour borders; many new features; big nursery sale on 23 June; refreshments available.

Owned by Lady King
Size 1.2ha (3 acres) approximately

Whatton House

LONG WHATTON, LOUGHBOROUGH LE12 5BG

Tel 01509 842225 **Fax** 01509 842268
Location Jct 24, Kegworth A6 towards Hathern.
Opening hours 2 pm – 6 pm; 31 March, 19 May & 23 June. And parties by arrangement.
Admission fee Adults £2.50; Children free.

Fifteen acres attached to a garden centre. Most of the features date from about 1900 but there has been much replanting in recent years. Two rose gardens, fine herbaceous borders and some magnificent specimen trees are among the attractions. There is also a mysterious 'bogey hole'.

Features Roses (ancient & modern); good herbaceous borders; arboretum; climbing plants; bark temple; canyon garden; bulbs; refreshments.

Owned by Lord Crawshaw
Number of gardeners 1
Size 6ha (15 acres)
English Heritage grade II

LINCOLNSHIRE

Lincolnshire, with which we include what was for a while south Humberside, has long been known for its horticultural industry based on bulb-growing, and it still has a high number of producers, both wholesale and retail. The show-garden at Springfields, together with its trade fairs and flower-parades, is one of the great attractions of Lincolnshire in spring. The county has its fair share of important historic gardens: Belton House and Grimsthorpe Castle are both open to the public, though the third Grade I garden at Brocklesby Park (Capability Brown, Humphry Repton, and Reginald Blomfield all worked there) remains strictly private. The National Gardens Scheme has a fair number of gardens opening for charity and the county is blessed with several specialist nurseries of national importance. In addition to the alpine experts Potterton and Martin near Caistor, there are two nurseries with significant National Collections – the fuchsia enthusiast Kathleen Muncaster on the north-west outskirts of Gainsborough and the auricula specialists Martin Nest Nurseries to the east of the same town. RHS members have free access for much of the year to Normanby Hall Country Park, one of the most interesting restoration projects on the East Coast of England.

Baytree Nurseries

HIGH ROAD, WESTON, SPALDING PE12 6JU

Tel 01406 370242   **Fax** 01406 372829
Website www.baytree-gardencentre.com
Location 1½ miles east of Spalding, on A151.
Opening hours 9 am – 6 pm; summer. 9 am – 5 pm; winter. Closed for Easter Day, Christmas Day & Boxing Day.

Baytree won the Garden Centre of Excellence Award some years ago: in 2000 it also won the growers' Retailer of the Year Award. Its six hectares include a pets and aquatic department, a leisure complex devoted to selling garden furniture and an owl centre. But it also aims to carry the largest selection of bulbs available at retail level anywhere in the country and a very large stock of plants, many of them grown on-site. Roses are a speciality: Baytree lists over 300 cultivars including some which it has bred and introduced itself.

Size 6.2ha (16 acres)

Belton House

GRANTHAM NG32 2LS

Tel 01476 566116   **Fax** 01476 579071
Website www.nationaltrust.org.uk
Location 3 miles north-east of Grantham on the A607.
Opening hours 11 am – 5.30 pm; Wednesday – Sunday plus Bank Holiday Mondays; 23 March to 3 November. Opens at 10.30 am in August. Closes at 4.30 pm on 20 July. 12 noon – 4 pm on Saturdays & Sundays from 4 November to 22 December.
Admission fee Adults £5.60; Children £2.80.

Grandeur and amenity go hand in hand at Belton. There are 1,000 acres of wooded deer park, a Wyattville orangery, a Dutch garden and an Italian garden with statues and parterres. But the adventure playground and other facilities make it popular with all ages.

Features Woodland garden; topiary; snowdrops; daffodils; bluebells; good herbaceous borders; biggest sugar maple *Acer saccharum* in the British Isles; gift shop; lunches, teas, licensed restaurant.

Owned by The National Trust
Number of gardeners 4
Size 14ha (35 acres)
English Heritage grade I

Doddington Hall

DODDINGTON, LINCOLN LN6 4RU

Tel 01522 694308   **Fax** 01522 685259
Website www.doddingtonhall.free-online.co.uk
Location Signed off the A46 Lincoln bypass.
Opening hours Garden only: 2 pm – 6 pm; Sundays; 24 February to 28 April. House & garden: Wednesdays, Sundays & Bank Holiday Mondays; May to September.
Admission fee Garden only: £3.10; Children £1.55.

Doddington is a ravishing Elizabethan house around which successive generations have made a successful Tudor-style garden. The owners keep it simple and open at the front, but in the walled garden (thickly and richly planted) are Edwardian knots and parterres, a modern herb garden and pleached hornbeams. Wonderfully harmonious and strongly recommended in early summer.

Features Good herbaceous borders; long succession of spring bulbs; irises; peonies; box-edged parterres, topiary; tea shop.

Owned by Antony Jarvis
Number of gardeners 2
Size 2.2ha (6 acres)
English Heritage grade II*

Grimsthorpe Castle

GRIMSTHORPE, BOURNE PE10 0NB

Tel 01778 591205   **Fax** 01778 591259
Website www.grimsthorpe.co.uk
Location On A151, 4 miles north-west of Bourne.
Opening hours 11 am – 6 pm; Thursdays, Sundays & Bank Holidays; April to September. Plus daily in August except Friday & Saturday.
Admission fee Adults £3; Concessions £2.50; Children £2.

Much is happening at Grimsthorpe. Recent researches have unearthed traces of the Stephen Switzer garden design from about 1700 and shown that it was probably a local engineer called John Grundy who designed the lake in 1771, not Capability Brown. Yew hedges have been planted to enclose the Victorian Italian garden, which is stylishly maintained with summer bedding among the topiary, urns and sculptures. The most interesting horticultural feature is a formal vegetable garden, made in the 1960s before the craze for *potagers*, right below the Italian garden. But new developments are planned for the near future.

 Features Topiary; roses (mainly modern); fine collection of trees; tea-room (licensed).

Owned by Grimsthorpe & Drummond Castle Trust Ltd
Number of gardeners 4
Size 10.7ha (27 acres)
English Heritage grade I

Gunby Hall

GUNBY, SPILSBY PE23 5SS

Tel 01909 486411 **Fax** 01909 486377
Website www.nationaltrust.org.uk
Location 2½ miles north-west of Burgh-le-Marsh.
Opening hours 2 pm – 6 pm; Wednesdays (plus Thursdays for garden only); 27 March to 30 September.
Admission fee Garden only: Adults £2.60.

Ignore the parkland and make for the two walled gardens. Here is all the action: rich herbaceous borders, an arched apple walk, shrub roses, herbs and vegetables.

 Features Roses (mainly old-fashioned); herbs; fruit; good herbaceous borders.

Owned by The National Trust
English Heritage grade II

Hall Farm & Nursery

HARPSWELL, GAINSBOROUGH DN21 5UU

Tel 01427 668412 **Fax** 01427 667478
Website www.hall-farm.co.uk
Location On A361, 7 miles east of Gainsborough.

Opening hours 10 am – 5 pm (or dusk, if earlier); daily; all year. Phone first in winter. For National Gardens Scheme: 10 am – 5.30 pm on 1 September.
Admission fee Adults £2.50; Children 50p on National Gardens Scheme day, otherwise free.

This small, modern garden is intensely planted and beautifully maintained as an adjunct to the nursery, and for the owners' pleasure. There are plants of every kind – trees, shrubs, bulbs and herbaceous plants – and over 100 different roses. The National Gardens Scheme day in September is a 'free seed collection' day.

 Features Roses (mainly old-fashioned) in a newly made rose garden; plantsman's collection of plants; good herbaceous borders; sunken garden; good nursery next door.

Owned by Pam & Mark Tatam
Size 0.4ha (1 acre)

Hippopottering Nursery

ORCHARD HOUSE, BRACKENHILL ROAD, EAST LOUND, HAXEY, DONCASTER DN9 2LR

Tel & Fax 01427 752185
Website www.hippopottering.com
Location Off A161 at Haxey on Owston Ferry road to East Lound.
Opening hours 10 am – 4 pm; Saturdays; April to September. And by appointment.

Hippopottering Nursery – the name has its origins in a family joke – are specialists in Japanese maples. They offer everything from selected colourful seedlings and bonsai material to mature specimens. Cultivars are selected from their collection of over 120; they also sell rootstocks.

Features Maples.

Owned by Margaret & Patricia Gibbons
Size 0.4ha (1 acre)

Kathleen Muncaster Fuchsias

18 FIELD LANE, MORTON,
GAINSBOROUGH DN21 3BY

Tel 01427 612329
Website www.kathleenmuncasterfuchsias.co.uk
Location North-west of Gainsborough: Field Lane is off the minor road to Walkerith.
Opening hours 10 am – 5 pm; Thursday to Tuesday; from February to mid-June. Phone first at other times.

This is the nursery of a fuchsia specialist who began as an amateur and now has a National Collection of hardy cultivars and one of the largest nurseries in the country which specialises in the genus. The hardy fuchsias can be seen in the garden, together with the stock plants: almost all the glasshouses may also be visited. The list is impressive, though not all the cultivars in the collection are propagated regularly – ask if they have a cutting available. They introduce new fuchsias every year: there are five introductions for 2002, including an exceptional new hardy cultivar called 'Remember Eric'.

Owned by Kathleen Muncaster
NCCPG National Collections Fuchsia (hardy)

Martin Nest Nurseries

GRANGE COTTAGE, HEMSWELL,
GAINSBOROUGH DN21 5UP

Tel 01427 668369   **Fax** 01427 668080
Location 6 miles east of Gainsborough on A631.
Opening hours 10 am – 4 pm; daily; all year. By appointment only at weekends from November to January.

Martin Nest Nurseries are wholesalers and retailers with a good business-like range of tough pot-grown hardy alpine plants. Primulas and auriculas are their speciality: some of their cultivars are unique to them. Visitors may be shown the National Collection of *Primula auricula* cultivars on request.

NCCPG National Collections *Primula auricula*

Normanby Hall Country Park

NORMANBY, SCUNTHORPE
DN15 9HU

Tel 01724 720588   **Fax** 01724 721248
Website www.northlincs.gov.uk/normanby
Location 3 miles north of Scunthorpe.
Opening hours 10.30 am – 5 pm (4.30 in winter) daily; all year. Closed 1 January, 25 & 26 December.
Admission fee Adults £3.50; Concessions £2.50. RHS members free from 25 March to 30 September.

The Victorian Walled Garden (actually built in 1817, before Queen Victoria was even born) has been restored and planted – with help from the National Lottery – as a living museum of 19th-century horticulture. Old varieties of fruit and vegetables are grown organically. The glasshouses have recently been rebuilt to house peaches and other fruit. Ferns and exotic ornamentals fill a display house. New this year (2002) are a bog garden along the base of the ha-ha (125m long) and a Christmas garden of hollies, ivies, hellebores and ferns.

 Features Fruit & vegetables are a special feature; herbaceous borders, woodland walks and parkland outside; deer park; shop; new nursery opens March 2002; refreshments.

Owned by North Lincolnshire Council
Number of gardeners 4
Size 0.4ha (1 acre), plus 16ha (39 acres) outside the walled garden.

Potterton and Martin

MOORTOWN ROAD, NETTLETON, CAISTOR LN7 6HX

Tel 01472 851714 **Fax** 01472 852580
Website www.users.globalnet.co.uk/~pottin
Location On B1205: leave A46 at Nettleton.
Opening hours 9 am – 4.30 pm; daily.
Admission fee Free.

This alpine and rock plant specialist has an interesting and extensive range of plants for sale, running from the easy to the unusual. All are propagated on-site, and most can be seen in the extensive display garden. The rock garden has a stream course, waterfalls and pools: elsewhere are raised beds, troughs, woodland and peat beds. The nursery holds many Chelsea gold medals, and has won the RHS Farrer Trophy (best alpine display) on several occasions. Satisfied customers praise not only the nursery's wide choice of plants, but also its cultivation skills and reasonable pricing policy.

 Features Large rock garden.

Owned by Robert & Jackie Potterton
Number of gardeners 3 part-time
Size 2ha (5 acres)

Springfields Show Gardens

CAMELGATE, SPALDING PE12 6ET

Tel 01775 724843 **Fax** 01775 711209
Website www.springfields.mistral.co.uk
Location 1 mile from Spalding, off new bypass.
Opening hours 10 am – 5 pm; daily; 15 March to 12 May.
Admission fee Adults £3.50; OAPs £3; Children free.

Originally (in 1966) a display garden for the Lincolnshire bulb trade, Springfields now offers fun and colour all through the season, with roses providing the midsummer display and bold bedding taking over until the autumn frosts. But it is still the bulbs which make the greatest impression – daffodils, tulips, hyacinths and many others, all donated by the industry. There are plans to develop and upgrade the garden as a major tourist attraction incorporating some retailing, but this depends upon a planning decision which is not expected until later in the year (2002). Meanwhile Springfields remains a real eyeful of a garden, splendidly maintained.

Features Woodland garden; roses (mainly modern); millions of bulbs; gift shop; restaurant & café.

Owned by Springfields Horticultural Society Ltd
Number of gardeners 3
Size 10ha (25 acres)

LONDON

London gardeners are much more fortunate than they would have you believe. They have a microclimate which enables them to grow plants that are tender anywhere except in the mildest corners of the south-west, and they enjoy a good choice of suitably stylish plants from garden centres and other outlets within the city itself. Some of the world's greatest gardens are within a short journey: among them are the Chelsea Physic Garden, Chiswick House, the Royal Botanic Gardens at Kew, Richmond Park and Syon Park. The Royal Parks Agency manages the inner-city green spaces like Hyde Park and Regent's Park with immense horticultural skill: almost all the parks contain acres of well-kept grass and trees of record size. London is of course the seat of the Royal Horticultural Society: the Chelsea Flower Show is traditionally regarded as the start of the London summer season. The Hampton Court Palace Flower show in July is, if possible, even more of a Londoners' show, while the regular London shows at the RHS's own halls in Westminster are attended by thousands of London gardeners keen to see plants and buy them. Nowhere has so many lectures and other educational garden events as London does. The RHS's Partner College at Capel Manor has a long programme of lectures, demonstrations and workshops throughout the year. Many of the specialist plant societies have their shows and administrative offices in London, too: if you want to see plants as diverse as orchids, carnations, vegetables, daffodils or camellias, London is the place to do so. The National Gardens Scheme thrives there; the Museum of Garden History is based there – just across the river from the Houses of Parliament; the Association of Gardens Trusts has its office in London and so does the Institute of Horticulture. The London Historic Parks & Gardens Trust is one of the country's most successful conservation societies. The greater part of the RHS's Lindley Library – Britain's largest collection of horticultural books and primary sources about gardening – is based in London and now housed in spacious purpose-built accomodation at 80 Vincent Square. Perhaps the only thing that a Londoner cannot do is to garden on a large scale. That apart, there is no better place to be a garden-lover.

Cannizaro Park

WEST SIDE COMMON, WIMBLEDON SW19

Tel 020 8545 3657
Location West side of Wimbledon Common.
Opening hours 8 am – sunset, Monday – Friday;
9 am – sunset, Saturday, Sunday & Bank Holidays; all year.
Admission fee Free.

Cannizaro is well-known among connoisseurs for its azaleas, planted about 40 years ago and a magnificent spectacle when in full flower. It is one of the best woodland gardens of its type in the country and especially beautiful when the underplantings of bulbs are in flower. There are some fine specimen trees, including birches, horse chestnuts and the tall sassafras.

Features Woodland garden; mature conifers; azaleas; magnolias; new fountain (2001); several *Sassafras albidum* 15m or more; some refreshments at summer weekends.

Owned by London Borough of Merton
Size 15.5ha (39 acres)
English Heritage grade II*

Capel Manor

BULLSMOOR LANE, ENFIELD EN1 4RQ

Tel 020 8366 4442   **Fax** 01992 717544
Website www.capel.ac.uk
Location A10 by Jct 25 on M25.
Opening hours 11 am – 6 pm (or dusk if sooner); daily;
March to October. But closed on Saturdays in March &
October. Weekdays only from November to February.
Admission fee £4 Adults; £3.50 OAPs; £2 Children.

There are three main areas at this high-profile demonstration garden attached to a horticultural college 'where the City meets the Countryside'. First there is the National Gardening Centre, where dozens of small model gardens are designed and planted to give people state-of-the-art ideas for their own gardens. Second, there are the trial grounds run by *Gardening Which?*, where this influential monthly magazine carries out all its trials and experiments, long-term and seasonal. Third, there is the series of themed gardens laid out for students to learn from: a walled garden, a herb garden, a knot garden, a disabled person's garden, a shade garden, an Italianate holly maze, a pergola, a Japanese garden, alpine beds and some historical recreations. Whatever your interests and whatever the time of the year, Capel Manor is a garden which educates and delights. And it is brilliant for new ideas, especially for small gardens.

Features Vegetables & fruit; topiary; plantsman's collection of plants; herbs; plants under glass; daffodils; good herbaceous borders; fine collection of trees; alpine plants; roses of every kind; small shop; restaurant.

Owned by Capel Manor Corporation
Number of gardeners 8
Size 12ha (30 acres)
NCCPG National Collections *Achillea; Sarcococca*

Chelsea Physic Garden

66 ROYAL HOSPITAL ROAD SW3 4HS

Tel 020 7352 5646   **Fax** 020 7376 3910
Website www.chelseaphysicgarden.co.uk
Location Entrance in Royal Hospital Road, towards the
Chelsea Embankment end.
Opening hours 11 am – 3 pm; 3 & 10 February for
snowdrops. 12 noon – 5 pm, Wednesdays; 2 pm – 6 pm,
Sundays; 7 April to 27 October. Plus 12 noon – 5 pm on

20 to 24 May for Chelsea Flower Show & 17 to 21 June for Chelsea Festival.
Admission fee Adults £4; Children £2.

This oasis of peace between Royal Hospital Road and the Chelsea Embankment started life in 1673 as a pharmacological collection, and has kept its original design – hence the word 'Physic' in its name. But it also has the oldest rock garden in Europe, the largest olive tree in Britain, extensive botanical order beds, a vast number of rare and interesting plants, and probably the last known specimen of the 1920s white Hybrid Tea rose 'Marcia Stanhope'. An historical walk emphasises the importance of the garden through the ages by drawing attention to the number of plants first introduced to Britain by the garden and its curators.

Features Herbs; plants under glass; good herbaceous borders; 18th-century rock garden; new Pharmaceutical Garden (1999); large olive tree growing outside; light refreshments.

Owned by Chelsea Physic Garden Company
Number of gardeners 5
Size 1.6ha (4 acres)
NCCPG National Collections *Cistus*
English Heritage grade I

Chiswick House

BURLINGTON LANE, CHISWICK
W4 2RP

Tel 020 8742 1225
Location South-west London on A4 & A316.
Opening hours 8 am – dusk; daily; all year.
Admission fee Free.

Laid out by Bridgeman and Kent for Lord Burlington, Chiswick is the best baroque garden in southern England, and the exquisite house is pure Palladian. The bachelor Duke of Devonshire added an Italian renaissance garden early in the 19th century, and a Camellia House with slate benches and huge bushes, mainly of old Japonica hybrids. But it is the lay-out and buildings which are so exceptional: the Ionic temple, the Inigo Jones gateway, the obelisk and the statues. Forget the dogs and the joggers – almost all free-entry gardens have a municipal heart – but explore the *pattes d'oie*, *allées* and ilex groves of the main garden on a hot July morning and you might be doing a Grand Tour of Italy 250 years ago.

Features Plants under glass; camellias; parterres; summer bedding; luxuriant evergreens; refreshments.

Owned by London Borough of Hounslow
Number of gardeners 8
Size 16ha (40 acres)
English Heritage grade I

Clifton Nurseries

CLIFTON VILLAS, LITTLE VENICE
W9 2PH

Tel 020 7289 6851
Location In Little Venice.
Opening hours 8.30 am – 6 pm; Monday – Saturday: 10.30 am – 4.30 pm; Sundays: March to September. 8.30 am – 5.30 pm; Monday – Saturday: 10 am – 4 pm; Sundays: October to February.

Clifton Nurseries were founded about 100 years ago and have grown to become one of the smartest and most stylish sources of good plants and designer sundries for Londoners. They concentrate on supplying town gardens with containers, statuary, climbers and shrubs in specimen sizes, indoor and conservatory plants. Topiary is one of their specialities: so are mature plants for instant gratification.

Fenton House

WINDMILL HILL, HAMPSTEAD
NW3 6RT

Tel & Fax 020 7435 3471
Website www.nationaltrust.org.uk
Location Entrances in Hampstead Grove near Hampstead Underground station.
Opening hours 2 pm – 5 pm; Saturdays & Sundays; 2 to 17 March. Then 2 pm – 5 pm; Wednesday – Sunday plus Bank Holiday Mondays but not Good Friday; 23 March to 3 November. Opens at 11 am on Saturdays, Sundays & Bank Holiday Mondays.
Admission fee Adults £4.40; Children £2.20.

Fenton House has a country garden in Hampstead, with neat, terraced gardens near the house, and a rather more informal design at the bottom. It is not outstandingly flowerful, but the hedges are good, plants are firmly trained, and there is something to see throughout the year: definitely worth knowing, and very popular with visitors.

Features Roses (mainly old-fashioned); herbs; good herbaceous borders; restored Edwardian garden; new greenhouse (1998); new scented border (2000).

Owned by The National Trust

Fulham Palace Garden Centre

BISHOPS AVENUE, FULHAM SW6 6EE

Tel 020 7736 9820   **Fax** 020 7371 8468
Website www.fulhamgardencentre.com
Location Off Fulham Palace Road.
Opening hours 9.30 am – 5.30 pm, Monday – Thursday; 9.30 am – 6 pm, Friday – Saturday; 10 am – 5 pm, Sundays. Shuts earlier in winter months.

Fulham Palace Garden Centre has everything for the town gardener, including specimen-sized plants, topiary and a good range of containers. The general range includes herbs, vegetables, fruit trees, herbaceous plants, climbers, ferns, grasses, olives, figs and oranges. The nursery will deliver seven days a week in London and further afield. It is owned by Fairbridge, the charity which arranges training for inner-city children. The Fairbridge Garden Society, based at the Fulham Palace Garden Centre, runs a lively programme of lectures, demonstrations, and garden visits at home and abroad. For details ring 020 7736 3210.

Ham House

RICHMOND TW10 7RS

Tel 020 8940 1950   **Fax** 020 8332 6903
Website www.nationaltrust.org.uk
Location On River Thames, signed from A307.
Opening hours 11 am – 6 pm (or dusk, if earlier); Saturday – Wednesday; all year except 1 January & 25/26 December.
Admission fee Adults £2; Children £1.

Ham is a modern re-creation of the original 17th-century garden. It is not a literal copy,

Hampton Court Palace

KT8 9AU

Tel 020 8781 9500
Website www.hrp.org.uk
Location North side of Kingston bridge over the Thames on A308 junction with A309.
Opening hours Park: dawn – dusk; daily; all year. King's Privy Garden: 9.30 am – 6 pm (4.30 pm from October to March). Opens at 10.15 am on Mondays.
Admission fee Privy Garden: Adults £2.80; Children £1.90. Maze: Adults £2.80; Children £1.90.

William III was responsible for the main features at Hampton Court today. His Privy Garden has recently been reconstructed as it was in 1702 and remains the outstanding example of a successful historic restoration from the 1990s. Even the planting is accurate – roses, fritillaries and other flowering plants chosen and cultivated exactly as they would have been 300 years ago. Note how widely spaced they are in their slightly raised beds, an exact copy of horticultural practices of the time. Next to the vast Privy Garden is the Pond Garden, a sunken formal garden with magnificent displays of bedding – tulips in spring and tender perennials in summer. Nearby is the Great Vine – actually 'Black Hamburgh' – planted in 1768 on the advice of Capability Brown: it is the world's oldest known vine and produces, on average, 300 kilos of grapes every year. To one side of the Privy Garden lies the great formal East Garden. Its central feature is the Long Water which cuts right through the deer park: the Hampton Court Palace Flower Show (organised by the Royal Horticultural Society) takes place astride its banks from 3 to 8 July: tickets may be puchased in advance on 0870 906 3790. The garden at the palace end of the long water was laid out as a parterre by William

III with 12 marble fountains: Queen Anne added the semi-circular canals in 1710. On the other side of the palace are the wilderness gardens, extending over a considerable area, and a mass of naturalised daffodils in spring. Here too is the famous Hampton Court Maze, which covers about one third of an acre and has yew hedges totalling nearly half a mile. Other areas in the Wilderness also have considerable horticultural interest, including the rose garden, a herbaceous garden, and walls covered with climbing plants. Hampton Court is large and you need several hours to appreciate all the gardens, their different styles and what they offer. The website is excellent – educational and helpful.

Features Topiary; roses (ancient & modern); herbs; fruit trees; good herbaceous borders; the famous maze; laburnum walk; knot gardens; the Great Vine; the Wilderness; shop.

Owned by Historic Royal Palaces
Number of gardeners 40
Size 22ha (60 acres) of formal gardens & 220ha (600 acres) of deer park
NCCPG National Collections Heliotropium
English Heritage grade I

but more of a free-handed re-interpretation. The best part is a grand series of hornbeam enclosures with white summerhouses and seats, known as the Wilderness. The borders are all planted, so far as possible, in the 17th-century style. There are plans to re-develop the kitchen garden in front of the orangery to contrast its 17th-century design and plantings with the better-known 19th-century ones that are commonly seen elsewhere.

 Features Formal gardens in 17th-century style; roses (mainly modern & climbers); herbs; fruit; parterres; holm oak avenue; National Trust shop; tea-room open 23 March to 3 November.

Owned by The National Trust
Number of gardeners 4
Size 8ha (20 acres)
English Heritage grade II*

Isabella Plantation

RICHMOND PARK, RICHMOND TW10 5HS

Tel 020 8948 3209   **Fax** 020 8332 2730
Location Richmond Park.
Opening hours Dawn – dusk; daily; all year.
Admission fee Free.

Ⓟ 🐦 ⓦⓒ ♿

The Isabella Plantation in Richmond Park is at last getting the recognition it deserves: these 42 acres of rhododendrons and azaleas under a mature deciduous canopy are one of the finest woodland gardens in the country. They are probably best visited in late April and May, when the azaleas are accompanied by lush streamside plantings of candelabra primulas, ferns and hostas. And it all gets better still: the new bog garden (opened in 2000) has been such a success that it will be extended during the course of 2002.

 Features Woodland garden; rhododendrons & azaleas; camellias and magnolias; good ornamental trees; primulas.

Owned by The Royal Parks Agency
Number of gardeners 5
Size 17.2ha (42 acres)
NCCPG National Collections *Rhododendron* (Kurume azaleas, the Wilson 50)
English Heritage grade I

Kenwood

HAMPSTEAD LANE NW3 7JR

Location North side of Hampstead Heath, off B519.
Opening hours 8 am to dusk (8.30 pm if sooner); daily; all year.
Admission fee Free (to park).

🐦 ⓦⓒ ♿ ☕

These 100 acres of superb 18th-century parkland around two glittering lakes were recently half-restored to Repton's original designs. There are splendid large plantings of rhododendrons, fine azaleas, and wonderful landscaped views to London and Westminster, but rather more could be done horticulturally.

 Features Woodland garden; good herbaceous borders; fine collection of trees; refreshments during the daytime.

Owned by English Heritage
English Heritage grade II*

Museum of Garden History

LAMBETH PALACE ROAD SE1 7LB

Tel 020 7401 8865 **Fax** 020 7401 8869
Website www.museumgardenhistory.org
Location Between Lambeth Bridge & Lambeth Palace.
Opening hours 10.30 am – 5 pm; daily; early February to mid-December
Admission fee £2.50 voluntary admission charge (£2 concessions).

The garden is small, and secondary to the Museum's fascinating collections and excellent exhibitions. Nevertheless it is neatly designed and planted – with a fair degree of historical correctness – as a 17th-century knot garden, using plants associated with the Tradescants. A garden for contemplation. But the events, exhibitions, lectures and courses are well worth knowing about: the Museum is undergoing major redevelopment with the aim of becoming a first-class information resource about the history of gardening in Britain.

Features 17th-century plants; good exhibitions; historic tool collection; books, cards and gifts; light refreshments.

Owned by Museum of Garden History
Number of gardeners 8 part-time volunteers

Myddelton House

BULLS CROSS, ENFIELD EN2 9HG

Tel 01992 702200 **Fax** 01992 651406
Location Off A10 onto Bullsmoor Lane: signed at Bulls Cross. Or train to Turkey Street Station.
Opening hours 10 am – 4.30 pm (3 pm from October to March); weekdays except Christmas Holidays; all year. Plus 2 pm – 5 pm; Sundays & Bank Holiday Mondays;

31 March to 27 October. And 12 noon – 4 pm for NGS on 24 February, 26 May & 28 July.
Admission fee Adults £2.10; Concessions £1.50.

Holy ground for plantsmen with a sense of history, E.A. Bowles's garden was abandoned for 30 years: Lee Valley Regional Park Authority has started to restore it. Thousands of naturalised bulbs have survived: snowdrops, crocus and narcissi in spring, and cyclamen, colchicums and sternbergias in autumn. The large wisteria planted in 1903 has also survived, while the rose garden has been replanted with varieties that Bowles grew. The iris borders are spectacular in May but it is true to say that, as with all plantsman's gardens, there is much to see throughout the year. A current project is to restore the Lunatic Asylum, Bowles's collection of freak plants like the double-flowered (but non-berrying) blackberry *Rubus ulmifolius* 'Bellidifolius'. The RHS thought so highly of this part of the garden that, even in the cash-strapped 1950s, it propagated the plants and created its own Lunatic Asylum corner at Wisley. And the Lee Valley Regional Park Authority has just re-acquired the kitchen garden and have plans to restore it too. There is a friends' group called the E.A. Bowles of Myddelton House Society which has an active programme of events: details from Mr A. Pettitt, 2(A) Plough Hill, Cuffley, Potters Bar, Hertfordshire EN6 4DR or from *michaelkingdom@aol.com*

Features Snowdrops; roses (mainly old-fashioned & climbers); plantsman's collection of plants; daffodils; good herbaceous borders; fine collection of trees.

Owned by Lee Valley Regional Park Authority
Number of gardeners 3
Size 2.2ha (6 acres)
NCCPG National Collections *Iris*
English Heritage grade II

Osterley Park

ISLEWORTH TW7 4RB

Tel 020 8232 5050   **Fax** 020 8232 5080
Website www.nationaltrust.org.uk
Location 5 miles west of central London on A4.
Opening hours 9 am – 7.30 pm (or dusk, if earlier);
daily; all year.
Admission fee Park & pleasure grounds free.

Osterley is a classical 18th-century landscape
with a fine semi-circular conservatory by
Robert Adam and some good trees –
especially cedars and oaks. Other highlights
include the Chinese Pavilion and the
Temple of Pan, but the greatest horticultural
interest comes some large specimens of
Magnolia grandiflora against the stable
block wall.

Features Woodland garden; herbs;
fruit; fine rare oaks; autumn colour;
tallest variegated chestnut *Castanea sativa*
'Albomarginata' (16m) in the British Isles;
National Trust shop; tea-room.

Owned by The National Trust
English Heritage grade II*

The Palm Centre

HAM NURSERY, HAM STREET, HAM,
RICHMOND TW10 7HA

Tel 020 8255 6191   **Fax** 020 8255 6192
Website www.palmcentre.co.uk
Location Near Ham House, on right hand side opposite
Riverside Drive.
Opening hours 9 am – 5 pm (or dusk, if earlier); daily;
all year.
Admission fee Free

The Palm Centre, close to Ham House, is a
5-acre nursery with one acre of glasshouses.
It specialises in hardy exotic plants,
especially palms, bamboos, tree ferns,
cordylines, cycads, yuccas and citrus. It lists
over 400 palm species. There are two
planted-out gardens, one with a good
number of mature palms of several different
species, which customers are encouraged to
wander through. They are intended to
illustrate the sheer number and range of
hardy exotics that may be grown outside this
way. The nursery's Japan 2001 exhibit will
remain in place until March 2002, majoring
on bamboos and Japanese garden
decorations.

Owned by Martin Gibbons
Size 1.6ha (4 acres)

Queen Mary's Gardens

INNER CIRCLE, REGENT'S PARK
NW1 4NR

Tel 020 7486 7905
Location In the middle of Regent's Park.
Opening hours Dawn – dusk; daily; all year.
Admission fee Free.

Queen Mary's Gardens are contained within Regent's Park's Inner Circle. Originally a display garden for the Royal Botanic Society (a 19th-century rival to the Royal Horticultural Society; Robert Marnock and William Robinson both worked there), the Japanese garden, the lake and the mound made from the excavations all date from the 1850s. The horticultural interest comes from the excellent herbaceous borders, tender bedding plants, displays of annuals and spring bulbs. Above all, Queen Mary's Gardens are known for their rose gardens, where large beds are planted each with just one cultivar – mainly modern Hybrid Teas and Floribundas, though there are English roses and old-fashioned ones too, often in mixed borders. At one end is a circular catenary of climbing and rambling roses around yet more beds of bright modern roses: a spectacular sight in early June – roses flower earlier in the London parks than anywhere else in England, and are worth a visit at any time after about the middle of May.

Features Roses (mainly modern); massed displays of roses; fine herbaceous borders.

Owned by Royal Parks Agency

Syon Park

BRENTFORD TW8 8JF

Tel 020 8560 0883 2   **Fax** 020 8568 0936
Website www.syonpark.co.uk
Location Between Brentford & Isleworth, north bank of River Thames.
Opening hours 10 am – 5.30 pm, or sunset if earlier; daily except 25 & 26 December; all year.
Admission fee Adults £3; Concessions £2.50.

Syon is a mixture of 18th-century landscape, 19th-century horticultural seriousness, 20th-century plantsmanship and 21st-century theme park. The Great Conservatory was designed by Charles Fowler in the 1820s; the formal terraces followed in the 1830s. But one of the nicest details about Syon is the way the water meadows along the banks of the Thames are still grazed by cows: it creates a unique rural prospect so close to the heart of London. There are fine trees too, the relic of a botanical collection dating back to the 1820s: some, including four species of oak, are record-breakers.

Features Spectacular Great Conservatory; woodland garden; mature conifers; good herbaceous borders; fine collection of trees; cacti; ferns; new walk around lake; tallest *Catalpa ovata* (22m) in the British Isles (and fourteen further record trees); tropical butterfly house; Wyevale Garden Centre on site: 020 8568 0134; shops, restaurants.

Owned by The Duke of Northumberland
Number of gardeners 7
Size 16ha (40 acres)
English Heritage grade I

Royal Botanic Gardens, Kew

KEW, RICHMOND TW9 3AB

Tel 020 8332 5655

Website www.rbgkew.org.uk

Location Kew Green (parking), tube to Kew Gardens Underground Station, or train from Waterloo to Kew Bridge.

Opening hours 9.30 am – 6.30 pm (7.30 pm at weekends), but closes at 5.30 pm from 9 February to 30 March and from 2 September to 26 October, & at 4.15 pm from 2 January to 8 February 2002 and from 27 October to 3 February 2003; daily; all year except Christmas & New Year's Day.

Admission fee Adults £6.50; Concessions £4.50; Children free.

Kew Gardens are enormous – the guide book advises that they take a whole day to visit – and have one of the largest collections of plants in the world. The emphasis is upon species rather than garden cultivars, but there is an immense amount for gardeners to see and admire and – of course – to learn from. There are seasonal features like the winter garden and historic areas like the Queen's garden behind Kew Palace which was designed in the 1960s as a reconstructed 17th-century garden. Nor should the famous pagoda and Japanese landscape gardens be forgotten. There are also many horticulturally themed gardens. The azalea garden divides azaleas into 12 distinct horticultural groups, e.g. the Ghent hybrids and the Knap Hill hybrids, and arranges them all systematically in historic order. The bamboo garden has over 120 cultivars arranged to maximise the contrast between their forms and leaf shapes. The berberis dell is a unique feature with a comprehensive collection of berberis and mahonia – the tallest is a 5m specimen of *Berberis lycoides*. Kew has one of the best bluebell woods in the London area, behind

Queen Charlotte's cottage. The grass garden has over 550 species and is being added to continuously: although the scientific purpose is to display the diversity and importance of grasses, the garden is arranged ornamentally. The holly walk was laid out in 1874 by Sir Joseph Hooker: the original specimens are therefore over 130 years old and as high as 30m. The collection has over 600 hollies. The juniper collection is the largest in Europe. The lilac garden ('Go down to Kew in lilac time') was renovated in 1993 and has over 100 specimens in ten separate beds. The rhododendron dell (700 plants) includes some unique Kew hybrids as well as hardy species. The rose garden was created in 1923 and is very popular in high summer: it has roses of all types and an area which illustrates the history of roses in cultivation. There is also a rose pergola running through the order beds, which were originally designed as a living library of flowering plants systematically arranged for students of botany. The pinetum has an important collection of conifers and there are many record breakers among the deciduous species at Kew too. The rock garden was rebuilt in the 1980s to include more micro-habitats. It has over 2,500 different plants roughly arranged in geographical areas, e.g. the mountains of Europe, the Mediterranean and Patagonia. The glasshouses also contain a vast collection of plants. The palm house was built in the 1840s to house tropical trees and shrubs – these include coconuts, bananas, bread-fruit, mangoes and paw-paws. The Princess of Wales conservatory opened in 1987 and has ten distinct climatic zones ranging from arid to moist tropical:

here are such plants as ginger, pineapple and orchids. The temperate house is set out geographically: among its most striking plants are proteas from South Africa. In the hot and humid waterlily house are tropical *Nymphaea* and *Victoria cruziana*, as well as such economic plants as rice and lemon grass. The alpine house was opened in 1981 and its systems of refrigeration and ventilation enable Kew to grow plants which would not otherwise survive the damp, mild climate of England. Other glasshouses to visit include the evolution house, which tells the story of plant evolution over the last 3,500 million years. Kew has every imaginable facility for visits by schools, groups, tourists and students of botany. In summer it also has very good bedding-out schemes, but the garden is somewhat bedevilled by Canada geese, which foul the grass, and by aircraft noise.

Features Woodland garden; sub-tropical plants; snowdrops; roses of every kind; rock garden; plantsman's collection of plants; herbs; plants under glass; fruit; mature conifers; good herbaceous borders; fine collection of trees; alpine plants; heather gardens; 138 record trees – more than any other garden in the British Isles – including 38 different oaks (*Quercus sp.*); gift & book shop; two restaurants & bakery.

Owned by Trustees of the Royal Botanic Gardens
Size 120ha (300 acres)
English Heritage grade I

NORFOLK

Norfolk has a large number of important historic gardens. Only a few are open to the public, but they include Blickling, Felbrigg, Holkham, Sheringham and the royal gardens at Sandringham – an impressive list. The garden with the finest collection of trees is Ryston Hall, but it is not open to the public. The same is true of Talbot Manor, which was planted from about 1950 onwards by the late Maurice Mason with advice from Sir Harold Hillier. Nevertheless, the National Gardens Scheme does fairly well in Norfolk and the county also has a good number of first-rate nurseries: Peter Beales Roses, Norfolk Lavender, P.W. Plants, Reads Nursery and the Romantic Garden Nursery are all of national importance and Bressingham Plant Centre was largely responsible for the enormous renewal of interest in herbaceous plants from about 1970 onwards. There are ten National Collections in the county, including a collection of *Elaeagnus* which is spread among several members of the Norfolk Group of the NCCPG. The Royal Horticultural Society has good links with Norfolk: Easton College near Norwich is a RHS Partner College and P.W. Plants is a RHS Partner Nursery, while Fairhaven Woodland & Water Garden and East Ruston Old Vicarage are RHS Free Access gardens. Many people consider that East Ruston Old Vicarage is the most important new garden to have been made in the UK during the last few years. And there is no doubt that both the Dell garden and Foggy Bottom at Bressingham continue to be immensely influential.

African Violet & Garden Centre

STATION ROAD, TERRINGTON ST CLEMENT, KING'S LYNN PE34 4PL

Tel 01553 828374 **Fax** 01553 828376
Website www.africanvioletcentre.ltd.uk
Location 3 miles west of King's Lynn, on A17.
Opening hours 9 am – 5 pm; daily; all year. Opens at 10 am on Sundays. Closed for New Year's Day, Christmas Day & Boxing Day.

Admission fee Free.

This nursery built its reputation on African violets, and its Chelsea exhibits have been memorable. Though it is now moving into other retail areas, it still has a fair selection of African violets on offer and displays to admire as well as hardy plants.

 Features African violets; house-plants; café.

Owned by Paul Crake & Mark Leach

Blickling Hall

BLICKLING, NORWICH NR11 6NF

Tel 01263 738030   **Fax** 01263 731660
Website www.nationaltrust.org.uk
Location 1 mile west of Aysham on B1354.
Opening hours 10.15 am – 5.15 pm; Wednesday –
Sunday & Bank Holiday Mondays; 23 March to
3 November. Plus Tuesdays in August. 11 am – 4 pm;
Thursday – Sunday; November & December.
Admission fee Adults £3.80; Children £1.90.

Blickling is the garden with everything: a
Jacobean mansion, handsomely
symmetrical; an early landscape lay-out (the
Doric Temple was built in about 1735); a
pretty conservatory by Samuel Wyatt; a large
mid-19th century parterre by Nesfield (note
the topiary pillars); and 1930s herbaceous
colour plantings by Norah Lindsay (her
masterpiece). And there are sheets of
bluebells in the woods.

Features Woodland garden;
rhododendrons & azaleas; good
herbaceous borders; bluebells; herbaceous
borders at peak July/August; National Trust
shop; light snacks, lunches & teas.

Owned by The National Trust
Number of gardeners 5
Size 20ha (50 acres)
English Heritage grade II*

Bradenham Hall

BRADENHAM, THETFORD IP25 7QR

Tel 01362 687243   **Fax** 01362 687669
Website www.bradenhamhall.co.uk
Location West of East Dereham, north of Bradenham.
Opening hours 2 pm – 5.30 pm; 2nd & 4th Sundays of
month; April to September.

Admission fee Adults £3; Children free.

This is an exceptional plant-lover's garden
for all seasons, made over the last 40 years in
a windy, open position at the top of what
passes in Norfolk for a hill. The first thing
you notice is that the house (early Georgian)
and garden walls are covered with unusual
shrubs, climbers and fruit. The flower
gardens are formally designed and richly
planted within beautiful yew hedges: formal
rose gardens, a paved garden, and
herbaceous and shrub borders. The
arboretum has a remarkable collection of
trees – more than 800 different species and
forms, many of them rare or very rare. All
are labelled. The walled kitchen gardens are
traditionally managed, with vegetables, cut
flowers, mixed borders, and 2 glasshouses.
In spring, the parkland and arboretum are
filled with daffodils – massed plantings of
more than 90 carefully chosen and graded
cultivars. A delight and an education.

Features Roses (mainly old-
fashioned); plantsman's collection of
plants; daffodils; good herbaceous borders;
fine collection of trees; tea-room.

Owned by Chris & Panda Allhusen
Number of gardeners 3
Size 8.3ha (21 acres)

Bressingham Plant Centre

BRESSINGHAM, DISS IP22 2AB

Tel 01379 687464
Website www.blooms-online.com
Location On A1066 3 miles west of Diss.
Opening hours 9 am – 5.30 pm; daily except
Christmas & Boxing Day.

The plant centre at Bressingham is no longer so closely associated with the Bloom family as it used to be. The retail range is strong on hardy perennials and shrubs, conifers and heathers, with a wide range of almost every type of garden plant. The owners are not just focused on plants, though: they say they 'also stock a wide range of gifts and lifestyle products'. The company also has other garden centres, for example at Dorney Court in Berkshire and Elton Hall in Cambridgeshire.

 Features Hardy plants; good garden centre.

Chanticleer

DEREHAM ROAD, OVINGTON, WATTON, THETFORD IP25 6SA

Tel 01953 881194
Location On A1075, 2 miles from Watton on the Dereham road.
Opening hours 10 am – 4 pm; 15 & 16 June, 3 & 4 August. And groups by appointment.
Admission fee Adults £2; OAPs £1; Children free.

Chanticleer is a former public house, converted to a private dwelling in the 1920s and since extended. The present owners have lived and gardened there for 20 years, originally in just under two acres, but then with three further acres for a small flock of Jacob sheep, Vietnamese pot-bellied pigs, goats, geese, chickens and ducks. The main garden includes a kitchen garden, greenhouses, orchard, herb garden and a large wildlife garden with a pond: all are managed organically. Great emphasis is placed on working with nature: the wildlife garden is frequented by birds, insects and small mammals, including breeding water voles. Most native shrubs and trees are represented, as are many wildflowers –

including two species of orchids, which have colonised parts of the wildlife area. There are demonstrations of how to make compost (including the use of wormeries) during both open weekends.

 Features Organic garden of great interest.

Owned by Mr & Mrs T. Rands
Number of gardeners owners only
Size 2ha (5 acres)

Dell Garden

BRESSINGHAM, DISS IP22 2AB

Tel 01379 688585 **Fax** 01379 688490
Location On A1066, 3 miles west of Diss.
Opening hours 10.30 am – 5.30 pm (4.30 pm in October); daily; April to October.
Admission fee Adults £7; OAPs £6; Children £5. Please note that this admission price includes joint entrance to Foggy Bottom garden. Unfortunately, Foggy Bottom is only open 12.30pm – 4.30pm, Tuesday – Friday, & Sundays & Bank Holiday Mondays.

There is no better place to learn about herbaceous plants – what they look like, how they grow and how to place them. The Dell is a 6-acre complex of about 50 island beds, which act as a trial ground and conservation resource for the herbaceous and alpine plants (over 5,000 of them) for which Alan Bloom is famous. The new Summer Garden was designed by Adrian Bloom to provide a new and more dramatic entrance to the garden. It has a stunning display of *Crocosmia* and *Miscanthus* cultivars interplanted with other perennials. The Blooms are keen to emphasise that the Dell Garden is not a museum piece but a carefully tended collection of perennials, developing and growing all the time.

East Ruston Old Vicarage

EAST RUSTON, NORWICH NR12 9HN

Tel 01602 650432   **Fax** 01692 651246
Website www.e-ruston-oldvicaragegardens.co.uk
Location Turn off A149 near Stalham – signed Walcott, Bacton, Happisburgh. Left at T-junction. On right after 2 miles, next to East Ruston church.
Opening hours 2 pm – 5.30 pm; Wednesdays, plus Friday-Sunday & Bank Holidays; 31 March to 25 October.
Admission fee Adults £3.80; Children £1. RHS members free in September & October.

This fine modern garden has been conceived on the grand scale. The owners combine the rare qualities of superb architectural design and exceptional plantsmanship. The house was built by a Surrey architect in 1913 in the Arts & Crafts style, which is uncommon in Norfolk. When the owners started to make their garden in 1988, it sat in an empty field. It was then that they planted the shelter belts, almost all tough evergreens. One of the most exciting things about the garden is to see so many tender exotics growing happily outside – literally thousands of them – which would not have been possible without the shelter belts. This is helped by the garden's location close to the North Sea with its maritime influence. The garden has been designed as a series of 'rooms', getting larger the further you move from the house. There are fine views borrowed from the landscape on two local churches and a whimsical porthole view of Happisburgh lighthouse. The 19 acres feature superb long borders abundantly and richly planted, a box parterre annually bedded out with unusual and original plant combinations, a gravelled forecourt with large groups of *Aeonium* 'Zwartkop' and various echeverias, a sunken garden containing many varieties including a large group of *Lobelia tupa*, and the newly relocated and much extended exotic garden with fabulously bold plantings of palms, bananas, shrubby salvias and many tender exotics. Much thought has gone into the design and preparation of beds for plants. The Mediterranean garden, for example, faces south and has a lot of brickwork and paving to preserve the warmth which plants need to survive through the winter. The beds are heavily mulched with gravel, and the result is that many plants survive which are typical of the Mediterranean *maquis*, the Californian chaparral and Australasia – clouds of yellow Australian mimosa, a very dark blue rosemary from the Mediterranean and *Beschorneria yuccoides* from Mexico. Even more impressive is the newly planted desert wash, made from over 200 tons of flints of varying sizes and covering at least an acre. It is intended to imitate the Arizona desert where the only rainfall is one of tumultuous thunderstorms every year. The plantings include some great specimens of palm trees, *Trithrinax campestris* from Argentina and *Brahea armata*, the Mexican blue palm, plus many agaves and aloes, some of which were grown from imported seed. East Ruston also has a pretty, no-nonsense vegetable garden, a cutting garden, woodland walks, wildflower meadows, a walled garden and a spectacular corn field, brimming with field poppies, cornflowers and corn marigold.

Features A young garden on a large scale; architectural plants; desert garden (2000); exotic garden (2001); tea-room.

Owned by Graham Robeson & Alan Gray
Size 7.6ha (19 acres)

Features Superb herbaceous borders; some alpine plants; beautiful plantings; island beds; refreshments in adjoining plant centre.

Owned by Alan Bloom
Number of gardeners 2
Size 2.2ha (6 acres)

East Lode

NURSERY LANE, HOCKWOLD,
THETFORD IP26 4ND

Tel 01842 827096
Location Down Church Lane in Hockwold, left at iron seat, then first house on right.
Opening hours By arrangement.
Admission fee Adults £2.

This is half-acre cottage garden is absolutely full of interest – shrubs, roses, clematis, and many unusual plants – all put together in the cottage style. Mrs Mansey fills it with colour throughout the year: many hellebores in spring, roses and clematis in summer, evergreens and silvers for autumn and winter, and tremendous underplantings of bulbs. There is a small pond, a greenhouse, some scree beds and a conservatory. It is also intended to be a haven for bees, birds and butterflies.

Features Plantsman's garden with many unusual plants; cottagey mix.

Owned by Mrs P. Mansey
Number of gardeners 1
Size 0.2ha (½ acre)

Fairhaven Woodland & Water Garden

SOUTH WALSHAM, NORWICH
NR13 6EA

Tel & Fax 01603 270449
Website www.norfolkbroads.com/fairhaven
Location Follow the brown signs off the A47 on to the B1140.
Opening hours 10 am – 5 pm; daily; all year except 25 December. Closes 9 pm on Wednesdays & Thursdays from May to August.
Admission fee Adults £3.50; OAPs £3; Children £1.25.
RHS members free from February to April & in October.

This is a vast woodland garden of naturalised rhododendrons under a canopy of ancient oaks – one vast pollarded specimen known as the King Oak is estimated to be 900 years old. In the 1960s, Lord Fairhaven laid two fairly narrow paths straight across a section of boggy Broads where sheets of candelabra primulas flourish in alder woodland. On the drier ground he planted masses of rhododendrons and azaleas among the naturalised *R. ponticum*. The garden is at its loveliest at the end of May, when the rhododendrons and candelabras are reflected in the still waters of the Broads. It is a bit short on follow-up later in the year, though there are effective plantings of *Osmunda regalis*, ligularias and gunneras. The snowdrops too are good in February, and the lysichitons in March. Many visitors use it as an access to South Walsham Broad, so that even in high season the horticultural visitor may be almost alone in the woodland garden. Good for wild life, too. And the garden is managed organically.

Features Woodland garden; bluebells; snowdrops; rhododendrons; lilies; candelabra primulas; boat trips on the

Elsing Hall

ELSING, DEREHAM NR20 3DX

Tel & Fax 01362 637224
Location B1110 to North Tuddenham, then follow signs.
Opening hours 2 pm – 6 pm; Sundays; June to
September; & by appointment.
Admission fee Adults £3; Children free.

David and Shirley Cargill bought Elsing Hall in 1984 and started to plant roses: their taste is both catholic and voracious. On the terracing in front of the house are cultivars as distinct as the shrub rose 'Centenaire de Lourdes' (a great favourite in France, but all too seldom seen in England), the lanky purple moss-rose 'William Lobb', pink 'Fimbriata' whose petals are fringed like a carnation's, the sumptuous 'Ardoisée de Lyon', and dainty white 'Katharina Zeimet'. Now the Cargills grow more than 500 different roses, and the number rises annually. They have a relaxed approach to the demands of maintenance, since most roses flourish on benign neglect and go on flowering year after year with little or no attention. The Cargills understand that there are better ways of passing your time as a gardener than following the conventional routines of spraying, pruning and training. There is no better place than Elsing Hall to enjoy the wild romantic way of growing roses. This is liberation gardening. Giant hogweeds seed around the front door, their outsize stateliness quite appropriate to the scale of the gabled hall. The huge grey thistle *Onopordum nervosum* self-seeds in the lawn below and is spared by the mower. But Elsing Hall is much more than a rose garden. The Cargills are enthusiastic plantsmen: their garden is a celebration of the sheer variety of the plant kingdom. Alongside the moat are bamboos, *Caltha polypetala*, a

patch of *Matteuccia struthiopteris* under a huge weeping ash, skunk cabbages, *Ligularia dentata* 'Desdemona', *Gunnera manicata* and *G. tinctoria* too: all are vigorous plants, lush growers, nudging each other for space. Some of their more recent additions – the garden is expanding all the time – include an avenue of ginkgos, a collection of willows, a small arboretum of trees chosen for their coloured bark, a formal garden with 64 yew pyramids and an old church steeple in the middle, a lime tunnel, and an autumn garden inspired by Piet Oudolf's use of autumn colour in his garden in Holland. Their latest project is a small 'theatre garden' with arches of variegated holly.

Features Roses (mainly old-fashioned); fruit; fine collection of trees; kitchen garden; otters; enlarged collection of old roses (1998); many rare trees planted (1999).

Owned by Mr & Mrs D.H. Cargill
Number of gardeners 1

broad; wild otters; shop; excellent plant sales area; tea-room.

Owned by Fairhaven Garden Trust
Number of gardeners 3
Size 36ha (90 acres)

Felbrigg Hall

FELBRIGG, NORWICH NR11 8PR

Tel 01263 837444   **Fax** 01263 837032
Website www.nationaltrust.org.uk
Location Entrance off B1436, signed from A148 & A140.
Opening hours 11 am – 5.30 pm; Saturday – Wednesday; 23 March to 3 November.
Admission fee Adults £2.30; Children £1.10.

There are fine trees in the park, but the best bit of Felbrigg is the walled kitchen garden, oriented on a large brick dovecote flanked by Victorian vineries. Fruit trees are trained against the walls (figs, pears, plums) and the garden laid to neatly-grown vegetables with herbaceous borders along the box-edged gravel paths.

Features Fruit; good herbaceous borders; National Trust shop; restaurant & tea-room.

Owned by The National Trust
Number of gardeners 3, plus 1 trainee
Size 2.2ha (6 acres)
NCCPG National Collections Colchicum
English Heritage grade II*

Foggy Bottom

BRESSINGHAM, DISS IP22 2AA

Tel 01379 688585   **Fax** 01379 688490
Location On A1066, 3 miles west of Diss.
Opening hours 12.30 pm – 4.30 pm; Tuesday – Friday, plus Sundays & Bank Holidays; April to October.

Admission fee Adults £7; OAPs £8; Children £5. Please note that admission price includes joint entrance to the Dell Garden.

Adrian Bloom started planting Foggy Bottom in about 1975 as a garden for year-round seasonal colour and interest. Its centrepiece was his unique collection of conifers, collected from all over the world and tested for English conditions. They were, for many years, the dominant plants in the garden, and he used them to show off the innumerable contrasts of form, colour, texture and shape between different cultivars. Then he began to use them in other plant combinations – with ornamental grasses, perennials and shrubs – chosen to give a succession of colour, texture and other interest throughout the year. Recently he overhauled the conifer bed and renamed it the 'All Seasons' bed. Some conifers were moved to other parts of the garden: others were heavily pruned. Some overgrown specimens were removed completely to make way for new planting schemes of shrubs, heathers, ornamental grasses and new young conifers. These new plantings are surrounded by an amphitheatre of mature beds. Adrian Bloom has also added a new woodland glade where shade- and moisture-loving plants surround a large pond. The net result is that Foggy Bottom continues to be an inspirational source of ideas for the smaller garden.

Features Plantsman's collection of plants; mature dwarf conifers; good herbaceous borders; Millennium planting scheme (2000); refreshments in adjacent plant centre.

Owned by Mr & Mrs Adrian Bloom
Number of gardeners 2
Size 2.2ha (6 acres)

Hoecroft Plants

SEVERALS GRANGE, HOLT ROAD,
WOOD NORTON, DEREHAM
NR20 5BL

Tel & Fax 01362 684206
Website www.hoecroft.co.uk
Location 2 miles north of Guist on B1110 (not in West
Norton village).
Opening hours 10 am – 4 pm; Thursday – Sunday; April
to September.

Hoecroft is a small but well-known specialist
nursery which began by concentrating upon
variegated and coloured foliage plants.
These range from the smallest alpines to
large shrubs. Perhaps more prominent now
is its list of ornamental grasses, rushes,
sedges and bamboos: it offers over 250
different cultivars, which may be seen in
the attached display garden.

 Features Grasses; mixed borders.

Owned by Jane Lister

Holkham Hall

HOLKHAM, WELLS-NEXT-THE-SEA
NR23 1AB

Tel 01328 710227   **Fax** 01328 711707
Location Off A149, 2 miles west of Wells.
Opening hours 1 pm – 5 pm; Sunday – Thursday; 26 May
to 30 September. Plus 11.30 am – 5 pm on 31 March,
1 April, 5 & 6 May, 2, 3 & 4 June, 25 & 26 August. Park
open from 9 am, Sunday to Friday, in summer; Monday to
Friday in winter.
Admission fee Park free.

Holkham is a big landscape garden, worked
on by Kent, Brown and Repton. Formal

terraces were added in the 1850s. The
garden centre known as Holkham Nursery
Gardens is in the 18th-century walled
garden and has several demonstration
gardens (including areas for herbs, roses
and perennials) along with a recently
restored fig house.

 Features Gift shop; garden centre
open daily all year 10 am – 5 pm;
refreshments.

Owned by The Earl of Leicester
English Heritage grade I

Hoveton Hall

WROXHAM, NORWICH NR12 8RJ

Tel 01603 782798   **Fax** 01603 784564
Location 9 miles from Norwich: brown tourist signs from
A1151.
Opening hours 11 am to 5.30 pm; Wednesdays, Fridays,
Sundays & Bank Holiday Mondays; Easter to 22
September. Also open on Thursdays in May.
Admission fee Adults £3.50; Wheelchair-bound £2;
Children £1.

The gardens are laid out around a series of
streams, with beautiful waterside plantings
and candelabra primulas. The walled
garden, built as late as 1936, is set out for
growing fruit and vegetable in the
traditional way, with fine herbaceous
borders too.

Features Rhododendrons & azaleas;
daffodils; good herbaceous borders;
water garden; light lunches & teas.

Owned by Mr & Mrs Andrew Buxton
Number of gardeners 3
Size 4ha (10 acres)

Lynford Arboretum

MUNFORD, THETFORD IP26 5HW

Tel 01842 810271
Location Turn right off A1065 just north of Munford.
Opening hours Dawn – dusk; daily; all year.
Admission fee Free.

The Lynford Arboretum was started in 1947 by students at the Forester Training School who at that time occupied nearby Lynford Hall. They planted about 100 species of conifers and broadleaves, some in forestry plots but mostly as individual specimens within the parkland and policies surrounding the house. The soil is thin and sandy, but some of those original plantings are already handsome specimens, including a *Nothofagus obliqua* and a *Pinus banksiana* each 20m tall. Rather simply maintained by the Forestry Commission, the arboretum has considerable potential for development. Lynford Hall is now an hotel: the extensive formal garden (rather gone back) was laid out by William Burn in the 1860s and was famous for its bedding until 1914. Beyond is a curving lake. Rather surprisingly, the Forestry Commission does not permit dogs in the arboretum.

Features Trees, deciduous & evergreen.

Owned by Forestry Agency

Mannington Gardens

MANNINGTON HALL, NORWICH NR11 7BB

Tel 01263 584175 **Fax** 01263 761214
Location Signed from B1149 at Saxthorpe.

Opening hours 12 noon – 5 pm; Sundays; May – September. And 11 am – 5 pm; Wednesday – Friday; June – August.
Admission fee Adults £3; Concessions £2.50; Children free.

The gardens at Mannington embrace a moated house, the ruins of Mannington church, two lakes (recently landscaped), a scented garden, an arboretum of native trees, genuine wildflower meadows and handsome herbaceous borders, but the best part is the Heritage Rose Garden, made in association with Peter Beales, where thousands of old-fashioned roses are planted to illustrate the history of roses in cultivation. The developments are represented by beds which display roses according to their periods, from the 15th century to 2002.

Features Roses (mainly old-fashioned & climbers); natural surroundings; colour borders; lakes; wildflowers; roses for sale; light refreshments, teas.

Owned by Lord Walpole
Number of gardeners 3½
Size 8ha (20 acres)
English Heritage grade II

Norfolk Lavender

CALEY MILL, HEACHAM, KING'S LYNN PE31 7JE

Tel 01485 570384 **Fax** 01485 571176
Location On A149, 13 miles north of Kings Lynn.
Opening hours 9.30 am – 6 pm; summer. 10.30 am – 4 pm; winter. Closed for about 2 weeks at Christmas & New Year.

This family-run nursery has grown into quite a business, and can be crowded when the fields of lavender (100 acres) flower in stripes across the surrounding fields. The nursery sells lavender (hardy and tender, bare root and potted), lavender products and other scented plants. Of most interest to the horticulturally aware will be the National Collection of *Lavandula* cultivars. And all will enjoy the f4-acre 'fragrant meadow' of plants chosen for their aromatic qualities.

NCCPG National Collections *Lavandula* (sect. Lavandula, Dentata, Pterostoechas & Stoechas)

Oxburgh Hall

OXBOROUGH, KING'S LYNN PE33 9PS

Tel 01366 328258   Fax 01366 328066
Website www.nationaltrust.org.uk
Location 7 miles south-west of Swaffham on Stoke Ferry road.
Opening hours 11 am – 4 pm; Saturdays & Sundays; 2 to 17 March. Then 11 am – 5.30 pm; Saturday – Wednesday; 23 March to 3 November. Daily in August.
Admission fee Adults £2.80; Children £1.40.

The baroque 19th-century parterre has been replanted by the National Trust with such herbs as rue and cineraria making permanent companions for annuals and bedding plants. Good fruit trees in the walled garden, especially medlars and quinces. Not a great garden, but a good one.

Features Roses (mainly modern); good herbaceous borders; French-style parterre; trained fruit trees; woodland walks; vegetable garden; gift shop; light lunches & teas.

Owned by The National Trust
Number of gardeners 2, plus volunteers
Size 6.2ha (15½ acres)
English Heritage grade II

P.W. Plants

SUNNYSIDE, HEATH ROAD, KENNINGHALL NR16 2DS

Tel & Fax 01953 888212
Location South-west of Norwich, just off B1113.
Opening hours 9 am – 5 pm; Fridays & Saturday; all year. But Fridays and only the last Saturday of the month between October & March.
Admission fee Free.

This RHS Partner Nursery offers a wide range of plants chosen for their general garden-worthiness, interesting foliage and shape. It is perhaps best known for its bamboos, which have won the nursery many medals at RHS shows, but P. W. Plants also stock grasses, shrubs, perennials and climbers. Most can be seen growing in the display gardens.

Features Bamboos.

Owned by Paul Whittaker
Size 0.6ha (1½ acres)

Peter Beales Roses

LONDON ROAD, ATTLEBOROUGH NR17 1AY

Tel 01953 454707   Fax 01953 456845
Website www.classicroses.co.uk
Location 2 miles south of Attleborough: leave A11 at Breckland Lodge. Follow Tourist Board signs.
Opening hours 9 am – 5 pm (4 pm in January); Monday – Friday. 9 am – 4.30 pm; Saturday. 10 am – 4 pm; Sunday.
Admission fee Free.

There is a small display garden attached to this well-known rose nursery and latest reports say that it is well maintained. A good range of older and classic roses is offered for sale, both at the nursery and from its mail-order catalogue which lists over 1,200 species and cultivars, many not available elsewhere in the United Kingdom.

 Features Roses (mainly old-fashioned).

Owned by Peter Beales
Number of gardeners 2
Size 1ha (2½ acres)
NCCPG National Collections *Rosa* (species)

Plantation Garden

4 EARLHAM ROAD, NORWICH
NR2 3DB

Tel 01603 455223/621868 **Fax** 01603 631166
Website www.plantationgarden.co.uk
Location Between Beeches Hotel and the Roman Catholic Cathedral.
Opening hours 10 am – 4 pm (9 am – 6 pm from April to October); daily; all year. On 14 April & 1 September for NGS.
Admission fee Adults £1.50; Children free. Honesty box.

The Plantation Garden was made in an abandoned chalk quarry by Henry Trevor, a successful Norwich businessman, between around 1856 until his death in 1897. In the ensuing years the garden passed through various hands until, in 1980, it was totally overgrown, abandoned and forgotten. In that year it was re-discovered and the Plantation Garden Preservation Trust formed to save and restore the garden. The area, nearly 3 acres in all, contains many features including woodland walkways, flower beds, lawns, a gothic fountain, Italianate terrace, 'Mediaeval' terrace wall and rustic bridge. There are many unique aspects to this very idiosyncratic garden making it a haven of peace and tranquillity –

a refuge from the hurly-burly of modern life and a glimpse into a bygone age. Sir Roy Strong is patron of the Trust and points out that the garden is 'something of a rarity, for in most cases it is usually only the grandest of gardens which survive from earlier periods'. The original house, designed by Edward Boardman for Henry Trevor, is now part of Beeches Hotel.

 Features Historic Victorian suburban garden undergoing restoration.

Owned by The Plantation Garden Preservation Trust
Number of gardeners 1 part-time, plus volunteers
Size 1.2ha (3 acres)
English Heritage grade II

Raveningham Hall Gardens

RAVENINGHAM, NORWICH
NR14 6NS

Tel 01508 548480 **Fax** 01508 548958
Website www.raveningham.com
Location Signed off A146 at Hales.
Opening hours 2 pm – 5.30 pm on Sundays, Wednesdays & Bank Holiday Mondays; April to September.
Admission fee Adults £2.50; OAPs £2; Children free.

The house at Raveningham is partly Georgian and partly 20th-century: the 14th-century church of St Andrew near the house is an integral part of the landscape. Both are set in a splendid 18th-century park and enhanced by 19th-century tree plantings. Despite all this history, the main attraction now is the modern plantings. These were largely the work of Priscilla, Lady Bacon, who collected rare plants and arranged them beautifully in areas like the long herbaceous border. She was also a keen dendrologist and planted the young arboretum. In the working walled garden (very pretty) is a recently restored Victorian glasshouse. Outside the walled garden are an orchard and herb garden. A new lake has been made in the park, and there are contemporary sculptures by the present owner's wife throughout. It is good to see this excellent modern garden open more often to the public again.

 Features Roses (mainly modern); good herbaceous borders; fine collection of trees; splendid 18th-century walled garden and Victorian glasshouses.

Owned by Sir Nicholas Bacon Bt.
Number of gardeners 2
English Heritage grade II

Reads Nursery

HALES HALL, LODDON NR14 6QW

Tel 01508 548395   **Fax** 01508 548040
Website www.readsnursery.co.uk
Location Off A146, 1 mile south of Loddon.
Opening hours 10 am – 5 pm (4 pm in winter); Tuesday – Saturday; all year. Plus 11 am – 4 pm; Sundays & Bank Holiday Mondays; April to October.
Admission fee Garden £1.50; Nursery free
Ⓟ ⓌⒸ ⓖ ⊛

This important and long-established family nursery specialises in citrus fruit-trees and conservatory plants. Its extensive list of *Citrus* cultivars is based upon the centuries-old collection made by Rivers of Sawbridgeworth. Rivers were famous fruit-breeders in the 19th century, and their citrus trees supplied the scions needed to start the California fruit industry. Reads acquired their stock when Rivers closed in 1983. They also grow and sell over 70 different grape cultivars, including many more English-raised vines than any other nursery: this is the place to find such Victorian delicacies as 'Lady Downe's Seedling' and 'Mrs Pince's

Black Muscat'. Their list of figs is equally extensive, and unparalleled among UK nurserymen: 'Goutte d'Or', 'Malcolm's Giant' and 'White Ischia' are among their specialities. But they also stock a large number of proper traditional conservatory plants – abutilons, bougainvilleas, brugmansias, gardenias, jasmines, passionflowers, sparmannias and hundreds more. In the adjoining 2-acre garden are the moated remains of a mediaeval hall, planted with topiary, a 'potted' fruit orchard, a *potager*, a vegetable garden and a plantsman's collection of shrubs, herbaceous plants and bulbs. Restoration on the Victorian glasshouse will be completed during the course of the year (2002).

 Features Conservatory plants; climbers.

Owned by The Read Family
Number of gardeners 1
Size 0.8ha (2 acres)
NCCPG National Collections *Citrus*; *Ficus*; *Vitis vinifera* (grapes)

The Romantic Garden Nursery

SWANNINGTON, NORWICH NR9 5NW

Tel 01603 261488   **Fax** 01603 864231
Website www.romantic-garden.demon.co.uk
Location 7 miles north-west of Norwich.
Opening hours 10 am – 5 pm; Wednesdays, Fridays & Saturdays.
Admission fee Free.
Ⓟ ⊛

The Romantic Garden Nursery sells topiary: ornamental standards, bobbles and pyramids in *Cupressus* and *Ilex*, as well as box in animal and other shapes. It is a specialist nursery holding one of the largest selections of topiary and ornamental standards in the country. It offers topiary packages too – these include a layout together with the necessary plants – and a range of wire frames for growing and shaping your own topiary. Also available are large specimens of conservatory plants and a 'plant hire' service, borrowing topiary and specimen plants for special occasions.

Owned by John Powles

Sandringham House

SANDRINGHAM, KING'S LYNN PE35 6EN

Tel 01553 772675   **Fax** 01485 541571
Website www.sandringhamestate.co.uk
Location Signed from A148.
Opening hours 10.30 am – 5 pm; daily; 30 March to 23 July & 7 August to 27 October. Closed 18 July.
Admission fee Adults £6; OAPs £4.50; Children £3.50.

The best of the royal gardens. The woodland and lakes are rich with ornamental plantings, and the splendid herbaceous borders were designed by Geoffrey Jellicoe, but it is the scale of it all that most impresses, and the grandeur too.

 Features Good herbaceous borders; rhododendrons; azaleas; maples; hydrangeas; gift shop; restaurant & tea-rooms.

Owned by H.M. The Queen
Number of gardeners 8
Size 22ha (60 acres)
English Heritage grade II*

Sheringham Park

SHERINGHAM NR26 8TB

Tel & Fax 01263 823778
Website www.nationaltrust.org.uk
Location Junction of A148 & B1157.
Opening hours Dawn – dusk; daily; all year.
Admission fee Cars £2.70.

This is one of the best Repton landscapes to have survived the last 200 years, but it was also fleshed out with a great 20th-century collection of rhododendrons. The elegant classical temple was designed by Repton but not actually built until 1975. Recent clearing and replanting have opened up the rhododendron woods very successfully.

 Features Woodland garden; mature conifers; rhododendrons; refreshments.

Owned by The National Trust
Number of gardeners 1
Size 20ha (50 acres)
English Heritage grade II*

Thorncroft Clematis Nursery

THE LINGS, REYMERSTON, NORWICH NR9 4QG

Tel 01953 850407   **Fax** 01953 851788
Website www.thorncroft.co.uk
Location Between Dereham & Wymondham on B1135.
Opening hours 10 am – 4.30 pm, daily, March to October. Closed Wednesdays. By appointment only in winter.
Admission fee Free.

This family-run specialist RHS Partner Nursery began as a hobby and has now developed into a substantial business. In the display garden attached to the nursery, the owners have set out some of the many ways that clematis may be grown – in borders and island beds, over shrub roses, through ornamental trees and in containers. There is also a formal sunken garden with clipped box hedges and classical obelisks (covered by yet more clematis, and roses). The nursery does not stock all clematis cultivars, but prefers to list those it regards as best, selected for such qualities as their length of flowering, colour, form, quantity of bloom, strength of growth and so on. These amount to some 300+ cultivars, including many new introductions from around the world.

Owned by Ruth & Jonathan Gooch

NORTHAMPTONSHIRE

Despite its industrial importance and its proximity to London, Northamptonshire is still a county of large estates. Three of the four Grade I historic gardens are open to the public (Althorp, Boughton House and Castle Ashby), while the fourth (Drayton) is occasionally open to groups from organisations like the Garden History Society. Althorp and Boughton also have good arboreta, each with a few champion trees. The National Gardens Scheme does well in Northamptonshire: it is particularly successful in persuading groups of gardens, as many as eight or nine in a village, to open together on the same day. It is therefore something of a paradox that there appear to be comparatively few nurseries in the county: certainly, the Royal Horticultural Society has no Partner Nurseries in Northamptonshire. On the other hand, its only Free Access garden – Cottesbrooke – is a modern classic, an historic landscape with a really good horticultural garden inserted into it.

Althorp

ALTHORP, NORTHAMPTON NN7 4HQ

Tel 01604 770107   **Fax** 01604 770042
Website www.althorp.com
Location Signed from M1, Jct 16.
Opening hours 10 am – 5 pm; daily; July to September. Closed 31 August.
Admission fee Adults £10.50; OAPs £8.50; Children £5.50 for tickets bought in advance from 0870 167 9000. Adults £11.50; OAPs £9.50; Children £5.50 on the gate.

Althorp is interesting more for its ex-royal associations than as a great garden. However, it is said to be undergoing some improvement under the direction of Dan Pearson. The 19th-century formal gardens are impressive and the traditional parkland deeply pastoral. In the 19th-century arboretum are some fine mature trees,

including a record-breaking Santa Lucia fir (*Abies bracteata*) over 30m high.

 Features Mature conifers; formal gardens; biggest *Abies bracteata* (38m) in the British Isles.

Owned by Earl Spencer
English Heritage grade I

Boughton House

KETTERING NN14 1BJ

Tel 01536 515731   **Fax** 01536 417255
Website www.boughtonhouse.org.uk
Location A43, three miles north of Kettering, signed through Geddington.
Opening hours 1 pm – 5 pm; Saturday – Thursday; 1 May to 1 September. Plus Fridays in August.
Admission fee Adults £1.50; OAPs & Children £1.

Boughton has a seriously important landscaped park (350 acres – 140ha) dating from the early 18th century. The lay-out is intact, and some of the plantings too – one of the lime avenues was planted in 1715. The original landscaping features have been purposefully restored over the last 20 years or so: rides, avenues, *allées*, lakes, canals and prospects. There is little of horticultural interest (even though Valerie Finnis lives in a wing of the house), but the sense of history is strongly felt.

   Features Roses (mainly modern); good herbaceous borders; good website; current holder of Sandford Award; shop; plant centre in walled garden; tea-rooms (weekdays only; daily in August).

Owned by The Duke & Duchess of Buccleuch & The Living Landscape Trust
Number of gardeners 5
Size 8ha (20 acres) garden
English Heritage grade I

Canons Ashby House

DAVENTRY NN11 3SD

Tel 01327 860044   **Fax** 01327 860168
Website www.nationaltrust.org.uk
Location Signed from A5 & A422.
Opening hours 11 am – 5.30 pm (4.30 pm in October & November); Saturday – Wednesday; 23 March to 3 November.
Admission fee Adults £1 (garden only).

Ⓟ ⓦⒸ ♿ 🌱 ☕

Canons Ashby is a rare survivor among gardens. The Drydens, who owned it, never really took to the landscape movement. The early 18th-century lay-out is intact and has been carefully restored by the National Trust. The terraces below the house (*very* pretty) are planted with clipped Portugal laurel (*Prunus lusitanica*) and period

fruit trees. A place to contemplate old Tory values.

    Features Topiary; fruit; good herbaceous borders; light lunches & teas.

Owned by The National Trust
Number of gardeners 2
Size 1.4ha (3½ acres)
English Heritage grade II*

Castle Ashby Gardens

CASTLE ASHBY, NORTHAMPTON NN7 1LQ

Tel & Fax 01604 696187
Location Off A428 between Northampton & Bedford.
Opening hours 10 am – 6 pm; daily; all year.
Admission fee Adults £2.50; OAPs & Children £1.50.

Ⓟ 🐕 ♿ 🌱 🏛 ☕

Much thought and money has recently been spent on restoring the gardens at Castle Ashby. The Italian formal gardens were among the first to be renewed, and the arboretum has been restocked. There are stylish terraces, an orangery and greenhouses built by Sir Matthew Digby Wyatt in the 1860s but perhaps the best thing about Castle Ashby is the park – 200 acres of it, designed by Capability Brown.

Features Topiary; plants under glass; fine collection of trees; gift shops; refreshments.

Owned by Marquess of Northampton
Number of gardeners 3
Size 8ha (20 acres)
English Heritage grade I

Coton Manor

GUILSBOROUGH NN6 8RQ

Tel 01604 740219 **Fax** 01604 740838
Website www.cotonmanor.co.uk
Location Signed from A5199 (formerly A50) & A428.
Opening hours 12 noon – 5.30 pm; Tuesday – Saturday &
Bank Holiday Mondays; April to September. Plus Sundays
in April & May.
Admission fee Adults £3.50; OAPs £3; Children £2.

The Pasley-Tylers have lived at Coton since
the 1920s, and every generation has left its
mark upon the garden. Among the best
features are a rose garden, a herb garden, a
woodland garden, colour plantings
(including a wonderful crimson and pink
border), a Mediterranean bank, a 5-acre
bluebell wood, an apple orchard with 80
English cultivars, and a wildflower meadow.
Water is everywhere: pools, streams and
ponds support hostas, primulas and the
black-and-yellow flowers of *Kirengeshoma
palmata*. There are surprises too: one might
suppose that the sweet-scented
Trachelospermum asiaticum and long-
flowering *Fremontodendron californicum*
were too tender for Northamptonshire, but
they both grow against the walls of the
house. Recent plantings include a herb
garden and a rose garden with pink 'Mary
Rose' and white 'Winchester Cathedral'. The
whole garden comes together nicely because
the plants are chosen for their overall
contribution as well as their intrinsic merits.
The standard of maintenance is excellent,
while the presence of a few ornamental birds
adds quite another dimension to a visit.

Features Woodland garden; roses
(mainly old cultivars); good
herbaceous borders; bluebells; waterfowl;
lots of pots; good garden nursery; home
produce & gifts; excellent small nursery;
light lunches & teas.

Owned by Ian Pasley-Tyler
Number of gardeners 3
Size 4ha (10 acres)

Cottesbrooke Hall

NORTHAMPTON NN6 8PF

Tel 01604 505808 **Fax** 01604 505619
Website www.cottesbrookehall.co.uk
Location 10 miles north of Northampton.
Opening hours 2 pm – 5 pm; Thursdays, Bank Holiday
Mondays & the first Sunday of each month; Easter to
September. Plus 2 pm – 5 pm; Tuesdays, Wednesdays &
Fridays; May to September.
Admission fee Garden only: Adults £3; Children £1.50.
RHS members free.

Cottesbrooke is the garden with everything:
a 2-mile drive, majestic parkland, a classical
bridge, a fabulously pretty house, an 18th-
century park, lakes, waterfalls, bluebell
woods, rhododendrons, acres of daffodils,
27 cultivars of naturalised snowdrops, half-
a-dozen garden rooms, Scheemaker's statues
from Stowe, an armillary garden, pergolas,
allées, 300-year old cedars, new
developments every year, immaculate
maintenance, an enlightened owner, plants
a-plenty, and the signatures of Geoffrey
Jellicoe and Sylvia Crowe among the
designers who have helped to develop it.

Features Roses (mainly old-
fashioned); good herbaceous borders;
harmonious design; thoughtful plantings;
water gardens; wild gardens; HHA/Christie's
Garden of the Year in 2000.

Owned by Captain & Mrs John Macdonald-Buchanan
English Heritage grade II

Holdenby House Gardens

HOLDENBY, NORTHAMPTON NN6 8DJ

Tel 01604 770074 **Fax** 01604 770962
Website www.holdenby.com
Location 6 miles north-west of Northampton, off A5199 or A428.
Opening hours 1 pm – 5 pm; Sunday – Friday; July & August. Plus Sundays from Easter to 30 September. Closes at 6 pm on Bank Holiday Sundays & Mondays.
Admission fee Adults £3; OAPs £2.50; Children £1.75. But Adults £5; OAPs £4.50; Children £3 at Bank Holidays when the house is open.

The outlines of the garden at Holdenby are Elizabethan: a bowling alley, some parterres and terraces which were built in 1580 to impress Queen Elizabeth on one of her progresses through England. They explain why Holdenby is so highly regarded as an historical garden. What we see now is modern and pretty. The Elizabethan-style garden was planted by Rosemary Verey, using only those plants which were available in 1580. Rupert Golby planted the 'fragrant border' and there is a charming 'silver border' made to display the owners' ever-growing collection of silver- and grey-leaved plants.

Features Roses (mainly old-fashioned); herbs; good herbaceous borders; Elizabethan-style garden; fragrant and silver borders; kitchen garden; current holder of Sandford Award; souvenirs and crafts for sale; tea-room in original Victorian kitchen.

Owned by Mr & Mrs James Lowther
Number of gardeners 3
Size 6ha (15 acres)
English Heritage grade II*

Kelmarsh Hall

NORTHAMPTON NN6 9LU

Tel 01604 686485 **Fax** 01604 686543
Website www.kelmarsh.com
Location On A508 at crossroads in Kelmarsh.
Opening hours 2 pm – 5 pm; Monday – Thursday & Sundays; Easter to 31 August. Opens at 2.30 pm on Sundays.
Admission fee Adults £2.

Kelmarsh is a handsome Palladian house: it looks out over a formal terrace to formalised parkland, designed by Geoffrey Jellicoe in 1936. The view extends across a meadow lined with horse chestnuts to a lake before wilder, open semi-parkland carries the eye to the horizon. Most of the horticultural interest is off to the side, around the outside of a triangular walled garden. First come lumpy box hedges, pleached limes and a pretty sunken garden, designed as a quincunx and planted with white and scented flowers. Further on, *Tropaeolum speciosum* clambers through the hedges which flank a sequence of narrow, intimate beds, designed by Nancy Lancaster with help from Norah Lindsay. Some of the yew hedges have been breached by cutting the yew trees back to the trunks and letting them grow into curious hump-backed shapes – a very effective and unique feature of the garden. At the furthest extremity, the narrow path bursts out into a fan-shaped old-fashioned rose garden, recently re-made, with a splendid view of the parish church across a paddock. On the way back (outside the walled garden again) is the long border, another Lancaster-Lindsay collaboration, which is currently being restored and replanted. This is a fine garden, which will be interesting to watch as it develops in years to come.

Features Spring bulbs; old hedges; lots of recent restoration; teas on Sundays.

Owned by Kelmarsh Hall Estate Preservation Trust
Number of gardeners 4
Size 5.6ha (14 acres)

The Menagerie

NEWPORT PAGNELL ROAD, HORTON NN7 2BX

Tel & Fax 01604 870957
Location One mile south of Horton on the B526.
Opening hours 2 pm – 5 pm; Mondays & Thursdays; April to September. Plus 2 pm – 6 pm on the last Sunday of those months.
Admission fee Adults £3.50; Children £1.50.

This folly, built in 1750 for the 2nd Earl of Halifax by Thomas Wright of Durham, stands above Grade II listed parkland. Derelict until 1975 – it was originally intended as a dining house with an attached zoo – it was completely restored by the architectural historian Gervase Jackson-Stops. The garden was conceived and laid out in the 1980s in a goosefoot pattern, with a central lime avenue leading to a spiral mount and obelisk, and two hornbeam-lined *allées* leading to restored 18th-century pools with fountains. The two thatched arbours are recent, one triangular and gothic, the other round and classical (now used as a chapel). Orpheus plays to the animals in the shell grotto beneath the house. The rose garden was designed by Vernon Russell-Smith and the exotic bog garden was by Jinny Blom in the spirit of Ian Kirby's original design. This is currently being expanded to reach the new 500 sq.m walled garden with its opulent central fountain. The plantings are bold and romantic. The nursery was designed by Charles Morris.

 Features Good modern design; inventive garden follies; pretty plantings.

Owned by Alexander Myers
Number of gardeners 2
Size 1.6ha (4 acres)

Old Rectory

SUDBOROUGH NN14 3BX

Tel 01832 733247   **Fax** 01832 733832
Location In village centre, by church, off A6116.
Opening hours 10 am to 4 pm; Tuesdays; April to September. Groups welcome at other times by appointment.
Admission fee Adults £3; Children free.

This immaculately maintained modern garden has been made around a handsome Georgian rectory with a bit of advice from Rosemary Verey and Rupert Golby. In front of the house, on the edge of the lawn, is a handsome and ancient *Robinia pseudoacacia*: everything else is fairly recent and extremely well grown. The garden is thickly and thoughtfully planted so that every season is rich in interest. Few of the plants are rare, but all are well chosen – some for their flowers, some for their foliage and others because they look good in mixed groups. Roses are much in evidence throughout the garden and in a dedicated rose garden. The best feature is an extensive and very pretty *potager*, which has an infinite number of box-edged beds and fairly narrow brick paths between them. Clematis and roses cover the framework of a tunnel: they are joined, in season, by ornamental gourds which are encouraged to grow up the same structure. The fruit trees are trained in many different ways and good use is made of flowers in pots to ensure that the *potager* has colour at all seasons.

Features Roses (ancient & modern); herbs; fruit; good herbaceous borders; handsome new *potager*; tea, coffee & biscuits.

Owned by Mr & Mrs A.P. Huntington
Size 1.2ha (3 acres)

Rockingham Castle

MARKET HARBOROUGH LE16 8TH

Tel 01586 770240 **Fax** 01586 771692
Location 2 miles north of Corby on A6003.
Opening hours 11.30 am – 5 pm; Sundays & Bank Holiday Mondays. Plus 1 pm – 5 pm Tuesdays & Thursdays in July & August.
Admission fee £3.50.

Rockingham has centuries of garden history in its layout: the park was landscaped in the 18th century but goes back to the 13th century as a deer park. The formal circular rose garden on the site of the old keep was added in the 19th century: it is surrounded by a billowing yew hedge 400 years old. The wild garden in a ravine was replanted 20 years ago as a mini-arboretum: all the modern plantings are very effective.

 Features Roses (mainly old-fashioned); good herbaceous borders (some new for 2002); fine collection of trees; gift shop; tea-room.

Owned by James Saunders Watson
Number of gardeners 3
Size 5ha (12 acres)
English Heritage grade II*

Sulgrave Manor

SULGRAVE, BANBURY OX17 2SD

Tel 01295 760205 **Fax** 01295 768056
Website www.stratford.co.uk/sulgrave
Location 7 miles from Banbury.
Opening hours 2 pm – 5.30 pm; daily; 29 March to 31 October.
Admission fee Adults £5; Children £2.50. But Adults £6.50; Children £3.25 for special events.

There are two reasons for visiting Sulgrave. The first is that it belonged to George Washington's family or, at least, to his ancestors. This places the Great American firmly among the English landed gentry. The second is that, after the estate was underwritten by the Colonial Dames in 1924, Sir Reginald Blomfield was called in to design a period garden. In his day, Blomfield was one of England's foremost architect-designers, and the garden he made for Sulgrave is formally laid out in the 17th-century style, to complement the old house. The plantings are suitably olde worlde, and the standard of maintenance unsurpassed. The Herb Society moved its headquarters to Sulgrave in October 2001 and work has now begun on a major new herb garden.

 Features Topiary; roses (mainly modern); herbs; fruit; good herbaceous borders; tea-room.

Owned by Sulgrave Manor Board
Number of gardeners 2
Size 2ha (5 acres)
English Heritage grade II

NORTHUMBERLAND AND TYNE & WEAR

Northumberland and Tyne & Wear are two sides of the same historical phenomenon: men made their fortunes in Newcastle or Sunderland, both now in Tyne & Wear, and then moved out to build houses and plant gardens in Northumberland. Belsay, Cragside and Lindisfarne all owe their gardens to this social pattern. Belsay is a Grade I garden: the only other one in Northumberland is Alnwick, where the Duchess of Northumberland has started to develop an extensive (and expensive) new water garden. The greatest 19th-century garden in Northumberland is Cragside, which now has a collection of champion conifers. There are record-breakers too at Alnwick, and a good arboretum at Howick, where many new plantings have also been made in recent years. The National Gardens Scheme does not have a large portfolio of gardens in Northumberland and Tyne & Wear, but there are several first-rate nurseries in the two counties, including Halls of Heddon, Herterton House and Hexham Herbs. The real interests of ordinary gardeners in Northumberland and Tyne & Wear are quite different: alpines and leeks. Both the Alpine Garden Society and the Scottish Rock Garden Club are well supported here, while the National Pot Leek Society could be described as a uniquely Geordie success story.

Alnwick Castle

ALNWICK NE66 1NQ

Tel 01665 510777
Website www.alnwickgarden.com
Location Signed in Alnwick.
Opening hours 10 am – 5 pm; daily; all year. Closed at Christmas.
Admission fee Adults £4; Concessions £3.50; Children free.

The Duchess of Northumberland is the driving force behind this imaginative new garden, and Jacques Wirtz is its designer. First open to the public in 2001, it is still only half-made, but the main feature is already impressive – a grand water cascade flanked by hornbeam tunnels. At the top, you enter the Ornamental Garden, a place of box-lined paths, pleached apples, old roses and mixed plantings, as dreamily English as the cascade is exotic. In due course the gardens – whose future depends upon funding – will be handed over to a charitable trust.

 Features Grand cascade; new gardens; garden café.

Owned by Duke & Duchess of Northumberland

Bede's World Herb Garden

BEDE'S WORLD, CHURCH BANK, JARROW NE32 3DY

Tel 0191 489 2106 **Fax** 0191 428 2361
Website www.bedesworld.co.uk
Location Signed from A185 & A19
Opening hours Dawn to dusk; daily; all year.
Admission fee Garden only: free.

Bede's World is an educational experience: one of its main parts is an 'Anglo-Saxon farm'. But there is also a herb garden, based on a plan of the 9th-century original at St Gall in Switzerland, where culinary, aromatic and medicinal herbs are grown. It is a small part of an ambitious enterprise which seeks to impart a feeling for the Anglo-Saxon world.

 Features Herbs; shop for herbal products; refreshments.

Owned by Jarrow 700 AD Ltd

Belsay Hall

BELSAY, NEWCASTLE-UPON-TYNE NE20 0DX

Tel 01661 881636 **Fax** 01661 881043
Location At Belsay on A696 Ponteland to Jedburgh road.
Opening hours 10 am – 6 pm (5 pm in October & 4 pm from November to March); daily except 1 January & 24 – 26 December.

Admission fee Adults £3.90; Concessions £2.90; Children £2.

The wildly Picturesque gardens at Belsay were created by Sir Charles Monck in the 19th century around his new Greek Revival house. The outstanding feature is 11 acres (4ha) of disused quarry with a sequence of gloomy chasms, corridors and pinnacles, which house all manner of exotic and rare plants. Rhododendron species flower here from November to August, climbers scramble 10m up the quarry faces, spring bulbs carpet the meadow and modern underplantings like lilies flower from May to September. The ravines create a microclimate which allows such plants as *Trachycarpus* palms and eucryphias to flourish in a cold upland site: Belsay is of great interest to plantsmen. The house is very plain – inspired by ancient Athens – but underpinned by fine formal terraces where the gardeners arrange magnificent displays of bedding. Down the valley are splendid woods planted with two acres of hardy hybrid rhododendrons: elsewhere are fine weed-free lawns (one is for croquet), intensive modern herbaceous plantings, a magnolia terrace, a recently restored rose border, tall heathers, brooding conifers (some of the earliest Douglas firs in England) and the ruins of Belsay Castle. The standard of maintenance is superb.

 Features Snowdrops; rhododendrons & azaleas (species & hardy hybrids); formal terraces; winter garden; unique quarry garden; gift shop; refreshments in summer.

Owned by Managed by English Heritage on behalf of the Belsay Trust
Number of gardeners 3, plus 1 trainee
Size 16ha (40 acres)
NCCPG National Collections *Iris spuria*
English Heritage grade I

Bide-a-Wee Cottage

STANTON, NETHERWITTON, MORPETH NE65 8PR

Tel 01670 772262
Location 7 miles north-west of Morpeth.
Opening hours 1.30 pm – 5 pm;
Wednesdays & Saturdays; 27 April to 31 August. Parties by arrangement at other times.
Admission fee £2. RHS members free.

The situation of the garden at Bide-a-Wee Cottage is extraordinary: most of the garden is hidden in a disused quarry on the edge of a 500ft (160m) ridge. The unusual site means that there are enormous variations within its 2 acres – variations of aspect, topography, soil-type and moisture. Mark Robson has seized on this natural diversity to plant a remarkably wide spectrum of plants. In the wet, shaded quarry bottom, by the ponds, are swathes of primulas, rodgersias, ostrich ferns, sensitive ferns and gunneras. Away from the water, on the north-facing slopes of the quarry and in the shade of trees, are meconopsis, rhododendrons and gentians. Quite a different type of plant grows on the south-facing slopes: abutilons, agapanthus, eremurus and eryngiums for example. Throughout the garden, the natural rock walls are contrasted with hedges and complemented by evergreens – conifers, rhododendrons and grasses. Then more ephemeral perennials and wildflowers are woven into the design, as are the more unusual plants that are the hallmark of a plantsman. Robson describes his garden as 'bold perennial plantings linked with a network of winding paths and steps, all associated with dramatic changes of level'. These are designed to create views across the garden or down onto lower levels, as well as into the countryside beyond. To the east,

above the quarry, drifts of late-flowering perennials (including lythrum, eupatorium and helianthus) melt into the ½-acre wildflower meadow that is also home to the beehives. Then the garden opens out and blends into the rough landscape of Northumberland – tough grassland grazed by sheep.

Features Rock garden; plantsman's collection of plants; excellent nursery selling plants from garden.

Owned by Mark Robson
Size 0.8ha (2 acres)

Birkheads Cottage Garden Nursery

BIRKHEADS LANE, CAUSEY ARCH, SUNNISIDE, NEWCASTLE-UPON-TYNE NE16 5EL

Tel 07778 447920   **Fax** 01207 232262
Website www.birkheadscottagegardennursery.co.uk
Location Follow brown sign on A6076 between Sunniside & Stanley.
Opening hours 10 am – 5 pm; daily; April to October. And by appointment at other times and seasons. Guided walks on the first Wednesday of the month.
Admission fee Donations welcome. Open for charity on 3 & 4 June.

This nursery offers a varied and informed selection of alpines, perennials and shrubs: the owner is a garden designer with a passion for plants. There are over 4,500 different plants growing in the adjoining garden: this is an remarkable number by any standards. Other features in the garden include a formal topiary garden made in the 19th century, a gravel garden with herbaceous beds, some rock gardens, a wildlife pond and wildflower garden, a mini arboretum, a spring garden and a grass garden.

 Features A plantsman's garden attached to a plantsman's nursery.

Owned by Christine Liddle

Cragside

ROTHBURY, MORPETH NE65 7PX

Tel 01669 620333   **Fax** 01699 620066
Website www.nationaltrust.org.uk
Location 15 miles north-west of Morpeth off A697 & B6341.

Opening hours 10.30 am – 7 pm (last admissions 5 pm). Tuesday – Sunday & Bank Holiday Mondays; 23 March to 3 November. Plus 11 am – 4 pm; Wednesday-Sunday; 6 November to 15 December.
Admission fee Adults £4.40; Children £2.20.

There are two gardens at Cragside. The newly-acquired Italianate formal garden has splendid carpet bedding, ferneries and a fruit house with rotating pots. Even more impressive are the rhododendron woods – hundreds and hundreds of acres of 19th-century hybrids, plus trusty *R. ponticum* and *R. luteum*, breathtaking in late May.

 Features Roses (mainly old-fashioned); rock garden; fruit; mature conifers; massive rock garden; tallest *Abies nordmanniana* (50m), *Cupressus nootkatensis* (33m) and *Picea glauca* (28m) in the British Isles; National Trust shop; refreshments.

Owned by The National Trust
Number of gardeners 4
English Heritage grade II*

Halls of Heddon

WEST HEDDON NURSERIES, HEDDON ON THE WALL, NEWCASTLE-UPON-TYNE NE15 0JS

Tel 01661 852445
Website www.hallsofheddon.co.uk
Location 1 mile north-west of Heddon, off the B6318.
Opening hours 9 am – 5 pm, Monday – Saturday; 10 am – 5 pm, Sundays.

Halls produced their first dahlia and chrysanthemum catalogue in 1931: now they offer cultivars for many purposes, including showing, cutting, garden display and greenhouse cultivation. Their extensive

list includes many cultivars which are unique to them – not offered by any other nursery. Their magnificent show fields are open from September until the plants are cut down by the frosts: they have over 10,000 plants on display. The garden centre carries a general range.

Herterton House Gardens & Nursery

HARTINGTON, CAMBO NE61 4BN

Tel 01670 774278
Location 2 miles north of Cambo (B6342).
Opening hours 1.30 pm – 5.30 pm; daily except Tuesdays & Thursdays; April to September. For National Gardens Scheme on 19 June, 17 July & 7 August.
Admission fee Adults £2.50; Children £1.

Ⓟ ⓦⓒ ⛲ 🏠

This excellent plantsman's garden is (rather unusually) firmly designed and meticulously planted. It is also attached to a small nursery – so firmly attached, in fact, that it is difficult to say whether this is a garden with a nursery or a nursery with a garden. The knot garden is famous, and much photographed, full of herbs and pharmacological plants. More impressive still are the herbaceous plantings, all weaving through each other in beautifully co-ordinated colours. In the gazebo at the top are photographs showing how the garden has developed, expanded, grown up and intensified over the years: a most inspirational display. The Lawleys added a new parterre to the 'fancy garden' last year: there are further plans for the future.

 Features Plantsman's collection of plants; small formal garden; physic garden; flower garden; fancy garden with a gazebo; nursery garden; first-class nursery attached.

Owned by Mr & Mrs Frank Lawley
Number of gardeners 2
Size 0.4ha (1 acre)

Hexham Herbs & Hardy Plants

CHESTERS WALLED GARDEN, CHOLLERFORD, HEXHAM NE46 4BQ

Tel 01434 681483
Location 6 miles north of Hexham, off B6318 near Chollerford.
Opening hours 10 am – 5 pm; daily; April to October. Telephone for winter opening times.
Admission fee Adults £2; Children (under 10) free.

Ⓟ ♿ ⛲ 🏠

This energetic and successful small modern nursery garden is strategically placed near the fort at Chesters. The herb collection is remarkable (over 900 cultivars) and the design within a 2-acre brick-walled garden is charming. Dye plants, a Mediterranean garden, an astilbe bed and a knot garden are just some of the features. In addition to their National Collections of *Origanum* and *Thymus*, the nursery has a very good collection of mint cultivars. The original name of the nursery was 'Hexham Herbs', and the addition of '& Hardy Plants' indicates a widening of its market. The garden has over 3,000 different plant cultivars growing in it, and the owners aim to propagate and sell them all in rotation, which means that if they do not have something just at the moment, you should be able to buy it from them in the future.

 Features Thyme bank; roses (mainly old-fashioned); herbs; 'Roman' garden; grass garden; wildlife ponds; nursery attached.

Owned by Mrs S. White
NCCPG National Collections *Origanum; Thymus*

Howick Hall

ALNWICK NE66 3LB

Tel & Fax 01665 577285
Location Off B1399 between Longhoughton & Craster.
Opening hours 1 pm – 6 pm; daily; April to October.
Admission fee Adults £2; OAPs & Children £1.

Rather an un-Northumbrian garden, because its closeness to the sea makes possible the cultivation of such tender plants as *Carpenteria* and *Ceanothus*. Formal terraces below the house are well planted, but the great joy of the garden at Howick is a small woodland which has acid soil. This was planted in the 1930s with a fine collection of rhododendrons and camellias: other plants are still being added. The result looks more west coast than east.

Features Roses (mainly old-fashioned); rhododendrons & azaleas; plantsman's collection of plants; mature conifers; spring bulbs; eucryphias; much new planting; biggest stone pine *Pinus pinea* in the British Isles.

Owned by Howick Trustees Ltd
Number of gardeners 5
English Heritage grade II

Kirkley Hall Gardens

PONTELAND NE20 0AQ

Tel 01670 841200   Fax 01661 860047
Location Signed in Ponteland.
Opening hours 10 am – 5 pm; daily; all year.
Admission fee free

The 3-acre, Victorian, walled garden at Kirkley Hall is one of the best in the north of England in which to learn how to garden.

The emphasis is on plants – their selection, cultivation and enjoyment. Along the front of the house are formal gardens with colourful containers in the modern style, and traditional bedding-out: a rising star among gardens.

Features Woodland garden; plantsman's collection of plants; plants under glass; fruit; mature conifers; good herbaceous borders; plant centre; light refreshments on weekdays.

Owned by Northumberland College at Kirkley Hall
Number of gardeners 3
Size 4ha (10 acres)
NCCPG National Collections *Fagus*

The Longframlington Centre for Plants

SWARLAND ROAD, LONGFRAMLINGTON, MORPETH NE65 8BE

Tel & Fax 01665 570382
Location Take B6345 1 mile east of Longframlington, then right down no through road for ¾ mile.
Opening hours 9 am – 7 pm (or dusk); daily; all year. Closed Christmas to New Year.
Admission fee Adults £2.50. Nursery free.

This is a very young garden (started in 1998), with lots of ambition. Hazel Huddleston is planting an arboretum for year-round interest to run it alongside her (equally young) plant centre and nursery – which she describes as 'probably the best in the north of England'. Her hope is that Longframlington will become 'a garden of national distinction' as well as 'a garden for today and the future'. The main problem at this stage is to acquire sufficient shelter on the green-field site to allow ornamentals to grow and establish well. The nursery is said to offer over 2,500 different plants, all of them suitable for the cold Northumbrian climate.

 Features Young nursery; new garden; coffee shop.

Owned by Hazel Huddleston
Size 5ha (12 acres)

Seaton Delaval Hall

SEATON SLUICE, WHITLEY BAY
NE26 4QR

Tel 0191 237 1493
Location ½ mile from coast between Whitley Bay & Blyth.
Opening hours 2 pm – 6 pm; Wednesdays & Sundays; June to September. Plus Bank Holidays in May.
Admission fee Adults £3; OAPs £2.50; Children £1.

The garden is modern: one of Jim Russell's earliest works, it dates from 1948. Parterres and topiary of yew and box are used to enclose old-fashioned roses, handsome ornaments and a fountain: a fair match for the sumptuous house – Vanbrugh's masterpiece. The horticultural interest comes from a fine weeping ash, good plantings of rhododendrons and azaleas, and a laburnum walk.

 Features Rhododendrons & azaleas; laburnum tunnel; ice house; roses.

Owned by Lord Hastings
English Heritage grade II*

St Luke's Cottage

NORTH ROAD, WOOLEY, HEXHAM
NE46 1TN

Tel 01434 673445
Location 3 miles south of Hexham (A69); 3 miles east of A68.
Opening hours By appointment.
Admission fee Donation to Multiple Sclerosis Society.

Alan Furness is a long-standing stalwart of the Alpine Garden Society, that most august of specialist horticultural societies. His garden in a cool valley in southern Northumberland illustrates the enormous opportunities for growing alpine plants which such a situation offers. Within his garden is a wide range of specially constructed habitats to suit an equally wide range of plants: a large limestone scree, and one for acid-loving plants; several high humus beds and meadow beds; a tufa rock bed; a pond, a bog and several damp areas; and three alpine houses. Celmisias, primulas, saxifrages, gentians and pulsatillas are especially well represented, but the whole garden is both a revelation and an inspiration.

 Features Alpine plants; screes; many different micro-habitats.

Owned by Mr & Mrs Alan Furness
Size 0.3ha (¾ acre)
NCCPG National Collections Celmisia (species)

Wallington

CAMBO, MORPETH NE61 4AR

Tel 01670 773600   **Fax** 01670 774420
Website www.nationaltrust.org.uk
Location 6 miles north-west of Belsay (A696).
Opening hours Walled garden: 10 am – 7 pm; daily;
all year. Closes at 6 pm in October & 4 pm between
November and March. Grounds open daily in
daylight hours.
Admission fee Adults £4.10.

There are three reasons to visit Wallington.
First, because Capability Brown was born in
nearby Kirkharle. Second, to gawp at the
ancient tree-like specimen of *Fuchsia* 'Rose
of Castile' in the conservatory. Third, to
admire the modern mixed borders (*very*
Graham Stuart Thomas) in the long,
irregular, walled garden, in a sheltered valley
far from the house. Worth the journey for
any of them, but prepare for a longish walk
to the walled garden.

Features Woodland garden; roses
(mainly old-fashioned & climbers);
rhododendrons & azaleas; plants under
glass; daffodils; good herbaceous borders;
tallest *Sorbus discolor* (7m) in the British
Isles; shop; restaurant.

Owned by The National Trust
Number of gardeners 5
NCCPG National Collections *Sambucus*
English Heritage grade II*

NOTTINGHAMSHIRE

For a county of such historic importance, Nottinghamshire has comparatively few historic gardens. Clumber Park has lost the house that was once at its centre, and Newstead Abbey has long lost its most famous owner, Lord Byron. Nevertheless there are some interesting 19th-century gardens in Nottinghamshire, including the curious little arboretum at Papplewick Pumping Station. One of the best civic parks in England is the Nottingham Arboretum, 8ha (20 acres) in extent, which opened in 1852: the architect Sir Joseph Paxton and the nurseryman Samuel Curtis both advised the founders. Nowadays there are few nurseries of national importance in the county. Nevertheless, the *RHS Plant Finder* had its origins in the list of nurseries prepared by the Nottingham Group of the Hardy Plant Society in the 1970s and early 1980s. The county also has some 12 National Collections. The National Gardens Scheme lists a fair number of gardens of all sizes which open in Nottinghamshire for charity: the RHS Free Access garden at Felley Priory is one of exceptional interest and beauty, and a good example of what can be achieved on an unpromising site in only a few years. One further sight should not be missed – the incredible hulk of the Major Oak, also known as Robin Hood's Oak, in Sherwood Forest.

Clumber Park

WORKSOP S80 3AZ

Tel 01909 476592/484977 Fax 01909 500721
Website www.nationaltrust.org.uk
Location Off A614 Nottingham Road, 4 miles south of Worksop.
Opening hours Park: dawn to dusk; every day; all year, but closed on 14 July, 18 August & 25 December. Walled garden: 10.30 am – 5.30 pm on Wednesdays & Thursdays & 10.30 – 6 pm on Saturdays, Sundays & Bank Holidays; April to September.
Admission fee Walled garden: Adults 70p. Cars & motorbikes £3.50; pedestrians, cyclists & coaches free.

Clumber has 3,800 acres of thickly wooded parkland with a Gothic chapel, classical bridge, temples, an avenue of cedars, a heroic double avenue of limes and masses of rhododendrons. There are good conservatories and a garden tools exhibition in the old walled garden. The main glasshouse range, at 150m, is the longest owned by the National Trust. But the scale of everything at Clumber is enormous: very impressive.

Features Woodland garden; autumn colour; vineries; old rhubarb cultivars; superb trees; tallest *Ilex aquifolium* 'Laurifolia' (20m) in the British Isles; National Trust shop; restaurant.

Felley Priory

UNDERWOOD NG16 5FL

Tel 01773 810230 **Fax** 01773 580440
Location ½ mile west of M1 Jct 27, on A608.
Opening hours 9 am – 12.30 pm; Tuesdays,
Wednesdays & Fridays; all year. Plus 9 am – 4 pm;
2nd & 4th Wednesday of every month; March to October.
And 11 am – 4 pm; every 3rd Sunday of month; March to
October. 11 am – 4 pm on 14 April for National Gardens
Scheme. NCCPG plants fairs 12 noon – 4 pm; 3 June &
7 October.
Admission fee Adults £2; Children free. RHS members
free from April to September.

Parts of the house at Felley Priory – a
wonderfully dark red sandstone
building – date back to 1557. One link with
the 16th century is a venerable pear-tree
which grows against the house: the Royal
Horticultural Society has identified it as
'Jargonelle', an ancient cultivar well-known
before 1600. Mrs Chaworth-Musters started
work on the garden in 1976 and was, from
the start, an adventurous gardener, willing
to try plants which might be considered
doubtfully hardy at 600ft (180m) so far
inland. The results are astonishing. Against
the garden walls are *Buddleja colvilei*,
nandinas, eucryphias, several hebes and
Drimys winteri: elsewhere in the garden are
Podocarpus salignus and *Correa
backhouseana*. Felley Priory is an excellent
garden for plants, with a very large number
of interesting ones in flower at every
season – enough to start a nursery where
everything is propagated from the garden.
Shrubs are a major interest, and Felley has
good collections of magnolias, cornus,
hydrangeas, *Paeonia suffruticosa* and
viburnums. Bulbs are planted in great
numbers: as well as snowdrops and
cyclamen there are massive displays of
daffodils in spring. The handsome yew
hedges are little more than 20 years old, yet
they fill the garden with their bulk: some
have been turned into objects of topiary,
with curvy tops and bobbles. In the rose
garden is a good display of well-grown old-
fashioned roses: some were imported
directly from French nurseries. The rarities
include a pink-and-white form of *Rosa
multiflora* which was collected in Korea by
Jamie Compton. The mediaeval garden
harks back to the original priory which was
lost at the time of the Reformation: it is
planted with plants that were known in the
15th century – among them are lilies, roses,
violas, columbines, irises, tulips and
Phillyrea latifolia. Everything at Felley is
charming, stylish and well-grown: and the
garden gets better all the time.

Features Old-fashioned rose-gardens;
good herbaceous borders; knot
gardens, two pergolas and thousands of
daffodils; new pleached hedge of *Crataegus
tanacetifolia*; unusual trees and shrubs;
nursery attached; tea-room.

Owned by The Hon. Mrs Chaworth-Musters
Size 1ha (2½ acres)

Owned by The National Trust
Size 1,500ha (3,800 acres)
English Heritage grade I

Hodsock Priory

BLYTH, WORKSOP S81 0TY

Tel 01909 591204   **Fax** 01909 591578
Website www.snowdrops.co.uk
Location Signed off the B6045 between Blyth & Worksop.
Opening hours 10 am – 4 pm; daily; 2 February to 10 March.
Admission fee Adults £3.50; Children 50p.

The gardens at Hodsock are unique in February when visitors can see a remarkable winter feature – snowdrops. There are thousands and thousands of them: they planted another 250,000 to celebrate the millennium alone and attracted more than 30,000 visitors last year. The Buchanans have also been planting ferns and lots of winter-flowering plants: *Cyclamen coum*, sarcococcas, daphnes and loniceras.

Features Aconites; hellebores; hepaticas; winter-flowering plants of all kinds; large *Catalpa* (Indian bean tree); tea-room.

Owned by Sir Andrew & Lady Buchanan
Number of gardeners 1 full-time, 3 part-time
Size 2ha (5 acres) plus woodland

Holme Pierrepont Hall

HOLME PIERREPONT, NOTTINGHAM NG12 2LD

Tel & Fax 0115 933 2371
Website www.holmepierreponthall.com
Location 3 miles east of Trent Bridge.

Opening hours 2 pm – 5.30 pm; Easter, Spring & Summer Bank Holiday Sundays & Mondays; Thursdays in June; Wednesdays & Thursdays in July; Tuesday – Thursday in August.
Admission fee House & gardens £4; Gardens £2.

The house at Holme Pierrepont is both beautiful and historic. The main attraction of the garden is a large courtyard garden, designed in 1875, whose box parterre is filled with modern plantings. But there are fine recent additions too: an old rose collection, splendid herbaceous borders and interesting fruit trees. The rare English tulip *Tulipa sylvestris* grows wild in a remote part of the estate.

Features Roses (mainly old-fashioned); formal gardens; teas in the long gallery.

Owned by Mr & Mrs Robin Brackenbury
English Heritage grade II

Mill Hill Plants

MILL HILL HOUSE, ELSTON LANE, EAST STOKE, NEWARK NG23 5QJ

Tel 01636 525460
Website http://come.to/mill.hill.plants&garden
Location 5 miles south-west of Newark. Leave A46 at East Stoke, for Elston; ½ mile down, on right.
Opening hours 10 am – 5.30 pm; Friday – Sunday & Bank Holiday Mondays; March to October. Closed November to February.
Admission fee Garden: £1.50. Nursery free.

This nursery offers a wide range of hardy perennials, including bearded irises. Many can be seen in the display garden, which is generously planted for year-round interest with hardy and half-hardy perennials, annuals and shrubs. It opens for the National Gardens Scheme.

Owned by Mr & Mrs R.J. Gregory
Size 0.2ha (½ acre)
NCCPG National Collections Berberis

Naturescape

COACH GAP LANE, LANGAR
NG13 9HP

Tel 01949 860592   **Fax** 01949 850431
Website www.naturescape.co.uk
Location Signed off A46 & A52.
Opening hours 11 am – 5.30 pm; daily; April to September.
Admission fee free

Naturescape is a significant nursery, specialising in British wild plants. These include wildflowers, bulbs, native shrubs and trees, pond and marsh species and cottage-garden favourites: many are available both as plants and as seeds. The principle behind the nursery is the realisation that many garden owners want to attract wildlife to their gardens, and that growing native plant species is the best way to do so. The visitor centre opened in 1990 and is set in a wildlife garden showing different habitats. Meadows, hedges, ponds, woodland edges and wetlands are supplemented by cottage gardens and such features as a bee garden.

 Features Wildflowers; native plants; tea-room.

Number of gardeners 2½
Size 18ha (45 acres)

Newstead Abbey

NEWSTEAD ABBEY PARK NG15 8GE

Tel 01623 455900   **Fax** 01623 455904
Website www.newsteadabbey.org.uk
Location 4 miles south of Mansfield on A60; 12 miles north of Nottingham.
Opening hours 9 am – dusk; daily; all year except the last Friday in November.
Admission fee Adults £2; Concessions £1.50.

Chiefly of interest for being the debt-ridden estate which Lord Byron the poet inherited and had to sell, Newstead has a good modern garden. Features include a Spanish garden, a tropical garden, an iris garden, a rose garden, a heather garden, ponds and lakes. Best are the Japanese garden and the substantial rockery. The Council has restored and extensively replanted it as a public amenity: lots of cheerful roses and summer bedding.

 Features Roses (ancient & modern); rock garden; herbs; Japanese garden; water features; restaurant & refreshments.

Owned by Nottingham City Council
Number of gardeners 5
Size 120ha (300 acres) of parkland
English Heritage grade I

Salley Gardens

SIMKINS FARM, ADBOLTON LANE,
WEST BRIDGFORD NG2 5AS

Tel 0115 923 3878
Location Just off the A52 from Nottingham to Grantham.
Opening hours By appointment.

Salley Gardens is a nursery which concentrates upon plants that are especially beneficial to mankind: all are organically grown. They include dye and beverage plants, and culinary and aromatic herbs and spices. The main emphasis however is on plants with medicinal properties. Three major herbal traditions are represented: North American, European, and Traditional Chinese Medicine. Plants used in homoeopathy, ayurveda, and conventional medicine are also listed.

 Features Herbal and medicinal plants.

OXFORDSHIRE

Oxfordshire is one of the best counties for keen gardeners. The natives may grumble about the cold, wet, heavy, clay soils of the Thames Valley, but they have some of the finest English gardens, ancient and modern, to show what those soils can do for them. There are no less than nine Grade I historic gardens in the county, and all are open to the public. Both the Oxford Botanic Garden and its country offshoot the Harcourt Arboretum at Nuneham Courtenay have seriously important plant collections, laid out to attract the ordinary garden-owner. It is in these two collections, too, that many of the county's record-breaking trees grow. Several 20th-century gardens were also laid out on a grand scale, including Sutton Courtenay, Buscot, Garsington, Waterperry and Pusey – the latter, alas, no longer open to the public. But the county also has a host of good small gardens: it has long been a matter for pride that Oxfordshire should have more gardens open for the National Gardens Scheme and raise more money for its charities than any other English county. Nevertheless it has only a handful of National Collections and comparatively few first-rate nurseries – Mattocks Roses, now part of the Notcutt chain, is perhaps the best known. It is as if Oxford were relying for its horticultural reputation more upon its past achievements than its present – rather like its university, some would say. Nevertheless it was at Oxford University that the Garden History Society was born, thanks to the energy and acumen of Mavis Batey. And the many college gardens which open to the public are another of the city's gifts to garden-lovers: Robin Lane-Fox looks after the Fellows' garden at New College. The Royal Horticultural Society has arranged free access for its members, albeit for only one month of the year, to a great teaching garden – Waterperry.

Blenheim Palace

WOODSTOCK, OXFORD OX20 1PX

Tel 01993 811091 **Fax** 01993 813527
Website www.blenheimpalace.com
Location 8 miles north of Oxford.
Opening hours 10.30 am – 5.30 pm; daily; 13 March to 31 October.

Admission fee Park & gardens: Adults £5.50; Children £2.75. Maze extra: £1.50 for adults & £1 for children.

Blenheim is the grandest of grand gardens. Vanbrugh, Bridgeman, Hawksmoor and Wise worked here: the grand bridge, the triumphal arch and the column of victory all date from the 1720s. The huge park

(2,000 acres – 800ha) was landscaped by Capability Brown. Achille Duchêne designed the formal gardens in the 1920s: the water terraces centre on a Bernini fountain and took five years to build. The Italian garden focuses on the neo-classical mermaid fountain and is decked with orange trees in summer. There is a pretty Victorian rose garden and, further away from the house, a maze and a lavender garden. The arboretum has some interesting trees, including four fine upright incense cedars (*Calocedrus decurrens*): in 1908, Winston Churchill proposed to his wife here.

 Features Formal gardens; new maze; current holder of Sandford Award; good shops; one restaurant & two self-service cafés.

Owned by The Duke of Marlborough
English Heritage grade I

Brook Cottage

WELL LANE, ALKERTON, BANBURY OX15 6NL

Tel 01295 670303/670590   **Fax** 01295 730362
Location 6 miles west of Banbury, ½ mile off A422.
Opening hours 9 am – 6 pm; Monday – Friday; Easter Monday to 31 October. Groups, evening & weekend visits by appointment.
Admission fee Adults £3; OAPs £2; Children free.

(P) (T) (WC) (🌳) (☕)

This first-rate modern garden has been made by the present owner and late architect husband since 1964 on 4 acres of sloping pasture. It has a wide variety of good plants and good planting but, above all, a fine sense of colour and form. Beautiful flowering trees in spring are followed by opulent old roses in summer and rich autumn colour. A recent addition is a border of blue and white agapanthus

interspersed with kniphofias in shades of lemon and lime. The yellow border is backed by a hedge of copper beech, while the white border is brought to life by a dark hedge of yew. The diversity of planting is supplemented by tender perennials displayed in numerous ornamental containers. But the garden is always changing and improving.

 Features Plantsman's collection of plants; roses (over 200, mainly species & shrubs); good herbaceous borders (colour co-ordinated); 50 different clematis; gravel & water gardens; DIY tea and coffee.

Owned by Mrs D.M. Hodges
Number of gardeners 1, plus some part-time help
Size 1.6ha (4 acres)

Broughton Castle

BANBURY OX15 5EB

Tel & Fax 01295 276070
Website www.broughtoncastle.demon.co.uk
Location 2½ miles west of Banbury on the B4035.
Opening hours 2 pm – 5 pm; Wednesdays & Sundays; 18 May to 14 September. Plus Thursdays in July & August & Bank Holiday Sundays & Bank Holiday Mondays (including Easter).
Admission fee Castle & gardens: Adults £5; OAPs & Students £4; Children £2.

(P) (T) (WC) (🌳) (☕)

The garden at Broughton Castle dates back to the 19th century: the neat knot garden with roses and lavender (best seen from the house) was designed by Lady Algernon Gordon-Lennox in the 1890s. The modern garden was established in 1970 with advice from Lanning Roper. It has two fine colour-themed borders. The blue-yellow-white border has roses like the pale yellow 'Mermaid', mid-yellow 'Golden Wings' and white 'Schneezwerg' growing with berberis, philadelphus and blue campanulas. The pink-and-silver one has shrub roses like 'Fantin Latour', 'Fritz Nobis' and *Rosa glauca*. The garden is probably at its best towards the end of June when all the roses are in full flower.

 Features Roses (mainly old-fashioned & climbers); good herbaceous borders; tea-room.

Owned by Lord Saye
Number of gardeners 1
Size 0.8ha (2 acres)
English Heritage grade II*

Buscot Park

FARINGDON SN7 8BU

Tel 01367 240786   **Fax** 01367 241794
Website www.faringdon-coll.com
Location On A417 west of Faringdon.
Opening hours Garden only: Monday – Friday (but not Bank Holidays). 29 March to 29 September.
Admission fee Adults £4 (garden only).

There are three fairly distinct gardens at Buscot. You enter through the newest – a series of colour plantings and horticultural features created by the National Trust over the last 20 years. Here is the 'Parents' Walk', a lush double herbaceous border designed by Peter Coats in the 1980s: it uses a lot of yellow foliage and contrasts it with purple, to create a sense of lightness and brightness even on the dullest of days. Next to it is the old kitchen garden which Tim Rees turned into a 'four seasons' garden in the early 1990s: each of the quadrants has plantings to represent one of the four seasons. It also has prettily trained fruit trees, vegetables used as climbing plants and gooseberries grown as standards. You climb out of the walled garden, up a steep staircase lined with yews, and walk past the front of the house on your way to the second of the gardens: a perfect *patte d'oie*, focused on the archway which leads into the service courtyard – it is pleasant to think that Lord Faringdon (who commissioned it in the 1890s) and his family used to go in and out of the kitchens on their way to the garden. The temptation is to explore all three avenues of the *patte d'oie* at once, but they are linked by cross-paths which run between further gardens cut out of the woodland: these include a circular sunken garden furnished in summer with orange- and lemon-trees in pots, and a pretty white-and-green garden which is known as the 'swinging garden' because of the swinging seats which surround it. But the third and best-known garden at Buscot is Harold Peto's water-garden, which dates from the 1900s and stretches down over hundreds of yards in a series of steps and then along a long, narrow, straight canal punctuated towards the end by a chunky Italianate bridge until it bursts out into the view of the lake at the bottom. The canal – little more than a rill really, and narrow enough to jump over in places – is framed first by Irish yews and then by clipped box hedges. It has an amazing dynamism and strength of design which makes it an entirely self-contained garden. The only downside to a visit is that the lake is actually the furthest point of the garden, and there is then no other way out except to re-trace your steps across the park and through the modern gardens. But Peter Coats's borders look even better as you approach them again from outside the walled gardens. And a word of warning: Buscot is a big garden, so allow lots of time for your visit.

 Features Topiary; roses (mainly old-fashioned); fruit; good herbaceous borders; tallest *Pinus nigra* var. *cebennensis* (32m) in the British Isles; light refreshments.

Owned by The National Trust
English Heritage grade II*

Greenways

40 OSLER ROAD, HEADINGTON, OXFORD OX3 9BJ

Tel 01865 767680 (after dark) **Fax** 01865 767922
Location Osler Road is off London Road, within Ring road.
Opening hours 2 pm – 6 pm; 12 May; 16 July; 11 August.
And groups by appointment.
Admission fee Adults £2; Children free.

This garden is totally different. The Cootes have emphasised the Provençal looks of the house by planting a rich Mediterranean garden – glittering evergreens, terracotta pots, old oil jars, gravel, parterres – with an exuberance of tender plants including olives, daturas, yuccas, oleanders, acanthus and *Albizia julibrissin*. It is quite the most stylish small garden in England, and intensively maintained to the highest standard.

Features Beautiful modern Italianate garden; sub-tropical plants; plantsman's collection of plants; good herbaceous borders; painted obelisks; long view to monumental classical vase.

Owned by Mr & Mrs N. H. N. Coote
Number of gardeners owners only
Size 0.3ha (¾ acre)

Harcourt Arboretum

NUNEHAM COURTENAY OX44 9PQ

Tel 01865 343501 **Fax** 01865 341828
Location On A423, just south of village of Nuneham Courtenay.
Opening hours 10 am – 5 pm; daily; May to October.
10 am – 4.30 pm; Monday – Friday; November to April.
Closed over the Easter weekend & 22 December – 4 January 2003.
Admission fee free: £2 for car park.

Though it belongs to the University of Oxford Botanic Garden, Harcourt Arboretum is best regarded as a stand-alone woodland garden with a distinct history and character. It has been developed since 1950 around a nucleus of magnificent American conifers planted about 1840 in a corner of the Nuneham Courtenay estate. The new plantings include 'plants from high places' (geographically arranged), conservation areas, an extensive glade of ornamental maples, and fine modern features like a collection of *Nothofagus*. This year (2002) sees more Kurume azaleas, a meadow garden and a chestnut coppice. The labelling is fairly good and there are useful information boards in front of specimens of particular interest. It is perhaps best visited in May, when the mature oak woodland which surrounds the conifers is filled with vast oceans of bluebells.

Features Woodland garden; rhododendrons & azaleas; mature conifers; camellias; fine collection of trees; bluebells.

Owned by University of Oxford
Number of gardeners 3
Size 32ha (80 acres)

Kelmscott Manor

KELMSCOTT, LECHLADE GL7 3HJ

Tel 01367 252486 **Fax** 01367 253754
Website www.kelmscottmanor.co.uk
Location Signed from B4449 & A4095.
Opening hours 11 am – 1 pm & 2 pm – 5 pm;
Wednesdays; April to September. Plus 2 pm – 5 pm on the 3rd Saturday of the month in April, May, June & September & 1st & 3rd Saturdays in July & August.
Admission fee Adults £7; Students £3.50. Gardens only: Adults £2; Children free.

Kelmscott Manor was the summer home of William Morris, an unspoilt Tudor farmhouse on the banks of the Thames. The surrounding countryside, river and garden were inspirational to Morris's designs and writings. Work on restoring the garden started in 1996 and the result is something that Morris would recognise being typical of the 1890s, with rustic fencing, herbaceous borders edged with box and an orchard and pergola. The planting reflects the rich botanical content of his designs – wild tulips (*T. sylvestris*) and fritillaries (*F. meleagris*) grow thickly under the original mulberry tree. Elsewhere are crocuses, aconites and snowdrops, followed by roses, hollyhocks, cottage annuals, poppies, pinks and China asters. Morris's original topiary dragon 'Fafnir' is currently being restored and the standard rose bushes flanking the garden path featured in his most famous book *News from Nowhere*.

 Features Gift shop; licensed restaurant for coffee, lunches & teas.

Owned by The Society of Antiquaries of London
Number of gardeners 1 part-time
Size 1.3ha (3¼ acres)
English Heritage grade II

Lime Close

35 HENLEY'S LANE, DRAYTON, ABINGDON OX14 4HU

Tel & Fax 01235 531231
Location Off main road through Drayton.
Opening hours 2 pm – 6 pm; 21 April & 9 June.
Admission fee Adults £2; Children 50p.

This modern garden has been much praised, and deservedly, for its wide range of plants and the way in which they are grouped. As well as rare trees, shrubs, alpines, perennials and bulbs, it can boast a recently-planted shade border, a pond, a pergola, some unusual topiary, an ornamental kitchen garden, a herb garden designed by Rosemary Verey and a wonderful selection of raised beds and troughs planted by the owner's aunt Miss C. Christie-Miller.

 Features Good mixed borders; unusual plants; cream teas.

Owned by Marie-Christine de Laubarède
Size 1.2ha (3 acres)

The Manor House

STANTON HARCOURT, WITNEY OX29 5RJ

Tel 01865 881928   **Fax** 01865 880117
Location In centre of Stanton Harcourt.
Opening hours 2 pm – 6 pm; 31 March; 1, 11, 14, 25 & 28 April; 2, 5, 6, 16, 19 & 30 May; 2, 3, 13, 16, 27 & 30 June; 11, 14, 25 & 28 July; 8, 11, 22, 25 & 26 August; 5, 8, 19 & 22 September.
Admission fee Garden only: Adults £3; OAPs & Children £2.

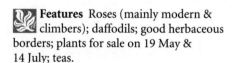

The remarkable late-mediaeval manor house at Stanton Harcourt is surrounded by Edwardian gardens in the Elizabethan style. Parts are romantically overgrown. Others have been spruced up in contemporary taste with David Austin roses and espaliered fruit trees.

 Features Roses (mainly modern & climbers); daffodils; good herbaceous borders; plants for sale on 19 May & 14 July; teas.

Owned by The Hon. Mrs Gascoigne
Size 5ha (12 acres)

Mattocks Roses

NUNEHAM COURTENAY, OXFORD
OX44 9PY

Tel 08457 585652 **Fax** 01865 343166
Website www.mattocks.co.uk
Location On B4015, Roundabout Golden Ball (A4074).
Opening hours 9 am – 5.30 pm (5 pm in winter);
Monday – Saturday. 11 am – 5 pm; Sundays.

This is one of the oldest nurseries in
England, founded in 1875 and now part of
Notcutts. Mattocks have been particularly
successful in promoting their 'County' series
of ground-cover roses. They offer a large
choice of all kinds of roses, and on-line
ordering too. One of their specialities, bred
by John Mattock and introduced in 1973, is
the yellow repeat-flowering climber
'Dreaming Spires'. A new rose garden has
just (2001) been opened and contains many
of the roses in the list.

Old Rectory

FARNBOROUGH, WANTAGE
OX12 8NX

Tel 01488 638298
Location In Farnborough village, opposite church.
Opening hours 2 pm – 6 pm; 21 April, 12 May & 23 June.
And by written appointment (£5, which includes tea,
coffee & cakes).
Admission fee Adults £2 for National Gardens Scheme.

This excellent modern garden has been
made by the owners on a high, cold, windy
site since 1965. Lots of hedges and thick
planting were the keys to survival, but the
effect now is of shelter and luxuriance.
There are splendid double herbaceous
borders, clever colour plantings, a collection

of small-flowered clematis, a kitchen garden,
a *boule* garden and an expanding arboretum
(150+ trees so far).

 Features Roses (mainly old-fashioned
& climbers); good herbaceous borders.

Owned by Mr & Mrs Michael Todhunter
Size 2.2ha (6 acres)

Oxford Botanic Garden

ROSE LANE, OXFORD OX1 4AZ

Tel 01865 286690 **Fax** 01865 286693
Location East end of High Street next to river, opposite
Magdalen College tower.
Opening hours 9 am – 5 pm (4.30 pm from October to
March); daily; all year except Good Friday & Christmas
Day. Glasshouses open 10 am – 4 pm.
Admission fee Donation box: £2 from April to August.

This is the oldest botanic garden in England,
first laid out in 1621: the handsome
gateways were added a few years later. It has
kept its original rectangular design and
many of the statues and garden ornaments.
It also has a calm that is far from the bustle
outside and has proved a refuge for
generations of undergraduates. There are
good and representative collections of
almost every type of plant, including a grass
garden, ferns, carnivorous plants, a water
garden, fernery, orangery and several
conservatories. Everything is well-labelled,
of course, and designed not only as an
aesthetically pleasing living collection of
plants for the university botanists but, much
more generally, as an educational resource.
In recent years the area outside the walled
garden has been developed as a garden to
inspire gardeners: here are a new water
garden, rock garden, herbaceous border and
autumn border. The palm house was re-
designed in 2000 so that visiting

schoolchildren could enjoy 'the ultimate rainforest experience'.

 Features Roses (mainly old-fashioned); rock garden; herbs; plants under glass; systematic beds; huge service tree; plants for sale in summer; *Victoria amazonica.*

Owned by University of Oxford
Number of gardeners 10
Size 1.8ha (4½ acres)
NCCPG National Collections *Euphorbia*
English Heritage grade I

Rousham House

STEEPLE ASTON, BICESTER OX6 3QX

Tel & Fax 01869 347110
Website www.information-britain.co.uk
Location A4260 then off the B4030.
Opening hours 10 am – 4.30 pm; daily; all year.
Admission fee Adults £3. No Children under 15.

Ⓟ ⓌⒸ ⓰

Rousham is the most perfect surviving example of William Kent's landscaping: *Kentissimo*, according to Horace Walpole. The main axis brings you to Scheemakers's statue of a lion devouring a horse, high above the infant River Cherwell. Follow the correct circuit: the serpentine landscape lies away to the side. Here are Venus's Vale, the Cold Bath and Townsend's Building, from which a lime walk will lead you to the Praeneste. Rousham is an Arcadian experience. The pretty herbaceous border in the walled garden and the modern rose garden by the dovecote seem almost an irrelevance.

 Features Early 18th-century landscape; important sculptures & garden buildings.

Owned by C. Cottrell-Dormer
Number of gardeners 4
Size 10ha (25 acres)
English Heritage grade I

The Skippet

MOUNT SKIPPET, RAMSDEN, WITNEY OX7 3AP

Tel 01993 868253
Location Turn off B4022 towards Finstock & immediately right again. After 500 yards, turn left.
Opening hours By appointment for individuals & groups.
Admission fee Donation to charity.

Ⓟ ⓌⒸ ⓰ ⓰

The Skippet is a Cotswold stone house, converted from four cottages. It has magnificent empty views and yet is almost entirely secluded. Against the walls of the house grow many climbers and wall-plants, including such tender plants as *Abutilon* 'Canary Bird' and *Solanum rantonnetii*. Adventurous plantsmen are always willing to try out plants which should not survive the winter's cold or wetness, and so The Skippet also has *Cuphea cyanaea* and many other abutilons flourishing outside. Though there are plants of every kind in the garden, from trees to bog plants, it is above all an alpine plantsman's collection, brimful with rarities in pots, troughs, screes, and raised beds. Every square inch is cultivated, which means that it has much of interest on every day of the year. Dr Rogers will be 91 years old during the year, and says that the first visitors to come on his birthday (date not disclosed) will be given a special present (in a pot, of course). But he is immensely generous to all visitors: 'tell them I *want* them to take cuttings', he says.

 Features Rock garden; plantsman's collection of plants; good herbaceous borders; alpine troughs; alpine house; tufa collection.

Owned by Dr M.A.T. Rogers
Number of gardeners ½
Size 0.8ha (2 acres)

Stansfield

49 HIGH STREET, STANFORD-IN-THE-VALE SN7 8NQ

Tel 01367 710340
Location Off A417 opposite Vale garage.
Opening hours 10 am – 4 pm; first Tuesday of month; April to September. And 2 pm – 6 pm on 9 June for National Gardens Scheme. And by appointment, including evenings.
Admission fee Adults £1.50; Children free.

Stansfield is a modern plantsman's garden, and a fascinating model of what an enthusiastic collector and cultivator of plants can achieve in a few years. Over 2,000 different plants grow in just over 1 acre. The special features include troughs, screes, open borders and endless micro-habitats.

 Features Plantsman's collection of plants; good herbaceous borders; Mediterranean garden.

Owned by Mr & Mrs D. Keeble
Number of gardeners owners only

Stonor

HENLEY-ON-THAMES RG9 6HF

Tel 01491 638587 **Fax** 01491 639348
Website www.stonor.com
Location 5 miles north of Henley-on-Thames.
Opening hours 2 pm – 5.30 pm; Sundays & Bank Holiday Mondays from April to September; Wednesdays in July & August.

Admission fee £3.50.

Stonor fills a hillside and can all be seen from the road below: classical parkland (with a deer park, too), the Elizabethan house, lawns, terraces, a 17th-century walled garden, and finally the wood with wonderful views at the top. Nothing appears to have changed for 200 years: the effect is miraculous.

Features Roses (mainly old-fashioned); rock garden; daffodils; tea-room.

Owned by Lord Camoys
Number of gardeners 1
English Heritage grade I

Waterperry Gardens

WHEATLEY, OXFORD OX33 1JZ

Tel 01844 339226 **Fax** 01844 339883
Website www.waterperrygardens.co.uk
Location Jct 8 or 8a on M40, well signed locally.
Opening hours 9 am – 5 pm; daily; all year except Christmas/New Year period.
Admission fee April to October: Adults £3.50; OAPs £3. Children £2. November to March: all £1.60. RHS members free in September.

The gardens at Waterperry are extensive, well-maintained and full of interesting plants. Much has been re-designed and replanted in recent years, with some fine formal features and pleasing plant combinations. The glasshouse in the walled garden is notable for a large Seville orange tree and there is a small gravel garden. The Virgin's Walk is a good place to study shade loving plants, but the main feature of this area is a long classical herbaceous border brilliantly colourful from late May until

October. The Mary Rose Garden, enclosed by yew hedges, illustrates both modern and older roses, and the formal garden is particularly neatly designed and colourful, with a small knot garden, herb border and wisteria tunnel. Nearby are some interesting ways of training apples and roses, but the main part of the garden is the extensive shrub borders, alpine beds and flower borders. Waterperry offers much to enjoy and learn from every season. The latest development is a long waterlily canal to be planted in Spring 2002.

 Features Roses; rock garden; herbs; good herbaceous borders; apple orchards; irises; home produce, stoneware, books; excellent plant centre; tea shop; wine licence.

Owned by School of Economic Science
Number of gardeners 3½
Size 2.8ha (7 acres)
NCCPG National Collections Saxifraga

Westwell Manor

BURFORD OX18 4JT

Location 2 miles from A40, west of Burford roundabout.
Opening hours 2 pm – 6.30 pm; 23 June. And by prior appointment for serious horticultural groups of more than 20.
Admission fee Adults £3; Children 50p.

Westwell is a large and peaceful Cotswold garden with several distinct 'rooms'. The features include rills, a water garden, herbaceous borders, an orchard, a lavender meadow, lots of hazel and willow fencing, a vegetable garden, a moonlight garden and a clematis wall.

Features Topiary; roses (mainly old-fashioned); good herbaceous borders; water.

Owned by Mr & Mrs T.H. Gibson
Number of gardeners 2
Size 2.8ha (7 acres)

SHROPSHIRE

Shropshire has the reputation of being a remote and quasi-feudal county. It is certainly true that very few of its historic gardens are ever open to the public. Hawkstone is the most notable exception, but this – the county's only Grade I garden – is now in multiple occupation: nevertheless its principal parts are still highly visitable and also have the best collection of trees, mainly conifers, in Shropshire. Among 20th-century gardens, Hodnet Hall is of national importance, and a sizeable achievement by modern standards. Three further recent gardens are also outstanding each in its own way – Burford House, the David Austin rose gardens and Wollerton Old Hall. Wollerton is a RHS Free Access garden, though the concession does not apply in the peak months of summer. The Royal Horticultural Society also has a good Partner Nursery in Hall Farm, in a county which is actually rather short on nurseries of any kind. Nevertheless, there are 16 National Collections in Shropshire; and the National Gardens Scheme is well supported, mainly by gardens which are large or medium-sized.

Attingham Park

SHREWSBURY SY4 4TP

Tel 01743 708162   **Fax** 01743 708123
Website www.nationaltrust.org.uk
Location 5 miles south-east of Shrewsbury on B4380.
Opening hours 9 am – 8 pm (5 pm from November to February); daily; all year except Christmas Day.
Admission fee Adults £2.20; Children £1.10.

No garden to speak of, but the classical late 18th-century parkland round the vast Georgian house is a joy to walk around at any time of the year.

 Features Rhododendrons & azaleas; daffodils; newly restored orangery; National Trust shop; light lunches & teas.

Owned by The National Trust
Number of gardeners 2
Size 20ha (50 acres)
English Heritage grade II*

Benthall Hall

BROSELEY TF12 5RX

Tel & Fax 01952 882159
Website www.nationaltrust.org.uk
Location 1 mile north-west of Broseley (B4375).
Opening hours 1.30 pm – 5.30 pm; Wednesdays, Sundays & Bank Holiday Mondays; 31 March to 29 September.
Admission fee Adults £2.30; Children £1.15.

The smallish garden has been well restored with a Graham Thomas rose garden. Home of the 19th-century botanist George Maw. His Mediterranean collection is still the backbone of the garden – crocus naturalised everywhere.

 Features Roses (mainly old-fashioned); herbs; good herbaceous borders; spring bulbs.

Owned by The National Trust
Number of gardeners 1
Size 1.2ha (3 acres)

Burford House Gardens

TENBURY WELLS WR15 8HQ

Tel 01584 810777   **Fax** 01584 810673
Location A456 between Tenbury Wells & Ludlow.
Opening hours 10 am – 5 pm (dusk in winter); daily; all year. Closed 1 January, 25 & 26 December.
Admission fee Adults £3.50; Children £1; Groups (10+) £3 (by prior arrangement).

This glamorous 7-acre garden, made to complement a stylish Georgian house, is now beautiful and mature. The fluid design is enhanced by interesting plants, imaginatively used and comprehensively labelled. There are good roses and herbaceous borders, and a magnificent series of water gardens, but Burford means *Clematis* – over 350 varieties – cleverly trained, grown and displayed among shrubs and in the new Clematis Maze near the coach house. Charles Chesshire has renewed and reordered much of the planting, and the results are excellent. There are new developments on the other side of the river, too: bulbs and wildflower plantings in particular.

 Features Clematis; roses (mainly old-fashioned & climbers); plantsman's collection of plants; mature conifers; good herbaceous borders; *Rosa* 'Treasure Trove';

new wildflower garden; new collection of bamboos; Georgian bridge restored (1999); café bar with morning coffee, homemade cakes, lunches, teas, licensed.

Owned by Treasures of Tenbury Ltd.
Number of gardeners 4
Size 2.8ha (7 acres)
NCCPG National Collections Clematis

David Austin Roses

BOWLING GREEN LANE, ALBRIGHTON, WOLVERHAMPTON WV7 3HB

Tel 01902 376300   **Fax** 01902 372142
Website www.davidaustinroses.com
Location Signed in Albrighton.
Opening hours 9 am – 5 pm; Monday – Friday. 10 am – 6 pm (or dusk if earlier); Saturdays & Sundays. All year except 25 December to 2 January. Open for National Gardens Scheme on last Sunday in June.
Admission fee Free.

David Austin has developed an entirely new strain of 'English' roses which combine the shape and scent of old-fashioned roses with the colours, health and floriferousness of modern types. The display gardens adjoining his nursery are impressive: five different sections, each extensive and thickly planted with old-fashioned roses and his own hybrids – nearly 1,000 different cultivars of English roses, 19th-century roses, climbers, ramblers and species, as well as some modern Hybrid Teas and Floribundas. In late June and early July it is a place of magic beauty. The garden is maintained to an extremely high standard: all the roses look happy and healthy, and flower profusely. Sculptures by David Austin's wife add a further dimension to a visit. Several new roses are introduced every year at Chelsea. Groups are sometimes allowed to see the breeding houses and trial grounds.

 Features Roses of every kind, especially 'English' roses; important rose nursery & plant centre; restaurant & light refreshments.

Owned by David Austin
Number of gardeners 1
Size 0.8ha (2 acres)

Dudmaston

QUATT, BRIDGNORTH WV15 6QN

Tel 01746 780866   **Fax** 01746 780744
Website www.nationaltrust.org.uk
Location 4 miles south-east of Bridgnorth on A442.
Opening hours 12 noon – 6 pm; Sunday – Wednesday; 31 March to 29 September.
Admission fee Adults £2.90.

Dudmaston has a fine collection of trees and shrubs, put together by several generations of keen plantsmen in the 19th and 20th centuries. Rhododendrons form the background: there are many magnolias, cherries, kalmias, maples and roses, underplanted with daffodils and primroses, which makes this a particularly fine garden in spring. But there is also a natural rock-garden made of the local red sandstone. Elsewhere are a bog garden and a good herbaceous border, recently replanted.

 Features Rhododendrons & azaleas; fine trees; sculptures; tea-room.

Owned by The National Trust
Number of gardeners 2
Size 3.2ha (8 acres)
English Heritage grade II

Hall Farm Nursery

VICARAGE LANE, KINNERLEY, OSWESTRY SY10 8DH

Tel & Fax 01691 682135
Website www.hallfarmnursery.co.uk
Location 2 miles from A5, between Shrewsbury & Oswestry.
Opening hours 10 am – 5 pm; Tuesday – Saturday; 1 March to 12 October.
Admission fee free

This RHS Partner Nursery (it won three gold medals at RHS shows in 2001) carries a good range of fashionable herbaceous perennials, including a great number of geraniums and ornamental grasses. Pulmonarias, hostas, astrantias, bog plants, sempervivums and aeoniums are other specialities. All its plants are grown and propagated on site: requests for cultural advice are therefore welcome. The display borders around the nursery are attractive and well maintained.

 Features Herbaceous plants; ornamental; grasses.

Owned by Christine & Nick Ffoulkes Jones

Hawkstone Historic Park & Follies

WESTON UNDER REDCASTLE, SHREWSBURY SY4 5UY

Tel 01939 200611   **Fax** 01939 200311
Location Off the A49 between Shrewsbury & Whitchurch.
Opening hours Gardens open at 10.30 am, but 10 am at weekends. Last admissions are 2.30 pm in January & February; 3 pm in March; 4 pm from 31 March to 1 July & from 1 September to 28 October; 5 pm between 2 July & 31 August. Open weekends only from January to March;

Wednesday – Sunday & Bank Holiday Mondays from 27 March to 1 July & 9 September to 27 October; daily between 1 June & 8 September; & closed between 28 October & 31 December.
Admission fee Adults £5.50; OAPs £4.50; Children £3. Reduced prices on all weekdays and at winter weekends.

Sir Rowland Hill began landscaping Hawkstone in the 1750s, but most of what remains was initiated by his elder son Sir Richard and completed by his grandson, another Sir Rowland Hill, best known for inventing the postage stamp. It is a fine example of the 'sublime' movement, which sought to create contrasts of emotion in the natural landscape. Hawkstone has deep ravines and gloomy chasms, accompanied by dizzying pinnacles, soaring sandstone rocks, and ornamental follies which fill the whole estate, once more than 700 acres in extent. It is the contrasts which make this landscape unique: the mosses, ferns, and dampness of its dark gullies turn suddenly into dramatic cliffs, tunnels, crags and bridges, while the peaks of the precipitous outcrops offer views across 13 counties. But allow lots of time for your visit – the owner recommends at least three hours.

 Features A remarkable series of landscaped follies; some good trees.

Owned by M.C. Boler
English Heritage grade I

Hillview Hardy Plants

WORFIELD, BRIDGNORTH WV15 5NT

Tel & Fax 01746 716454
Website www.hillviewhardyplants.com
Location Between Worfield & Albrighton, off B4176.
Opening hours 9 am – 5 pm, Monday – Saturday, March to mid-October. And by appointment.

This is a good nursery for hardy herbaceous perennials. Its range of primulas and auriculas, aquilegias and South African plants is especially noteworthy. Guided tours can be arranged for groups.

Owned by John & Ingrid Millington

Hodnet Hall Gardens

HODNET, MARKET DRAYTON TF9 3NN

Tel 01630 685202   **Fax** 01630 685853
Location Near junction of A53 & A442.
Opening hours 12 noon – 5 pm; Tuesday – Sunday & Bank Holiday Mondays; April to September.
Admission fee Adults £3.50; OAPs £3; Children £1.50.

In the 1950s, *The RHS Journal* (forerunner of *The Garden*) described Hodnet as a 'small modern garden'. Now it has more than 60 acres of woodland garden around a chain of ornamental pools. The woodlands are planted with exotic trees like magnolias, maples and davidias against a background of native oaks, sycamores, limes and beech-trees. Underneath are rhododendrons, azaleas, camellias, prunus and berberis, themselves underplanted when they flower in spring with a wide variety of herbaceous plants, especially hostas, primulas, daffodils and bluebells. The spacious mixed borders near the house are particularly interesting in July, when they are complemented by the beds of old-fashioned roses and modern floribundas. But Hodnet is a garden for everyone and every season – good in late summer too, when the hydrangeas and astilbes flower. Allow lots of time for a thorough visit to one of the greatest 20th-century gardens.

 Features Woodland garden; roses (mainly old-fashioned); good herbaceous borders; camellias; primulas; rhododendrons; HHA/Christie's Garden of the Year in 1985; 17th-century tea-rooms.

Owned by A.E.H. Heber-Percy
Number of gardeners 4
Size 22+ha (60+ acres)
English Heritage grade II

Lingen Nursery and Gardens

LINGEN, BUCKNELL SY7 0DY

Tel 01544 267720
Website www.lingennursery.co.uk
Location Follow brown tourist signs from the A4113 & A4362, north-east of Presteigne.
Opening hours 10 am – 5 pm; Thursday – Monday; Easter to September. Nursery opens from February to October.
Admission fee Garden £2. Nursery free.

Lingen specialises in unusual alpine and herbaceous plants. In addition to their two National Collections, the owners have put together notable collections of auriculas and penstemons (both alpine and herbaceous) and have a number of interesting aquilegias and irises too. But it is true to say that you will not visit Lingen without seeing a plant that you have never seen before. The gardens are worth a visit in their own right: one acre is intensively planted with a rock garden and cottage garden, supplemented by an alpine house and raised beds. Two more acres are now (2002) under development to create a bog garden, further herbaceous borders, a scree and a rock outcrop.

 Features Auriculas; penstemons; tea-room.

Owned by Kim & Maggie Davis
NCCPG National Collections *Iris sibirica*; *Campanula*

Lower Hall

WORFIELD, BRIDGNORTH WV15 5LH

Tel 01746 716607   **Fax** 01746 716325
Location In centre of village of Worfield.
Opening hours 29 & 30 June for Worfield church. And by appointment. Groups welcome.
Admission fee Adults £3; Children free.

Lanning Roper helped to get this splendid garden going in the 1960s. It bestrides the River Worfe and every part has a distinct character. There are lush streamside plantings, infinite colour schemes, and a woodland area at the bottom. These contrast with formal designs, straight brick paths, a pergola and more colour themes in the old walled garden. It is one of the best gardens to be made since World War II, and neatly kept.

 Features Roses (all sorts); plantsman's collection of plants; good herbaceous borders; water; tea & coffee.

Owned by C.F. Dumbell
Number of gardeners 1
Size 1.7ha (4¼ acres)

Preen Manor

CHURCH PREEN, CHURCH STRETTON SY6 7LQ

Tel 01694 771207
Location Signed from B4371 Much Wenlock/Church Stretton.
Opening hours 2 pm – 6 pm; 5 May, 13 June; 11 & 25 July; 6 October (closes at 4.30 pm for Harvest Thanksgiving). And parties by appointment.
Admission fee Adults £3; Children 50p.

Preen has a stylish new garden with some original ideas to complement the historic old site. These include a chess garden, a collection of plants in handsome old pots, a pebble garden, a fern garden and that symbol of the 1990s – a gravel garden. Down in the woodland garden are rhododendrons and candelabra primulas. And it gets better every year.

 Features Woodland garden; fruit; fern garden; homemade teas.

Owned by Mrs Philip Trevor-Jones
Number of gardeners 2½
Size 2.2ha (6 acres), plus woodland

Ruthall Manor

DITTON PRIORS, BRIDGNORTH
WV16 6TN

Tel 01746 712608
Location Take Weston road from church then 2nd left.
Opening hours For National Gardens Scheme.

This 1-acre plantsman's garden, some 250m (800ft) up, has been made over the last 20 years. It has good trees, rare shrubs, lots of groundcover, and a pretty pool with aquatics and marginals.

 Features Plantsman's collection of plants.

Owned by Mr & Mrs G.T. Clarke

Swallow Hayes

RECTORY ROAD, ALBRIGHTON,
WOLVERHAMPTON WV7 3EP

Tel 01902 372624   **Fax** 01902 373151
Location M54, Jct 3, then A41 towards Wolverhampton & first right after garden centre.

Opening hours 10.30 am – dusk on 20 January.
2 pm – 5 pm on 26 May. And groups by appointment.
Admission fee Adults £2.50; Children 10p. £3 per head for groups, to include light refreshments.

Swallow Hayes is a plantswoman's garden (3,000 plants) entirely made since 1968 and a model of its kind, where groundcover helps to minimise labour and maximise enjoyment. The garden started life as a stock-ground and trial-ground for the owner's wholesale nursery. Mrs Edwards has more than 100 different cultivars of *Geranium* in a garden which is packed with different micro-habitats, each of them themed and exploited as fully as possible. There is much to see and enjoy at every time of the year – hence the National Collection of winter-flowering witch-hazels *Hamamelis* of which there are over 50 cultivars.

 Features Rock garden; herbs; fruit; mature conifers; good herbaceous borders; ferns; geraniums; trees & shrubs; teas on open days.

Owned by Mrs P. Edwards
Number of gardeners Owner, plus some very part-time help
Size 0.8ha (2 acres)
NCCPG National Collections *Hamamelis*; *Lupinus* (Russell strains)

Wollerton Old Hall

WOLLERTON, MARKET DRAYTON
TF9 3NA

Tel 01630 685760   **Fax** 01630 685583
Website www.wollertonoldhallgarden.com
Location Follow brown tourist signs from A53 in Hodnet.
Opening hours 12 noon – 5 pm; Fridays, Sundays & Bank Holidays; 29 March to 30 August. Plus Fridays in September.

Admission fee Adults £3.50; Children £1. RHS members free in April, May & September.

Started in 1984, this outstanding garden creation seeks to combine horticultural excellence with unrestrained planting of perennials, careful colour design with strong contrasts, and intimacy with bold design structure. As the site is centuries old, the dominant theme is of linear formality but this gradually gives way to total informality where the garden meets the Shropshire countryside.

Features Plantsman's collection of plants; good herbaceous borders; deciduous euonymus; salvias; clematis; shrub roses; crocosmias; lunches & teas.

Owned by Lesley Jenkins
Number of gardeners 2
Size 1.2ha (3 acres)

SOMERSET

Like its neighbour Devon, Somerset is rich in both gardens and nurseries: it is a county where gardeners are well served. Four of its five Grade I historic gardens – Dunster, East Lambrook, Hestercombe and Montacute – are regularly open to the public. Somerset also has an exceptional number of good small and medium-sized gardens, often made by the present owners – as witness the large number (in quite a small county) which open in aid of the National Gardens Scheme. The mild climate – warm and wet – and the rich soils are famous for cider and dairying: they also induce good growth in gardens. It has long been recognised that along the coast – at Porlock and Cannington, for example – plants flourish which would not survive in any but the mildest parts of Devon and Cornwall. Nevertheless the county has no arboreta of note and few trees which are thought to be among the tallest or largest of their kind. Somerset has many nurseries and among them are several of national or international importance: Avon Bulbs and Broadleigh Gardens for bulbs, Kelways for peonies, Mallet Court for rare trees, P.M.A. Plants for Japanese maples, Thornleigh for fruit trees. And, though not mentioned in the *RHS Plant Finder* – she has a reputation for reticence – Patricia Marrow's Kingsdon Nursery at Somerton has long enjoyed renown for first-rate plants of the sort you cannot find elsewhere. Somerset also has a large number (over 20) of National Collections, which is always a good indicator of the general level of interest in gardening. And it has long been well served by the county horticultural college at Cannington, which is one of the leading centres in all England for the teaching of amenity horticulture. Cannington is also a RHS Partner College, with a programme of public lectures, demonstrations and workshops all through the year.

The American Museum

CLAVERTON MANOR, BATH
BA2 7BD

Tel 01225 460503 **Fax** 01225 480726
Website www.americanmuseum.org
Location Off A36 south of Bath.

Opening hours 1 pm – 6 pm, Tuesday – Friday;
12 noon – 6 pm, Saturdays, Sundays & Bank Holiday
Mondays; 23 March to 3 November.
Admission fee Adults £3.50; OAPs £3; Children £2.
Private tours by prior arrangement.

The 15 enchanting acres of garden at
Claverton Manor were created by two

artistic Americans, Dallas Pratt and John Judkyn, from about 1960 onwards. They bought the handsome classical house, built in 1820, to hold their collection of early American domestic arts and artefacts: the American Museum is now the largest of its kind outside the USA and well worth a visit. The house has a stunning situation with wide views across to the west-facing slopes of the Avon valley, yet sheltered and screened from all but the prettiest eye-catchers on the other side. Tea is served on the terrace in front of the house, next to the little Colonial herb garden ('Colonial' = pre-1778). Sloping lawns lead to the Mount Vernon garden, a box-edged re-creation of George Washington's own original. The first enclosure has beds of old roses: the main section is a herbaceous garden. Despite a little historical latitude with the choice of 18th-century plants, it is all very neat and instructive, and prettily enclosed by white picket fencing. Also of horticultural interest is a young arboretum which opened in 1985 on the slopes below. This celebration of hardy American trees and shrubs adds up to a fine, well-labelled collection, and includes (among many other rarities) *Alnus rhombifolia*, *Salix mackenziana* and *Philadelphus insignis*. Also worth discovering are a ferny dell at the bottom of the arboretum and a collection of American apple cultivars, with such names as 'Smokehouse' and 'Sheep's Nose'. The American Museum is a well-endowed foundation and its gardens are very well maintained, which adds enormously to the pleasure of a visit, though rabbits are a problem.

 Features Topiary; roses (mainly old-fashioned); herbs; fruit; good herbaceous borders; fine collection of trees.

Owned by Trustees of the American Museum in Britain
English Heritage grade II

Ammerdown Park

KILMERSDOWN, RADSTOCK, BATH
BA3 5SH

Tel 01761 432227   **Fax** 01761 433094
Location West of Terry Hill crossroads: A362/A366.
Opening hours 11 am – 5 pm; 1 April, 6 May, 3 June, 26 August.
Admission fee Adults £3; £1 OAPs; Children free.

Ammerdown's lay-out is Lutyens at his most ingenious. The lie of the land precludes right angles, but long straight views cover up the irregularities. It has some nice plants, particularly trees, but the design is everything and there are good spring bulbs. A restoration plan has recently got under way.

  Features Major Lutyens garden; good design; refreshments.

Owned by The Hon. Andrew Joliffe
Number of gardeners 2½
English Heritage grade II*

Ashfield Court Nurseries

FARRINGDON, NORTH PETHERTON
TA6 6PE

Tel 01278 663438
Location Turn left at northern end of Farringdon.
Opening hours By appointment.

Ashfield Court Nurseries specialise in *Verbena* cultivars. Their remarkable collection has over 100 of them.

 Features Verbenas; light refreshments.

Owned by Michael Michieli
NCCPG National Collections *Verbena*

Avon Bulbs

BURNT HOUSE FARM, MID-
LAMBROOK, SOUTH PETHERTON
TA13 5HE

Tel & Fax 01460 242177
Website www.avonbulbs.co.uk
Location Turn south, down 'no through road', halfway
between West Lambrook & East Lambrook.
Opening hours 9 am – 4.30 pm; Thursday – Saturday;
mid-February to end March & mid-September to end
October.

Avon Bulbs offers an impressive variety of
bulbs (and close relatives) of all sizes, types
and seasons – mainly by mail order. The
nursery is well-run and the plants are
beautifully grown. It is well worth a visit
early in the year to see the wide range of its
stock, including much which is not listed
in the catalogue. The opening hours are
limited because of the seasonal nature of
the business and the nursery's show
commitments. It is a good idea to check
with them before visiting.

 Features Hardy bulbs of every kind.

Barrington Court

BARRINGTON, ILMINSTER TA19 0NQ

Tel 01460 241938
Website www.nationaltrust.org.uk
Location In Barrington village.
Opening hours 11 am – 4.30 pm; Thursday – Sunday;
March & October. 11 am – 5.30 pm; Saturday – Thursday;
April to September & daily in July & August.
Admission fee Adults £5.20; Children £2.50.

There is still an Edwardian opulence about
Barrington. Massive plantings of irises, lilies
and rich dark dahlias. And good design

detail too: the patterns of the brick paving
are a study in themselves.

 Features Roses (mainly old-
fashioned); fruit; fine collection of
trees; tea-room & licensed restaurant.

Owned by The National Trust
Number of gardeners 3, plus 1 trainee
Size 4ha (10 acres)
English Heritage grade II*

Bath Botanic Gardens

ROYAL VICTORIA PARK, BATH,
BA1 2NQ

Tel 01225 448433   **Fax** 01225 480072
Location West of city centre by Upper Bristol Road.
Opening hours 9 am – dusk; daily; all year except
Christmas Day.
Admission fee Free.

Bath's Botanic Gardens were founded in
1887, extended in 1926 and again in 1987. It
has 9 acres of trees, shrubs, borders,
limestone-loving plants and scented walks.
It has never been attached to a university or
institute, so it is more of a horticultural
collection than a botanic garden, and
public amenity is its main function. The
central feature is a rocky pool designed in
the Japanese style, surrounded by venerable
not-so-dwarf maples. Standards are high,
maintenance is good, and the seasonal
highlights of bulbs and bedding are among
the best. The excellent guidebook is a model
of visitor-friendliness.

 Features Rock garden; fine collection
of trees; autumn colour; fine bedding
displays; good *Scilla* collection; tallest tree of
heaven *Ailanthus altissima* (31m) and tallest
hornbeam *Carpinus betulus* (27m) in
England (and eleven other record trees).

Owned by Bath City Council
Number of gardeners 4
Size 3.8ha (9½ acres)
English Heritage grade II

Blackmore & Langdon

STANTON NURSERIES, PENSFORD,
BRISTOL BS39 4JL

Tel 01275 332300 **Fax** 01275 331207
Location 8 miles south of Bristol on B3130, between A37
Wells road & A38.
Opening hours 9 am – 5 pm; Monday – Friday.
10 am – 4 pm; Saturdays & Sundays.

This family business, started in 1901 and
still run by the founder's grandchildren,
celebrated its centenary last year. Blackmore
& Langdon has a long tradition of breeding
and growing showy border plants – huge
begonias and tall delphiniums, in particular.
The nursery's immaculately grown flowers
have been a feature of RHS Flowers Shows –
and especially the Chelsea Flower Show – for
many years. What is not so well known is
that the nursery also produces phlox,
aquilegias and polyanthus. All its plants are
grown on site. The nursery will be holding a
special sale weekend and a preview of the
plants prepared for the Chelsea Flower Show
on 10, 11 & 12 May 2002.

 Features Dephiniums; begonias.

Owned by The Langdon family

Broadleigh Gardens

BISHOPS HULL, TAUNTON TA4 1AE

Tel 01823 286231 **Fax** 01823 232464
Website www.broadleighbulbs.co.uk
Location At Barr, 1½ miles north-west of Bishops Hull.
Opening hours 9 am – 4 pm; Monday – Friday.
Viewing & collection of pre-booked orders.
Admission fee Charity donation.

This nursery, with strong RHS connections,
is best known for its small bulbs, though it
now grows almost as many foliage and
woodland perennials. Look out for the
agapanthus, crocosmias, snowdrops, the
many miniature narcissus and species tulips,
and Broadleigh's own Pacific Coast hybrid
irises. The nursery and 3-acre garden are
open for viewing only.

 Features Spring bulbs (especially
miniature narcissus); agapanthus.

Owned by Christine Skelmersdale
Number of gardeners 4
Size 2ha (5 acres)
NCCPG National Collections *Narcissus* (miniature)

Cannington College Heritage Garden

CANNINGTON, BRIDGWATER
TA5 2LS

Tel 01278 655000 **Fax** 01278 655055
Website www.cannington.ac.uk
Location 3 miles west of Bridgwater on A39.
Opening hours 9 am – 5 pm; daily; April to October.
Admission fee Adults £2; OAPs & Children £1.50.

There have been changes at Cannington's
Heritage Gardens recently: gone is the

nursery, gone are the plant sales, and gone are the four National Collections. But the gardens are still worth visiting and the college can still claim to have one of the largest collections of rare and unusual plants in the south-west of England, with '10,000 named plant varieties'. This makes it highly attractive to all plantsmen and gardeners, whatever their particular interest. Originally intended as a teaching resource (Cannington was for long the leading West Country college for ornamental horticulture), the garden was strongly promoted in the 1980s for its visitor attractions. Within a mediaeval wall next to Cannington Court are five individual walled gardens, each planted with its own botanical theme. One has Australian plants, another Mediterranean. The collections are indeed very extensive and beautifully displayed and, although the collections of tender *Abutilon*, *Argyranthemum* and *Osteospermum* cultivars are much smaller than before, the garden still has a good number of different *Wisteria* cultivars.

 Features Plantsman's collection of plants; good herbaceous borders.

Owned by Cannington College

Cothay Manor

GREENHAM, WELLINGTON TA21 0JR

Tel 01823 672283   **Fax** 01823 672345
Location Off A38, 1½ miles from Greenham.
Opening hours 2 pm – 6 pm; Wednesdays, Thursdays, Sundays & Bank Holiday Mondays; May to September. Group (20+) by appointment.
Admission fee £3.50.

Cothay is an exciting old/new garden on either side of the River Tone. The 7 acres of formal gardens designed in the 1920s by

Reggie Cooper (a friend of Lawrence Johnston, and Harold & Vita too) have now been completely replanted, room by room, colour by colour, since the Robbs came here in 1993. Cothay makes a model study of how a garden can be rejuvenated. It is now in the prime of life, brimming with vigour. New for 2001 were an avenue of the mop-headed acacia (*Robinia pseudoacacia* 'Umbraculifera') nearly 100m long, underplanted with nepeta and a thousand white tulips.

 Features 1920s design; 1990s plants; cream teas.

Owned by Mr & Mrs Alastair Robb
Number of gardeners 1½
Size 2.8ha (7 acres); plus 2ha (5 acres) of new trees
English Heritage grade II*

Crowe Hall

WIDCOMBE HILL, BATH BA2 6AR

Tel 01225 310322
Location Off A36 up Widcombe Hill.
Opening hours 2 pm – 6 pm; 7 April, 12 May, 9 June, 14 July & by appointment.
Admission fee Adults £2.50; Children £1.

Crowe Hall is a most extraordinary and exciting garden. It looks straight out at the Capability Brown landscape at Prior Park, and 'borrows' it. Below the house is an Italianate terrace, which leads to a ferny rock garden (real rocky outcrops here) and down into a semi-woodland garden. Here there are mown grass paths and semi-wild, flowery plantings of great beauty, especially in late spring. Recent developments include a 'Sauce' garden, in memory of Lady Barratt, a former owner, and a 'Hercules' garden.

Features Roses (mainly old-fashioned); fine greenhouse & grotto; 'Teazle' garden (2001); teas.

Owned by John Barratt
Number of gardeners 2
Size 4.2ha (11 acres)
English Heritage grade II

Dunster Castle

MINEHEAD TA24 6SL

Tel 01643 821314   **Fax** 01643 823000
Website www.nationaltrust.org.uk
Location 3 miles south-east of Minehead on A39.
Opening hours 11 am – 4 pm; daily; January to 22 March, & 28 September to December. 10 am – 5 pm; daily; 23 March to 27 September. Closed 25 to 27 December.
Admission fee Adults £3; Children £1.50.

Dunster is a Victorian woodland on a steep slope, terraced in places and planted with tender exotica – mimosa, *Beschorneria* and a 150-year-old lemon tree in an unheated conservatory.

 Features Woodland garden; sub-tropical plants; *Arbutus* grove; tallest *Taxodium ascendens* (23m) in the British Isles; National Trust shop; tea-room at Dunster Mill.

Owned by The National Trust
Number of gardeners 4
Size 6.7ha (17 acres)
NCCPG National Collections *Arbutus*
English Heritage grade I

East Lambrook Manor

EAST LAMBROOK, SOUTH PETHERTON TA13 5HL

Tel 01460 240328   **Fax** 01460 242344
Website www.eastlambrook.com
Location Signed from A303 at South Petherton.
Opening hours 10 am – 5 pm; daily; February to October. Plus special openings for National Gardens Scheme.
Admission fee Adults £2.95; OAPs £2.50; Children & Students £1 (subject to review).

East Lambrook is the archetypal cottage garden, made by Margery Fish, the popular gardening writer, and charmingly restored in recent years. Margery Fish was an important influence in British gardening in the 1950s and 1960s. She learnt about gardening not from books but from her own observations, so that she developed her own unselfconscious style of gardening. As a journalist, she knew how to communicate, and her books about the garden she made at East Lambrook have been very influential. The new owners are continuing the work of restoration begun in the 1980s, and have updated the plantings while respecting the original spirit. They have returned Margery Fish's nursery to its original site, made a special bed for the National Collection of hardy geraniums and restored the malthouse. They also run courses for gardeners all through the year.

 Features Margery Fish's garden; plantsman's collection of plants; good herbaceous borders; 150 different snowdrops; hellebores; euphorbias; geraniums; cottage garden plants; lunches & teas from Easter to September.

Owned by Marianne & Robert Williams
Number of gardeners 3
Size 0.8ha (2 acres)
NCCPG National Collections *Geranium*
English Heritage grade I

Elworthy Cottage Plants

ELWORTHY COTTAGE, ELWORTHY,
LYDEARD ST LAWRENCE, TAUNTON
TA4 3PX

Tel 01984 656427
Website www.elworthycottage.care4free.net
Location 10 miles north-west of Taunton, on B3188 in
Elworthy village centre.
Opening hours 10 am – 4 pm, Tuesdays, Thursdays &
Fridays, mid-March to the end of September. And by
appointment.
Admission fee £1.50.

Elworthy offers a pleasant selection of
perennials and cottage garden plants,
including quite a number which are
uncommon or hard-to-find, as well as old
favourites. The nursery is strong on
geraniums (over 200), clematis (over 90),
pulmonarias (over 50), violas (over 40), as
well as crocosmias and grasses. Some of the
plants the nursery offers are not available
from any other source. It has also
introduced a number of new plants,
including *Geranium* × *oxonianum* 'Elworthy
Misty'. Most of the plants can be seen
growing in the display garden, which is
neatly laid out with island beds and themed
colours for year-round interest but also to
blend into the surrounding countryside
(Exmoor National Park) and to encourage
wildlife. Recent additions include a hedge of
native species and a wildflower bank, a
rockery and gravel area for shade-tolerant
plants, and a new orange-and-yellow border
for autumn. A formal vegetable garden is
planned this year.

 Features Raised beds; troughs;
wildflowers.

Owned by Mike & Jenny Spiller
Number of gardeners owners only
Size 0.4ha (1 acre)

Gaulden Manor

TOLLAND, LYDEARD ST LAWRENCE
TA4 3PN

Tel 01984 667213
Location 1 mile east of Tolland church, off B3224.
Opening hours 2 pm – 5 pm; Thursdays, Sundays & Bank
Holidays; 2 June to 26 August. And groups by appointment
at other times.
Admission fee £3.50.

Gaulden is a modern garden, well designed
and well planted. It has a series of small
garden rooms, each devoted to a different
theme (roses, herbs etc.) which makes it
seem much larger than it really is and a
pleasure to explore. The stream garden –
very pretty – is below the monks' pond, its
sides planted with candelabra primulas,
ferns and gunneras.

Features Woodland garden; roses
(ancient & modern); herbs; good
herbaceous borders; scent gardens; secret
garden; book & gift shop.

Owned by James Starkie
Number of gardeners 2
Size 0.8ha (2 acres)

Greencombe Gardens

PORLOCK TA24 8NU

Tel 01643 862363
Location ½ mile west of Porlock on left of road to
Porlock Weir.

Opening hours 2 pm – 6 pm; Saturday – Wednesday; April to July & October to November.
Admission fee Adults £4; Children (under 16) 50p.

Greencombe is an organic showpiece of international renown. The garden stretches across a sheltered hillside which looks up to the tree-covered slopes of Exmoor behind and down across ancient fields to Porlock Bay and an uninterrupted view of the sea. It is a woodland garden, long and narrow, with a rich underplanting of ornamental plants beneath an outstanding canopy of oaks, hollies, conifers and sweet chestnuts. Camellias, rhododendrons, azaleas, maples, lilies, roses, clematis, and hydrangeas are in turn underplanted with many ferns and the garden's four National Collections: *Erythronium*, which are small mountain-lilies; *Vaccinium*, which the curator Joan Loraine calls 'whortleberries worldwide'; *Gaultheria*, which she refers to as 'whortleberries for bears'; and *Polystichum*, the 'thumbs-up' fern. The garden is completely organic, with compost heaps and leaf mould pits on show, and a riot of birds, butterflies and lesser insects. But, like all good plantsman's gardens, Greencombe is absolutely stuffed with interesting plants and has lots to interest the visitor at every time of the year.

Features Woodland garden; plantsman's collection of plants; good herbaceous borders; organically run; tea.

Owned by Greencombe Garden Trust
Number of gardeners 2 part-time
Size 1.4ha (3½ acres)
NCCPG National Collections *Erythronium*; *Gaultheria*; *Polystichum*; *Vaccinium*

Hadspen Garden

CASTLE CARY BA7 7NG

Tel & Fax 01749 813707
Website www.hadspengarden.co.uk
Location 2 miles east of Castle Cary on A371.
Opening hours 10 am – 5 pm; Thursday – Sunday & Bank Holiday Mondays; March to September.
Admission fee Adults £3; Children 50p.

Part garden, part nursery specialising in colour-plantings and unusual plants. Little remains of Penelope Hobhouse's first garden: the Popes have re-made it in the modern idiom, using a wide range of rare plants to create decorative effects. Most visitors speak highly of it. The Popes' book *Colour by Design*, published by Conran Octopus and based on their work at Hadspen, has also been praised.

Features Roses (mainly old-fashioned); plantsman's collection of plants; good herbaceous borders; Eric Smith's *Hosta* collection; tulips; excellent nursery; colour gardening; thousands of *Tulipa*; nursery; light lunches & teas.

Owned by N. & S. Pope
Number of gardeners 2½
Size 2ha (5 acres)
NCCPG National Collections *Rodgersia*

Hestercombe Gardens

CHEDDON FITZPAINE, TAUNTON
TA2 8LQ

Tel 01823 413923   **Fax** 01823 413747
Website www.hestercombegardens.com
Location 4 miles north of Taunton.
Opening hours 10 am – 5 pm; daily; all year.
Admission fee Adults £4.30; OAPs £4; Children £1.

Ignore the house – a Victorian mansion now used as Council offices – and look at the famously restored garden. Lutyens's hallmarks are everywhere: iris-choked rills, pergolas, seats, relieved staircases and pools where reflections twinkle on recessed apses. Gertrude Jekyll's planting is bold and simple, which adds to the vigour. The combination of Lutyens design and Jekyll plants is extremely photogenic: Hestercombe is a highly rewarding garden to learn about symmetry, balance and proportion. The secret landscape garden which Copleston Warre Bampfylde laid out in the late 18th century re-opened in 1997: 40 acres of lakes, temples, combes and woodlands which have not been seen for over 100 years.

 Features Good herbaceous borders; classical landscaping; Lutyens design & Jekyll planting; refreshments.

Owned by Hestercombe Gardens Project Ltd
Number of gardeners 8
Size 20ha (50 acres)
English Heritage grade I

Kelways Ltd

BARRYMORE FARM, LANGPORT
TA10 9EZ

Tel 01458 250521   **Fax** 01458 253351
Website www.kelways.co.uk
Location On B3153, just east of Langport.
Opening hours 9 am – 5 pm; Monday – Friday.
10 am – 4 pm; Saturday – Sunday.

Ⓟ 🐕 🚾 ♣

Long famous for its herbaceous and tree peonies, Kelways also has a large range of irises, and an expanding range of perennials, shrubs and bedding plants. The nursery has undergone a number of changes in recent years. An orchid house displays and sells English-grown orchids.

 Features Peonies; irises.

Owned by C. Johnson
NCCPG National Collections Paeonia lactiflora

Lower Severalls Gardens & Nursery

CREWKERNE TA18 7NX

Tel 01460 73234   **Fax** 01460 76105
Website www.visitourgardens.co.uk
Location 1 mile east of Crewkerne.
Opening hours 10 am – 5 pm; daily; 1March to 19 October. Closed Thursdays & Sundays, but open 2 pm – 5 pm on Sundays in May & June.
Admission fee Adults £2.50.

Ⓟ 🚾 ♿ ♣

Both the garden and nursery started in 1985. At first, the nursery specialised in herbs, of which it still has a wide range. However, there are also good selections of hardy geraniums and salvias. The garden is set in front of an 18th-century farmhouse: it has fine herbaceous borders, island beds and an area for bog plants.

 Features Herbaceous borders; island beds; herbs.

Size 1.2ha (3 acres)

Lytes Cary Manor

CHARLTON MACKRELL, SOMERTON
TA11 7HU

Tel & Fax 01458 224471
Website www.nationaltrust.org.uk
Location Near A303 junction with A372 & A37.
Opening hours 2 pm – 6 pm; Mondays, Wednesdays & Saturdays; 23 March to 30 October. Plus Fridays from June to August

Admission fee Adults £4.60; Children £2.20.

Lytes Cary has a neo-Elizabethan garden to go with the prettiest of manor houses: yew hedges, hornbeam walks, alleys and lawns, medlars, quinces and a simple Elizabethan flower border. Further away is a new river walk.

 Features Topiary; good herbaceous borders.

Owned by The National Trust
Number of gardeners 1
English Heritage grade II

Mallet Court Nursery

CURRY MALLET, TAUNTON TA3 6SY

Tel 01823 480748   **Fax** 01823 481009
Website www.malletcourt.co.uk
Location In middle of Curry Mallet.
Opening hours 10 am – 4 pm; Mondays to Fridays. Other days by appointment.
Admission fee free

This is a wonderful specialist tree nursery with an excellent list of unusual trees. Its displays at RHS flower shows, including Chelsea and Hampton Court, have been a delight and a revelation over many years now. Many of the species it sells are offered by no other nursery anywhere in the world. It is particularly good for *Quercus* and *Acer*, and strong on species from China and Korea, but the nursery's list is full of species of every imaginable genus of rare trees. Every dendrophile in Britain knows of it and buys from it: the array of plants to be seen at the nursery is itself an education.

Owned by J.G.S. Harris & Mrs P.M.E. Mallet-Harris

The Manor House

WALTON-IN-GORDANO, CLEVEDON BS21 7AN

Tel 01275 872067
Location North side of B3124 on Clevedon side of Walton-in-Gordano.
Opening hours 10 am – 4 pm; Thursday; May & June. And by appointment, at any time.
Admission fee Adults £2; Children free.

This is a really interesting plantsman's garden on a substantial scale, offering something for every taste, from autumn-flowering bulbs to rare conifers. Many of the trees and shrubs are grown from seeds brought back from the travels of Caryl Wills's parents, but it is not just the range of his parents' interests which is breath-taking: plants are used to create endless contrasts and harmonies of colour, form, light and shade. Every habitat is an opportunity: they have recently been clearing and planting two very dry acres of ilex and conifer shade – and most successfully. Moreover, as with all good plant collections, there is always much for the visitor to learn and enjoy, whatever the season. The garden is beautifully maintained, too.

Features Woodland garden with herbaceous understorey; climbing roses; formal ponds; hellebores & snowdrops in spring; 6–8 weeks autumn colour; plantsman's collection of plants.

Owned by Mr & Mrs Caryl Wills
Number of gardeners 1
Size 1.6ha (4 acres)

Mill Cottage Plants

HENLEY MILL, WOOKEY BA5 1AW

Tel 01749 676966
Location 2 miles from Wells, off A371. Left into Henley Lane, then 50 yards on left.
Opening hours Nursery: 10 am – 5.30 pm, Wednesdays, March to September. Garden also open by appointment.
Admission fee Garden £1; Nursery free.

The nursery grows a selection of unusual perennials, including a wide range of geraniums, hellebores, oriental poppies, dieramas, ferns and grasses. It also has a good line in rare hydrangea cultivars. The garden is well worth seeing, though it is best to ask in advance if you can visit. It includes a sunny formal garden, a shaded 'folly' garden; kitchen garden, 'hot red' borders, and a late summer bed (mainly grasses and perennials). Groups are especially welcome.

 Features Beautiful waterside setting; hardy perennials.

Owned by Peter & Sally Gregson
Number of gardeners 2½
Size 1ha (2½ acres)

Milton Lodge

OLD BRISTOL ROAD, WELLS BA5 3AQ

Tel 01749 672168
Location Old Bristol road off of A39.
Opening hours 2 pm – 5 pm; Tuesdays, Wednesdays, Sundays & Bank Holidays; Easter to 31 October.
Admission fee Adults £2.50; Children (under 14) free. Groups by arrangement.

This impressive Edwardian garden is terraced down a hillside against a backdrop of Wells Cathedral. Most of the plantings are modern, and look good against the walls and bulky yew hedges. In a combe, across the main road, is an 8-acre 19th-century arboretum. Both parts are full of interesting plants, excellently maintained and constantly improving, with considerable new planting in recent years.

Features Roses (mainly modern); good herbaceous borders; fine collection of trees; teas on Sundays (May to August); tallest *Populus alba* (20m) in the British Isles.

Owned by D.C. Tudway Quilter
Size 1.6ha (4 acres)
English Heritage grade II

Montacute House

MONTACUTE, YEOVIL TA15 6XP

Tel & Fax 01935 823956
Website www.nationaltrust.org.uk
Location In Montacute village.
Opening hours 11 am – 5.30 pm (dusk if earlier); daily except Tuesday; 31 March to 4 November. Then 11.30 am – 4 pm; Wednesday – Sunday; 7 November to March 2002.
Admission fee Adults £3.30; Children £1.60. Reduced rates in winter.

The sunken gardens at Montacute are a perfect foil for the amazing Elizabethan mansion and beautifully maintained. They cannot be beaten for the sense of English renaissance grandeur they impart. The National Trust has recently had the courage to replant the borders not as they were originally planned by Vita Sackville-West, nor as subsequently laid out by Graham Thomas in pretty pastel shades, but using the brilliant colours devised by Phyllis Reiss of nearby Tintinhull in the 1950s. The vivid colours of 'Frensham' roses, purple berberis and late-summer dahlias are the ideal complement to the Ham-stone house.

 Features Roses (mainly old-fashioned); good herbaceous borders; exquisite gazebos; light lunches & teas, licensed restaurant.

Owned by The National Trust
Number of gardeners 4
Size 5ha (12 acres), plus 10.2ha (26 acres) parkland
English Heritage grade I

National Collection of Passiflora

GREENHOLM NURSERIES LTD, KINGSTON SEYMOUR, CLEVEDON BS21 6XS

Tel 01934 833350 **Fax** 01934 877255
Website www.passiflora-uk.co.uk
Location In the middle of Kingston Seymour, just to the west of the M5.
Opening hours 9 am – 1 pm & 2 pm – 5 pm; Monday – Saturday.
Ⓟ ✿

This nursery is testimony to John Vanderplank's commitment to these Central and South American climbing plants. It is a good example of what an enthusiast can achieve single-handed in promoting a genus by raising its profile and making it more widely grown and popular. One glance at the *RHS Plant Finder* makes clear the measure of that achievement: over 100 species and forms are listed by this nursery and by nobody else. Vanderplank has collected many in the wild: his regular exhibits at RHS flower shows (often in the NCCPG tent at Hampton Court) invariably contain several new species, as yet unnamed. Naturally his nursery is of international importance, and he supplies material to

pharmaceutical companies and botanical institutes studying the chemical make-up of plants. The catalogue (it also exists on-line) is detailed, and includes precise temperature and cultivation requirements.

NCCPG National Collections *Passiflora*

P.M.A. Plant Specialities

JUNKER'S NURSERY, LOWER MEAD, WEST HATCH, TAUNTON TA3 5RN

Tel 01823 480774 **Fax** 01823 481046
Website www.junker.net
Location West Hatch is 4 miles south of Taunton.
Opening hours By appointment only.
Ⓟ ✿

P.M.A. has some interesting container-grown trees and shrubs. It is particularly strong on Japanese and snakebark acers, daphnes, magnolias and the ornamental tree *Cornus*. Some plants are available in larger sizes for instant impact. The display borders are particularly instructive.

Owned by Nick & Karan Junker

Prior Park

RALPH ALLEN DRIVE, BATH BA2 5AH

Tel & Fax 01225 833422
Website www.nationaltrust.org.uk
Location 1½ miles south of Bath city centre.
Opening hours 12 noon – 5.30 pm (or dusk, if earlier); Wednesday – Monday; February to Easter. 11 am – 5.30 pm (or dusk, if earlier); Wednesday – Monday; Easter to November. 11 am – dusk; Friday – Sunday; December to January 2003.

Admission fee Adults £4; Children £2.

The classical landscape at Prior Park was laid out between 1734 and 1764 by a property developer called Ralph Allen, who was a friend of Pope and Burlington. Pope advised extensively on the original lay-out and buildings before Capability Brown gave them a make-over in the early 1760s. The park is no more than 28 acres, stretching from the extremely handsome Palladian house (not National Trust) at the top of the steep valley to the Palladian bridge right at the bottom, which is the focus of the entire landscape. It is reached by a rugged and sometimes slippery path through the woods on either side, quite unfitted for wheelchairs and buggies and only suitable for the sure-footed and confident. There is nothing of horticultural interest, but some fine trees – mainly beech, with some yew, sycamore and seedling ashes – underplanted with ferns and laurels. Nevertheless it is hard to imagine a more elegant landscape than this one, which uses the busy and fashionable city of Bath as its background. Photographers may wish to visit it early in the afternoon, when the sun shines on the Palladian bridge. There is one snag, however: the Trust can offer no on-site parking. Badgerline runs buses (Nos. 2 & 4) from the Grand Parade or Dorchester Place, every 20 minutes.

 Features Palladian bridge; handsome parkland.

Owned by The National Trust
Number of gardeners 2, plus volunteers
Size 11.1ha (28 acres)
English Heritage grade I

Scotts Nurseries (Merriott) Ltd

MERRIOTT TA16 5PL

Tel 01460 72306   **Fax** 01460 77433
Location 2 miles north of Crewkerne between the A30 & the A303.
Opening hours 8 am – 5 pm; Monday – Friday. 9 am – 5 pm; Saturdays. 10.30 am – 4.30 pm; Sundays.

Scotts of Merriott is a first-rate, long-established and respected nursery-cum-garden centre, offering a very wide range of field- and container-grown plants. It is particularly strong on old-fashioned roses, ornamental trees, top fruit and shrubs.

Sherborne Garden

PEAR TREE HOUSE, LITTON BA3 4PP

Tel 01761 241220
Location On B3114, ½ mile west of Litton village.
Opening hours 11 am – 6 pm; Mondays; June to September. Plus 9 June & 21 July for the NGS.
Admission fee Adults £2; Children free. Groups welcome by appointment.

This plantsman's garden started in a modest enough way in 1964 but now extends to more than 6 acres. It is long and thin, and very thickly planted, yet it also seems to sit very well in the countryside. The owners are particularly interested in trees and plant them closely in groups for comparison: hence the 'prickly wood' (of hollies), the larch wood, the pinetum and a new acer glade, as well as some 50 different oaks. But there are good herbaceous plantings and bulbs, as well as the trees, which makes it an excellent garden to dawdle in and learn from.

Features Woodland garden; roses (ancient & modern, plus many species); plantsman's collection of plants; small pinetum; collection of hollies (180 varieties) and hardy ferns (250 varieties); 29 different waterlilies; new millennium 'wadi'; tea/coffee.

Owned by Mr & Mrs John Southwell
Number of gardeners 1, part-time
Size 2.2ha (6 acres)

Tintinhull House

TINTINHULL, YEOVIL BA22 8PZ

Tel & Fax 01935 822545
Website www.nationaltrust.org.uk
Location In Tintinhull village.
Opening hours 12 noon – 6 pm; Wednesdays – Sunday; April to September.
Admission fee Adults £3.80; Children £1.80.

Ⓟ ⓌⒸ ☕

This small garden – less than 2 acres – is the most famous example of a Jekyll-style garden on a small scale. It combines great design with a wide range of plants and the most skilful use of colour combinations in planting them. The garden looks larger than it really is because it has been divided into a sequence of small rooms of different size, all of them hedged or walled. Perhaps the most famous part is the largest, around a formal rectangular pool in front of a pillared summerhouse. The borders on either side are in complete contrast to each other: one is made in the bright bold colours of scarlet, yellow, orange and white, while the other is dominated by pastel pinks, mauves, blues and pale yellows. Yet they are also mirror images of each other because each uses grey-leaved plants and striking leaf shapes as well as colour. No garden employs such a wide palette of plants so rigorously as elements of design. There has been much cutting back,

clearing, renewal and replanting recently. The jury is out on whether this has been successful: preliminary reports suggest that the work represents an example of National Trust simplification at the expense of personal touch.

Features Topiary; roses (mainly old-fashioned); good herbaceous borders; colour borders; kitchen garden.

Owned by The National Trust
English Heritage grade II

Wayford Manor

CREWKERNE TA18 8QG

Tel 01460 73253　**Fax** 01460 76365
Location 3 miles south-west of Crewkerne off A30 or B3165.
Opening hours 2 pm – 6 pm; 5, 6 & 19 May, 2 & 16 June, for National Gardens Scheme. Parties by appointment.
Admission fee Adults £2; Children 50p.

Ⓟ 🐾 ⓌⒸ ⚘ ☕

Wayford is one of the best gardens designed by Harold Peto: terraces and courtyards, pools and arbours, balustrades and staircases, Tuscan and Byzantine. In the wild garden is an extensive collection of mature acers and magnolias, as well as many rhododendrons, bog plants and daffodils. The whole garden is being restored by the enthusiastic and knowledgeable owners. Last year the pergola with stone Tuscan columns was reinstated as Peto originally designed it.

Features Good herbaceous borders; rhododendrons; spring bulbs; maples; tallest *Photinia davidiana* (13m) in the British Isles; teas.

Owned by Mr & Mrs R.L. Goffe
Number of gardeners 1
Size 1.6ha (4 acres)
English Heritage grade II

STAFFORDSHIRE

Staffordshire has three historic gardens to which English Heritage has accorded Grade I status: Alton Towers, Biddulph Grange and Shugborough. All are open to the public. The county is not, however, a magnet for garden-visitors with horticultural interests. The Dorothy Clive Garden is the only really first-rate garden in Staffordshire to have come out of the 20th century. The National Garden Scheme has comparatively little success within the county and there are no nurseries of national standing. Why this should be remains a puzzle: the county is fairly wealthy, its soils are fertile, and its climate is not too subject to extremes. Staffordshire's historic gardens trust is however very active and its historic gardens are well-visited – Shugborough, Weston and Trentham have all enjoyed long traditions of popular participation in their public programmes events. There are few arboreta of note and practically no record-sized trees anywhere in the county. Even the Royal Horticultural Society seems unable to stir up enthusiasm for gardening: Staffordshire is one of the few counties where it has no partnership arrangement with any nursery, garden or college.

Alton Towers

ALTON, STOKE-ON-TRENT ST10 4DB

Tel 0870 5204060 **Fax** 01538 704099
Website www.alton-towers.co.uk
Location Signed for miles around.
Opening hours 9.30 am – 5/6/7 pm depending on season; daily; March to October.
Admission fee Tickets vary in cost according to season but are always fairly expensive: Alton offers much more than gardens to visit.

Alton has 300 acres of dotty and exuberant display, best seen from the cable-car. Ignore the theme park: the gardens are by and large detached from the razzmatazz. There are splendid Victorian conifers and gaudy bedding, magnificently done. The highlights include a Swiss Cottage, a Roman bridge, a Chinese pagoda, a flag tower, and a corkscrew fountain. It is seriously important to garden historians and excellent entertainment still – but not for contemplative souls. Best in term time.

Features Woodland garden; roses (mainly modern); rock garden; mature conifers; good herbaceous borders; many restaurants.

Owned by Tussauds Group
Size 120ha (300 acres)
English Heritage grade I

Biddulph Grange

BIDDULPH, STOKE-ON-TRENT
ST8 7SD

Tel 01782 517999   **Fax** 01782 510624
Website www.nationaltrust.org.uk
Location ½ mile north of Biddulph, 3½ miles south-east
of Congleton.
Opening hours 12 noon – 5.30 pm, Wednesday – Friday
(closed Good Friday); 11 am – 5.30 pm; Saturdays,
Sundays & Bank Holiday Mondays; 23 March to
3 November. Also 12 noon – 4 pm; Saturdays & Sundays;
11 November to 22 December.
Admission fee Adults £4.50; Children £2.40 (but free
from 11 November to 22 December).

The garden at Biddulph was made in the
middle of the 19th century by James
Bateman – an important amateur garden
designer, plantsman and writer. His garden
has dozens of different microclimates,
compartments, follies and whimsies: it is, in
fact, the earliest example of a garden being
divided into a series of smaller rooms, each
designed and planted to a different theme.
Some are so original and inventive that they
still strike us as frankly rather wacky – the
Dragon Parterre, for example, which is
dominated by a golden cow, or the stumpery
where carefully excavated and inverted tree
stumps and roots form a framework for
trailing ivies and other plants. One of the
more eccentric novelties is the 'upside-down
tree' replanted with its roots in the air
between the Rhododendron Ground and the
Lime Avenue. Others are the Egyptian
courtyard with its own pyramid, a bowling
green and quoits ground, the Chinese
garden (surprisingly large and beautiful,
with a joss house, temple and section of the
Great Wall) and the ferny Scottish glen.
Elsewhere are areas devoted to collections of
plants – a wellingtonia avenue, a pinetum
and the dahlia walk. The estate suffered

years of neglect when the house (fairly ugly,
mid-Victorian and neo-Jacobean) was used
as a hospital but the National Trust has
restored it energetically since 1988 and
many of the quirkier features are as good as
ever again. The trees survived best: some of
the conifers are very large handsome
specimens in the prime of middle age now.

 Features Victorian garden with many
different styles & rooms; excellent
plants & plantings; mature conifers; mosaic
parterre; Mrs Bateman's Garden replanted
(1998); gift shop; tea-room.

Owned by The National Trust
Number of gardeners 5, plus 2 part-timers
Size 6ha (15 acres)
English Heritage grade I

Dorothy Clive Garden

WILLOUGHBRIDGE, MARKET
DRAYTON TF9 4EU

Tel 01630 647237   **Fax** 01630 647902
Website www.dorothyclivegarden.co.uk
Location A51, midway between Nantwich & Stone.
Opening hours 10 am – 5.30 pm; daily; April to October.
Admission fee Adults £3.20; OAPs & Groups (20+) £2.70;
Children £1. RHS members free in July & August.

Meticulously maintained and still
expanding, this garden was begun in 1940
but seems ageless. It was made on an
unpromising site, a cold windy hilltop, but
advice on plants and planting came from
Frank Knight, then director of Wisley. The
lay-out is informal, yet full of incidents, each
with a distinct character: they include a
superb woodland garden, an alpine scree, a
damp garden, a conifer collection and
spectacular summer flower borders. The
Dorothy Clive Garden is best perhaps in
May, when the woodland quarry is brilliant

with rhododendrons, but the scree (replanted in 1998) and rock garden (reflected in the lake) are hard to beat at any season. And, since it has many well-grown but unusual plants of all kinds, there is always much to see whatever the season.

 Features Woodland garden; mature conifers; camellias; good herbaceous borders; heather; cyclamen; new fernery (2000); tea-room with beverages & home-baked food.

Owned by Willoughbridge Garden Trust
Number of gardeners 3
Size 3.2ha (8 acres)

Moseley Old Hall

MOSELEY OLD HALL LANE, FORDHOUSES WV10 7HY

Tel & Fax 01902 782808
Website www.nationaltrust.org.uk
Location South of M54 between A449 & A460.
Opening hours 1 pm – 5 pm (but 11 am to 5 pm on Bank Holiday Mondays); Wednesdays, Saturdays, Sundays, Bank Holiday Mondays & the following Tuesdays; 23 March to 3 November.
Admission fee Adults £4.20.

This is a modern reconstruction of a 17th-century town garden: neat box parterres, a nut walk and an arched pergola hung with clematis. The plantings are all of a period, including the fruit trees: quietly inspirational.

 Features Topiary; snowdrops; herbs; current holder of Sandford Award; gift shop; tea-room.

Owned by The National Trust
Number of gardeners 2 part-time
Size 0.4ha (1 acre)

Oulton House

OULTON, STONE ST15 8UR

Tel 01785 813556   **Fax** 01785 816252
Location From Stone take Oulton Road & turn left after Oulton sign. 3rd driveway on right.
Opening hours By appointment, February to July.
Admission fee Adults £2; Children 75p.

This 3-acre garden has been made by Mrs Fairbairn over many years, essentially for private enjoyment not for public display. It is full of good plants – roses, rhododendrons, geraniums and clematis – arranged in colour groupings.

Features Snowdrops; roses (mainly old-fashioned); rock garden; plants under glass; good herbaceous borders; hellebores; spring bulbs.

Owned by Mr & Mrs W.A. Fairbairn
Number of gardeners owners, plus part-time help
Size 1.4ha (3½ acres)

Shugborough Hall

MILFORD, STAFFORD ST17 0XB

Tel 01889 881388   **Fax** 01889 881323
Website www.nationaltrust.org.uk
Location Signed from Jct 13 M6.
Opening hours 11 am – 5 pm; Tuesday-Sunday & Bank Holiday Mondays; 30 March to 29 September, plus first three Sundays in October, and parties by appointment. Last admissions 4.15 pm. Times may vary: please ring to check.
Admission fee Parkland: Vehicles £2; Coaches free.

This classical and neo-classical landscape has Chinese additions; a handsome Nesfield terrace dominated by dumplings of clipped golden yew; 50 oaks in the new arboretum;

and a rose garden restored by Graham Thomas. All very popular with the locals.

 Features Woodland garden; roses (mainly old-fashioned); good herbaceous borders; formal terraces with rhododendrons; current holder of Sandford Award; garden centre; lunches, snacks, tea & evening dinners.

Owned by The National Trust
Number of gardeners 4
Size 4ha (10 acres)
English Heritage grade I

Trentham Gardens

STONE ROAD, STOKE-ON-TRENT
ST4 8AX

Tel 01782 657341
Location Signed from M6.
Opening hours 10 am – 5 pm (4 pm in winter); daily; all year. Garden may close for redevelopment after July 2002.
Admission fee Adults £1; Children 50p.

The future of this, the grandest of grand Victorian gardens, lies in the balance. It is to be hoped that its essential amenities will be preserved for posterity: the terraces were designed by Sir Charles Barry and set within a Capability Brown park. Until recently, colourful summer bedding recalled its 19th-century heyday.

 Features Important Italianate formal gardens; summer bedding; coffee lounge; plus a diner in summer.

Owned by Trentham Leisure Ltd.
English Heritage grade II*

Weston Park

WESTON-UNDER-LIZARD, SHIFNAL
TF11 8LE

Tel 01952 852100   **Fax** 01952 850430
Website www.weston-park.com
Location Off the A5 to Telford.
Opening hours 11 am – 7 pm (last admissions 5 pm); Easter, then every weekend until 30 June. Thereafter, daily until 1 September & every weekend until 15 September. Closed 5 June, 13 July, 4 August & 15-23 August.
Admission fee Adults £2.50; OAPs £2; Children £1.50.

Weston has a fine 18th-century landscape (Capability Brown worked there) and a 19th-century Italianate parterre, a temple of Diana and a handsome orangery by James Paine. It is not of major horticultural interest, but best for its fine collection of trees, some of them record-breakers, and the collection of *Nothofagus* planted by the late Lord Bradford.

 Features Woodland garden; fine collection of trees; landscaped park; rhododendrons; gift shop; restaurant.

Owned by The Weston Park Foundation
Number of gardeners 3
English Heritage grade II*

SUFFOLK

Suffolk has comparatively few historic gardens of national importance but, such as they are, they are of great interest to the garden-lover. Both Helmingham and Shrubland are rated as Grade I gardens, while Euston, Ickworth and Somerleyton are all Grade II*. There is a particularly fine collection of trees at East Bergholt Place, which has recently opened up as a visitor-friendly garden with a good general nursery attached. Suffolk is a rich county but was, until recently, rather cut off from London and its markets, which may help in part to explain why it has so many good nurseries. Notcutts is one of the largest quality nurseries in the country, with a long and distinguished history of plant introductions and exhibits at RHS flower shows. The leading seedsmen Thompson & Morgan have been at Ipswich for over 100 years: their trial grounds may also be visited in season. But it is the sheer number of good small modern nurseries which is so surprising: we list Goldbrook, Mills Farm, Paradise Centre, Park Green and Rougham Hall among others – but Gardiner's Hall Plants at Braiseworth (over 3,000 different plants) and North Green Snowdrops (sent 'in the green') are also worth knowing. Siskin Plants, which we listed last year, has since opted to become 'mail order only'. Suffolk has many good modern gardens like Wyken Hall (made by RHS Council Member Sir Kenneth Carlisle), and others which we do not list, including the Blakenham Woodland Garden at Little Blakenham (made by the late Lord Blakenham, Treasurer of the RHS). The National Garden Scheme does well in the county and there is an active historic gardens trust too. The NCCPG is represented by about a dozen National Collections, including some horticulturally important genera like lilacs (*Syringa*), delphiniums and fuchsias. Otley College near Ipswich is a RHS Partner College, with lectures, workshops and garden walks throughout the year: further details from 020 7821 3408.

East Bergholt Place

EAST BERGHOLT CO7 6UP

Tel & Fax 01206 299224
Location 2 miles east of A12, on B1070, east-north-east of East Bergholt.
Opening hours 10 am – 5 pm; daily; March to September, except for the Charity days: (2 pm – 5 pm; 1, 14 & 28 April, 12 & 26 May, 2 June & 20 October).
Admission fee Adults £2.50; Children free.

Features Topiary; rhododendrons & azaleas; camellias; fine collection of trees; specialist plant centre in walled garden.

Owned by Mr & Mrs Rupert Eley
Number of gardeners 1
Size 6ha (15 acres)

East Bergholt has a wonderful woodland garden planted by Charles Eley, the present owner's great-grandfather, at the start of the 20th century. It is the home of *Malus × pupurea* 'Eleyi' and has been called a 'Cornish Garden in Suffolk'. Unfortunately, not all of it is always open to the public, except on charity open days. At other times visitors can see a collection of trees known as the 'Swale', around a gentle valley with a small brook running down the middle. Many of the older trees and shrubs were grown from original collections by George Forrest: others represent modern plantings and re-plantings. The collection is well-labelled and well-maintained – a fine place to see a wide range of trees and shrubs. Good specimens include a very handsome variegated cherry-laurel *Prunus laurocerasus* 'Castlewellan' 5m high, a magnificent *Quercus castaneifolia* and a fine 3-stemmed *Davidia involucrata* var. *vilmoriniana*. Some are record-breakers, including a *Lithocarpus densiflorus* 12m tall. The valley is sheltered by hedges of holly and yew and a mature collection of hardy rhododendrons. And it is good for insects and wildlife too. Restoration and replanting continue. The much-praised nursery in the walled garden has a good general stock, most of it bought in.

Euston Hall

EUSTON, THETFORD IP24 2QP

Tel 01842 766366 **Fax** 01842 766764
Location On A1088 3 miles south of Thetford & 12 miles north of Bury St Edmunds.
Opening hours 2.30 pm – 5 pm; Thursdays; 6 June to 26 September, plus 30 June & 1 September. NCCPG Plant Sale on 26 May.
Admission fee £2.

The classical 18th-century landscaping at Euston is very beautiful. William Kent made the serpentine lake, though it was later modified by Capability Brown. Kent also built the elegant banqueting house. There are avenues of beech and lime, and clumps, spinneys and belts of mature trees. The formal terraces by the house lead to herbaceous borders and rose gardens. It all adds up to a most satisfying composition where horticulture plays second fiddle to landscaping.

 Features Roses (mainly old-fashioned); William Kent temple and summerhouse; new 'Monet' bridge on lake; river walk & watermill.

Owned by The Duke of Grafton
Number of gardeners 2
Size 28ha (70 acres)
English Heritage grade II*

Goldbrook Plants

HOXNE, EYE IP21 5AN

Tel & Fax 01379 668770
Location On south-east edge of Hoxne.
Opening hours 10 am – 5 pm; Thursday – Sunday; April to September. Other days by appointment. Closed January & around Chelsea & Hampton Court Shows.

Goldbrook's exhibits at Chelsea and other RHS flower shows have won them much praise – and an impressive run of gold medals. Their collection of hostas is quite exceptional – over 1,000 cultivars, of which a great many are available from no other nursery. The same is true of their hemerocallis. Look out for their American introductions too – many of the hemerocallis bear the prefix 'Siloam' (e.g. *H.* 'Siloam Fairy Tale') – while the hostas they have raised themselves are often prefixed by 'Goldbrook'.

 Features Hostas; hemerocallis.

Haughley Park

STOWMARKET IP14 3JY

Tel 01359 240701 **Fax** 01359 240546
Location Signed from A14.
Opening hours 2 pm – 5.30 pm; Tuesdays; May to September, plus 28 April & 5 May for bluebells.
Admission fee Adults £3; Children free.

Haughley has a Jacobean mansion with well-kept modern flower gardens and fine trees (especially a *Magnolia grandiflora* which is one of the largest we know – 8m high and 11m across). In the walled garden are vegetables, trained fruit trees, a rose arbour and other ornamental features. But the acres of lily-of-the-valley and bluebells in the woodland garden are worth the journey no matter how far. There is a choice of three woodland walks, from 1½–2½ miles long: the camellias are good in May and the rhododendrons in June. In the West Woods, the owners have been carrying out an interesting experiment since the great gale of 1987. This arises from the different way in which each part was subsequently managed. Some areas were undamaged and remain 'natural'; one area of damaged woodland

Helmingham Hall

STOWMARKET IP14 6EF

Tel 01473 890363   **Fax** 01473 890776
Website www.helmingham.com
Location 9 miles north of Ipswich on B1077.
Opening hours 2 pm – 6 pm; Sundays; 5 May to
15 September; plus individuals & groups on Wednesday
afternoons by prior arrangement.
Admission fee Adults £3.75; Children £2.

A visit to Helmingham is a step back into history, to a time of ancient certainties, order and peace. The Tollemaches have lived here since 1487. The house is a moated manor, half-timbered when built in 1480, but given a cladding of bricks and tiles in the 18th century. It is set in the most spacious 400-acre deer-park, loosely studded with vast centennial oaks grown to their full spread. Helmingham's formal garden lies beyond the moat to the south of the house. It is surrounded by 60 hybrid musks, lightly pruned and allowed to billow out, to fill the beds. The entire garden, about 100m long, is edged with 'Hidcote' lavender, underplanted with variegated London pride, and complemented by *Campanula lactiflora*, alstroemerias, foxgloves and peonies. This is gardening on a large scale, and makes its impact through simplicity and repetition: it is immensely grand. Beyond the formal garden is the walled garden proper, built of brick in 1745. On either side of the central grassy path runs a broad and stately double herbaceous border perhaps 120m long. Climbing roses are tied to straining wires all along its back: they include 'Guinée', 'Long John Silver', and *Rosa multiflora* var. *cathayensis*. The roses are underplanted with herbaceous plantings chosen to blend with the soft colours of the roses: pinks, blues, mauves, whites and the palest of creamy yellows. Not until the main rose-flowering has finished in mid-August do yellows, bronzes, oranges and reds come to the fore. A spring border runs the whole way along one of the outer walls of the walled garden and is planted mainly with irises, tulips and peonies, backed by more climbing roses, vines, clematis, chaenomeles, ceanothus and myrtle from Queen Victoria's wedding posy. Nearer the house is a new series of knot gardens planted in 1982, which look as if they have been here for hundreds of years. The knots include the Tollemaches' heraldic device, a fret or interlacing pattern of bands, which has been made to interweave by pruning the strips of box at different levels. It leads to another rose garden: albas and species roses, centifolias and mosses, a large choice of gallicas and so on, underplanted with spring bulbs, white foxgloves, *Campanula persicifolia*, *Alchemilla mollis*, purple violas and geraniums. One reason why the garden is so successful is that the roses and their companion plantings all fall within a narrow colour range: it is a discipline from which every garden-owner can learn. But everything here is carefully thought through and controlled: you see this firmness too in the immaculately edged lawns and weedless borders. Everywhere at Helmingham, order prevails over anarchy.

Features Roses (mainly old-fashioned); good herbaceous borders; deer park; moat; fine walled garden; good parterres and knots; shop; tea-room.

Owned by Lord Tollemache
English Heritage grade I

has been left in place to recover naturally; one area had the stumps left in place to shoot as coppice timber and several areas were cleared and replanted between 1992 and 1996.

Features Woodland garden; rhododendrons & azaleas; good herbaceous borders; bluebells; lily-of-the-valley; 1,000-year-old oak.

Owned by Robert Williams
Number of gardeners 3½
Size 3.2ha (8 acres), plus 105ha (265 acres) of park & woods.

Ickworth

HORRINGER, BURY ST EDMUNDS IP29 5QE

Tel 01284 735270 **Fax** 01284 735175
Website www.nationaltrust.org.uk
Location 3 miles south-west of Bury St Edmunds.
Opening hours 10 am – 5 pm (4 pm in winter); daily; all year except Christmas period. Closed at weekends from 2 January to 23 March and from 3 November to 21 December.
Admission fee Adults £2.70.

Ickworth is an extraordinary garden for an extraordinary house: the main borders follow the curves of the house. There are also an Italian garden and long vistas in the park, but the old kitchen garden is bare.

Features Autumn colour; Italian garden; Victorian 'stumpery'; display of lemon trees in orangery; tallest *Quercus pubescens* (29m) in the British Isles.

Owned by The National Trust
NCCPG National Collections *Buxus*
English Heritage grade II*

Mills Farm Plants and Gardens

NORWICH ROAD, MENDLESHAM IP14 5NQ

Tel & Fax 01449 766425
Website www.millsfarmplants.co.uk
Location On A140 just south of Mendlesham village turning.
Opening hours 9 am – 5.30 pm; Wednesday – Sunday, plus Bank Holiday Mondays; all year. Closed all January.
Admission fee Free.

Mills Farm specialises in *Dianthus* (new and old hybrids, species and rock garden types) and roses: there is a list for each genus. The roses are mostly old-fashioned varieties, in a well-chosen selection – about 100 different cultivars. This RHS Partner Nursery also lists about 500 herbaceous perennials out of a total of 1,100 at any time. The owners claim to have one of the widest commercial collection of pinks (*Dianthus*) in the UK. They also breed their own and have introduced quite a number of *Dianthus* cultivars with the prefix 'Mendlesham', including 'Mendlesham Frilly', 'Mendlesham Glow' and 'Mendlesham Maid'. The garden is well worth visiting – designed entirely for the owners' pleasure as a formal and restrained place for contemplation, with a limited colour palette and the sound of falling water. It is surrounded by yew hedges and planted so that something is in flower throughout the year. Everything has good, strong foliage, too. The owners have just (2002) added a demonstration bed for dianthus, planted with all the cultivars they grow.

 Features Dianthus.

Owned by Dr & Mrs P.L. Russell

Notcutts Nurseries

IPSWICH ROAD, WOODBRIDGE
IP12 4AF

Tel 01394 383344 **Fax** 01394 445307
Website www.notcutts.co.uk
Location On the Ipswich Road.
Opening hours 9 am – 6 pm; Monday – Saturday.
10.30 am – 4.30 pm; Sundays.

Notcutts are large wholesale nurseries with a garden centre chain and branches in Norwich, Oxford (Mattocks roses), Staines, Peterborough, St Albans, Bagshot, Maidstone, Tunbridge Wells, Cranleigh, Booker, Solihull and Ardleigh. The company as a whole is strongest on flowering shrubs and trees and their large, beautifully colour-co-ordinated displays of these at the Chelsea Flower Show have been a source of wonder and praise for many years. But they offer every type of plant in all their branches and the quality of their stock is first class. They list over 3,000 different plants. Staff are also extremely helpful and knowledgeable. It is difficult for even the most experienced gardener not to come away from a visit to a branch of Notcutts without several new additions to his garden.

 Features Flowering trees & shrubs; rhododendrons; hibiscus; large restaurant.

NCCPG National Collections *Hibiscus syiacus* cvs.

Paradise Centre

TWINSTEAD ROAD, LAMARSH, BURES
CO8 5EX

Tel & Fax 01787 269449
Website www.paradisecentre.com
Location Signed in Lamarsh.

Opening hours 10 am – 5 pm; Saturday – Sunday & Bank Holidays; Easter to October. Other times by appointment.
Admission fee Free.

This garden-nursery specialises in bulbs, herbaceous plants, shade-plants and damp-lovers, almost all of which are grown at the nursery. The adjoining gardens are superb: five acres of light woodland with thousands and thousands of bulbs giving colour at every season. Many are unusual. There is also a natural spring, whose water provides an ideal habitat for *Gunnera manicata*, lysichitons and other damp-loving plants.

 Features Shade-lovers and damp-lovers.

Owned by Cees & Hedy Stapel-Valk

Park Green Nurseries

WETHERINGSETT, STOWMARKET
IP14 5QH

Tel 01728 860139 **Fax** 01728 861277
Website www.parkgreen.co.uk
Location 6 miles north-east of Stowmarket.
Opening hours 10 am – 4 pm; Monday – Friday;
1 March to 22 September. Plus 10 am – 1 pm on Saturdays in same period.
Admission fee Free.

This RHS Partner Nursery specialises in ornamental grasses and other hardy perennial plants, but its most important line is hostas. It stocks over 200 different cultivars and introduces new ones every year. Recent home-raised releases include 'Delia', 'Knave's Green', 'Sarah Kennedy' and 'Gay Search'.

Owned by Richard & Mary Ford

Rougham Hall Nurseries

A14 ROUGHAM, BURY ST EDMUNDS
IP30 9LZ

Tel 01359 270577 **Fax** 01359 271149
Website www.roughamhallnurseries.co.uk
Location Off the west-bound carriageway of the A14.
Opening hours 10 am – 4 pm; daily; March to October.

Rougham Hall Nurseries – always very popular when they come to RHS flower shows – are breeders, introducers and growers of an extensive and interesting range of perennials. Their selection of asters is particularly good, as is their list of delphiniums, of which they have a National Collection. Their other National Collection is of gooseberries: they have by far the most extensive list anywhere in the world. The whole history of this most highly prized of dessert fruits is contained within the hundreds of cultivars which they list. The range is always increasing, too: it is worthwhile enquiring if they do not appear to have one that you are looking for.

NCCPG National Collections *Delphinium*; gooseberries

Shrubland Park Gardens

CODDENHAM, IPSWICH IP6 9QQ

Tel 01473 830221 **Fax** 01473 832202
Website www.shrublandpark.co.uk
Location Between Claydon & Coddenham: come by A14 or A140.
Opening hours 2 pm – 5 pm; Sundays & Bank Holiday Mondays; 31 March to 1 September.
Admission fee Adults £3; OAPs & Children £2.

This grand Victorian garden was designed by Charles Barry and has been famous ever since for the spectacular Italianate staircase which connects the terrace around the house with the formal gardens below. William Robinson later helped with the planting, both around the formal garden and in the park and woodland gardens beyond. Much restoration and recovery has been completed in recent years: Shrubland is getting better and better.

Features Spectacular garden architecture; woodland garden; roses (mainly modern); good herbaceous borders; box maze; Swiss châlet.

Owned by Lord de Saumarez
Number of gardeners 5
Size 16ha (40 acres)
English Heritage grade I

Somerleyton Hall

SOMERLEYTON, LOWESTOFT
NR32 5QQ

Tel 01502 730224 **Fax** 01502 732143
Website www.somerleyton.co.uk
Location 4 miles north-west of Lowestoft on B1074.
Opening hours 12.30 pm – 5.30 pm; Thursdays, Sundays & Bank Holidays, plus Tuesdays & Wednesdays in July & August; 31 March to 30 September. Ring for details of openings planned for October.
Admission fee Adults £5.20; OAPs £5; Children £2.60. (2001 prices).

Somerleyton is a splendid place to visit: there is much for the garden- and plant-lover to see and enjoy. In front of the house (palatial, Victorian) is an extremely grand formal garden. William Andrews Nesfield laid out the terraces and the yew maze, which was planted in 1846: it is not too difficult to get to the centre – less than 400m from the entrance, provided you make no mistakes on the way. The gardens are full of topiary and good statuary, including a great equatorial sundial, encircled by signs of the Zodiac. Near the house are quantities of roses, herbaceous borders and seasonal bedding. Further afield are large plantings of rhododendrons and azaleas. Though none is actually a record-breaker, Somerleyton has some very fine specimen trees, including a giant redwood (*Sequoiadendron giganteum*), *Eucalyptus gunnii*, Monterey pine (*Pinus radiata*), Atlas cedar (*Cedrus atlantica*) and a particularly good maidenhair tree (*Ginkgo biloba*). There has been much replanting since the hurricane of 1987 and the new plantings are already making quite an impact. The walled garden was once the kitchen garden but is now planted with flowers: on the walls are many different climbers including roses, clematis, figs, climbing hydrangeas and such wall-shrubs as *Hoheria sexstylosa*. The glasshouses and peach-cases were designed by Sir Joseph Paxton, architect of the Crystal Palace, with his characteristic ridge-and-furrow roofs. They are now planted with tender ornamentals like Meyer's lemon, abutilons, *Cassia (Senna) corymbosa* and the sweetly-scented *Dregea sinensis*. An old boiler house has a collection of old garden equipment in it. Other good features include an elegant, long, metal pergola with lots of different wisterias and a young avenue of lime trees along the driveway, planted in 1981.

Features Roses (mainly modern); plants under glass; maze; new bamboo bed; fine statues; magnificent trees; pergola; formal garden; walled garden; souvenir gift shop; light lunches & teas.

Owned by Lord & Lady Somerleyton
Number of gardeners 4½
Size 5ha (12 acres)
English Heritage grade II*

Wyken Hall

STANTON, BURY ST EDMUNDS
IP31 2DW

Tel 01359 250287   **Fax** 01359 252256
Location 9 miles north-east from Bury St Edmunds; follow brown signs from A143 at Ixworth to Wyken Vineyards.
Opening hours 2 pm – 6 pm; Sunday – Friday; Easter to 1 October. Plus 8 June for National Gardens Scheme.
Admission fee Adults £2.50; OAPs £2; Children free.

The garden at Wyken is ingeniously designed: a series of old-style gardens to complement the Elizabethan house. These include a knot garden, a herb garden, a traditional English kitchen garden, wildflower meadows, a nuttery and a copper beech maze. All are in scale with the house and the farmland around. Stylish and well maintained, this is one of the best modern private gardens in the country. The restaurant features in the *Good Food Guide* and is a Michelin *Bib Gourmand*. The 'Giant Stride' (a sort of revolving maypole) was added to commemorate the millennium.

Features Woodland garden; roses (ancient & modern); plantsman's collection of plants; herbs; fruit; good shrubs; good herbaceous borders; award-winning 7-acre vineyard; country store shop; Vineyard Restaurant.

Owned by Sir Kenneth & Lady Carlisle
Number of gardeners 2
Size 1.6ha (4 acres)

SURREY

A Martian could be excused for thinking that Surrey was the centre of the horticultural universe. It is the county with everything that gardeners could ever want. Its six Grade I gardens include two very important landscapes – Claremont and Painshill – and two highly influential 20th-century gardens – Munstead Wood and the Savill Garden. Because of its closeness to London, it has become a very rich county during the last 100 years, which means that people have the time and money to garden on a large scale. The National Gardens Scheme does extremely well in Surrey, with a large number of medium-sized gardens opening for charity, as well as a handful of intensely cultivated smaller gardens. It is the county where the National Gardens Scheme has its headquarters and where its chairman lives – her garden at Vale End is itself open to the public. Surrey has many of the country's best known nurseries – the light soils being poor for agriculture but excellent for growing plants: the floral mile along the A30 is a famous landmark, where some of the trees and shrubs in the old Waterer nurseries have grown to exceptional size. There are good trees too – and many record-breakers – at Winkworth Arboretum, the Savill Garden and the RHS Garden Wisley. Surrey still has a large number of first-class nurseries: we include the important Knap Hill Nursery, Millais Nurseries and the newer star Toobees Exotics. Brian & Heather Hiley, from whose nursery at Wallington some of the best exhibits to be seen at RHS shows were mounted in the 1990s, have now moved to Cornwall to plant a garden which will doubtless merit a visit as soon as it is open. There are other nurseries which we do not have space to list but which are well worth visiting – Secretts near Godalming, Lincluden at Bisley and Pantiles at Chertsey for example. The Surrey Gardens Trust and the Surrey group of the NCCPG are both very active in the county: the NCCPG has its base at Wisley. There are over 30 National Collections in Surrey, including seven at Wisley and eight at the Savill Garden. And of course the Royal Horticultural Society's own flagship garden at Wisley dominates every aspect of gardens and gardening in the county: as many as 20% of the society's members live in Surrey.

Brook Lodge Farm Cottage

BLACKBROOK, DORKING RH5 4DT

Tel 01306 888368
Location Signed from A24 past Plough Inn in Blackbrook.
Opening hours 2 pm – 5 pm; 9 & 12 June, 4 & 17 July,
7 & 14 August, 4 September. And by appointment.
Admission fee Adults £2; Children free.

Planted by the present owner over many
years, this garden has matured into a fine
plantsman's garden with much variety:
shrub roses, a rockery, a woodland walk,
herbaceous borders and a cottage garden.

 Features Woodland garden; roses
(mainly old-fashioned); plantsman's
collection of plants; mature conifers; good
herbaceous borders; homemade teas.

Owned by Mrs Basil Kingham
Number of gardeners 2
Size 1.4ha (3½ acres)

Cadenza

BUTTERFLY WALK, WARLINGHAM
CR6 9JA

Tel 01883 623565
Location M25 Jct 6; north up A22 for 4 miles; fourth exit
at large roundabout; uphill & turn right.
Opening hours By appointment only.
Admission fee Free.

This is the private garden of keen
plantsmen. Their special interest is small
bulbs, and they have one of England's most
interesting collections of hardy cyclamen.

Features Cyclamen; fritillaries; bulbs.

Owned by Mr & Mrs Ronald Frank
Number of gardeners part-time help
Size 0.3ha (¾ acre)

Chilworth Manor

CHILWORTH, GUILDFORD GU4 8NL

Tel 01483 561414
Location In middle of village, up Blacksmiths Lane.
Opening hours 2 pm – 6 pm; 6–10 April, 11–16 May,
9–13 June, 15–19 June, & 11 July. And by appointment.
Admission fee £2.

This is a remarkable garden, tiered up over
seven distinct levels. The top three date from
about 1700 and are walled around with
beautiful brickwork. There are good
climbers and shrubs against the walls, and a
bog garden in the woods at the bottom. The
main herbaceous border has recently been
replanted by a Dutch designer.

Features Woodland garden; good
herbaceous borders; rhododendrons;
interesting new shrub plantings; sculpture
exhibitions; tallest *Ilex aquifolium*
'Bacciflava' (10.5m) and largest *Ilex
aquifolium* 'Pendula' in the British Isles.

Owned by Lady Heald
Number of gardeners 1

Clandon Park

WEST CLANDON, GUILDFORD
GU4 7RQ

Tel 01483 222482 **Fax** 01483 223479
Website www.nationaltrust.org.uk
Location Off the A247 at West Clandon.
Opening hours 11 am – 5 pm; daily; all year.
Admission fee Free.

Capability Brown's magnificent mature beeches are now underplanted with sombre Victorian shrubberies and slabs of comfrey, bergenias and *Geranium macrorrhizum* – the apotheosis of National Trust groundcover. There is a modern pastiche of a Dutch garden at the east end of the grounds but the daffodils in spring are breathtaking.

 Features Parterres; grotto; Dutch garden; Maori meeting-house; Clandon Park Garden Centre is nearby.

Owned by The National Trust
Number of gardeners 1
Size 3.8ha (9½ acres)
English Heritage grade II

Claremont Landscape Garden

PORTSMOUTH ROAD, ESHER KT10 9JG

Tel 01372 467806 **Fax** 01372 464394
Website www.nationaltrust.org.uk
Location On southern edge of town (A307).
Opening hours 10 am – 6 pm (but dusk from November to March & 7 pm or sunset if earlier on Saturdays, Sundays & Bank Holiday Mondays from April to October); daily, all year, but closed on Mondays from November to March. Closed 18, 19 & 22 July & 25 December. Closed at 2 pm on 20 & 21 July.
Admission fee Adults £3.80; Children £1.75.

This vast historic landscape – now much reduced – was worked over by Vanbrugh, Bridgeman, Kent and Capability Brown and has been energetically restored in recent years. The elegant green theatre is best seen flanked by spreading cedars from across the dark lake. Very popular locally, it is apt to get crowded at summer weekends.

 Features Laurel lawns; tallest service tree *Sorbus domestica* (23m) in the British Isles, and two further record trees.

Owned by The National Trust
Number of gardeners 3, plus volunteers
Size 19.6ha (49 acres)
English Heritage grade I

Hannah Peschar Sculpture Garden

BLACK AND WHITE COTTAGE, STANDON LANE, OCKLEY RH5 5QR

Tel 01306 627269 **Fax** 01306 627662
Website www.hannahpescharsculpture.com
Location Turn off A29 down Cathill Lane, left at T junction, over bridge & drive is 400 yards on right.
Opening hours 11 am – 6 pm; Fridays & Saturdays. 2 pm – 5 pm; Sundays & Bank Holidays. May to October. And by appointment.
Admission fee Adults £8; Concessions £6; Children £5.

The lush water-gardens and woodlands surrounding a black-and-white cottage are the setting for this remarkable and ever-changing collection of contemporary British sculpture. The water-garden was originally made by Anthony Paul but has been revamped with lots of architectural plants. There are pools and a stream, and surprisingly few flowers – the structure of the background is more important for sculpture than any transient colour. Nevertheless, an earlier owner was the distinguished horticulturist Dick Trotter, Mr Bowles's 'nephew Dick' and sometime Treasurer of the RHS.

Owned by Hannah Peschar
Number of gardeners 1
Size 4ha (10 acres)

Hatchlands

EAST CLANDON, GUILDFORD
GU4 7RT

Tel 01483 222482   **Fax** 01483 223176
Website www.nationaltrust.org.uk
Location Off A246 Guildford to Leatherhead.
Opening hours 2 pm – 5.30 pm; Tuesday – Thursday,
Sundays & Bank Holiday Mondays; April to October. Also
Fridays in August. Park walks in Repton Park open daily
11 am – 6 pm from April to October.
Admission fee Adults £2.50; Children £1.25.

Apart from the Jekyll garden (roses, lupins,
box and columbines) Hatchlands is an 18th-
century landscape with parkland. But the
garden buildings are charming and the
National Trust has made good progress with
restoration and replanting.

 Features Woodland garden; National
Trust shop; restaurant.

Owned by The National Trust
Number of gardeners 2
Size 180ha (450 acres) of parkland

Herons Bonsai Ltd

WIRE MILL LANE, NEWCHAPEL,
LINGFIELD RH7 6HJ

Tel 01342 832657
Location Turn left off the A22, ½ mile south of junction
with B2028.
Opening hours 9.30 am – 5.30 pm; Monday – Saturday.
10.30 am – 4.30 pm on Sundays. Closes at dusk in winter.

This bonsai nursery has a string of gold
medals behind it from Chelsea Flower
Shows. As well as trees for indoors and
outdoors, there are pots, tools and
accessories. They also run bonsai classes
and offer Japanese garden design.

Hydon Nurseries

CLOCK BARN LANE, HYDON HEATH,
GODALMING GU8 4AZ

Tel 01483 860252   **Fax** 01483 419937
Location 2 miles east of A3, Milford exit. Near Cheshire
Home.
Opening hours 8 am – 5 pm, Monday – Friday. Plus
Saturdays 9 am – 12.45 pm (5 pm from 1 March to 15 June
and from late September to October). Sundays by
appointment. Closed for lunch 12.45 pm – 2 pm.
Admission fee Free. Parties by arrangement.

These rhododendron and azalea specialists
have an extensive range of all classes,
including some tender species and their own
Rhododendron yakushimanum hybrids. They
have a comprehensive stock of evergreen
azaleas, and also sell companion trees and
shrubs, especially camellias (another
speciality). The nursery extends over
25 acres: among the many fine trees are
five large trees of the dark pink form of
Magnolia campbellii and fine mature
specimens of *Nothofagus dombeyi* and *N.
antarctica*, as well as the two record-
breakers. Visitors are particularly welcome
to see the magnolias in early spring.

Features Rhododendrons & azaleas;
tallest *Eucalyptus pauciflora* subsp.
niphophila and *Sorbus* 'Joseph Rock' in the
British Isles.

Number of gardeners 5
Size 10ha (25 acres)

Knap Hill Nursery Ltd

BARRS LANE, KNAPHILL, WOKING
GU21 2JW

Tel 01483 481214   **Fax** 01483 797261
Website www.knaphillrhododendrons.co.uk
Location 2½ miles west of Woking, off A322.
Opening hours 9 am – 5 pm; Monday – Friday.
Closed on bank holidays.

This large and famous rhododendron
nursery is also one of England's oldest,
founded over 200 years ago: members of the
Slocock family have been hybridising
rhododendrons for several generations and
their nursery covers more than 200 acres.
Their extensive list includes hybrids, dwarf,
semi-dwarf and *R. yakushimanum* hybrids,
as well as deciduous and evergreen azaleas.
The display area has about 600 different
cultivars: not all are listed at any one time,
but they will propagate to request. Over the
years, the nursery has won 28 gold medals at
the Chelsea Flower Show and was awarded
the Rothschild Cup in 1997 and 1999.

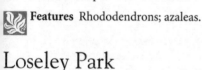 **Features** Rhododendrons; azaleas.

Loseley Park

GUILDFORD GU3 1HS

Tel 01483 304440   **Fax** 01483 302036
Website www.loseley-park.com
Location Off B3000 at Compton, south of Guildford.
Opening hours 11 am – 5 pm; Wednesday – Sunday; 6
May to 29 September.
Admission fee Adults £3; OAPs £2.50; Children £1.50.
RHS members free in May & September.

The walled garden attached to this fine
Elizabethan house has recently been re-made
and re-planted with 1,000 old-fashioned roses
framed by long, low, box hedges. The new
herb garden is divided into six sections,
respectively devoted to culinary, medicinal,
ornamental, dye plants, cosmetic plants and
an area of native wildflowers to attract
wildlife. The fiery herbaceous borders come
into their own in July and August, while the
moat walk makes for a quiet amble at any
season. The peaceful fountain garden is filled
with plants of a cream, white and silver
theme. The newest addition is the vegetable
garden and moat walk.

 Features Roses (mainly old-
fashioned); herbs; fruit; lakeside walk;
gift shop; courtyard tea-room; restaurant.

Owned by Michael More-Molyneux
Number of gardeners 3
Size 1ha (2½ acres)

Millais Nurseries

CROSSWATER FARM, CHURT,
FARNHAM GU10 2JN

Tel 01252 792698   **Fax** 01252 792526
Website www.rhododendrons.co.uk
Location In Crosswater Lane, signed from Churt village.
Opening hours Nursery: 10 am – 1 pm & 2 pm – 5 pm;
Monday – Friday. Also Saturdays in spring & autumn.
And daily in May. Garden: late April to early June.
Admission fee Garden £2; Nursery free.

This important and dynamic rhododendron
and azalea nursery has an extensive range of
species and hybrids, including some new
Himalayan species, late-flowering cultivars
chosen to avoid the frost, large-leaved
species for sheltered gardens, scented
deciduous azaleas, *R. yakushimanum*
hybrids for the smaller garden, dwarf
cultivars for the rock garden and Maddenia
series rhododendrons for the conservatory.
In addition to the garden (6 acres, ponds,

stream and companion plantings) there is a trials garden where hundreds of new cultivars from around the world are labelled and tested.

 Features Rhododendrons; sorbus.

Owned by The Millais family
Size 2.2ha (6 acres)

Munstead Wood

HEATH LANE, BUSBRIDGE, GODALMING GU7 1UN

Tel 01483 417867 **Fax** 01483 425041
Location 1 mile south of Godalming on B2130: turn along Heath Lane. Parking in field 300 yards along on left.
Opening hours 2 pm – 6 pm; 14 April, 19 May & 2 July.
Admission fee Adults £3; OAPs £1.50; Children free.

Munstead Wood is important for being Gertrude Jekyll's own garden. Here she worked out the principles she expounded in her best-known books *Wood and Garden* (1899) and *Colour in the Flower Garden* (1908). Her garden has now been split into several smaller holdings each in separate ownership, but the main parts are still attached to the house which Lutyens designed in 1896. The wood garden is fairly intact: the views up and down its main path to and from the lawn in front of the house seem just as they were a hundred years ago: birches underplanted mainly with rhododendrons and azaleas. Closer to the house is a block of borders full of good plantings – herbaceous plants, in particular. The nut walk and its nearby borders have recently been replanted: the Clarks have spent many years restoring the garden – and the results are admirable.

 Features Woodland garden; roses (mainly old-fashioned); sunken rock

garden; good herbaceous borders; rhododendrons & azaleas; spring garden; new orchard (1999); cream teas.

Owned by Sir Robert & Lady Clark
Number of gardeners 2
Size 4ha (10 acres)
English Heritage grade I

Painshill Park

PORTSMOUTH ROAD, COBHAM KT11 1JE

Tel 01932 868113 **Fax** 01932 868001
Website www.painshill.co.uk
Location Signed from M25 Jct 10 & A3.
Opening hours 10.30 am – 6 pm (last tickets 4.30 pm); Tuesday – Sunday & Bank Holiday Mondays; April to October. 11 am – 4 pm (last tickets 3 pm) Tuesday – Thursday, Saturdays & Sundays; November to March. Closed 25 & 26 December.
Admission fee Adults £4.50; Concessions £4; Children (under 16) £2.

Charles Hamilton was the plantsman, painter and designer who created Painshill between 1738 and 1773, when he finally went bankrupt. His lasting achievement was to transform a barren heathland into ornamental pleasure grounds and parkland of dramatic beauty. A 14-acre lake is at the centre of the design: it offers a focus for the garden's most famous features, the white gothic temple and the grotto, which is approached across a 'Chinese' bridge. Hamilton sought to provoke the greatest variety of moods: other features included a ruined abbey and a Turkish tent. Hamilton was a pioneer of the naturalistic landscape style, and very influential, but never a rich man: he leased Painshill from the Crown and had little to spend, which makes his achievement all the more remarkable. He was also a great plantsman, importing many new species from North America for his shrubberies. After 1948 the garden fell into dereliction. Over the past 20 years it has been meticulously restored and the Painshill Trust has made enormous progress in raising the substantial funds needed. The Heritage Lottery Fund is a major supporter and has grant-aided the new Visitor and Education Centre which was completed last year (2001).

 Features 'American' garden; grotto; Turkish tent; tallest *Juniperus virginiana* (26m) in the British Isles.

Owned by Painshill Park Trust
Number of gardeners 4
Size 63ha (158 acres)
English Heritage grade I

Pantiles Plant & Garden Centre

ALMNERS ROAD, LYNE, CHERTSEY KT16 0BJ

Tel 01932 872195   **Fax** 01923 874030
Website www.pantiles-nuseries.co.uk
Location 5 mins from M25 Jct 11.
Opening hours 9 am – 6 pm (5 pm in winter); Monday – Saturday; all year. Plus 10 am – 4 pm on Sundays.

The nursery specialises in outsize container-grown specimens up to eight metres high. It is popular with professionals and impatient amateurs alike – anyone, in fact, in search of that instant air of maturity which a large and well-grown tree can bring. The range of specimen trees is very impressive, and includes tree ferns like *Dicksonia antarctica* as well as large specimens of yew and box, cloud-pruned in the Japanese style.

 Features Large plants; bonsai; aquatics; coffee shop.

Planta Vera

LYNE HILL NURSERY, LYNE CROSSING ROAD, CHERTSEY KT16 0AT

Tel & Fax 01932 563011
Location Just south of junction of M3 & M25; map in catalogue.
Opening hours 9 am – 5 pm, last weekend of each month & Bank Holidays, April to October; other times by appointment.

Morris May took over Richard Cawthorne's *Viola* collection in 1995. He continues Cawthorne's work by maintaining the world's largest collection of violas (*Melanium* section): some of the collection is in display beds at the nursery. Plants are propagated from autumn cuttings, ready for sale in spring. Planta Vera's business is mainly wholesale, though there is a range of herbaceous perennials available as well as the violas.

Polesden Lacey

GREAT BOOKHAM, DORKING RH5 6BD

Tel 01372 458203   **Fax** 01372 452023
Website www.nationaltrust.org.uk
Location Off A246 between Leatherhead & Guildford.
Opening hours 11 am – 6 pm (or dusk, if earlier); daily; all year.
Admission fee Adults £4; Children £2.

Polesden Lacy is best for the long terraced walk, laid out by Sheridan, and the return through an Edwardian-style rose garden whose pergolas drip with ramblers. The park is good and there are fine views and walks around the estate.

Features Snowdrops; roses of every kind; good herbaceous borders; lavender garden; large National Trust shop.

Owned by The National Trust
Number of gardeners 6, plus 1 trainee
Size 12ha (30 acres), plus landscaped park
English Heritage grade II*

Ramster

CHIDDINGFOLD GU8 4SN

Tel 01428 654167 **Fax** 01428 658345
Location 1½ miles south of Chiddingfold on A283.
Opening hours 11 am – 5 pm; daily; 13 April to 7 July. Parties by appointment at other times.
Admission fee Adults £3; Children free.

Ramster was first laid out in 1890, with help from a local nursery, Gauntletts of Chiddingfold, who were known for their interest in flowering shrubs and especially for Japanese plants and planting. From this original influence date the ornamental stone lanterns, the large plantings of bamboos, and the avenue of *Acer palmatum* var. *dissectum* seedlings, now over 100 years old. In 1922 the property was bought by Miranda Gunn's grandparents Sir Henry and Lady Norman. Lady Norman was a keen gardener, the sister of the second Lord Aberconway, who was a past President of the RHS. She had been brought up at Bodnant, where she imbibed the family's great love of rhododendrons: many of the plants at Ramster came from Bodnant, and some of the rhododendrons and azaleas are her own hybrids. Ramster is an important garden for rhododendrons and, in the part known as Ant Wood, the Gunns have been building up a comprehensive collection of the old Hardy Hybrids – over 200 plants. But the garden is full of other projects and developments: the bog garden has come

together very quickly since it was planted in 1998, and there is a new Millennium Garden. The garden is maintained in such a way as to allow meadow grasses, wildflowers and orchids to flourish and flower later in the year, but Ramster is essentially a garden for spring and early summer.

 Features Mature woodland garden with rhododendrons, magnolias, camellias, azaleas; bluebells; largest *Euonymus europaeus* (6m) in the British Isles; homemade teas in May & at weekends.

Owned by Mr & Mrs Paul Gunn

Titsey Place

OXTED RH8 0SD

Tel 01273 407056 **Fax** 01273 478995
Location Off the B269 north of Limpsfield.
Opening hours 1 pm – 5 pm; Easter Monday, then on Wednesdays, Sundays & Bank Holiday Mondays from 15 May to 30 September.
Admission fee Adults £2; Children £1.

The historic garden at Titsey has been well restored with advice from Elizabeth Banks since it first opened to the public in 1993. The lay-out is gardenesque and most of the plantings date from the middle of the 19th century. The large triple-trunked horse chestnut (*Aesculus hippocastanum*) on the upper terrace dates from that time. A stream which rises in the grounds has been dammed to make two lakes. The formal gardens are planted with roses and herbaceous plants, while the old walled kitchen garden has been planted as an example of how fruit, vegetables and flowers were grown in Victorian times.

Owned by The Trustees of the Titsey Place Foundation
Number of gardeners 5
Size 5ha (12 acres)

RHS Garden Wisley

WOKING GU23 6QB

Tel 01483 224234 **Fax** 01483 211750
Website www.rhs.org.uk
Location M25 Jct 10. Follow brown tourist signs.
Opening hours 10 am (but 9 am at weekends) to 6 pm;
daily; all year except Christmas Day. Sundays from March
to October reserved for RHS members and their guests
only. Closes at 4.30 pm from November to February. Last
admissions one hour before closing.
Admission fee Adults £6; Children £2. RHS Members
free. Discounts for groups (pre-booked 21 days) – ring
01483 212307.

Wisley is the most important horticultural demonstration garden in Europe – perhaps in the world. It has many incidents of great intrinsic value – the vast Pulhamite rock garden which fills an entire hillside, for example – but its true worth lies in its comprehensiveness: everything that a gardener could possibly want to see and learn from is here within its 200 acres. The only problem is its very size: Wisley is not a garden you could ever hope to get round properly in just a day, let alone a few hours. It is somewhere to explore over many visits at different times of the year, until the lay-out and the principal features become familiar and you learn where you should go to see what is good and instructive at the time of your visit.

The Royal Horticultural Society moved its experimental garden from Chiswick in 1903 when Sir Thomas Hanbury bought the Wisley estate and gave it to the Society for 'the encouragement and improvement of the science and practice of horticulture in all its branches.' Wisley was then in a remote part of Surrey with no public transport to serve it. The move would not have been possible without the invention of the motor car:

6,000 Fellows (as members were then called) visited it during its first 12 months. Now more than 700,000 visitors come to the garden every year. Wisley was unashamedly a trials garden where the Society practised the perfect cultivation of every type of plant that could be grown in the British Isles from alpines to hothouse orchids, whether in the open ground or in artificial conditions. This was backed up – then, as now – by an important system of trials which grew, tested, examined and made awards to flowers, fruit and vegetables. Those trials remain one of the garden's most important activities. Wisley was, above all, conceived as a scientific garden: to this day, the main building which dominates the formal garden near the entrance is known as the laboratory and contains scientific and administrative offices.

Sir Simon Hornby, president of the RHS until 2001, describes Wisley as 'a garden to delight, instruct and inspire.' His assertion is true at every time of the year. For many visitors the pulling power of Wisley is greatest in the short, dark days of winter. That is the time when such plants as cyclamen and narcissi fill the alpine pan house: there is always colour and interest here because suitable pots are brought from the growing-frames and plunged into its sandy benches specifically to maintain the display through every week of the year. In the landscaped alpine house, too, there is much of interest even in deep mid-winter. The main glasshouses certainly come into their own in winter. The display range has three sections – cool, warm and hot. Each is landscaped and supports a large number of plants growing in the soil that are suitable for greenhouses and conservatories at home. Sometimes the seasonal display is augmented by pots brought from the growing areas behind and placed on the benches: 'Charm' and 'Cascade' chrysanthemums in November, for example. There are many other houses open to visitors: the orchid collections and the cacti house are among the most popular.

Wisley really begins to come into its own in spring. The alpine meadow is the best of its kind anywhere in Britain: from about the middle of March onwards, for at least four weeks, it is completely carpeted with hoop-petticoat narcissi (forms of *N. bulbocodium*). Clearly the conditions and the regime of cultivation suit them, because the narcissi continue to spread and increase every year. In September, the same meadows are thick with autumn-flowering crocus. Beyond them is the pulhamite rock garden, constructed in 1911–12 which is probably the finest in Britain. It does not provide the variety of habitats which more modern rock gardens offer, but it is a majestic and beautiful construction. It covers the whole hillside from the 'monocot border' (full of such plants as agapanthus, daylilies, amaryllis, nerines and kniphofias – best in late summer) at the top to the stream at the bottom of the valley, whose margins are thick with such plants as *Lobelia cardinalis* and lysichitons. Beyond is an area of light woodland where magnolias and tall rhododendrons give shelter to such woodlanders as meconopsis, hellebores and snowdrops and huge patches of candelabra primulas.

By late spring, one of the best areas is Battleston Hill, the highest point in the gardens, where winding paths take you through a beautifully laid out woodland garden underplanted with rhododendrons, azaleas, magnolias and camellias. Crocuses in late winter, lilies in high summer and colchicums in autumn extend the season so that this is always an area of colour and interest. Here, and throughout the garden, are many unusual rare and interesting plants which add so much to the horticultural quality of Wisley. Also on Battleston Hill is a 'Mediterranean' garden where an extensive collection of plants with a reputation for tenderness shows what can be grown successfully on light, well-drained soil when trees provide shelter and frost rolls away downhill.

Wisley has a fine collection of roses, from such rare and tender species as the plant of *R. gigantea* on the wall of the Laboratory to the massed ranks of modern roses which fill the beds around the Bowes-Lyon pavilion and in behind the mixed borders. Wisley is, in short, one of the best places in Britain to see roses of every sort, including some which are not seen elsewhere in English gardens open to the public. The mixed borders also come into their own from midsummer onwards: there are two of them, and they face each other on either side of the broad, grass ride which leads up to Battleston Hill. These borders are 130m long, backed by beech hedges and have a light framework of shrubs as a background for deep plantings of all the traditional perennials of the English herbaceous border.

Wisley has many other areas dedicated to the cultivation and display of particular plants. The pinetum is one example – an under-visited area of stately conifers, some of them record-breakers and all of them interesting at every season. The heather garden in Howard's Field is another dedicated garden with probably the best collection of heathers in England. The fruit fields too are a part of the garden that far too few venture into: over 1,400 cultivars of top, bush and soft fruit are grown here. The Society has been associated with the cultivation of fruit ever since its foundation in 1804, and displays of Wisley fruit have long been a feature of RHS London shows.

Wisley has its formal gardens too. These centre upon the long rectangular canal in front of the Laboratory and the walled gardens beyond. Designed by Geoffrey Jellicoe and Lanning Roper, the canal is a formal setting for waterlilies while the walled enclosures have spectacular summer and winter bedding displays. Rare and tender climbers cover their walls. Formal in a different sense are the model gardens which seem to grow and develop every year. The first were model fruit gardens, which showed people how to grow a great variety of fruit (and grow it well) in a small area. Nearby are model vegetable and herb gardens, now supplemented by many ornamental model gardens, which serve the same function – to show visitors what may be achieved in their own gardens. A new Town Garden reflects the mood of today's urban gardeners. There have been other new developments in this area recently – part of the gardens' rolling programme of development – including a country garden by Penelope Hobhouse, and the loan of some fine garden sculpture on Battleston Hill. New for the millennium was the renovation of the Walled Garden (west) to create a plantsman's corner filled with a mixture of hardy and tender plants.

For many people, one of the most fascinating areas is the main Trials area in Portsmouth Field – over the brow of Battleston Hill and down towards the furthest boundary with the old Portsmouth road. This is where the Royal Horticultural Society runs most of its trials (some temporary and some permanent) of a very wide selection of annuals, perennials, shrubs, bulbs, fruit and vegetables. Trials of woody plants take place nearby at Deers Farm. The permanent trials are conducted (among others) with border carnations, chrysanthemums, daffodils, dahlias, daylilies, delphiniums, garden pinks, irises and sweet peas. These trials continue from year to year with periodic replanting, at which time additions and removals are made. They are of exceptional interest to visitors, and often of remarkable beauty too. There can be few horticultural experiences more exciting than to walk through the massed ranks of thickly planted delphiniums or sweet peas that tower over you in July or August.

The Wisley Plant Centre is also exceptionally good, especially as a source of rare and new plants.

Features Woodland garden; snowdrops; roses (ancient & modern); rock garden; plantsman's collection of plants; plants under glass; fruit; mature conifers; good herbaceous borders; fine collection of trees; heather garden; herb garden; horticultural trials; vegetable gardens; tallest *Ostrya virginiana* (15.5m) in the British Isles, and 25 further record trees; marvellous bookshop and gift shop; restaurant & café.

Owned by The Royal Horticultural Society
Number of gardeners 79
Size 96ha (240 acres)
NCCPG National Collections *Calluna vulgaris*; *Crocus*; *Daboecia*; *Epimedium*; *Erica*; *Galanthus*; *Rheum*
English Heritage grade II*

Savill Garden

THE GREAT PARK, WINDSOR SL4 2HT

Tel 01753 847518   **Fax** 01753 847536
Website www.savillgarden.co.uk
Location In Wick Lane at Englefield Green, 3 miles west
of Egham off the A30 & 5 miles from Windsor.
Opening hours 10 am – 6 pm (4 pm from November to
February); daily except 25 & 26 December.
Admission fee Adults £5; OAPs £4.50; Children £2 in
April & May. Less in other months.

This is quite simply the finest woodland garden in England, developed since 1932 on an undulating site framed by magnificent deciduous trees. There are, in fact, several gardens here, some formal and some informal, but all are seamlessly linked together. The woodlands contain unrivalled spring plantings with masses of camellias, rhododendrons, azaleas, maples and flowering dogwoods underplanted with subtle drifts of bulbs, ferns and herbaceous plants. Recent refurbishment of the bog garden has allowed the development of stunning associations of meconopsis, primulas, astilbes, hostas and wild narcissi. The primulas have just been replanted, and come in monospecific masses, from the earliest *P. rosea* and *P. denticulata* through to *P. florindae* in July and August. In high summer, the rose garden and tremendous set-piece double herbaceous borders are worth a long trip to see. The nearby gravel garden is one of England's oldest and largest: parts of it have recently been replanted with a fine display of drought-tolerant plants – many of them rare – and plants which benefit from the mulching effect of the gravel. Extensive and intelligent use is made of a wide range of summer perennials in the borders and in containers. A new summer garden is under development for 2002:

formal structure, informal planting, pastel shades. By late summer the woods are filled with hydrangeas, whose cool blues and whites are stunningly effective. Then the deciduous broad-leaved trees begin their autumn spectacle. From November to March the newly created winter beds display flowers, stems and berries in effective colour groupings. But there are many reasons to visit the Savill Garden at other times of the year – the drifts of *Narcissus bulbocodium* (second only in their splendour to the alpine meadow at Wisley) in March, for example, and the floods of lysichitons in April. The collections of maples, camellias, rhododendrons and azaleas are also exemplary. The raised beds, the cool greenhouse and the monocot border are each full of interest in due season. The guide book, the plant centre and the website are all alike – excellent.

Features Roses (mainly modern); camellias; fine collection of trees; mahonias; magnificent late summer borders; tallest silver birch *Betula pendula* (30m) in the British Isles (& 13 other record trees); gift and plant shop; licensed restaurant.

Owned by Crown Estate
Number of gardeners 12
Size 14ha (35 acres)
NCCPG National Collections *Ilex*; *Magnolia*; *Mahonia*; *Pernettya*; *Pieris*; *Rhododendron* (species & Glen Dale azaleas); ferns; dwarf conifers
English Heritage grade I

Toobees Exotics

BLACKHORSE ROAD, WOKING
GU22 0QT

Tel 01483 797534 **Fax** 01483 751995
Website www.toobees-exotics.com
Location Off A324 between Woking & Brookwood.
Opening hours 10 am – 5 pm; Thursday – Sunday & Bank
Holiday Mondays; 18 April to 29 September. And by
appointment.

Ⓟ ♿ 🌱

Toobees are well known to visitors to RHS
London shows: they have a constant flow of
new and rare succulents from Africa and
Madagascar. These include species of
euphorbia, pachypodium, carnivorous
plants, air-plants, palms and cycads. Visitors
are always welcome to inspect the
propagation areas and the amazing display
of large stock plants. The address for
correspondence is 20 Inglewood, Woking,
Surrey GU21 3HX.

Vale End

ALBURY, GUILDFORD GU5 9BE

Tel & Fax 01483 202296
Website www.ngs.org.uk
Location 500 yards west of Albury on A248.
Opening hours 10 am – 5 pm; 16 June & 28 & 29 July.
Plus 6 pm – 9 pm on 20 June. Groups by arrangement.
Admission fee Adults £2.50; Children free. £3.50 on
20 June.

Ⓟ 🐕 ⓌⒸ 🌱 🍽

Vale End is a modern plantsman's garden,
one of the best on Bagshot sand, where a
love of plants has not been allowed to
obscure either the design or the landscape
beyond. It is walled around, and made on
many levels, on a site that faces south-west:
the owners have taken the opportunity to

grow sun-loving and Mediterranean plants.
Daphne Foulsham is chairman of the
National Gardens Scheme and can take
much of the credit for the scheme's
exponential success in recent years.

 Features Plantsman's collection of
plants; good herbaceous borders; roses
(mainly old-fashioned); vegetables; fruit;
herbs; new water feature on steep bank
(2001); refreshments.

Owned by Mr & Mrs John Foulsham
Size 0.4ha (1 acre)

Vann

HAMBLEDON, GODALMING GU8 4EF

Tel & Fax 01428 683413
Location 2 miles from Chiddingfold. Signs from A283 at
Hambledon on NGS days.
Opening hours 10 am – 5 pm; daily; 2 to 7 April;
7 to 12 May; 17 to 23 June. Also 2 pm – 7 pm on 6 May
for the National Gardens Scheme. And by appointment.
Admission fee Adults £3; Children 50p. Pre-booked
groups welcome.

Ⓟ ⓌⒸ ♿ 🏛 ☕

This high-profile Jekyll garden has been well
restored and meticulously maintained by the
present Caroes, the third generation to live
here. Start with the old cottage garden at the
back of the house and move along the Arts
& Crafts pergola straight to the lake. This is
the heart of the garden, from which several
distinct gardens lead from one to the next
and melt into the Surrey woods: among
them, a yew walk (1909), island beds, mixed
borders, the Jekyll water garden (1991), a
woodland cherry walk, and a woodland
garden under vast oaks leading to a hazel
coppice. The plantings are dense and
thoughtful.

 Features Woodland garden; good
herbaceous borders; bluebells;

Valley Gardens

THE GREAT PARK, WINDSOR SL4 2HT

Tel 01753 847518   **Fax** 01753 847536
Location At Englefield Green, 5 miles from Windsor,
off A30: follow signs for Savill Garden.
Opening hours 8 am – 7 pm (3.30 pm in winter);
daily; all year.
Admission fee Cars £3.50 (£5 in April & May);
occupants free.

This is a woodland garden on a royal scale. The Valley Garden has over 200 acres of plantings across a site of great natural beauty which falls in vast sweeps to the open expanse of Virginia Water. As in the Savill Garden, huge trees of oak, beech, sweet chestnut and Scots pine provide a magnificent framework and have been used with great sensitivity. The whole composition conveys the feeling of a flowering forest from some far-off corner of Asia. From March and April until the end of June, a succession of camellias, rhododendrons and azaleas provide an unbelievable kaleidoscope of colour, most notably in the Punch Bowl where a natural combe is filled with terrace upon terrace of brightly coloured Japanese Kurume azaleas. Giant magnolias garland themselves overhead with thousands of chalice-shaped blooms. A huge array of supporting trees, shrubs and perennials jostles for attention. Enormous groups of hydrangeas provide late summer colour, from the white foaming flowers of *H. paniculata* to the blues and pale pinks of the lacecaps and mopheads. In autumn the hillsides light up in a spectacle unrivalled this side of the Appalachian Mountains. In the nearby heather garden an old gravel pit has been transformed into a horticultural wonder to rival the Punch Bowl: ostensibly dominated by heathers and dwarf conifers (there is a National Collection here), the garden contains unrivalled collections of exotic and native birches, whitebeams and rowans, wild roses, cotoneasters and cistus. Recent plantings have made extensive use of ornamental grasses to provide relief amongst the stolid conifers. On the next hillside is to be found the National Collection of *Rhododendron* species, brought here in the 1950s from the famous garden of Tower Court near Ascot. A sweeping valley also contains a pinetum of some note, carpeted by countless thousands of dwarf narcissi in March and April. All in all, a garden of the blue-stocking variety.

Features Outstanding collection of trees; hydrangeas; heathers; primulas; magnolias; rhododendrons & azaleas; refreshments at the Savill Garden.

Owned by Crown Estate
Number of gardeners 16
Size 87ha (220 acres)
NCCPG National Collections *Ilex*; *Magnolia*; *Mahonia*; *Pernettya*; *Pieris*; *Rhododendron* (species & Glen458 Dale azaleas); dwarf conifers

fritillaries; wood anemones; plants for sale at weekends; teas on 6 May; other refreshments for groups by arrangement.

Owned by Mrs Martin Caroe
Number of gardeners ½
Size 2ha (5 acres)
English Heritage grade II

The Vernon Geranium Nursery

CUDDINGTON WAY, CHEAM, SUTTON SM2 7JB

Tel 020 8393 7616 **Fax** 020 8786 7437
Website www.geraniumsuk.com
Location South-west of Cheam.
Opening hours 9.30 am – 5.30 pm; Monday – Saturday. 10 am – 4 pm; Sundays. March to July.

As it names indicates, this is a specialist pelargonium nursery. The number of pelargonium cultivars here speaks for itself – over 1,100 doubles and semi-doubles, Deacons, stellars, rosebuds, finger-flowered, fancy-leaved, speckled, uniques, dwarfs, miniatures, angels and regals – the list seems endless. Guided tours are given daily at 11 am and 2.30 pm between 14 and 29 July.

 Features Pelargoniums.

Winkworth Arboretum

HASCOMBE ROAD, GODALMING GU8 4AD

Tel 01483 208477 **Fax** 01483 208252
Website www.nationaltrust.org.uk
Location 2 miles south-east of Godalming, off B2130.
Opening hours All year; dawn – dusk. Groups *must* pre-book in writing.
Admission fee Adults £3.50.

Winkworth is a true arboretum in the sense that it has a large collection of full-sized trees – as many taxa as possible – planted liberally over a large area. Many of the plantings are now in their prime. The acres of red oak (*Quercus coccinea*), *Nyssa sylvestris* and *Liquidambar styraciflua* are quite spectacular in autumn.

Features Woodland garden; fine collection of trees; bluebells; wood anemones; autumn colour; tallest *Acer davidii* (19m) in the British Isles, and 5 further record trees; shop; tea-room.

Owned by The National Trust
Number of gardeners 3
Size 40ha (100 acres)
NCCPG National Collections *Sorbus* (Aria & Micromeles groups)

SUSSEX, EAST

The two historic gardens in East Sussex which English Heritage has rated Grade I could not be more different – Great Dixter and Sheffield Park. Yet they have one thing in common which is typical of East Sussex gardens generally – they are gardens whose historic features have been overlaid with plants. Few of the other historic gardens in the county are open to the public, but garden-visitors are almost spoiled for choice. Every corner of East Sussex seems to brim with good modern gardens – those like Pashley Manor and Merriments have been widely recognised for their beauty and invention – and good collections of trees, including those at Sheffield Park and Stanmer Park, near Brighton. The National Gardens Scheme does well in East Sussex, especially in the area around Crowborough where there are many medium-sized gardens to see. Nurseries, too, are good and fairly plentiful: some of the best are attached to gardens, like Great Dixter, or have a fine display garden attached to them, like Merriments. There are comparatively few National Collections: one of the most interesting is the collection of lilacs (*Syringa* cvs.) kept by the City of Brighton & Hove Parks Department. Members of the Royal Horticultural Society have free access to Sheffield Park throughout the year.

Bateman's

BURWASH, ETCHINGHAM TN19 7DS

Tel 01435 882302   **Fax** 01435 882811
Website www.nationaltrust.org.uk
Location Signed at west end of village.
Opening hours 11 am – 5.30 pm; Saturday – Wednesday; 3 March to 4 November.
Admission fee Adults £5; Children £2.50.

These 10 acres on the banks of the River Dudwell were Rudyard Kipling's home from 1902 until his death in 1936. The garden is fun for children, because there is a working flour mill, but not spectacular for the knowledgeable gardener, except for the

Campis grandiflora on the house and the herbaceous borders designed by Graham Thomas.

Features Roses (mainly old-fashioned); herbs; good herbaceous borders; Kipling pear arch; National Trust shop; tea-room.

Owned by The National Trust
Number of gardeners 2
Size 4ha (10 acres)
English Heritage grade II

Bates Green Farm

ARLINGTON, POLEGATE BN26 6SH

Tel & Fax 01323 482039
Location 3 miles south-west of Hailsham.
Opening hours 10.30 am – 6 pm; 8 April, 13 May & 10 June for National Gardens Scheme. And by appointment.
Admission fee Adults £2; Children free.

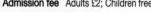

Made by the present owners since the mid-1970s, the garden at Bates Green Farm has several different areas: a large rock garden, a shady garden, and wonderful mixed borders planted for year-round colour associations. The owners say they seek perfection, but wonder if they will ever achieve it.

Features Woodland garden; good herbaceous borders; colour borders; bluebells; rockery; pond; refreshments by arrangement.

Owned by Mr & Mrs J.R. McCutchan
Size 0.8ha (2 acres)

Brickwall House & Gardens

FREWEN COLLEGE, NORTHIAM TN31 6NL

Tel 01797 252001
Location Off B2088.
Opening hours 2 pm – 4.30 pm; Bank Holidays. Plus Wednesdays in school holidays. And by appointment for groups (01797 253388).
Admission fee £3.50.

This important historic garden, with 17th-century features which were re-worked in the 19th century, has recently been re-designed as a Stuart garden, to match the house. Brickwall now has borders planted exclusively with old-fashioned plants and a chess garden where green and yellow yew shapes are grown in squares of black or white chips. The bluebells in the arboretum are magnificent.

Features Topiary; herbs; good herbaceous borders; fine collection of trees; bluebells; extensively re-designed since 1980; postcards and guide books but no shop; refreshments by arrangement.

Owned by Frewen Educational Trust
English Heritage grade II*

Cabbages & Kings Garden

WILDERNESS FARM, WILDERNESS LANE, HADLOW DOWN TN22 4HU

Tel 01825 830552   **Fax** 01825 830736
Location ½ mile south of A272.
Opening hours 2 pm – 6 pm; Friday – Monday (including Bank Holiday Mondays); Easter – September.
Admission fee Adults £4; Concessions £3.50: Children £2. RHS members free in April & September.

Subtitled 'The Centre for Garden Design', this is the show garden of a leading contemporary garden designer. It is conceived as a series of interlinking garden-rooms, terraces and incidents, lushly and vividly planted. The idea is to give visitors lots of ideas for their own gardens – how to transform them, how to create garden rooms, and how to design sitting areas, features and focal points.

Features Good modern design & planting; tea, coffee, homemade cakes.

Owned by Andrew & Ryl Nowell

Clinton Lodge

FLETCHING, UCKFIELD TN22 3ST

Tel 01825 722952   **Fax** 01825 723967
Location In main village street.
Opening hours 2 pm – 5.30 pm; 16, 17 & 26 June,
5 July & 2 August for NGS. And by appointment.
Admission fee NGS days: Adults £3.50; Children £2. £4
for groups (minimum 25 people).

Ⓟ ⓦⓒ ⓖ ⓨ

Clinton Lodge is a rising star among new
gardens, designed round a handsome 17th-
century house. There are formal gardens of
different periods, starting with a 'mediaeval'
potager and an Elizabethan-style herb
garden. The most successful parts are the
pre-Raphaelite walk of lilies and pale roses,
and the Victorian-style herbaceous borders
in soft pastel shades. A canal garden and an
allée of fastigiate hornbeams were added in
2001 and the garden has recovered well from
recent flood damage.

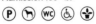 **Features** Roses (mainly old-
fashioned); herbs; good herbaceous
borders; yew hedges; lime walks; *potager*;
knot gardens.

Owned by Mr & Mrs H.R. Collum
Number of gardeners 1½
Size 2.2ha (6 acres)

Latchetts

FRESHFIELD LANE, DANEHILL,
HAYWARDS HEATH RH17 7HQ

Tel 01825 790237   **Fax** 01825 790085
Location 1 mile south-west of Danehill along Freshfield
Lane.
Opening hours 2 pm – 5.30 pm; 16 & 17 August.
Admission fee £3

Ⓟ ⓗ ⓦⓒ ⓖ ⓨ

Latchetts is a garden of plenty, put together
with enthusiasm since 1991 and full of good
things to enjoy: trees, shrubs, roses and
herbaceous plants. These are supplemented
by bedding plants, a fact which explains why
it opens in mid-August and indicates that it
is maintained to a very high standard. In the
new walled garden (a millennium project)
are beautifully trained fruit trees, but this is
a garden which is still developing as new
features are added every year.

Owned by Mr & Mrs Laurence Hardy
Number of gardeners 2
Size 1.6ha (4 acres)

Merriments Gardens

HAWKHURST ROAD, HURST GREEN
TN19 7RA

Tel 01580 860666   **Fax** 01580 860324
Website www.merriments.co.uk
Location On A229.
Opening hours 10 am – 5 pm; daily; 1 April to
mid-October. Opens at 10.30 am on Sundays.
Admission fee Adults £3.50; Children £2.

Ⓟ ⓦⓒ ⓖ

The gardens at this nursery are young –
started in 1991 on a bare clay field – but the
tail is already wagging the dog. Four
remarkable acres of imaginative design and
striking planting are kept meticulously tidy.
The planting has been chosen so that each
area blends seamlessly into the next and
creates a satisfying and harmonious whole.
The deep sweeping borders are designed and
planted to combine colour, form and
texture in endlessly imaginative planting
schemes. The features include foliage
borders, two ponds, a border for spring,
several borders designed to peak in summer
and autumn, a blue garden – and dozens
more. Recent developments include a dry
area which has been transformed into a

Great Dixter

DIXTER ROAD, NORTHIAM TN31 6PH

Tel 01797 252878 **Fax** 01797 252879
Website www.greatdixter.co.uk
Location Off A28 at Northiam Post Office.
Opening hours 2 pm – 5 pm; Tuesday – Sunday; 1 April
to 28 October, plus Bank Holiday Mondays. Open at 11 am
on the Sundays & Mondays of Bank Holiday weekends.
Admission fee Adults £4.50; Children £1. (2001 prices).

Christopher Lloyd's father Nathaniel bought Great Dixter in 1910: Lutyens did a conversion job on the house and laid out part of the gardens. Most of the brickwork, yew hedges, steps, walls, doorways and arts-and-crafts details date back to the original design – contemporary with Hidcote and earlier than Sissinghurst. The topiary was Nathaniel Lloyd's contribution – he wrote a book about it. But the main reason for the garden's pre-eminent reputation is the decades of horticultural skill which 'Christo' Lloyd himself has put into its planting. He is a knowledgeable plantsman who once taught horticulture at Wye College and has a remarkable eye for combining plants in harmonious groupings throughout the year. His books – especially the compilation of articles from *Country Life* published as *The Well-Tempered Garden* – have been popular and influential, so that the Lloyd style of planting and maintaining a garden is probably more widely copied now than any other. The heart of the garden is the Long Border, about 65m long and 4½m deep, which has become a showcase and trial ground for his experiments. It is a series of compositions loosely strung together with a wide variety of weaving colours, heights and textures but unified as much by good foliage as by flowers. Every section of it teaches you

something new that could be made to work in your own garden. One of Lloyd's strengths is his fondness for change – his desire to refine and improve his garden all the time. He was one of the first garden-owners to use lots of annuals and tender perennials to extend the summer season right through into autumn. He shocked the country's rosarians by replacing his parents' collection of old-fashioned roses with a late-summer explosion of dahlias, cannas and exotic foliage. And nobody has practised the gentle, patient art of long-term meadow-gardening so successfully as Christopher Lloyd: indeed, he has written so eloquently and prolifically about the principles and practices of meadow gardening that, even if he had never penned a word on any other aspect of ornamental horticulture, he would be established as a great apostle of this charming and relaxed art form which he sometimes refers to as 'tapestry gardening'. Visiting Great Dixter should be a compulsory part of every gardener's ongoing education.

Features Topiary; sub-tropical plants; plantsman's collection of plants; good herbaceous borders; meadow garden; colour schemes; gift shop.

Owned by Christopher Lloyd & Olivia Eller
Number of gardeners 5
Size 2ha (5 acres)
English Heritage grade I

Mediterranean-inspired scree garden and a waterlogged area which has been turned into a bog garden and planted with moisture-loving plants. The nursery is good, too.

 Features Plantsman's collection of plants; good herbaceous borders; brilliant modern design; tropical border (2001); golden border (2002); first-rate nursery attached; garden café.

Owned by The Weeks & Buchele families
Size 1.6ha (4 acres)

Michelham Priory

UPPER DICKER, HAILSHAM
BN27 3QS

Tel 01323 844224 **Fax** 01323 844030
Website www.sussexpast.co.uk
Location Signed from A22 & A27.
Opening hours 10.30 am – 4 pm; Wednesday – Sunday; March & October. 10.30 am – 5 pm; Wednesday – Sunday; April – July & September; 10.30 am – 5.30 pm; daily; August.
Admission fee Adults £4.80; OAPs £4.20; Children £2.50.

The old Augustinian priory has an Elizabethan barn, a blacksmith shop, a rope museum, a working watermill and England's largest mediaeval water-filled moat. Within the garden are several distinct areas, including a physic garden and cloister garden, with mediaeval plantings (faithful, if a little dull), some very good borders, a bog garden, a kitchen garden and several wildflower areas. It all makes for an enjoyable visit, highly educational for children and interesting for parents too.

 Features Roses (ancient & modern); herbs; mature conifers; good herbaceous borders; sculpture trail; dovecote gift shop; licensed restaurant & tea-room.

Owned by The Sussex Archaeological Society & Sussex Past
Number of gardeners 3
Size 2.8ha (7 acres)

Moorlands

FRIARS GATE, CROWBOROUGH
TN6 1XF

Tel 01892 652474
Location 2 miles north of Crowborough, off B2188.
Opening hours 11 am – 5 pm; Wednesdays; 1 April to 1 October. Plus 19 May & 14 July, & by appointment.
Admission fee Adults £3; Children free.

The garden at Moorlands was begun by Dr Smith's parents in 1929: Dr Smith took over in 1974, made a lake and ponds, and planted a lot of woodland and bog-loving plants. The garden now combines mature trees with modern herbaceous plantings. By the house, on a sloping site, is a long herbaceous border. This leads to the main stream, red with iron ore but clean enough for trout and protected enough for kingfishers. It is spring-fed, full of waterfalls, and planted with grasses and bamboos. Moorlands is a plantsman's garden of fine trees, rhododendrons and collectors' shrubs, underplanted with bog plants as well as wildflowers such as native daffodils (*Narcissus pseudonarcissus*) and orchids.

 Features Good plants for plantsmen; bog plants; rhododendrons; teas.

Owned by Dr & Mrs Steven Smith
Number of gardeners 3 part-time
Size 1.6ha (4 acres)

Paradise Park

AVIS ROAD, NEWHAVEN BN9 0DH

Tel 01273 512123   **Fax** 01273 616005
Website www.paradisepark.co.uk
Location Signed from A26 & A259.
Opening hours 10 am – 6 pm (but 5.30 pm in winter); daily; all year except 1 January & 25 December.
Admission fee Adults £4.99; OAPs & Children £3.99.

Part of a leisure complex attached to a garden centre, the most interesting features are a tropical house and a cactus house, each landscaped with handsome plant collections chosen for display. There are some imaginative garden designs – Caribbean, seaside, desert, oriental and rainforest gardens, for example. It is a haven in winter, and the outside gardens are a pleasure to explore in summer, full of contrasting designs and splendid water features. They contain a Sussex history trail – beautiful models of important historic buildings in the county, each in a different setting. Other attractions include a hemerocallis collection, a fuchsia border and an alpine rock garden.

 Features Plants under glass; hydroponic demonstration area; *Streptocarpus* collection; plant centre; large coffee-shop.

Owned by Jonathan Tate
Number of gardeners 5
Size 1ha (2½ acres) of garden and 0.1ha (¼ acre) under glass

Pashley Manor Gardens

TICEHURST, WADHURST TN5 7NE

Tel 01580 200888   **Fax** 01580 200102
Website www.pashleymanorgardens.com
Location On B2099 between A21 & Ticehurst village.

Opening hours 11 am – 5 pm; Tuesday – Thursday, Saturday & Bank Holiday Mondays; 9 April to 28 September.
Admission fee Adults £6; OAPs & Children £5.

Pashley Manor is a new/old garden, made or re-made in the Victorian style over the last ten years or so with advice from the brilliant Anthony du Gard Pasley. The original structure came from fine old trees, fountains, springs and large ponds or small lakes. The modern plantings have added gentle shapes, spacious expanses, harmonious colours and solid plantings. There is a sumptuous series of new enclosed gardens where colour-gardening is practised to brilliant effect. And it gets better every year.

 Features Roses (mainly old-fashioned & climbers); mature conifers; Victorian shrubberies; hydrangeas; irises; HHA/Christie's Garden of the Year in 2000; fresh produce for sale; lunches & teas.

Owned by James & Angela Sellick
Number of gardeners 5
Size 5ha (12 acres)

Rotherview Nursery with Coghurst Camellias

IVY HOUSE LANE, THREE OAKS, HASTINGS TN35 4NP

Tel 01424 756228   **Fax** 01424 428944
Location Follow brown tourist signs to Coghurst Hall Holiday Village (next door).
Opening hours 9 am – 5 pm; daily; March to October. 10 am – 4 pm; daily; November to February.

Rotherview Nursery with Coghurst Camellias is an inter-nursery hybrid – two specialist nurseries recently combined on one site. Rotherview produces a wide range of alpines and perennials (especially hardy ferns) whilst Coghurst has a list of over 200 camellias, including the autumn-flowering *C. sasanqua* cultivars. Both nurseries have been regular exhibitors at RHS Flower Shows. The list of camellias is being expanded and the garden is already much improved, with raised beds for Rotherview's alpines and an area of trough gardens, as well as a camellia walk.

Sheffield Park Garden

UCKFIELD TN22 3QX

Tel 01825 790231   **Fax** 01825 791264
Website www.nationaltrust.org.uk
Location Between East Grinstead & Lewes on A275.
Opening hours 10.30 am – 4 pm (or dusk, if earlier); Saturdays & Sundays; January & February. 10.30 am – 6 pm; Tuesday – Sunday plus Bank Holidays; March to October. 10.30 am – 4 pm; Tuesday – Sunday; November & December.
Admission fee Adults £4.80; Children £2.40. RHS members free.

Sheffield Park is a beautiful 120-acre garden around four lakes. These were laid out in the 18th century by Capability Brown and Humphry Repton. The result is landscaping on the grandest of scales, though the lakes now reflect the 20th-century plantings of exotics. Carpeted with daffodils and bluebells in spring, its rhododendrons, azaleas and stream garden are spectacular in early summer. In autumn, the garden is ablaze with wonderful leaf colours, and long beds of gentians. But the collection of rare trees and shrubs makes it a fascinating visit at any time of year.

 Features Mature conifers; fine collection of trees; bluebells; daffodils;

kalmias; autumn crocuses; rhododendrons; tallest *Nyssa sylvatica* (21m) in the British Isles, plus two other record trees.

Owned by The National Trust
Number of gardeners 5
Size 50ha (120 acres)
NCCPG National Collections *Rhododendron* (Ghent azaleas)
English Heritage grade I

Standen

EAST GRINSTEAD RH19 4NE

Tel 01342 323029   **Fax** 01342 316424
Website www.nationaltrust.org.uk
Location 2 miles south of East Grinstead, signed from B2110.
Opening hours 11 am – 6 pm; Wednesday – Sunday & Bank Holiday Mondays; 23 March to 3 November. 11 am – 3 pm; Friday – Sunday; 8 November to 15 December.
Admission fee Adults £3; Children £1.50.

This Edwardian garden has magnificent views across the valley. A series of enclosed gardens around and below the house gives way to woodland slopes and an old quarry furnished with ferns. Parts are rather overgrown (and are being restored) but there is much to trigger the imagination here – not least, how the National Trust achieves so much with only one gardener.

Features Roses (mainly Rugosas & old-fashioned); rock garden; mature conifers; good herbaceous borders; rhododendrons; azaleas; woodland shrubs.

Owned by The National Trust
Number of gardeners 1
Size 5ha (12 acres)

SUSSEX, WEST

West Sussex is even better endowed with fine gardens and interesting nurseries than East Sussex. All five Grade I gardens are open to the public – Goodwood, Leonardslee, Parham, Petworth House and Stansted Park – though only Leonardslee and Parham are of great horticultural interest. However there is also a glut of Grade II* gardens open to the public, and all of them chiefly of importance for their plant collections – Borde Hill, Cowdray, Gravetye, Highdown, Nymans, High Beeches, Wakehurst and West Dean. These are matched by a great number of good medium-sized gardens which open for the National Gardens Scheme and a large number of good nurseries and garden centres. Architectural Plants, Coghurst Camellias (now part of Rotherview Nursery), Croftway and Ingwersens are all nurseries of national or international status and often seen at RHS Flower Shows. Apuldram Roses, however, decided last autumn (2001) to close its retail site and operate only as a mail order business. The NCCPG has a good number of National Collections in the county. Borde Hill and Nymans offer free access to RHS members, though Borde Hill extends this privilege only in September and October. The old county horticultural society at Brinsbury is a RHS Partner College with a series of public lectures, demonstrations and workshops throughout the year: details from 020 7821 3408.

Architectural Plants

Cooks Farm, Nuthurst, Horsham
RH13 6LH

Tel 01403 891772   Fax 01403 891056
Website www.architecturalplants.com
Location 3 miles south of Horsham, behind the Black Horse pub in Nuthurst.
Opening hours 9 am – 5 pm; Monday – Saturday.
Admission fee Free

Somewhat out of the ordinary, Architectural Plants specialises in exotic-looking, evergreen foliage plants, often with architectural or sculptural shapes. 'Architectural' means that the plants themselves have their own architecture – strong, sometimes spectacular, shapes which bring a distinctive year-round presence to a garden. Examples include eucalyptus, bamboos, hardy palms, hardy bananas and evergreen magnolias. Larger specimens are available for immediate impact. The display area around the nursery is stylishly laid out and a pleasure to visit in its own right. The nursery also has a branch at Lidsey Road, Woodgate, near Chichester (open 10 am – 4 pm, Sunday to Friday): it has phillyreas, arbutus and many rare trees, plus seaside exotics, but no display garden.

Features Architectural plants; large specimens.

Owned by Angus White
Size 1.2ha (3 acres)

Borde Hill Garden

HAYWARDS HEATH RH16 1XP

Tel 01444 450326   **Fax** 01444 440427
Website www.bordehill.co.uk
Location 1½ miles north of Haywards Heath.
Opening hours 10 am – 6 pm (or dusk); daily; all year.
Admission fee Adults £5.50; OAPs £5; Children £3.
RHS members free except 16 March to 30 September.

This important woodland garden has been significantly developed and improved in recent years. It was originally planted in the early 1900s with exotic trees and a large collection of rhododendron species grown from such introducers as Forrest and Kingdon Ward. Some of those trees are now record-breakers, including a rare Chinese tulip tree (*Liriodendron chinense*) now 19m tall, a Greek beech (*Fagus orientalis*) of the same height, and a splendid *Pinus muricata* now 31m high. The garden has recently been substantially re-developed for the recreation market and is all the better for the new capital. The gardens surrounding the house are divided into 'rooms'. These include the Garden of Allah with a new (1999) wildlife pool; a ring of Knap Hill azaleas backed by rhododendrons from Farrer and Cox's expedition to Burma and China in 1919; the newly-restored Victorian greenhouses, one of which is a peach house and another devoted to South African plants; a new Mediterranean garden designed by Robin Williams; a new rose garden planted mainly with David Austin roses; the Italian garden and two dells with *Trachycarpus* palms. The garden also has all sorts of family-friendly facilities like an adventure playground and a smart restaurant.

 Features Woodland garden; plantsman's collection of plants; fine collection of trees; rhododendrons; azaleas; magnolias; plants from original seed; 48 different record trees, one of the largest collections in the British Isles; small gift shop; plant centre; tea-room, restaurant & pub.

Owned by Borde Hill Garden Ltd
Number of gardeners 5
Size 4.2ha (11 acres) of formal gardens, plus 16ha (40 acres) of woodland and 150 acres of parkland
English Heritage grade II*

Champs Hill

COLDWALTHAM, PULBOROUGH RH20 1LY

Tel 01789 831868   **Fax** 01789 831536
Location West of Coldwaltham, on road to Fittleworth.
Opening hours 2 pm – 6 pm on 10, 17 & 24 March; 5, 12 & 19 May; and 4, 11 & 18 August.
Admission fee Adults £2.50; Children free.

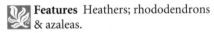

This garden has been developed around three disused sand-quarries since 1960. The woodlands are full of beautiful azaleas and rhododendrons, but the most striking feature is the collection of heathers – over 300 cultivars – interplanted with dwarf conifers. The garden also has some interesting sculptures, and stupendous views.

 Features Heathers; rhododendrons & azaleas.

Owned by Mr & Mrs David Bowerman
Size 10.7ha (27 acres), including woodland

Cowdray Park

MIDHURST GU29 0AQ

Tel 01730 812461   **Fax** 01730 812122
Location South of A272, 1 mile east of Midhurst.
Opening hours For NGS, and by appointment.
Admission fee Adults £2.50; Children free.

Cowdray is seldom open, but worth a long journey to see the ornate house and its contemporary (100-year-old) collection of trees, particularly conifers – don't miss the avenue of wellingtonias up at the top. Some are now record-breakers, and the sweeps of rhododendrons and azaleas, especially the hardy hybrids down 'the dell', are on the grand scale too. There are also two lakes, waterfalls, wildflower areas and a lot of new planting.

Features 300-year-old Lebanon cedar; wellingtonia avenue; rhododendrons; grapes & fruit in the glasshouses; valley garden; tallest *Abies concolor* f. *violacea* (28m) and *Chamaecyparis pisifera* (29m) in the UK; refreshments.

Owned by Viscount & Viscountess Cowdray
English Heritage grade II*

Croftway Nursery

YAPTON ROAD, BARNHAM, BOGNOR REGIS PO22 0BQ

Tel 01243 552121   **Fax** 01243 552125
Website www.croftway.co.uk
Location Between Yapton & Barnham, on B2233.
Or 10 minutes walk from Barnham station.
Opening hours 9 am – 5 pm; daily. Closed December to February.

There has been a nursery on the site of Croftway for many years: *Monarda* 'Croftway Pink' was raised here in the 1930s. The present owners have been in business – it is a *family* business – since 1988. Their most important specialities are irises and hardy geraniums – they think very highly of the geraniums which Alan Bremner breeds in Orkney – but they are also good for other herbaceous perennials. They have a wide choice of achilleas, astrantias, crocosmias, daylilies, hostas, nepetas, penstemons, phlox, salvias, and other labiates. The show garden is excellent – there are many new plants on trial there.

Features Hardy geraniums; a wide selection of herbaceous plants; bearded irises.

Owned by Malcolm Spencer

Denmans

FONTWELL, ARUNDEL BN18 0SU

Tel 01243 542808   **Fax** 01243 544064
Website www.denmans-garden.co.uk
Location Off A29 or A27, near Fontwell racecourse.
Opening hours 9 am – 5 pm; daily; March to October.
Or by appointment.
Admission fee Adults £2.95; OAPs £2.65; Children (over 5) £1.75.

This modern garden is a showpiece for John Brookes's ideas and commitment to easy care. He uses foliage, gravel mulches, contrasts of form, coloured stems, winter bark and plants as elements of design. The garden's design is so fluid that you feel carried along by its momentum and, of course, it is a brilliant source of ideas for your own garden.

Features Excellent modern design; gravel and grass; roses (mainly old-fashioned); herbs; good herbaceous borders; spring bulbs; shop; garden centre; lunches & teas.

Size 1.6ha (4 acres)

Floraldene

FINDON ROAD, WORTHING
BN14 0BW

Tel 01903 261231
Location West side on Findon Road, next to Durrington Cemetery, opposite Mayfield Close.
Opening hours For local charities in March, August & September.

This garden, started in the early 1950s, is particularly good for heathers – hundreds of different cultivars grown in a small garden by a true devotee. Amazingly, the garden is on chalk, and also supports some camellias and azaleas.

 Features Heathers; free teas.

Owned by John Tucker
Number of gardeners owner only
Size 0.2ha (½ acre)

Gravetye Manor Hotel

EAST GRINSTEAD RH19 4LJ

Tel 01342 810567   **Fax** 01342 810080
Location 4 miles south-west of East Grinstead.
Opening hours Hotel & restaurant guests only; all year. The perimeter path is open to the public free of charge from 10 am to 5 pm on Tuesdays & Fridays.

Gravetye is William Robinson's own garden, very influential about 100 years ago, and scrupulously maintained by Peter Herbert as it was in its prime. It was here that Robinson put into practice the natural style of gardening which he promoted so vigorously in his magazines and books. Robinson's own original woodland garden has many of the trees he planted – fine davidias and nyssas, for example. And the meadows below the house are planted with naturalised bulbs in the style that Robinson made popular through his writings. Gravetye is still a garden to learn from: there is much to admire and copy.

 Features William Robinson's woodland garden; topiary; roses (mainly old-fashioned); plantsman's collection of plants; good herbaceous borders; fine collection of trees; alpine meadow; gazebo.

Owned by Peter Herbert
Number of gardeners 4
Size 12ha (30 acres)
English Heritage grade II*

High Beeches

HANDCROSS RH17 6HQ

Tel 01444 400589   **Fax** 01444 401543
Website www.highbeeches.com
Location South of B2110, 1 mile east of M23 at Handcross.
Opening hours 1 pm – 5 pm; daily, except Wednesdays; 28 March to 30 June, September & October. Plus Sunday to Tuesday in July & August.
Admission fee Adults £4.50. Reductions for groups of 30+. Coaches by appointment.

One of the best (and most magical) of the famous Sussex woodland gardens, High Beeches was originally laid out by Colonel Giles Loder, a cousin of the Loders of Wakehurst. In 1966 it was acquired by Anne and Edward Boscawen, who have devoted many years to its maintenance and improvement. Now it is now managed by a non-profit-making charitable trust. The original woodland has been thinned and underplanted with exotics, many of them rare. Some are trees like nyssas, magnolias, *Tetracentron sinense* and davidias; others are shrubs – there is a Loderi Walk planted with *Rhododendron × loderi* cultivars. A valley of ponds and woodland glades is beautifully planted with splendid rhododendrons, azaleas and camellias for spring, and swathes of native bluebells. The garden has wonderful autumn colours too, and a policy of letting good plants naturalise – cowslips, wild orchids, willow gentians and *Primula helodoxa*. The clock in the Clock Tower (now the restaurant) was installed to commemorate Colonel Loder's Derby winner, Spion Cop.

Features Woodland garden; plantsman's collection of plants; mature conifers; fine collection of trees; rhododendrons; 5-acre natural wildflower meadow; tallest *Stewartia monodelpha* (11m) in the British Isles; restaurant open from noon.

Owned by High Beeches Gardens Conservation Trust
Number of gardeners 2
Size 10ha (25 acres)
NCCPG National Collections *Stewartia*
English Heritage grade II*

Highdown

LITTLEHAMPTON ROAD,
GORING-BY-SEA BN12 6NY

Tel 01903 239999 ext 2539   **Fax** 01903 821384
Location Signed from A259.
Opening hours 10 am – 6 pm (4.30 pm in February, March, October & November, & 4 pm in January & December); daily (but not weekends from October to March); all year.

Admission fee free – donations welcome.

This is the most famous garden to be made on chalk, and one of the best. It was actually laid out in a disused chalk quarry and on the surrounding, south-facing downland. Its maker, Sir Frederick Stern, was determined to try anything that might grow in these unusual conditions. Eighty years on, the results are some handsome trees, vigorous roses, and long-forgotten peony hybrids. The gardens are designed on a large grid and planted mainly as mixed borders. Mediterranean plants do especially well: hellebores, tulips, daffodils and anemones have naturalised over large areas. Stern was a fine plantsman and scholar, and wrote the classic book *A Chalk Garden* as a memoir of his gardening experiences. He was also a distinguished plant breeder: Highdown has given us two very fine roses in *Rosa* 'Highdownensis' and 'Wedding Day'. The garden is now well maintained by Worthing Borough Council and a pleasure to visit at any season, but perhaps especially in spring.

Features Woodland garden; roses (mainly old-fashioned); rock garden; plantsman's collection of plants; mature conifers; good herbaceous borders; fine collection of trees; tallest specimen of *Carpinus turczaninowii* in the UK, a handsome tree; refreshments from March to September.

Owned by Worthing Borough Council
Number of gardeners 4
Size 4ha (10 acres)
NCCPG National Collections plants introduced by Sir Frederick Stern
English Heritage grade II*

Holly Gate Cactus Nursery

BILLINGSHURST ROAD, ASHINGTON
RH20 3BA

Tel 01903 892930
Website www.hollygatecactus.co.uk
Location ½ mile from Ashington, on B2133 to Billingshurst.
Opening hours 9 am – 5 pm; daily. Closed 25 – 26 December.
Admission fee Adults £2; OAPs & Children £1.50.

Holly Gate specialises in cacti and succulents. It carries over 50,000 plants of all types in stock and sells them both retail and wholesale. Many are also planted in the cactus garden, which has some fine specimens and a wide range of taxa – fascinating for the *cognoscenti* and an eye-opener for the uninitiated, whatever the weather.

 Features Cacti; succulents.

Owned by T.M. Hewitt
Number of gardeners 2
Size 930 sq.m. (10,000 sq.ft.)

W.E.Th. Ingwersen Ltd

BIRCH FARM NURSERY, GRAVETYE,
EAST GRINSTEAD RH19 4LE

Tel 01342 810236
Website www.ingwersen.co.uk
Location 4 miles south-west of East Grinstead.
Opening hours 9 am – 1 pm & 1.30 pm – 4 pm; daily, except Sundays & Bank Holidays; March to September. Weekdays only from October to February. Closed for 2 weeks at Christmas.
Admission fee free

This was the first alpine nursery in the south of England: when it started in March 1927 (the company is celebrating its 75th birthday this year), Mr Ingwersen was a tenant of William Robinson at nearby Gravetye Manor. The company's exhibits at RHS Flower Shows have been a source of much praise. It still has one of the best collections in the country of traditional alpines, especially European primulas, sempervivums and autumn-flowering gentians, but it is also a good place to find less common rock plants, the smaller perennials, dwarf shrubs and conifers. There are many raised beds and troughs to see at the nursery (which is in a most beautiful setting): one can spend a long and very happy time here looking at alpines and browsing through possible purchases.

 Features Rock plants; troughs; lots of small plants for interested plantsmen.

Owned by Paul Ingwersen

Parham

PARHAM HOUSE, PULBOROUGH
RH20 4HS

Tel 01903 742021   **Fax** 01903 746557
Website www.parhaminsussex.co.uk
Location On A283 midway between Pulborough & Storrington.
Opening hours 12 noon – 6 pm; Wednesdays, Thursdays, Sundays & Bank Holiday Mondays; Easter to October.
Admission fee Gardens only: Adults £4; Children 50p.

Parham is an ethereal English garden for the loveliest of Elizabethan manor houses. In the deer park are a landscaped lake and a cricket ground. The fun for garden-lovers is in the old walled garden: four acres of lush borders, colour plantings in yellow, blue and

Leonardslee Gardens

LOWER BEEDING, HORSHAM RH13 6PP

Tel 01403 891212   **Fax** 01403 891305
Website www.leonardslee.com
Location 4 miles south-west of Handcross at junction of B2110 & A281.
Opening hours 9.30 am – 6 pm; daily; April to October.
Admission fee Adults £5, but £6 on week-days and £7 at weekends in May; Children £3 at all times.

Leonardslee is a plantsman's garden on an enormous scale: it was begun in 1889 by Sir Edmund Loder and still belongs to his descendants. It is important historically as one of the earliest examples of a collection of rare plants in a designed setting – a series of woodland valleys with panoramic views on the edge of the Wealden Forest. The gardens are beautiful when they first open in April with magnificent magnolias and camellias. Autumn colour is another feature: from the middle of September onwards maples, azaleas, liquidambars, carryas and nyssas produce one of the finest arrays of autumn colour in England. But Leonardslee is famous above all for its rhododendrons which line the many miles of paths up and down the hillsides and around the seven lakes. Sheets of bluebells accompany their main flowering in May, while the banks of the lakes and streams are densely planted with candelabra primulas, lysichitons and gunneras. There are many other fascinating features: magnificent conifers (but never in sufficient quantities to spoil the impression that this is a deciduous woodland garden); large plantings of modern *Rhododendron yakushimanum* hybrids; several original plants of *Rhododendron × loderi* hybrids; a large area naturalised by *Scilla liliohyacinthus*; rare shrubs like *Ilex dipyrena*; a European cork oak (*Quercus suber*) and the Amur cork oak (*Phellodendron amurense*); a tree fern (*Dicksonia antarctica*) growing outside but protected in winter; a Pulhamite rock garden about 100 years old, which has a very striking clump of the hardy Chusan palm (*Trachycarpus fortunei*) and a bright mixture of evergreen azaleas; and a truly beautiful valley on the other side of the main lake which is filled from top to bottom with a flood of sweet-scented yellow azaleas (*Rhododendron luteum*).

Features Rock garden; plantsman's collection of plants; mature conifers; new Millennium plantings (100 oak species; 100 maple species; many flowering *Cornus*); bonsai; tallest fossil tree *Metasequoia glyptostroboides* (28m) and *Magnolia campbellii* (27m) in the British Isles, and 5 further champion trees; gift shop; licensed restaurant & café.

Owned by R.R. Loder
Number of gardeners 7
Size 100ha (250 acres)
English Heritage grade I

Nymans

HANDCROSS, HAYWARDS HEATH RH17 6EB

Tel 01444 400321   **Fax** 01444 400253
Website www.nationaltrust.org.uk
Location Handcross, off the main road on B2114
Opening hours 11 am – 6 pm; Wednesday – Sunday,
plus Bank Holiday Mondays; 1 March to 3 November.
11 am – 4 pm; Saturdays & Sundays; November to March
2002. Closed 28 & 29 December.
Admission fee Adults £6; Children £3. Reductions in
winter. RHS members free.

Features Woodland garden; topiary; roses (mainly old-fashioned); plantsman's collection of plants; good herbaceous borders; fine collection of trees; eight different record-breaking trees; shop; plant centre open daily 11 am – 6 pm; licensed restaurant.

Owned by The National Trust
Number of gardeners 7
Size 12ha (30 acres)
English Heritage grade II*

The garden at Nymans was made in the early years of the 20th century by Leonard Messel, and his head gardener James Comber. Although it is now owned by the National Trust, there is still a substantial input from latter-day members of the Messel family, including Lord Snowdon and Alistair Buchanan of Hillbarn House (*q.v.*). Nymans is a stupendous plantsman's garden with a wonderful collection of plants of every type which have been marshalled with a fair degree of artistry and made to fit within a strong overall design. It is one of the best gardens of the Sussex hills, and one which retains much of the distinctive style dictated by its historic collection of shrubs and trees. In the walled garden are opulent yellow-and-blue herbaceous borders, a pioneering collection of old roses, a stupendous wisteria pergola and vast collections of magnolias and camellias. Further afield, the woodland and wild garden have a great collection of rare trees and shrubs. Nymans suffered very severely from the Great Storm of 1987, but has since made a brilliant recovery and many would say now that the garden looks better than ever.

mauve, old and new fruit trees, and all maintained to the highest standard. The aim is to achieve 'Edwardian opulence … without being too purist'. There are striking colour combinations too within the vegetable garden, while extensive cutting borders supply material for the arrangements of cut flowers for which the house is famous.

 Features Roses (mainly old-fashioned); trained fruit; good herbaceous borders; organic kitchen garden; HHA/Christie's Garden of the Year in 1990; shop; light lunches & teas.

Owned by Parham Park Trust
Number of gardeners 4½, plus volunteers
Size 4.2ha (11 acres)
English Heritage grade I

Petworth House

PETWORTH GU28 0AE

Tel 01798 343929/342207   **Fax** 01798 342963
Website www.nationaltrust.org.uk
Location At Petworth, well signed.
Opening hours Garden: 11 am – 6 pm; Saturday – Wednesday; 23 March to 3 November. Plus 9, 10, 16 & 17 March (12 noon – 4 pm) for spring bulbs. Plus Good Friday. Park: 8 am – dusk if sooner; daily; all year (but closes at 12 noon for concerts).
Admission fee Garden ('Pleasure grounds'): £1.50. Park free.

One of the best Capability Brown landscapes in England sweeps right up to the windows of Petworth House. The National Trust has decided to add modern attractions: herbaceous borders and acres of azaleas in a new woodland garden. Both park and garden have enjoyed a renaissance since the Great Gale of 1987.

 Features Capability Brown landscape; woodland garden; good herbaceous borders; deer park; one million daffodils; shop; restaurant; tea-rooms.

Owned by The National Trust
Number of gardeners 4
Size 12ha (30 acres) of pleasure grounds; 280ha (700-acre) park.
English Heritage grade I

Stonehurst

ARDINGLY RH17 6TN

Tel 01444 892052
Location 1 mile north of Ardingly on B2028.
Opening hours For NGS, and by appointment.
Admission fee Adults £2.50; Children £1.

The garden at Stonehurst was designed by Thomas Mawson in about 1910. In front of the house is a croquet lawn, which leads through a brick-and-tile pergola to a rose garden containing a swimming pool. Elsewhere is a tennis court surrounded by low brick walls and a viewing bastion at the corner. All of this makes the garden very interesting for the social and garden historian. But the horticultural joys are below the house, in a thick woodland garden: Stonehurst is in a rock-lined secret valley, where springs issue to form a series of small lakes, and rare liverworts have special scientific interest. The Strausses have made it known as a garden for rhododendrons, camellias and rare trees and shrubs which regularly win prizes at RHS shows in London. It is very well maintained.

Features Rock outcrops; good herbaceous borders; camellias; magnolias; azaleas; lakes; orchids, rhododendrons & camellias for sale; teas.

Owned by D.R. Strauss
Number of gardeners 2½
Size 12ha (30 acres)
English Heritage grade II

Wakehurst Place

ARDINGLY, HAYWARDS HEATH
RH17 6TN

Tel 01444 894066 Fax 01444 894069
Website www.kew.org
Location On B2028 between Turners Hill & Ardingly.
Opening hours 10 am – 7 pm (6 pm in March, 5 pm in February & October, & 4 pm from November to January); daily except Christmas Day & New Year's Day; all year.
Admission fee Adults £6.50; OAPs £4.50; Children free. Free to National Trust members.

Wakehurst Place, now managed by the Royal Botanic Gardens at Kew as a country outlier, has a long horticultural history. Most of the planting, however, began after Gerald Loder bought the estate in 1903 and began to introduce exotic trees and shrubs – a development which continued throughout the mid-20th century under the next owner Sir Henry Price. The planting suffered badly in the great storm of 1987 but the survivors include many rare trees including the King William pine (*Athrotaxis selaginoides*). Among the record-breaking trees which survived the gales are *Cornus nuttallii* and *Torreya nucifera* both 17m high, *Carya tomentosa* at 27m, and two cultivars of *Chamaecyparis lawsoniana* – 'President Roosevelt' at 15m and 'Winston Churchill' slightly shorter at 13m. A recent addition has been the 'iris dell', planted with authentic Japanese cultivars of water iris (*Iris ensata*), against a brilliant background of Kurume azaleas – Wakehurst has significant connections with Japan. The water garden is surrounded by sheets of blue meconopsis and the giant Himalayan *Cardiocrinum giganteum*. Wakehurst also has its botanic collections, including a Monocot border – wonderful ginger plants (*Hedychium*) in autumn – and specimen beds with especially comprehensive collections of hypericums, hydrangeas and agapanthus. Many parts of the woodland garden are underplanted with rhododendrons, which are at their best in April and May. Wakehurst has also benefited from major funding by the Millennium Commission, which has enabled it to develop the world's largest seed bank: it aims to collect and conserve some ten per cent of the world's flora – 24,000 species – by the year 2010.

Features Ornamental woodland garden; roses (mainly old-fashioned & climbers); rhododendrons & azaleas; plantsman's collection of plants; daffodils; camellias; fine collection of trees; alpine plants; bluebells; Asian heath garden; pinetum; cardiocrinums; good autumn colour; *Iris ensata* dell; water garden; tallest *Ostrya japonica* (15m) in the British Isles, plus 25 further tree records; gift-shop; plant sales (March to October); light refreshments & restaurant.

Owned by RBG Kew, on lease from National Trust
Number of gardeners 40
Size 67ha (170 acres)
NCCPG National Collections Betula; Hypericum; Nothofagus; Skimmia
English Heritage grade II*

West Dean Gardens

WEST DEAN, CHICHESTER PO18 0QZ

Tel 01243 811210 & 811301 Fax 01243 811342
Website www.westdean.org.uk
Location 6 miles north of Chichester on A286.

Opening hours 11 am – 5 pm; daily; March to October. Opens at 10.30 am from May to September.

Admission fee Adults £4.50; OAPs £4; Children £2.

Laid out in the 1890s and 1900s, West Dean has now been extensively restored. Harold Peto's 100m pergola has been replanted with roses. Much of the damage to the 50-acre St Roche's arboretum caused by the 1987 storm has been made good. The great range of glasshouses in the walled garden has been repaired and the garden itself planted as a working kitchen garden which is now the crowning glory of West Dean. A huge variety of plants – from peaches to peppers, cucumbers to coleus, aubergines to orchids – grow in the 16 glasshouses and frames. Out of doors are orderly rows of cabbage, carrots, lettuce and beetroot, alongside herbaceous borders in rich reds, oranges and yellows. No space is wasted: the kitchen garden has over one mile of walls covered in trained fruit trees – over 200 different apples, pears and plums. No private garden has so many beautifully grown fruit and vegetables. Beyond the walled garden are 35 acres of ornamental gardens, the St Roche's arboretum and 240 acres of landscaped park. Herbaceous borders and annual bedding schemes have been reinstated, rustic summer houses rebuilt and the arboretum taken in hand. The redevelopment of the spring garden, including the 1820s rustic thatched summer house with its moss- and heather-lined interior and its floor of knapped flints and horses' molars is now complete. New plantings for the wild garden are planned for 2003.

Features Roses (mainly old-fashioned & climbers); plants under glass; museum of old lawn mowers; long pergola with roses & clematis; tallest *Cupressus goveniana* (22m) and *Ailanthus vilmoriniana*

(26m) in UK; amazing kitchen garden; licensed restaurant.

Owned by The Edward James Foundation
Number of gardeners 9
Size 36ha (90 acres) in all
NCCPG National Collections *Aesculus*; *Liriodendron*
English Heritage grade II*

Yew Tree Cottage

BANKTON HILL, CRAWLEY DOWN, CRAWLEY RH10 3EB

Tel 01342 714633
Location Opposite Grange Farm on B2028.
Opening hours By appointment from May to September.
Admission fee Adults £1.50; OAPs £1.

This miraculous small garden has been designed, planted and maintained by the nonagenarian owner over many years. For much of the 1980s and 1990s, there was no better example of the cottage-garden style. It won infinite plaudits for its display of plants, including a *BBC Gardener's World* interview with Gay Search in 1998. Then, in 1999, Mrs Hudson decided to replace it with a gravel-and-grasses garden inspired by Piet Oudolf. The result is fascinating.

Features Good herbaceous borders; cottage garden style; colour borders; new ornamental grass garden (2000); refreshments for small parties.

Owned by Mrs K. Hudson
Number of gardeners 1
Size 0.15ha (⅓ acre)

WARWICKSHIRE

Warwickshire has for centuries been a prosperous county: it has the rich clay soils, the country estates and the gardens to prove it. Many of its historic gardens are open to the public throughout the season, including such top attractions as Arbury Hall, Charlecote Park, Farnborough Hall, Packwood House, Upton House and Warwick Castle. The National Gardens Scheme is very successful in persuading the owners of modern gardens to open them to the public, especially by grouping several together within a village. Last year, for example, no less than 11 gardens in the village of Dorsington opened simultaneously for the Scheme, and the same number (on a different Sunday in June) in the up-market Earlsdon area of Coventry. Warwickshire has many first-rate garden centres and a few top-class specialist nurseries too – notably Fibrex Nurseries, who specialise in pelargoniums, ivies, hardy ferns and hellebores. Fibrex also has two of the county's National Collections. The Henry Doubleday Research Association, the organic gardening organisation, has its headquarters at Ryton near Coventry: it offers free access to RHS members throughout the year.

Arbury Hall

NUNEATON CV10 7PT

Tel 024 7638 2804   **Fax** 024 7664 1147
Location 3 miles south-east of Nuneaton off the B4102.
Opening hours 2 pm – 6 pm; Bank Holiday Sundays & Mondays; Easter Sunday to September.
Admission fee Adults £4; Children £2.50.

Arbury is more important historically than horticulturally: Sanderson Miller was involved in some 18th-century improvements and there is a wonderfully landscaped sequence of canals and lakes. During the 19th century, many good trees were planted, now in the full-grown beauty of their maturity: purple beeches and a golden sycamore for example. Then there are bluebell woods, pollarded limes, a large rose garden, a walled garden and a huge wisteria. Nothing is outstanding in itself, but the ensemble is an oasis of peace on the edge of industrial Daventry and worth the journey from far away.

Features Woodland garden; roses (mainly modern); rhododendrons & azaleas; daffodils; bluebells; gift & crafts shop; tea-room.

Owned by Viscount Daventry
English Heritage grade II*

Baddesley Clinton

KNOWLE, SOLIHULL B93 0DQ

Tel 01564 783294 **Fax** 01564 782706
Website www.nationaltrust.org.uk
Location 1 mile west of A4141
Opening hours 12 noon – 5.30 pm; Wednesday –
Sunday; 6 March to 15 December. Also open on Bank
Holiday Mondays and Jubilee Bank Holiday. Closes at
5 pm in March, April, October & 1-3 November; closes at
4.30 pm from 6 November to 15 December.
Admission fee Adults £2.90.

The walled garden at Baddesley Clinton has
fine mixed plantings, including a good
collection of shrub roses, herbaceous plants,
herbs and annuals. One of the Victorian
lean-to glasshouses has recently been
restored. In front of the house (an ancient
manor house) is a formal courtyard garden.
Further away are woodland walks, a lake and
wildflower meadows.

Features Formal courtyard garden;
walled garden; restaurant.

Owned by The National Trust
Number of gardeners 2
Size 4.5ha (11 acres)
English Heritage grade II

Charlecote Park

WELLESBOURNE, WARWICK
CV35 9ER

Tel 01789 470277 **Fax** 01789 470544
Website www.nationaltrust.org.uk
Location Signed from A429.
Opening hours 11 am – 6 pm; Friday – Tuesday; 23
March to 3 November. Also 11 am – 4 pm on Saturdays &
Sundays from 2 February to 17 March and from
9 November to 15 December.

Admission fee £3 (garden only).

Fine cedars and a Capability Brown park are
the main claims to Charlecote's fame, but
the young William Shakespeare is reputed to
have poached deer from the park, so the
National Trust has planted a border with
plants mentioned in his works.

Features Topiary; parterre; mature
conifers; deer park; orangery; National
Trust shop; restaurant.

Owned by The National Trust
Number of gardeners 2
English Heritage grade II*

Coughton Court

ALCESTER B49 5JA

Tel 01789 400777 **Fax** 01789 765544
Website www.coughtoncourt.co.uk
Location 2 miles north of Alcester on A435.
Opening hours 11 am – 5.30 pm; Wednesday – Sunday;
23 March to 30 September. Plus Bank Holiday Mondays &
Tuesdays, and Tuesdays in July & August. Plus Saturdays
& Sundays only in October. Closed 22 June & 20 July.
Admission fee Adults £6.95; Children £3.45.

The garden at Coughton has all been made
since 1992, designed by Christina Williams,
the owner's daughter. An Elizabethan-style
knot garden fills the courtyard, and
extensive new plantings beyond lead the eye
out to the distant landscape. There is a new
rose labyrinth in the walled garden and a
herb garden, as well as an orchard planted
with local varieties of fruit. The bog garden,
planted in 1997, has come together well.

Features Interesting historic gardens
(new) around the house (old); pretty
plants and plantings; gift shop & plant
centre; restaurant/café.

Owned by Mrs Clare Throckmorton & the National Trust
Number of gardeners 4
Size 10ha (25 acres)

Farnborough Hall

BANBURY OX17 1DU

Tel 01295 690002
Website www.nationaltrust.org.uk
Location Off A423, 6 miles north of Banbury.
Opening hours 2 pm – 6 pm; Wednesdays & Saturdays;
April to September. Also 5 & 6 May. Terrace walk also
open on Thursdays & Fridays.
Admission fee Grounds £1.75; Terrace Walk £1
(Thursdays & Fridays by prior arrangement only).

Farnborough Hall is Sanderson Millar's
masterpiece – grand vistas, classical temples
and a dominating obelisk, together with a
long curving terraced walk to the adjoining
estate of Mollington. No flowers, but space
and peace.

 Features Woodland garden; topiary;
roses (mainly old-fashioned).

Owned by The National Trust
English Heritage grade I

Fibrex Nurseries Ltd

HONEYBOURNE ROAD, PEBWORTH,
STRATFORD-UPON-AVON CV37 8XT

Tel 01789 720788   **Fax** 01789 721162
Website www.fibrex.co.uk
Location South-east edge of village, on road to Broad
Marston.
Opening hours 10.30 am – 5 pm; Monday – Friday; all
year. Plus weekends (12 noon – 5 pm) from March to July.
Closed for last two weeks of December & first week of July.

Fibrex is a family nursery, built up over
more than 40 years and a regular prize-
winner at RHS Flower Shows. It has four
specialities – pelargoniums, ivies, hardy
ferns and hellebores – and holds National
Collections in two of them. The National
Collection of pelargoniums has over 2,000
different species and cultivars and claims to
be the largest in the world. The National
Collection of ivies (*Hedera*) has over 300
different species and cultivars. The ferns are
planted out in the show garden in a natural
manner using mature plants: the hellebores
too are planted out for viewing when they
are in flower.

 Features Pelargoniums; ivies; hardy
ferns; hellebores.

NCCPG National Collections *Hedera*; *Pelargonium*

The Mill Garden

55 MILL STREET, WARWICK
CV34 4HB

Tel 01926 492877
Location Off A425, beside castle gate.
Opening hours 9 am – 6 pm; Friday – Sunday, plus Bank
Holiday Mondays; Easter to September.
Admission fee Adults £1; Children free.

No garden has such an idyllic setting, on the
banks of the Avon at the foot of Warwick
castle: the views in all directions are superb.
The garden is planted in the cottage style
and seems much larger than its 1 acre: it
burgeons with plants, and the use of annuals
to supplement the varied permanent
planting enables it to have colour and form,
contrasts and harmonies, at every season.
This garden was made by Arthur Measures
over a long period: his son and daughter
continue to open it in his memory.

Features Plantsman's collection of plants; water plants; magnificent riverside position.

Owned by D.G. & J. Measures

Packwood House

GROVE ROAD, LAPWORTH, SOLIHULL B94 6AT

Tel 01564 783294 **Fax** 01564 782706
Website www.nationaltrust.org.uk
Location 2 miles east of Hockley Heath: signed from A3400.
Opening hours 11 am – 5.30 pm; Wednesday – Sunday, plus Bank Holiday Mondays & 3 & 4 June; 6 March to 3 November. Closes at 4.30 pm in March, October & November.
Admission fee Garden only: Adults £2.60.

Long famous for its topiary, Packwood also has magnificent herbaceous borders which make a visit in July or August particularly rewarding.

 Features National Trust shop; refreshments available at peak times.

Owned by The National Trust
Number of gardeners 3½
Size 2.8ha (7 acres)
English Heritage grade I

Ryton Organic Gardens

COVENTRY CV8 3LG

Tel 024 7630 3517 **Fax** 024 7663 9229
Website www.hdra.org.uk
Location 5 miles south-east of Coventry off A45.
Opening hours 9 am – 5 pm; daily; all year except Christmas week.

Admission fee Adults £3; Children free. RHS members free.

Ryton is the UK centre of excellence for organic gardening. It is very well laid out and landscaped, with 35 different small gardens, all highly instructive. The staff's commitment is also impressive. The gardens include herb gardens, rose gardens, fruit and vegetable displays plus wildlife and conservation areas. A children's trail and guided tours are available. Gardening courses and special events are held throughout the year. The excellent restaurant and substantial shop will add considerably to your enjoyment. The website is full of interest.

 Features Herbs; plants under glass; considerable educational interest; shop with gardening products, books, food, wine & gifts; organic whole-food restaurant.

Owned by Henry Doubleday Research Association
Number of gardeners 7
Size 4ha (10 acres)

Upton House

BANBURY OX15 6HT

Tel & Fax 01295 670266
Website www.nationaltrust.org.uk
Location A422, 7 miles north-west of Banbury & 12 miles south-east of Stratford-upon-Avon.
Opening hours 12.30 pm – 5 pm; Saturday – Wednesday, plus Good Friday; 23 March to 3 November. Opens at 11 am on Saturdays, Sundays & Bank Holidays. Then from 12 noon to dusk on Saturdays & Sundays only from November to 15 December.
Admission fee Adults £3.

High on a ridge near the site of the battle of Edgehill, Upton is terraced right down to the pool at the bottom. The centrepiece is a kitchen garden, reached by flights of Italianate stairs. There are also modern formal gardens, one with standard *Hibiscus syriacus* 'Bluebird' underplanted with eryngiums, another a rose garden. Further down are a bog garden, a cherry garden and grand herbaceous borders to lead you back to the house. The garden is fascinating, and not at all what you expect when you first see the house.

 Features Good herbaceous borders; bog garden; National Trust shop; licensed restaurant.

Owned by The National Trust
Number of gardeners 5, plus 2 students
Size 14ha (35 acres)
NCCPG National Collections Aster
English Heritage grade II*

Warwick Castle

WARWICK CV34 4QU

Tel 01926 495421   **Fax** 01926 401692
Website www.warwick-castle.co.uk
Location In town centre.
Opening hours 10 am – 6 pm (5 pm in winter); daily; all year except 25 December.
Admission fee Adults £11.50; OAPs £8.20; Children £6.75. Subject to review and usually less out-of-season.

This classic 18th-century landscape looks good after some recent restoration, as do the late 19th-century formal garden, the Backhouse rock garden, and a Victorian-style rose garden.

Features Topiary; roses (mainly old-fashioned); rhododendrons & azaleas; mature conifers; Capability Brown landscape; handsome conservatory; shop; refreshments.

Owned by Tussauds Group
Number of gardeners 8
Size 23ha (62 acres)
English Heritage grade I

WEST MIDLANDS

As an administrative entity, West Midlands was a short-lived county: created in 1974 from parts of Warwickshire and Staffordshire: it is now entirely split up into unitary authorities. Its historic gardens are few, but they include what is left of the poet Shenstone's The Leasowes, together with the Birmingham Botanical Gardens and Castle Bromwich Hall. The latter are both highly visitable and highly visited – excellent gardens, deservedly popular still. Being such an urban county, West Midlands is short on old estates, landscaped parks and arboreta, but full of large villa-gardens like the one in Edgbaston which became the University of Birmingham Botanic Garden. This is the area too where the National Gardens Scheme does best. The county also has some good nurseries: Ashwood is one of the most innovative in the British Isles. The biggest RHS event in the Midlands takes place at the NEC from 19 to 23 June 2002: BBC *Gardener's World* Live is very different from such shows as Chelsea and Hampton Court, though the great draw is the enormously long floral marquee which the Royal Horticultural Society runs with great aplomb. The county, though small, also has a surprisingly large number of National Collections, including three (*Ceanothus*, *Gladiolus* and *Rudbeckia*) held by Dudley Borough Council.

Ashwood Nurseries Ltd

ASHWOOD LOWER LANE,
KINGSWINFORD DY6 0AE

Tel 01384 401996   **Fax** 01308 401108
Website www.ashwood-nurseries.co.uk
Location 2 miles west of Kingswinford, near A449.
Opening hours 9 am – 6 pm; Monday – Saturday.
9.30 am – 6 pm; Sundays. All year, except
25 & 26 December.

Ashwood is a rising star among nurseries. The owners have the happy knack of anticipating trends in horticultural fashion: they then put a lot of thought into developing new plants and, thus, new markets. They began in the 1970s with lewisias, crossing and selecting them until they could offer a remarkable range of colours. In 1996 they were awarded a gold medal for their lewisias at the Chelsea Flower Show, their first ever exhibit at the Royal Horticultural Society's most prestigious show. Next they began to breed hellebores – strains of *H. orientalis* in particular. The Ashwood hybrids are remarkable for their purity of colour, vigour and form – but, above all, for the new developments that they have brought to the genus: doubles, anemone-centred and upright forms. Now they are turning their attention to hybrids of *H. niger*. More recent, but no less promising, has been their involvement with hardy cyclamen, auriculas, and hepaticas. Hepaticas are extremely fashionable in Japan, where rare cultivars may cost the equivalent of several hundred pounds, and there is clearly money to be made from developing this genus yet further. Above all, Ashwood means quality: the exhibits the nursery brings to RHS Flower Shows are beautifully grown. A visit to their nursery is strongly recommended. It is, of course, a RHS Partner Nursery.

 Features Hellebores; cyclamen; lewisias; hepaticas; auriculas.

Birmingham Botanical Gardens & Glasshouses

Westbourne Road, Edgbaston, Birmingham B15 3TR

Tel 0121 454 1860   **Fax** 0121 454 7835
Website www.birminghambotanicalgardens.org.uk
Location Follow brown tourist signs in Edgbaston.
Opening hours 9 am (10 am on Sundays) – 7 pm, or dusk if earlier; daily; all year except Christmas Day.
Admission fee Adults £5 (£5.50 on summer Sundays); Concessions £2.70.

Part botanic garden, part public park, wholly delightful, the Birmingham Botanical Gardens boasts an historic lay-out (John Claudius Loudon), rare trees and shrubs, gardens for rhododendrons, roses, herbs and alpines, and four glasshouses (tropical, palm house, orangery and cacti house). The plant highlights are innumerable, but include water hyacinths (the weed that is choking the Nile), rice plants, papyrus plants, coffee and sugar, bananas and pineapples, many cycads, insectivorous plants, 'living stones', *Paulownia tomentosa*, good herbaceous plants (phlox, euphorbias, geraniums,

delphiniums) and the National Collection of Bonsai housed in a secure courtyard. New in 2002 are six BBC *Gardener of the Year* gardens, an organic garden, and a 'discovery' garden for children.

 Features Roses (ancient & modern); rock garden; plantsman's collection of plants; plants under glass; fruit; mature conifers; good herbaceous borders; alpine yard; bonsai; three 'historic' gardens – Roman, Mediaeval & Tudor.

Owned by Birmingham Botanical & Horticultural Society
Number of gardeners 10, plus students
Size 6ha (15 acres)
NCCPG National Collections Bonsai
English Heritage grade II*

Castle Bromwich Hall Gardens

Chester Road, Castle Bromwich B36 9BT

Tel & Fax 0121 749 4100
Website www.cbhgt.swinternet.co.uk
Location 5 miles from city centre just off B4114.
Opening hours 1.30 pm – 4 30 pm; Tuesday – Thursday. 2 pm – 6 pm; Saturdays, Sundays & Bank Holiday Mondays. 31 March to 31 October.
Admission fee Adults £3.50; OAPs £2.50; Children £1.50.

Castle Bromwich Hall is garden archaeology at work. The gardens are being restored as they were in about 1700 by a privately funded trust. Work began in 1985 and has been very successful: the result is beautiful, inspiring and educational. The gardens contain a large collection of unusual period plants, and a 19th-century holly maze. There is also a holly walk – a broad path lined with variegated hollies. At its end, an elegant summer house looks across to an early greenhouse. Nearby is the formal vegetable garden, made to the design of Batty Langley's *New Principles of Gardening* (1728). Many historic vegetables and herbs are grown, along with unusual varieties like the black 'Congo' potato and white carrot. Fruit trees are formally trained – apples, pears, apricots, figs and cherries. The Upper and Lower Wildernesses have grown to maturity, but they have been underplanted well. The north garden has just been restored to the design shown in Henry Beighton's Prospect of 1726, its parterre outlined with yew, mown grass and gravel.

 Features Walled gardens; historic vegetables, fruit and herbs; holly maze.

Owned by Castle Bromwich Hall Gardens Trust
Number of gardeners 3, plus volunteers
Size 4ha (10 acres)
English Heritage grade II*

University of Birmingham Botanic Garden

58 EDGBASTON PARK ROAD, EDGBASTON B15 2RT

Tel 0121 414 4944   **Fax** 0121 414 5619
Website www.birmingham.ac.uk
Location Off A38 Bristol Road, ½ mile.
Opening hours 11 am – 4 pm; Monday – Friday. Closed Bank Holidays, Easter & Christmas holidays.
Admission fee Adults £2.

This was originally a private garden, belonging to one of Birmingham's great-and-good families: it was given to the university in 1943 but still has the 'feel' of a private garden – one with an exceptional collection of plants. The rhododendrons and naturalised bulbs are very pretty: even the roses, chosen to illustrate their history in cultivation, fit well into an ornamental garden. Perhaps the most interesting plants are the collection of alpines in troughs, in the sandstone rockery and in the scree beds. There are some geographic beds which put together plants that combine naturally in the wild, but everything else about the garden is horticultural, rather than botanic.

 Features Roses of every kind; a good collection of plants of every kind.

Owned by University of Birmingham
Number of gardeners 3
Size 2.2ha (6 acres)
NCCPG National Collections Rosa (History of European roses)

Wightwick Manor

WIGHTWICK, WOLVERHAMPTON WV6 8EE

Tel 01902 761108   **Fax** 01902 764663
Website www.nationaltrust.org.uk
Location 3 miles west of Wolverhampton on A454.
Opening hours 11 am – 6 pm on Wednesdays, Thursdays, Saturdays & Bank Holidays (plus 4 June); March to December.
Admission fee Adults £2.50.

Wightwick is a substantial Victorian garden, designed by Alfred Parsons and Thomas Mawson. It has topiary, a rose arbour, avenues of Irish yews and a Poets' Corner where all the plants were taken as cuttings from the gardens of literary men – Keats, Tennyson and Dickens among them.

Features Topiary; roses (mainly old-fashioned & climbers); rock garden; good herbaceous borders; current holder of Sandford Award; coffee & soft drinks.

Owned by The National Trust
Number of gardeners 3½
Size 16.8ha (42 acres)

WILTSHIRE

Wiltshire is the county that people travel through on their way to somewhere else. For gardeners, this is a mistake. Unlike so many counties whose great Grade I historic gardens are often rather dull, Wiltshire's are all supremely beautiful – Bowood, Iford, Longleat, Stourhead and Wilton. All are open to the public, as are many of the other graded gardens. Wiltshire also has a number of very good plantsman's gardens – notably Broadleas and Home Covert near Devizes, and the Old Vicarage at nearby Edington. It has some fine arboreta: tree-enthusiasts should also try to see the record-breaking multi-stemmed specimen of *Zelkova carpinifolia* at Wardour Castle – 35m high when last officially measured in 1977. The National Gardens Scheme does well in the county, particularly among the owners of medium-sized and large gardens. The Wiltshire Gardens Trust is active in conservation and also represents the NCCPG in the county: there is a sprinkling of National Collections among its members. Wiltshire does not, however, do so well for nurseries: perhaps only the Botanic Nursery at Atworth can be said to have a national profile. Geoffrey Jellicoe's masterpiece at Shute House, Donhead St Mary, has recently been open to groups by prior appointment. It is worth noting that, contrary to widespread belief, both Shute House and Larmer Tree Gardens are actually in Wiltshire, not in Dorset.

The Abbey House

MARKET CROSS, MALMESBURY
SN16 9AS

Tel 01666 822212 **Fax** 01666 822782
Website www.abbeyhousegardens.co.uk
Location In town centre, behind abbey. Public car-parks nearby.
Opening hours 11 am – 6 pm; daily; 21 March to 21 October.
Admission fee Adults £5; Concessions £4; Children £2. RHS members free in March & October.

This remarkable 5-acre garden has all been made by the Pollards since 1995. They have planted 2,000 different roses to celebrate the millennium, and 2,000 different herb cultivars. Other features include an arcaded fruit walk, a knot garden, huge herbaceous borders, a striking laburnum tunnel and a formal garden. But it is the design and planting which are so distinctive: bold, varied and inspirational. The woodland garden running down to the river is home to thousands of spring bulbs. Look out for a *BBC Gardeners World* half-hour feature film on the garden, planned for screening in late spring 2002.

Features Plantsman's collection of plants; herbaceous borders; roses of every kind; good design; colour contrasts; refreshments.

Owned by Ian Pollard

Avebury Manor

AVEBURY, MARLBOROUGH SN8 1RF

Tel 01672 539203 **Fax** 01672 539388
Website www.nationaltrust.org.uk
Location In the village, well signed.
Opening hours 11 am – 5.30 pm; daily except Mondays & Thursdays; April to October. Open Bank Holiday Mondays.
Admission fee Adults £2.70; Children £1.30.

The National Trust is continuing the work of restoration at this great Edwardian garden and the 'garden rooms' are being revived and replanted: the results are well worth another visit.

 Features Topiary; roses (mainly old-fashioned); good herbaceous borders; double lavender walk; shop just outside the garden; refreshments in village.

Owned by The National Trust
Number of gardeners 2
Size 2.2ha (6 acres)

Bolehyde Manor

ALLINGTON, CHIPPENHAM SN14 6LW

Tel 01249 652105 **Fax** 01249 659296
Location 2 miles west of Chippenham.
Opening hours 2.30 pm – 6 pm; 23 June. And by appointment.
Admission fee Adults £2.50; Children 50p.

This charming house is surrounded by outbuildings and walls of old Cotswold stone, which form the background to a series of enclosed gardens. Each is very prettily designed and planted in the modern style – using plants for their contrasts and combinations of flower, shape, colour and form. The gardens seem to brim over with flowers and an abundance of beauty. If only it were open more often.

 Features Roses (mainly old-fashioned); pretty *potager*, good herbaceous borders; climbing roses.

Owned by Earl & Countess Cairns
Number of gardeners 1
Size 1.2ha (3 acres)

The Botanic Nursery

COTTLES LANE, ATWORTH, MELKSHAM SN12 8NU

Tel 07850 328756 **Fax** 01225 700953
Location Just south of the A365 at the western end of Atworth.
Opening hours 10 am – 5 pm; Fridays & Saturdays; all year except January. And by appointment.
Admission fee Free.

The Botanic Nursery built its reputation on growing lime-tolerant plants, but has become better known as a plantsman's nursery, where a long browse will winkle out all sorts of rarities. It is best known at RHS Flower Shows for its spectacular displays of foxgloves (*Digitalis*) from its National Collection, though it also has very good collections of unusual shrubs, eryngiums and dieramas. The 1-acre display garden (mainly trees and shrubs) is well worth a visit, too.

 Features 2,000 different plants, many rare, all lime-tolerant.

Owned by Terence & Mary Baker
Size 0.8ha (2 acres)

Bowood House & Gardens

CALNE SN11 0LZ

Tel 01249 812102   **Fax** 01249 821757
Website www.bowood-estate.co.uk
Location Off A4 in Derry Hill village between Calne & Chippenham.
Opening hours 11 am – 6 pm; daily; 23 March to 3 November. Separate charge of £3.30 for rhododendron walks, open from mid April to early June (telephone for exact dates, which depend upon the flowering season).
Admission fee Adults £5.90; OAPs £4.90; Children £3.70.

Beautifully maintained and welcoming, Bowood has something from every period of English garden history. Capability Brown made the lake and planted many of the trees and lawns which give such a beautiful setting to the house. Charles Hamilton added the famous cascade below the lake in the picturesque style. There is an important 19th-century pinetum and laid out on pre-Linnaean principles – geographically – with oceans of grass to separate the continents. It is not just a collection of magnificent conifers, but contains many rare and beautiful deciduous trees too, including the tallest specimen of the cut-leaved horse-chestnut (*Aesculus hippocastanum* 'Laciniata') in the British Isles. By the house are handsome Italianate formal gardens designed by Smirke and Kennedy in the 19th century and recently replanted by Lady Mary Keen. Up in the woods in a separate part of the estate, and entered directly from the A342, is a magnificent display of modern rhododendrons around the Robert Adam mausoleum. The oceans of bluebells which surround these rhododendron drives is one of the finest in the south of England. Be sure to miss the reclining nude above the formal gardens.

Features Lake; 100-acre Capability Brown landscaped parkland; famous old arboretum; topiary; mature conifers; modern borders; rhododendrons, azaleas & bluebells (separate garden); tallest *Thuja occidentalis* 'Wareana' in the UK; gift shop; buffet lunches & afternoon teas in licensed restaurant.

Owned by The Marquis of Lansdowne
Number of gardeners 4
English Heritage grade I

Broadleas

DEVIZES SN10 5JQ

Tel 01380 722035
Location 1 mile south of Devizes.
Opening hours 2 pm – 6 pm; Wednesdays, Thursdays & Sundays; April to October.
Admission fee Adults £3; Children £1.

Lady Anne Cowdray started to make this garden – now owned by a charitable trust – in 1947. Since then it has grown into a very fine plantsman's garden, with lots of different kinds of plant but an especially good collection of ornamental trees and shrubs. Broadleas has a rose garden, a grey border, a rock garden and a 'secret' garden, all near the Regency house. But the main attraction is the Dell, a greensand combe that stretches down to the valley below, its sides just stuffed with good things. At the top are two tall magnolias, thought to be *M. sprengeri* var. *diva* and *M. sargentiana* var. *robusta*. Pass between them, and past a very tall paulownia, and you come into a world of rare trees, vast magnolias, sheets of *Primula whitei* and cyclamen. And Broadleas has two characteristics common to all good plantsman's gardens: it is worth visiting at any time of the year and it gets better all the time. The nursery sells surplus plants, many grown from wild-collected seed by members of the International Dendrology Society.

 Features A plantsman's collection of plants; woodland garden; roses (ancient & modern); good herbaceous borders; fine ornamental trees; excellent small nursery for rare plants; teas on summer Sundays.

Owned by Broadleas Gardens Charitable Trust
Number of gardeners 2½
Size 3.6ha (9 acres)
English Heritage grade II

Conock Manor

DEVIZES SN10 3QQ

Tel 01380 840227
Location 5 miles south-east of Devizes off A342.
Opening hours 2 pm – 6 pm; 26 May.
Admission fee Adults £2.50; Children free.

Beautiful parkland surrounds this covetable Georgian house. Behind the copper-domed stables, an elegant shrub walk meanders past *Sorbus*, maples and magnolias. Some of the trees which have been planted in recent years are already making a good show. A recent addition is a Persian garden – brickwork in stylised script with water runnels and small fountains.

 Features *Cottages orneés*; fine trees and mixed borders; good *Sorbus* and *Eucalyptus*; woodland walk; cream teas.

Owned by Mrs Bonar Sykes
Number of gardeners 1 part-time
Size 0.8ha (2 acres), plus parkland
English Heritage grade II

Corsham Court

CORSHAM SN13 0BZ

Tel & Fax 01249 701610
Location Signed from A4 Bath to Chippenham.
Opening hours 2 pm – 5.30 pm; Tuesday – Sunday & Bank Holiday Mondays; 20 March to 30 September. Plus 2 pm – 4.30 pm; Saturdays & Sundays; 1 January to 19 March & October to December.
Admission fee Adults £2; OAPs £1.50; Children £1. RHS members free.

Corsham is a major 18th-century landscape garden, one of the few where both Capability Brown and Humphry Repton worked. Then the flower garden was developed in the middle of the 19th century: box-edged borders and a pretty fountain, all kept up with some good modern planting. An 18-acre (7ha) arboretum was planted in the 1980s which is growing up well and is already well worth exploring. There are plans to landscape it and enlarge its collections in the near future.

 Features Fine trees; designed by Capability Brown and Humphry Repton; young arboretum; magnolias; amazing oriental plane *Platanus orientalis* whose sweeping limbs have rooted over a huge area.

Owned by James Methuen-Campbell
Number of gardeners 4
English Heritage grade II*

The Courts

HOLT, TROWBRIDGE BA14 6RR

Tel & Fax 01225 782340
Website www.nationaltrust.org.uk
Location In the middle of Holt village.

Opening hours 12 noon – 5.30 pm; Sunday – Friday; 24 March to 14 October.
Admission fee Adults £4; Children £1.50.

Holt Court (as it used to be called) is a 1920s masterpiece in the Hidcote style. It has rich colour plantings in a series of garden rooms and excellent plants, beautifully used. It is also well maintained by the Head Gardener, who came from Sissinghurst. Expect lots of improvements in the course of 2002, including a new kitchen garden, a sculpture exhibition and a new tea-room.

Features Topiary; plantsman's collection of plants; good herbaceous borders; fine collection of trees.

Owned by The National Trust
Number of gardeners 2
Size 10ha (25 acres)
English Heritage grade II

Heale House Garden

MIDDLE WOODFORD, SALISBURY
SP4 6NT

Tel 01722 782504
Location Signed off the western Woodford valley road, & from A345 & A360.
Opening hours 10 am – 5 pm; daily; all year. Closed on Mondays, except Bank Holidays.
Admission fee Adults £3.25; Children £1.50.

Many would agree that Heale is the prettiest garden in southern England. It sits at the bottom of a broad, chalk valley, with the River Avon and its leats flowing through. The house is Carolean, with substantial additions so sympathetically designed by Detmar Blow that it is difficult to know which parts belong to the original house. Harold Peto laid out the garden: you see his handiwork in the formal gardens which run up towards the south along an avenue of *Robina pseudoacacia* 'Umbraculifera' (recent replacements for the original laburnums). There are formal pools, terraces, balustrades and Italianate garden architecture on the way. Alongside the river are more balustrading, old rambling roses and a lawn which is richly planted with hybrid musk roses and herbaceous plants. On an island in the river is a Japanese garden, laid out in 1901 and much altered by the sheer growth of the original Japanese maples: however, the scarlet lacquered bridge and the neat tea-house seem almost new. Perhaps the best part of the garden is the old kitchen garden, surrounded by cob walls and designed around topiary and pergolas. Here, over 30 years from the mid-1960s onwards, Lady Anne Rasch developed a wonderful series of mixed borders, exuberantly planted with roses, clematis and herbaceous plants which is one of the best examples of the genre in England. But the garden and its excellent nursery are open all through the year, and there is always something to see, including swarms of cyclamen in autumn, and woodlands full of snowdrops and aconites in winter.

Features Roses (mainly old-fashioned); fruit; good herbaceous borders; Japanese gardens; good plant associations; first Christie's/HHA Garden of the Year in 1984; plant centre; garden & gift shop; tea & coffee shop.

Owned by Mr & Mrs Guy Rasch
Number of gardeners 2, plus owners
Size 3.2ha (8 acres)
English Heritage grade II*

Hillbarn House

GREAT BEDWYN, MARLBOROUGH
SN8 3NU

Tel 01672 870207 **Fax** 01672 871015
Location In High Street, opposite garage.
Opening hours 2 pm – 6 pm; 14 July.
Admission fee £2 Adults; 50p Children.

Many consider Hillbarn to be Lanning
Roper's masterpiece. It was a difficult site –
small and steep – in which he created an
illusion of size by dividing it up into small
compartments. One is a French-style
potager: among the first to be made in
England, it has helped to create a fashion.
Another compartment is a chequer-board
with herbs and bulbs. Alistair Buchanan's
topiary has become a major feature in recent
years. The hornbeam hedges and arbours
are exceptionally stylish, and there are
handsome plantings throughout the garden,
which is very well maintained with a lot of
family input.

Features Pleached limes; hornbeam
tunnel & stilted hedge; topiary; good
modern design; tea & biscuits.

Owned by Alistair J. Buchanan
Number of gardeners 1
Size 0.8ha (2 acres)

Home Covert

ROUNDWAY, DEVIZES SN10 2JA

Tel 01380 723407
Location 1 mile north of Devizes in Roundway Village.
Opening hours 2 pm – 6 pm; 17 April, 19 May, 19 June,
17 July & 21 August.
Admission fee Adults £2.50; Children free.

Home Covert is one of the most influential
and largest plantsman's gardens in England.
The knowledge and taste of the owners –
together with their generosity towards
visitors – have made it a cult garden among
cognoscenti and learner-gardeners alike. The
Phillips describe it as 'a botanical
madhouse': it would be truer to call it a
horticultural treasure-house. Every type of
plant is grown but, above all, rare trees:
Cercis racemosa, for example, and hundreds
of plants – perhaps thousands – grown from
seeds collected by such friends as Roy
Lancaster, Martyn Rix and Maurice Foster.
An older generation of plantsman is also
commemorated here – Maurice Mason,
Norman Haddon and Margery Fish, for
example. Home Covert is a large garden,
informally laid out within natural oak
woodland, and it needs a long time to see
round. Down in the bog garden are
collections of willows and alders, naturalised
Lathraea clandestina and swathes of
candelabra primulas. Near the house is an
enormous lawn, completely free of weeds,
with a view for miles down the Avon valley.
Raised beds, a rock garden, shade borders,
protected beds for tender plants, swarms of
erythroniums, fat clumps of lilies, old-
fashioned roses and wild species – there
seems no end to the number and variety of
what is grown here.

Features Woodland garden;
plantsman's plants of every kind;
extensive new plantings (2001); teas on
19 May.

Owned by Mr & Mrs John Phillips
Number of gardeners owners only
Size 13ha (33 acres)

Iford Manor

BRADFORD-ON-AVON BA15 2BA

Tel 01225 863146 **Fax** 01225 852364
Website www.ifordmanor.co.uk
Location 7 miles south-east of Bath, signed from
A36 & Bradford-on-Avon.
Opening hours 2 pm – 5 pm; Sundays & Easter Monday;
April & October. Plus Tuesday – Thursday, Saturdays,
Sundays & Bank Holiday Mondays from May to
September.
Admission fee Adults £3; OAPs & Children (over 10)
£2.50. Children under 10 free on weekdays but not
admitted at weekends.

Harold Peto's own Italianate garden on a
steep wooded hillside is meticulously
maintained and a delight to visit. Peto was a
fashionable architect with a passion for
classical Italian architecture and
landscaping. When he returned from
working in France and Italy, he bought Iford
to house his collections of statues and
architectural marbles. He planted phillyreas,
Italian cypresses and other Mediterranean
species and laid out the garden as a series of
formal terraces on the steep hillside behind
the house. The architectural highlights
include a Romanesque cloister, an octagonal
gazebo, and a gloriously colonnaded terrace.
Every detail is wonderfully photogenic,
especially when contrasted with wisterias,
roses or the well-chosen National Collection
of acanthus. The woodland garden is worth
exploring (it hides a recently restored
Japanese garden) and there is much of
horticultural interest too at Iford, notably a
meadow of naturalised martagon lilies.

 Features Harold Peto's own garden;
opulent Edwardian design; Italian
cypresses and handsome *Phillyrea*; martagon
lilies; cyclamen; roses; teas on Bank Holidays
and some weekends.

Owned by Mrs E. Cartwright-Hignett
Number of gardeners 3
Size 0.6ha (1½ acres) plus 5ha (12 acres) of woodland
NCCPG National Collections *Acanthus*
English Heritage grade I

Lacock Abbey

LACOCK, CHIPPENHAM SN15 2LG

Tel 01249 730141 **Fax** 01249 730501
Website www.nationaltrust.org.uk
Location 3 miles south of Chippenham, just east of A350.
Opening hours 11 am – 5.30 pm; daily; 16 March to
3 November. Closed 29 March.
Admission fee Adults £4; Children £2.40.

The National Trust has recently recreated
the 'botanic garden' planted by Lacock's
most famous past owner, William Fox
Talbot, the 'inventor' of photography. It was
he who planted many of the mature trees in
the park, including the tulip tree
(*Liriodendron tulipifera*), swamp cypress
(*Taxodium distichum*) and walnut (*Juglans
nigra*).

Features Snowdrops; crocus;
parkland.

Owned by The National Trust

Larmer Tree Gardens

TOLLARD ROYAL, SALISBURY
SP5 5PT

Tel 01725 516228 **Fax** 01725 516449
Website www.rushmore-estate.co.uk
Location Follow brown signs from A354 or B3081.
Opening hours 11 am – 6 pm; daily except Saturdays;
Easter Sunday to 31 October. Closed throughout July.
Admission fee Adults £3.75; OAPs £3; Children £2.50.

The Larmer Tree Gardens were laid out by General Augustus Pitt-Rivers as a public amenity. He put up a series of eccentric garden buildings around a spacious lawn of perhaps two acres: they include the Singing Theatre, the Indian Room, the Roman Temple and the Lower Indian Building in the Nepalese style, brought here in 1880 after the Colonial Exhibition in London. In the 1880s and 1890s, trainloads of East Enders were brought there by the philanthropic owner for a jolly cultural day in the country. His descendants have entirely restored the gardens since about 1990 and added some modern horticultural features. The best of these is a series of artificial pools in an artificial dell, surrounded by multi-coloured hydrangeas. All is set in light oak woodland with splendid thickets of cherry laurel. It is not a garden of the highest horticultural interest, though there are some venerable eucryphias, crinodendrons and stewartias. It is however spaciously laid out and very enjoyable to visit.

 Features Hydrangeas; woodland gardens; remarkable series of follies.

Owned by W. Gronow-Davies & Trustees
Number of gardeners 2
Size 4.2ha (11 acres)
English Heritage grade II

Admission fee Grounds & gardens: Adults £3; OAPs & Children £2.

Forget the lions and the loins, Longleat has a classic 18th-century landscape by Capability Brown, a home park of 600 acres best seen from Heaven's Gate and a grand Victorian garden reworked by Russell Page in the 1930s. Capability Brown's landscape has been carefully managed and replanted over many years, so that it keeps its intended form. The Victorian garden between the house and the elegant conservatory built by Wyatville in the 1820s is now a very beautiful rose garden. The plantings of ornamental trees and rhododendrons woodlands have been thickened and updated with many new introductions. In short, Lord Bath (like his father before him) has conserved the best of Longleat and reinvigorated the rest. Worth another visit.

Features Woodland garden; topiary; rhododendrons & azaleas; good herbaceous borders; fine collection of trees; orangery; 'love labyrinth' with saucily-named roses; sun maze & lunar labyrinth; shops; cafeterias & restaurants.

Owned by 7th Marquess of Bath
Number of gardeners 8
English Heritage grade I

Longleat House

WARMINSTER BA12 7NW

Tel 01985 844400 **Fax** 01985 844885
Website www.longleat.co.uk
Location Off A362 Warminster to Frome road.
Opening hours 10 am – 4 pm; daily; 16 March to 31 December. Closed 25 December. Closes at 5 pm at weekends, Bank Holidays and during school holidays.

The Mead Nursery

BROKERSWOOD, WESTBURY BA13 4EG

Tel 01373 859990
Location Near Rudge, off A36 or A361.
Opening hours 9 am – 5 pm, Wednesday – Saturday, & Bank Holiday Mondays; 12 noon – 5 pm, Sundays, 1 February to 10 October. 12 noon – 5 pm on 18 August for NGS.

Admission fee Adults £2 & Children £1.50 (tea & cake included) on 18 August. Otherwise free.

The Mead Nursery specialises in alpine plants (including varieties suitable for trough plantings), pot-grown bulbs and (mainly short-growing) herbaceous perennials. All plants are grown in peat-free compost. The display garden is excellent: raised alpine beds, a sink garden, a bog bed, a newly developed pond, and herbaceous borders planted with colour combinations in mind.

 Features Perennials; alpines; bulbs; all plants grown on site; pretty demonstration garden.

Owned by Stephen & Emma Lewis-Dale
Size 0.3ha (¾ acre)

Oare House

OARE, MARLBOROUGH SN8 4JQ

Tel 01672 562428
Location In village, west side of A345.
Opening hours 2 pm – 6 pm; 21 April & 28 July.
Admission fee Adults £2; Children free.

Oare has an approach along lime avenues and tall hedges whose grandeur is echoed by the main garden behind: a huge apron of walled lawn, with majestic mixed borders at the sides, lead the eye over a half-hidden swimming pool to a grand ride and on to the Marlborough Downs beyond. Intimacy exists only in some small enclosed gardens to the side and in the kitchen garden. Here are a magnificent herbaceous border in reds and yellows, a tunnel of fruit trees and vegetables in neat rows. Half a mile or so away, alongside the minor road to West Stowell, is the arboretum, with clumps of

Sassafras albidum at the entrance and about 20 different record-breaking trees – quite a surprise in this rustic backwater.

 Features Good herbaceous borders; fine collection of trees; tall hedges of field maple; extensive new plantings in arboretum; light refreshments.

Owned by Henry Keswick
Number of gardeners 3
Size 2.2ha (5½ acres), excluding arboretum
English Heritage grade II

Old Vicarage

EDINGTON, WESTBURY BA13 4QF

Tel & Fax 01380 830512
Location On B3098 in Edington village.
Opening hours 2 pm – 6 pm; 9 June.
Admission fee Adults £3.50; Children free.

John d'Arcy bought the Old Vicarage in 1982: it is now one of the best examples of a plantsman's garden in southern England. The site offers a surprising range of mini-habitats, and d'Arcy took advantage of their potential to grow the widest possible number of plants. The features now include a sunken garden, a shady pergola, an avenue of fastigiate hornbeams *Carpinus betulus* 'Fastigiata', a gravel garden where *Morina afghanica* and *Ptilostemon afer* seed around, hot walls, raised beds, peat beds and shady beds – all blended with the rest of the garden so that no feature dominates any part of it. d'Arcy's great skill is as a cultivator: the fact that there is so much colour and interest at every time of the year proves that good plantsmanship can produce effects to challenge the most carefully designed and planted of gardens. Trees are underplanted with shrubs, which are underscored in turn by herbaceous plants and bulbs, several different plants being placed together to give a succession of interest throughout the year. d'Arcy's special interests include mahonias, cyclamen, nerines and hollies. He is also well known as a plant collector. *Corydalis flexuosa* came from Sichuan in 1989; several new species of *Dierama* came from South Africa, together with such new species of *Geranium* as *G. harveyi* and *G. pulchrum*. All are still here, together with the living holotype of *Salvia darcyi*.

Features Plantsman's plants – a collector's collection; herbaceous borders; alpine plants; shade plants; gravel garden; small arboretum.

Owned by John d'Arcy
Number of gardeners 1
Size 1ha (2½ acres)
NCCPG National Collections *Oenothera*

Pound Hill House

WEST KINGTON, CHIPPENHAM
SN14 7JG

Tel 01249 782822 **Fax** 01249 782953
Location Follow signs from A420 between 'The Shoe' & Marshfield (Nettleton & West Kington turning).
Opening hours 2 pm – 5 pm; daily; April to October. On 7 July for NGS and on 7 & 8 September for Greenfinger Appeal.
Admission fee Adults £2.50; Children free. RHS members free from July to October.

The garden has been laid out and planted since 1988 by Barbara and Philip Stockitt, with advice from their daughter, garden-designer Bunny Guinness, a Chelsea gold medal-winner. They supplemented the Cotswold dry-stone walls with hedges of yew and box to make a series of neat rooms, in scale with the substantial Cotswold farmhouse. Barbara is a nurserywoman, the owner of the highly successful wholesalers

West Kington Nurseries and, incidentally, a sister of David Austin the rose-breeder. You approach the garden through an excellent small retail nursery which is beautifully laid out with a most inviting selection of plants, especially topiary and architectural plants, and well-integrated into the overall design. Inside the garden proper you encounter first a neat, formal kitchen garden, full of interesting vegetables, and a small rose garden of polyanthas 'The Fairy' and 'Little White Pet' grown as standards. The main part of the garden lies behind the house, most instructively laid out with structure given by box edging, yew cones and architectural plants at key points in the design. The plantings offer a stylish selection of plants, including many of the best modern cultivars, thickly planted and very well grown. Two particularly good features are a short avenue of Spanish chestnuts clipped to keep the trees small and the leaves large, and another of *Betula jacquemontii* entirely underplanted on both sides by pulmonarias – very striking in spring. But this excellent 2-acre showcase-garden is interesting throughout the year.

Features Woodland garden; roses (ancient & modern); fruit; alpine plants; walled area for topiary & specimen plants; adjacent to West Kington Nurseries Plant Centre; refreshments.

Owned by Mr & Mrs Philip Stockitt
Number of gardeners 1
Size 0.8ha (2 acres)

Sharcott Manor

PEWSEY SN9 5PA

Tel 01672 563485
Location Off A345, one mile south-west of Pewsey.
Opening hours 11 am – 5 pm; first Wednesday of every month; April to October. Plus 2 pm – 6 pm; 8 April & 8 July.

Admission fee Adults £2; Children free.

This extensive modern garden has been quite transformed over the last 20 years into a densely planted plantsman's paradise. There is much to see as you move gently between the garden rooms near the house and out into the spacious lawns and woodland garden. There are harmonies and contrasts to please the most colour-conscious, while the dark shady lake at the bottom is a haven of romantic broodiness. Sharcott is an excellent garden which deserves to be better known.

 Features Plantsman's collection of plants; good herbaceous borders; woodland garden and stream garden; good plant sales area, all propagateded from garden; homemade teas.

Owned by Captain & Mrs David Armytage
Number of gardeners 2 part-time
Size 2.2ha (6 acres)

Sherston Parva Nursery Ltd

MALMESBURY ROAD, SHERSTON SN16 0NX

Tel 01666 841066   **Fax** 01666 841132
Website www.sherstonparva.com
Location On B4040, 3 miles south of Westonbirt.
Opening hours 10 am – 5 pm; daily; all year. Closed in January.

Sherston Parva is an established nursery specialising in clematis and other climbing plants and wall shrubs. It also sells herbaceous plants. It has a stock of about 300 different clematis, though not all are propagated and available at one time so it is always worth asking if you want a particular

cultivar. The nursery in any event makes it fairly clear that 'we feel it is more beneficial to our customers to remove from our list those varieties which have been so obviously superseded'. But there is always an excellent selection and their other climbers and wall shrubs are well-chosen. They look wonderful against the nursery's own Cotswold stone walls.

 Features Clematis; climbing plants; wall shrubs.

Stourhead

STOURTON BA12 6QD

Tel 01747 841152   **Fax** 01747 842005
Website www.nationaltrust.org.uk
Location 3 miles north of Mere, signed off the A303/B3092.
Opening hours 9 am – 7 pm, or dusk if earlier; daily; all year.
Admission fee Adults £4.90; Children £2.70. Reductions in winter.

Whatever the weather or season, Stourhead conveys a sense of majesty and harmony. Try it early on a May morning, when the air is sweet with azaleas. Or scuff the fallen leaves in late November. Think of it 200 years ago, without the rhododendrons or exotic trees, when all the beech trees were interplanted with spruces and the colours came all from shades of green. Ponder the 18th-century aesthetic, which esteemed tones and shades more highly than colours, and follow the iconographic tour inspired (they say) by Virgil. Spot the change from classical to gothic, from Pope to Walpole, and wonder at the National Trust's ability to maintain it so well with only six gardeners.

 Features Snowdrops; rhododendrons & azaleas; mature conifers; fine collection of trees; good autumn colour; tallest tulip tree *Liriodendron tulipifera* (37m) in the British Isles, and seven other record tree species; new National Trust shop & plant centre; famous hotel/pub opposite gate.

Owned by The National Trust
Number of gardeners 6
Size 40ha (100 acres)
English Heritage grade I

Stourton House Flower Garden

STOURTON, WARMINSTER BA12 6QF

Tel 01747 840417
Location Next to Stourhead, 2 miles north of A303 at Mere.
Opening hours 11 am – 6 pm; Wednesdays, Thursdays, Sundays & Bank Holiday Mondays; April to November. Groups at other times by appointment.
Admission fee Adults £3; Children 50p.

This 5-acre garden next to Stourhead is famous for its dried flowers, thanks to the energy and personality of Elizabeth Bullivant. It also has a strong design and some beautiful plant combinations. The baroque curves to the hedges are completely original. Stourton is also a garden with a tremendous number of different and unusual plants and some particular favourites – hence the enormous collection of hydrangeas, the split-corona daffodils and the plantings of rhododendrons, azaleas and camellias. Mrs Bullivant has also been successful in plant competitions at RHS shows, bringing up a great variety of plants to show to a wider audience. But Stourton is not a garden for show – rather, it is a well-loved private garden with a sideline in dried flowers. It is also very good at all seasons –

and especially in early autumn when it is frankly stunning. The garden suffered somewhat from the weather in 2001, but Mrs Bullivant hopes to get it up to scratch again this year.

Features Good herbaceous borders; Victorian greenhouse; elegantly curving hedges of Leylandii; 270 different hydrangeas; delphiniums; hosts of daffodils, in innumerable shapes, sizes and colours; plants & dried flowers for sale all year; homemade teas; light lunches; sticky cakes.

Owned by Mrs Anthony Bullivant
Size 2ha (5 acres)

Westdale Nurseries

HOLT ROAD, BRADFORD-ON-AVON BA15 1TS

Tel & Fax 01225 863258
Location 1 mile east of Bradford town centre; left-hand side.
Opening hours 9 am – 6 pm; daily except Christmas.

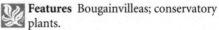

Westdale has made quite an impact at RHS Flower Shows in recent years with its wonderful displays of bougainvilleas. It lists over 100 different cultivars, which are available in different sizes. All can be seen growing in their extensive glasshouses outside Bradford-on-Avon. But their range of other conservatory plants is very wide, and they are enthusiastic plantsmen, willing to try any plant which may have value as an ornament to the conservatory or greenhouse. Well worth a visit.

Features Bougainvilleas; conservatory plants.

Wilton House

WILTON, SALISBURY SP2 0BJ

Tel 01722 746720   **Fax** 01722 744447
Location In village, 3 miles west of Salisbury on A30.
Opening hours 10.30 am – 5.30 pm; daily;
27 March – 27 October.
Admission fee Adults £4; Children £3.

Wilton has a sublime 18th-century park around its classical Inigo Jones house, which is famous for its paintings. It is this stupendous parkland setting above the river Nadder which is the chief delight of visiting the gardens at Wilton. There are comparatively few horticultural excitements, though the house has pleasant mixed borders along one of its sides and a stylish modern garden, rather formal, in the entrance court designed by Lady Tollemache. On the edge of the park are a pretty new rose garden and an oriental water garden: opinions are divided as to the merits of the new millennium water feature.

 Features Roses; handsome cedars; famous Palladian bridge; magnificent golden-leaved oak; self-service restaurant.

Owned by Earl of Pembroke/Wilton House Trust
Number of gardeners 4
Size 8.3ha (21 acres)
English Heritage grade I

Wiltshire College Lackham

LACOCK, CHIPPENHAM SN15 2NY

Tel 01249 466800   **Fax** 01249 444474
Website www.lackham.co.uk
Location 3 miles south of Chippenham on A350.

Opening hours 10 am – 5 pm; Sundays & Bank Holiday Mondays; May to August.
Admission fee Adults £2; Concessions £1.50; Children free.

Lackham is among the best of the old county college gardens and now better known, following its appearance last year on the 'Roots & Shoots' TV gardening programme. A major extension was opened in 1996 – an Italian-style garden, an historic rose garden, a sensory garden, herbaceous borders and illustrations of English gardens over each of the last four centuries. The heart of Lackham is its walled garden of flowers, ornamentals, herbs, fruit and vegetables, beautifully laid out to educate and delight. In one of the glasshouses is the champion plant of *Citrus medica* which grew the largest citron ever seen in Britain (according to the Guinness Book of Records). The grounds are good for an exploration too, especially in bluebell time: there has been a lot of attractive companion planting for the National Collection of poplars.

 Features Plantsman's collection of plants; herbs; fruit & vegetables; plants under glass; daffodils; good herbaceous borders; fine collection of trees; alpine plants; bluebells; roses of every kind; sensory garden; laurel maze; woodland walk; souvenirs for sale; refreshments.

Owned by Wiltshire College Lackham
Number of gardeners 4, plus students
Size 8ha (20 acres)
NCCPG National Collections *Populus*

WORCESTERSHIRE

Worcestershire has been reconstituted not as a county (which it was until 1974) but as a District Council. But such is the feeling of distinct identity that we have treated it in this book as a legal county again: the same applies to Herefordshire, to which it was yoked for 25 years. In fact, from a horticultural standpoint, Worcestershire has rather more going for it than its ex-partner: a flourishing National Gardens Scheme, the site of the only dedicated horticultural college in England at Pershore (a RHS Partner College), the headquarters of the Alpine Garden Society, ten National Collection holders, and two of the most popular gardening shows in the country – the Spring Gardening Show (10–12 May 2002) and the Autumn Garden & Country Show (28–29 September 2002), both at the Three Counties Showground at Malvern. Worcestershire also has some excellent specialist nurseries, including Cotswold Garden Flowers, Old Court Nurseries and Stone House Cottage Garden. Though few of its historic parks and gardens are open to the public, they include that great plantsman's garden Spetchley Park (substantially re-made by a great-nephew of Miss Ellen Willmott) and Witley Court (now undergoing extensive renovation by English Heritage).

Cotswold Garden Flowers

SANDS LANE, BADSEY, EVESHAM
WR11 5EZ

Tel 01386 422829 **Fax** 01386 49844
Website www.cgf.net
Location On south-east edge of village.
Opening hours 9 am – 5.30 pm; Monday – Friday. 10 am – 5.30 pm; Saturday – Sunday. Other times by appointment. Closed at weekends from mid-October to March.
Admission fee Free.

Though it was founded as recently as 1991, Cotswold Garden Flowers is already the market leader for rare perennials and small shrubs: over 8,000 different cultivars are grown in the fascinating garden. The nursery's catalogue is both amusing and informative, but it is nothing compared to the joy of visiting the nursery and having the opportunity to see so many new and interesting plants. The owner has a knack for seeking out and introducing plants which are highly 'garden-worthy'.

Owned by Bob Brown
NCCPG National Collections *Lysimachia*

Eastgrove Cottage Garden

SANKYNS GREEN, SHRAWLEY, LITTLE WITLEY, WORCESTER WR6 6LQ

Tel 01299 896389
Website www.eastgrove.co.uk
Location On road between Great Witley (on A443) & Shrawley (on B4196).
Opening hours 2 pm – 5 pm; Thursday – Sunday, plus Bank Holiday Mondays; April to July. Also Thursday – Saturday; 1 September to 12 October.
Admission fee Adults £2.50 (£3 in June & July).

Eastgrove is a very pretty, 17th-century, half-timbered, black-and-white cottage, with an equally pretty cottage garden that has been entirely made by the Skinners since they bought the near-derelict property in 1975. The scale is small, but the quality and variety of the plantings are stunning. There are herbs, dwarf conifers, a developing collection of trees which they call an arboretum, a bog garden, a raised bed (known as the 'Great Wall of China') and, above all, thickly planted herbaceous plants. The design and planting of the borders is carefully thought through: the 'secret garden' concentrates on mauves, pinks, silvers and crimsons. Although perhaps best in high summer, the garden is good enough to visit at any time of the year and beautifully maintained. The nursery propagates only plants from the garden and has a list of over 1,000 different varieties. Specialities include aquilegias, hardy chrysanthemums, dianthus, heleniums, irises, peonies, penstemons, rosemary, salvias, violas, pelargoniums, and other tender perennials.

 Features Cottage garden; rose arches; plantsman's plants; herbaceous borders; wall plantings; pots & containers; attached to good small nursery.

Owned by Malcolm & Carol Skinner
Number of gardeners 2
Size 0.6ha (1½ acres)

Gorsehill Abbey Farm

COLLIN LANE, BROADWAY WR12 7PB

Tel 01386 852208   **Fax** 01386 858570
Location 1 mile north of Broadway, off A44 roundabout; east for 400 yards, farm on left.
Opening hours 2.30 pm – 6 pm; Thursday; July & August. And by appointment.
Admission fee Adults £2; Children free.

Gorsehill Abbey Farm is an organic garden surrounded by perry orchards and open countryside, made since 1992 and still developing. The owners are keen plantsmen, so they grow a wide variety of interesting and unusual plants with the aim of providing year-round interest. Features include a large mixed border, pergolas, ponds and water features, wildlife areas, and extensive fruit and vegetable gardens. The garden was featured in *The Garden* in August 2000.

Features Organic garden in an organic dairy farm.

Owned by Mike & Diane Stacey
Number of gardeners owners only
Size 0.8ha (2 acres)

The Manor House

BIRLINGHAM, PERSHORE WR10 3AF

Tel 01386 750005   **Fax** 01386 751288
Location At south-east end of Birlingham.

Opening hours 11 am – 5 pm; 9 June (Plant Fair), 13, 16, 20, 23 & 27 June.

Admission fee Adults £2.50; Children free. £3 on 9 June.

The garden was first set out in the late 1780s: relics of these original plantings include giant box hedges and a very fine *Phillyrea*, as well as the ha-ha which allows the eye an unhindered sweep to the River Avon and the magnificent views of Bredon Hill. Jane Williams-Thomas has replanted the garden with a designer's eye, making terraces and using hedges to create enclosed intimate areas. One important element of the design has been the use of many benches to encourage repose and create a peaceful atmosphere. Roses are a particular love – the garden has over 100 different cultivars – and they are interplanted with silver plants and perennials that will respond to the dry, warm site. The white garden is particularly successful: it has brick paths surrounded by yew hedges and the lush, romantic planting which characterises the whole garden. Rare plants are used in unusual combinations to bring out contrasts and harmonies of form and colour. The garden is a member of the Quiet Garden Trust.

 Features Plantsman's collection of plants; good herbaceous borders; walled garden; white garden; teas.

Owned by Mr & Mrs David Williams-Thomas
Number of gardeners owners, plus part-time help
Size 0.7ha (1¾ acres)

The Priory

KEMERTON, TEWKESBURY GL20 7JN

Tel 01386 725258
Location In Kemerton village.
Opening hours Parties by appointment between 17 June & 27 September.

Admission fee Adults £2.50; Children free.

The Priory is a late-summer comet, brilliant in August and September when annuals and tender plants supplement the perennial colour planting. Mrs Healing has many spent years studying plants and perfecting her colour gradings. The results are worth a long journey to see and to study: the crimson border is the best there has ever been.

 Features Very good, colour-themes herbaceous borders; roses (mainly old-fashioned); plants for plantsmen; knot garden; newly designed millennium vegetable garden (2000); teas on open Sundays.

Owned by The Hon. Mrs Healing
Number of gardeners 1
Size 1.6ha (4 acres)

Rickard's Hardy Ferns Ltd

KYRE PARK, TENBURY WELLS WR15 8RP

Tel 01885 410282   **Fax** 01885 410729
Location Off B4214 Bromyard road, 4 miles south of Tenbury Wells.
Opening hours 11 am – 5 pm; Wednesday – Monday; April to October. And by appointment.

Rickard's is probably the best-known nursery specialising in ferns in the British Isles. It has won a succession of gold medals at the Chelsea Flower Show in recent years. A great number are offered for sale, including some of the fashionable half-hardy tree ferns. Nearly 1,000 different species and cultivars grow in the collection at the nursery. Kyre Park is an historic landscape – mainly a classical 18th-century landscape with lakes, but some of its elements date back to the 17th century.

 Features Ferns of every kind and size.

NCCPG National Collections Cystopteris; Polypodium; Thelypteridaceae
English Heritage grade II

Spetchley Park

WORCESTER WR5 1RS

Tel 01905 345224 **Fax** 01453 511915
Website www.spetchleygardens.co.uk
Location 2 miles east of Worcester on A422.
Opening hours 11 am – 5 pm; Tuesday – Friday & Bank Holiday Mondays, (plus 2 pm – 5 pm on Sundays); April to September.
Admission fee Adults £3.50; Children £1.70.

In a classic English landscaped park, three generations of Berkeleys have created one of the best plantsman's gardens in the Midlands. Ellen Willmott was the owner's great aunt and many of the most exciting trees and shrubs date from her time – a gnarled specimen of the laciniate walnut (*Juglans nigra* 'Laciniata'), for example. In the Fountain Gardens, *Tulipa sprengeri* has seeded and naturalised over a large area. Other spring flowers include peonies, columbines and masses of bulbs. In summer, there are hundreds of different roses – old-fashioned roses, tea roses, David Austin roses, floribunda roses – every type of rose is here. Martagon lilies have naturalised in large quantities. The conservatory is crammed with unusual plants. The planting continues: everywhere in the garden are new designs, new plants and new combinations. A whole new garden has been planted to commemorate the millennium, with tunnels of *Cercis*

canadensis 'Forest Pansy' and *Robinia hispida* 'Macrophylla'. Because of its scale and variety, this garden offers something to everyone, but most especially to the plantsman.

 Features Many good plants of every kind for plantsmen; roses (ancient & modern); rhododendrons & azaleas; daffodils; good herbaceous borders; fine trees; a deer park; good new plantings in the kitchen garden; naturalised lilies; teas & refreshments.

Owned by R.J. Berkeley
Number of gardeners 4
Size 12ha (30 acres)
English Heritage grade II*

Stone House Cottage Garden

STONE, KIDDERMINSTER DY10 4BG

Tel 01562 69902 **Fax** 01562 69960
Website www.shcn.co.uk
Location In village, 2 miles from Kidderminster on A448.
Opening hours 10 am – 5.30 pm; Wednesday – Saturday; March to September. Plus Bank Holiday Mondays. And by appointment between October & March.
Admission fee Adults £2.50; Children free.

This is the garden of a famous nursery, which it matches for the range of beautiful and unusual plants it offers. The owners are compulsive plantsmen and, as the garden is small, they have to move plants around or replace them altogether to make room for new arrivals. This means that the garden is constantly developing and improving – especially since much thought is given to the way each plant will associate with its neighbours. Around the walls is an eccentric collection of follies built as towers, which makes this garden quite unique.

Features Plantsman's plants; herbs; good herbaceous borders; alpine plants; unusual climbing plants; roses (mainly old-fashioned & climbers); excellent nursery attached.

Owned by James & Louisa Arbuthnott
Number of gardeners 1
Size 0.3ha (¾ acre)

The Walled Garden

6 ROSE TERRACE, WORCESTER
WR5 1BU

Tel & Fax 01905 354629
Location Off Fort Royal Hill (which is off A44); ½ mile from Cathedral.
Opening hours For NGS, and by appointment.
Admission fee Adults £2; Children 50p.

This all-organic private garden is a centre for the study of herbs. The owners have reclaimed the walled garden, dating from Victorian times, and planted a series of gardens for sitting and thinking.

 Features Herb gardens.

Owned by William & Julia Scott
Number of gardeners owners only
Size 0.3ha (¾ acre)

Webbs of Wychbold

WYCHBOLD, DROITWICH WR9 0DG

Tel 01527 860000 **Fax** 01527 861284
Website www.webbsofwychbold.co.uk
Location 1 mile from M5, Jct 5: follow brown tourist signs.
Opening hours 9 am – 6 pm; Monday – Friday (8 pm April – September). 9 am – 6 pm; Saturdays & Bank Holidays. 10.30 am – 4.30 pm; Sundays.

Webbs are a major garden centre, a regional heavyweight with several trade awards for excellence. They have an extremely large stock of plants of every kind, as well as a wide range of in-house retail opportunities of interest to gardeners and non-gardeners alike. They have a reputation as plant-introducers too: a form of *Nemesia denticulata* which they call 'Confetti' and *Coreopsis* 'Calypso' are two of their plant introductions. Their display gardens (over an acre of them) include a herb garden, a series of patio gardens and a sequence of other model lay-outs which they call the Riverside Gardens. Tours of the nurseries and their National Collection of shrubby potentillas are also available. Webbs will be hosting a two-day 'Garden Enthusiasts' Summer Spectacular' in conjunction with the RHS on 28 & 29 June 2002: details from the RHS Event Finder www.rhs.org.uk

 Features Model gardens; prize-winning garden centre; gift shop; restaurant & café.

Size 20ha (50 acres)
NCCPG National Collections *Potentilla fruticosa* cvs.

Witley Court

GREAT WITLEY WR6 7JT

Tel 01299 896636
Website www.english-heritage.org.uk
Location 10 miles north of Worcester on A443.
Opening hours 10 am – 6 pm (5 pm in October); daily; April to October. 9 am – 4 pm; Wednesday – Sunday; November to March. Closed 1 January & 24–26 December.
Admission fee Adults £3.80; Concessions £2.90; Children £1.90.

The gardens at Witley Court are undergoing extensive restoration and are increasingly in good condition, thanks to English Heritage.

You enter through the rhododendron woods, planted mainly with hardy hybrids under a canopy of American conifers. At the bottom of the valley, below the cascade which runs from the lake, is an Elizabeth Frink statue – one of eight sculptures in the woods. More interesting, though, is the spectacular ruined mansion and the immense formal gardens behind. They are one of William Andrews Nesfield's masterpieces, built on a monumental scale by the first Earl of Dudley: English Heritage has plans to restore them during the course of the year (2002) and to add some new contemporary gardens too. The sheer size of the roofless conservatory and the fountains is remarkable: a place to fantasise about life among the plutocrats 100 years ago.

 Features Victorian formal garden; rhododendron woodlands; café.

Owned by English Heritage
Number of gardeners 2
Size 16ha (40 acres)
English Heritage grade II*

YORKSHIRE, EAST RIDING OF

Since the demise of much-disliked Humberside, the East Riding has been reconstituted as an administrative area. Many of the Yorkshire's gardening institutions are organised on an all-Yorkshire basis: thus, for example, the Yorkshire Gardens Trust and the Yorkshire Group of the NCCPG are county-wide societies. Sledmere House is the outstanding historic garden in East Yorkshire, though Burton Constable is also well-known for its Capability Brown landscape garden. There are comparatively few good modern gardens in East Yorkshire, apart from the charming water-gardens at Burnby, where a National Collection of waterlilies (*Nymphaea*) is displayed in a beautifully landscaped site. There are four further National Collections in East Yorkshire, including a collection of *Crataegus laevigata* and *C. monogyna* cultivars at the University of Hull's garden at Cottingham – a botanic garden which has lost the botany department that was once the reason for its existence. There is a sprinkling of gardens that open for the National Gardens Scheme in East Yorkshire, which has its own county organiser. There are few nurseries of national repute: one which is not listed below is Swanland Nurseries, which has a good collection of *Pelargonium* cultivars – over 800 of them. Burnby Hall offers free entry to RHS members – and a very enjoyable garden it is.

Bishop Burton Botanic Garden

BISHOP BURTON COLLEGE, BEVERLEY
HU17 8QG

Tel 01964 553000   **Fax** 01964 553101
Location In Bishop Burton: entrance off village green.
Opening hours 9 am – 5 pm; Monday to Friday; all year.

Admission fee Free.

Bishop Burton is a college where horticulture is taught, so this is not so much a botanic garden as a demonstration garden to teach students about plants. The walled garden has areas where fruit, vegetables and herbs are grown, together with a display of good herbaceous plants and shrubs. There are also several glasshouses. Outside, in the park, is a 19th-century landscape with good wellingtonias, cedars and a cucumber tree (*Magnolia acuminata*).

 Features A good collection of plants; fine trees in park.

Owned by Bishop Burton College
Number of gardeners 4, plus students
Size 0.8ha (2 acres) walled garden, plus park

Burnby Hall Gardens

POCKLINGTON YO42 2QF

Tel 01759 302068 **Fax** 01759 388272
Website www.burnbyhallgardens.co.uk
Location Off A1079 13 miles east of York.
Opening hours 10 am – 6 pm; daily; 29 March to 29 September.
Admission fee Adults £2.50; OAPs £2; Children £1. RHS members free.

Burnby Hall is famed for its waterlilies, planted by Amos Perry in the 1930s and now totalling over 80 different cultivars. They are grown in two long, landscaped lakes. But there is much more to Burnby: a rock garden, heather beds, a 'secret garden', seasonal bedding and a good collection of conifers all contribute to its visitor-friendly air. There is a new woodland walk, and the walled garden is being restored as a Victorian garden. Follow the tarmac path around the lakes: Burnby is a grand place for a promenade, especially when a brass band is playing on Sunday afternoons in summer.

 Features Rock garden; mature conifers; good herbaceous borders; café; gift shop.

Owned by Stewarts Trust
Number of gardeners 3
Size 3.2ha (8 acres)
NCCPG National Collections *Nymphaea*

Burton Agnes Hall Gardens

BURTON AGNES, DRIFFIELD YO25 0ND

Tel 01262 490324 **Fax** 01262 490513
Location On A166 Driffield-Bridlington road.
Opening hours 11 am – 5 pm; daily; April to October.
Admission fee Adults £2.40; OAPs £2.15; Children £1. RHS members free.

The old walled garden has been re-designed in a neo-Elizabethan style to complement the house. As well as a *potager* and herb garden it has such unconventional features as a life-size games board for snakes & ladders, a jungle garden and a maze with a riddle. Rather more conventional are the plantings of shrub roses (lots of them), clematis and herbaceous plants. It is most enjoyable to visit.

 Features Good modern plantings; new pebble mosaic (2000); café & ice-cream parlour.

Owned by Burton Agnes Hall Preservation Trust Ltd
Number of gardeners 3½
NCCPG National Collections *Campanula*

Burton Constable

SKIRLAUGH, HULL HU11 4LN

Tel 01964 562400 **Fax** 01964 563229
Website www.burtonconstable.com
Location Via Hull B1238 to Sproatley follow brown tourist signs.
Opening hours 12.30 pm – 5 pm (last admission 4.15); Saturday – Thursday; Easter Sunday to 31 October.
Admission fee Adults £1; Children 50p.

The main feature around the massive house is a Capability Brown landscape: his original plans are still shown. However, the foundation has recently received lottery funding for a major restoration of the gardens, including the four acres of 19th-century pleasure grounds, so this is a garden to watch in future.

Features Woodland garden; good herbaceous borders; fine 18th-century orangery; Victorian parterre; shop; light snacks.

Owned by Burton Constable Foundation
Number of gardeners 3
English Heritage grade II

Sledmere House

SLEDMERE, DRIFFIELD YO25 3XG

Tel 01377 236637   **Fax** 01377 236500
Location Off A166 between York & Bridlington.
Opening hours 11 am – 4.30 pm; daily except Mondays & Saturdays; Easter weekend, then from 6 May to 22 September.
Admission fee Adults £2; Children £1.

Sledmere has a classical Capability Brown landscape: his originals plans can be seen in the museum. An Italianate formal garden was added in 1911, with Greek and Roman busts swathed in climbing roses. In recent years, since the arrival of the head gardener from Castle Howard, Sledmere has seen extensive replanting in the 18th-century walled garden and around the house. A new knot garden is growing up quickly.

Features Climbing roses; mature conifers; deer park; Capability Brown landscape; craft & gift shop; tea-terrace & cafeteria.

Owned by Sir Tatton Sykes
Number of gardeners 3
English Heritage grade I

YORKSHIRE, NORTH

North Yorkshire corresponds with the old North Riding of Yorkshire: it is a county of large estates and small market towns. Among its historic gardens are some of the grandest landscapes in England: Castle Howard, Duncombe Park and Studley Royal are all Grade I gardens. North Yorkshire also has three very important modern gardens – Harlow Carr, Newby Hall and Thorpe Perrow – each quite different in character but all horticultural heavyweights. The Cockpit Garden at Richmond Castle will open later this year as the fourth in English Heritage's Contemporary Heritage Gardens initiative. Harlow Carr, for years the flagship the Northern Horticultural Society, joined the RHS's growing fleet of top gardens in 2001 and has now embarked on substantial redevelopment and improvement at the RHS's hands. The National Gardens Scheme does well in North Yorkshire and so does the NCCPG, which has over 20 National Collections in the county. The best nurseries are also in North Yorkshire, including R.V. Roger Ltd, which has a good line in exotic 'architectural' plants, and the *Pulmonaria* and rare plant specialist Stillingfleet Lodge Nurseries: Stillingfleet also has a good garden which RHS members can visit free. Newby Hall, Millgate House and Harlow Carr are also free-access gardens for RHS members. The Royal Horticultural Society has a Partner College at Askham Bryan, the old county horticultural college: it has about a dozen public lectures and workshops throughout the year – details from the School Secretary on 01904 772230.

Beningbrough Hall & Gardens

BENINGBROUGH, YORK YO30 1DD

Tel 01904 470666   **Fax** 01904 470002
Website www.nationaltrust.org.uk
Location 8 miles north-west of York off the A19.
Opening hours 11 am – 5.30 pm; Saturday – Wednesday, plus Good Friday & Fridays in July & August; 23 March to 3 November.

Admission fee Adults £3.60; Children £1.80.

Beningbrough is approached by an avenue of limes through stately parkland. Apart from a gloomy Victorian shrubbery, the gardens are modern and pretty. Two small formal gardens, one with reds and oranges and the other with pastel shades, lie on either side of the early Georgian house. A sumptuous mixed border, graded from hot colours to cool, runs right to the gate of the walled kitchen garden.

Castle Howard

YORK YO6 7DA

Tel 01653 648444 **Fax** 01653 648501
Website www.castlehoward.co.uk
Location 15 miles north-east of York, off A64.
Opening hours 10 am – 4.30 pm (last entry); daily;
15 March to 3 November. Ray Wood on Wednesdays &
at weekends.
Admission fee Adults £5; Children £3.

Be prepared to spend all day at Castle Howard: it is essential visiting both for plantsmen and for anyone with a sense of history. At every time of the year, there are really good walks through woodlands and formal gardens, along the terraces and beside the water, and views of the buildings and sculptures in the landscape. The heroic megapark was first laid out by the 3rd Earl of Carlisle in 1700. Vanbrugh filled the five axes with landscapings and important buildings: the south lake, the terraces, the statues and the waterfalls down to the new river are all his. Vanbrugh's masterpiece, built in 1724-6, is the Temple of the Four Winds. The Mausoleum was designed by Hawksmoor in 1728. In front of the house are the remains of a vast 19th-century parterre, whose centre point is the Atlas fountain built by Nesfield in the 1850s. Within a walled garden is a series of grand 1980s rose gardens (slightly Surrey) designed by Jim Russell, with every type of rose from ancient to modern. Of more interest to gardeners and plantsmen is Ray Wood, where a fine and historic collection of rhododendrons and other ericaceous plants (all meticulously labelled) is destined to develop as one of the greatest woodland gardens in Europe. The rhododendrons and other plants of 20th-century plant hunters are here in abundance – collections by Forrest, Rock, Kingdon Ward, Ludlow and Sheriff are all here, as are more recent collections from Nepal, Bhutan, Japan, and China. Since 1999 the wood has been managed jointly by Castle Howard and the Royal Botanic Gardens at Kew: there is a small additional charge to visit it.

Features Important buildings; impressive landscape; sculptures; woodland garden; roses (ancient & modern); good herbaceous borders; tallest elm *Ulmus glabra* (37m) in British Isles; shop and plant centre; cafeteria.

Owned by Castle Howard Estates Ltd
Size 400ha (1,000 acres)
English Heritage grade I

Features Fruit; good herbaceous borders; American garden; good conservatory on house; traditional Victorian kitchen garden undergoing restoration; 'Lady Downe's Seedling' grape, raised at Beningbrough in 1835; vast Portuguese laurel *Prunus lusitanica*; National Trust gift shop; morning coffee; hot & cold lunches; afternoon teas.

Owned by The National Trust
English Heritage grade II

Daleside Nurseries

RIPON ROAD, KILLINGHALL,
HARROGATE HG3 2AY

Tel 01423 506450   **Fax** 01423 527872
Website www.dalesidenurseries.co.uk
Location 4 miles north of Harrogate (A61).
Opening hours 9 am – 5 pm, Monday – Saturday; 10 am – 12 noon, 1.30 pm – 4.30 pm, Sundays.
Admission fee Free.

Daleside is a well-established (founded 1958) general nursery with a wide range of plants available including clematis, conifers, rhododendrons and azaleas, roses, trees and shrubs, soft fruit and fruit trees.

Duncombe Park

HELMSLEY YO62 5EB

Tel 01439 770213   **Fax** 01439 771114
Website www.duncombepark.com
Location Off A170; signed from Helmsley.
Opening hours 11 am – 5.30 pm or dusk if earlier; Sunday – Thursday; 28 April – 27 October.
Admission fee Adults £3; Children £1.50.
RHS members free.

Christopher Hussey wrote that 'the grass terraces of Duncombe and Rievaulx are unique, and perhaps the most spectacularly beautiful among English landscape conceptions of the 18th century'. They were probably completed between 1713 and 1730 to the designs of either Charles Bridgeman or Stephen Switzer, or both. The gardens were created on a virgin plateau 56m above Helmsley Castle and the Arcadian valley of the River Rye, and determined the site for the Duncombes' great house. There are classical temples, vast terraces, woodland walks, parterres and a secret garden – and all so spacious and tranquil.

 Features Stately 18th-century landscape; gift shop; licensed tea-room.

Owned by Lord Feversham
Number of gardeners 1
Size 14ha (35 acres), within 160ha (400 acres) of parkland
English Heritage grade I

Millgate House

RICHMOND DL10 4JN

Tel 01748 823571   **Fax** 01748 850701
Website www.millgatehouse.com
Location Bottom of Market Place; first house in Millgate on left.
Opening hours 10 am – 6 pm; daily; April to October. Plus 10 am – 4 pm on 24 February & 3 March for snowdrops.
Admission fee Adults £1.50; Children free.
RHS members free in June & July.

This is a walled garden in the middle of the town, and thus remarkably sheltered. Since starting work in the garden in 1980, the owners' aim has been to create structure, bulk, year-round interest and a sense of profusion. They have achieved this by re-designing the garden to suggest that it is much larger than it really is, and by planting only the best plants of every type. The most prominent are roses, clematis, hostas, snowdrops, hellebores, ferns and foliage shrubs. By 1995 the owners had won the National Garden Competition, against 3,200 other entries. The garden continues to improve: this year (2002) sees many new plantings and a re-design of part. Professor David Stevens calls it 'a sophisticated study in both the manipulation of spatial concepts and [in] planting design'. It is immensely stylish, a model for all town gardens.

Owned by Tim Culkin & Austin Lynch
Number of gardeners owners only
Size 0.15ha (one-third of an acre)

Mount Grace Priory

OSMOTHERLEY, NORTHALLERTON DL6 3JG

Tel 01609 883494   **Fax** 01609 883361
Website www.nationaltrust.org.uk
Location 12 miles north of Thirsk on A19.
Opening hours 10 am – 6 pm; daily; April to September. 10 am – 5 pm; daily; October. 10 am – 1 pm & 2 pm – 4 pm; Wednesday – Sunday; November to March.
Admission fee Adults £3; Concessions £2.30; Children £1.50.

The herb garden, designed by Stephen Anderton in 1994, is of most interest to gardeners. It is a recreation of a 15th-century monastic garden. Around the house, the 1920s flower borders are being restored: there are terraces, acers, rhododendrons and azaleas. It is not a garden in which to dally, but an interesting add-on to the whole experience of a visit to the property.

 Features Herbs.

Owned by The National Trust (managed by English Heritage)
Number of gardeners 2

Newby Hall

RIPON HG4 5AE

Tel 01423 322583   **Fax** 01423 324452
Website www.newbyhall.co.uk
Location Off B6265, 2 miles from A1 between Boroughbridge & Ripon.
Opening hours 11 am – 5.30 pm; Tuesday – Sunday & Bank Holiday Mondays; 29 March to 29 September.
Admission fee Adults £5.50; OAPs £4.50; Children £4. RHS members free.

Newby is the garden with everything: firm design, an endless variety of features, great plantsmanship and immaculate maintenance. Its axis is a bold, wide, double border stretching gently down to the River Ure. The National Collection of *Cornus* now extends to 37 species and 70 cultivars, planted to give colour, beauty and interest. Newby also has a large number of other rare trees and shrubs and a comprehensive collection of shrubby salvias, many of them collected in central and southern America by the owner's brother Dr James Compton. Newby is second only to Hidcote as an example of 20th-century gardening, but very much grander: visit it at any season and expect to spend all day there.

 Features Woodland garden; roses (mainly old-fashioned & climbers); rock garden; plantsman's collection of plants; daffodils; good herbaceous borders; new sculpture park (May 2002); HHA/Christie's Garden of the Year in 1986; tallest *Acer griseum* (15m) in UK; adventure playground; shop and plant stall; licensed restaurant.

Owned by Richard Compton
Number of gardeners 7
Size 10ha (25 acres)
NCCPG National Collections *Cornus*
English Heritage grade II*

Parcevall Hall Gardens

Skyreholme, Skipton BD23 6DE

Tel 01756 720311   **Fax** 01756 720441
Website www.parcevallhallgardens.co.uk
Location Off B6160 from Burnsall.
Opening hours 10 am – 6 pm; daily; April to October;
winter visits by appointment.
Admission fee Adults £3; Children 50p. RHS members
free from May to August.

The gardens at Parcevall Hall have a
breathtaking architectural layout and views
of the Yorkshire dales. They were largely
designed and planted by Sir William Milner
in 1927 and benefit from a great variety of
soils (limestone and gritstone) which means
that rhododendrons and camellias grow
alongside limestone outcrops. It is
something of a plantsman's garden too: the
naturalised daffodils in the orchard include
'W.P. Milner' while the *Primula florindae*
given by Kingdon Ward has now naturalised
around the lily pond. Within the grounds
are 14 Stations of the Cross.

Features Woodland garden; climbing
roses; rock garden; rhododendrons &
azaleas; water features; candelabra primulas;
tea-room.

Owned by Walsingham College (Yorkshire Properties) Ltd
Number of gardeners 3
Size 6.4ha (16 acres)

RHS Garden Harlow Carr

Beckwithshaw, Harrogate
HG3 1QB

Tel 01423 565418   **Fax** 01423 530663
Website www.rhs.org.uk
Location Crag Lane off Otley Road (B6162), 1½ miles
from Harrogate centre.
Opening hours 9.30 am – 6 pm, or dusk if earlier; daily;
all year.
Admission fee Adults £4.50; OAPs £3.50; Students £2;
Children (under 11) free. RHS members free.

Not for nothing is Harlow Carr known as
'the Wisley of the North': for more than 50
years, it has set itself the challenge of
educating, inspiring and delighting northern
gardeners. The gardens are comprehensive
and spectacular. The features include rock
gardens, heathers, alpine houses, streamside
and water gardens, woodland gardens, a
rhododendron collection, peat terraces, a
winter garden, a shrub rose border,
vegetable and fruit plots, and an extensive
arboretum. New features appear every year:
look out for the new kitchen garden and
fruit garden, the re-designed and replanted
herb garden, and the new border which
mixes herbaceous plants with ornamental
grasses. The Royal Horticultural Society also
ensures that Harlow Carr is an important
centre for horticultural learning, with a
splendid list of events and courses all
through the year for amateurs and
professionals alike.

Features Vegetables; rock garden;
herbs; fruit; daffodils; fine collection of
trees; heathers and alpines; good autumn
colour; gift shop; plant centre open every
day 9 am – 6 pm; licensed restaurant.

Owned by Royal Horticultural Society
Number of gardeners 10
Size 23ha (58 acres)
NCCPG National Collections *Calluna* (provisional); *Dryopteris*; *Fuchsia* section Quelusia (provisional); *Polypodium*; *Rheum*

Ripley Castle

RIPLEY, HARROGATE HG3 3AY

Tel 01423 770152 **Fax** 01423 771745
Website www.ripleycastle.co.uk
Location 3½ miles north of Harrogate, off A61.
Opening hours 9 am – 5 pm (or dusk if earlier); daily; all year.
Admission fee Adults £3; OAPs £2.50; Children £1.50. RHS members free.

Ripley has a garden with something for everyone: a 14th-century castle (restored); temples; a landscape designed by Capability Brown; a fine Regency conservatory; a Victorian formal garden; evergreen shrubberies (handsome yews); rare vegetables from Henry Doubleday Research Association in the traditional Victorian walled garden; colour at every season; over 2,000 hyacinths in 40 varieties; woodland walks; herbaceous borders; and hundreds of thousands of bulbs – daffodils in hosts.

Features Hyacinths; sub-tropical plants; good herbaceous borders; bluebells; gift shop with plants, fruit and vegetables; castle tea-room.

Owned by Sir Thomas Ingilby Bt.
Number of gardeners 4
NCCPG National Collections *Hyacinthus orientalis*
English Heritage grade II

R.V. Roger Ltd

THE NURSERIES, PICKERING
YO18 7HG

Tel 01751 472226 **Fax** 01751 476749
Location 1 mile south of Pickering, on A169.
Opening hours 9 am – 5 pm; Monday – Saturday. 1 pm – 5 pm; Sundays.

There has been a change of emphasis at Roger's since this excellent nursery was founded in 1913. It used to be best-known for its all-round range of alpines, bulbs, conifers, perennials, roses, trees and shrubs. Then it started to develop a speciality for trained fruit trees – everything from espaliered apples to gooseberries grown as standards (it still lists 72 different apples and an incredible 59 gooseberries). Now it is also one of the top places for architectural plants like bamboos from China and tree ferns from Australia. The list of Australian natives is also expanding – clematis, kennedias and hardenbergias among the climbers, and xanthorrhoeas and macrozamias among the woody plants. Excellence and variety remain the nursery's guiding principles.

 Features Exotic specimen trees; Australian plants; trained fruit trees.

Sleightholmedale Lodge

FADMOOR, KIRKBYMOORSIDE
YO62 7JG

Tel 01751 431942 **Fax** 01751 430106
Location Signed from Fadmoor.
Opening hours 2 pm – 6 pm; 26 May, 20 & 21 July. And by written appointment at any time.
Admission fee Adults £2; Children 50p.

This family garden – Mrs James is the third generation to garden here – is a plantsman's paradise right on the edge of the moors. The walled garden was built on a south-facing slope, which makes it possible to grow a wide range of plants that might not otherwise survive. As well as magnificent meconopsis and hardy herbaceous plants it has Mexican and Mediterranean rarities (a cistus walk, for example) which are a triumph for good cultivation and manipulation of the microclimate. The herbaceous borders are held together by repeating certain plants throughout: foxgloves, campanulas, martagon lilies, for example. Outside the walled garden is an orchard underplanted with snowdrops and narcissi. Up at the top is a hollyhock walk. And there are roses of every sort – hundreds of them, perhaps thousands.

 Features Roses (ancient & modern); plantsman's collection of plants; good herbaceous borders; teas in July.

Owned by Mrs R. James
Number of gardeners 1, plus 2 very part-time
Size 1.2ha (3 acres)

Stillingfleet Lodge Nurseries

STILLINGFLEET, YORK YO19 6HP

Tel & Fax 01904 728506
Website www.stillingfleetlodgenurseries.co.uk
Location 6 miles south of York: turn opposite the church.
Opening hours 1 pm – 4 pm; Wednesdays; May to September. Plus Fridays in May & June.
Admission fee Adults £2; Children 50p.
RHS members free.

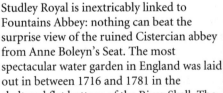

Stillingfleet is a series of small gardens surrounding a late 18th-century farmhouse. The emphasis is on a cottage garden style of

planting, for ease of maintenance. Foliage is used to add interest and texture: the result is a sequence of sumptuous herbaceous borders – a living lesson in how to plant a garden. The collection of pulmonarias is fascinating: 13 species and over 150 cultivars flower over a long period. A wildflower walk leads to a pond planted for natural effect. The nursery has an excellent herbaceous list with a high proportion of unusual plants: the catalogue changes each year but is always good for geraniums and pulmonarias. Worth a long journey to visit.

 Features Herbaceous plants; wildflower walk.

Owned by Vanessa Cook
Number of gardeners Owner, plus a little part-time help
Size 0.6ha (1½ acres)
NCCPG National Collections *Pulmonaria*

Studley Royal

FOUNTAINS, RIPON HG4 3DZ

Tel 01765 608888 **Fax** 01765 608889
Website www.nationaltrust.org.uk
Location 3 miles west of Ripon off B6265, via the Visitor Centre.
Opening hours 10 am – 5 pm (6 pm in summer) or dusk if sooner; daily; all year, except Fridays from November to January & 24 & 25 December. Closes at 4 pm on 12 & 13 July.
Admission fee Adults £4.80; Children £2.50.

Studley Royal is inextricably linked to Fountains Abbey: nothing can beat the surprise view of the ruined Cistercian abbey from Anne Boleyn's Seat. The most spectacular water garden in England was laid out in between 1716 and 1781 in the sheltered flat bottom of the River Skell. The abbey is at one end, the deer park at the other. The combination of the formal canal, moon pools, grotto springs, rustic bridge, sculptures and the Temple of Piety against a dark background of trees is a supreme example of 18th-century landscaping at its most individual.

 Features Topiary; snowdrops; World Heritage site; 400-acre deer park; water garden; biggest *Prunus avium* (bird cherry) in British Isles; National Trust visitor centre shop; tea-room.

Owned by The National Trust
English Heritage grade I

Sutton Park

SUTTON-ON-THE-FOREST, YORK YO6 1DP

Tel 01347 810249 **Fax** 01347 811251
Website www.statelyhome.co.uk
Location 8 miles north of York on B1363.
Opening hours 11 am – 5 pm; daily; 29 March to 29 September.
Admission fee Adults £2.50; OAPs £1.50; Children 50p. (2001 prices).

Ⓟ ⓦⓒ 🏠 ☕

Capability Brown was here in the 18th century, but the joy of Sutton is the formal garden laid out on terraces below the house by Percy Cane in the 1960s and planted by the late Nancie Sheffield with exquisite taste. It was one of the first to throw off the austerity of the post-war years and insist upon floral profusion and segregated colour schemes. It is still quite the prettiest garden in Yorkshire. In the grounds are a Georgian ice-house and a woodland walk which takes you round some of the best trees on the estate – oaks, wellingtonias, and some fine Victorian conifers.

 Features Fine formal gardens; woodland garden; roses (mainly old-fashioned); plantsman's collection of plants;

good herbaceous borders; walled pond garden; plants for sale occasionally; refreshments on Wednesdays & Sundays in summer.

Owned by Sir Reginald & Lady Sheffield
Number of gardeners 2½
Size 3.2ha (8 acres), plus parkland

Thorp Perrow Arboretum

BEDALE DL8 2PR

Tel & Fax 01677 425323
Website www.thorpperrow.com
Location On the Bedale–Ripon road, 2 miles south of Bedale.
Opening hours Dawn to dusk; daily; all year.
Admission fee Adults £5.25; OAPs & Students £4; Children £2.75. RHS members free from Monday to Friday (excluding Bank Holidays).

Ⓟ 🍴 ⓦⓒ ♿ 🌼 🏠 ☕

Thorp Perrow is the most important arboretum in the north of England, with more than 20 record-breaking trees among the thousands planted since Sir Leonard Ropner started work in 1931. There was already a pinetum on the estate, planted by Lady Augusta Milbank in the 1840s and 1850s. Ropner surrounded it with his new plantings – over 1,000 different taxa still survive, to which his son Sir John has added at least another 300. There are handsome avenues to walk along, often lined with a single genus or species – red oaks, rowans, cherries or cypresses, for example. Many are thickly lined with daffodils in spring, as are the glades and bays where you can study a particular collection like acers or hollies. The only downside to Thorp Perrow is that all the trees are identified only with a number, which you then have to look up in the catalogue of plantings. This minor irritation apart, Thorp Perrow is in every way an inspiring and enjoyable place to visit.

 Features The best collection of trees in northern England; daffodils; bluebells; new Millennium Glade; information centre; licensed tea-room.

Owned by Sir John Ropner Bt.
Size 34ha (85 acres)
NCCPG National Collections *Fraxinus*; *Juglans*; *Tilia*
English Heritage grade II

Valley Gardens

HARROGATE

Tel 01423 500600   **Fax** 01423 556720
Website www.harrogate.gov.uk
Location Signed from town centre.
Opening hours Dawn – dusk; daily; all year.
Admission fee Free.

The Valley Gardens at Harrogate are one of the best examples of plantsmanship in a public garden in England, first laid out between 1880 and 1900. The Sun Pavilion has recently been refurbished with a grant from the Lottery. The gardens have alpine rarities in spring, a romantic rhododendron dell, good roses, a magnificent dahlia display in late summer and the best colour bedding in Yorkshire.

 Features Rock garden; good herbaceous borders; wonderful primulas alongside the stream; small cafeteria.

Owned by Harrogate Borough Council
Size 6.7ha (17 acres)
English Heritage grade II

YORKSHIRE, SOUTH

The county of South Yorkshire was invented in 1974 and is, in effect, Greater Sheffield. Nevertheless it has a couple of good historic gardens which are open to the public – Wentworth Castle and Brodsworth Hall. The Sheffield Botanical Gardens too are of great horticultural interest, having been planted and maintained over many years as a garden of ornamental plants of every kind. Both the Sheffield Botanical Gardens and the gardens at Wentworth Castle have benefited from lottery funding in recent years and are very visitor-friendly as a result, though it is still possible to visit Wentworth only as part of a guided tour. The National Gardens Scheme has very few gardens opening for it in the county and, though it is well provided with garden centres, South Yorkshire has no specialist nurseries of national importance. There are eight NCCPG National Collections – including two at Sheffield Botanical Gardens and three at Wentworth Castle.

Brodsworth Hall & Gardens

ENGLISH HERITAGE, BRODSWORTH, DONCASTER DN5 7XJ

Tel 01302 722598   **Fax** 01302 337165
Location 6 miles north-west of Doncaster.
Opening hours 12 noon – 6 pm; Tuesday – Sunday & Bank Holiday Mondays; 29 March to 27 October. Then 11 am – 4 pm; weekends only.
Admission fee Garden only: Adults £3.50; OAPs £2.60; Children £1.80. Cheap rates in winter.

Brodsworth was unkempt for 50 years, acquired by English Heritage in 1990, and is now being restored as first laid out in the 1860s. It offers Italianate terraces, statues and classical follies, a rose garden where ramblers are trained on ironwork arcades, magnificent trees including monkey puzzles and 10m *Arbutus* trees, and bright Victorian bedding. A fine fern collection has recently been planted in the restored rock garden.

Features Good specimen conifers; Victorian spring & summer bedding; large fern collection; significant clipped evergreen shrubberies; statuary; shop.

Owned by English Heritage
Number of gardeners 4
Size 5.2ha (13 acres)
English Heritage grade II*

Sheffield Botanical Gardens

CLARKEHOUSE ROAD, SHEFFIELD S10 2LN

Tel & Fax 0114 267 6496
Website www.sbg.org.uk
Location Jct 33 of M1, follow A57 signs to Glossop, left at Royal Hallamshire Hospital, 500yds on left.

Opening hours 8 am (10 am at weekends) – 7.45 pm (4 pm in winter); daily; all year.
Admission fee Free.

The Sheffield Botanical Gardens were founded in 1833 by public subscription and still burgeon with civic pride. The garden has been awarded a £5.06m lottery grant and has a phased programme of work leading up to September 2004. This summer, the glass pavilions built by Robert Marnock are being repaired. The lay-out of the garden is a good example of the 'gardenesque' style made popular by John Claudius Loudon but there is much to interest the plantsman, too. The features include good camellias and magnolias; heathers; a peat garden; a rock garden; a lilac collection; good trees. The garden has splendid summer bedding too, and lots of seats: an exemplary combination of botany and amenity.

Features Roses (mainly modern); rock garden; mature conifers; good herbaceous borders; historic conservatories; peat garden; heath garden; restaurant.

Owned by Sheffield Town Trust
Number of gardeners 7, plus 2 part-time
Size 7.6ha (19 acres)
NCCPG National Collections Diervilla; Weigela
English Heritage grade II

Wentworth Castle Gardens

LOWE LANE, STAINBOROUGH, BARNSLEY S75 3ET

Tel 01226 731269
Location Signed 'Northern College'. 3 miles south of Barnsley; 2 miles from M1.
Opening hours Mainly by guided tours from mid-April to the end of June. Also open on selected Sunday afternoons in May. Annual open days 2 & 3 June. Details from 01226 731269.
Admission fee Adults £2.50; Concessions £2 (£2.50 on 2 & 3 June); Children free.

Wentworth Castle has a major landscape garden, one of the earliest in England, which accounts for the amazing series of buildings in the grounds – among them are an Ionic rotunda, the gothic folly of Stainborough Castle, an obelisk to Queen Anne and another to Lady Mary Wortley-Montagu to commemorate her introduction of smallpox inoculation to England. The garden was then overlaid with a seriously important collection of hardy hybrid rhododendrons at the end of the 19th century. This has been the basis of its current development as an educational and cultural resource. Lottery funding, if successful, will allow restoration of the pleasure grounds and walled gardens. Wentworth Castle is twinned with the Kunming Academy of Sciences, China. There is only one problem about visiting it – you have to go with a guided tour.

Features Historic landscape; woodland garden; newly excavated 19th-century rock garden; educational collection of rhododendrons.

Owned by Barnsley Metropolitan Borough Council
Number of gardeners 5
Size 16ha (40 acres)
NCCPG National Collections Rhododendron species; Magnolia species; Camellia × williamsii
English Heritage grade I

YORKSHIRE, WEST

West Yorkshire corresponds to the old West Riding. It is a county of great contrasts, from the industrial and commercial cities of Bradford and Leeds to the wool towns of Huddersfield and Halifax, with a chunk of the Peak District in the south-west and some large agricultural estates in the north. The most important historic gardens are Bramham Park – a remarkable pre-landscape garden on a big scale – and the opulent Harewood House. But they are matched for sheer horticultural value by four gardens which all have an historic past but are now owned and managed by Leeds City Council as gardens for public recreation – Lotherton Hall, Temple Newsam, The Hollies, and the Canal Gardens & Tropical World in Roundhay Park. The NCCPG has no less than 11 National Collections in the care of the Leeds City Parks Department. There are rather few specialist nurseries of national standing in the county, though it is well served by garden centres. The standards of horticultural displays in both private and public gardens are greatly aided by the activities of the Yorkshire in Bloom competition.

8 Dunstarn Lane

ADEL, LEEDS LS16 8EL

Tel 0113 267 3938
Location Off Long causeway, Adel.
Opening hours 2 pm – 7 pm; 30 June, 7 July, 4 August.
Admission fee Adults £1.50; Children free.

The house at 8 Dunstarn Lane is modern, built as a retirement house in the grounds of his old family home (The Heath) by Richard Wainwright, the retired member of parliament who is now president of the Delphinium Society. The part of the garden which he retained includes the area where he (and his father before him) have grown delphiniums for more than half a century. It is probably the finest and most extensive collection of delphiniums in private hands, with nearly seventy cultivars. They are interplanted with their traditional border companions – roses (mainly modern), phlox, dahlias, Michaelmas daisies and many unusual perennials.

 Features Roses; delphiniums; fine trees.

Owned by Mr & Mrs Richard Wainwright
Number of gardeners 1
Size 1.2ha (3 acres)

Bramham Park

WETHERBY LS23 6ND

Tel 01937 846002   **Fax** 01937 846001
Location 5 miles south of Wetherby on A1.

Opening hours 10.30 am – 5.30 pm; daily; April to September. Closed for horse trials from 6 to 9 June & occasionally for other events. Ring before visiting.
Admission fee Gardens only: Adults £4; OAPs £2; Children £2.

Bramham has very important pre-landscape formal gardens, laid out in the grand manner in the style of Le Nôtre in the early 18th century. Long straight rides cut through dense woodland, with ornamental ponds, cascades, loggias, temples and an obelisk. The standard of maintenance is exemplary: all credit to the Lane Foxes for the care they have lavished upon Bramham over such a long period.

 Features Very important pre-landscape park; daffodils; good herbaceous borders; light refreshments.

Owned by George Lane Fox
Number of gardeners 3
Size 27ha (66 acres)
English Heritage grade I

Canal Gardens & Tropical World

ROUNDHAY PARK, PRINCES AVENUE, LEEDS LS8 2ER

Tel 0113 266 1850   **Fax** 0113 237 0077
Website www.leeds.gov.uk
Location 3 miles north-west of city centre, off A6120 ring road.
Opening hours Open 10 am all year. Close at 4 pm in January & December; 5 pm in February & November; 6 pm in March & October; 7 pm in April & September; 8 pm from May to August.
Admission fee Tropical World: Adults £2; Children £1. Gardens free.

Tropical World's glasshouses contain South American rain forest plants, bromeliads, hoyas, cacti and a butterfly house. It is said to have the largest collection of tropical plants outside Kew. It is in any event a wonderful retreat from a Yorkshire winter and a triumph of municipal horticultural excellence. Roundhay Park has a £6.1m project to preserve and enhance the gardens which has received support from the Heritage Lottery Fund. Tropical World is visited by over 1,000,000 people every year.

 Features Sub-tropical plants; roses (mainly modern); plants under glass; good carpet bedding; orchids; desert house; souvenirs; cafeteria by lakeside.

Owned by Leeds City Council
Number of gardeners 40
Size 220ha (600 acres)
English Heritage grade II

Golden Acre Park

OTLEY ROAD, BRAMHOPE, LEEDS LS16 5NZ

Tel 0113 267 3729
Website www.leeds.gov.uk
Location 6 miles north-west of Leeds city centre on A660 Otley Road.
Opening hours Dawn – dusk; daily; all year.
Admission fee Free.

Golden Acre is part historic park, part botanic collection, part demonstration garden and part test ground for Fleuroselect and *Gardening Which?*. It began life in the 1930s as an amusement park, but the City Council decided after the war to develop it as a public garden with a strong botanical interest. Perhaps the best of the five impressive public gardens in Leeds, it is certainly the most popular.

Features Rock garden; large heather garden; new 'harmony' garden; herb garden; limestone rock garden; sandstone rock garden; arboretum; pinetum; display houses; rhododendrons & azaleas; cherry orchard; gifts/souvenirs; restaurant.

Owned by Leeds City Council
Size 54ha (137 acres)
NCCPG National Collections *Primula auricula*; *Syringa*

Harewood House

MOOR HOUSE, HAREWOOD, LEEDS
LS17 9LQ

Tel 0113 218 1010   **Fax** 0113 218 1002
Website www.harewood.org
Location Between Leeds & Harrogate on A61.
Opening hours 10 am – 6 pm; daily; 7 March to 3 November, then Saturdays & Sundays until 15 December.
Admission fee Grounds: Adults £6.50; OAPs £5.50; Children £4. RHS members free from 7 March to 28 June, excluding weekends & Bank Holidays.

Capability Brown was the first famous landscaper to work at Harewood for the Lascelles family: he was followed by Humphry Repton, J.C. Loudon and Sir Charles Barry. The latter came in the 1840s, to build the stupendous Italianate terrace which was restored in 1994 with a European Commission grant. Its grand parterre and ornate fountains are the perfect link between the house and the landscaped park. Around the lake are hundreds of rhododendrons, unusual shrubs and bulbs, particularly daffodils. The waterfall at the lake head feeds a rocky garden where primulas, astilbes, hostas and gunneras grow rampantly in the damp. The rose garden at the end of the lakeside walk is an extra delight in early summer. The large, traditional walled garden displays a wide selection of vegetables and economic crops from around

the world: Harewood is a registered Seed Library garden.

 Features Formal terraces; woodland garden; Japanese garden; rhododendrons; current holder of Sandford Award; two shops; licensed café selling light lunches.

Owned by Harewood House Trust Ltd.
Number of gardeners 12
Size 56ha (140 acres)
English Heritage grade I

The Hollies Park

WEETWOOD LANE, LEEDS LS16 5NZ

Tel 0113 278 2030   **Fax** 0113 247 8277
Website www.leeds.gov.uk
Location 3 miles north of city off A660.
Opening hours Dawn – dusk; daily; all year.
Admission fee Free.

Ⓟ Ⓗ ⓦⓒ

This public park is made in a plantsman's garden, and is well run by a hard-pressed and enthusiastic team. Visitors wishing to see the National Collections are advised to make a prior appointment.

Ⓦ **Features** Woodland garden; rhododendrons; eucryphias.

Owned by Leeds City Council
Size 37ha (93 acres)
NCCPG National Collections *Deutzia*; *Hemerocallis* (Coe hybrids); *Hosta* (large-leaved); *Philadelphus*; *Syringa*

Land Farm Gardens

COLDEN, HEBDEN BRIDGE, HALIFAX HX7 7PJ

Tel 01422 842260
Location On right, 2 miles from Hebden Bridge on Colden road.
Opening hours 10 am – 5 pm; Saturdays, Sundays & Bank Holiday Mondays; May to August.
Admission fee Adults £3.

This is a pioneering plantsman's garden, high in the Pennines and facing north. The range of plants that can successfully be grown in such an unpromising situation is an eye-opener – lots of hardy rhododendrons, shrubs, trees and alpines. There is also a good collection of sculpture, with more pieces arriving all the time.

Features Garden created by owners on green field site; good conifers and herbaceous borders; new woodland garden (2 acres); *Meconopsis*; *Tropaeolum*; art gallery.

Owned by John Williams
Size 1.6ha (4 acres)

Lotherton Hall

ABERFORD, LEEDS LS25 3EB

Tel 0113 281 3259   **Fax** 0113 281 3068
Website www.leeds.gov.uk
Location Off A1, ¾ mile east on B1217.
Opening hours 8 am – 8 pm or dusk, if earlier; daily; all year.
Admission fee Garden free, but charges for parking.

This showpiece garden was laid out about 1885-1915 by a friend of Ellen Willmott. It was given to the Council in 1968 and has been well restored in recent years. It offers gazebos, walks, yew hedging, rose gardens, and a lily pond recently replanted with period varieties. The rock garden known as the Dell is especially good. The formal garden is laid out with gravel paths and lots of bedding. Lotherton is a garden that is on the move again, with a woodland trail recently added for disabled users.

Features Edwardian plantswoman's garden; roses (mainly modern); good trees; fine hedges; mature layout; shop; cafeteria.

Owned by Leeds City Council
Number of gardeners 2
Size 4ha (10 acres)
English Heritage grade II

Temple Newsam Park

LEEDS LS15 0AE

Tel 0113 264 5535
Website www.leeds.gov.uk
Location 3 miles south-east of city, off A63 Selby Road.
Opening hours Dawn – dusk; daily; all year.
Admission fee Free. Admission charge to house.

This prodigious house on a windy bluff, surrounded by 1,200 acres of parkland, has been a 'green lung' for Leeds since 1923. Somewhat dilapidated in the past, the garden is now improved by some recent plantings. These include a traditional herb garden; a spring garden full of bulbs; the Italian garden with formal flower beds; box, yew and beech hedges; pleached laburnum walks; and a clipped hornbeam stilt hedge. A fine rhododendron and azalea walk runs down to the lakes. Nearby is an arboretum and a bog garden. Further on still, the old walled kitchen garden is planted with roses and wide herbaceous borders. The long conservatory has a fine display of flowering plants, ivies and cacti: its back wall (1788) still has the flues which were used to keep it warm with hot air.

 Features Roses (ancient & modern); plants under glass; good herbaceous borders; rhododendrons; souvenirs; tea-room open daily from 10.30 am.

Owned by Leeds City Council
NCCPG National Collections Aster; Delphinium; Phlox paniculata
English Heritage grade II

York Gate

BACK CHURCH LANE, ADEL, LEEDS LS16 8DW

Tel 0113 267 8240
Website www.gardeners-grbs.org.uk
Location 2½ miles south-east of Bramhope and ½ mile east of A660, behind Adel Church, off A660.
Opening hours 2 pm – 5 pm; Thursdays, Sundays & Bank Holiday Mondays; May to September. And on Fridays & Saturdays by appointment.
Admission fee Adults £3 (£4.50 for private visits); Children free.

This 1-acre masterpiece – a modern cult garden – was made by the Spencer family between 1951 and 1994. It is of equal interest to the designer and the plantsman. Its marvels include shrub and herbaceous borders, an orchard with pool, an arbour, a miniature pinetum, a dell with stream, a folly, a nut walk, a peony bed, iris borders, a fern border, the famous herb garden, a pretty summerhouse, an alley, a white and silver garden (due to be replanted in 2002), a kitchen garden, and a pavement maze. This masterpiece of tight design, invention, colour sense and sheer creative opportunism is now safely in the care of the Gardeners' Royal Benevolent Society.

Features Brilliant design; plantsman's collection of plants; famous herb gatrden; an espaliered *Cedrus atlantica* 'Glauca'; endless inventive details; plants for sale occasionally; tea & biscuits.

Owned by The Gardeners' Royal Benevolent Society
Number of gardeners part-timers & volunteers
Size 0.4ha (1 acre)

SCOTLAND

Scottish gardens are very variable – this is a factor of their soil and climate. All along the west coast, from Dumfries & Galloway up to Ullapool and beyond, are fine, subtropical woodland gardens, where one can enjoy acres of large-leaved rhododendrons and eucalyptus trees and all manner of curiosities like *Myosotidium hortensia*, which would not be hardy in any but the most favoured parts of England. There is no better place to go visiting gardens in May or June – provided the weather is kind. There are comparatively few good gardens in inland Scotland. Historically, the big estates were (and still are) in remote places where the land is unsuitable for agriculture and, in consequence, their gardens tend to be few and disappointing. In the Borders, for example, there are several estates along the valleys of the Tweed and the Teviot whose gardens are open to the public: all have collections of 19th-century conifers underplanted with hardy hybrid rhododendrons or common *R. ponticum*, but little else in the way of horticultural interest. On the East Coast, however, there are once again many worthy gardens, above all the superb botanic garden at Edinburgh, which (like all botanic gardens nowadays) is laid out to please visitors, and other good botanic gardens at Dundee, St Andrews and Aberdeen. There are interesting gardens too near Edinburgh (especially Malleny at Balerno) and on Deeside (Crathes, Kildrummy and Drum).

Trees flourish in much of Scotland – especially those North American conifers for which the cool, damp west coast provides perfect growing conditions: many of the tallest pines, firs and spruces in Britain are in Scotland. The largest collection of record-breaking trees is at the Royal Botanic Gardens in Edinburgh, which has 45.

We have listed the gardens to visit in Scotland under the old 1974 regions, rather than the historic counties or the plethora of more recent local councils. The regions divide the country into areas of acceptable size for the purpose of this book, though there is a preponderance of gardens in the old region of Strathclyde – as indeed there still is in Argyll & Bute. If readers can suggest a better way than the old regions to list gardens, we would be pleased to hear from them. Scotland's Garden Scheme divides the country into areas which are even more confusing – 'Etterick & Lauderdale', for example, and 'Lochaber, Badenoch & Strathspey'. The 1974 regions do at least have the advantage of having been administrative areas until very recently.

Scotland has many great historic gardens. The basis of the protection they enjoy is the *Inventory of Gardens & Designed Landscapes in Scotland* which was published in 1987. The Inventory listed 275 sites, which are graded in a more specific way than the gardens on the English register, for example, according to the value of their horticultural content or historic importance. Historic Scotland has recently begun to extend the Inventory.

Nobody has done more to acquire, save, restore and redevelop Scotland's great gardens than the National Trust for

Scotland. Its portfolio of properties includes many of the best historic and horticultural gardens in the country: Branklyn, Brodick, Crathes, Culzean and Inverewe are gardens of international renown. The Royal Botanic Garden at Edinburgh too has developed four of the finest gardens anywhere in the world – Dawyck, Logan, Benmore (Younger Botanic Garden) and its own incomparable garden in north Edinburgh.

Members of the Royal Horticultural Society have free access for at least some months of the year to a dozen Scottish gardens: Abriachan, Cawdor Castle, Dundee Botanic Garden, Dunrobin Castle, Geilston Garden, Glenwhan, Harmony Garden, Hill of Tarvit, Kellie Castle, Leith Hall, St Andrews Botanic Garden, Scone Palace, Torosay Castle and the great teaching garden at Threave. More may be added during the course of the year: see the Society's website www.rhs.org.uk for the latest news. Scotland also has its own Yellow Book called *The Gardens of Scotland*, available from Scotland's Gardens Scheme, 31 Castle Terrace, Edinburgh EH1 2EL. It lists over 350 gardens throughout Scotland and, like its English equivalent, is the essential starting point for choosing more gardens to visit than this book recommends.

Scotland is well served by garden centres, especially by such chains as Dobbie's in the Lowlands. It has some excellent specialist nurseries too: Jack Drake is Britain's premier alpine nursery; nobody has bred more or better new rhododendrons than Peter Cox at Glendoick; and Cally in Dumfries & Galloway has a great reputation for rare plants. However, it is fair to say that there are fewer nurseries *per capita* in Scotland as a whole than in England.

Scotland also has its own rather basic horticultural structure: these include, for example, such societies as the Scottish Rock Garden Club, the Scottish Rhododendron Society, the Royal Caledonian Horticultural Society and the Scottish Orchid Society. All are excellent organisations and some, like the Scottish Rock Garden Club and the Scottish Rhododendron Society, are substantial societies with good programmes of events and publications of record. Scotland also has a number of horticultural training colleges, notably Threave, Oatridge and the Scottish Agricultural College at Auchincruive – the latter is a RHS Partner College.

BORDERS

Abbotsford

MELROSE TD6 9BQ

Tel 01896 752043 **Fax** 01896 752916
Location On B6360, two miles west of Melrose.
Opening hours 9.30 am – 5 pm (but 2 pm – 5 pm on
Sundays in March, April, May & October); daily; 18 March
to 31 October. Walled garden open from June onwards.
Admission fee Adults £4; Children £2.

Sir Walter Scott laid out the gardens at
Abbotsford in the 1820s: he designed the
formal Court garden by the house and
planted the surrounding woodlands. The
walled garden centres on a handsome
orangery, with roses, fruit trees and
herbaceous borders planted for late
summer effect.

Features Fine walled garden;
orangery; topiary; herbaceous borders;
gift shop; self-service tea-room.

Owned by Dame Jean Maxwell-Scott DCVO
Number of gardeners 2
Size 0.4ha (1 acre)

Dawyck Botanic Garden

STOBO EH45 9JU

Tel 01721 760254 **Fax** 01721 760214
Website www.rbge.org.uk
Location 8 miles south-west of Peebles on B712.
Opening hours 9.30 am – 6 pm; daily; 14 February to
17 November.
Admission fee Adults £3; Concessions £2.50;
Children £1.

Dawyck is a woodland garden, run as a
regional garden of the Royal Botanic Garden
Edinburgh. It is very different from
Edinburgh's other outliers: its 60 acres are
high in the hills where the climate is more
continental than temperate. The trees for
which the garden is famous were first
planted in the 1830s: the owners subscribed
to the great plant-hunting expeditions of the
day, including those of David Douglas. This
explains the many fine North American
conifers in the garden. In the early 20th
century, the owners received plants from the
early Chinese collections of E.H. Wilson.
The gardens are also famous for their
rhododendrons, berberis and cotoneasters
and – of course – the upright Dawyck beech,
an upright, fastigiate form of the common
beech, first found in the policies in the
mid-19th century.

Features Good herbaceous borders;
meconopsis; Chinese conifers; Dawyck
beech; Douglas fir from original seed; tallest
Abies mariesii (21m) in the British Isles, and
12 further record trees; gift shop; light
refreshments.

Owned by Royal Botanic Garden Edinburgh
Size 22ha (60 acres)

Edrom Nurseries

COLDINGHAM, EYEMOUTH TD14 5TZ

Tel & Fax 01890 771386
Location A1107, 5 minutes from A1.
Opening hours 9 am – 5.30 pm; Monday – Friday;
March to October.

This nursery specialises in alpine primulas, gentians and meconopsis. The list of these three genera is particularly comprehensive, and includes many forms that are not available elsewhere. As with the other alpines it lists, many are new to commerce or grown under collectors' numbers.

Floors Castle

KELSO TD5 7SF

Tel 01573 223333   **Fax** 01573 226056
Location Signed in Kelso.
Opening hours 10 am – 4.30 pm; daily; all year.
Admission fee £3.

Floors has handsome traditional herbaceous borders in the walled garden and the castle is impressively sited in its parkland. But change and restoration continue too: a new 2-acre parterre in front of the castle is surmounted by a ducal coronet, while the 'star plantation' was entirely replanted with azaleas and rhododendrons in 1998. There are some good trees in the park, including a holm oak (*Quercus ilex*) and a Dawyck beech (*Fagus sylvatica* 'Fastigiata'), and a venerable holly on the spot where King James II of Scotland was blown up while besieging Roxburgh Castle in 1460.

Features Good borders; French-style parterre for Millennium (2000); garden centre in walled garden; licensed restaurant & shop.

Owned by The Duke of Roxburghe
Number of gardeners 5

Harmony Garden

ST MARY'S ROAD, MELROSE TD6 9LJ

Tel 01721 722502
Website www.nts.org.uk
Location In Melrose, opposite the abbey.
Opening hours 10 am – 5.30 pm; daily; 25 March to 27 October. But 1.30 pm – 5 pm on Sundays.
Admission fee £2. RHS members free.

'Harmony' takes its name from the Jamaican pimento plantation where its original builder James Waugh made his fortune. It is a modest, quiet walled garden with lawns, herbaceous and mixed borders, vegetable and fruit areas, and a rich display of spring bulbs. The views of Melrose Abbey and the Fildon Hills are a bonus.

Owned by The National Trust for Scotland
Number of gardeners 1
Size 0.8ha (2 acres)

Kailzie Gardens

KAILZIE, PEEBLES EH45 9HT

Tel & Fax 01721 720007
Location On B7062 2 miles east of Peebles.
Opening hours 11 am – 5.30 pm; daily; all year.
Admission fee Adults £2.50; Children 75p (but £2 & 50p respectively from November to Maundy Thursday).

Kailzie has been revived over the last 20 years. The large walled garden has a mixture of flowers and produce: a laburnum alley, a rose garden and double herbaceous borders are some of the attractions. There are meconopsis and primulas in the rhododendron woodland walks outside. There will be a special week in June 2002 for the sale of geraniums and fuchsias.

Features Woodland garden; snowdrops; daffodils; shop; restaurant & teas.

Owned by Angela, Lady Buchan-Hepburn
Number of gardeners 3
Size 8ha (20 acres)

Lilliesleaf Nursery

GARDEN COTTAGE, LINTHILL, LILLIESLEAF TD6 9HU

Tel & Fax 01835 870415
Location On B6359 between Midlem & Lilliesleaf.
Opening hours 10 am – 5 pm, Monday – Saturday; 10 am – 4 pm, Sundays. December to March, phone first.
Admission fee Free.

This nursery, in a pretty position on the bank of the River Ale, has a general plant range, with an emphasis on perennials and hard-to-find plants of every kind. It is particularly good for epimediums, and offers a number of hybrids listed by no other nursery. The demonstration garden is also worth seeing: attractive mixed borders in a walled garden.

Owned by Teyl de Bordes
Number of gardeners 2
Size 0.4ha (1 acre)
NCCPG National Collections *Epimedium*

Manderston

DUNS TD11 3PP

Tel 01361 883450   **Fax** 01361 882010
Website www.manderston.co.uk
Location On A6105 2 miles east of Duns.
Opening hours 2 pm – dusk; Sundays & Thursdays; 9 May to 29 September, plus 27 May & 26 August.
Parties at any time by appointment.

Admission fee Gardens only: Adults £3.50; Children £1.50.

The house is Edwardian, built in classical neo-Georgian style. Below it are four expansive terraces with rich planting around clipped yews and hollies and fountains on the upper terrace. Below is a small lake with an ornamental boathouse and an 18th-century Chinese-style bridge. On the other side of the lake are the woodland gardens with a large collection of unusual species of trees and shrubs: the extensive collection of rhododendrons and azaleas dates back 100 years. This woodland garden is criss-crossed with numerous paths so that visitors can see all parts of it. On the north side of the house, after crossing wide lawns set about with mature trees, visitors reach the formal garden and herbaceous borders, both at their best in summer.

 Features Woodland garden with rhododendrons & azaleas; mature conifers; good herbaceous borders; good bedding out on the formal terraces; cream teas & ice-cream.

Owned by Lord Palmer
Number of gardeners 2
Size 22ha (56 acres)

Mellerstain

GORDON TD3 6LG

Tel 01573 410225   **Fax** 01573 410636
Website www.scottishborders.com/mellerstain
Location 1 mile west of A6089 Kelso – Edinburgh road.
Opening hours 11.30 pm – 6 pm; daily, except Saturdays; Easter to 30 September.
Admission fee £3.

The house has extensive views south to the Cheviots: it was built by the Adams (father and son) between 1725 and 1778. It is set off by Sir Reginald Blomfield's formal garden, balustraded and terraced, but now rather covered by lichen. The garden is planted with floribunda roses and lavender. Beneath it runs the landscaped park, also laid out by William and Robert Adam, sauntering down to a lake. The whole picture is uncompromisingly grand.

 Features Topiary; roses (mainly modern); Italian terraced garden by Sir Reginald Blomfield; lake restored (1997/98); tweed and gift shop; licensed restaurant.

Owned by Mellerstain Trust
Number of gardeners 1
Size 1.8ha (4½ acres)

Mertoun Gardens

St Boswells, Melrose TD6 0EA

Tel 01835 823236 **Fax** 01835 822474
Location B6404, 2 miles north-east of St Boswells.
Opening hours 2 pm – 6 pm; Saturdays, Sundays & Public Holiday Mondays; April to September.
Admission fee Adults £2; OAPs £1.50; Children 50p.

Originally part of the Duke of Sutherland's estates, Mertoun is best known for its immaculately maintained, traditional, 3-acre kitchen garden with its range of heated glasshouses and frames. A long herbaceous border within it has recently been replanted. There is also a young arboretum, established since 1975, with a good selection of conifers and hardwoods, most of which have grown away very well. For many years now, the Dukes have grown a strain of pea which is said to have come from one found by Lord Carnarvon in the tomb of Tutenkhamen.

 Features Vegetables; herbs; plants under glass; daffodils; good herbaceous borders.

Owned by Mertoun Gardens Trust
Number of gardeners 3
Size 10.3ha (26 acres)

Monteviot House Gardens

Jedburgh TD8 6UQ

Tel 01835 830380 **Fax** 01835 830288
Location Off A68 north of Jedburgh & B6400 to Nisbet.
Opening hours 12 noon – 5 pm; daily; April to October.
Admission fee Adults £2; Children free.

The gardens at Monteviot lie along a dramatic slope of the Teviot valley. The box-hedged herb garden and terrace along the front of the house have a breathtaking view of the river below. The sheltered terraced rose garden is Victorian: the river garden at the bottom was originally designed in the 1930s by Percy Cane. Italianate in inspiration, this sheltered garden slopes down between curved borders of herbaceous plants, shrubs, bulbs and roses, to a broad stone landing stage above the waters of the Teviot itself. In the nearby water garden, fed by a natural spring, three islands are linked by elegant curved wooden bridges. Here are bog plants and bamboos. The dramatic impact of the garden as a whole is heightened by the contrast between formal and the informal and by the way that the planting leads seamlessly through the different parts. The trees in the arboretum are exceptional: recent clearing has displayed them in their glory. *Fagus sylvatica* 'Riversii' is 30m high.

 Features Fine collection of trees; water garden; Victorian rose garden; new plantings in arboretum (2000); refreshments for pre-booked groups.

Number of gardeners 3

Priorwood Garden

MELROSE TD6 9PX

Tel 01896 822493
Website www.nts.org.uk
Location Next to Melrose Abbey.
Opening hours 10 am (1.30 pm on Sundays) – 5 pm; daily; 25 March to 27 October. 10 am (1 pm on Sundays) – 4 pm; daily; October to 24 December.
Admission fee Adults £2; Concessions £1.50. Honesty box.

Priorwood is best known for its shop, which was recently extended and improved. Everything in the garden is geared towards dried flowers. Most of the plants are chosen because they are suitable for drying, but they are also very colourful. Courses on drying flowers are also held here. In the orchard is a collection of historic apple cultivars, all organically grown.

 Features Herbs; fruit; good herbaceous borders; dried flower shop and NTS gift shop.

Owned by The National Trust for Scotland
Number of gardeners 1

Traquair House

INNERLEITHEN EH44 6PW

Tel 01896 830323   **Fax** 01896 830639
Website www.traquair.co.uk
Location Signed from Innerleithen.
Opening hours 10.30 am – 5.30 pm; daily; 30 March to 31 October.
Admission fee Grounds only: Adults £2.50; Children £1.

The main attraction is a large maze, planted in 1980 of beech and Leyland cypress. The house is a Catholic time-warp, said to be the oldest inhabited and most romantic house in Scotland. The Bear Gates in the park, once the main entrance to the estate, have been closed ever since Bonnie Prince Charlie passed through them for the last time in 1746.

Features Woodland garden; roses (mainly old-fashioned); good herbaceous borders; gift shop; restaurant serving lunch & tea; Traquair ale.

Owned by Mrs Maxwell Stuart
Number of gardeners 3
Size 12ha (30 acres)

DUMFRIES & GALLOWAY

Broughton House Gardens

12 HIGH STREET, KIRKCUDBRIGHT DG6 4JX

Tel & Fax 01557 330437
Location Signed in centre of Kirkcudbright.
Opening hours 12 noon – 5 pm; daily; 25 March to 31 October. Opens at 10 am and closes at 6 pm in July & August. Open 11 am – 4 pm on 23 & 24 February for snowdrops.
Admission fee Adults £3.50; Concessions £2.50.

E.A. Hornel the artist laid out the Japanese-style garden in the 1900s: it is the best known part of the garden here and featured in many of his portraits. Most of the rest is a 'Scottish' garden with a fine position above the River Dee. The house contains many of Hornel's works and an extensive collection of Scottish books.

Owned by National Trust for Scotland
Number of gardeners 1
Size 0.8ha (2 acres)

Cally Gardens

GATEHOUSE OF FLEET, CASTLE DOUGLAS DG7 2DJ

Tel none **Fax** 01557 815029
Location 12 miles west of Castle Douglas, on Gatehouse road off A75.
Opening hours 10 am – 5.30 pm; Saturdays & Sundays; plus 2 pm – 5.30 pm from Tuesday to Friday. Easter to early October.
Admission fee Adults £1.50; Children free.

Cally is a nursery for the horticultural *avant-garde*. It specialises in new and rare perennials, including some from wild-collected and botanic garden seed. Many are culled from a collection of over 3,500 plants, which makes it one of the most interesting in Scotland – the owner, Michael Wickenden, has an excellent eye for quality. The walled garden has 30 large borders where all these novelties and rarities can be seen growing. It is particularly good in September but in 2002 the most spectacular time will be early June, when new plantings of 1,000 *Meconopsis betonicifolia* and 1,000 *M. × sheldonii* come into flower for the first time. The list of what is for sale changes by as much as half each year.

Owned by Michael Wickenden
Number of gardeners 2, plus students
Size 1.2ha (3 acres)

Castle Kennedy Garden

STAIR ESTATES, REPHAD, STRANRAER DG9 8BX

Tel 01776 702024   **Fax** 01776 706248
Location 5 miles east of Stranraer on A75.
Opening hours 10 am – 5 pm; daily; April to September.
Admission fee Adults £3; OAPs £2; Children £1
(2001 prices).

Castle Kennedy is a ruined keep, destroyed in the first half of the 18th century when the bedding which was being aired for the return of the master, the 2nd Earl of Stair, caught fire. Its imposing bulk overlooks the walled garden, which is a riot of herbaceous colour in the summer, with gnarled old apple trees heavy with lichen in its midst, and some interesting tender shrubs, including bottle-brushes (*Callistemon* species) against its walls. The main horticultural interest lies outside, although the romantic planting continues. The 2nd Earl was a military man, and bequeathed to the garden its highly original structure of dashing rides, ridges and earthworks which represent battle encampments. They were made by the Royal Scots Greys and the Inniskilling Fusiliers when they should have been occupied suppressing religious dissent in the area. The extensive gardens now occupy an isthmus bounded by two lochs, with the ruined castle at one end, and its 19th-century replacement Lochinch Castle at the other – the place where *Buddleja* 'Lochinch' originated. There is a 2-acre round pond, from which an ancient, slightly decrepit avenue of monkey puzzle trees leads off. These trees, *Araucaria araucana*, were grown from original seed sent from Chile: elsewhere are plants garnered by Stair forbears who subscribed to the collecting expeditions of Sir Joseph Hooker (*Rhododendron arboreum* for

example). The gardens generally are well stocked with rhododendrons, at their best in April and May. Later in the season, in an area known as the dancing green, a semi-circle of crimson *Embothrium coccineum* (June) is interplanted with flower-decked *Eucryphia* × *nymansensis* (August). There are more conventional flower borders in the area beside Lochinch Castle. In gardens as old as these, time has started to take its toll, but restoration and replanting is underway. The gardens recommend visitors to follow one of four graded walks to get the most out of their visit. For the energetic, this is a marvellous place just to wander at will.

Features Woodland garden; good herbaceous borders; rhododendrons; embothriums; eucryphias; monkey puzzle avenue; tallest *Pittosporum tenuifolium* (17m) in the British Isles, tallest *Rhododendron arboreum* (16m) and 3 other record-breaking trees; plant centre; tea-room.

Owned by Lochinch Heritage Estate
Size 30ha (75 acres)

Craigieburn Classic Plants

BY MOFFAT DG10 9LF

Tel & Fax 01683 221250
Location 2½ miles east of Moffat, on A74. On the left, beyond Craiglochan signs.
Opening hours 12 noon – 6 pm; Saturdays & Sundays; Easter to September.
Admission fee Charity donation.

The nursery at Craigieburn is now playing second fiddle to the garden, which is undergoing substantial development and improvement as a collection of Himalayan plants. It is particularly good for *Meconopsis*, of which the Wheatcrofts used to have a National Collection. The mild climate means that *Lobelia tupa* grows to 2.5m. The nursery now sells mainly surplus plants from the garden.

 Features Meconopsis; woodland plants; Himalayan plants.

Owned by Andrew & Janet Wheatcroft
Size 3.2ha (8 acres)

Elizabeth MacGregor

ELLENBANK, TONGLAND ROAD, KIRKCUDBRIGHT DG6 4UU

Tel & Fax 01557 330620
Location On A711, 1 mile north of Kirkcudbright.
Opening hours 10 am – 5 pm; Mondays, Fridays & Saturdays; 26 April to 7 October.

Violas – over 100 of them – are the speciality at this excellent nursery: some are not available from any other source. They are complemented by a lively selection of perennials and shrubs for cottage gardens and mixed-border planting. The walled garden is worth a visit in its own right.

 Features Violas; perennials.

Galloway House Gardens

GARLIESTON, NEWTON STEWART DG8 8HF

Tel & Fax 01988 600680
Website www.garlieston.net/gardens
Location Off B7004 at Garlieston.
Opening hours 9 am – 5 pm; daily; March to October.
Admission fee £1.

Galloway House is where Neil McEacharn learnt to garden, before moving to Lake Maggiore to create the great gardens of Villa Taranto. A vast *Davidia involucrata* dates from his ownership, as do many of the tender trees and shrubs which he planted to take advantage of the mild maritime climate – eucryphias, for example. The fine conifers date back to the Earls of Galloway in the 19th century, while most of the *Rhododendron* species were planted after the war. The garden is still undergoing restoration, but is already a great pleasure to visit, especially in late spring.

 Features Snowdrops; rhododendrons & azaleas; daffodils; camellias; bluebells; camellia house restored (1999); extensive new plantings.

Owned by Galloway House Gardens Trust
Number of gardeners 1
Size 26ha (65 acres)

Glenwhan Garden

DUNRAGIT, BY STRANRAER DG9 8PH

Tel & Fax 01581 400222
Website www.glenwhan.co.uk
Location 1 mile off A75 at Dunragit Village. Follow brown tourist signs.
Opening hours 10 am – 5 pm; daily; April to September. And by appointment.
Admission fee Adults £3; OAPs £2.50; Children £1.
RHS members free from August to October.

Glenwhan is a plantsman's garden which has been created since 1979 by its present owners, starting from wild fields and scrub. Ambitious in scale, the heart of the garden is a pair of lochans or bog lakes. Above them rises a series of roped terraces, planted with heathers, azaleas, small conifers, golden elders, hardy fuchsias and massed Rugosa roses. A small folly stands at the peak. In prospect, the whole design is beautifully composed and tranquil. From the folly there are extensive views across the garden to Luce Bay and the Mull of Galloway beyond. Tessa Knott's first plantings were a sturdy shelter belt of small trees, including native Scots pines, English oaks and mountain ashes. Now 20 years old, there are occasional glimpses through these lichen-stained ancients to the gorse scrub and bog which surround the garden. The shelter belt is a transitional feature: it is a refinement of the more primitive vegetation beyond the perimeter fence, and it introduces planting themes which are then developed within the garden, in the form, for example, of collections of choicer *Sorbus* and *Quercus* species (including *Q. × bushii* and *Q. dentata*). Pools have been cut out of the blackest peat to make an attractive sequence of grassy water gardens, planted with primula and meconopsis cultivars.

Glenwhan is very much a plantsman's garden, but Tessa Knott also uses plants to create effects, and she has capitalised upon the lie of the land to produce different habitats. The new plantings include large-leaved rhododendrons (*R. fictolacteum* for example), and some interesting southern hemisphere plants, including eucalyptus and olearias around the summerhouse. Another highlight is the dappled woodland walk with yet more new planting. Indeed many parts of this garden are 'work in progress' which will be worth returning to see again as they mature.

Features Woodland garden; roses (mainly old-fashioned); plantsman's collection of plants; bluebells; cistus; camellias; primulas; bog plants; trees and shrubs; many new *Rhododendron* species from collected seed; shop; nursery with interesting plants; licensed garden restaurant.

Owned by Mr & Mrs William Knott
Number of gardeners 2
Size 5ha (12 acres)

Logan Botanic Garden

PORT LOGAN, STRANRAER DG9 9ND

Tel 01776 860231   **Fax** 01776 860333
Website www.rbge.org.uk
Location 14 miles south of Stranraer on B7065.
Opening hours 9.30 am – 6 pm; daily; March to October.
Admission fee Adults £3; Concessions £2.50; Children £1; Family £7.

This extraordinarily exotic garden, started by the McDouall family in the 19th century, is now part of the Royal Botanic Garden Edinburgh. Logan's sheltered aspect and proximity to the warming waters of the Atlantic enable a wide range of tender and southern hemisphere plants to be grown out of doors. The bedding out of thousands of half-hardy perennials makes the garden a blaze of colour on bright sunny days. In the walled garden, overlooked by the slender remains of Castle Balzieland, there is a fine collection of established tree ferns (*Dicksonia antarctica*). They are underplanted with the smaller fern, *Blechnum chilense*, which creates an impression of lush fertility, as if the dicksonias have seeded themselves everywhere. The formal lily pond is partly framed by a diagonal avenue of cabbage palms (*Cordyline australis*) 10m high. Around the pond are waving wands of *Dierama pulcherrimum* and *Kniphofia*, and the air glints with dragonflies in summer. Among the trees which flower in the sheltered walls are a tall *Metrosideros umbellatus* and the flame tree, *Embothrium coccineum*. Also flowering freely here, as it does in other gardens in south-west Scotland, is *Eucryphia* × *nymansensis* 'Nymansay'. Beyond the brilliance of the walled garden, and past an avenue of Chusan palms (*Trachycarpus fortunei*), lies Logan's woodland garden. Some of its pleasures are more hidden than others, but a spectacular specimen of *Magnolia campbellii* 'Charles Raffill' stands on the edge, in flower in April, and decked with swollen red pods by August. Look out in particular for plants from the southern hemisphere, including *Leptospermum lanigerum, Crinodendron hookerianum,* and the Chatham Island daisy bush, *Olearia semidentata* (also known as *O.* 'Henry Travers'). Do not miss the gunnera bog either, where this giant rhubarb-like plant grows so tall and thick that you can lose yourself under its prickly, slightly sinister canopy. In the Discovery Centre there are reference books, computers and microscopes which the visitor can use, perhaps to learn more about the Maddenia section of the genus *Rhododendron,* in which the garden specialises. Visitors can borrow innovative free audio guides, which are keyed to numbers marked on labels throughout the gardens. It is slightly surreal to see your fellow visitors wandering around clasping these futuristic wands, but the guide is informative and chatty.

Features Sub-tropical plants; good herbaceous borders; tree ferns; cardiocrinums; gunnera; cordylines; trachycarpus palms; tender perennials (diascias, fuchsias, salvias); eucalyptus; shop selling books, gifts and local crafts; light meals & refreshments.

Owned by Royal Botanic Garden Edinburgh
Size 12ha (30 acres)

Threave Garden

CASTLE DOUGLAS DG7 1RX

Tel 01556 502575   **Fax** 01556 502683
Website www.nts.org.uk
Location Off A75, 1 mile west of Castle Douglas.
Opening hours 9.30 am – sunset; daily; 1 March to 23 December. Walled garden & glasshouses close at 5 pm.
Admission fee Adults £5; Concessions £3.75; Children £1. RHS members free in April, May, September & October.

Threave is a teaching garden with a very wide range of attractions – something to interest every gardener, in fact. It has been developed since 1960 with the needs of students at the School of Horticulture, garden-owners and tourists all in mind. Threave has quickly acquired the reputation of a Scottish Wisley. There are over 200 daffodil cultivars to admire in spring; a fine collection of old roses in the summer; colourful herbaceous borders; and good autumn colour. The modern designs are inspirational and a new Victorian-style conservatory has recently been built in the walled garden.

Features Woodland garden; roses (ancient & modern); rock garden; plantsman's collection of plants; plants under glass; fruit; good herbaceous borders; fine collection of trees; peat garden; heath garden; tallest *Alnus rubra* (23m) in the British Isles, and two other record trees; shop; restaurant & snacks.

Owned by The National Trust for Scotland
Number of gardeners 2, plus 3 instructors
Size 26ha (64 acres)

FIFE

Cambo Gardens

KINGSBARNS, ST ANDREWS
KY16 8QD

Tel 01333 450054   **Fax** 01333 450987
Website www.camboestate.com
Location On A917 between Kingsbarns & Crail.
Opening hours 10 am – dusk; daily; all year. Guided tours by arrangement.
Admission fee Adults £2.50; Children free.

Cambo's large romantic Victorian walled garden is built around the Cambo Burn, a most unusual feature which gives the garden its unique character. The burn is lined with willows, traversed by elegant wrought-iron bridges, and incorporates a waterfall. The garden also has a very fine display of annuals and perennials as well as fruit and vegetables for the handsome Victorian house. Outside are 70 acres of woodland walks leading down to the sea, spectacular in early spring when carpeted with snowdrops, snowflakes and aconites. Elsewhere are an ornamental *potager*, masses of spring bulbs, a lilac walk (26 cultivars), over 250 different roses, fine herbaceous borders for summer and autumn, and a meadow of colchicums. New planting schemes are planned for 2002.

Features Roses (mainly old-fashioned); daffodils; snowflakes; aconites; colchicum meadows; autumn colour.

Owned by Mr & Mrs T.P.N. Erskine
Number of gardeners 3
Size 1ha (2½ acres), plus 28ha (70 acres) woodland

Falkland Palace

FALKLAND, CUPAR KY15 7BU

Tel 01337 857397   **Fax** 01337 857980
Website www.nts.org.uk
Location On A912, 11 miles north of Kirkcaldy. 10 miles from M90, Jct 8.
Opening hours 11 am (1 pm on Sundays) – 5.30 pm; daily; April to October. Opens at 10 am on weekdays from June to August.
Admission fee Adults £3; Concessions £2.25.

The palace at Falkland is old: it dates from the first half of the 16th century. Today's garden was built in about 1950 by Percy Cane: his reconstruction of a Scottish renaissance garden has a herb garden in the Jacobean style, an astrolabe walk and formal parterres prettily planted in pastel colours.

Features Fruit; good herbaceous borders; autumn colour; spectacular delphinium border; gift shop.

Owned by The National Trust for Scotland
Number of gardeners 2
Size 4.2ha (11 acres)

Hill of Tarvit

CUPAR KY15 5PB

Tel & Fax 01334 653127
Website www.nts.org.uk
Location Off A916, 2½ miles south of Cupar.
Opening hours 9.30 am – sunset; daily; all year.
Admission fee Adults £2; Concessions £1 in honesty box. RHS members free.

Hill of Tarvit is an established plantsman's garden, formally designed but opulently planted and maintained, in keeping with the Lorimer house. The Edwardian plantings, now splendidly mature, are complemented by modern additions. The Trust has begun to restore and replant the borders on the top terrace in the Edwardian style.

 Features Woodland garden; roses (mainly old-fashioned); plantsman's collection of plants; good herbaceous borders; heathers; tea-room in house (open in summer).

Owned by The National Trust for Scotland
Number of gardeners 2
Size 8ha (20 acres)

Kellie Castle

PITTENWEEN KY10 2RF

Tel 01333 720271   **Fax** 01333 720736
Website www.nts.org.uk
Location On B9171, 3 miles north-west of Pittenween.
Opening hours 9.30 am – sunset; daily; all year.
Admission fee Adults £2; Concessions £1. Pay & display.
RHS members free.

Ⓟ ⓦⓒ ⓖ ⊕ ⓦ

Kellie Castle was Sir Robert Lorimer's own family house: it was he who re-made the garden in its present form and designed both the 'secret garden' and 'Robin's corner'. It is no more than 1 acre in extent, but strong lines and thick planting create a sense of both space and enclosure. Much of the planting is modern. The organic walled garden contains a fine collection of old-fashioned roses, fruit trees and herbaceous plants: there are displays in the summerhouse about the history of the walled garden. The yew hedges are threaded with scarlet *Tropaeolum speciosum*.

 Features Roses (mainly old-fashioned); fruit; good herbaceous borders; strong design; extended collection of historic vegetables; gift shop; tea-room.

Owned by The National Trust for Scotland
Number of gardeners 2
Size 6.4ha (16 acres)

St Andrews Botanic Garden

THE CANONGATE, ST ANDREWS KY16 8RT

Tel 01334 477178   **Fax** 01334 476452
Website www.st-and.ac.uk/standrews/botanic
Location A915, Largo Road, then entrance in The Canongate.
Opening hours 10 am – 7 pm (4 pm October to April); daily; all year.
Admission fee Adults £2; OAPs & Children £1. RHS members free.

Ⓟ ⓦⓒ ⓖ ⊕ ⓦ

The botanic garden at St Andrews is currently undergoing much improvement. The garden's main asset, the peat, rock and water complex (crag, scree, moraine, alpine meadow and bog) is being repaired and replanted. Work on the cactus house has been completed, a new alpine house is now open, and the orchid house re-opened recently. There is also a tropical house and a house for Maddenia rhododendrons. The garden caters particularly well for children.

 Features Woodland garden; rock garden; rhododendrons & azaleas; plants under glass; fine collection of trees; peat beds; ferns; heath garden; order beds; herbaceous borders.

Owned by St Andrews University
Number of gardeners 5
Size 7.2ha (18 acres)

GRAMPIAN

Blackhills

BY ELGIN, MORAY IV30 3QU

Tel 01343 842223   **Fax** 01343 843136
Website www.blackhills.co.uk
Location 1 mile south of Lhanbryde, near Elgin on the B9103.
Opening hours Last two Sundays in May, & by appointment.
Admission fee Donation.

Blackhills is a magnificent collection of rhododendrons in two steep-sided glacial valleys: these possess a microclimate which allows many plants to grow that are normally considered too tender for the north-east coast of Scotland. The rhododendrons were planted throughout the 20th century by successive generations of the Christie family, along with many other Himalayan and Chinese plants, in a woodland garden which is now fully mature. There are about 360 different rhododendron species growing at Blackhills, all of wild origin: most were collected in the Himalayas, some came from North America, Central Asia and Northern Europe. The garden now contains one of the finest and most extensive private collections of species rhododendrons in the world. Some of the species self-seed.

 Features Rhododendrons.

Owned by T.S. Christie
Number of gardeners 1
Size 20ha (50 acres)

Brodie Castle

BRODIE, FORRES, MORAY IV36 2TE

Tel 01309 641371   **Fax** 01309 641600
Website www.nts.org.uk
Location Signed from A96.
Opening hours Grounds: 9.30 am – sunset; daily; all year.
Admission fee £1 in honesty box.

Brodie Castle came to the National Trust for Scotland in 1980. It sits in a landscaped park and there are rhododendrons in the woodland policies, but Brodie is famous, above all, for its daffodils. Many were bred here at the turn of the 19th century and the Trust has tried assiduously to identify, propagate and distribute them more widely. They are a glorious sight when they bloom in the lawns around the baronial battlements.

Features Woodland garden; rhododendrons & azaleas; daffodils; NTS shop; tea-room in castle (closes at 4.30 pm).

Owned by The National Trust for Scotland
Number of gardeners 6, plus 2 part-time
Size 32ha (80 acres)
NCCPG National Collections Narcissus

Crathes Castle

BANCHORY AB31 5QJ

Tel 01330 844525   **Fax** 01330 844797
Website www.nts.org.uk
Location On A93, 15 miles west of Aberdeen.
Opening hours 9 am – sunset; daily; all year.

Admission fee Adults £5; Concessions £3.75.

Crathes is famous for its walled garden, which started as a kitchen garden and was substantially developed as a flower garden in the 1920s and 1930s. It is divided into eight distinct gardens, each with its own character. These include a white border, a yellow enclosure known as the Golden Garden, a misty blue garden, and a dreamy high summer border with pastel shades for long Highland evenings. The garden is intensively planted to give colour all the year round. Some of the topiary yew hedges date back to 1702.

Features Woodland garden; roses (ancient & modern); plantsman's collection of plants; mature conifers; two ice houses; specimen trees; colour borders; current holder of Sandford Award; tallest *Zelkova* × *verschaffeltii* in the British Isles, and four further tree records.

Owned by The National Trust for Scotland
Number of gardeners 5
Size 1.5ha (3¾ acres)
NCCPG National Collections *Viburnum*; *Dianthus* (Malmaison carnations)

Cruickshank Botanic Garden

ST MACHAR DRIVE, ABERDEEN AB24 3UU

Tel 01224 272704   **Fax** 01224 272703
Location Follow signs for Aberdeen University and/or Old Aberdeen.
Opening hours 9 am – 4.30 pm; Monday – Friday; all year. Plus 2 pm – 5 pm; Saturdays & Sundays; May to September.
Admission fee Free.

Cruickshank Botanic Garden was founded in 1898 for the teaching and study of botany at the University of Aberdeen. Its 12 acres still have an educational element but also serve as an amenity for the wider public. Its leading features include: a rock garden for alpine plants and bulbs, where wild orchids seed around; an arboretum, planted quite recently – in about 1970 – with natives, exotics and garden cultivars, many of them now semi-mature; collections of native plants, including all the endemic *Sorbus* species of the British Isles; and a rose garden which has been laid out to illustrate the history of the rose in cultivation. The garden is well-maintained and – like all botanic gardens – worth visiting at any time of the year. It is also supported by an enthusiastic Friends organisation. The latest development is a wildflower meadow.

Features Lots of plants; roses (mainly old-fashioned); rock garden; good herbaceous borders; fine collection of trees; stone troughs; peat beds; Scottish upland plants; *Meconopsis* × *sheldonii*.

Owned by Aberdeen University
Number of gardeners 3

Drum Castle

DRUMOAK, BANCHORY AB31 3EY

Tel 01330 811204   **Fax** 01330 811962
Website www.nts.org.uk
Location Off A93, 10 miles west of Aberdeen.
Opening hours Grounds: 9.30 – sunset; daily; all year. Garden: 10 am – 6 pm; daily; 25 March to 27 October, plus weekends in October.
Admission fee Adults £1; honesty box or ticket machine.

The gardens at Drum are modern – begun in 1991 with the intention of providing an appropriate historic setting for the castle and a place where old Scottish roses could be grown. There is a knot garden planted with herbs in the style of the early 17th century and a formal garden with *allées* and topiary to represent the early 18th century. Most of the borders are designed and planted in the 20th-century style as mixtures of roses, other shrubs and perennials. Scattered all around the gardens is the best collection of Scottish roses (hybrids of *Rosa pimpinellifolia*) in Britain.

 Features Roses (mainly old-fashioned); small tea-room.

Owned by The National Trust for Scotland
Number of gardeners 2
Size 8ha (20 acres)

Kildrummy Castle

KILDRUMMY, ALFORD AB33 8RA

Tel 01975 571203/571277
Location On A97, off A944.
Opening hours 10 am – 5 pm; daily; 29 March to October.
Admission fee Adults £2.50; Children free.

Kildrummy has a glen-garden, laid out about 100 years ago. The richly planted pools and ponds are complemented by a plantsman's collection on the hillside, and a large mature rock garden made from the natural sandstone. It is one of the most romantic gardens in Scotland.

 Features Roses (mainly old-fashioned); plantsman's collection of plants; fine collection of trees; autumn colour; heathers; water garden & rock garden replanted (1998); tea & coffee.

Owned by Kildrummy Castle Garden Trust
Number of gardeners 2.5
Size 8ha (20 acres)

Leith Hall

KENNETHMONT, HUNTLY AB54 4NQ

Tel 01464 831216   **Fax** 01464 831594
Website www.nts.org.uk
Location On B9002 west of Kennethmont.
Opening hours 9.30 am – sunset; daily; all year.
Admission fee Adults £2.50; Concessions £1.90. RHS members free.

From this garden's historic past come two ponds and an ice house, but richly planted borders are the pride of Leith Hall today: they are full of colour all through the summer. Also impressive is the rock garden, restored and replanted by that most successful of societies, the Scottish Rock Garden Club. Leith gets better and better.

 Features Roses (mainly modern); rock garden; good herbaceous borders; bluebells; ice house; sculptures in woodland walk; refreshments from May to October, 1.30 pm – 5.30 pm.

Owned by The National Trust for Scotland
Number of gardeners 2
Size 2.2ha (6 acres)

Pitmedden

ELLON, ABERDEEN AB4 7PD

Tel 01651 842352   **Fax** 01651 843188
Website www.nts.org.uk
Location 1 mile west of Pitmedden on A920.
Opening hours 10 am – 5 pm; daily; May to September. Last entry 5.30 pm.
Admission fee Adults £5; Concessions £4.

The spectacular formal garden at Pitmedden was meticulously created in the 1950s by the National Trust for Scotland, using

17th-century Scottish designs. Three of the four parterres came from patterns associated with Holyrood House: the fourth is an heraldic design based on the coat-of-arms of Sir Alexander Seton, who first laid out a garden here in 1675. The result has three miles of box hedging and uses 40,000 bedding plants every summer. It may not be completely authentic, but it certainly looks genuine enough, as well as being both impressive, satisfying and peaceful.

 Features Herbs; gazebos; parterres; tea-room.

Owned by The National Trust for Scotland
Number of gardeners 5
Size 6ha (15 acres)

HIGHLAND

Abriachan Gardens

LOCH NESS SIDE, BY INVERNESS
IV3 8LA

Tel & Fax 01463 861232
Location Just off the A82.
Opening hours 9 am – 7 pm (5 pm from October to March); daily; all year.
Admission fee Adults £2; OAPs £1; Children 20p.
RHS members free from March to October.

These unique gardens on the shores of Loch Ness wind their way through the native hazel and oak woodland and offer spectacular views down the Great Glen. Many choice plants are grown here: their specialities are hardy perennials and shrubs. There are extensive garden walks among dry stone dykes and raised beds.

 Features Good modern garden; herbaceous plants; geraniums, helianthemums and Barnhaven primulas; hot drinks machine.

Owned by Mr & Mrs D. Davidson
Number of gardeners 2
Size 1.6ha (4 acres)

Allangrange

MUNLOCHY, BLACK ISLE IV8 8NZ

Tel 0146 3811249   **Fax** 0146 3811407
Location Signed off A9, 5 miles north of Inverness.
Opening hours 2 pm – 5.30 pm; 5 May & 16 June; or by appointment.
Admission fee £2.

Colour gardening by Mrs Cameron, a botanical artist, has made this one of the loveliest summer gardens in the British Isles. The spring flowers are good, too.

Features Woodland garden; roses (mainly old-fashioned); primulas; rhododendrons; colour borders; teas in house.

Owned by Major Allan Cameron
Number of gardeners 1
Size 1.2ha (3 acres)

Ardfearn Nursery

BUNCHREW, INVERNESS IV3 6RH

Tel 01463 243250
Location Off A862 west of Inverness.
Opening hours 9 am – 5.30 pm; daily.

Alpines and small ericaceous shrubs in quantity are produced at this nursery in a lovely Highland setting. It is particularly good for celmisias, gentians and above all, primulas. But the stock is always changing, which is what draws back the nursery's discriminating clientèle year after year.

Attadale Gardens

STRATHCARRON, WESTER ROSS
IV54 8YX

Tel 01520 722217   **Fax** 01520 722546
Website www.attadale.com
Location On A890 between Strathcarron & South Strome.

Opening hours 10 am – 5.30 pm; Monday – Saturday; April to October. Coaches by prior arrangement only.
Admission fee Adults £3; Children £1.

The gardens at Attadale were started in the 1890s: many rhododendrons, azaleas and specimen trees date from that time. The recent expansion of planting began in the 1980s, with over 2,000 trees and shrubs, which are now underplanted with irises, candelabra primulas, gunneras and bamboos. The ponds and waterfalls are spanned by bridges and richly planted with marginals and waterlilies. A fern garden is backed by dripping black rocks. There is also a vegetable garden and herb garden. The nursery specialises in bog plants – among them, meconopsis, primulas and rodgersias.

 Features Rhododendrons; meconopsis; primulas; bog plants; nursery.

Owned by Mr & Mrs Ewen Macpherson
Number of gardeners 3½
Size 8ha (20 acres)

Cawdor Castle

CAWDOR, NAIRN IV12 5RD

Tel 01667 404615 **Fax** 01667 404674
Website www.cawdorcastle.com
Location Between Inverness & Nairn on B9090.
Opening hours 10 am – 5 pm; daily; 1 May to 13 October.
Admission fee £3.30. RHS members free in May, June, September & October.

Cawdor Castle could claim to be the most romantic castle in the Highlands – the 14th-century home of the Thanes of Cawdor. It has several gardens: the earliest dates from the 16th century and has the maze. There is

also an 18th-century flower garden with large herbaceous borders and roses and a 19th-century wild garden with a good collection of rhododendrons and spring bulbs as well as splendid trees. Recent additions include a holly maze, a laburnum walk and coloured planting schemes. Earth, Purgatory and Paradise are somehow represented in the new plantings, but they are best enjoyed as colours and shapes. The effect is neither cranky nor grand, just extremely charming. The Auchindoune garden, originally planted in the 1920s with plants brought back by Lord Cawdor from his expedition to the Himalayas with Frank Kingdon Ward, is being restored with almost all the plants they brought back from the Tsangpo Gorges: open for the first time in 2002, by appointment only.

 Features Woodland garden; roses (mainly old-fashioned); fruit; good herbaceous borders; good late summer plantings; gift shop; licensed restaurant in castle.

Owned by The Dowager Countess Cawdor
Number of gardeners 4
Size 1.4ha (3½ acres)

Coiltie Garden

DIVACH, DRUMNADROCHIT IV63 6XW

Tel 01456 450219
Location Take the small uphill road out of Drumnadrochit to Divach.
Opening hours 12 noon – 7 pm; daily; 10 June to 4 August.
Admission fee Adults £2.50; Children free.

There was little except a few old trees and a 30m waterfall when the Nelsons came to Coiltie in 1980 and took on the neglected and overgrown Victorian garden. They decided not to reconstruct it, but to lay a new informal one on the sloping site, and planted it with hedges, shrubs, climbers, herbaceous plants and lots of roses. The views are stupendous.

 Features Roses; trees; mixed borders.

Owned by Mr & Mrs David Nelson
Number of gardeners 1
Size 1.6ha (4 acres)

Dochfour Gardens

INVERNESS IV3 6JY

Tel 01463 861218 **Fax** 01463 861366
Location 5 miles south-west of Inverness on the A82.
Opening hours 10 am – 4 pm; Monday – Friday; April to September. Coach parties by appointment.
Admission fee Adults £1.50; Concessions £1.

Ⓟ &

Dochfour is a substantial garden, landscaped and terraced down to the Loch Dochfour. Though best when the daffodils and rhododendrons colour the hillside, it is most famous for the size and number of its 19th-century conifers.

 Features Conifers; rhododendrons & azaleas; naturalised daffodils; parterres; water gardens; tallest *Thuja occidentalis* 'Lutea' in the British Isles, plus two further tree records; no shop, but pick-your-own fruit in season.

Owned by The Hon. Alexander Baillie
Number of gardeners 1½
Size 7.6ha (19 acres)

Dunrobin Castle Gardens

GOLSPIE, SUTHERLAND KW10 6SF

Tel 01408 633177 **Fax** 01408 634081
Website www.great-houses-scotland.co.uk
Location 1 mile north of Golspie on A9.
Opening hours Dawn to dusk; daily; all year round. Castle gardens: 10.30 am (4.30 pm in April, May & October); 1 April to 15 October. Last entry 30 minutes before closing.
Admission fee Castle & garden: Adults £6.25; OAPs £4.50. RHS members free. Reductions for groups. Gardens open free when castle closed.

The grand terraced gardens at Dunrobin were laid out in 1850 by Sir Charles Barry, architect of the Houses of Parliament. Their formal style, striding down to the Dornoch Forth, is appropriate to the French-style *château*. Three parterres surround the fountains, two bedded out traditionally and one planted with hardy geraniums and underplanted with tulips and lilies. Recent restoration and re-planting have produced a line of whitebeams, gunneras, new rhododendrons and three herbaceous borders. Another addition has been some 20 wooden pyramids planted with clematis and climbing roses – very pretty.

 Features Woodland garden; topiary; roses (mainly modern); good herbaceous borders; formal gardens; gift shop; tea-room in castle.

Owned by The Sutherland Trust
Number of gardeners 3
Size 2ha (5 acres)

The Hydroponicum

ACHILTIBUIE, ULLAPOOL IV26 2YG

Tel 01854 622202   **Fax** 01854 622201
Location Signed off A835, 25 miles north of Ullapool.
Opening hours 10 am – 6 pm; daily; 2 April to 30
September. Guided tours on the hour (last one at 5 pm).
Plus tours at 12 noon & 2 pm from Monday to
Friday in October.
Admission fee Adults £4.75; Concessions £3.50;
Children £2.75.

The Hydroponicum has three growing
houses, each individually heated and
featuring plants from different climatic
zones. Salads, herbs and tree fruits grow in
the 'cottage garden' house. Tomatoes, citrus
fruit and olives fill the 'South of France'
house. And the 'Canary Island zone' is
planted with vines, figs, tamarillos and
bananas. 'Planted' is not quite the right
word: hydroponics are all about soilless
cultivation – essential in places like Saudi
Arabia but a small miracle here in the
north-west of Scotland.

 Features Hydroponic culture; fruit
under glass.

Owned by Viscount Gough
Number of gardeners 2
Size 0.1ha (¼ acre) glasshouses & 0.8ha (2 acres) grounds

Inverewe

POOLEWE, ROSS AND CROMARTY IV22 2LQ

Tel 01445 781200   **Fax** 01445 781497
Website www.nts.org.uk
Location On A832, 6 miles north of Gairloch.
Opening hours 9.30 am – 9 pm; daily; 25 March to
31 October.
Admission fee Adults £7; Concessions £5.25.

Inverewe is one of the wonders of the
horticultural world, a sub-tropical garden
in the north-west Highlands. Its position
on a sheltered peninsular, warmed by the
Gulf Stream, explains the luxuriance of its
plantings. It is also the reason why, even
so far north, it has much to interest the
plantsman at every time of the year. The
garden owes its origins to Osgood
Mackenzie, who from 1862 to 1922 planted
windbreaks to protect more delicate exotics
within. Spectacular large-leaved Himalayan
rhododendrons, magnolias, eucalyptus,
tree ferns, palms and tender rarities are
underplanted with drifts of blue poppies and
candelabra primulas. Among Inverewe's
record trees are specimens of *Eucalyptus
cordata* and *Salix magnifica*, neither of
which would be fully hardy in the home
counties of England. Inverewe is
exceptionally well maintained, though
perhaps best on a sunny, dry day in May,
before the midges breed.

Features Woodland garden; sub-
tropical plants; rock garden;
plantsman's collection of plants; mature
conifers; good herbaceous borders; fine
collection of trees; autumn colour;
meconopsis; candelabra primulas; lilies;
tallest *Eucalyptus cordata* (30m) in the
British Isles, and three further record trees;
large shop; excellent new restaurant.

Owned by The National Trust for Scotland
Number of gardeners 8
Size 20ha (50 acres)
NCCPG National Collections *Olearia*; *Brachyglottis*; *Rhododendron* (Barbatum, Glischra & Maculifera sections)

Jack Drake

INSHRIACH ALPINE NURSERY, AVIEMORE, INVERNESS-SHIRE PH22 1QS

Tel 01540 651287   **Fax** 01540 651656
Website www.kincraig.com/drakesalpines
Location 4 miles south of Aviemore. Take B970 to Inverdruie. Turn right, ¾ mile after the Spey Bridge.
Opening hours 10 am – 5 pm; Monday – Friday.
10 am – 4 pm; Saturdays. March to October.
Admission fee free.

This is a Mecca for devotees of alpine and rock garden plants. It offers a large number of selected or collected forms. True alpines rub shoulders with species for wild and bog gardens. The nursery is laid out with demonstration gardens – screes, peat walls, wild gardens and bog gardens.

Features Scotland's premier alpine nursery; primulas; meconopsis; gentians; heathers.

Owned by John & Gunnbjørg Borrowman
Size 0.8ha (2 acres)

Leckmelm Arboretum

BY ULLAPOOL IV23 2RH

Location 3 miles south of Ullapool on the A835.
Opening hours 10 am – 6 pm; daily; April to September.
Admission fee Adults £2; Children free.

The Leckmelm Arboretum was laid out in the 1870s, and it is from those days that many of the finest trees date – wellingtonias, cedars, monkey puzzles and a huge weeping beech (*Fagus sylvatica* 'Pendula'). The record-breakers include an *Abies amabilis* 40m high, a good *Chamaecyparis lawsoniana* 'Wisselii' and a *Kalopanax pictus*. The Troughtons have taken advantage of the position on the shores of Loch Broom to make new plantings: they have put in such large-leaved rhododendrons as *R. sinogrande* and *R. macabeanum*, and even a selection of dicksonias, palms and olive trees.

Features Ancient trees; good rhododendrons.

Owned by Mr & Mrs Peter Troughton
Number of gardeners 1
Size 5ha (12 acres)

Lochalsh Woodland Garden

BALMACARA, BY KYLE OF LOCHALSH, ROSS IV40 8DN

Tel 01599 566325   **Fax** 01599 566359
Website www.nts.org.uk
Location On A87, 3 miles from Kyle.
Opening hours 9 am – sunset; daily; all year.
Admission fee Adults £2; Concessions £1. Honesty box.

This woodland garden is becoming much better known, and deservedly. The structure is about 100 years old – tall pines, oaks and larches with ornamental underplantings started in the late 1960s. Rhododendrons from Euan Cox at Glendoick came first: newer plantings include ferns, bamboos, fuchsias, hydrangeas and Maddenia rhododendrons, as well as plants from Tasmania and New Zealand.

Features Woodland garden; sub-tropical plants; plantsman's collection of plants; mature conifers.

Owned by The National Trust for Scotland
Number of gardeners 1
Size 5.2ha (13 acres)

Royal Botanic Garden Edinburgh

20A INVERLEITH ROW, EDINBURGH EH3 5LR

Tel 0131 552 7171　**Fax** 0131 248 2901
Website www.rbge.org.uk
Location 1 mile north of Princes Street.
Opening hours 9.30 am – 7 pm; daily; April to August.
Closes at 6 pm in March & September, 5 pm in
February & October, 4 pm from November to January.
Closed 1 January & 25 December.
Admission fee free. Voluntary donation at the
glasshouses. Guided tours available (£3) at 11 am
& 2 pm, daily from April to September.

The gardens at the Royal Botanic Garden
Edinburgh have an important amenity
function for both tourists and local people,
but they are principally a collection of plants
of scientific and educational importance.
They are internationally renowned for: their
plants from the Himalaya, west China and
Japan; their rhododendron collection – the
best in the world; their collection of orchids
from south-east Asia; their alpines; and their
flora of Arabia. So far as possible, these have
been displayed within the gardens in a
naturalistic setting which hints at their
native habitats. The landscaping in the
glasshouses is particularly good and
recreates a whole series of different
environments from arid deserts to humid
tropics. It goes without saying that
everything is extremely well labelled and the
standard of maintenance is among the
highest in any garden anywhere in the
world. The members of staff are also
invariably courteous and helpful. The rock
garden is over two acres in extent and
composed of many different micro-habitats,
most of them helped by the naturally light
sandy soil and low rainfall. More than 5,000
species (from areas as different as high
mountains, the arctic regions and the
Mediterranean) flourish in the mounds and
gullies of sandstone and conglomerate
alongside the stream and in the screes. The
heath garden has just been restored (2001)
as a Scottish moorland complete with
Landrover tracks. The arboretum has nearly
2,000 different trees, many of them seldom
seen in cultivation – the sort that visitors
consider attractive but are then disappointed
to find unavailable commercially. There are
also extensive areas dedicated to azaleas and
to systematic demonstration gardens. A
must for any visitor to Scotland.

Features Woodland garden; sub-
tropical plants; roses (ancient &
modern); rock garden; rhododendrons &
azaleas; herbs; plants under glass; mature
conifers; good herbaceous borders; fine
collection of trees; alpine plants; peat beds;
45 UK record-breaking trees, more than any
other Scottish garden; shop; recently
enlarged plant sales area; licensed café.

Owned by Board of Trustees
Size 31ha (77 acres)

LOTHIAN

Binny Plants

ECCLESMACHAN ROAD, BROXBURN
EH52 6NL

Tel 01506 858931 **Fax** 01506 858155
Location 2 miles north of Uphall.
Opening hours 10 am – 5 pm; Thursday – Monday;
mid-March to 31 October.
Admission fee Free.

This excellent nursery has an expanding
range. Its original specialities were
euphorbias, geraniums, hostas and small
shrubs, but it has now added a good range
of grasses and ferns. The catalogue has good,
helpful plant descriptions, with some
shrewd observations that give the reader
confidence.

Owned by Billy Carruthers

Dalmeny House

ROSEBERY ESTATES, SOUTH
QUEENSFERRY EH30 9TQ

Tel 0131 331 1888 **Fax** 0131 331 1788
Website www.dalmeny.co.uk
Location B924 off A90.
Opening hours 2 pm – 5.30 pm; Sunday – Tuesday;
July & August. And for SGS in snowdrop time.
Admission fee Grounds only: free.

The grounds at Dalmeny are extensive, and
visitors are encouraged to see the valley walk
with rhododendrons, wellingtonias and
other conifers. But the estate concentrates
upon the house and its remarkable

collections rather than promoting the
gardens and grounds.

 Features Woodland garden;
snowdrops; mature conifers;
rhododendrons & azaleas; wellingtonias;
refreshments.

Owned by The Earl of Rosebery

Inveresk Lodge

24 INVERESK VILLAGE, MUSSELBURGH
EH21 7TE

Tel 01721 722502
Website www.nts.org.uk
Location A6124 south of Musselburgh, 6 miles east
of Edinburgh.
Opening hours 10 am – 6 pm, Monday – Friday;
12 noon – 6 pm, Saturdays & Sundays; April to October.
10 am – 4.30 pm, Monday – Friday; 2 pm – 5 pm, Sundays;
November to March.
Admission fee Adults £2; Concessions £1. Honesty box.

This modern, terraced garden has been
tailor-made for a modest estate and is
maintained to a high standard. In its fine
Edwardian conservatory are an aviary and
some tree ferns. Elsewhere are good
herbaceous borders and interesting climbing
plants. Graham Thomas designed the
rose borders.

Features Roses (mainly old-
fashioned); good herbaceous borders;
raised beds; peat beds.

Owned by The National Trust for Scotland
Number of gardeners 1
Size 5.2ha (13 acres)

Malleny House Garden

BALERNO EH14 7AF

Tel 0131 449 2283
Website www.nts.org.uk
Location In Balerno, south-west of Edinburgh, off A71.
Opening hours 9.30 am – 7 pm (4 pm from November to March); daily; all year.
Admission fee Adults £2; Concessions £1. Honesty box.

Malleny is one of the National Trust for Scotland's best gardens, much praised for its 'personal' quality. The 19th-century shrub roses are richly underplanted with herbaceous plants which carry the display through into the autumn: there is a sense of opulence about the garden throughout the summer and autumn. The bonsai collection creates quite another dimension, as do the magnificent conservatory and the huge cones of yew topiary, relics of a 17th-century formal garden. It is, above all, a very peaceful garden – and far too little visited.

Features Topiary; roses (mainly old-fashioned & climbers); plants under glass; good herbaceous borders; Scottish National Bonsai Collection.

Owned by The National Trust for Scotland
Number of gardeners 1
Size 1.2ha (3 acres)
NCCPG National Collections *Rosa* (19th-century shrubs)

Suntrap Garden

43 GOGARBANK, EDINBURGH EH12 9BY

Tel 0131 339 7283
Location 1 mile west of Edinburgh bypass, between A8 & A71.
Opening hours 10 am – 4.30 pm; daily; all year, but with limited facilities at weekends.
Admission fee Adults £1; Children free.

Suntrap has 3 acres of demonstration gardens attached to Oatridge Agricultural College: it is one of the best places in Lothian to learn how to be a better gardener. It is now being developed as a life-long learning centre, with courses and events throughout the year. The features include island beds, a rock garden, a peat garden, sculptures, vegetable plots, a rose garden, annual borders – and much more.

Features Woodland garden; vegetables; roses (mainly modern); plants under glass; daffodils; good herbaceous borders; alpine plants; 'Italian' garden; peat walls.

Owned by Oatridge Agricultural College
Size 1.2ha (3 acres)

STRATHCLYDE

Achamore Gardens

ISLE OF GIGHA PA41 7AD

Tel 01583 505254   **Fax** 01583 505244
Website www.isle-of-gigha.co.uk
Location Take Gigha ferry from Tainloan (20 mins) then easy walking for 1½ miles.
Opening hours Dawn – dusk; daily; all year.
Admission fee Adults £2; Children £1.

Ⓟ 🐕 (wc)

Achamore is one of the best rhododendron gardens in the British Isles, and started as recently as 1944. Despite such a short existence (many rhododendron gardens date well back into the 19th century) Achamore has also had its fair share of ups and downs. It was largely planted by Sir James Horlick, with advice from Jim Russell. It has about 20 distinct areas cut out of the woodland (overgrown with *R. ponticum*) but they all have rhododendrons in common: their names include the Loderi garden, Thomson Garden and Macabeanum Wood. Camellias, eucalyptus and nothofagus also grow well here, as do many of the Surrey-type trees recommended by Russell – flowering cherries, sorbus and birches. And there are good herbaceous plantings too, from daffodils through to pulmonarias and primulas.

 Features Woodland garden; sub-tropical plants; rhododendrons; azaleas; biggest *Larix gmelinii* in the British Isles.

Owned by Holt Leisure Parks Ltd (Mr D.N. Holt)
Number of gardeners 2
Size 16ha (40 acres)

Achnacloich

CONNEL, OBAN PA37 1PR

Tel 01631 710221   **Fax** 01631 710796
Location On A85, 3 miles east of Connel.
Opening hours 10 am – 6 pm; daily; April to October.
Admission fee Adults £1.50; OAPs £1; Children free.

Ⓟ 🐕 (wc) 🌷

Achnacloich is a substantial woodland garden, made in three stages. First there were the Scots pine and European larch, which have grown to great heights. Then came the large-scale plantings of rhododendrons, particularly the *triflora* species which have begun to naturalise. The latest stage has been the creation of a plantsman's garden using the tender shrubs and trees which flourish on the west coast on Argyll. Some of the embothriums are taller than the native oaks.

 Features Woodland garden; rhododendrons & azaleas; good shrubs.

Owned by Mrs J. Nelson
Number of gardeners 1
Size 14ha (35 acres)

An Cala

ISLE OF SEIL PA34 4RF

Tel & Fax 01852 300237
Location In village of Easdale.
Opening hours 10 am – 6 pm; daily; April to September.
Admission fee Adults £1.50; Children free.

Ⓟ 🐕

This sheltered garden on the wild west coast was designed by Thomas Mawson and planted by the actress Faith Celli: it still has a 1930s feel to it. There is a natural rock garden and several streams which have been dammed and planted with moisture-loving species. The result is a garden of great lushness with splendid views across the islets of the Inner Hebrides. A flock of Rupert Till wire-sculpted sheep complement the straying real ones outside the garden.

 Features Rock garden; wild garden; bog garden; waterfalls & streams.

Owned by Mrs T. Downie
Number of gardeners 1
Size 2ha (5 acres)

Angus Garden

BARGUILLEAN, TAYNUILT PA35 1HY

Tel 01866 822254 **Fax** 01866 822048
Location Turn south off A85 at Taynuilt: 3 miles on right.
Opening hours Dawn – dusk; daily; March – October.
Admission fee Adults £2; Children free.

This young garden in a beautiful setting on the shores of Loch Etive has a particularly fine collection of modern rhododendrons in light oak woodland. It doubles up as a test ground for new hybrids introduced from USA. There are plans for a substantial expansion of the gardens to create more summer and autumn interest. Rather short on labels, but a garden to watch.

 Features Woodland garden; rhododendrons & azaleas; newly installed Peace Bell.

Number of gardeners 1
Size 4.2ha (11 acres) plus 6ha (15-acre) lake

Ardanaiseig Hotel Garden

ARDANAISEIG, KILCHRENAN, BY TAYNUILT PA35 1HE

Tel 01866 833333 **Fax** 01866 833222
Website www.ardanaiseig-hotel.com
Location On Loch Awe, 4 miles up from Kilchrenan.
Opening hours 9 am – 5 pm; daily; all year.
Admission fee Adults £2; Children free.

Ardanaiseig has a fine woodland garden with an important collection of rhododendrons and azaleas. Most were planted about 100 years ago. The hotel is in a stunning position on a promontory. The 19th-century walled garden is now undergoing restoration.

 Features Woodland garden; rhododendrons & azaleas; daffodils; good herbaceous borders; bluebells; maples; magnolias; hotel open to garden visitors.

Owned by Bennie Gray
Number of gardeners 2
Size 2ha (5 acres)

Ardchattan Priory

CONNEL, OBAN PA37 1RQ

Tel 01796 481355 **Fax** 01796 481211
Website www.gardens-of-argyll.co.uk
Location 5 miles east of Connel Bridge, on the north shore of Loch Etive.
Opening hours 9 am – 6 pm; daily; April to October.
Admission fee Adults £2; Children free.

Best in spring, when daffodils flower in light ornamental woodland, Ardchattan is also planted for high summer, with an emphasis on roses and herbaceous borders. The autumn colour, too, is surprisingly good for a west coast garden.

Features Roses (mainly old-fashioned); daffodils; good herbaceous borders; good collection of *Sorbus* species; huge *Hebe* bushes; tea-room, 11 am – 5 pm, May to August.

Owned by Mrs Sarah Troughton
Number of gardeners 1½
Size 1.6ha (4 acres)

Ardkinglas Woodland Garden

CAIRNDOW PA26 8BH

Tel 01499 600261   **Fax** 01499 600241
Website www.ardkinglas.com
Location On A83 at Cairndow.
Opening hours Daylight hours; daily; all year.
Admission fee £3.

Ⓟ 🐕 ⓦⓒ 🌼 ♿

Formerly known as Strone Gardens, Ardkinglas is famous for its magnificent conifers. As well as the tallest tree in Britain, it has the 'mightiest conifer in Europe', a specimen of *Abies alba* with a huge girth. The garden has been substantially improved by recent restoration and new plantings: this year (2002) will see an extension to the woodland garden itself and a new bridge across the River Kinglas to a 17th-century mill. Among the rhododendrons are many hybrids bred by Michael Noble, Lord Glenkinglas, when he was Secretary of State for Scotland. The nearby Tree Shop, run by the Ardkinglas Estate, is a nursery specialising in trees and shrubs – especially rhododendrons. It is open seven days a week and has a handsome list of unusual plants.

Features Woodland garden; rhododendrons & azaleas; mature conifers; tallest tree in Britain *Abies grandis* (63m), and 8 further UK record trees; excellent nursery.

Owned by S.J. Noble Esq.
Number of gardeners 2
Size 10ha (25 acres)
NCCPG National Collections *Abies*; *Picea*

Ardtornish Garden

LOCHALINE, MORVERN BY OBAN PA34 5VZ

Tel 01967 421288   **Fax** 01967 421211
Location 2 miles north of Lochaline.
Opening hours 10 am – 5 pm; daily; April to October.
Admission fee £3.

Ⓟ 🐕 ⓦⓒ 🌼

This is Faith Raven's other garden – see Docwra's Manor in Cambridgeshire – and a complete contrast: 28 acres of rocky hillside full of rhododendron species and Edwardian hybrids like 'Pink Pearl' and 'Cynthia'. Mrs Raven has actively improved it with a great range of interesting plants.

Features Plantsman's collection of plants; mature conifers; bluebells; kitchen garden; gunnera; rhododendrons; autumn colour.

Owned by Mrs John Raven
Number of gardeners 1
Size 11ha (28 acres)

Arduaine Garden

ARDUAINE, BY OBAN, ARGYLL
PA34 4XQ

Tel & Fax 01852 200366
Website www.nts.org.uk
Location On A816 between Oban & Lochgilphead.
Opening hours 9.30 am – sunset; daily; all year.
Admission fee Adults £3.50; Concessions £2.60.

Arduaine is a luxuriant woodland garden in a sheltered, south-facing valley at the edge of the sea. Stout conifers and 12m thickets of *Griselinia* protect the spectacular rhododendrons which two nurserymen planted in the 1970s. *Primula denticulata* and *Narcissus cyclamineus* have naturalised in grassy glades. *Cardiocrinum giganteum* and *Myosotidium hortensia* grow vigorously. There are several outsize and champion trees, including *Eucryphia glutinosa, Gevuina avellana, Trochodendron araliodes* and the upright form of the tulip tree known as *Liriodendron tulipifera* 'Fastigiatum'. Some of the giant rhododendrons (*R. arboreum* subsp. *zeylanicum*) are 100 years old: the plant of *R. griffithianum* too must be one of the largest in existence. But the sheer variety of the plantings is an education, while the whole garden is handsomely maintained.

 Features Sub-tropical plants; rhododendrons; tallest *Nothofagus antarctica* (26m) in the British Isles and 6 further records; no refreshments in the garden, but Loch Melfort Hotel is next door.

Owned by The National Trust for Scotland
Number of gardeners 3
Size 8ha (20 acres)

Barwinnock Herbs

BARRHILL, GIRVAN KA26 0RB

Tel & Fax 01465 821338
Website www.barwinnock.com
Location Off B7207, 12 miles north-west of Newton Stewart.
Opening hours 10 am – 5 pm; daily; April to October.

Although not far from such tourist destinations as Galloway Forest Park, Barwinnock Herbs is set among wonderfully wild scenery, which forms a spectacular backdrop to this beautifully laid out nursery. Primarily a nursery which specialises in organically-grown culinary, medicinal and aromatic herbs, there is a small garden too, in which these plants are prettily displayed. The plant yard itself is most attractive, with the pots arranged on rustic tables amidst a collection of agricultural bygones. There is a small rural museum attached, with some local produce and seed on sale and, for those who want to venture further afield, there are some enticing walks mapped out from the nursery. If you do not want to take your purchases with you, they are happy to post them for you.

Owned by Dave & Mon Holtom
Number of gardeners 1

Benmore Botanic Garden

DUNOON PA23 8QU

Tel 01369 706261 **Fax** 01369 706369
Website www.rbge.org.uk
Location 7 miles north of Dunoon on A815.
Opening hours 9.30 am – 6 pm; daily; March to October.

Admission fee Adults £3; OAPs £2.50; Children £1;
Family £7.

Benmore Botanic Garden has been a
regional annexe of the Royal Botanic Garden
Edinburgh since 1929, having been given to
the nation a few years earlier by the brewer
Harry Younger. The stupendous redwood
avenue which greets the visitor at the
entrance dates from 1863 and was the start
of a systematic programme of planting
conifers on the estate, into which the
Youngers introduced ornamental trees and
shrubs. The mild, wet climate makes
possible the cultivation of tender plants
from lower altitudes of the Sino-Himalaya,
Bhutan, Japan and the New World.
Benmore is a living textbook of the genus
Rhododendron: over 350 species and sub-
species grow at Benmore, and a further 300
hybrids and cultivars. Their background is
of conifers planted early in the 19th century,
perhaps the best collection in Scotland. The
conifers are at the heart of RBGE's
conservation programme and have been
supplemented by new ecological plantings
including a Bhutanese glade and a Chilean
glade. But the whole garden is spacious,
educational and beautifully maintained.

 Features Woodland garden; mature
conifers; fine collection of trees; giant
redwood avenue planted in 1863;
rhododendrons; ferns; new Chilean plant
collection; ten record-breaking trees,
including *Nothofagus betuloides* at over 20m;
gift shop; tea-room.

Owned by Board of Trustees/Royal Botanic Garden,
Edinburgh
Size 52ha (125 acres)

Biggar Park

BIGGAR ML12 6JS

Tel 01899 221085
Location ¼ mile south-west of Biggar on A702:
black iron gates & a lodge on the north side.
Opening hours By appointment for groups, May to
August; & for SGS.
Admission fee Adults £2; Children 50p.

Biggar Park garden is a mixture of woodland
(formal and informal), spacious lawns, and
unusual trees, shrubs and rhododendrons. It
is 225m above sea-level, so somewhat
susceptible to late spring frosts. In the
traditional working walled garden are fine
herbaceous borders, vegetables, fruit-trees
and a greenhouse. Shrub Roses are a special
interest: there are good collections of both
old and modern cultivars. The gardens also
have a good collection of meconopsis. A
small Japanese Garden is in the process of
development. Several ornamental ponds are
landscaped into the garden.

 Features Herbaceous borders; spring
bulbs, especially fritillaries;
rhododendrons & azaleas; meconopsis; old
roses; good collection of shrubs and trees;
plants for sale on SGS days.

Owned by Captain & Mrs David Barnes
Number of gardeners 1
Size 4ha (10 acres)

Brodick Castle

ISLE OF ARRAN KA27 8HY

Tel 01770 302202   **Fax** 01770 302312
Website www.nts.org.uk
Location Ferry from Ardrossan to Brodick, follows signs.
Opening hours 9.30 am – sunset; daily; all year. Walled
garden closes at 5 pm.

Admission fee Adults £3.50; Concessions £2.65.

This lush rhododendron garden was begun by Molly, Duchess of Montrose, in 1923. The climate at Brodick is mild and wet: the sloping hillside is almost frost-free. Some of the Duchess's plantings are now record-breakers, including *Embothrium coccineum* at more than 20m, the seldom-seen *Euonymus tingens*, the wild form of *Leptospermum scoparium* more than 10m high, and the rare *Nothofagus nervosa* which is over 30m high. In the woodland are fine magnolias, camellias, crinodendrons and olearias too, but none of these plantings is a match for the rhododendrons, many of which were grown from collectors' seed. The work of collectors Forrest, Ludlow and Kingdon Ward are all represented here. The walled garden has been restored as it might have been in Victorian times. For those with longer to dally, Brodick also has a fine park with further features including a restored ice-house.

Features Sub-tropical plants; good herbaceous borders; fine trees; candelabra primulas; meconopsis; lilies; good bedding; tallest *Drimys winteri* (21m) and *Embothrium coccineum* (20m) in the British Isles (& three further records); NTS shop; restaurant & tea-rooms.

Owned by The National Trust for Scotland
Number of gardeners 6, plus 2 part-time
Size 32ha (80 acres)
NCCPG National Collections *Rhododendron* (subsections Falconera, Grandia and Maddenia)

Colzium Walled Garden

OFF STIRLING ROAD, KILSYTH, GLASGOW G65 0PY

Tel 01236 828150 **Fax** 01236 826322
Location Signed from Kilsyth on B803.
Opening hours 12 noon – 7 pm; daily; Easter to mid-September. 12 noon – 4 pm; Saturdays & Sundays; rest of year.
Admission fee free.

Colzium Walled Garden is an up-and-coming young garden, which the Council has developed on an ancient site since 1976. A wide range of plants is grown within the protection of high walls, particularly conifers, rhododendrons and ornamental trees and shrubs of dwarf habit. They are intended to offer colour and interest throughout the year. The standards of maintenance and labelling are excellent.

Features Snowdrops; over 100 different *Galanthus* cultivars.

Owned by North Lanarkshire Council
Number of gardeners 3
Size 0.2ha (½ acre)

Culzean Castle & Country Park

MAYBOLE, AYRSHIRE KA19 8LE

Tel 01655 884455 **Fax** 01655 884503
Website www.nts.org.uk
Location Off A719, west of Maybole & South of Ayr.
Opening hours 10 am – 5 pm; daily; all year.
Admission fee Park & garden only: Adults £4.50; Concessions £3.40.

Culzean is the flagship of the National Trust for Scotland, thoroughly restored and seriously open to the public (more than 400,000 visitors a year). The gardens are important and include a deer park, a ruined arch, a viaduct, an ice house, a beautiful gothic camellia house, gazebos, a pagoda and a vinery. The three areas of horticultural interest are the walled garden, the fountain court and 'Happy Valley', which is a woodland garden with fine specimen trees. Record-breakers include an upright Irish yew (*Taxus baccata* 'Fastigiata') at 19m, and the rare southern Japanese hemlock *Tsuga sieboldii* at 25m.

 Features Woodland garden; herbs; plants under glass; good herbaceous borders; deer park; formal garden; tallest Irish yew *Taxus baccata* 'Fastigiata' in the British Isles (plus two further tree records); current holder of the Sandford Award; good shop; self-service restaurant.

Owned by The National Trust for Scotland
Number of gardeners 7, plus 4 groundsmen
Size 50ha (120 acres)

Finlaystone

LANGBANK PA14 6TJ

Tel & Fax 01475 540 285
Website www.finlaystone.co.uk
Location On A8, 10 mins west of Glasgow.
Opening hours 10 am – 5 pm; daily; all year.
Admission fee Adults £3; OAPs & Children £2.

Much of the garden at Finlaystone was laid out in about 1900. The formal garden dates from this period: it is enclosed within a yew hedge which was castellated by 'an enthusiastic family governess and a French aunt' in about 1920. But most of today's imaginative and beautiful garden is more

recent. The New Garden dates from 1959: the banks of a burn are lined with hostas, *Darmera peltatum* – spectacular in autumn – and azaleas which blend into the woodland beyond. In fact, throughout Finlaystone, the woodland areas are thick with azaleas, as well as rhododendrons, bluebells and snowdrops. Celtic themes have inspired the MacMillans to construct several new gardens on the hillside above the house. The Celtic Garden has an intricate pattern of paving set into grass: the design is based on one from the *Book of Kells*. In the walled garden is a 'garden oasis' in the form of a Celtic cross with a pool at the centre but all enclosed by a circular brick rose pergola. There is also a garden of scented plants for blind visitors which is sometimes known as the 'Fragrant Garden' and on other occasions as the 'Smelly Garden'.

 Features Rhododendrons & azaleas; daffodils; bluebells.

Owned by Arthur Macmillan
Number of gardeners 1, plus family members
Size 4ha (10 acres)

Geilston Garden

CARDROSS, DUMBARTON G82 5EZ

Tel 01389 841867
Location On A814, at western end of Cardross.
Opening hours 9.30 am – 5 pm; daily; 25 March to 27 October.
Admission fee £2.50. RHS members free.

Ⓟ ⓦⒸ

Geilston is a nice example of the many small country houses, villas and estates which were put together by successful Glasgow industrialists along the banks of the Clyde. The garden retains a sense of being a private space in which the visitor is an invited guest. The many attractive features include a fruit and vegetable garden with a central 'dipping pond', a walled garden with traditional glasshouses and a burn which winds through the wooded glen.

Owned by The National Trust for Scotland
Number of gardeners 1
Size 2.8ha (7 acres)

Glasgow Botanic Garden

730 GREAT WESTERN ROAD, GLASGOW G12 0UE

Tel 0141 334 2422   **Fax** 0141 339 6964
Location On A82, 2 miles from city centre.
Opening hours Grounds: 7 am – dusk; daily; all year. Glasshouses & Kibble Palace: 10 am – 4.45 pm (4.15 pm in winter); daily; all year. Special opening for SGS on 8 & 9 September.
Admission fee Free.

Most of the elements of the traditional botanic garden are here, including chronological beds, but the glory of Glasgow is its two glasshouses – the Kibble Palace and the Main Range. The Kibble Palace is a fine 19th-century cast-iron and steel structure, now in need of the restoration which will start in 2002. It houses collections from South Africa, China, South America and the Canaries: a walk around its outer circle takes the visitor round the horticultural globe. There is no better place to enjoy a winter's day in Glasgow. The Main Range is a more conventional construction – though also showing signs of disrepair – with good glasshouse collections of plants arranged by family and use, from tree ferns to palms and from cacti to orchids. A new herb garden was completed in 2001 and a new species rose garden will open this year (2002).

Features Roses (ancient & modern); herbs; plants under glass; mature conifers; good herbaceous borders; fine collection of trees; beautiful glasshouse (the 'Kibble Palace').

Owned by Glasgow City Council
NCCPG National Collections *Begonia*; *Dendrobium*; *Dicksoniaceae*

Glenarn

RHU, HELENSBURGH G84 8LL

Tel 01436 820493   **Fax** 0141 221 8450
Location Turn up Pier Road at Rhu Marina, first right is Glenarn Road.
Opening hours Dawn to dusk; daily; 21 March to 21 September.
Admission fee Adults £2; OAPs & Children £1.

Glenarn's 10 acres of woodland garden has at least one venerable old rhododendron dating from Sir Joseph Hooker's Himalayan expedition in the 1860s and many others from the 1930s trips of Kingdon Ward and Ludlow & Sheriff. The garden owes its present outline to the Gibson family who owned it from 1927 to 1982, and many of their original rhododendron hybrids still flourish here, though there are plenty of magnolias, camellias, pieris, and other good plants too. The Thornleys took over in 1983 – both of them professional architects whose gardening was moulded by the formal gardens of Italy – but their commitment to the woodland nature of the garden is remarkable. They have re-laid the steps, re-cut the paths, restored the vegetable garden and added a pond with a water chute. Work is progressing in the rock garden, where the owners are excavating and restoring the quarry face. Meanwhile they have also propagated the unique plants, renewed the plantings, created spaces, and maintained the balance between individual specimens. It is a remarkable achievement and worth a visit at any season, though especially in spring. There will be a special opening on 5 May for Scotland's Gardens Scheme.

Features Rock garden; plantsman's collection of plants; mature conifers; rhododendrons; embothriums; refreshments may be booked in advance for groups.

Owned by Mr & Mrs Michael Thornley
Number of gardeners owners only
Size 4ha (10 acres)

Greenbank Garden

FLENDERS ROAD, CLARKSTON, GLASGOW G76 8RB

Tel 0141 639 3281
Website www.nts.org.uk
Location One mile along Mearns Road from Clarkston Toll, take 1st left.
Opening hours Garden: 9.30 am – sunset; daily; all year. Walled garden closes at 5 pm. Closed 1 & 2 January, 25 & 26 December.
Admission fee Adults £3.50; Concessions £2.50.

Greenbank is a demonstration garden: it was left to the National Trust for Scotland in 1976 on condition that it was developed as a teaching resource for people with small gardens. The walled garden has therefore been divided into a great number of sections which represent different interests and skills: a rock garden, fruit garden, dried flower plot, raised beds, winter garden, and so on.

Features Woodland garden; rock garden; fruit in the walled garden; good herbaceous borders; a garden for the disabled; roses of every kind; NTS gift shop; light refreshments & drinks.

Owned by The National Trust for Scotland
Number of gardeners 3
Size 1ha (2½ acres) walled garden; 6ha (15 acres) of policies

Mount Stuart

ISLE OF BUTE PA20 9LR

Tel 01700 503877 **Fax** 01700 505313
Website www.mountstuart.com
Location 5 miles south of Rothesay.
Opening hours 10 am – 6 pm; daily except Tuesdays & Thursdays; May to 29 September. Plus Easter weekend, and Saturdays & Sundays in April & October.
Admission fee Adults £4; Children £2.

Mount Stuart has a vast and fascinating garden to accompany the sumptuous house. Its 300 acres include: a mature Victorian pinetum; a 2-acre rock garden designed by Thomas Mawson and thickly planted with rare collected plants; a 'wee' garden of 5 acres, planted with tender exotics from Australia and New Zealand; and a kitchen garden re-designed by the late Lord Bute with help from Rosemary Verey. Add in the relics of an 18th-century landscape, a tropical greenhouse, acres of bluebells and established rhododendrons, and you have the measure of a long and fascinating visit.

Features Woodland garden; rhododendrons & azaleas; plants under glass; mature conifers; bluebells; important rock garden; tender plants; fine new visitor centre; restaurant & café.

Owned by The Mount Stuart Trust
Number of gardeners 8
Size 120ha (300 acres)

Torosay
Castle & Gardens

CRAIGNURE, ISLE OF MULL
PA65 6AY

Tel 01680 812421   **Fax** 01680 812470
Website www.holidaymull.org/members/torosay
Location 1½ miles from Craignure on A849 to Iona.
Opening hours Gardens: 9 am – dusk; daily; all year.
Admission fee Adults £5; Concessions £4; Children
£1.75. RHS members free from April to June.

The best feature of the gardens at Torosay is
the Italian Statue Walk, lined with 19 figures
by Antonio Bonazza. The formal terraces
(attributed to Lorimer) are covered with
rambling roses, other climbers and
perennials. The Japanese garden, bog
garden, greenhouses and rock garden add
to the sheer variety. The woodland garden
is stuffed with interesting specimens:
Eucryphia, *Embothrium* and *Crinodendron*
among many Chilean plants, underplanted
with old daffodil cultivars, meconopsis
and primulas.

Features Rock garden; water garden;
Eucalyptus walk; new conservation
plantings with conifers from Royal Botanic
Garden at Edinburgh; eucalyptus walk;
shop; tea-room (April to mid-October)
with light lunches.

Owned by Mr C. James
Number of gardeners 2½, plus seasonal extras
Size 5ha (12 acres)

TAYSIDE

Bell's Cherrybank Centre

CHERRYBANK, PERTH PH2 0PF

Tel 01738 627330   **Fax** 01738 472823
Location Take Perth road from M90 Jct 11 & first right onto B9112.
Opening hours 10 am – 5 pm; daily; May to September. Plus 12 noon – 4 pm on Sundays. By appointment at other times.
Admission fee Adults £3.

These immaculately maintained show gardens make good use of water and incorporate some striking modern sculptures. They are best known for the collection of heaths and heathers, the most comprehensive in the British Isles with over 900 cultivars.

 Features Heathers; heathers for sale; light refreshments & drinks.

Owned by Guinness UDV
Number of gardeners 2
Size 2.6ha (6½ acres)
NCCPG National Collections Erica

Bolfracks Garden

ABERFELDY PH15 2EX

Tel 01887 820207
Location 2 miles west of Aberfeldy on A827.
Opening hours 10 am – 6 pm; daily; mid-March to October.
Admission fee Adults £2.50; Children free.

Bolfracks is a plantsman's garden, unusual among Scottish gardens for having a good display of flowers throughout the year. There are rhododendrons and azaleas, of course, but they are principally dwarf species and hybrids, and joined by a large number of daphnes, phyllodoces, pieris, quinces and berberis. Midsummer sees the shrub roses, of which there is a good collection, with everything from gallicas through to modern shrub roses. But Bolfracks is particularly good for its herbaceous borders: the perennials make an effective display by June and continue through until autumn, when gentians, cyclamen and colchicums take over.

 Features Herbaceous plants; roses; lots of plants at every season.

Owned by The Hutchinson Trustees
Number of gardeners 1
Size 1.2ha (3 acres)

Branklyn Garden

116 DUNDEE ROAD, PERTH PH2 7BB

Tel 01738 625535
Website www.nts.org.uk
Location Off Dundee Road, on eastern edge of Perth, ½ mile from Queen's Bridge.
Opening hours 9.30 am – sunset; daily; March to October.
Admission fee Adults £3.50; OAPs £2.60.

The apotheosis of Scottish rock gardening, Branklyn is a suburban garden absolutely crammed with rare plants growing in a series of artificial micro-habitats. This is a garden to go round slowly, looking at all the plants – small rhododendrons, alpines, herbaceous plants and peat-lovers. It was built up between 1922 and 1967 by John Renton, who bequeathed it to the National Trust for Scotland on his death. This sort of garden depends for its success upon the understanding and plantsmanship of the gardeners who work in it, and the Trust has been fortunate with their employees at Branklyn since they took it on.

 Features Rock garden; plantsman's collection of plants; rhododendrons; alpines; *Meconopsis* × *sheldonii* 'Branklyn'; small NTS gift shop.

Owned by The National Trust for Scotland
Number of gardeners 2
Size 0.8ha (2 acres)
NCCPG National Collections *Cassiope*

Christie's Nursery

DOWNFIELD, WESTMUIR, KIRRIEMUIR
DD5 8LP

Tel & Fax 01575 572977
Website www.christiealpines.co.uk
Location On A926 1 mile west of Kirriemuir.
Opening hours 10 am – 5 pm; daily except Sundays & Tuesdays; March to October.

This alpine nursery – a RHS Partner Nursery – has an impressive list, particularly strong on gentians, hardy orchids, corydalis and lewisias. The owners reckon to have about 1,000 different items in stock at any time, and about 2,000 growing in their pretty display garden.

Features Meconopsis; trilliums; lilies; new limestone scree (2002).

Owned by Ian & Ann Christie
Size 0.6ha (1½ acres)
NCCPG National Collections *Gentiana*

Cluny House

BY ABERFELDY, PERTHSHIRE
PH15 2JT

Tel 01887 820795
Location 3½ miles from Aberfeldy, on the Weem – Strathtay Road.
Opening hours 10 am – 6 pm; daily; March to October.
Admission fee Adults £3; Children under 16 free.

Cluny is a plantsman's garden, largely made in the 1950s by Mrs Mattingley's father, who subscribed to the Ludlow and Sherriff expeditions. Some older trees date from the 19th century – notably two vast wellingtonias – and the Mattingleys have continued to develop the garden since they took over in 1987. It is very much a woodland garden, with a natural appearance, except that the canopy is now of rhododendrons, acers, sorbus, euonymus, and birches. It has superb rhododendrons and many other ornamental trees and shrubs from the Himalayas and North America, as well as an underplanting of meconopsis, trilliums, gentians, nomocharis, cardiocrinums, erythroniums, lilies, arisaema and hellebores. But it is memorable, above all, for primulas – starting with the early-flowering petiolarid species – *P. whitei*, *P. tanneri*, *P. sonchifolia* and *P. nana*, for example. Then come sheets of candelabra species: the first is yellow *P. chungensis*, followed by purple *P. pulverulenta*, the dark pink and white forms of *P. japonica*, purple *P. beesiana*, orange *P. bulleyana*, yellow *P. sikkimensis* and yellow *P. florindae* – as well as naturally occurring hybrids between them. Many exotic species – and not just primulas – seed and regenerate freely in the acid, humus-rich soil. The whole garden is hand-weeded and chemical-free: interesting seedlings are thereby spotted and protected.

Features Plantsman's collection of plants; fine collection of trees; meconopsis; primulas; cardiocrinums; wellingtonia (*Sequoiadendron giganteum*) with the widest girth in the British Isles.

Owned by Mr J. & Mrs W. Mattingley
Size 2.2ha (6 acres)
NCCPG National Collections *Primula* (Asiatic species)

Drummond Castle Gardens

MUTHILL, CRIEFF PH7 4HZ

Tel 01764 681257   **Fax** 01764 681550
Location South of Crieff on A822.
Opening hours 2 pm – 6 pm; daily; Easter weekend, then from May to October.
Admission fee Adults £3.50; OAPs £2.50; Children £1.50.

Drummond has probably the most important formal garden in Scotland, laid out in about 1830 as a St Andrew's cross, with complex parterres filled since the 1950s with roses, statues, clipped cones, herbaceous plants, gravel and lots more beside. The result is order, shape, structure, mass, profusion and colour. There is also a copper beech planted by Queen Victoria to commemorate her visit in 1842. Parts of the film *Rob Roy* were shot in the gardens.

 Features Fruit; important formal garden.

Owned by Grimsthorpe & Drummond Castle Trust Ltd
Number of gardeners 5
Size 5ha (12 acres)

Dundee Botanic Garden

RIVERSIDE DRIVE, DUNDEE DD2 1QH

Tel 01382 647190   **Fax** 01382 640574
Location Signed from Riverside Drive (A85), near its junction with Perth Road.
Opening hours 10 am – 4.30 pm (3.30 pm from November to February); daily; all year. Closed 1 & 2 January, 25 & 26 December.
Admission fee Adults £2; OAPs & Children £1. RHS members free.

Dundee has a fine modern botanic garden which caters well for visitors: its gentle south-facing slopes are just above the banks of the River Tay. Founded in 1971, it can now boast fine collections of conifers and broad-leaved trees, good shrubs, tropical and temperate glasshouses, a water garden and a herb garden. There are also systematic and chronological borders and a whole series of native plant communities from montane to coastal habitats. These include a collection of *Sorbus* species native to Britain. There are also plant groupings which demonstrate adaptations for survival, such as drought resistance (the Mediterranean garden) and specialised pollination. Among the more surprising collection are *Nothofagus* species from South America and a large collection of *Eucalyptus* trees from Australia.

 Features Sub-tropical plants; herbs; plants under glass; mature conifers; drought-resistant plants; carnivorous plants; shop; café.

Owned by University of Dundee
Number of gardeners 3
Size 9.2ha (23 acres)

Edzell Castle

EDZELL, ANGUS DD9 7VE

Tel 01356 648631
Website www.historic-scotland.gov.uk
Location On B966 to Edzell Village, then signed for 1 mile.
Opening hours 9.30 am – 6.30 pm; April to September.
9 am – 4 pm; October to March. Closed on Thursdays after
12 noon, and all day on Friday. Not open until 2 pm on
Sundays.
Admission fee Adults £2.80; OAPs £2; Children £1.

Edzell has a 1930s formal garden in the
17th-century style, designed to be seen from
the ruined keep. It is shaped like a quincunx
of sorts, with yew bobbles, box edging and
roses in the beds. The four main segments
have the motto of the Lindsey family *DUM
SPIRO SPERO* ('While I breathe, I hope')
cut round their edges in box.

 Features Topiary; bedding; formal
garden; shop.

Owned by Historic Scotland
Number of gardeners 1

Glendoick Gardens

GLENDOICK, PERTH PH2 7NS

Tel 01738 860205   **Fax** 01738 860630
Website www.glendoick.com
Location A90 between Perth & Dundee.
Opening hours 2 pm – 5 pm; 5 & 19 May. And
pre-booked parties of 20+ during May.
Admission fee £2.

Everyone knows of the Glendoick nursery,
but the garden is even more important.
Started by Farrer's friend Euan Cox in the
1920s, it has one of the best collections of
plants, especially rhododendron species,
forms and hybrids, in the British Isles. The
nursery started in 1953, and all its stock is
propagated on site. Peter Cox has specialised
in breeding low-growing rhododendrons
for small gardens: his successes include
'Curlew', 'Razorbill' and 'Egret', as well as
the evergreen azalea 'Panda'. He has also
continued to hunt for plants in China, as
his father did before him. There is a good
demonstration garden in the garden centre
which is open all year.

 Features Woodland garden; fine trees;
plantsman's collection of plants;
primulas; meconopsis; lilies; famous garden
centre attached.

Owned by Mr & Mrs Peter A. Cox
Number of gardeners owners, with (very) part-time help
Size 4ha (10 acres), including nursery

House of Dun

MONTROSE, ANGUS DD10 9LQ

Tel 01674 810264   **Fax** 01674 810722
Website www.nts.org.uk
Location On A395, halfway between Montrose & Brechin.
Opening hours 9.30 am – sunset; daily; all year.
Admission fee £1 in honesty box.

The first thing you notice at House of
Dun is the magnificent line of mature
wellingtonias, but there are sheets of spring
bulbs, a Victorian rose garden for summer, a
border of *Nerine bowdenii* over 100m long,
and a collection of old fruit trees of interest
in autumn. The walled garden (rather small)
has been restored as it might have been in
the late 19th century and planted with
cultivars that date back to the 1880s.

Features Woodland garden;
snowdrops; roses (mainly old-
fashioned); fruit trees; daffodils; mature
conifers; ice house.

Owned by The National Trust for Scotland
Number of gardeners 1
Size 18ha (45 acres)

House of Pitmuies

BY FORFAR, ANGUS DD8 2SN

Tel 01241 828245
Location Off A932 Forfar to Arbroath Road.
Opening hours 10 am – 5 pm; daily; April to October.
Admission fee Adults £2.50; Children free.

House of Pitmuies is one of the most beautiful modern gardens in Scotland, and still expanding. Laid out and planted in the Hidcote style, Pitmuies has wonderful shrub roses in mixed plantings, clever colour schemes, and innumerable different gardens within the garden: a delphinium border, cherry walk, an alpine meadow for wildflowers, rhododendron glades, vast hollies, *Acer griseum* and a splendid monkey puzzle inherited from Victorian times. Enchanted and enchanting.

 Features Roses (ancient & modern); plants under glass; fruit; herbaceous borders; alpine meadow; ferns; new woodland garden; tallest *Ilex aquifolium* 'Argenteomarginata' in the British Isles.

Owned by Mrs Farquhar Ogilvie
Number of gardeners 1, plus 1 groundsman
Size 10.3ha (26 acres)

Kinross House

KINROSS KY13 7EU

Tel 01577 863467
Location In Kinross.
Opening hours 10 am – 7 pm; daily; April to September.

Admission fee Adults £2; Children 50p.

Kinross is one of the most beautiful houses in Scotland, with extensive views across Loch Leven. It is approached along a magnificent avenue of lime trees. The elegant walled garden has herbaceous borders and roses and a 17th-century sense of proportion. It is one of the few Scottish gardens which are genuinely at their best in July and August.

 Features Walled garden; mixed borders; lime avenue.

Owned by Sir David Montgomery Bt.

Scone Palace

PERTH PH2 6BD

Tel 01738 552300   **Fax** 01738 552588
Website www.scone-palace.co.uk
Location Signed from A93.
Opening hours 9.30 am – 5.45 pm; daily; April to October. 10 am – 4 pm in winter.
Admission fee Gardens only: Adults £3.10; OAPs £2.50; Children £1.70. RHS members free in September & October.

Scone is best known for its pinetum and for the Douglas firs (*Pseudotsuga menziesii*) grown from original seed sent back by their discoverer David Douglas, who was born on the estate. Lord Mansfield has the largest private collection of orchids in the country.

 Features Established pinetum; woodland walks; rhododendrons & azaleas; daffodils; new 'Murray' maze; tallest *Tilia platyphyllos* (37m) in the British Isles, and 4 other record trees; orchids.

Owned by The Earl of Mansfield
Number of gardeners 7
Size 40ha (100 acres)

WALES

Most of the best-known gardens of Wales are close to the sea – as, indeed, are most of its larger centres of population. This gives the principality a reputation for being able to grow tender plants that would not be hardy – say – in Surrey. There is some truth in this, though no Welsh garden is truly sub-tropical in the way that Tresco and Inverewe are. The National Gardens Scheme offers gardens to visit in every part of Wales, and in respectable numbers. The Royal Horticultural Society has negotiated free access for its members, for some or all of the year, to Bodnant, the National Botanic Garden of Wales and Picton Castle.

This book lists gardens in Wales under the old 1974 counties, rather than the historic counties or the present administrative units. The 1974 counties are a useful size for the purpose of this book, and their names are readily recognised.

Wales has many historic gardens, made mainly in the 18th and 19th centuries and usually in the styles that were fashionable in England at the time. The National Trust has played an important part in preserving and restoring some of the finest. Bodnant, Plas Newydd and Powis Castle are gardens of the utmost international importance. By and large, however, they share with other Welsh gardens the characteristic of having acquired their horticultural importance during the 20th century: the same is true of other classic Welsh gardens like Portmeirion and Dyffryn. Much of that horticultural input came from England and there was until quite recently a sense among some that gardening was a hobby either for very rich or

anglicised Welshmen or for the English who came to live in Wales. Though it cannot rival such major botanic gardens as Kew and Edinburgh, the new National Botanic Garden of Wales does give a new focus to Welsh horticulture.

Wales's historic gardens are well supported by the Welsh Historic Gardens Trust which has taken action to identify, evaluate and conserve the principality's heritage. Its declared aims are to initiate and assist in the conservation of gardens, parks and designed landscapes that are of historic, cultural and aesthetic importance in the Welsh heritage, and to raise public awareness of the decline in particular places. Comparatively few historic gardens in Wales are open to the public.

CADW, the Welsh Historic Monuments Commission in Cardiff, publishes a Register of Parks and Gardens of Special Historic Interest in Wales. This is the work of Elisabeth Whittle who wrote the standard modern work on the subject *The Historic Gardens of Wales* (HMSO, 1992). The Register is modelled on English Heritage's list for England and the criteria for selection and grading gardens are comparable.

The best collection of trees in Wales is at Bodnant, which has a large number of rarities and some 20 champions among them. There are good tree collections also at Dyffryn and Margam in Glamorgan. The NCCPG has 21 National Collections in Wales, of which seven are in National Trust gardens and four in the care of the gardens belonging to the City of Swansea.

Wales has comparatively few top-class nurseries, and practically none in South Wales near Cardiff or Swansea. However, the outstanding examples elsewhere in the principality are among Britain's best. Celyn Vale has a unique list of Australasian trees; Dibleys Nurseries are the leading nursery for *Streptocarpus* and other house plants; and Crûg Farm Plants is a true plantsman's nursery which introduces more new collected plants into cultivation than any other in Britain.

The two principal horticultural colleges are at opposite ends of Wales. Both the Welsh College of Horticulture at Mold (Tel: 01352 841000) and Pencoed College at Bridgend (Tel: 01656 302600) are RHS Partner Colleges with a good number of public lectures and workshops throughout the year. The Royal Horticultural Society has also arranged special events during 2002 at its Partner Nursery Crûg Farm Plants in Gwynedd and at Dyffryn Gardens in South Glamorgan.

CLWYD

Aberconwy Nursery

GRAIG, GLAN CONWY, COLWYN BAY
LL28 5TL

Tel 01492 580875
Location South of Glan Conwy, 2nd right off A470.
Turn right at top of hill: nursery is on the right.
Opening hours 10 am – 5 pm; Tuesday – Sunday;
February to October.

This nursery is best known as one of our
leading nurseries for alpine plants and a
steady introducer of new cultivars, especially
autumn-flowering gentians. But it also offers
unusual shrubs, and herbaceous and
woodland plants, including many dwarf
rhododendrons and small ericaceous plants.
Other specialities are cistus, dieramas,
epimediums and hybrids of *Helleborus niger*.

Owned by Keith Lever

Celyn Vale Nurseries

ALLT-Y-CELYN, CARROG, CORWEN
LL21 9LD

Tel & Fax 01490 430671
Website www.eucalyptus.co.uk
Location 3 miles east of Corwen & 1 mile from Carrog,
near A5.
Opening hours 9 am – 4 pm; Monday – Friday;
January to November.
Admission fee free

Specialist growers of eucalyptus and acacias:
they use seed from high altitude specimens
to maximise hardiness and will advise also
on suitable species for coppicing, poor
drainage, alkaline soils, hedging, salt
tolerance and so on. They say that the
hardiest gum trees are *E. archeri*, *E. coccifera*,
E. pauciflora subsp. *debeuzevillei*, *E.
kybeanensis*, *E. pauciflora* subsp. *niphophila*,
E. parvifolia and *E. subcrenulata*.

 Features *Eucalyptus.*

Owned by Andrew McConnell

Chirk Castle

CHIRK LL14 5AF

Tel 01691 777701 **Fax** 01691 774706
Website www.nationaltrust.org.uk
Location 1½ miles west of Chirk off A5.
Opening hours 11 am – 6 pm (last admission 4.30 pm);
Wednesday – Sunday, plus Bank Holiday Mondays;
28 March to 28 October. Closes at 5 pm in October.
Admission fee Adults £2.80; Children £1.40.

Chirk has handsome 19th-century formal
gardens, one planted with roses and another
with billowing yew topiary. There is also a
good 1930s collection of trees and shrubs,
the relics of a garden by Norah Lindsay. The
National Trust has done much to provide
shelter from the wind, so that more tender
plants may be grown.

 Features Woodland garden; topiary;
snowdrops; roses (ancient & modern);
rock garden; rhododendrons & azaleas;
good herbaceous borders; eucryphias;
hydrangeas; lime avenue.

Owned by The National Trust

Bodnant Gardens

TAL-Y-CAFN, COLWYN BAY LL28 5RE

Tel 01492 650460   **Fax** 01492 650448
Website www.nationaltrust.org.uk
Location 8 miles south of Llandudno & Colwyn Bay
on A470. Entrance ½ mile along Eglwysbach Road.
Opening hours 10 am – 5 pm; daily; 16 March to
3 November.
Admission fee Adults £5.20; Children £2.60.
RHS members free.

Two Lords Aberconway, both past-Presidents of the Royal Horticultural Society, and three generations of the Puddle family, as Head Gardeners, have made Bodnant compulsory visiting. From its position above the valley of the River Conwy, Bodnant combines dramatic formal terraces with extensive woodland plantings on the grandest of scales. A deep herbaceous border, backing onto a high wall, is instantly striking, with mature, often tender climbers rampant above bold, warm plantings. Although this is North Wales, and the views from the lawns are across the valley to the Carneddau mountains and Snowdonia National Park, parts of the garden feel distinctly Italianate. Beside the house, two enormous cedars overshadow a formal lily pond, on the first of five terraces, where hydrangeas abound. A crisply shaved yew hedge curves above a mezzanine rose pergola, and there are specimens of *Magnolia grandiflora* everywhere. Below is a stately gazebo from the early 18th century, the Pin Mill, which looks across a flat pool to a grassy stage at the opposite end of its terrace, edged with cut cubes of topiary. Plantings of pencil-thin cypresses, and *Cistus* and *Potentilla* cultivars, help to create an intensely Mediterranean feel on clear summer days. Behind the Pin Mill, the

mood changes, as the grassy valley fills with tall specimen trees, marching beside a fast flowing mill stream and a stern old mill. Along the stream there are hostas, bergenias and meconopsis. Some of the massive *Sequoiadendron* specimens bear planting plaques which show them to be in their second century. Winding back in an extended arc towards the house, there are gentler woodland plantings, with shrubbery borders, and smaller trees growing in grass. There is a magnificent collection of magnolias, rhododendrons and camellias. Other good plantings include *Viburnum* × *bodnantense*, hybrid camellias, huge rhododendrons, white wisterias, a vast *Arbutus* × *andrachnoides*, flaming embothriums and the famous laburnum tunnel. The garden is admirably maintained, and is popular with visitors, too. The walled plant-yard is strong on many of the tender climbers from the garden, and reasonably priced.

 Features An important collection of plants; good herbaceous borders; fine collection of trees; good autumn colour; laburnum arch; tallest Californian redwood *Sequoia sempervirens* (47m) in the British Isles and 18 further record-breaking tree species – more than any other garden in Wales; plant centre; light lunches, teas, refreshments 11 am – 5 pm.

Owned by The National Trust
Number of gardeners 18
Size 32ha (80 acres)
NCCPG National Collections Embothrium; Eucryphia; Magnolia (spp.); Rhododendron forrestii

Dibleys Nurseries

LLANELIDAN, RUTHIN LL15 2LG

Tel 01978 790677   **Fax** 01978 790668
Website www.dibleys.com
Location 6 miles south of Ruthin, off the B5429.
Opening hours 10 am – 5 pm; daily; April to September.
Plus weekdays in March & October
Admission fee Garden £2; Glasshouses free.

Dibleys is the leading British nursery for gesneriads – especially streptocarpus, of which they have a comprehensive collection of cultivars, from 'Constant Nymph' to the latest modern hybrids like the ever-blooming 'Crystal Ice'. They will be introducing three new cultivars this year (2002). They have made a great impact on RHS Flower Shows in recent years, and won 13 consecutive gold medals at Chelsea. Dibleys also have a long list of other gesneriads like *Kohleria* and *Columnea*, and a good line in foliage begonias. An excellent nursery, in top form. The garden has a wide range of trees and shrubs, and extensive views over the Vale of Clwyd.

Owned by The Dibley family
Size 0.4ha (1 acre) glasshouses; 4ha (10 acres) garden
NCCPG National Collections *Streptocarpus*

Erddig

WREXHAM LL13 0YT

Tel 01978 355314   **Fax** 01978 315151
Website www.nationaltrust.org.uk
Location Signed from A483 & A525.
Opening hours 11 am – 6 pm; Saturday – Wednesday;
23 March to 3 November. Opens at 10 am in July &
August; closes at 5 pm in October.
Admission fee Gardens only: Adults £3.40;
Children £1.70.

More of a re-creation than a restoration, Erddig today majors on domestic life in the early 18th century. There are old-fashioned fruit trees (an excellent collection of apples, plums, pears and cherries, beautifully trained), an avenue of pleached limes, and a long canal to frame the house, but all are slightly awed by the Victorian overlay – avenues of monkey puzzles and wellingtonias.

Features Woodland garden; roses (mainly old-fashioned); fruit; spring bulbs; restaurant, tea-room.

Owned by The National Trust
Size 5.2ha (13 acres)
NCCPG National Collections *Hedera*

DYFED

Aberglasney Gardens

LLANGATHEN SA32 8QH

Tel & Fax 01558 668998
Website www.aberglasney.org.uk
Location 4 miles west of Landeilo, signed from A40.
Opening hours 10 am – 6 pm; daily; April to October.
Phone for winter times. Coaches by appointment only.
Admission fee Adults £5; OAPs £4; Children £2.50.

Aberglasney has a garden that lay dormant
for about 400 years, until plans were made
to restore it in the style of the 16th and 17th
centuries. The structure remains fairly intact
from that time – including a cloister and
parapet walk – and reproduction gardens
have been inserted within that framework.
There are six gardens in all, including three
walled gardens. Hal Moggridge and
Penelope Hobhouse have both been
involved with the project: work continues.
The modern plantings include meconopsis,
primulas, trilliums and lilies. The dense yew
tunnel dates from about 1700.

 Features Important historic garden;
yew tunnel; pool garden.

Owned by Aberglasney Restoration Trust
Number of gardeners 4
Size 3.6ha (9 acres)

Cae Hir

CRIBYN, LAMPETER SA48 7NG

Tel & Fax 01570 470839
Location In village.
Opening hours 1 pm – 6 pm; daily except Mondays (but
open on Bank Holiday Mondays). Closed in winter.

Admission fee Adults £2.50; OAPs £2; Children 50p.

This vigorous and expanding garden was
begun in 1985 and has already been featured
many times on television. Mr Akkermans'
energy and achievement are an inspiration.
He has taken six acres from the surrounding
meadows and made them into a series of
beautiful colour-conscious gardens. All
different types of plants are here: trees,
shrubs and herbaceous plants, often used in
original ways. Mr Akkermans is now
experimenting with half-hardy trees and
shrubs, allowing wildflowers to mix with
cultivated ones in some parts of his
immaculately tidy garden.

Features Colour gardens; bonsai;
mature ornamental trees; bog garden;
light refreshments.

Owned by Wil Akkermans
Number of gardeners owner only
Size 2.6ha (6½ acres)

Colby Woodland Garden

AMROTH, NARBERTH SA67 8PP

Tel 01834 811885
Website www.nationaltrust.org.uk
Location Signed from A477.
Opening hours 10 am – 5 pm; daily; 1 April to
31 October. Walled garden opens at 11 am.
Admission fee Adults £2.80; Children £1.40.

Colby is an attractive woodland garden, best
in May when the rhododrons and

azaleas are in full flower. Among the 19th-century plantings are vast cryptomerias, clumps of *Embothrium coccineum* and a huge specimen of *Rhododendron falconeri* subsp. *eximium*, planted in 1883. In the walled garden, a rill runs down from the *trompe l'oeil* gazebo to a pool. There have been many new plantings recently throughout the garden.

 Features Woodland garden; rhododendrons & azaleas; mature conifers; shop; light refreshments.

Owned by The National Trust
Number of gardeners 2
Size 11.1ha (28 acres)

The National Botanic Garden of Wales

MIDDLETON HALL, LLANARTHNE, CARMARTHEN SA32 8HG

Tel 01558 668768   **Fax** 01558 668933
Website www.gardenofwales.org.uk
Location 7 miles east of Carmarthen, off A48.
Opening hours From 10 am, daily, except Christmas Day. Closing times vary from 4.30 pm to 6 pm according to the time of year.
Admission fee Adults £6.50; Concessions £5; Children £3. RHS members free from January to March.

(P) (WC) (&) (⚘) (🎁) (☕) (🍴)

The landscaped park and gardens of the original 18th-century Middleton Hall estate are the setting for this new national botanic garden which opened to the public in 2000 amid great public acclamation. The Gardd Fotaneg Genedlaethol Cymru near Llanarthne in the Vale of Towy sees itself as the Welsh Kew, and will carry out research into conservation and biology. Near the entrance to the garden is a 'Welsh landscape' with native meadows and woodlands. Then comes the Broadwalk, 220m long, with a rill

which runs down through a geological display of Welsh rocks. The garden's collection of herbaceous plants is planted along its edges, with narrow paths leading into the plantings to facilitate access. There is also a herb garden, named after the Physicians of Myddfai, with an ethnobotanical collection of native pharmacological Welsh plants. Last winter they added the 'Real Japanese Garden', the display which won the top award at the Chelsea Flower Show in 2001. However, it is the Great Glasshouse which has received most of the adulation, and rightly so, because it is a stunning piece of architecture – the largest single-span glasshouse in the world. It concentrates upon the Mediterranean floras of the world – cheaper to maintain than tropical floras – including Chile, California, south-west Australia, South Africa, the Mediterranean basin and the Canary Isles.

 Features Good glasshouses; herbaceous plants; herbs; shop; café; restaurant.

Owned by Trustees of the NBG, Wales
Number of gardeners 12
Size 72ha (180 acres)

Picton Castle

PICTON, HAVERFORDWEST, PEMBROKESHIRE SA62 4AS

Tel & Fax 01437 751326
Website www.pictoncastle.co.uk
Location 4 miles east of Haverfordwest off A40.
Opening hours 10.30 am – 5 pm; Tuesday – Sunday & Bank Holiday Mondays; April to October.
Admission fee Adults £3.95; OAPs £3.75; Children £1.95. RHS members free from April to September.

(P) (🐕) (WC) (&) (⚘) (🎁) (☕)

This 13th-century castle has been the home of the Philipps family for some 400 years, and the 40 acres of grounds include fine collections of rhododendrons, azaleas, magnolias, camellias, myrtles, embothriums and eucryphias, some of which have been bred by the castle gardeners. Older specimens like a vast multi-trunked *Abies alba* have been joined by new plantings of recent introductions – *Taiwania cryptomerioides* and *Calocedrus formosana* among them. The climate is mild, and supports normally tender plants like *Pittosporum tobira* 'Variegatum' and *Vestia foeteda*. The display is at its best in May to June: summer and autumn bring woodland walks among the massive oaks and giant redwoods. Recent additions include a fern walk and a collection of bamboos. The walled garden has a fish pond, an indoor fernery, rose beds, herbaceous borders and a fountain in the centre.

Features Woodland garden; rhododendrons & azaleas; camellias; garden shop selling surplus garden produce; restaurant.

Owned by Picton Castle Trust
Number of gardeners 4, plus 2 part-time
Size 16ha (40 acres)

GLAMORGAN

Clyne Gardens

MILL LANE, BLACK PILL, SWANSEA
SA3 5BD

Tel 01792 298637/401737 **Fax** 01792 297394
Website www.swansea.gov.uk/leisure/allparks.html
Location 3 miles west of Swansea on coast road.
Opening hours Dawn to dusk; daily; all year.
Admission fee free. Pre-arranged tours at £1 a head.

(P) (🐕) (wc) (&) (🌿) (☕)

Clyne is a stupendous woodland garden, the best in South Wales, well cared for by enthusiastic and knowledgeable staff. It is supreme as a magic rhododendron valley in May, but the range of rare and tender plants provides interest all year. Bluebells, lysichitons and gunneras are among its other features. It was planted between 1921 and 1952 by a local landowner called Algernon Walker-Heneage-Vivian, who subscribed to many of the Himalayan and Chinese plant-hunting expeditions of the day. The forms and hybrids of *Rhododendron niveum* which the head gardener brought to the RHS flower shows in 1996 and 1997 are still remembered by the London rhododendron fraternity. The mild climate means that *R. fragrantissimum* grows happily outside, and there is a group of *R.* 'Loderi King George' 16m high. The car park is small, and tends to fill up early in the day. There are band concerts on Sunday afternoons in summer. Also worth visiting are the Swansea Botanical Gardens at Singleton Park.

Features Woodland garden; rhododendrons & azaleas; good herbaceous borders.

Owned by City & County of Swansea
NCCPG National Collections *Pieris*; *Enkianthus*; *Rhododendron* (Triflora & Falconera subsections)

Dyffryn Botanic Garden

ST NICHOLAS, CARDIFF CF5 6SU

Tel 029 2059 3328 **Fax** 029 2059 1966
Location Jct 33 M4 on A48 then follow signs.
Opening hours 10 am – 5.30 pm; daily; mid-April to October.
Admission fee Adults £3; OAPs & Children £2.50. Subject to review.

(P) (🐕) (wc) (&) (🌿) (🎁) (☕)

Dyffryn has 55 acres of sumptuous gardens designed by Thomas Mawson for Reginald Cory around an Edwardian prodigy house. They are now being restored with a chunky £3.23m millennium grant. Originally intended partly for display – there is even a Roman garden with a temple and fountain – and partly for the Corys' own pleasure, Dyffryn has a huge collection of good plants built up in the early years of the 20th century. Watch it revive over the next year or so: the garden as a status symbol.

 Features Woodland garden; roses (mainly modern); rhododendrons & azaleas; good herbaceous borders; spring bulbs; summer bedding; tallest purple birch *Betula pendula* 'Purpurea' in the British Isles (and ten other record trees); plants for sale on Bank Holidays; refreshments.

Owned by Vale of Glamorgan Council

Margam Park

PORT TALBOT SA13 2TJ

Tel 01639 881635   **Fax** 01639 895897
Location Follow directions from M4 Jct 38.
Opening hours 10 am – 7 pm (5 pm in winter); daily;
all year.
Admission fee Free.

Margam is a popular country park with lots
to interest the garden historian and
plantsman: a wonderful range of
conservatories and glasshouses, including
the orangery for which Margam is famous,
big trees and rhododendrons (some grown
from Kingdon Ward's seed), and cheerful
bedding out. The orangery gardens have just
been completely restored, using some of the
large grant which the garden has received
from the European Regional Fund. Recent
additions include Tudor and monastic
gardens and a new pergola 410m (450 yards)
long: further work is promised. Margam is
also the seat of Fuchsia Research
International, where almost all the *Fuchsia*
species are grown under glass in a
naturalistic landscape: it is probably the
largest collection in the world, complete
with humming-birds.

Features Roses (mainly modern); fine
collection of trees; bedding out;
daffodils; rhododendrons; orangery; tallest
bay tree *Laurus nobilis* (21m) in the British
Isles; gift shop; restaurant & light
refreshments.

Owned by Neath Port Talbot County Borough Council
Number of gardeners 4
Size 22ha (60 acres)

Plantasia

PARC TAWE, SWANSEA SA1 2AL

Tel 01792 298637/474555   **Fax** 01792 297394
Website www.swansea.gov.uk/leisure/allparks.html
Location Off main Eastern approach to Swansea.
Opening hours 10 am – 5 pm; Tuesdays – Sundays &
Bank Holidays; all year. Closed 1 January, 25 & 26
December.
Admission fee Adults £2.20; Concessions £1.50.
Subject to review.

Plantasia is a large glasshouse with three
climatic zones – arid, tropical, and rain
forest. Each is full with exotic plants –
palms, strelitzias, tree ferns, nepenthes,
cacti and such economic plants as coconuts
and pineapple. The authorities say that some
of the 5,000 plants represent species which
are actually extinct in the wild. It is the
perfect goal for a winter expedition, and
not expensive, but you may not enjoy the
insects, birds, monkeys and reptiles as
much as the flowers.

Features Tropical & arid glasshouses;
good collection of exotic plants;
educational facilities; souvenirs; soft drinks.

Owned by City & County of Swansea
Number of gardeners 2

GWENT

Penpergwm Lodge

ABERGAVENNY NP7 9AS

Tel & Fax 01873 840208
Website www.penplants.com
Location 3 miles from Abergavenny on B4598, opposite King of Prussia pub.
Opening hours 2 pm – 6 pm; Thursday – Sunday; end of March to end of September.
Admission fee Adults £2.50; Children free.

Catriona Boyle has developed the garden at Penpergwm over the last 20 years, using some of the structure created when the house was built in Edwardian times – mature trees, open lawns, formal areas and old hedges. She has added two exuberant terraces, each planted to a colour theme and linked by a parterre and vine walk. The original vegetable garden has been re-designed and renamed a *potager*, with flowers, standard roses and vegetables. The result is both clever and satisfying – Mrs Boyle runs a well-regarded garden school. The nursery has lots of home-propagated plants, mostly unusual herbaceous plants, bulbs, climbers and shrubs, but also half-hardy perennials which extend the garden season. Specialities include *Aconitum*, euphorbias, cistus, philadelphus, clematis, loniceras, camassias, erythroniums, *Melianthus major* and salvias.

Features New vine walk, planted for autumn colour; new purple and apricot border (2000); nursery for unusual plants; teas on Sundays.

Owned by Mrs C. Boyle
Number of gardeners 1
Size 1.6ha (4 acres)

The Veddw

DEVAUDEN NP6 6PH

Tel 01291 650836 **Fax** 01291 650948
Location Signed from the pub on the green at Devauden.
Opening hours 2 pm – 5 pm; Sundays & Bank Holiday Mondays; April to September
Admission fee Adults £2.50; Children £1.

This is a young and expanding garden – enjoyable to see now, and to watch as the owners' ideas for its expansion develop. It is also interesting because it is a low-budget garden and the owners are happy to tell you about their mistakes as well as their successes. For example, the front garden was at first planted as a careless, random 'cottage garden': then they decided that it 'looked a mess' and started to add structural elements like clipped box. The main garden includes a magnolia walk, a 'Buff Beauty' garden and a crescent-shaped border which is planted with pastel colours to provide flowers from spring to autumn. Much attention is given to colour planting: pinks, mauves, whites and purples in some parts, but reds, oranges and yellows in the front garden. There is much variety and good design and many good plants too. The 2-acre woodland is destined to become part of the garden proper, but the owners are finding it difficult to get the ornamental underplantings established. All in all, a garden of great charm – and promise.

Features New garden; colour gardening; young woodland garden; new reflecting pool and grass paterre.

Owned by Anne Wareham & Charles Hawes
Number of gardeners owners only
Size 1.6ha (4 acres)

GWYNEDD

Bodysgallen Hall

LLANDUDNO LL30 1RS

Tel 01492 584466 **Fax** 01492 582519
Location On right, off A470 to Llandudno.
Opening hours Daily; all year.
Admission fee Open only to Hotel Guests.
Children over 8 welcome.

These are good gardens and good grounds for a good hotel. Partly 1920s and partly modern, the gardens include a knot garden divided into eight segments, an extremely busy kitchen garden, woodland walks, a little sunken garden with a lily pond and a modern parterre with white floribundas in the old walled garden. And it is handy for Bodnant, too.

 Features Woodland garden; roses (mainly old-fashioned); rock garden; herbs; fruit; knot garden; parterres; refreshments at hotel.

Owned by Historic House Hotels Ltd
Number of gardeners 4
Size 87ha (220 acres), including parkland

Cefn Bere

CAE DEINTUR, DOLGELLAU LL40 2YS

Tel 01341 422768
Location At Cae Deintur, behind primary school, up short steep hill, left half way up, 4th house.
Opening hours By appointment from early spring to late autumn.
Admission fee Contribution to National Gardens Scheme.

Cefn Bere is a plantsman's garden within a disciplined design: the owners say that it encapsulates their own development as gardeners over the last 40 years. It has a great variety of rare plants within a small compass, especially alpines, perennials, grasses, ferns and evergreens. And wonderful views.

 Features Plantsman's collection of plants; plants under glass; troughs; roses (mainly old-fashioned); cuttings & seeds available.

Owned by Mr & Mrs G.M. Thomas
Number of gardeners owners only
Size 0.08ha ($\frac{1}{5}$ acre)

Crûg Farm Plants

GRIFFITH'S CROSSING, CAERNARFON LL55 1TU

Tel & Fax 01248 670232
Website www.crug-farm.co.uk
Location 2 miles north-east of Caernarfon, off A487, follow signs to Bethel.
Opening hours 10 am – 6 pm; Thursday – Sunday & Bank Holidays; 23 February to 29 September.
Admission fee Garden open for NGS on 31 March, 2 & 3 June, 14 July, & 25 August.

This RHS Partner Nursery is unusual in specialising in plants for shade: perennials, shrubs and climbers. The range is extensive and interesting. The selection of hardy geraniums equals many specialists in the genera. The owners' collecting expeditions to Korea, Sikkim, Japan, China, Vietnam, Laos, the Philippines and Taiwan are making an impact on the gardens of many discerning plantsmen: new-to-science names a-plenty. The display garden and private garden are worth seeing when they are open for the National Gardens Scheme.

Owned by Bleddyn & Sue Wynn-Jones
NCCPG National Collections *Coriaria*; *Paris*

Penrhyn Castle

BANGOR LL57 4HN

Tel 01248 353084   **Fax** 01248 371281
Website www.nationaltrust.org.uk
Location 3 miles east of Bangor on A5122, signed from A55 – A5 junction.
Opening hours 11 am – 5 pm; daily except Tuesday; 23 March to 3 November. Open at 10 am – 5.30 pm in July & August. Last admission 4.30 pm.
Admission fee Adults £4; Children £2.

A neo-Norman castle with a distant walled garden of parterres and terraces merging into the slopes of rhododendrons and camellias. There is much of dendrological interest (ancient conifers, holm oaks, champion eucryphias and naturalised arbutus trees) and a 'dinosaur landscape' of tree ferns, gunneras and aralias.

 Features Woodland garden; sub-tropical plants; mature conifers; 1920s walled garden; rhododendrons; trees planted by royals; *Fuchsia* pergola walk; light lunches in licensed tea-room.

Owned by The National Trust
Size 19ha (47 acres)

Plas Brondanw Gardens

LLANFROTHEN, PANRHYNDEUDRAETH LL48 6SW

Tel 01766 770484
Location On Croesor road off A4085.
Opening hours 9 am – 5 pm; daily; all year.
Admission fee Adults £2; Children 50p.

Plas Brondanw is the highly original and architectural Edwardian garden laid out by Sir Clough Williams-Ellis 17 years before he began Portmeirion, and now assiduously restored by his granddaughter Menna. It is one of the best-kept secrets in North Wales, full of slate stonework and such original design ideas as the arbour of four red-twigged limes. The garden rooms are inward looking and almost cottagey in their planting, but the mountain peaks are ever present.

Features Arts & Crafts garden; topiary; follies.

Owned by Trustees of the Second Portmeirion Foundation
Number of gardeners 2

Plas Newydd

LLANFAIRPWLL, ANGLESEY LL61 6EQ

Tel 01248 714795   **Fax** 01248 713673
Website www.nationaltrust.org.uk
Location 2 miles south-west of Llanfairpwll on A4080.
Opening hours 11 am – 5.30 pm; Saturday – Wednesday; 23 March to 3 November.
Admission fee Adults £2.60; Children £1.30.

Plas Newydd has a grand collection of rhododendrons (plus azaleas, magnolias and acers) within a Repton landscape on a spectacular site above the Menai Straits. Its many other horticultural attractions include an avenue of *Chamaecyparis pisifera* 'Squarrosa' running down to the sea, an arboretum of Australian plants (lots of eucalyptus and nothofagus) and 'hot & cold' borders. Some of the rhododendrons came as a wedding present to Lord and Lady Anglesey from Lord Aberconway at Bodnant: many others followed. There are examples of the more tender species of considerable size, including a *R. montroseanum* which is probably the largest in Britain. Late-flowering hybrids like 'Polar Bear' extend the season well into July. The fine Italianate garden below the house is 1930s, most surprising.

 Features Mature conifers; azaleas; magnolias; rhododendrons; maples; spectacular agapanthus; eucalyptus; National Trust shop; tea-room.

Owned by The National Trust
Number of gardeners 4
Size 12.3ha (31 acres)

Plas-yn-Rhiw

RHIW, PWLLHELI LL53 8AB

Tel & Fax 01758 780219
Website www.nationaltrust.org.uk
Location 16 miles from Pwllheli. Turn off B4413 at Botwnnog and follows signs along lanes & through village.
Opening hours 12 noon – 5 pm; daily except Tuesday; 23 March to 30 September. Also on Saturdays & Sundays in October and 21–25 October. Closed on Wednesdays until 13 May.
Admission fee Adults £2; Children £1. £2.50 for snowdrops in February (telephone for exact times & dates).

This pretty garden is small and fairly formal: it is divided into a series of rooms which are hedged with cherry laurel and bay to protect them from the sea-gales. Box-edged parterres are filled with rambling roses and billowing cottage garden flowers. Tender trees and shrubs flourish in the mild coastal climate.

 Features Good herbaceous borders; formal gardens; gifts shop.

Owned by The National Trust
Number of gardeners 1, plus 1 trainee
Size 0.4ha (1 acre)

Portmeirion

PENRHYNDEUDRAETH LL48 6ET

Tel 01766 770000   **Fax** 01766 771331
Website www.portmeirion.com
Location Between Penrhyndeudraeth & Porthmadog.
Opening hours 9.30 am – 5.30 pm; daily; all year.
Admission fee Adults £5.30; OAPs £4.20; Children £2.60.

Portmeirion is where the architect Sir Clough Williams-Ellis worked out his Italianate fantasies. The television series *The Prisoner* was filmed here. The gardens are carved out of a rhododendron woodland but formal, with a mixture of Mediterranean plants and exotic palms, and full of architectural bric-a-brac of every period. Other attractions include tree ferns, gunneras, phormiums, ginkgos and holm oaks. Williams-Ellis began to lay out the garden at Portmeirion as soon as he made his first purchase of land along the coastline of north-west Wales in 1926. He bought up further estates in later years, by which he acquired one of the chief attractions of the gardens at Portmeirion today – the collection of rhododendrons and azaleas which is known as the Gwyllt gardens. *Rhododendron arboreum* has grown to enormous size and in parts of the garden is still impenetrable. The peak display comes in May: the mainstay of late summer and autumn is thousands of hydrangeas throughout the Portmeirion estate. The gardens have been further developed in the last 20 years, taking advantage of the mild climate. One garden – almost at the furthest end of the estate and planted with a background of eucalyptus trees – is known as the 'ghost garden' because of the way the wind whistles in the leaves.

Features Woodland garden; sub-tropical plants; rhododendrons & azaleas; giant yuccas; exuberant summer bedding; tallest *Maytenus boaria* (18m) in the British Isles; several shops; refreshments, and hotel.

Owned by Portmeirion Ltd
Number of gardeners 11
Size 28ha (70 acres)

POWYS

Ashford House

TALYBONT-ON-USK, BRECON
LD3 7YR

Tel 01874 676271
Location 1 mile east of Talbont along B4588.
Opening hours 2 pm – 6 pm; Tuesdays; April to September.
Admission fee Adults £2; Children free.

There are two parts to the garden at Ashford: both have been made by the Andersons. First there is the walled garden, about an acre in extent, with raised beds (lots of alpines), and a plantsman's collection of plants of every kind in fine mixed borders. Then there is the woodland garden, which the Andersons have underplanted with suitable shrubs, especially rhododendrons, camellias and bulbs.

 Features Alpines; woodland with rhododendrons; tea, coffee & biscuits.

Owned by Mr & Mrs D.A. Anderson
Number of gardeners 1 part-time
Size 1.4ha (3½ acres)

The Dingle

WELSHPOOL SY21 9JD

Tel 01938 555145 **Fax** 01938 555778
Location Left turn to Nurseries off A490 to Llanfyllin.
Opening hours 9 am – 5 pm; daily except Tuesdays; all year except Christmas week.
Admission fee Adults £1.50; Children free.

This steep garden attached to a successful nursery is essentially a plantsman's private garden. It is mainly made up of unusual trees and shrubs, but it has some herbaceous plantings too. The beds are put together with a carefully co-ordinated colour mixtures and designed to look good all through the year.

 Features South-facing bank; pool; north-facing woodland garden; unusual trees & shrubs; first-rate nursery attached; cold drinks & ice-creams.

Owned by Mr & Mrs Roy Joseph
Number of gardeners 1
Size 1.6ha (4 acres)

Dolwen

CEFN COCH, LLANRHAEADR-YM-MOCHNANT SY10 0BU

Tel & Fax 01691 780411
Location Right at Three Tuns Inn, ¾ mile up lane.
Opening hours 2 pm – 4.30 pm; Fridays, plus last Sunday of month; May to August. And by appointment.
Admission fee Adults £2; Children free.

Old garden: new owners. This plantsman's garden on a steep site was energetically made by Mrs Denby in the 1980s: it continues to be open under the enthusiastic guidance of the new owners who have started replanting some of the beds and adding features of their own. There are stupendous views and beautiful plantings around three large ponds, fed by natural springs and connected by waterfalls. It remains one of the best modern gardens in Wales, of ever-growing interest.

Features Woodland garden; roses (mainly old-fashioned); plantsman's collection of plants; good herbaceous borders; water features; tea-room.

Owned by Bob Yarwood & Jeny Marriott
Number of gardeners 4 part-time
Size 1ha (2½ acres)

Glansevern Gardens

GLANSEVERN, BERRIEW, WELSHPOOL SY21 8AH

Tel 01686 640200   **Fax** 01686 640829
Location On A483, 4 miles south-west of Welshpool.
Opening hours 12 noon – 6 pm; Fridays, Saturdays & Bank Holiday Mondays; May to September. And parties by appointment.
Admission fee Adults £3; OAPs £2; Children free.

The handsome Greek-revival house at Glansevern sits in a landscaped park (1802), complete with its lake, rhododendrons and splendid Victorian specimen trees. The 1840s rock garden incorporates a spooky grotto. The 'Smoker's Walk' runs down through woodland to the banks of the River Severn. But it is the modern planting which really distinguishes Glansevern: luxuriant primulas in the water-garden, island beds around the house and roses in one of the walled gardens. Another walled garden, exactly one acre in size, was re-designed and replanted last winter (2001–2002).

 Features Rock garden and grotto; roses (mainly modern); water garden; lake; good herbaceous borders; good trees.

Owned by Gerran & Meriel Thomas
Number of gardeners 3
Size 7.2ha (18 acres)

Powis Castle

WELSHPOOL SY21 8RF

Tel 01938 551920   **Fax** 01938 554336
Website www.nationaltrust.org.uk
Location 1 mile south of Welshpool off the A483.
Opening hours 11 am – 6 pm; Wednesday – Sunday plus Bank Holiday Mondays; 23 March to 3 November. Plus Tuesdays in July & August.
Admission fee Adults £5; Children £2.50.

The hanging terraces draped with bulky overgrown yews and exuberant summer bedding are famous. If you visit Powis in summer or early autumn, you will be completely distracted by the rare and tender plants on the walls – they include Banksian roses, pomegranates and a hefty *Acca sellowiana* – and by the containers brilliantly planted with annuals and tender plants. At other times it is the structure which impresses: the 17th-century terraces, lead statues, planters and clipped yews. The views are always a big draw, but especially when the rhododendrons and azaleas are in flower on the ridge opposite the castle. There is much wonderfully rich colour planting by Graham Thomas and in early autumn the maples colour the lower slopes, as does an Edwardian garden of roses and hollyhocks in summer. The aspect is south-east, so Powis is best seen in the morning light: photographers please note.

 Features Famous terraces gardens; woodland garden; topiary; good herbaceous borders; tender plants; colour plantings; good autumn colour; plant shop & gift shop.

Owned by The National Trust
Number of gardeners 8
Size 9.6ha (24 acres)
NCCPG National Collections *Aralia*; *Laburnum*

NORTHERN IRELAND

Northern Ireland has some fine historic landscapes dating back to the 18th century: Florence Court in Co. Fermanagh and Castle Ward in Co. Down are two that we list. However, there is no doubt that the two best gardens in Northern Ireland are the 20th-century masterpieces – Mount Stewart and Rowallane. Both are in the care of the National Trust, which has maintained them as major tourist attractions. It is a pity that so few people from Britain know them at first hand. Given good weather, they are among the most enchanting and extensive gardens anywhere in the British Isles – and especially lovely in late spring.

Many trees and shrubs flourish in the mild, damp climate of Co. Down and Co. Antrim. The National Arboretum at Castlewellan has a very fine collection of mature tress: 38 of them are record-breakers. Nevertheless, it is fair to say that gardening and garden visiting are not such popular activities in Northern Ireland as on the mainland of the United Kingdom. Prices reflect this: the cost of admission to National Trust properties in Northern Ireland is substantially less than one would pay to visit a garden of equivalent quality in England.

The most comprehensive list of historic parks, gardens and demesnes in Northern Ireland was written by Belinda Jupp and published in 1992 as *The Heritage Gardens Survey*. The Northern Ireland Gardens Committee is keen to complete a more formal register.

The Ulster Gardens Scheme raises funds every year for work in National Trust gardens which would not otherwise be possible. The scheme is run by the Northern Ireland region of the National Trust at Rowallane. The gardens tend to be small and private ones made by the present owners: the Ulster Gardens Scheme also issues a second list of gardens which are open only for group visits by appointment. The Northern Ireland Tourist Board publishes a handsome brochure called *An Information Guide to Gardens and Historic Demesnes* which describes some 26 parks and gardens in considerable detail. It is available free from tourist offices in Northern Ireland or directly from NITB, 59 North Street, Belfast BT1 1NB.

Northern Ireland has a few gardening clubs and societies of its own: there is, for example, a Northern Ireland Daffodil Group and a Rose Society of Northern Ireland. Daffodils have for long been a Northern Irish speciality: Brian Duncan and Carncairn Daffodils are two of the world's leading breeders, and their owners follow in the footsteps of other great Ulster daffodil men like Sir Frank Harrison and Guy Wilson. Roses are very popular: the roses in the Sir Thomas & Lady Dixon Park in south Belfast are a great draw in summer and the

Dickson roses nursery – now only wholesale – has been at Newtownards for over 100 years. Since the closure of the Slieve Donard nursery, there has been no outstanding plantsman's nursery in Northern Ireland, though Gary Dunlop at Ballyrogan comes close to it, and Patrick Ford at Seaforde is a particularly good source of rare trees and shrubs. There are eight National Collections in Northern Ireland, most of them held by corporate owners like the National Trust.

Northern Ireland's only horticultural college is Greenmount College of Agriculture & Horticulture in Antrim, which is a RHS Partner College and is running public lectures and demonstrations in 2002: details are available from the college on 028 9442 6661. RHS members also have free access to a number of gardens in Northern Ireland during the summer, most notably Benvarden Garden and Carnfunnock Country Park in Co. Antrim.

Benvarden Garden & Grounds

BENVARDEN, DERVOCK, BALLYMONEY
BT53 6NN

Tel 028 2074 1331   **Fax** 028 2074 1955
Location Follow the brown signs on B67 Coleraine–Ballycastle road.
Opening hours 1.30 pm – 5.30 pm; Tuesday – Sunday, plus Bank Holiday Mondays; June to August.
Admission fee Adults £2.50; Children free. RHS members free from June to August.

The main feature of the 2-acre walled garden is a spectacular curved red brick wall, nearly 4m high, dating from approximately 1780. Around the walls are espalier-trained apples and pear trees. Other features include a splendid rose garden, several herbaceous borders, a new box parterre, and a fully working kitchen garden. There are also walks around a small lake planted with rhododendrons, azaleas, magnolias and fine trees.

Features Roses; herbaceous plants; kitchen garden; rhododendrons & azaleas.

Owned by Mr & Mrs Hugh Montgomery
Number of gardeners 2
Size 2ha (5 acres)

Carnfunnock Country Park

DRAINS BAY, COAST ROAD, LARNE
BT40 2QG

Tel 028 2827 0541   **Fax** 028 2827 0852
Website www.larne.gov.uk
Location On Antrim Coast Road (A2), 3½ miles north of Larne.

Opening hours 10 am – dusk; daily; all year. Closed 1 January & 25 December.
Admission fee Parking fees. Free for RHS members in July & August.

The walled garden is set within Carnfunnock Country Park on the Antrim Coast, an Area of Outstanding Natural Beauty. It was originally the cottage garden of the Cairndhu Estate owned and run by Sir Thomas & Lady Dixon. The gardens contain a wide collection of plants from all over the world and enjoy a microclimate which allows plants such as the bottle brush (*Callistemon*) and eucalyptus to flourish. The gardens also boast an amphitheatre, while one of the central features to the walled garden is a unique collection of sundials tracing the history of time. The park also has a hornbeam maze in the shape of Northern Ireland.

Features Rhododendrons & azaleas; tender plants; café (Easter to September).

Owned by Larne Borough Council
Number of gardeners 3
Size 190ha (473 acres)

Castle Ward

STRANGFORD, DOWNPATRICK
BT30 7LS

Tel 028 4488 1204   **Fax** 028 4488 1729
Website www.nationaltrust.org.uk
Location On A25, 7 miles from Downpatrick & 1½ miles from Strangford.
Opening hours 10 am – 4 pm (8 pm from May to September); daily; all year.
Admission fee Grounds free.

It is the position of the house at Castle Ward which makes it so special – set among rolling parkland with stupendous views across Strangford Lough – while the house itself intrigues the visitor by having one façade in the Georgian style and the other in Gothick. There are fine trees in the park, including embothriums and an avenue of ancient limes. In the walled garden are stately cordylines, dwarf palms, pittosporums and the rare *Mitraria coccinea*.

 Features Sub-tropical plants; bluebells; cordylines; landscaped park; daffodils.

Owned by The National Trust
Size 16ha (40 acres)

Castlewellan National Arboretum

CASTLEWELLAN BT31 9BU

Tel 028 4377 8664 **Fax** 028 4377 1762
Location 30 miles south of Belfast, 4 miles west of Newcastle.
Opening hours 9 am – dusk; daily; all year.
Admission fee £3.80 per car (2001 price).

Castlewellan means trees: 35 record-breakers and many rarities. The heart of the collection is in a 12-acre walled garden, interplanted with rhododendrons and other shrubs. The central path has mixed borders at the top: dwarf rhododendrons are prominent even here. Much has been restored in recent years: the two fountains have been restored and lost views of the Mountains of Mourne opened up again. Labelling is good, both here and in the adjoining 6-acre woodland garden, and the standard of maintenance high. There are plans to make the collections of *Taxus* and *Eucryphia* comprehensive. In the Forest Park is the newly planted Peace Maze,

representing the journey to peace in Northern Ireland. It is said to be the longest and largest hedge-maze in the world.

 Features Woodland garden; mature conifers; fine collection of trees; autumn colours; embothriums; eucryphias; tallest *Chamaecyparis nootkatensis* 'Lutea' (22m) in the British Isles, plus 34 other tree records; new 'fragrant garden' around a Lutyensesque tea house.

Owned by Dept. of Agriculture & Rural Development, Forest Service
Number of gardeners 4
Size 40ha (100 acres)

Florence Court

ENNISKILLEN BT92 1DB

Tel 028 6634 8249 **Fax** 028 6634 8873
Website www.nationaltrust.org.uk
Location 8 miles south-west of Enniskillen.
Opening hours Grounds: 10 am – 8 pm (4 pm from October to April); daily; all year.
Admission fee £2.50 per car from March to September.

Florence Court has an 18th-century parkland, with stupendous views of Lough Erne and some magnificent trees. These include the original Irish Yew (*Taxus baccata* 'Fastigiata') and many specimens of a beautiful form of weeping beech with a broad curving crown. The rhododendrons are, for the most part, huge ancient hybrids of *R. arboreum*, but there has been much new planting in recent years and the horticultural interest is now considerable.

 Features Woodland garden; fine collection of trees; ice-house; rhododendrons; picnics welcome.

Owned by The National Trust
Size 3.6ha (9 acres)

Mount Stewart

GREY ABBEY, NEWTOWNARDS, CO. DOWN BT22 2AD

Tel 028 4778 8387   **Fax** 028 4278 8569
Website www.nationaltrust.org.uk
Location East of Belfast on A20.
Opening hours Lakeside gardens & walks: 10 am – 8 pm
(4 pm from October to April); daily; all year. Formal
gardens; 10 am – 8 pm (4 pm from October to April); 16–18,
23–24 & 29–31 March, April to September daily and
October to December 11 am – 4 pm at weekends only.
Admission fee Adults £3.75; Children £2.

Mount Stewart is the greatest garden in
Northern Ireland, arguably in all
Ireland. There are two factors which have
made this possible: the exceptionally mild
climate which allows plants to thrive that
would not survive in all but the mildest parts
of the British Isles; and the willingness of the
garden's principal maker, Edith,
Marchioness of Londonderry, to spend
money on a large scale on design, plants and
staff. The formal garden in front of the
house is grandly laid out with all manner of
inventive details: best known are the stone
carvings of animals known as the dodo
terrace. Beyond the formal garden is a
sunken Spanish garden and off to one side is
the shamrock garden where a bed designed
by Lady Londonderry to represent the Red
Hand of Ulster has been surrounded in these
more politically correct times by a green
shamrock. The rare plants begin on the walls
of the house itself: *Rosa gigantea* covers a
large area and there are huge plants of
Ceanothus arboreus 'Trewithen Blue'. Here
too are the wonderfully flowing beds of the
lily wood where exotic myrtles,
pittosporums and phormiums are
underplanted with primulas, cyclamen,
narcissi and lilies, but here – as in every part
of the garden – one is never far from

amazing large-leaved rhododendrons,
cordylines and tree ferns. Better still is the
walk around the lake, where rhododendrons
flood the woodlands: for many visitors in
spring it is the highlight of a tour of Mount
Stewart. The views across the lake are
dominated by the mausoleum and the
exceptional collection of rhododendrons is
interplanted with rare shrubs like mimosas,
clianthus, prostantheras, pittosporums and
grevilleas. They are underplanted in places
with meconopsis and candelabra primulas
and, at one point, you catch a glimpse of a
white stag in a glade. The outstanding area is
the Jubilee Glade where plants in shades of
red, white and blue provide colour all
through the year. For design, variety, plants
and plantings, Mount Stewart is a place of
miracles. Allow lots of time for your visit.

Features A remarkable plantsman's
garden; woodland walks; topiary;
snowdrops; good herbaceous borders; fine
collection of trees; bluebells; rare and tender
shrubs galore; souvenir shop; refreshments
from 12.30 pm.

Owned by The National Trust
Size 31ha (78 acres)
NCCPG National Collections *Phormium; Dianella; Libertia*

Rowallane Garden

SAINTFIELD, BALLYNAHINCH, CO. DOWN BT24 7LH

Tel 028 9751 0131   **Fax** 028 9751 1242
Website www.nationaltrust.org.uk
Location One mile south of Saintfield on A7.
Opening hours 10 am – 8 pm (4 pm between October & April); daily; all year. Closed 24 December to 1 January.
Admission fee Adults £3. Reductions in winter.

The extensive gardens at Rowallane can be dated back to 1903, when Hugh Armytage Moore inherited the estate from his uncle John Moore. Uncle John had planted some of the larger trees – wellingtonias, beeches and rhododendrons – but everything else you see today dates from the 20th century. Hugh Armytage Moore was a great plantsman – not just a collector of horticultural curiosities, but a selector of good forms. As his appetite for plants grew, so the garden expanded into the little fields which pattern the estate. The seedlings grew and needed to be planted. The hedges and walls which surround these enclosures remain as the boundary features of each compartment, so that you still have the impression of walking from field to field although each is thickly planted with ornamental trees and shrubs. Moore subscribed to the plant collecting expeditions of E.H. Wilson and Frank Kingdon Ward. It is to those expeditions, that the vast collection of rhododendrons owes its origins. No garden can match it on a sunny day in April or May, as you amble from a glade of *R. augustinii* forms to a line of *R. macabeanum* or back through *R. yakushimanum* hybrids: the large-leaved species are particularly prominent. Because of the mild climate, many other good plants flourish here which are rare elsewhere – *Lomatia ferruginea, Grevillea rosmarinifolia*

and *Nothofagus cunninghamii*, for example. Other rarities include *Helwingia japonica* and *Cupressus duclouxiana*, the latter a record-breaking specimen. Rowallane has also given us some good garden hybrids (e.g. *Hypericum* 'Rowallane') and selected forms (e.g. *Viburnum plicatum* 'Rowallane'). Another notable feature is the rock garden – an outcrop of natural whinstone rock which actually has few plants growing in it, but many around the base of the boulders, including the striking candelabra primula 'Rowallane Rose'. And the walled garden too is a treasure-house of rare plants, including *Feijoa (Acca) sellowiana* and the National Collection of *Penstemon* species, which gives colour long after the rhododendrons have faded. But it is still the rhododendrons and azaleas for which the garden is best remembered.

Features Rhododendrons & azaleas; a great plantsman's collection of plants; fine collection of trees; good autumn colour; snowdrops; rock garden; tallest *Cupressus duclouxiana* (14m) in the British Isles and three other record trees; National Trust shop; new Information Centre; light refreshments 2 pm – 6 pm May to August & weekends in April & September.

Owned by The National Trust
Size 20ha (50 acres)
NCCPG National Collections *Penstemon*

Guy Wilson Daffodil Garden

UNIVERSITY OF ULSTER, COLERAINE
BT52 1SA

Tel 028 7044 4141
Location Signed from sports centre, or entry via Portstewart Road.
Opening hours Dawn – dusk; daily; all year.
Admission fee Free.

The name says it all – this is both a celebration of Guy Wilson as a daffodil breeder and a museum of his hybrids. Drifts of his cultivars, and others of Irish raising, sweep through the university gardens.

 Features An exceptional collection of daffodils, best in second half of April.

Owned by University of Ulster at Coleraine
NCCPG National Collections *Narcissus*

Seaforde Gardens

SEAFORDE, DOWNPATRICK BT30 8PG

Tel 028 44 81 1225   **Fax** 028 44 81 1370
Location Between Belfast & Newcastle.
Opening hours 10 am – 5 pm; Monday – Saturday.
1 pm – 6 pm; Sundays.

Seaforde is an important nursery for trees and shrubs, including Irish specialities (*Eucryphia* × *intermedia* 'Rostrevor') and tender taxa. The list now includes a growing number of rhododendrons grown from Patrick Forde's own collecting expeditions to Bhutan, Yunnan, Tibet and Vietnam. The gardens – open all year – are extensive and important: they have drifts of primulas, camassias and bluebells, as well as both pink forms of *Eucryphia lucida*.

Features Rare trees; eucryphias; lots of interesting plants.

Owned by Patrick Forde
Number of gardeners 2
Size 2ha (5 acres)
NCCPG National Collections *Eucryphia*

REPUBLIC OF IRELAND

Until quite recently, gardens were widely thought of in Ireland as part of the culture of the Anglo-Irish: real Irishmen possessed neither the resources nor the cultural points of reference to occupy themselves with horticulture. There was a grain of truth in this: one of the consequences of the troubles and the land reforms has been the disappearance of many of the historic gardens, parks and demesnes which accompanied the houses of the landed gentry. It is a problem of which the Irish are acutely aware and where such groups as the Irish Georgian Society have done much to change people's perceptions. The new wealth and confidence which Ireland has found within the European Union have helped to dispel the notion that gardens are yet another manifestation of British superiority: now they are seen as something which the Irish can seize upon and adapt to their own cultural styles, traditions, needs and conditions.

The old order is still there, of course. Most of the big gardens attached to big houses and open to the public date back to the 19th century – examples are Lismore, Derreen, Tullynally and Powerscourt. But a number were also made in the middle of the 20th century, often with English pounds (Birr and Malahide) or American dollars (Glenveagh and Mount Congreve). And the best modern gardens in Ireland have most

certainly been made by Irishmen – one has only to think of Jim Reynolds's amazing combination of plantsmanship, artistry and style at Butterstream to wonder what further wonders we can expect from Irish horticulture in the years ahead.

Irish gardens tend to be tagged on at the end of guidebooks to UK gardens. The truth is that they are one of the best reasons for visiting Ireland in the first place. This has been made clear from time to time by books that do not always receive the currency they deserve. Two recent titles with a heavy photographic input are *Glorious Gardens of Ireland* with pictures by Melanie Eclare (Kyle Cathie, 1999) and *Irish Gardens* by Olda Fitzgerald (Conran Octopus, 1999). And the Irish Tourist Board (PO Box 273, Dublin 8) publishes a handsomely illustrated guide to *Great Houses, Castles & Gardens of Ireland*. In addition to some 80 of the best places in Eire, it lists about 20 Country House Hotels. The guide is invaluable, and whets the armchair visitor's appetite.

Ireland is well supplied with garden centres, but has few specialist nurseries. Good garden plants are more difficult to come by. Irish gardeners sometimes say that their best herbaceous plants tend to come from Britain and are then more widely distributed through an informal system of gifting. The NCCPG is represented by the

Irish Garden Plant Society: there are only three National Collections in the country – *Garrya* and *Potentilla fruticosa* (cultivars) at National Botanic Gardens, Glasnevin, and *Olearia* in the care of Fingal County Council at Malahide Castle. It is also to be hoped that the new Irish interest in gardening will benefit the Royal Horticultural Society of Ireland, whose 'Royal' title hints at its ties to the United Kingdom but which has less than 2,000 members.

Garden restoration is a growth industry in Ireland today. During the last ten years, Dúchas – which calls itself 'the Heritage Service' – has helped to rescue the Lutyens gardens at Heywood in Co. Laois and taken over the administration of Fota. Private enterprise has come to the rescue of other gardens: Nicholas and Susan Mosse have made a grand job of restoring the romantic landscape garden at Kilfane in Co. Kilkenny while Benedictine nuns have started to restore the high Victorian gardens at Kylemore Abbey in Connemara. But perhaps the greatest measure of the popularity of gardening in Ireland today is the success of Helen Dillon as a garden-owner, horticultural guru and media star – a success which is very well deserved, for her Dublin garden is an inspiration and her ability to communicate by the written and spoken word is legendary.

Altamont Garden

ALTAMONT, TULLOW, CO. CARLOW

Tel 00 353 503 59444   **Fax** 00 353 503 59510
Location Signed from N80 & N81.
Opening hours All year. Phone for opening times.

Altamont is a charming and romantic woodland garden, full of rare plants, together with lakes, islands, a bog garden and a shady glen. A new double herbaceous border, 75m long within the walled garden, was opened in 2000 with a plant sales area next to it. The woodland garden is a place of contemplation and wonder, and very old-world Irish.

 Features Woodland garden; rhododendrons & azaleas; cyclamen.

Owned by Dúchas, The Heritage Service
Number of gardeners 4
Size 16ha (40 acres)

Annes Grove Gardens

CASTLETOWNROCHE, MALLOW, CO. CORK

Tel & Fax 00 353 22 26145
Location 1 mile north of Castletownroche on N72.
Opening hours 10 am – 5 pm, Monday – Saturday; 1 pm – 6 pm, Sundays; mid-March to 30 September.
Admission fee Adults €4; OAPs & Students €3; Children €1.

Annes Grove has long been famous for its 30-acre garden, begun in 1907: 'Robinsonian' is the word most often used to describe it. The walled garden is a flower garden, with a 17th-century mount and a Victorian gothic summer house on top. The river garden is lushly wild with lysichiton, gunnera and candelabra primulas around the pools. In the glen garden lies a wonderfully dense collection of rhododendrons and azaleas, many from Kingdon Ward's seed.

 Features Woodland garden; plantsman's collection of plants; good herbaceous borders; rhododendrons from wild seeds; rare trees; tallest *Azara microphylla* (11m) in the British Isles; lunches & teas by arrangement for groups.

Owned by Patrick Annesley
Number of gardeners 4
Size 12ha (30 acres)

Ardgillan Park

BALBRIGGAN, CO. DUBLIN

Tel 00 353 1 890 5629   **Fax** 00 353 1 890 5649
Website www.fingalcoco.ie
Location Off the coast road between Skerries & Balbriggan in Co. Dublin.
Opening hours 10 am – 5 pm; daily; all year.
Admission fee Free.

Although referred to as a castle, Ardgillan is a large country house with castellated embellishments. It was built in 1738 by Robert Taylor, with later additions, and has always been famous for its magnificent views of the coastline north of Dublin. The original gardens were all but lost in the troubles, but were restored by the Council and opened to the public as a Regional Park in June 1985. The gardens at Ardgillan are in two main parts: the formal rose garden and *Potentilla* collection to the west of the house and the walled garden to the north-west. The formal garden has been restored to its layout on the Ordnance Survey map of 1865. The Victorian conservatory at one end of the rose garden has also been restored: it was originally constructed at Malahide in the 1880s by the Scottish firm of McKenzie & Moncur. Work has now begun on restoring further outbuildings to incorporate a Museum of Gardening.

 Features Roses (ancient & modern); potentillas (nearly 200 cvs.); walled garden; herb garden; *potager*; good herbaceous borders; ice house; 200-year-old yew walk; Victorian conservatory.

Owned by Fingal County Council
Size 1.6ha (4 acres)
NCCPG National Collections *Potentilla*

Ardnamona

LOUGH ESKE, CO. DONEGAL

Tel 00 353 73 22650   **Fax** 00 353 73 22819
Website www.ardnamona.com
Location On Lough Eske, 5 miles north-east of Donegal.
Opening hours 10 am – 6 pm; daily; all year.

Ardnamona is masterpiece of huge arborescent rhododendrons, some as much as 20m high, like a Himalayan forest on the lower slopes of the Blue Stack mountains. A few date back to the introductions of Sir Joseph Hooker in the 1860s. Others were brought by Sir Arthur Wallace as seeds or cuttings from the imperial gardens in Peking and the palace gardens in Kathmandu. All are covered in moss and ferns that revel in the soft climate. Rocky outcrops add to the sense of awesome wilderness, but reclamation and replanting are well under way: the owners have made a big impact on the 40 acres of *Rhododendron ponticum*.

 Features Woodland garden; mature conifers; ancient rhododendrons; bed & breakfast offered.

Owned by Mr & Mrs Kieran Clarke

Ballymaloe Cookery School Garden

BALLYMALOE, SHANAGARRY, CO. CORK

Tel 00 353 21 4646785   **Fax** 00 353 21 4646909
Website www.cookingisfun.ie
Location Ballymaloe, signed from Castlemartyr & Shanagarry.
Opening hours 10 am – 6 pm; daily; 1 April to 1 October.
Admission fee Adults €5; OAPs €2.50; Children €2.

The garden attached to the famous Ballymaloe cookery school is full of unusual fruit, vegetables and herbs. Seldom is a functional garden so stylishly designed and planted, or so extensive. And it is organic.

 Features Vegetables; roses (mainly old-fashioned); fruit; good herbaceous borders; magnificent formal parterres for herbs; Celtic maze; shell house; garden shop.

Owned by Tim & Darina Allen
Number of gardeners 3
Size 1.2ha (3 acres)

Ballynacourty

BALLYSTEEN, CO. LIMERICK

Tel 00 353 61 396409   **Fax** 00 353 61 396733
Location 3 miles from Askeaton, on River Shannon.
Opening hours By appointment.
Admission fee €5.

Ballynacourty is a fine modern family garden: six densely planted acres won from open farmland. It is interesting for its selection of lime-tolerant trees and shrubs and to see how a garden of this size may be maintained with minimum help.

Features Shrub roses (mainly old-fashioned); herbaceous borders.

Owned by George & Michelina Stacpoole
Number of gardeners 1 part-time
Size 2.2ha (6 acres)

Birr Castle Demesne

BIRR, CO. OFFALY

Tel 00 353 509 20336   **Fax** 00 353 509 21583
Website www.birrcastle.com
Location Rosse Row in Birr, Co. Offaly.
Opening hours 9 am – 6 pm or dusk; daily; all year.
Admission fee Adults €7; OAPs €5; Children €3.50.

The best garden in the Irish Midlands, Birr has a huge collection of trees and shrubs and a wonderful walled garden with a tunnel down the middle. Many of the plants are grown from original collectors' material: some were collected in the wild by the owner's parents, Michael and Anne Rosse. Birr also has the tallest box hedges in the world. In the grounds is the famous telescope, once the largest in the world, now fully restored and witness to the polymath abilities of the owner's family over the generations. Three new features were added for the millennium: a *teatro verde*, a winter garden and a new river garden.

 Features Topiary; roses (mainly old-fashioned); plantsman's collection of plants; herbs; good herbaceous borders; fine collection of trees; *Paeonia* 'Anne Rosse'; *Magnolia* 'Anne Rosse'; tallest *Acer monspessulanum* (15m) and boxwood *Buxus sempervirens* (12m) in the British Isles, plus 49 other record species.

Owned by Earl of Rosse
Number of gardeners 6
Size 52ha (125 acres)

Butterstream

KILDALKEY ROAD, TRIM, CO. MEATH

Tel 00 353 46 36017   **Fax** 00 353 46 31702
Location Outskirts of Trim on Kildalkey Road.
Opening hours 11 am – 6 pm; daily; May to September.

Ireland's Sissinghurst is just over 20 years old, and still expanding. Jim Reynolds has made a series of garden rooms (13 at the last count) in the modern style around an old farmhouse. Each is different but connected to the next. They include a green garden, a white garden, a hot-coloured garden, a Roman garden, a pool garden (with Tuscan portico reflected in it), an obelisk garden, and many others. The latest and largest feature is two vast canals in the 17th-century Dutch style. The plants are determined by the soil – heavy, cold, limy clay.

 Features Roses (ancient & modern); plantsman's collection of plants; fruit; good herbaceous borders; colour borders; canals; lime *allées*.

Owned by Jim Reynolds
Number of gardeners 3
Size 3.2ha (8 acres), plus semi-parkland

Coolcarrigan Gardens

COOLCARRIGAN, NAAS, CO. KILDARE

Tel 00 353 45 863512   **Fax** 00 353 45 8641400
Location 12 miles north of Naas.
Opening hours By appointment only, from April to August.
Admission fee €5.

This garden owes everything to a gale which knocked the heart out of the established plantings in 1974. Harold Hillier advised on the replanting and the result is one of the best modern collections of trees and shrubs in Ireland – over 1,100 different species and cultivars. The owners, keen plantsmen, have added late summer borders and a rock garden.

 Features Snowdrops; rock garden; rhododendrons & azaleas; plantsman's collection of shrubs & trees; daffodils; bluebells; refreshments by arrangement.

Owned by Mr & Mrs John Wilson-Wright
Number of gardeners 1
Size 4ha (10 acres)

Curraghmore

PORTLAW, CO. WATERFORD

Tel 00 353 51 387102 **Fax** 00 353 51 387481
Location 14 miles west of Waterford: enter by Portlaw gate.
Opening hours 2 pm – 5 pm; Thursdays & Bank Holidays; Easter to mid October. Also (jointly with House) 9 am – 1 pm; Monday – Friday; January, May & June.

Lord Waterford's family has lived at Curraghmore since 1170, which is a long time even by Irish standards. It has fine terraced gardens with balustrades and an excellent collection of trees and shrubs, dating mainly from the 19th and early 20th centuries. The outstanding feature is the Shell Grotto which was built in 1754 by the heiress to the property, Catherine Poer, Countess of Tyrone. She personally decorated the interior walls with shells which were collected from all round the world. Curraghmore is a magnificent estate which deserves to be better known.

Features Fine collection of trees; landscaped park.

Owned by The Marquess of Waterford

Derreen

LAURAGH, KILLARNEY, CO. KERRY

Tel 00 353 64 83588
Location 15 miles from Kenmare on the Castletown Road.
Opening hours 11 am – 6 pm; daily; April to October.
Admission fee Adults €4; Children €2.

Derreen is quite extraordinary. The rocky outcrops come right to the front door, but the fast lush growth of its trees and shrubs is boundless. Tree ferns *Dicksonia antarctica* and myrtles *Luma apiculata* have gone native, and seed themselves everywhere. Moss, lichen and ferns abound. Large-leaved rhododendrons grow to great heights. It is a place of wonder on a sunny day in late April.

Features Woodland garden; subtropical plants; tree ferns; rhododendrons; two ponds (1999).

Owned by The Hon. David Bigham
Number of gardeners 2
Size 22ha (60 acres)

The Dillon Garden

RANELAGH, DUBLIN 6, CO. DUBLIN

Tel 00 353 1 4971308 **Fax** 00 353 1 4971308
Website www.dillongarden.com
Location 45 Sandford Road.
Opening hours 2 pm – 6 pm; daily; March, July & August. Plus Sundays, April to June, & September. Groups by appointment.
Admission fee Adults €5.

This much acclaimed plantsman's garden offers a fantastic range of rarities, from snowdrops and hellebores in spring, to tropaeolums in autumn. Unlike some collectors' gardens, Helen Dillon's is immaculately maintained, strictly planted according to colour and beautifully designed as a series of garden rooms. Two years ago (2000), she replaced the lawn with a canal with formal beds and small cascades set in limestone paving: more major changes are planned for 2002. This must be the most intensively gardened garden in the British Isles – a source of constant admiration and inspiration.

 Features Plantsman's collection of plants; plants under glass; good herbaceous borders.

Owned by Helen & Val Dillon
Number of gardeners 1
Size 0.2ha (½ acre)

Earlscliffe

BAILY, CO. DUBLIN

Tel 00 353 1 8322556   **Fax** 00 353 1 8323021
Website http://homepage.tinet.ie/~earlscliffe/
Location At the end of Ceanchor Road, off the L86 on the south side of the Howth peninsular.
Opening hours By appointment for groups only.
Admission fee Prices on application.

Dr & Mrs Robinson have developed Earlscliffe since 1969 as a low-maintenance garden devoted to rare and tender plants. The secret is the microclimate which the garden enjoys on a south-facing slope above the sea. Nothing is protected and the Robinsons have concentrated on woody plants to facilitate maintenance. The range of plants which have succeeded is frankly staggering: among them are some 60 *Eucalyptus* species from Australia, *Beschorneria yuccoides* from Mexico, *Sonchus arboreus* from the Canary Islands, *Itoa orientalis* from Vietnam, *Metrosideros robustus* from New Zealand and *Puya*

alpestris from Chile. The Ryukyu Island banana *Musa basjoo* fruits most years. *Luma apiculata* and *Escallonia rubra* var. *macrantha* are weeded out in their hundreds. Other self-seeders include *Echium pininana* and *Euphorbia mellifera* from the Canary Islands, *Erica lusitanica* from Iberia and *Cordyline australis* from New Zealand. The planting continues. And the website is excellent.

 Features Australian and South African plants.

Owned by Dr & Mrs David Robinson
Number of gardeners owners only
Size 4.4ha (11 acres)

Fairfield Lodge

MONKSTOWN AVENUE, MONKSTOWN, CO. DUBLIN

Tel & Fax 00 353 1 2803912
Location In Monkstown village.
Opening hours By appointment.

Fairfield is a small town garden, made to appear much larger by division into a series of outdoor rooms. Its formal design, informal planting and clever colour combinations have made it a modern classic.

 Features Roses (mainly old-fashioned & climbers); good herbaceous borders; colour combinations; refreshments.

Owned by John Bourke

Fernhill

SANDYFORD, CO. DUBLIN

Tel 00 353 1 295 6000
Location 7 miles south of central Dublin on the Enniskerry Road.
Opening hours 11 am – 5 pm (2 pm – 6 pm on Sundays & Bank Holidays); Tuesday – Sunday (& Bank Holidays); March to September.
Admission fee Adults €5; OAPs €4; Children €2.

This popular garden on the outskirts of Dublin has a good collection of rhododendrons and other woodland plants and some magnificent trees 150 years old. There are steep woodland walks and an excellent nursery which sells plants on Saturday afternoons in April and September.

Features Woodland garden; rock garden; good herbaceous borders; fine collection of trees; sculpture exhibitions; rhododendrons; new fern plantings (2000).

Owned by Mrs Sally Walker
Number of gardeners 2
Size 12ha (30 acres)

Fota Arboretum & Garden

FOTA ISLAND, CARRIGTWOHILL, CO. CORK

Tel & Fax 00 353 21 4812728
Location 9 miles from Cork city, off Cobh road.
Opening hours 9 am (11 am on Sundays) – 6 pm (5 pm from November to March); daily; all year. Closed for Christmas holidays.
Admission fee Cars €2; pedestrians free.

Fota is famous above all for its trees, most of them planted by the Smith-Barry family towards the end of the 19th century. As well as a fine collection of Victorian conifers (huge redwoods and wellingtonias), the garden and arboretum are notable for the collection of flowering mimosas (*Acacia*), a beautiful *Styrax japonica*, a magnificent collection of mature magnolias, and a spectacular specimen of *Phoenix canariensis* which was planted out over 100 years ago. Some of the record-breaking trees have been lost in recent years but many of Fota's very rare trees still survive, including *Juniperus bermudiana* and *Phyllocladus tricomanoides*. The garden and arboretum were transferred to the State in 1996 and have since undergone much restoration, regeneration and improvement. New plants have been added, often as part of international conservation programmes. The old walled kitchen garden has been converted to a formal rose garden, with themed borders of monocots, shade-loving and South American plants, a large selection of climbers on the walls, and a collection of Irish-bred daffodils. The original formal gardens, known as the 'pleasure gardens' are presently undergoing restoration.

Features Woodland garden; mature conifers; 160 Irish-bred daffodil cultivars; Victorian garden.

Owned by Dúchas, The Heritage Service
Number of gardeners 5
Size 11ha (27 acres)

Gash Gardens

GASH, CASTLETOWN, PORTLAOISE, CO. LAOIS

Tel 00 353 502 32247   **Fax** 00 353 502 32857
Location ½ mile from N7 at Castletown.

Opening hours 10 am – 5 pm; daily; May to September. Opens at 2 pm on Sundays.
Admission fee €3.50. Group rates by appointment. Not suitable for children.

Gash is a young, award-winning plantsman's garden, started in 1984, full of unusual plants and maintained to very high standard. It has four acres, alongside the River Nore, with streams and other water features. There is a large rock and alpine garden, colourful herbaceous borders and an extensive collection of trees and shrubs. The garden bursts into life with a display of alpine plants and rhododendrons in spring and early summer. In June comes the laburnum arch, followed by the herbaceous borders which carry through to autumn – autumn colour is particularly good. The garden was initially laid out and developed by Noël Keenan as a complement to his nursery business: his daughter is continuing to develop and maintain it.

 Features Herbaceous perennials; rock garden; rhododendrons; plantsman's collection of plants; new mixed border (2000); nursery at entrance, open all year.

Owned by Mary Keenan
Number of gardeners 1, plus part-time
Size 1.6ha (4 acres)

Glenveagh Castle

CHURCHILL, LETTERKENNY, CO. DONEGAL

Tel 00 353 74 37090   **Fax** 00 353 74 37072
Location 14 miles north-west of Letterkenny on R251.
Opening hours Daily; dawn to dusk; all year.

Glenveagh was built for its view down the rocky slopes of Lough Veagh, and part of the garden is known as the View Garden. Lanning Roper laid out a formal Italianate courtyard garden. Jim Russell advised on planting. There are wonderful borders and conservatories as well as rhododendrons and camellias. The unusual shrubs are magnificent: tree-like griselinias and *Michelia doltsopa*, for instance. There are new plantings from the Royal Botanic Garden at Edinburgh and a trip to Yunnan in 1996.

 Features Sub-tropical plants; roses (mainly old-fashioned); plantsman's collection of plants; plants under glass; fruit; good herbaceous borders; fine collection of trees; restaurant at visitor centre; tea-room.

Owned by Dúchas, The Heritage Service

Glin Castle

GLIN, CO. LIMERICK

Tel 00 353 68 34173   **Fax** 00 353 68 34364
Website www.glincastle.com
Location On N69, 32 miles west of Limerick.
Opening hours By appointment.
Admission fee Adults ×6.

Simple formal gardens run down towards the park and merge with the surrounding woodland. The walled kitchen garden has recently received a make-over: cutting borders, herbs, herbaceous borders and such vegetables as sea-kale and asparagus. In the pleasure gardens are some fine ornamental trees – dogwoods, magnolias, cherries and parrotias, as well as rhododendrons and camellias. Taken with the gothicised castle and its magnificent position on the Shannon estuary, Glin is a place of rare enchantment.

Features Vegetables; sub-tropical plants; rhododendrons & azaleas; daffodils; camellias; bluebells; grotto &

Victorian hermitage recently restored; gate shop.

Owned by Desmond Fitzgerald, Knight of Glin
Number of gardeners 2
Size 2ha (5 acres)

Heywood Gardens

BALLINAKILL, CO. LAOIS

Tel 00 353 502 33563
Location In grounds of Ballinakill College.
Opening hours Dawn – dusk; daily; all year.
Admission fee Free.

The formal garden (circular and walled) was originally designed by Lutyens in 1912, then taken into State care in 1993 and has since been carefully restored and replanted with advice from Graham Thomas. Go now, to see what an Edwardian garden looked like when newly made. Around it are lakes and woodland gardens with fine trees.

 Features Lutyens garden; Graham Thomas plantings; woodland garden.

Owned by Office of Public Works

Hillside

ANNMOUNT, GLOUNTHANE, CO. CORK

Tel & Fax 00 353 21 4353119
Location From Cork, turn left at Glounthane Church, up hill, under bridge, 100 yards on right.
Opening hours By appointment between May & September.

This is an intensely cultivated plantsman's garden in a setting of mature trees (beech and pines) and rhododendrons, azaleas,

pieris and woodland plants. It burgeons with alpine plants in every part – stone troughs, a scree bed and gravel areas. It also won the Top Garden in Ireland award in 2000 for its all-season attractions. And it is forever changing and improving.

 Features Rhododendrons & azaleas; plantsman's collection of plants; alpine plants; woodland plants.

Owned by Mrs Mary Byrne
Number of gardeners owner only
Size 1.6ha (4 acres)

Japanese Gardens & St Fiacre's Garden

TULLY, KILDARE TOWN, CO. KILDARE

Tel 00 353 45 521617   **Fax** 00 353 45 522964
Website www.irish-national-stud.ie
Location Signed in Kildare.
Opening hours 9.30 am – 6 pm; daily; 12 February to 12 November.
Admission fee €8.50 Adults; €6.50 OAPs; €4.50 Children.

The Japanese garden is a sequence which symbolises Man's journey through life. It was made for Lord Wavertree by Japanese gardeners in the early years of the 20th century. A very substantial new garden, dedicated to St Fiacre the patron saint of gardeners, was opened in 1999, and provides a grand contrast.

 Features Famous Japanese garden; souvenir shop; light refreshments.

Owned by Irish National Stud
Number of gardeners 3
Size 1.6ha (4 acres)

John F. Kennedy Arboretum

NEW ROSS, CO. WEXFORD

Tel 00 353 51 388171 **Fax** 00 353 51 388172
Location 8 miles south of New Ross off R733.
Opening hours 10 am – 8 pm, May to August;
10 am – 6.30 pm, April & September; 10 am – 5 pm,
October to March. Closed 29 March & 25 December.
Admission fee Adults €2.50; OAPs €1.90;
Children & Students €1.20.

This is a memorial arboretum founded in 1968 with financial help from Irish/American citizens on 623 acres near the Kennedy homestead. Thirty years on, the statistics are impressive: 4,500 types of trees and shrubs arranged taxonomically, and 200 plots by geographical distribution. All are meticulously labelled, and planted with artistry. There is one circuit for broadleaves and another for conifers, interwoven at times to improve the overall appearance of the collection. Special features include an 'ericaceous garden' with 500 different rhododendrons, and many varieties of azaleas and heathers. There is also a slow-growing conifer collection, a hedge collection, a display of groundcover plants and a selection of climbing plants on a series of stone and timber shelters. In summer a miniature railway runs through plantings that represent each continent.

Features Mature conifers; fine collection of trees; eight different tree records for the British Isles; souvenirs; cafeteria for teas/refreshments in summer.

Owned by Dúchas, The Heritage Service
Number of gardeners 14
Size 247ha (623 acres)

Johnstown Castle Gardens

WEXFORD, CO. WEXFORD

Tel 00 353 53 42888 **Fax** 00 353 53 42004
Location 4 miles south-west of Wexford.
Opening hours 9 am – 5.30 pm; daily; all year except Christmas day.

Johnstown Castle has 50 acres of ornamental grounds with good trees, tall cordylines, three lakes and the Irish Agricultural Museum. There is a section in the museum devoted to old lawnmowers and antique garden equipment.

Features Woodland garden; mature conifers; walled gardens; ornamental lakes; tallest *Cupressus macrocarpa* (40m) in the British Isles; coffee-shop with snacks, July and August only.

Owned by TEAGASC (Food & Agriculture Development Authority)
Number of gardeners 4
Size 20ha (50 acres)

Kilfane Glen & Waterfall

THOMASTOWN, CO. KILKENNY

Tel 00 353 56 24558 **Fax** 00 353 56 27491
Website www.NicholasMosse.com
Location Off N9, 2 miles north of Thomastown.
Opening hours 2 pm – 6 pm; Sundays; April to June & September. 11 am – 6 pm; daily; July & August.
Admission fee Adults €5.50.

A romantic landscape garden laid out in the 1790s and vigorously restored by the present owners. Sit in the tiny *cottage ornée*, admire the exquisite form of the waterfall across the ravine, and dream of Rousseau.

 Features Woodland garden; bluebells; new grass garden (2000); excellent modern art pieces; teas by arrangement.

Owned by Nicholas & Susan Mosse
Number of gardeners 2
Size 8ha (20 acres)

Lismore Castle

LISMORE, CO. WATERFORD

Tel 00 353 58 54424   **Fax** 00 353 58 54896
Website www.lismorecastle.com
Location Centre of Lismore.
Opening hours 1.45 pm – 4.45 pm; daily; 30 March to 29 September. Opens at 11 am in high season.
Admission fee Adults €4; Children €2.

Lismore is best for the castellated house: the gardens are interesting rather than exceptional, but there is a pretty grove of camellias and a double yew walk planted in 1707. The upper enclosure is even older, a Jacobean survivor. The herbaceous border aligned on the cathedral spire has recently been replanted to give colour throughout the summer. Visit the walled garden for some fine traditional kitchen gardening: the vinery was designed by Paxton – this is the Irish Chatsworth.

 Features Woodland garden; roses (mainly old-fashioned); magnolias; spring bulbs; interesting modern sculptures (including Anthony Gormley).

Owned by Lismore Estates
Number of gardeners 4
Size 2.8ha (7 acres)

Lodge Park Walled Garden

STRAFFAN, CO. KILDARE

Tel 00 353 1 628 8412   **Fax** 00 353 1 627 3477
Location Follow sign to Steam Museum Straffan from Maynooth & Kill.
Opening hours 2.30 pm – 5.30 pm; Tuesday – Friday (plus Sunday in June/July only); June to August.
Admission fee €4.

As it did in the 18th century, the walled garden at Lodge Park continues to produce fruit and vegetables with much more besides. The edible crops grow alongside an ever-increasing collection of lesser-known ornamental plants. Coloured borders of white, blue and yellow greet the visitor and a pink border begins the main walk of the garden, near a collection of peonies. Behind a new classical entrance, the original cold greenhouse allows semi-tender plants to be displayed. A more modern heated greenhouse gives protection for such plants as cymbidiums and daturas. The main walk of the garden is lined with box hedges, interrupted by topiary yews: behind the box lies a south-facing border of shrubs and perennials. In the centre is an ornamental salad garden, a fruit garden and a more conventional vegetable garden. The main herbaceous border has a backdrop of roses and is spectacular in July. The rose garden includes a circular iron structure clad in climbing roses topped by a copper rosebud. The north-facing border allows for a collection of shade-loving plants, especially hellebores and pulmonarias.

 Features Roses; good herbaceous borders; newly restored Victorian greenhouse (1998); gift shop at Museum.

Owned by Mr & Mrs Robert Guinness
Number of gardeners 1
Size 0.8ha (2 acres)

Mount Usher Gardens

ASHFORD, CO. WICKLOW

Tel 00 353 404 40205 **Fax** 00 353 404 40116
Location Ashford, 30 miles south of Dublin on the N11.
Opening hours 10.30 am – 6 pm; daily; 15 March to
3 November.
Admission fee Adults €5; OAPs & Children €4. Guided
tours for groups available.

These twenty acres of garden have the River
Vartry running through their middle: both
sides of the river are crowded with unusual
trees and shrubs – 5,000 different species
and cultivars, some of them *very* rare. The
self-sown *Pinus montezumae* are justly
famous. There are good herbaceous plants
too, and lilies in July. It is a truly remarkable
plantsman's garden made in the
Robinsonian style by four generations of
Walpoles from 1868 to 1980 and extensively
restored by the present owner.

Features Woodland garden; sub-
tropical plants; plantsman's collection
of plants; mature conifers; fine trees; spring
bulbs; pretty bridges across the river; new
millennium arboretum (2000); tallest
Cornus capitata (18m) in the British Isles,
plus 28 other record tree species.

Owned by Mrs Madelaine Jay
Number of gardeners 4
Size 8ha (20 acres)

Muckross House & Gardens

MUCKROSS, KILLARNEY, CO. KERRY

Tel 00 353 64 31440 **Fax** 00 353 64 33926
Location 4 miles south of Killarney on N71.
Opening hours Dawn – dusk; daily; all year except one
week at Christmas.
Admission fee Free.

Killarney National Park provides a most
beautiful setting for the gardens and ancient
parkland of Muckross House. The walled
garden has just been restored: so has the
range of Richardson greenhouse which will
be open to visitors in spring 2002. There are
a young arboretum (now fully open to
visitors) and some enormous old
rhododendrons, but the woodland is of oak,
yew, Scots pines and arbutus trees and, even
more exciting for a garden-visitor, the rock
garden is a natural one, of carboniferous
limestone. Well maintained.

Features Woodland garden; rock
garden; mature conifers; fine collection
of trees; rhododendrons; azaleas;
greenhouse collection; extensive young
conifer plantings in arboretum; lunches,
hot & cold snacks daily.

Owned by Dúchas, The Heritage Service
Size 6ha (15 acres), plus 10ha (25-acre) arboretum

National Garden Exhibition Centre

KILQUADE, KILPEDDER, CO. WICKLOW

Tel 00 353 1 2819890 **Fax** 00 353 1 2810359
Website www.clubi.ie/calumet
Location Signed from the N11, 7 miles south of Bray.

National Botanic Gardens

GLASNEVIN, DUBLIN 9, CO. DUBLIN

Tel 00 353 1 837 4388   **Fax** 00 353 1 836 0080
Website www.irelandseye.com
Location 3 miles north of City Centre between N1 & N2:
exit from M 50 to City Centre at Jct X or Y.
Opening hours 9 am – 6 pm (10 am – 4.30 pm in winter);
daily except 25 December. Open at 11 am on Sundays.
Admission fee Free.

Glasnevin was founded in 1795 to promote a scientific approach to the practice of agriculture: education remains a priority at the gardens which have a flourishing school of horticulture. The design of the botanic garden is classically Victorian, laid out as a beautiful public park in undulating ground on the south bank of the River Tolka: plants are comprehensively documented, labelled and classified. Notable trees include a magnificent Caucasian ironwood (*Zelkova carpinifolia*) near the new Herbarium building, good specimens of *Tetradium daniellii*, *Gymnocladus dioica* and *Davidia involucrata* and notable plants of a prostrate form of maidenhair tree (*Ginkgo biloba*) and the weeping Atlantic cedar (*Cedrus atlantica* 'Pendula'). Recent years have seen a dramatic programme of restoration and renewal. The elegant curvilinear range of glasshouses, built by Richard Turner between 1843 and 1868, has been magnificently restored. It has – among many tropical plants – a good collection of cycads. The cactus and fern houses – the borders around them are planted with arum lilies and white watsonias – each have extensive collections, including a 400-year-old tree fern presented by the Melbourne Botanic Garden in the 1890s. Now the restoration of the great palm house is under way. The gardens are a focal point for

horticulture in Ireland and still fulfil the function of distributing new introductions among the gardens of Ireland. New education and visitor facilities have recently been added and it remains the finest collection of plants in Ireland. Allow a full day to do justice to the garden and its attractions.

Features Large collection of trees including conifers; plant families collection; rock garden and alpine yard; rose garden; vegetable garden; native plants; arboretum; herbaceous borders; seasonal bedding and displays; serpentine pond and heather garden; four ranges of public glasshouses; tropical waterlilies; succulents; tender conifers and cycads; Vireya rhododendrons; house plants; palms; orchids; tallest variegated Plane tree *Platanus × hispanica* 'Suttneri' (21m) in the British Isles, plus 25 other tree records; refreshments by arrangement.

Owned by Office of Public Works
Number of gardeners 18
Size 20ha (50 acres)
NCCPG National Collections *Garrya*; *Potentilla fruticosa*

Opening hours 10 am (1 pm on Sundays) – 6 pm (dusk in winter); daily; all year.
Admission fee Adults €4.50; OAPs €3.50; Groups (10+) €4.

This is a permanent exhibition of contemporary style attached to a garden centre. It has 20 linked but distinct gardens: the Herb Garden; 'Oriental Reflections'; 'Shady Secrets'; the Contemplative Garden; the Celtic Garden; the 'Pythagoras at Play' Garden; and so on. Each was made by a different designer and construction team. It adds up to the best of modern Irish design for small gardens: a shop window for ideas on style, plants and materials.

 Features Model gardens; garden centre; restaurant.

Owned by Tim & Suzanne Wallis

Powerscourt Gardens

POWERSCOURT ESTATE, ENNISKERRY, CO. WICKLOW

Tel 00 353 1 204 6000 **Fax** 00 353 1 204 6900
Website www.powerscourt.ie
Location 12 miles south of Dublin off N11.
Opening hours 9.30 am – 5.30 pm (dusk in winter); daily except 25 & 26 December; all year.

Powerscourt is a wonderful mixture of awesome grandeur and sheer fun. It is also extremely well organised for visitors. The main Italianate garden, a stately 1860s staircase down to a lake, has Great Sugarloaf Mountain as an off-centre backdrop. It is lined with bedding plants, statues and urns (look out for the sulky cherubs). To one side is the Japanese garden – not strongly Japanese – but full of twists and hummocks. In the arboretum, Alan Mitchell designed a

tree trail. Powerscourt is busy in summer, but you can escape into solitude along the avenue of monkey puzzles. The magnificent house is now open to visitors again.

 Features Woodland garden; mature conifers; fine collection of trees; much recent restoration, including the Bamberg gates, and a remodelling of the Japanese garden; tallest *Abies spectabilis* (32m) in the British Isles, plus 10 other record tree specimens.

Owned by Powerscourt Estate
Number of gardeners 6
Size 19ha (47 acres)

Primrose Hill

PRIMROSE LANE, LUCAN, CO. DUBLIN

Tel 00 353 1 6280373
Location Lucan village, at top of Primrose Lane, through black iron gates.
Opening hours 2 pm – 6 pm; daily; February, then June to the beginning of August. And by appointment.
Admission fee Adults €4; Children €2.

Primrose Hill is a plantsman's garden, particularly interesting for its rare forms of herbaceous plants and its snowdrops. The planting continues, and includes a small arboretum, but this is a garden which gets better every year.

Features Snowdrops; plantsman's collection of plants; good herbaceous borders; new small formal garden (2000).

Owned by Robin & Cicely Hall
Number of gardeners owners only
Size 2.2ha (6 acres)

Ram House Garden

COOLGREANY, GOREY, CO. WEXFORD

Tel 00 353 402 37238   **Fax** 00 353 402 37238
Location N11 to Inch & turn inland 1½ miles to Coolgreany.
Opening hours 2.30 pm – 6 pm; Fridays to Sundays & Bank Holidays; 27 April to 9 September. And by appointment.
Admission fee Adults €4; Children €2.

Ram's is a romantic, scented garden, laid out in the modern style, as a series of garden rooms, full of good plants and clever plantings. The owners are keen plantsmen, so that the garden and its collections are forever expanding and improving. *Pseudopanax arboreus* and *Acacia pravissima* flourish in the woodland and a large-flowered fuchsia against the walls of the house has reached the roof. Lots of changes and improvements are planned for 2002.

Features Woodland garden; climbing roses; good herbaceous borders; water garden; over 70 clematis; paintings for sale; seeds for sale; tea-room.

Owned by Godfrey & Lolo Stevens
Number of gardeners owners only
Size 0.8ha (2 acres)

Talbot Botanic Gardens

MALAHIDE CASTLE, MALAHIDE, CO. DUBLIN

Tel 00 353 1 8727777   **Fax** 00 353 1 8727530
Location 10 miles north of Dublin on Malahide Road.
Opening hours 2 pm – 5 pm (or by appointment); daily; May to September.
Admission fee Adults €3; Groups €2.50.

The Talbot Botanic Garden at Malahide Demesne was the work of Milo Talbot, a passionate amateur botanist with a particular interest in southern hemisphere plants, notably the flora of Tasmania and Chile. He built up a collection of 5,000 different taxa and, since the soil is limy, they are mostly calcicole plants. The gardens include a 4-acre walled garden, divided into seven distinct areas which give the impression of a series of secret gardens each with its own particular range of plants. It is in this walled garden that the rarer and tender species will be found. There are seven small glasshouses including a Victorian Conservatory at the end of the central path – a prominent focal point. Each house is very different in its style and in its plantings. The smallest has a collection of *Primula auricula* cultivars, while the Victorian house has a collection of Australasian plants. There are extensive collections of escallonias, *Syringa*, philadelphus, nothofagus and pittosporum as well as the National Collection of *Olearia*. Malahide is best visited at 2 pm on Wednesday afternoons when guided tours are offered of the walled garden (not otherwise open).

Features Woodland garden; plantsman's collection of plants; mature conifers; fine collection of trees; alpine plants; Tasmanian plants; restaurant.

Owned by Fingal County Council
Size 8.7ha (22 acres)
NCCPG National Collections *Olearia*

Tullynally Castle

CASTLEPOLLARD, CO. WESTMEATH

Tel 00 353 44 61159   **Fax** 00 353 44 61856
Location Signposted from Castlepollard.
12 miles from Mullingar.
Opening hours 2 pm – 6 pm; daily; May to August.

Admission fee Adults €5; Children €2.

Tullynally has a romantic Loudonesque garden for a rambling Gothic Revival house. Formal terraces overlook the park and lead to the woodland gardens, enriched with recent plantings of maples and magnolias. A fine avenue of Irish yews is the centrepiece of the walled garden: they are thought to be about 200 years old and thus among the oldest in existence. The owner Thomas Pakenham wrote the acclaimed *Meetings with Remarkable Trees* (Weidenfeld, 1996), some of whose photographs were taken at Tullynally: a sequel is expected soon – perhaps in the autumn of 2002. And he has introduced some interesting exotics to Tullynally from his travels abroad.

Features Woodland garden; grotto; lake; new Chinese & Tibetan gardens; plants collected by owners; several of the largest beech trees *Fagus sylvatica* in the British Isles.

Owned by Mr & Mrs Thomas Pakenham
Number of gardeners 2
Size 10ha (25 acres)

Valclusa Gardens & Nursery

WATERFALL ROAD, ENNISKERRY, CO. WICKLOW

Tel 00 353 1 286 9485   **Fax** 00 353 1 286 1877
Location Follow signs to waterfall from Kilmacanogue on N11 or from Enniskerry. Last house on left before waterfall gates.
Opening hours 10 am – 7 pm; Saturdays, Sundays & Bank Holiday Mondays; Easter to October. Plus Wednesdays & Fridays in May & June.

The garden has a fine position by the famous waterfall. Among its established trees (huge specimens of redwood, embothriums, *Cornus capitata* and a weeping form of *Liriodendron tulipifera*) is a modern plantsman's garden of rhododendrons, grasses, hostas and over 100 geraniums.

Features Plantsman's collection of plants; fine collection of trees; wildflower meadow; butterfly garden; good nursery attached.

Owned by Duncan & Susan Forsythe
Number of gardeners 1
Size 1.2ha (3 acres)

PLANT-
LOVER'S
GUIDES

NCCPG NATIONAL COLLECTIONS

ABELIA
Pleasant View Nursery & Garden, Devon, England

ABIES
Ardkinglas Woodland Garden, Strathclyde, Scotland

ACACIA
Tresco Abbey, Cornwall, England

ACANTHUS
Iford Manor, Wiltshire, England

ACER
Hergest Croft Gardens, Herefordshire, England

ACER (Japanese cvs.)
Westonbirt The National Arboretum, Gloucestershire, England

ACHILLEA
Capel Manor, London, England

ADIANTUM
Tatton Park, Cheshire, England

AESCULUS
West Dean Gardens, West Sussex, England

ALCHEMILLA
Cambridge University Botanic Garden, Cambridgeshire, England

ANEMONE NEMOROSA
Kingston Lacy, Dorset, England

ANEMONE (Japanese)
Broadview Gardens, Kent, England
Heathlands, Hampshire, England

AQUILEGIA
Hardwicke House, Cambridgeshire, England

ARALIA
Powis Castle, Powys, Wales

ARBUTUS
Dunster Castle, Somerset, England

ARGYRANTHEMUM
Lower Icknield Farm, Buckinghamshire, England

ARTEMISIA
Elsworth Herbs, Cambridgeshire, England

ASPLENIUM SCOLOPENDRIUM
Sizergh Castle, Cumbria, England

ASTER
Temple Newsam Park, West Yorkshire, England
Upton House, Warwickshire, England

ASTER (autumn-flowering)
The Picton Garden, Herefordshire, England

ASTILBE
Holehird, Cumbria, England
Marwood Hill Gardens, Devon, England

ASTRANTIA
Warren Hills Cottage, Leicestershire, England

AUBRIETA
University of Leicester Botanic Garden, Leicestershire, England

AZARA
Exeter University Gardens, Devon, England
Trelissick Garden, Cornwall, England

BEGONIA
Glasgow Botanic Garden, Strathclyde, Scotland
Rhodes & Rockliffe, Essex, England

BERBERIS
Mill Hill Plants, Nottinghamshire, England

BERGENIA (species & primary hybrids)
Cambridge University Botanic Garden, Cambridgeshire, England

BETULA
Hergest Croft Gardens, Herefordshire, England
Wakehurst Place, West Sussex, England

BONSAI
Birmingham Botanical Gardens & Glasshouses, West Midlands, England

BRACHYGLOTTIS
Inverewe, Highland, Scotland

BUDDLEJA
Longstock Water Gardens, Hampshire, England

BUXUS
Ickworth, Suffolk, England
Langley Boxwood Nursery, Hampshire, England

CALLUNA (provisional)
RHS Garden Harlow Carr, North Yorkshire, England

CALLUNA VULGARIS
RHS Garden Wisley, Surrey, England

CAMELLIA
Mount Edgcumbe Gardens, Cornwall, England

CAMELLIA JAPONICA
Antony Woodland Garden, Cornwall, England

CAMELLIA × WILLIAMSII
Wentworth Castle Gardens, South Yorkshire, England

CAMPANULA
Burton Agnes Hall Gardens, East Yorkshire, England
Lingen Nursery and Gardens, Shropshire, England

CARPINUS
The Sir Harold Hillier Gardens & Arboretum, Hampshire, England

CARPINUS BETULUS cvs.
Beale Arboretum, Hertfordshire, England

CASSIOPE
Branklyn Garden, Tayside, Scotland

CATALPA
Cliveden, Buckinghamshire, England

CEANOTHUS (deciduous)
Knoll Gardens, Dorset, England

CELMISIA (species)
St Luke's Cottage, Northumberland, England

CHAMAECYPARIS LAWSONIANA
University of Leicester Botanic Garden, Leicestershire, England

CHAMAECYPARIS LAWSONIANA cvs.
Bedgebury National Pinetum, Kent, England

CIMICIFUGA
Bridgemere Garden World, Cheshire, England

CISTUS
Chelsea Physic Garden, London, England

CITRUS
Reads Nursery, Norfolk, England

CLEMATIS
Burford House Gardens, Shropshire, England

CLEMATIS VITICELLA
Longstock Water Gardens, Hampshire, England

COLCHICUM
Felbrigg Hall, Norfolk, England

CONOPHYTUM
Abbey Brook Cactus Nursery, Derbyshire, England

CONVALLARIA
Kingston Lacy, Dorset, England

COPROSMA
County Park Nursery, Essex, England

CORIARIA
Crûg Farm Plants, Gwynedd, Wales

CORNUS
Newby Hall, North Yorkshire, England
RHS Garden Rosemoor, Devon, England
The Sir Harold Hillier Gardens & Arboretum, Hampshire, England

CORYLUS
The Sir Harold Hillier Gardens & Arboretum, Hampshire, England

CORYLUS (cobnuts & filberts)
Brogdale, Kent, England

COTONEASTER
The Sir Harold Hillier Gardens & Arboretum, Hampshire, England

CROCUS
RHS Garden Wisley, Surrey, England

× CUPRESSOCYPARIS
Bedgebury National Pinetum, Kent, England

CYDONIA OBLONGA
Norton Priory Museum & Gardens, Cheshire, England

CYSTOPTERIS
Sizergh Castle, Cumbria, England
Rickard's Hardy Ferns Ltd, Worcestershire, England

DABOECIA
RHS Garden Wisley, Surrey, England

DAPHNE
Brandy Mount House, Hampshire, England

DELPHINIUM
Temple Newsam Park, West Yorkshire, England
Rougham Hall Nurseries, Suffolk, England

DENDROBIUM
Glasgow Botanic Garden, Strathclyde, Scotland

DEUTZIA
The Hollies Park, West Yorkshire, England

DIANELLA
Mount Stewart, Co. Down, Northern Ireland

DIANTHUS
Kingstone Cottage Plants, Herefordshire, England

DIANTHUS (Malmaison carnations)
Crathes Castle, Grampian, Scotland

DICKSONIACEAE
Glasgow Botanic Garden, Strathclyde, Scotland

DIERVILLA
Sheffield Botanical Gardens, South Yorkshire, England

DRYOPTERIS
RHS Garden Harlow Carr, North Yorkshire, England
Sizergh Castle, Cumbria, England

DWARF CONIFERS
Savill Garden, Surrey, England
Valley Gardens, Surrey, England

ECHINOPSIS hybrids
Abbey Brook Cactus Nursery, Derbyshire, England

ELAEAGNUS
Beale Arboretum, Hertfordshire, England

EMBOTHRIUM
Bodnant Gardens, Clwyd, Wales

ENKIANTHUS
Clyne Gardens, Glamorgan, Wales

EPIMEDIUM
RHS Garden Wisley, Surrey, England
Lilliesleaf Nursery, Borders, Scotland

ERICA
RHS Garden Wisley, Surrey, England
Bell's Cherrybank Centre, Tayside, Scotland

ERYTHRONIUM
Greencombe Gardens, Somerset, England

EUCALYPTUS
Meon Orchard, Hampshire, England

EUCRYPHIA
Bodnant Gardens, Clwyd, Wales
Seaforde Gardens, Co. Down, Northern Ireland

EUPHORBIA
Oxford Botanic Garden, Oxfordshire, England

FAGUS
Kirkley Hall Gardens, Tyne & Wear, England

FALLOPIA
Rowden Gardens, Devon, England

FERNS
Savill Garden, Surrey, England

FICUS
Reads Nursery, Norfolk, England

FRAGARIA × *ANANASSA*
Brogdale, Kent, England

FRAXINUS
Thorp Perrow Arboretum, North Yorkshire, England
The Quinta, Cheshire, England

FRITILLARIA (European species)
Cambridge University Botanic Garden, Cambridgeshire, England

FUCHSIA
Croxteth Hall & Country Park, Merseyside, England
University of Leicester Botanic Garden, Leicestershire, England

FUCHSIA (hardy)
Kathleen Muncaster Fuchsias, Lincolnshire, England

FUCHSIA section Quelusia (provisional)
RHS Garden Harlow Carr, North Yorkshire, England

GALANTHUS
Brandy Mount House, Hampshire, England
RHS Garden Wisley, Surrey, England

GARRYA
National Botanic Gardens, Co. Dublin, Republic of Ireland

GAULTHERIA
Greencombe Gardens, Somerset, England

GENTIANA
Christie's Nursery, Tayside, Scotland

GERANIUM
East Lambrook Manor, Somerset, England
Catforth Gardens, Lancashire, England

GERANIUM (species & primary hybrids)
Cambridge University Botanic Garden, Cambridgeshire, England

GREVILLEA
Pine Lodge Gardens & Nursery, Cornwall, England

GYMNOCALYCIUM
Abbey Brook Cactus Nursery, Derbyshire, England

HAMAMELIS
The Sir Harold Hillier Gardens & Arboretum, Hampshire, England
Swallow Hayes, Shropshire, England

HAWORTHIA
Abbey Brook Cactus Nursery, Derbyshire, England

HEDERA
Erddig, Clwyd, Wales
Fibrex Nurseries Ltd, Warwickshire, England

HELIOTROPIUM
Hampton Court Palace, London, England

HELLEBORUS
Broadview Gardens, Kent, England

HELLEBORUS (part)
White Windows, Hampshire, England
Longthatch, Hampshire, England

HEMEROCALLIS
Antony House, Cornwall, England

HEMEROCALLIS (Coe hybrids)
The Hollies Park, West Yorkshire, England

HEMEROCALLIS cvs. post-1970
Rosewood Daylilies, Kent, England

HESPERIS
University of Leicester Botanic Garden, Leicestershire, England

HIBISCUS SYIACUS cvs.
Notcutts Nurseries, Suffolk, England

'HILLIER' PLANTS
The Sir Harold Hillier Gardens & Arboretum, Hampshire, England

HOHERIA
Abbotsbury Sub-tropical Gardens, Dorset, England

HOSTA (large-leaved)
The Hollies Park, West Yorkshire, England

HOSTA (modern hybrids)
Ann & Roger Bowden, Devon, England

HOSTA (small leaved)
Apple Court, Hampshire, England

HYACINTHUS ORIENTALIS
Ripley Castle, North Yorkshire, England

HYDRANGEA
Holehird, Cumbria, England

HYPERICUM
Wakehurst Place, West Sussex, England

ILEX
RHS Garden Rosemoor, Devon, England
Savill Garden, Surrey, England
Valley Gardens, Surrey, England

IRIS
Myddelton House, London, England

IRIS (species)
The Harris Garden, Berkshire, England

IRIS ENSATA
Marwood Hill Gardens, Devon, England

IRIS SIBIRICA
Lingen Nursery and Gardens, Shropshire, England

IRIS SPURIA
Belsay Hall, Tyne & Wear, England

IRIS UNGUICULARIS
Great Barfield, Buckinghamshire, England

JUGLANS
Thorp Perrow Arboretum, North Yorkshire, England
Wimpole Hall, Cambridgeshire, England

JUNIPERUS
Bedgebury National Pinetum, Kent, England

KNIPHOFIA
Barton Manor, Isle of Wight, England

LABURNUM
Powis Castle, Powys, Wales

LAVANDULA
Downderry Nursery, Kent, England

LAVANDULA (sect. Lavandula, Dentata, Pterostoechas & Stoechas)
Norfolk Lavender, Norfolk, England

LEUCOJUM
Great Barfield, Buckinghamshire, England

LIBERTIA
Mount Stewart, Co. Down, Northern Ireland

LIGUSTRUM
The Sir Harold Hillier Gardens & Arboretum, Hampshire, England

LIRIODENDRON
West Dean Gardens, West Sussex, England

LITHOCARPUS
The Sir Harold Hillier Gardens & Arboretum, Hampshire, England

LITHOPS
Abbey Brook Cactus Nursery, Derbyshire, England

LONICERA (species & primary hybrids)
Cambridge University Botanic Garden, Cambridgeshire, England

LUPINUS (Russell strains)
Swallow Hayes, Shropshire, England

LYSIMACHIA
Cotswold Garden Flowers, Worcestershire, England

MAGNOLIA
Savill Garden, Surrey, England
Valley Gardens, Surrey, England

MAGNOLIA (species)
Bodnant Gardens, Clwyd, Wales
Wentworth Castle Gardens, South Yorkshire, England

MAHONIA
Savill Garden, Surrey, England
Valley Gardens, Surrey, England

MALUS
Granada Arboretum, Cheshire, England

MALUS (apples, ornamental cvs. & cider apples)
Brogdale, Kent, England

MECONOPSIS
Houghall, Co. Durham, England

MENTHA
Iden Croft Herbs, Kent, England

MONARDA
Leeds Castle, Kent, England

NARCISSUS
Brodie Castle, Grampian, Scotland
Guy Wilson Daffodil Garden, Co. Derry, Northern Ireland

NARCISSUS (miniature)
Broadleigh Gardens, Somerset, England

NERIUM OLEANDER
Elsworth Herbs, Cambridgeshire, England

NOTHOFAGUS
Wakehurst Place, West Sussex, England

NYMPHAEA
Burnby Hall Gardens, East Yorkshire, England
Stapeley Water Gardens, Cheshire, England
Bennetts Water Lily Farm, Dorset, England
Kenchester Water Gardens, Herefordshire, England

OENOTHERA
Old Vicarage, Wiltshire, England

OLEARIA
Inverewe, Highland, Scotland
Talbot Botanic Gardens, Co. Dublin, Republic of Ireland

ORIGANUM
Hexham Herbs & Hardy Plants, Northumberland, England
Iden Croft Herbs, Kent, England

OSMUNDA
Sizergh Castle, Cumbria, England

PAEONIA LACTIFLORA
Kelways Ltd, Somerset, England

PAEONIA
Hidcote Manor, Gloucestershire, England

PAPAVER ORIENTALE
Water Meadow Nursery and Herb Farm, Hampshire, England

PARAHEBE
County Park Nursery, Essex, England

PARIS
Crûg Farm Plants, Gwynedd, Wales

PASSIFLORA
National Collection of Passiflora, Somerset, England

PELARGONIUM
Fibrex Nurseries Ltd, Warwickshire, England

PENSTEMON
Kingston Maurward Gardens, Dorset, England
Rowallane Garden, Co. Down, Northern Ireland

PERNETTYA
Savill Garden, Surrey, England
Valley Gardens, Surrey, England

PERSICARIA
Rowden Gardens, Devon, England

PHILADELPHUS
The Hollies Park, West Yorkshire, England

PHLOMIS
Just Phlomis, Gloucestershire, England

PHLOX PANICULATA
Temple Newsam Park, West Yorkshire, England

PHORMIUM
Mount Stewart, Co. Down, Northern Ireland
Charney Well, Cumbria, England

PHOTINIA
The Sir Harold Hillier Gardens & Arboretum, Hampshire, England
Trelissick Garden, Cornwall, England

PHYGELIUS
Knoll Gardens, Dorset, England

PICEA
Ardkinglas Woodland Garden, Strathclyde, Scotland

PIERIS
Clyne Gardens, Glamorgan, Wales
Savill Garden, Surrey, England
Valley Gardens, Surrey, England

PINUS
The Quinta, Cheshire, England

PINUS (excl. dwarf cvs.)
The Sir Harold Hillier Gardens & Arboretum, Hampshire, England

PLATANUS
Mottisfont Abbey, Hampshire, England

PLEIONE
Butterfields Nursery, Buckinghamshire, England

POLYPODIUM
RHS Garden Harlow Carr, North Yorkshire, England
Rickard's Hardy Ferns Ltd, Worcestershire, England

POLYSTICHUM
Greencombe Gardens, Somerset, England
Holehird, Cumbria, England

POPULUS
Wiltshire College Lackham, Wiltshire, England

POTENTILLA FRUTICOSA
National Botanic Gardens, Co. Dublin, Republic of Ireland

POTENTILLA FRUTICOSA cvs.
Webbs of Wychbold, Worcestershire, England

POTENTILLA
Ardgillan Park, Co. Dublin, Republic of Ireland

PRIMULA AURICULA
Golden Acre Park, West Yorkshire, England
Martin Nest Nurseries, Lincolnshire, England

PRIMULA (Asiatic species)
Cluny House, Tayside, Scotland

PRIMULA (Cortusoides section)
Plant World Botanic Gardens, Devon, England

PRUNUS (cherry)
Brogdale, Kent, England

PRUNUS (plums)
Brogdale, Kent, England

PSEUDOPANAX
Ventnor Botanic Garden, Isle of Wight, England

PULMONARIA
Stillingfleet Lodge Nurseries, North Yorkshire, England

PYRUS
Brogdale, Kent, England

QUERCUS
The Sir Harold Hillier Gardens & Arboretum, Hampshire, England

RANUNCULUS FICARIA
Rowden Gardens, Devon, England

RHEUM
RHS Garden Harlow Carr, North Yorkshire, England
RHS Garden Wisley, Surrey, England

RHODODENDRON
Highclere Castle, Hampshire, England

RHODODENDRON (Barbatum, Glischra & Maculifera sections)
Inverewe, Highland, Scotland

RHODODENDRON (subsections Falconera, Grandia and Maddenia)
Brodick Castle, Strathclyde, Scotland

RHODODENDRON (Ghent azaleas)
Sheffield Park Garden, East Sussex, England

RHODODENDRON (Knap Hill azaleas)
Sherwood, Devon, England

RHODODENDRON (Kurume azaleas, the Wilson 50)
Isabella Plantation, London, England

RHODODENDRON species
Wentworth Castle Gardens, South Yorkshire, England

RHODODENDRON (species & Glen Dale azaleas)
Savill Garden, Surrey, England
Valley Gardens, Surrey, England

RHODODENDRON (Triflora & Falconera subsections)
Clyne Gardens, Glamorgan, Wales

RHODODENDRON FORRESTII
Bodnant Gardens, Clwyd, Wales

RIBES (gooseberries)
Rougham Hall Nurseries, Suffolk, England

RIBES (species & primary hybrids)
Cambridge University Botanic Garden, Cambridgeshire, England

RIBES GROSSULARIA (gooseberries)
Brogdale, Kent, England

RIBES NIGRUM (blackcurrants)
Brogdale, Kent, England

RIBES SATIVUM (currants other than blackcurrants)
Brogdale, Kent, England

RODGERSIA
Hadspen Garden, Somerset, England

ROHDEA JAPONICA
Apple Court, Hampshire, England

ROSA
Mottisfont Abbey, Hampshire, England

ROSA (19th-century shrubs)
Malleny House Garden, Lothian, Scotland

ROSA (History of European roses)
University of Birmingham Botanic Garden, West Midlands, England

ROSA (species)
Peter Beales Roses, Norfolk, England

ROSA (species & cultivars)
The Gardens of the Rose, Hertfordshire, England

ROSMARINUS
Downderry Nursery, Kent, England

RUSCUS
Cambridge University Botanic Garden, Cambridgeshire, England

SALIX
Westonbirt The National Arboretum, Gloucestershire, England

SALVIA
Kingston Maurward Gardens, Dorset, England
Pleasant View Nursery & Garden, Devon, England

SAMBUCUS
Wallington, Northumberland, England

SARCOCOCCA
Capel Manor, London, England

SAXIFRAGA
Waterperry Gardens, Oxfordshire, England

SAXIFRAGA (European species)
Cambridge University Botanic Garden, Cambridgeshire, England

SCABIOSA CAUCASICA
Hardwick Hall, Derbyshire, England

SKIMMIA
University of Leicester Botanic Garden, Leicestershire, England
Wakehurst Place, West Sussex, England

SORBUS
Granada Arboretum, Cheshire, England
Houghall, Co. Durham, England

SORBUS (Aria & Micromeles groups)
Winkworth Arboretum, Surrey, England

SIR FREDERICK STERN, PLANTS INTRODUCED BY
Highdown, West Sussex, England

STEWARTIA
High Beeches, West Sussex, England

STREPTOCARPUS
Dibleys Nurseries, Clwyd, Wales

STYRACACEAE (incl. Halesia, Pterostyrax, Styrax, Sinojackia)
Holker Hall, Cumbria, England

SYRINGA
Golden Acre Park, West Yorkshire, England
The Hollies Park, West Yorkshire, England

TAXUS
Bedgebury National Pinetum, Kent, England

THELYPTERIDACEAE
Rickard's Hardy Ferns Ltd, Worcestershire, England

THUJA
Bedgebury National Pinetum, Kent, England

THYMUS
Hexham Herbs & Hardy Plants, Northumberland, England

TILIA
Thorp Perrow Arboretum, North Yorkshire, England

TRILLIUM
Spinners, Hampshire, England

TULBAGHIA
Marwood Hill Gardens, Devon, England

TULIPA (species & primary hybrids)
Cambridge University Botanic Garden, Cambridgeshire, England

VACCINIUM
Greencombe Gardens, Somerset, England

VERBENA
Ashfield Court Nurseries, Somerset, England

VIBURNUM
Crathes Castle, Grampian, Scotland
RHS Garden Hyde Hall, Essex, England

VICARY GIBBS PLANTS
Lyme Park, Cheshire, England

VINCA
Monksilver Nursery, Cambridgeshire, England

VITIS VINIFERA
Brogdale, Kent, England

VITIS VINIFERA (grapes)
Reads Nursery, Norfolk, England

WEIGELA
Sheffield Botanical Gardens, South Yorkshire, England

WOODWARDIA
Apple Court, Hampshire, England

YUCCA
Renishaw Hall, Derbyshire, England

ZELKOVA
Hergest Croft Gardens, Herefordshire, England

WHERE TO SEE PARTICULAR PLANTS

ALPINES

Cambridge University Botanic Garden
Cambridgeshire, England
Hillside
Co. Cork, Republic of Ireland
W.E.Th. Ingwersen Ltd
West Sussex, England
Jack Drake
Highland, Scotland
National Botanic Gardens
Co. Dublin, Republic of Ireland
Potterton and Martin
Lincolnshire, England
RHS Garden Wisley
Surrey, England
Royal Botanic Garden Edinburgh
Lothian, Scotland
Royal Botanic Gardens, Kew
London, England
St Luke's Cottage
Northumberland, England
University of Durham Botanic Garden
Co. Durham, England
University of Leicester Botanic Garden
Leicestershire, England

ARBORETA

Bath Botanic Gardens
Somerset, England
Batsford Arboretum
Gloucestershire, England
Bicton Park Gardens
Devon, England
Cambridge University Botanic Garden
Cambridgeshire, England
Cruickshank Botanic Garden
Grampian, Scotland
Dawyck Botanic Garden
Borders, Scotland

Earlscliffe
Co. Dublin, Republic of Ireland
Exeter University Gardens
Devon, England
Fota Arboretum & Garden
Co. Cork, Republic of Ireland
Granada Arboretum
Cheshire, England
Lynford Arboretum
Norfolk, England
Marwood Hill Gardens
Devon, England
National Botanic Gardens
Co. Dublin, Republic of Ireland
Nymans
West Sussex, England
RHS Garden Wisley
Surrey, England
RHS Garden Hyde Hall
Essex, England
RHS Garden Rosemoor
Devon, England
Rowallane Garden
Co. Down, Northern Ireland
Royal Botanic Garden Edinburgh
Lothian, Scotland
Royal Botanic Gardens, Kew
London, England
Saling Hall
Essex, England
Sheffield Park Garden
East Sussex, England
Talbot Botanic Gardens
Co. Dublin, Republic of Ireland
Torosay Castle & Gardens
Strathclyde, Scotland
Winkworth Arboretum
Surrey, England

BEGONIA
Blackmore & Langdon
Somerset, England

BLUEBELLS
Emmetts Garden
Kent, England
Haughley Park
Suffolk, England
Hole Park
Kent, England
Leonardslee Gardens
West Sussex, England
Lydney Park Gardens
Gloucestershire, England
Royal Botanic Gardens, Kew
London, England
Sheffield Park Garden
East Sussex, England
Stourhead
Wiltshire, England
Winkworth Arboretum
Surrey, England

CACTI
Abbey Brook Cactus Nursery
Derbyshire, England
Birmingham Botanical Gardens & Glasshouses
West Midlands, England
Cambridge University Botanic Garden
Cambridgeshire, England
Holly Gate Cactus Nursery
West Sussex, England
National Botanic Gardens
Co. Dublin, Republic of Ireland
RHS Garden Wisley
Surrey, England
Royal Botanic Garden Edinburgh
Lothian, Scotland
Royal Botanic Gardens, Kew
London, England
Toobees Exotics
Surrey, England
University of Durham Botanic Garden
Co. Durham, England

CAMELLIAS
Bodnant Gardens
Clwyd, Wales
Burncoose Gardens & Nurseries
Cornwall, England
Glendurgan Gardens
Cornwall, England
Greenway
Devon, England
Lydney Park Gardens
Gloucestershire, England
Marwood Hill Gardens
Devon, England
Mount Edgcumbe Gardens
Cornwall, England
RHS Garden Wisley
Surrey, England
Rotherview Nursery with Coghurst Camellias
East Sussex, England
Trehane
Cornwall, England

CARNATIONS
RHS Garden Wisley
Surrey, England

CHRYSANTHEMUMS
Halls of Heddon
Tyne & Wear, England
RHS Garden Wisley
Surrey, England
Philip Tivey & Son
Leicestershire, England

CLEMATIS
J. Bradshaw & Son
Kent, England
Burford House Gardens
Shropshire, England
Sherston Parva Nursery Ltd
Wiltshire, England
Thorncroft Clematis Nursery
Norfolk, England

CONIFERS

Batsford Arboretum
Gloucestershire, England

Benmore Botanic Garden
Strathclyde, Scotland

Clumber Park
Nottinghamshire, England

Cragside
Northumberland, England

Dawyck Botanic Garden
Borders, Scotland

Dochfour Gardens
Highland, Scotland

Foggy Bottom
Norfolk, England

Fota Arboretum & Garden
Co. Cork, Republic of Ireland

Mount Stuart
Strathclyde, Scotland

National Botanic Gardens
Co. Dublin, Republic of Ireland

Nymans
West Sussex, England

RHS Garden Wisley
Surrey, England

Royal Botanic Gardens, Kew
London, England

Scone Palace
Tayside, Scotland

Sheffield Park Garden
East Sussex, England

Trelissick Garden
Cornwall, England

Winkworth Arboretum
Surrey, England

CYCLAMEN

Ashwood Nurseries Ltd
West Midlands, England

Cadenza
Surrey, England

RHS Garden Wisley
Surrey, England

Tile Barn Nursery
Kent, England

DAFFODILS

Acorn Bank Garden
Cumbria, England

Broadleigh Gardens
Somerset, England

Brodie Castle
Grampian, Scotland

Clandon Park
Surrey, England

Erddig
Clwyd, Wales

Fota Arboretum & Garden
Co. Cork, Republic of Ireland

Guy Wilson Daffodil Garden
Co. Derry, Northern Ireland

Petworth House
West Sussex, England

RHS Garden Wisley
Surrey, England

Stourhead
Wiltshire, England

Threave Garden
Dumfries & Galloway, Scotland

DAHLIAS

Biddulph Grange
Staffordshire, England

Butterfields Nursery
Buckinghamshire, England

Halls of Heddon
Tyne & Wear, England

Spinners
Hampshire, England

Philip Tivey & Son
Leicestershire, England

Valley Gardens
North Yorkshire, England

DELPHINIUMS

8 Dunstarn Lane
West Yorkshire, England

Blackmore & Langdon
Somerset, England

Falkland Palace
Fife, Scotland

Godington Park
Kent, England

Haddon Hall
Derbyshire, England
RHS Garden Wisley
Surrey, England
Rougham Hall Nurseries
Suffolk, England

FERNS
The Abbey House
Wiltshire, England
Brodsworth Hall & Gardens
South Yorkshire, England
National Botanic Gardens
Co. Dublin, Republic of Ireland
Rickard's Hardy Ferns Ltd
Worcestershire, England
Royal Botanic Garden Edinburgh
Lothian, Scotland
Royal Botanic Gardens, Kew
London, England
Sherborne Garden
Somerset, England
Sizergh Castle
Cumbria, England

FUCHSIAS
Duchy of Cornwall Nursery
Cornwall, England
Margam Park
Glamorgan, Wales
The Vernon Geranium Nursery
Surrey, England

GLADIOLI
RHS Garden Wisley
Surrey, England

GLASSHOUSES
Birmingham Botanical Gardens & Glasshouses
West Midlands, England
Cambridge University Botanic Garden
Cambridgeshire, England
Canal Gardens & Tropical World
West Yorkshire, England

The Eden Project
Cornwall, England
The Living Rainforest
Berkshire, England
The National Botanic Garden of Wales
Dyfed, Wales
National Botanic Gardens
Co. Dublin, Republic of Ireland
Ness Botanic Gardens
Cheshire, England
Plantasia
Glamorgan, Wales
RHS Garden Wisley
Surrey, England
Royal Botanic Garden Edinburgh
Lothian, Scotland
Royal Botanic Gardens, Kew
London, England
Sir George Staunton Country Park
Hampshire, England
University of Durham Botanic Garden
Co. Durham, England
University of Leicester Botanic Garden
Leicestershire, England

HEATHERS
The Abbey House
Wiltshire, England
The Bannut
Herefordshire, England
Bell's Cherrybank Centre
Tayside, Scotland
Bicton Park Gardens
Devon, England
Blencathra
Berkshire, England
Champs Hill
West Sussex, England
Exeter University Gardens
Devon, England
Floraldene
West Sussex, England
Jack Drake
Highland, Scotland
National Botanic Gardens
Co. Dublin, Republic of Ireland
Ness Botanic Gardens
Cheshire, England

RHS Garden Wisley
Surrey, England
Royal Botanic Garden Edinburgh
Lothian, Scotland
Threave Garden
Dumfries & Galloway, Scotland
Valley Gardens
Surrey, England

HEBES
University of Bristol Botanic Garden
Gloucestershire, England

HEMEROCALLIS
Antony House
Cornwall, England
Apple Court
Hampshire, England
Ann & Roger Bowden
Devon, England
Goldbrook Plants
Suffolk, England
Rosewood Daylilies
Kent, England

HERBACEOUS PLANTS
Barrington Court
Somerset, England
Beningbrough Hall & Gardens
North Yorkshire, England
Beth Chatto Gardens
Essex, England
Buscot Park
Oxfordshire, England
The Courts
Wiltshire, England
The National Botanic Garden of Wales
Dyfed, Wales
National Botanic Gardens
Co. Dublin, Republic of Ireland
Ness Botanic Gardens
Cheshire, England
Nymans
West Sussex, England
Packwood House
Warwickshire, England

RHS Garden Wisley
Surrey, England
RHS Garden Hyde Hall
Essex, England
Royal Botanic Gardens, Kew
London, England
Savill Garden
Surrey, England
Tintinhull House
Somerset, England
Upton House
Warwickshire, England
Wallington
Northumberland, England

HERBS
The Abbey House
Wiltshire, England
Acorn Bank Garden
Cumbria, England
The National Botanic Garden of Wales
Dyfed, Wales
RHS Garden Wisley
Surrey, England
RHS Garden Rosemoor
Devon, England
Royal Botanic Gardens, Kew
London, England
Salley Gardens
Nottinghamshire, England
University of Leicester Botanic Garden
Leicestershire, England
The Walled Garden
Worcestershire, England

HOSTAS
Apple Court
Hampshire, England
Ann & Roger Bowden
Devon, England
Goldbrook Plants
Suffolk, England
Mill Hill Plants
Nottinghamshire, England
Park Green Nurseries
Suffolk, England

IRISES

The Abbey House
Wiltshire, England
Broadleigh Gardens
Somerset, England
Croftway Nursery
West Sussex, England
Kelways Ltd
Somerset, England
Marwood Hill Gardens
Devon, England
Mill Hill Plants
Nottinghamshire, England

MAGNOLIAS

Batsford Arboretum
Gloucestershire, England
Bodnant Gardens
Clwyd, Wales
Caerhays Castle Gardens
Cornwall, England
Glendurgan Gardens
Cornwall, England
Lanhydrock
Cornwall, England
Marwood Hill Gardens
Devon, England
RHS Garden Wisley
Surrey, England
Savill Garden
Surrey, England
Sherwood
Devon, England
Spinners
Hampshire, England
Valley Gardens
Surrey, England

ORCHIDS

Butterfields Nursery
Buckinghamshire, England
Glasgow Botanic Garden
Strathclyde, Scotland
Kelways Ltd
Somerset, England
RHS Garden Wisley
Surrey, England

Royal Botanic Garden Edinburgh
Lothian, Scotland
Royal Botanic Gardens, Kew
London, England
Scone Palace
Tayside, Scotland

PLANTSMAN'S GARDENS

Beth Chatto Gardens
Essex, England
Biddulph Grange
Staffordshire, England
Birkheads Cottage Garden Nursery
Tyne & Wear, England
Bluebell Cottage Gardens & Lodge Lane Nursery
Cheshire, England
Cally Gardens
Dumfries & Galloway, Scotland
Cambridge University Botanic Garden
Cambridgeshire, England
Cannington College Heritage Garden
Somerset, England
Copton Ash Gardens
Kent, England
Cotswold Garden Flowers
Worcestershire, England
The Courts
Wiltshire, England
Crûg Farm Plants
Gwynedd, Wales
Cruickshank Botanic Garden
Grampian, Scotland
Dell Garden
Norfolk, England
The Dillon Garden
Co. Dublin, Republic of Ireland
Dundee Botanic Garden
Tayside, Scotland
Earlscliffe
Co. Dublin, Republic of Ireland
The Garden House
Devon, England
Great Dixter
East Sussex, England
Greencombe Gardens
Somerset, England

The Harris Garden
Berkshire, England

Heathlands
Hampshire, England

Hinton Ampner House
Hampshire, England

Home Covert
Wiltshire, England

Killerton
Devon, England

Longthatch
Hampshire, England

The Manor House
Somerset, England

Marwood Hill Gardens
Devon, England

National Botanic Gardens
Co. Dublin, Republic of Ireland

Nymans
West Sussex, England

Oxford Botanic Garden
Oxfordshire, England

RHS Garden Harlow Carr
North Yorkshire, England

RHS Garden Hyde Hall
Essex, England

Rowallane Garden
Co. Down, Northern Ireland

Royal Botanic Garden Edinburgh
Lothian, Scotland

Royal Botanic Gardens, Kew
London, England

Savill Garden
Surrey, England

Scotney Castle Garden
Kent, England

Sheffield Park Garden
East Sussex, England

Sherborne Garden
Somerset, England

Spetchley Park
Worcestershire, England

St Andrews Botanic Garden
Fife, Scotland

Talbot Botanic Gardens
Co. Dublin, Republic of Ireland

University of Birmingham Botanic Garden
West Midlands, England

University of Durham Botanic Garden
Co. Durham, England

Valley Gardens
Surrey, England

PRIMROSES

Edrom Nurseries
Borders, Scotland

RHODODENDRONS AND AZALEAS

Achamore Gardens
Strathclyde, Scotland

Angus Garden
Strathclyde, Scotland

Benmore Botanic Garden
Strathclyde, Scotland

Blackhills
Grampian, Scotland

Bodnant Gardens
Clwyd, Wales

Borde Hill Garden
West Sussex, England

Cannizaro Park
London, England

Clyne Gardens
Glamorgan, Wales

Dawyck Botanic Garden
Borders, Scotland

Dorothy Clive Garden
Staffordshire, England

Glenarn
Strathclyde, Scotland

Glendoick Gardens
Tayside, Scotland

Glendurgan Gardens
Cornwall, England

Highclere Castle
Hampshire, England

Hodnet Hall Gardens
Shropshire, England

Hydon Nurseries
Surrey, England

Isabella Plantation
London, England

Knap Hill Nursery Ltd
Surrey, England
Lanhydrock
Cornwall, England
Leonardslee Gardens
West Sussex, England
Lydney Park Gardens
Gloucestershire, England
Marwood Hill Gardens
Devon, England
Millais Nurseries
Surrey, England
Mount Stewart
Co. Down, Northern Ireland
Muncaster Castle
Cumbria, England
National Botanic Gardens
Co. Dublin, Republic of Ireland
Ness Botanic Gardens
Cheshire, England
Nymans
West Sussex, England
The Old Glebe
Devon, England
Petworth House
West Sussex, England
Plas Newydd
Gwynedd, Wales
Ramster
Surrey, England
RHS Garden Wisley
Surrey, England
Rowallane Garden
Co. Down, Northern Ireland
Royal Botanic Gardens, Kew
London, England
Savill Garden
Surrey, England
Scotney Castle Garden
Kent, England
Sheffield Park Garden
East Sussex, England
Sherwood
Devon, England
Stourhead
Wiltshire, England
Trengwainton Gardens
Cornwall, England

Valley Gardens
Surrey, England
Wentworth Castle Gardens
South Yorkshire, England

ROCK GARDENS

Cambridge University Botanic Garden
Cambridgeshire, England
Cruickshank Botanic Garden
Grampian, Scotland
Dorothy Clive Garden
Staffordshire, England
Mount Stuart
Strathclyde, Scotland
National Botanic Gardens
Co. Dublin, Republic of Ireland
Ness Botanic Gardens
Cheshire, England
RHS Garden Wisley
Surrey, England
Royal Botanic Garden Edinburgh
Lothian, Scotland
Royal Botanic Gardens, Kew
London, England

ROSES, MODERN

The Abbey House
Wiltshire, England
Benvarden Garden & Grounds
Co. Antrim, Northern Ireland
Chartwell
Kent, England
David Austin Roses
Shropshire, England
The Gardens of the Rose
Hertfordshire, England
Mattocks Roses
Oxfordshire, England
RHS Garden Wisley
Surrey, England
RHS Garden Hyde Hall
Essex, England
RHS Garden Rosemoor
Devon, England
Royal Botanic Gardens, Kew
London, England
University of Birmingham Botanic Garden
West Midlands, England

ROSES, OLD

Cruickshank Botanic Garden
Grampian, Scotland

David Austin Roses
Shropshire, England

Drum Castle
Grampian, Scotland

The Gardens of the Rose
Hertfordshire, England

Hardwick Hall
Derbyshire, England

Hunts Court
Gloucestershire, England

Kiftsgate Court
Gloucestershire, England

Mottisfont Abbey
Hampshire, England

Nymans
West Sussex, England

Peter Beales Roses
Norfolk, England

RHS Garden Hyde Hall
Essex, England

RHS Garden Rosemoor
Devon, England

Royal Botanic Gardens, Kew
London, England

University of Birmingham Botanic Garden
West Midlands, England

Westbury Court
Gloucestershire, England

Wiltshire College Lackham
Wiltshire, England

SNOWDROPS

Benington Lordship
Hertfordshire, England

Cambo Gardens
Fife, Scotland

East Lambrook Manor
Somerset, England

Heale House Garden
Wiltshire, England

Hodsock Priory
Nottinghamshire, England

Monksilver Nursery
Cambridgeshire, England

Plas-yn-Rhiw
Gwynedd, Wales

Snape Cottage
Dorset, England

SUB-TROPICAL PLANTS

Abbotsbury Sub-Tropical Gardens
Dorset, England

Achamore Gardens
Strathclyde, Scotland

Derreen
Co. Kerry, Republic of Ireland

Dunster Castle
Somerset, England

Earlscliffe
Co. Dublin, Republic of Ireland

The Eden Project
Cornwall, England

Exeter University Gardens
Devon, England

Fota Arboretum & Garden
Co. Cork, Republic of Ireland

Greenway
Devon, England

Knoll Gardens
Dorset, England

Logan Botanic Garden
Dumfries & Galloway, Scotland

Meon Orchard
Hampshire, England

Mount Stewart
Co. Down, Northern Ireland

Mount Stuart
Strathclyde, Scotland

The Palm Centre
London, England

Penrhyn Castle
Gwynedd, Wales

Rowallane Garden
Co. Down, Northern Ireland

Royal Botanic Gardens, Kew
London, England

Talbot Botanic Gardens
Co. Dublin, Republic of Ireland

Torosay Castle & Gardens
Strathclyde, Scotland

Trelissick Garden
Cornwall, England

Trengwainton Gardens
Cornwall, England
University of Bristol Botanic Garden
Gloucestershire, England
Ventnor Botanic Garden
Isle of Wight, England
Westdale Nurseries
Wiltshire, England

TOPIARY
Abbotsford
Borders, Scotland
Athelhampton
Dorset, England
Chirk Castle
Clwyd, Wales
Drummond Castle Gardens
Tayside, Scotland
Graythwaite Hall
Cumbria, England
Herterton House Gardens & Nursery
Northumberland, England
Langley Boxwood Nursery
Hampshire, England
Levens Hall
Cumbria, England
Packwood House
Warwickshire, England
Pitmedden
Grampian, Scotland
The Romantic Garden Nursery
Norfolk, England

VIOLAS
Church Hill Cottage Gardens
Kent, England
Elizabeth MacGregor
Dumfries & Galloway, Scotland
Planta Vera
Surrey, England

WILDFLOWERS
The Garden House
Devon, England
Naturescape
Nottinghamshire, England

WOODLAND GARDENS
Hodnet Hall Gardens
Shropshire, England
Leonardslee Gardens
West Sussex, England
Mount Stewart
Co. Down, Northern Ireland
RHS Garden Wisley
Surrey, England
Rowallane Garden
Co. Down, Northern Ireland
Savill Garden
Surrey, England
Valley Gardens
Surrey, England

**UNITED KINGDOM &
REPUBLIC OF IRELAND**

ATLANTIC

OCEAN

NORTH SEA

MAP 20

SCOTLAND

MAP 19

NORTHERN
IRELAND

MAP 18

MAP 22

MAP 17

ENGLAND

Irish Sea

MAP 16

REPUBLIC
OF
IRELAND

MAP 15

MAP 12

MAP 13

MAP 14

MAP 21

MAP 11

MAP 10

WALES

MAP 8

MAP 9

MAP 7

Celtic Sea

MAP 6

MAP 5

MAP 2

MAP 3

MAP 4

MAP 1

English Channel

| 0 | 40 | 80 Km |
| 0 | 20 | 40 Miles |

N

Key To Garden Location Maps

——————	Coastline	**M1**	Motorway		Urban Area
⬤⬤⬤⬤⬤	International Border	**A5**	Dual Carriageway		Settlement
——————	Regional Border	**A15**	Main Road		
——————	County Border	——————	Minor Road	✹	Garden Location

MAP 2 • 481

MAP 4 • **483**

MAP 6 • **485**

MAP 8 • 487

MAP 10 • **489**

MAP 12 • **491**

MAP 14 • **493**

The Wash

Holbeck Marsh

Wisbech

March

A141

Isle of Ely

Ely

A142

A1065

Mildenhall

A11

Bury St Edmunds

A14

Newmarket

Cambridge

M11

A11

A10

Royston

Haverhill

Saffron Walden

Audley End

M11

Amberden Hall

Easton Lodge

Saling Hall

Braintree

A120

Langthorns Plantery

A131

Bishop's Stortford

A10

Ware

Harlow

Sawbridgeworth

The Gibberd Garden

Rhodes & Rockliffe

Cheshunt

Chelmsford

A414

Waltham Abbey

Chipping Ongar

RHS Garden, Hyde Hall

A10

M25

A12

Billericay

A130

Brentwood

Basildon

Rayleigh

Hornchurch

County Park Nursery

LONDON

Grays

A13

M25

Dartford

A226

Gravesend

Gillingham

Chatham

Sittingbourne

Isle of Sheppey

Herne Bay

A299

Margate

Ramsgate

Canvey Island

Southend-On-Sea

Foulness Island

Southminster

Tillingham

Maldon

Glen Chantry

Witham

Coggeshall

Olivers

Colchester

Bath Chatto Gardens

Paradise Centre

Sudbury

East Bergholt Place

A12

Clacton-on-Sea

Harwich

Felixstowe

A14

Ipswich

A12

Woodbridge

Orford Ness

Aldeburgh

Saxmundham

Framlingham

Notcutts Nurseries

Helmingham Hall

Shrubland Hall

Needham Market

Stowmarket

Rougham Hall Nurseries

Ickworth

A134

A14

Haughley Park

Mills Farm Plants & Gardens

Wyken Hall

SUFFOLK

Fisk's Clematis Nursery

Halesworth

Southwold

Park Green Nurseries

A140

Goldbrook Plants

Harleston

Diss

Dell Garden

Foggy Bottom

A1066

Euston Hall

A134

Thetford

PW Plants

Bressingham Plant Centre

A143

Reads Nursery

Lowestoft

A12

Raveningham Hall

Somerleyton Hall

Loddon

A146

Plantation Garden

ESSEX

A131

Chelmsford

East Lode

Brandon

A1065

A10

Peter Beales Roses

A134

Hilborough

Watton

Attleborough

A11

Chanticleer

Oxburgh Hall

A1065

Swaffham

Thorncroft Clematis Nursery

Bradenham Hall

Dereham

A47

Litcham

Elsing Hall

The Romantic Garden Nursery

NORWICH

Fairhaven Woodland & Water Garden

Great Yarmouth

NORFOLK

A140

Hoveton Hall

A1065

Hoecroft Plants

Blickling Hall

Melton Constable

North Walsham

The Broads

East Ruston Old Vicarage

King's Lynn

A17

African Violet Centre

A1101

A10

A47

A1122

Fakenham

A148

Sandringham House

A149

Norfolk Lavender

Hunstanton

Holkham Hall

Wells-next-the-Sea

Mannington Gardens

Sheringham Park

Felbrigg Hall

Sheringham

Blakeney Point

Blakeney

Cromer

Mundesley

| 0 | 10 | 20 Km |
| 0 | 10 | 20 Miles |

N

MAP 16 • **495**

MAP 18 • 497

MAP 20 • **499**

MAP 22 • 501

Islay

North Channel

Kintyre

Dunfanaghy

Guy Wilson Daffodil Garden
Ballycastle

Bunbeg
Buncrana
Coleraine
Benvarden Garden and Grounds

Glenveagh Castle
Dungloe
Londonderry
Carnlough

Letterkenny
NORTHERN
Carnfunnock Country Park

Ballybofey
IRELAND

Glencolumbkille
Ardnamona

Killybegs
Donegal
Omagh
Ballyrogan Nurseries

Ballyshannon
Lower Lough Erne
Lough Neagh
BELFAST
Mount Stewart

Manorhamilton
Enniskillen
Portadown
Lisburn
Rowallane Garden

Florence Court
Monaghan
Lurgan
Castle Ward

Sligo
Armagh
Castlewellan
Seaforde Gardens

Ballina
Belturbet
Castleblayney
National Arboretum
Newcastle

Lough Conn
Boyle
Carrick-on-Shannon
Cavan
Rostrevor

Westport
Carrick-macross
Dundalk

Lough Mask
REPUBLIC
Tullynally Castle
Drogheda

Cleggan
Moyard
Cong
Roscommon
OF
Butterstream
Trim
Ardgillan Park

Clifden
Oughterard
Ardagh
National Botanic Gardens
Talbot Botanic Gardens

Lettermore
IRELAND
Mullingar
Primrose Hill
Earlscliffe

Galway
Athlone
Lodge Park Walled Garden
DUBLIN

Galway Bay
Japanese Gardens
The Dillon Garden
Fernhill

Kilronan
Kinvarra
Portumna
Birr
Birr Castle Demesne
Kildare
Powerscourt Gardens

Whitegate
Lough Derg
Portlaise
Valclusa Gardens
National Garden Exhibiton Centre

Ennis
Roscrea
Heywood Gardens
Mount Usher Gardens
Wicklow

Killaloe
Gash Gardens
Carlow
Altamont Garden
Arklow

Kilrush
Ballynacourty
Kilfane Glen & Waterfall
Ram House Gardens

Askeaton
Limerick
Gorey

Glin Castle
Adare
Clonmel
New Ross
John F Kennedy Arboretum
Enniscorthy

Tralee
Curraghmore
Wexford

Ballyferriter
Dingle
Kanturk
Annes Grove Gardens
Lismore Castle
Waterford
Johnstown Castle Gardens

Dingle Bay
Killorglin
Killarney
Mallow
Lismore
Dunmore East

Cahirciveen
Muckross House and Gardens
Cork
Youghal
Ardmore

Kenmare
Hillside
Cobh
Fota
Ballymaloe Cookery School Garden

Derreen
Clonakilty
Kinsale

Castletown

Crookhaven
Baltimore

Celtic Sea

ATLANTIC OCEAN

St George's Channel

0   20   40 Km
0   20   40 Miles

N

INDEX